Anthropology

T

Anthropology

Theoretical Practice in Culture and Society

Michael Herzfeld

BLACKWELL PUBLISHING
350 Main Street, Malden, MA 02148-5020, USA
9600 Garsington Road, Oxford OX4 2DQ, UK
550 Swanston Street, Carlton, Victoria 3053, Australia

First published 2001

5   2006

Library of Congress Cataloging-in-Publication Data

Herzfeld, Michael, 1947–
    Anthropology : theoretical practice in culture and society / Michael Herzfeld
      p. cm.
    Includes bibliographical references and index
    ISBN 0-631-20658-2 (alk. paper)—ISBN 0-631-20659-0 (pb. : alk. paper)
    1. Ethnology—Philosophy.   2. Ethnology—Methodology.   I. Title

    GN345.H47 2001
    301—dc21

                                                              00-057915

ISBN-13: 978-0-631-20658-3 (alk. paper)—ISBN-13: 978-0-631-20659-0 (pb. : alk. paper)

A catalogue record for this title is available from the British Library.

Set in 10.5 on 12 pt Sabon
by Best-set Typesetter Ltd, Hong Kong
Printed and bound in India
by Gopsons Papers Ltd, Noida

The publisher's policy is to use permanent paper from mills that operate a sustainable forestry policy, and which has been manufactured from pulp processed using acid-free and elementary chlorine-free practices. Furthermore, the publisher ensures that the text paper and cover board used have met acceptable environmental accreditation standards.

For further information on
Blackwell Publishing, visit our website:
www.blackwellpublishing.com

This work is grounded in a collective endeavor.

The other contributors to the project that generated it are:

Marc Abélès, Nurit Bird-David, John Borneman,
Constance Classen, David Coplan, Veena Das, Sara Dickey,
Arturo Escobar,
Néstor García Canclini, Don Handelman,
Ulf Hannerz, Václav Hubinger, Kay Milton, Juan Ossio,
Michael Roberts,
Don Robotham, David Scott,
and Nicholas Thomas.

Their original formulations may be found in UNESCO's
International Social Science Journal, issues 153 (September 1997)
and 154 (December 1997).

Contents

Foreword

Created in the aftermath of World War II for the "purpose of advancing, through the educational and scientific and cultural relations of the peoples of the world, the objectives of international peace and of common welfare,"[1] the United Nations Educational, Scientific and Cultural Organisation (UNESCO) is the only UN Agency with a mandate to develop and promote the social sciences.

Working for over fifty years to meet this objective in countries stretching across the globe, the Organisation remains committed to the social science community and to demonstrating how social science work is a fundamental pillar of social and economic development. In conceptualising this volume, we wish to emphasise the importance of the discipline of anthropology and anthropological methods for comprehending societal dynamics in an increasingly globalised world. Initially planned as a disciplinary textbook, the volume has, in fact, far surpassed our original expectation. The book that you are about to read plunges you into a thought-provoking voyage that sweeps across the discipline and delves into key issues that challenge society today. It is intended not only for an academic audience, although it represents a comprehensive and lively picture of the discipline. Any non-specialist interested in contemporary issues will find delightful and insightful reflection on a diverse array of topics. I also urge the community of development practitioners to pay particular attention to this volume, as it questions global assumptions that increasingly dominate political and economic decision-making.

The preface of this book provides a comprehensive overview of the process that led to its production, and I will not repeat that story here. Instead, I wish to pay special tribute to the fine international team of anthropologists who have contributed their writings to this volume. They generously accepted the "unity in diversity teamwork" format that we proposed, which makes this collective work so unique. Their original contributions are published in UNESCO's *International Social Science Journal*, issues 153 and 154, and I am grateful to the Editor, David Makinson, and his assistant, Glynis Thomas, for having taken responsibility for the work related to this publication.

[1] Constitution of UNESCO, London, 16 November 1945

Finally, I would like to comment on the author of this project. Professor Michael Herzfeld's academic qualities are well-known. This volume is yet another testimony to his masterful capacities to analyse and challenge, to interact with the contributors to this volume and with the reader, through skilful and witty writing. Beyond academia, his personal qualities of commitment, perfectionism, enthusiasm and generosity really have transformed this project into a particular delight.

In offering this volume, we at UNESCO hope to continue to demonstrate the importance of the social and human sciences world-wide.

Nadia Auriat, Ph.D.
Project Officer
Division of Social Science Research & Policy
UNESCO

Ali Kazancigil
Assistant Director General, p.i.
Sector of Social and Human Sciences
UNESCO

Preface

This is an overview of social and cultural anthropology, a discipline within the social sciences that, broadly speaking, covers the relationship between society and culture. This discipline might best – and not a little mischievously – be defined as the comparative study of common sense, both in its cultural forms and in its social effects.

The tactic used in developing the present work derives from earlier publications but reflects some peculiarities of both the author and the discipline. I have built the text around a set of essays previously commissioned and published in the *International Social Science Journal* by authors whom I happen to admire and whose work fits, in my view, two key requirements. The first of these is a skeptical distance from the solipsistic extremes, the Scylla and Charybdis, of modern sociocultural theory: postmodernism and positivism in their more dogmatic excesses. This is the critical position that I have elsewhere described as the "militant middle ground" – a space that at once is strongly resistant to closure and that is truly grounded in an open-ended appreciation of the empirical (Herzfeld 1997a). It is a space in which anthropologists can learn to move away from what Nicholas Thomas has argued is their inflated sense of the importance of their theories in the larger world, a space defined by what he in very similar language to my own has called an "intermediate point of view."

The other key requirement is a sense of what I would call the pedagogical imperative of anthropology – the insistence that all its many obvious discomfitures offer the student a pragmatic understanding of what epistemology is all about. Here, again, the modesty of a discipline concerned with practice rather than with grand theory may ultimately have a more lasting effect in the world. This is a view of anthropology as a model for critical engagement with the world, rather than as a distanced and magisterial explanation of the world. This engagement may take many forms, from critiques of policy (e.g., Ferguson 1992) and professional practice (Balshem 1993; Kleinman 1995) to ethnographically oriented phenomenology (e.g., M. Jackson 1989), but its key feature is a clear understanding that even the very marginality of so much of what anthropologists study offers grist to a critical mill – and a humbling awareness of how much of it will always remain marginal from the perspective of those who control and define the centers of power.

Where is that middle ground – between what poles does it provide a space for reflection? It lies between the sometimes crass extremes of positivism and deconstruction, with their deliciously similar panoplies of self-justifying and self-referential rhetoric; between the disembodied abstractions of grand theory and the ingrown self-absorption of local interests and "national" studies; between self-satisfied rationalism and equally self-satisfied nihilism. It straddles other binarisms as well, making nonsense of the distinction – of which so much used to be made – between social and cultural anthropology, and relocating that debate where it properly belongs: as a proxy war, in which supposedly theoretical paradigms fought out the mutual (but sometimes also willful?) incomprehension of British and American academic communities. This middle ground, moreover, is not to be confused with compromise or complaisance. To the contrary, it is a call to capitalize on the discipline's peculiar capacity for critical insight on the human condition and its interpretation, and to recognize that some of the dominant binarisms of modern rhetoric – that pitting science against the humanities, for example – may reflect political actuality but offer little help otherwise in deciphering the lived, experienced, and socially engaging world we inhabit. It is above all a call to seize reality by rejecting any single, dominant representation of what constitutes Reality.

This does not make for easy answers. When I was a student at Oxford over two decades ago, a favorite examination question was to ask whether a textbook of anthropology could be written. One was expected, I think, to express a proper awe of the subject by saying that this was impossible. And indeed, so it is – and for reasons that are more compelling today than they were a quarter of a century ago. This volume is consequently not intended as a textbook. Consistent with the pedagogical model I have just described, however, it is a teaching tool – though not necessarily for classroom use; we are all students. And it is written less in awe of the terrible comprehensiveness of the discipline than in hopes of participating in some thoughtful reassessments of what matters in our world, and to whom. It is a provocation, not a prescription: that is the kind of teaching that anthropology offers, which is why it is so disapproved by normativists of all stripes – official ideologues, econometric modelers, champions of western (or any other) cultural dominance.

That approach is well served, I suggest, by the book's peculiar genesis. The chapters emerged from my colleagues' fine, if riotously diverse, programmatic, and state-of-the-art assessments. Rather than simply absorb those chapters in my own text, I have preserved distinct segments as quotations from those original statements, absorbing only the more "mechanical" elements – for which I was certainly also dependent on the expert help of the authors of the articles – in my own prose. I have added and subtracted a great deal beyond these operations as well: interested readers can consult the original articles in order to gauge the process whereby textual unity has been attempted in order to emphasize rather than suppress the variety of points of view. Within the middle ground, there are nuances and disagreements. This book is an attempt to make those disharmonies work for the reader as provocations to further thought – although, to be sure, they are unlikely to be as radical as those one encounters in the larger "culture wars."

So this is indeed not a textbook if that term implies any degree of comprehensiveness or normativity. There is, it is true, an element of prescription in the very notion of a militant middle ground. But this would seem inevitable if we are to retain the possibility of treating as culturally and historically contingent such taken-for-granted phenomena as the capitalist economy, the logic of democracy, or the claims of science.

Part of the tactic of keeping the discussion off balance at all times concerns the chapter headings. Gone from the surface are such familiar old warhorses as kinship, ethnicity, and religion. But they are still emphatically present in the text – indeed, they pervade virtually all the chapters in one way or another. The history of a discipline is not so easily dismissed; nor are its central preoccupations so trivial. Rather, they have become part of its own peculiar "common sense." At the same time, we can contribute most usefully to an understanding of the troubled world around us – and ethnicity, for example, is very much one of its "troubles" – by challenging the categorical certainty that leads people to assume that these topics are intellectually unproblematic. Ethnicity, for example, is all too easily assumed to possess such irreducible essence that the very act of challenging its centrality must seem either demented or, and this is my hope, provocatively wise. If the reader of this book conscientiously follows through all the scattered but systematically interrelated discussions of ethnicity and other forms of identity, those concepts will never again seem so seductively crystalline – so conceptually innocent of ambiguity, manipulability, or rhetorical padding masking a dangerous vacuity.

For related reasons I have not devoted a special chapter to law or medicine – not, that is, because these are unimportant, but because, to the contrary and in a very real sense, they pervade everything written here. Thus, for example, the interests of medical anthropology are refracted here through discussions of suffering, symbolism, epistemology, sexuality, ritual, politics, aesthetics. The interests of legal anthropology have a venerable history, and again questions of normativity and its enforcement – and subversion – pervade this account. Here I simply signal the transcendent ubiquity of the two areas. The alert reader will soon discover how ill-advised it would have been to try to summarize them in single chapters.

As for that old chestnut, kinship, it is no less pervasive. The lingering importance of kinship is not merely the outcome of a now outmoded professional obsession. Rather, the present situation is one in which its complex interweavings appear everywhere. Is the Bosnian horror best seen as a tale of collapsed civility? of religious intolerance? of ethnicity run riot? of the humiliation and the agony of mothers and daughters, victims of a code of male vengeance now beyond any pacific mediation? or even of patrilineal kinship and the agnatic feud acted out, finally, in a global endgame, at the most destructively inclusive level yet known to humankind? It is all these things and more. But to ignore the last-named dimension, that of kinship (today coupled with that of gender), would be to revert to the journalistic sensationalism of the inexplicable and the atavistic, themselves rhetorics of otherness with which the West consoles itself for what it, in part, has wrought; while to isolate kinship as a *Ding an sich* in the manner of the textbooks of an earlier age would be to perpetuate the western myth that, as the primary basis for sociality, kinship is a peculiarity of exotic societies, rather than a pervasive feature of all and especially of the cosmology we call "nationalism." On the other hand, if are going to continue using it as a key concept, newly developed attention to feminism and gay concerns must necessarily alter its significance in sometimes startling ways. Too much, for too long, has been taken for granted – and it is social anthropology's business to question the obviousness that we call common sense.

In the chapter headings, following a convention originally developed for the *ISSJ* essays, I have chosen a plural format (e.g., "economies") and a focus on ideological claims as opposed to established facts (e.g., "environmentalisms") in order to emphasize that anthropologists generally view critically the exclusive claims often made for received ways of organizing the world. Pluralization is a fine way to destabilize the authority of received categories. The 1992 US presidential election was fought around the slogan, "It's the economy, stupid!" – a remarkable surrender by a self-proclaimedly democratic and pluralistic nation to the idea that a single issue, with a single logic, would determine the future course of events (and even that "the economy" was a single phenomenon!). In English the use of the singular with a definite article – "the typical native," for example – is a clear play for conceptual closure. The same usage – "the Italian" (*l'italiano*) does not respect the law," for example – can be used in pronouncements of tantalizing ambiguity: are they self-congratulatory, self-ironizing, or an equally ironic challenge to the preceived judgmentalism of critical outsiders (including anthropologists)? Anthropologists, having written books about "the" members of this or that people, have nevertheless long observed the human desire for such closure with a critical eye, and may especially appreciate its more self-ironic manifestations. But the appearance of this pattern, far from validating the claims of western economic rationality, confirms all the more forcefully, if only we remain open to the idea, the highly constructed, meaning-laden, and contingent character of such dominant "facts" – which would thus be better interpreted as key symbols and which, as such, are no less appropriate an object of anthropological study than the esoterica of any remote, exotic society.

Anthropology is clearly a gadfly discipline, and this does not always make it popular. Castigated in many ex-colonial states as the repository of imperialism, reviled by nationalists in the sites of newly resurgent irredentism and fascism, it clashes, perhaps inevitably, with any attempt to model the world on a single cultural design. Its radically comparativist concerns automatically render it suspect in totalitarian eyes, yet its practitioners' relentless inquisitiveness may make them the object of ordinary people's deepest misgivings: I have myself been suspected of being a spy for foreign powers and for the local bureaucracy. Occasionally, too, things go wrong, as when a book rather heedlessly titled *Yanomamö: The Fierce People* (Chagnon 1968) apparently became an excuse for the attempted cultural and demographic extirpation of the Yanomamö, or when anthropologists have allowed themselves to be seduced into serving some repressive political interest as the price of admission. But these cases, too, become, for those of good faith and an open mind, part of the discipline's historically grounded self-awareness and collective conscience.

Writing a book about social and cultural anthropology – even one that seeks to sample rather than to summarize – poses a special challenge: where even to begin? UNESCO's two-step format, however, also suggested a viable solution. I have presented the chapters as a recension – my own, necessarily idiosyncratic recension – of the thoughts of the international team of colleagues whose articles in the two special issues of *International Social Science Journal* thus form the starting-point of this book, as well as an opportunity to expand the space for ideas that I have found to be helpful in my own areas of specialization. In this way I have been able to lean on my colleagues' wisdom and knowledge and to let their positions (I trust) be clear, while attempting to derive from this complex discussion a more or less internally coherent picture of one possible anthropological vision. I am grateful for their agreement to this scheme and for consenting to crystallize their expertise in the *ISSJ* articles in the first place, and I accept full responsibility for the shortcomings that my own intervention must inevitably have introduced in the individual topics or in the book overall. Many of these colleagues responded to an early draft of this book with further observations and criticisms, some of them several times, and I have tried to preserve as much of the flavor of the ongoing conversation as the format would permit.

Readers (and authors) may notice that I have incorporated quite different proportions of the *ISSJ* team's original texts (although I have marked the more significant verbatim passages as quotations); engaged in different ways with their respective ideas; and in some cases rearranged materials so that there is no longer a direct and unmodified identification of each chapter with one of the articles. (When any of these individuals is quoted verbatim without an in-text citation, the quotation is from that person's *ISSJ* article, except where I have indicated that a particular remark occurred in the course of the subsequent conversations in which we variously engaged.) In this way, rather than simply using each article as a template for my own prose, I have tried through substantive changes and careful quotation to engage all the contributors' work in a more active form of discussion. They have commented on the final draft, and I have incorporated those reactions as well – to keep myself honest but also, what is more important, to draw the reader into the community of discussion that this book represents. Moreover, I hope in this way to engage the interest of a wide range of nonspecialists while at the same time presenting to the discipline itself a lively version of its current "conversation."

Indeed, this mode of authorship is consistent with the current understanding of ethnography – the field practice of anthropology and the genre in which it is described – as the product of a negotiated collaboration. The original texts are available to anyone who wants to see how far I may have recast the thoughts, including my own, that emerged in the first stage of this project. But in the present text, I hope to offer a vision that may not be completely unified or internally consistent but that at least constitutes a consolidation of sorts. It is a working out of common concerns, an act of what French countryfolk call *débrouillardise* (Reed-Danahay 1996) – a creative coping and groping through the obfuscation created by layer upon layer of cultural "obviousness." It is as a critique of the assumptions of that obviousness – of what is everywhere called common sense, and that is everywhere different and distinctive to its own setting – that the anthropology conceived here should always be heard as the critical voice of insistent puzzlement (see Fernandez 1986).

This work is in every sense the result of a collective endeavor. In these interactive days, there seems little point in attempting to reproduce the magisterial formulations of yesteryear, even supposing that one author might have proved equal to the task. Let me be quite clear about this: I could not have crafted many of the chapters in this book without the articles and discussions that preceded them. (I have intentionally left in place some embedded citations of works I could not have read for linguistic or other reasons.) Thus, in writing these antecedent texts into a single work, I have tried at once to let the original ideas appear but in the clearest possible articulation with my own sense of anthropology, a sense that is, I believe, largely shared in its broad implications, if not always in every detail, by these colleagues around the world. Their help has been something of an inoculation against the tempting parochialism of powerful centers – the ethnocentrism that forever threatens to seduce anew those of us who have grown up in the old colonizing countries, which are, not coincidentally, the birthplaces of social and cultural anthropology. Aided by this deliberate internationalization, which has its own circumstantial limitations and challenges (the genealogy of knowledge still goes back to the same colonial centers), the anthropology presented in these pages is in quite a literal sense, I hope, a social and cultural practice. I intend it to be read as a constructive and historically sensitive critique of social institutions and as a productive irritant – its "pedagogical" role – in the flesh of today's dominant structures of knowledge. As such, it should enjoy a special engagement with the other disciplines of human society. Readers may also note that I make almost exaggeratedly frequent use of certain texts. These serve as an informal indexing device: their recurrence marks conceptual links across what otherwise too easily become parochial zones of specialization. In this way, I have tried to emphasize anthropology's curious capacity for illuminating parallels and connections between areas of social life commonly – in the dominant mode of "common sense" – held to be discrete.

This work is very much more of a collective venture than most volumes that appear under the name of a single author. The development of a new, more interactive format meant a lot of hard work for all of us, but from my perspective, at least, it was worth every bit of the extra effort and time involved. I therefore want to express my deep gratitude, appreciation, and affection for the collegial group of scholars whose work formed the fertile grounds for what for me was a very new kind of authorship: Marc Abélès, Nurit Bird-David, John Borneman, Constance Classen, David Coplan, Veena Das, Sara Dickey, Arturo Escobar, Néstor García Canclini, Don Handelman, Ulf Hannerz, Václav Hubinger, Kay Milton, Juan Ossio, Michael Roberts, Don Robotham, David Scott, and Nicholas Thomas. This was an adventure that their good-natured tolerance and intellectual forthrightness made both possible and enjoyable. Some of them continued to argue and to offer often provocative and always helpful suggestions almost up to the final completion of the manuscript; I could not have asked for better stimulation. I strongly urge readers to consult these colleagues' original essays, published in issue 153 (September 1997) and 154 (December 1997) of *International Social Science Journal*, in order to appreciate more directly the remarkable synergy involved in the overall production of the ideas represented here. In the preparation of the manuscript, I relied heavily on the tactful efficiency and intellectual engagement of Yu-son Jung, and I am also deeply indebted to Thomas Malaby and Saipin Suputtamongkol for their editorial and substantive input. At UNESCO, Nadia Auriat and David Makinson, ably assisted by Glynis Thomas, were a source of inspiring support during the journal phase, while at Blackwell Publishers I not only delightedly found myself once again working with my old comrade-in-arms from *American Ethnologist* days, Jane F. Huber – a special pleasure indeed – but also rapidly came to appreciate the professional thoroughness as well as the compassion and friendship of Tony Grahame and the steady support of Simon Eckley: few authors can have been the beneficiaries of such a fortunate convergence!

1

Orientations: Anthropology as a Practice of Theory

Anthropology: A critique of common sense

Social and cultural anthropology is "the study of common sense." Yet common sense is, anthropologically speaking, seriously mis-named: it is neither common to all cultures, nor is any version of it particularly sensible from the perspective of anyone outside its particular cultural context. It is the socially acceptable rendition of culture, and is thus as variable as are both cultural forms and social rules – those twin axes that define the formal objects of anthropological theory. Whether viewed as "self-evidence" (Douglas 1975: 276–318) or as "obviousness," common sense – the everyday understanding of how the world works – turns out to be extraordinarily diverse, maddeningly inconsistent, and highly resistant to skepticism of any kind. It is embedded in both sensory experience and practical politics – powerful realities that constrain and shape access to knowledge. How do we know that human beings have really landed on the moon? We are (usually) convinced of it – but how do we know that our conviction does not rest on some misplaced confidence in the sources of our information? If we have reason to doubt that others are entirely successful in making sense of the world, how do we know – given that we cannot easily step outside our own frame of reference – that we are doing any better?

To be sure, this challenge to what we might call scientific and rational credulity was not what the earliest anthropologists (in any professionally recognizable sense) had in mind. To the contrary, they were convinced of their own cultural superiority to the people they studied, and would have reacted with astonishment to any suggestion that science could be studied in the same way as "magic." They did not see that distinction as itself symbolic; they thought it was rational, literal, and real. But their thinking was no less mired in the structures and circumstances of colonial domination than were those of the colonized peoples they studied, although their angle of perspective was necessarily different – so that it is hardly surprising that they reached different conclusions, whether or not these had any empirical validity. In recognizing this embarrassing ancestry for our field, I want to suggest more than an intellectual exercise in imagination or atonement for collective past sins. I want to suggest that anthropology has learned as much – and can therefore teach as much – by attention to its mistakes as by the celebration of its achievements. That is, after all, what we urge students of anthropology to do in the field – so much so that the responses to solecisms and poor judgement can often be more informative than responses to the most carefully crafted interview protocol. The achievements are largely matters of factual recording (and even these are often in dispute); but the social character of the most abstract theory has begun to be much more apparent to us, and, paradoxically, this awareness of entailment has allowed us to be much more rigorously comparative than ever before – to see our own worldview, with anthropology its instrument and its expression, in the same terms as we view those distant others on whom we have for so long fixed our gaze. So why not study science as an ethnographic object?

Much recent anthropological work has indeed inspected the claims of modern technology, politics, and science. Notably, the entire field of medical anthropology (see especially Kleinman 1995) has challenged the claims of a crass scientism that – as Nicholas Thomas observes in a somewhat different context – has failed to keep pace with developments in science itself. There has clearly been an enormous expansion of the discipline's topical range since the Victorians' preoccupation with what they called savage societies. That expansion, moreover, entails much more than a mere broadening of factual or even theoretical horizons. It is a rearrangement of the very principles of intellectual perspective.

Anthropology, a discipline that has thus developed an ironic sense of its own social and cultural context, is particularly well equipped to challenge the separation of modernity from tradition and rationality from superstition – perhaps, ironically, in part because it played an enormously influential role in the creation of this antinomy. The constant exposure of anthropologists in the field to the cultural specificity of their own backgrounds undoubtedly played an important part in generating a sense of – and discomfort with – the cultural vainglory of the centres of world power. Indeed, a famous spoof by Horace Miner (1956), an article in which he analysed the curious body rituals of the "Nacirema" (a well-known tribal group, spelled backwards), makes fun of scholars' formal way of theorizing everyday matters. Instead of merely poking fun at the ease with which scholars are seduced by the vanity of expertise, however, Miner raised a serious question of epistemology: why should the supposed rationality of western lifestyles escape the sardonic eye of the anthropologist? The question is serious because it is fundamentally political, and the evidence for this confronts anthropologists in the field at every turn. A study (Ferreira 1997) of Amazonian responses to Western-imposed mathematical conventions, for example, shows that the denial of natives' cognitive capacities may be an integral part of their exploitation and even extirpation by the local agents of international commercial interests. Anthropology is often about misunderstandings, including anthropologists' own misunderstandings, because these are usually the outcome of the mutual incommensurability of different notions of common sense – our object of study.

Yet the task becomes correspondingly more difficult as the politics and worldview under study move closer not only to home but to the centers of effective power. Anthropology entails the unveiling of intimate practices that lie behind rhetorical protestations of eternal truth, ranging from "that's always been our custom", in almost every village and tribal society studied by the anthropologists of the past, to the evocation of science and logic by every modern political elite (see, e.g., Balshem 1993; Zabusky 1995). We should not be surprised if those whose authority may be compromised by such revelations do not take too kindly to becoming the subjects of anthropological research. Calling themselves modern, they have claimed above all to have achieved a rationality capable of transcending cultural boundaries (see Tambiah 1990). They have characterized other societies as pre-modern, and have attributed to these a lack of specialization in domains requiring mental activity. Thus, the political was held to be inextricably embedded in kinship and more generally in the social fabric of such societies. In the same way, art was not distinguished from craft or from ritual production; economic life was sustained by social reciprocities and belief systems; and science could not emerge as an autonomous field because human beings had not yet found efficient ways of disentangling the practical from the religious (or the superstitious, as this domain was sometimes called, presupposing a besetting incapacity to separate cosmological belief from pure philosophy on the one hand and practical knowledge on the other). Thus, anthropology's main task was seen as the study of domains of the social – politics, economics, kinship, religion, aesthetics, and so on – in those societies the members of which had not learned to make such abstract distinctions. Long after the demise of evolutionism as the dominant theory of society and culture, this evolutionist assumption sustained the categories of modernity and tradition as the basis for teaching anthropology, and hence also the illusion that societies that had announced themselves to be modern and advanced had somehow managed to rise above the inability to conceptualize the abstract and so had succeeded in rationalizing the social through the specialization of tasks.

Yet such assumptions could not be long sustained. They quickly clashed with the direct experience of field research, as Thomas observes: long immersion among the populations towards which such condescension was directed undermined the sense of absolute superiority and empirically discredited basic presuppositions. Indeed, as Stocking (1995: 123, 292) has noted, the turn to fieldwork – even before Malinowski – was crucial in undermining evolutionist perspectives even though their organizing framework was to prove disturbingly persistent: knowing those about whom one writes as neighbors and friends makes lofty ideas about the hierarchy of cultures both untenable and distasteful. Increasingly anthropologists began to apply at home what they had found helpful in supposedly simple societies. Mary Douglas (1966), in arguing for a cultural and social definition of dirt against a purely biochemical one, profoundly challenged the hygiene-centered preoccupations of European and North American societies that Miner had so mercilessly satirized. Marc Abélès perceives politics in modern Europe, at least in part, as a resuscitation of local-level values and relations, to the interpretation of which the anthropologist's grass-roots perspective affords especially immediate access.

Yet we should not expect too great a role for anthropology in the future: that "the foreign relativizes the familiar" is less useful and startling today, when the knowledge that anthropologists produce is immediately open to criticism by those about whom it is produced as they come to share an increasingly large range of communications technology with us. Nevertheless, this assessment might itself be cause for optimism about the potential for anthropology to contribute usefully to current social and political criticism. Hand-wringing about the crisis of representation should not obscure the fact that some of the more considered critiques themselves generated important new insights and departures. Even the disillusionment with fieldwork that began to appear in the 1960s – and especially with its claims to theoretically objective rigor – had the effect of strengthening this rejection of the radical separation between the observer and the observed and so created more, not less, empirically grounded forms of knowledge.

It is especially telling that, as Néstor García Canclini has emphasized, the rapid growth of urban social forms has dealt a decisive blow to that separation between observer and observed (and to the exclusive focus of some of the more traditional or "exoticizing" forms of anthropology on "salvage" work). As he points out, anthropologists are themselves subject to most of the forces that affect the urban populations they study. By the same token, however, the distinction between the urban and the rural, which (in the binary form in which it is often articulated) is to some extent simply an artefact of the history of anthropology itself, is also now increasingly difficult to sustain. Such insights underscore the importance of being fully aware of the discipline's historical entailments. This more fluid relationship with our subject-matter emerges as a result of increasingly reflexive approaches. As a basic orientation in anthropology, it is both analytically more useful and historically more responsible than rejecting the whole enterprise as fatally and irremediably flawed either by observer "contamination" (a symbolic construct found with surprising frequency in writings claimed as scientific) or by its indisputably hegemonic past (which it shares with the entire range of academic disciplines). Both the pragmatic and the rejectionist responses can certainly be found in the ethnographic literature, sometimes curiously conjoined in a single work. In such contradictory moments, in fact, we can sometimes see the first stirrings of a more flexible approach to the categorical confusions that, as Néstor García Canclini observes, proliferate in the complexity of urban life.

Take, for example, two roughly contemporaneous studies of Moroccan society, both of which carry introspection to lengths that many have found to be excessive. Against the grim rejectionism of Kevin Dwyer's *Moroccan Dialogues* (1982), a work in which a single ethnographer-informant relationship is made to do the work of destabilizing a whole discipline, Paul Rabinow's distinctly nihilistic *Reflections on Fieldwork in Morocco* (1977) makes a very different case: its contribution to current anthropological thought comes less through the author's disgust with traditional method (or rather with the lack of it) than through his perceptive recognition that the jaded ex-colonialist French hôtelier was at least as good a subject for ethnographic investigation as the romantic Berber denizens of the kasbah and the suq. Such moves help to make the "unmarked" carriers of modernity both visible and interesting and to dismantle their rhetoric of cultural neutrality. Even as some European critics, for example, assail anthropologists for daring to study Europeans themselves on the same terms as exotic savages, thereby exposing a cultural hierarchy that is indeed worth studying in its own cultural and social context, the recent, rapid intensification of this focus on "the West" has also helped to dissolve much of the residue of anthropology's own embarrassingly racist origins. Fortunately, the absence of so-called Western societies from the roster of generally acknowledged ethnographic sites, a situation that implicitly represented such societies as transcending culture itself, is now being trenchantly redressed.

In Rabinow's book, moreover, we see one of the most perverse strengths of anthropology: that its capacity for even quite destructive self-examination has provided a pedagogical tool of considerable value. Furthermore, anthropology's now skeptical view of rationalism offers a healthy corrective to the more universalistic assumptions common in other social-science disciplines, while its persistent localism provides a strong vaccine against universalizing the particularistic values of cultures that happen to be politically dominant. Whenever the end of anthropology has been proclaimed from within there has been a renewal of both external interest and internal theoretical energy. This, I suggest, is because anthropology provides a unique critical and empirical space in which to examine the universalistic claims of common sense – including the common sense of Western social theory.

While I am cautious about the risk of inflated ideas about what the discipline can do for the world at large, I would also argue that – at least in the classroom, hardly an unimportant place, but also in all the other arenas of opinion formation to which anthropologists have access from time to time – there is great value in the destabilization of received ideas both through the inspection of cultural alternatives and through the exposure of the weaknesses that seem to inhere in all our attempts to analyze various cultural worlds including our own. We need such a counterweight to the increasingly bureaucratic homogenization of the forms of knowledge.

I would argue, furthermore, that the characteristic stance of this discipline has always been its proclivity for taking marginal communities and using that marginality to ask questions about the centers of power. Indeed, some of the most exciting ethnographic studies are those which challenge the homogenizing rhetoric of nation-states. Recent work on Indonesia – a country of riotous variety – makes the point with especially dramatic force, both topically and conceptually (Bowen 1993; George 1996; Steedly 1993; Tsing 1993). But even in the world of European power, there are marginal spaces that complicate the representation of nationhood, culture, and society in ways that challenge long-cherished assumptions within the discipline (see Argyrou 1996a, 1997 on Cyprus; Herzfeld 1987 on Greece).

Field research, often in a tension-laden collaboration with respectably grand theory, has always been the cornerstone of anthropology. It generates an intimacy of focus – changing ways of framing ethnographic fieldwork make the more spatial image of a bounded community somewhat out-dated – that permits the recognition of indeterminacy in social relations. This is an empirical concern that too easily escapes the broader view but that nonetheless has enormous consequences for the larger picture (in the prediction of electoral patterns, for example, where isolated communities with very specific proclivities may hold the casting vote in a tight race). The nature of ethnographic research, Nicholas Thomas has argued, may now be changing, in response to new ways of organizing social and cultural life. Indeed, there is a pragmatically sensible shift from insistence on the local focus of ethnography – a tiny unit often situated within an equally arbitrary "culture area" and defined by the supposed peculiarities of that area – and toward new efforts at finding the intimacy necessary to successful fieldwork in large cities, electronic encounters, offices and laboratories, on buses and trains (see Gupta and Ferguson, eds., 1997; Herzfeld 1997a).

Yet this shift does not invalidate the anthropological preference for microscopic analysis. Curiously enough, in fact, the huge increase in scale of global interaction has intensified rather than attenuated the need for such an intimate perspective, as Thomas notes, and as we shall see particularly in the chapter on Media. If anthropologists still want to be "participant observers," hiding in villages while the villagers themselves are busily commuting (see Deltsou 1995), tracking old friends through the communications superhighway, or refusing to engage with the myriad national and international agencies that assist and confound people's everyday lives, will not suffice.

History and the Myth of Theoretical Origins

Most summaries of anthropology start with an account of its history, or at least place that history before any discussion of such contemporary themes as that of reflexivity. My thought in partially reversing that convention here is to highlight, as an example of what I am describing, the tendency to see the growth of the discipline as one of unilinear progress – in other words, as an example of one of the discipline's earliest master narratives, that of evolutionism (sometimes also known as social Darwinism or survivalism). It also makes it easier to emphasize a related point: that, far from being arranged in a tidy sequence beginning at some mythical point of origin, the "stages" of anthropological thought often overlap, confound the usual predictions of their order of appearance, and reappear as embarrassing anachronisms amidst supposedly progressive theoretical developments. Thus, for example, the seemingly very "modern" and postcolonial insight that key analytic categories such as kinship and marriage may not be as universally applicable as we had once imagined is anticipated in the writings of explorers who had wrestled practically with the inadequacies of these categories in the field a century ago, notably in Australia (see Stocking 1995: 26). Conversely, however, some key ideas associated with the evolutionism of Victorian Britain and the functionalist modes of explanation systematized by Malinowski in the 1920s often reappear in the structuralism of the 1960s and even in its successors, including the reflexive historiography of the 1990s. Let me elaborate on this by briefly commenting on the characteristic instance of Lévi-Strauss' structuralism.

Among his many contributions to anthropological theory, Claude Lévi-Strauss advanced the view that myth was "a machine for the suppression of time" and that it had the effect of concealing the contradictions raised by the very existence of social life (see discussion and further references in Leach 1970: 57–8, 112–19). Thus, for example, society prohibits incest, but how to explain reproduction except through a primal act of incest? (By extension, we might say that the birth of a new nation – an entity that characteristically lays claim to pure origins – must presuppose an act of cultural or even genetic miscegenation. And indeed Lévi-Strauss' views on myths of origin are especially apposite for the analysis of nationalistic histories.) How different is this from Malinowski's (1948) celebrated definition of myth as a "charter" for society? Or again, if incest taboos reflect the importance of maintaining clear categorical distinctions between insiders and outsiders and so enable each society to reproduce itself by marrying out (exogamy), how far does this escape the teleological implication – typical of most forms of functionalism – that such is the goal of rules prohibiting incest?

The sobering evidence of such intellectual recidivism has an important corollary. Once we see theories as expressions of a social and political orientation and as heuristic devices for exploring social reality, rather than as the instruments of pure intellect, the theories become visible in hitherto unsuspected places. We begin to realize, in other words, that informants are themselves engaged in theoretical practices – not, for the most part, in the sense of a professional engagement, but through the performance of directly comparable intellectual operations. Lévi-Strauss's (1966) celebrated distinction between "cold" and "hot" societies thus turns out to be one of scale rather than of kind.

It is one thing to recognize informants as producers of abstract social knowledge, but, as Thomas remarks, quite another to use it as the basis of our own theoretical understanding. Nevertheless, the increasing porosity of the contemporary world means that we shall be ever more dependent on our informants' intellectual tolerance and will therefore, willy-nilly, find ourselves doing just that. For, to an increasing degree, they "read what we write" (Brettell, ed., 1993). Moreover, they, too, write, and some of them write anthropology. This makes their ratiocination more perceptible (see especially Reed-Danahay 1997 [ed.]), although it also perhaps means that the domination of "modern" writing systems might occlude other modes of reasoning. The rise of a few dominant languages and ways of representing them is a development that would limit rather than expand our intellectual possibilities.

The extension of "sense" from "common sense" to "the sensorium" and the concomitant rejection of an a priori commitment to the Cartesian separation of mind from body is vital to expanding our capacity to appreciate the practical theorizing of social actors (M. Jackson 1989). (As with some of the complex kinship systems studied by early anthropologists, whether we realize it or not it is our own intellectual incapacity that is at issue.) Insights into those areas of the sensorium that resist reduction to verbal description are challenges to our capacity to suspend disbelief but, for that very reason, they demand a less solipsistic response than either the kind of objectivism that only accepts as significant the limited compass of understanding already circumscribed by the values of one culture (see Classen 1993a), or the surprisingly parallel self-indulgence of writing about culture from the safety of pure introspection. The latter is indeed a return to Victorian "armchair anthropology" in the name of a "postmodern" equivalent such as cultural studies.

The dearth of older studies of the sensory is especially surprising when one considers that evolutionists propounded at an early date the view that human beings became progressively less dependent on physical sensation as the life of the active mind took over. Yet these self-satisfied Victorians were, for example, deeply interested in ritual – one of the discipline's hardiest perennials. As Don Handelman remarks, ritual may engage all the senses to an extent not usually realized in (modern forms of) spectacle. Yet there has not until recently been much anthropological curiosity about the role of senses other than the visual and the auditory in ritual practices, and only rather modest attempts have been made to analyse these aspects as anything more than appendages to the main business of ritual action.

Raising questions about such matters reveals the limits of purely verbal channels of enquiry, and consequently poses a productive challenge to all the social sciences, especially those in which there is some recognition of social actors' own theoretical capacities. Don Handelman has raised the issue of theory that is implicit in ritual, yet he argues that we then construct a different theoretical framework that allows us to disembed the indigenous theory from its manifestations as ritual. Well and good – but this demands a dramatic increase in our ability both to record and to analyze those nonverbal semiotics through which the actors' conceptual assumptions and insights are expressed, manipulated, and, to use Handelman's terminology, transformed. For it is at least conceivable that in transforming the condition of a group or an individual, the performance of a ritual may also transform the way in which its underlying assumptions are perceived or conceptualized – something of the sort is presupposed in the idea that rituals, often associated with the reproduction of systems of power, may also serve as vehicles of change.

Here it seems especially vital to avoid the common error of assuming that all meaning can be rendered accurately in linguistic form. Much of what passes for translation should more accurately be called exegesis. Paradoxically this awareness of the limits of language entails a considerable command of the language of the culture in which one is working. It is crucial to be able to identify irony, to recognize allusion (sometimes to politically significant shifts in language use), and to go beyond simplistic assumptions that a language that appears grounded in social experience is "less" capable of carrying abstract meaning than one's own (see Labov 1972).

So, too, is a willingness to recognize that informants' ideas about meaning may not correspond to the verbocentric assumptions usually held by western intellectuals. In my own work in a rural Cretan community, for example, I have found that the inhabitants' ability to decode the semiotics of their own discourse as well as that of the encompassing bureaucratic nation-state is fueled by an acute sense of political marginality. Other examples are given in this book. Local usage in some societies appears to conflate linguistic meaning with casual observations that something "matters" (or "is meaningful," as we might say). But if such views do reflect local usage, perhaps they can also do something to loosen the hold that the language-centered model of meaning has over our intellectualist imagination.

The idea of illiterate village theorists is not especially astounding when one considers that these people must contend with enormous social complexities. Their situation, enmeshed in sometimes mutually discordant allegiances to entities larger than the local community, requires adroit decoding skills as a matter of sheer political survival. As a result, informants may display an exegetical virtuosity and a conceptual eclecticism that would, in a professional anthropologist, appear as signs of inconsistency, but in the local context simply display the pragmatic deployment of theory at its most varied. One can find the equivalent of functionalists, evolutionists, and even structuralists among one's informants: types of explanation respond to the needs of the situation. This becomes an even more complex issue when dealing with populations whose reading has been, perhaps unbeknownst to them, suffused with the vocabulary of past anthropologies – and that includes an increasing share of the world's populations. Local explanations of "custom" are frequently legitimated with a heavy dose of "scientific" evolutionism, for example – and, since theory often draws on currently popular notions, it is empirically unsound in such cases to treat popular discourse and anthropological theory as two wholly separate domains. Only a historical account of the relationship between them makes it possible to disentangle them for analytic purposes.

This is why I would welcome a disciplinary history that paid far greater attention than was hitherto acceptable to the role our informants play in the development of our ideas. For there is some evidence for this role. In the 1960s, for example, a major dispute pitted the structuralists (as "alliance theorists") against structural-functionalists (as "descent theorists") in the explanation of kinship. It turns out that – with a few, albeit notable, exceptions – most of the former had worked in South America and South East Asia, while the majority of the latter had conducted their research in Africa and the Middle East. Could this not be the result of the impact of local traditions of exegesis on the thinking of anthropologists? Ethnographic reports are replete with intimations of local theorizing; an early, and famous, example is that of Evans-Pritchard's experience with Nuer who drew diagrams in the ground in order to explain the lineaments of their ideal-typical lineage structure to him (Evans-Pritchard 1940: 202). To treat these exercises as ethnographic vignettes rather than as theoretical contributions seems ungenerous by the standards of today's more reflexive ethos.

Anthropology, framed in these terms, is perhaps unusual among the social sciences in the degree to which its practitioners acknowledge the collapse of the once axiomatic separation of theorizing scholar and ethnographic "subject." Does this mean that their models are fatally flawed? On the contrary, I suggest, their claims to intellectual rigor are strengthened by such acknowledgements of intellectual debt – acknowledgements that simultaneously undercut the arbitrariness of the scientistic (as opposed to scientific) insistence on perfect replicability and the equally self-referential nihilism towards which some – but not all – forms of postmodernism threaten to propel the discipline.

Among the latter, the assessments of ethnography in *Writing Culture* (Clifford and Marcus, eds., 1986) have been especially and appropriately criticized by feminists (Mascia-Lees, Sharpe, and Cohen 1987–8; Behar and Gordon, eds., 1995). Especially in the light of such criticisms from those who might have been expected to be sympathetic, it would be easy to dismiss the postmodern trend as simply another exploitative discourse. But that would be to repeat, yet again, the offense that is most commonly laid at its door. In fact, however, these instances of what Don Robotham has called "moderate" postmodernism have served as provocations to expand the space of ethnographic investigation, thereby, I would argue, rendering it more rather than less empirical – a judgment with which extremists of both the positivist and the postmodern persuasions would probably be equally unhappy.

But can a discipline so often forced to examine itself in this way contribute anything to human understanding, or are its internal squabbles simply too distracting or paralyzing? Certainly some of them seem dangerously silly. But the available evidence suggests that in fact the result has been an increase in ethnographic work, held to a higher standard of both scientific (in the most general sense) and moral accountability. If that is so, there are at least two major gains to be discussed: first, in the realization of the intellectual riches that scholars' increased humility might make generally available, and, second, and by extension, in the pedagogical task of fighting racism and other pernicious essentialisms in a world that seems increasingly inclined to return to them.

Anthropology and the Politics of Identity

The emphasis on agency has led to a partial dissolution of the once clear-cut divisions among anthropological topics, defined in terms of institutional significance (kinship, politics, religion, economics and so on). Kinship, for example, today enjoys a more organic entailment in other areas of research. Whether as a dimension of the relationship between gender and state power (e.g., Borneman 1992; Yanagisako and Delaney, eds., 1995) or as the guiding metaphor of nationalism, in losing its former autonomy it has gained a pervasive sociocultural significance far in excess of what its erstwhile prominence allowed it. Today, as we shall see, it may be sorely in need of reframing; but it remains surprisingly central.

Ethnicity, too, has achieved a new ubiquity. The concept itself has come in for a good deal of deconstruction, but it dies hard. Although anthropologists have contributed massively to its analysis, moreover, they have been especially alive to its political adoption by incipient nationalisms (e.g., J. Jackson 1995). It therefore constitutes an especially clear illustration of the difficulty of analytically separating the anthropological enterprise from its object of study – a difficulty that (as I am arguing here), far from invalidating the discipline, corresponds especially closely to the empirical realities. Indeed, it is not only the case that anthropologists increasingly find themselves repeating knowledge that local actors already possess, in a form that the locals may not find particularly revealing of new insights. That knowledge may also – to the extent that anthropological production is still taken seriously – serve to legitimize emergent identities and practices.

This situation is something of a test case for the strengths and weaknesses of a postmodern perspective. On the one hand, awareness of being in the picture offers a salutary corrective to the usual image of "cultures" as hermetically and unambiguously bounded entities – whether as physically isolated tribal communities or as industrial states severely defined (and often literally fenced in) by national borders. But it also suggests that any attempt to deny the reality of such borders for the actors themselves is indefensible, and may, as Jean Jackson (1995) in particular has noted, undercut their attempts at self-determination in the face of state brutality. It also forces scholars to confront the inevitable problem that today's liberation of one population may bring in its train the extermination or enslavement of others. At the very least, anthropologists can sound warnings about the reality of such slippage.

In conformity with this vision of the interconnectedness of things, the discussion of ethnicity and nationalism percolates through numerous other focal themes. For example, we inspect connections among ritual, bureaucracy, nationalism, and the production of spectacle in religious and nationalist contexts – two domains that themselves exhibit revealing similarities, notably in the relationship between nationalism and myth-making. Here it may be useful to note Sara Dickey's brief but illuminating mention of the national-character studies that relied on media as their principal source of data and that, I would add, themselves shared a long history with nationalistic folklore studies (see Cocchiara 1952; Caro Baroja 1970). Anthropology was once powerfully implicated in the nation-building and related enterprises of which its present-day practitioners are now implicated in the "constructivist" critique – to the distress of many host communities, as Argyrou (1996b), J. Jackson (1995), Thomas, and others have observed. The constructivist position not only questions present-day unities, but does so through the disaggregation of a nominally unified past. In particular, it entails questioning the idea of a single point of departure that we meet in both myths of origin and nationalistic histories, and this may pose deeply serious threats to new entities that have not yet adequately covered their heterogeneous traces (perhaps including anthropology itself?): time is commonly a source of validation – a means of establishing cosmic rights of use, as it were.

Ethnicity and nationalism are thus ubiquitous themes in anthropology: they circumscribe both its intellectual agenda and its potential for meaningful political engagement. They demand of all anthropologists a willingness to consider in good faith the potential consequences of what they write and publish, placing the moral burden of responsibility – a burden that cannot be assuaged by pat ethical prescriptions – squarely on the anthropologists' shoulders. They are, in many senses, the very ground on which anthropology as a discipline must make its case – whether as the object of its study, the basis for historical reflection and reassessment, or the political context for action.

In this project I have therefore, consistently with the theme of anthropology as a systematic critique of notions of common sense, opted at the organizational level to emphasize instead such less "obvious" domains as the senses, modernities, and media; but there is no cause for concern, for the "obvious" themes demonstrate their hardiness by reappearing in new guises within the framework adopted here. Such rearrangements are not merely cosmetic, nor merely accidental: they are intentionally designed to encourage theoretical reassessment as well.

One important area on which this entire project focuses quite deliberately is that of modernity – or, rather, a plethora of modernities. Two themes are central. First, there is the question of whether modernity is radically different or whether, viewed as a plurality in accordance with Don Robotham's formulation (with its attendant rejection of older and now clearly simplistic antinomies pitting subaltern against colonial perspectives), one can view "it" as a distinctive entity at all. This is methodologically important because on it depends how far we treat in the same framework such pairs as state bureaucracy and the symbolic classification of tribal rituals; moiety systems of kinship and competing legal regimes of family law and political ideology (as in pre-1989 Berlin: see Borneman 1992); and scientific rationalities and religious practice. Is Miner's Nacirema spoof merely an elegant joke, or does it prompt serious reflection on the extent to which we can make claims equating modernity with some universal notion of rationality? What does it mean to treat the political elites of modern industrialized societies in terms of kinship and other face-to-face idioms of identity, as Abélès recommends? And why has kinship returned so decisively to center-stage, in studies ranging from nationalism to reproductive technologies and ideologies (Strathern 1989; Ginsburg and Rapp, eds., 1996; Ginsburg 1989; Kahn 2000)? If such studies are grounded on a metaphorical use of the "archaic" term in each pair, so are the modernities that they analyze. The kinship metaphors used in nation-state construction will be especially familiar to most readers of this book.

The second question concerns the plurality of possible "modernities." For modernity is not a universalizing trend. Thus, if its riotous variety allows plenty of play to human agency, we may ask whether there have in fact ever been societies as conformist as those portrayed by the evolutionist and functionalist imaginations. The evidence suggests, not only that such uniformity and boundedness are gross oversimplifications, but also that the persistence of social and cultural diversity in the so-called global village of the new millennium portends an important role for an anthropology newly sensitized to agency and practice. It will be a valuable corrective to social analyses latterly co-opted by the discourses of state and supra-state power.

The theoretical turn to concepts of agency and practice (see Ortner 1984) signaled an important moment in the discipline's self-realization. At the very time when some observers – gleefully or sadly according to their own perspectives – were predicting that the crisis of ethnographic representation and the partially self-inflicted critique of anthropology would destroy its credibility, three important developments led in the opposite direction.

First, many scholars interpreted the criticisms as a challenge to deepen and broaden the purview of ethnography rather than to abandon ship; the result was a significant rise in the publication of theoretically engaged ethnography. Second, many of those who agreed with the criticisms nevertheless felt that they could be built back into the discipline's theoretical framework, thereby permitting greater sensitivity to issues that, in the final analysis, still had to do with the depth and richness of ethnographic description. Third, the rise of a text metaphor for ethnography was found to have severe limits (see, e.g., Asad 1993), yet it may be that some awareness of these was what forced discussion back to the social actors themselves – a development that counteracted the disembodied and over-generalized visions of society and culture generated by both the textualist and the positivistic extremes.

Textualism was also associated with a debilitating over-dependence on language-based models of meaning. Yet language itself provided an escape route: the realization, still too partial, that ordinary language insights – the shift from reference to use – can be applied as much to all other semiotic domains as they can to language. The new anthropological emphasis on visual media and on multisensory analysis underscores the importance of avoiding a referential view of meaning that reduces everything to pure text – the practice of anthropology included.

It is nonetheless important not to throw the baby out with the bathwater: the textual turn in anthropology, especially as pioneered by Clifford Geertz (1973a), did much to force anthropologists' attention on meaning as opposed to an objectified form, even though it did so in ways that were to prove almost as deterministic as what they had displaced. Malcolm Crick's (1976) early critique of literalism, a now neglected but fundamentally important text, can serve as a useful and well-argued introduction to these concerns. And such a critique of literalism entails recognizing that an act (verbal or otherwise) can be profoundly historical, yet in no sense reducible to the enumeration of events that we might therefore expect. History can be danced, felt, smelled, and, yes, spoken; and every act and every sensory experience is a potential carrier of links with the recent and the more distant past.

A Sense of Application

I have suggested that anthropology might provocatively be defined as the comparative study of common sense. This is an important tool to deploy against the insistent rationalism of a wide range of international agencies that seek to impose their particular renditions of common sense on societies that do not endorse those ideas, on problems to which they are ill-suited because of local values and practices, and on people who respond in unexpected ways. To some extent, of course, this is simply a remediable practical issue: it is no use sending food aid to people whose religion will not permit them to touch the gift. But in another sense it shows that a practice-oriented anthropology can and must also be a critique of practicality. In this regard, I would particularly note recent work by Arturo Escobar (1995), James Ferguson (1990), and Akhil Gupta (1998), among many others – work that does not deny the importance of various forms of aid in a world struggling to survive extreme poverty and rapid demographic expansion, but that seeks to illuminate its abuses and misuses. These features sometimes promote great suffering, as Veena Das has noted, in the name of rationality.

To the extent that ideas of the sensible are increasingly presented in global terms, we can now thus also say that anthropology may serve as a discourse of critical resistance to the conceptual and cosmological hegemony of this global common sense. Much of the work discussed in this book illustrates how anthropology can protect a critically important resource: the very possibility of questioning the universal logic of "globalization" and exposing its historically narrow and culturally parochial base by hearing other voices, is preserved through the critical investigations of anthropology. If, for example, economic rationality can be seen as the driving force behind current representations of rationality, local conceptions of economic wisdom make it clear why many of the world's people will not be persuaded. What from the perspective of the dominant discourse looks like irrational traditionalism emerges, on closer inspection, as an alternative logic. The comparison may also coincide with evidence that state global agencies do not necessarily act in accordance with their own stated rationality, an observation that underscores the importance of maintaining a strong sense of the conceptual and social diversity that still exists in the world.

Such concerns are practical as well as academic. The isolation of the "ivory tower" from the "real world" has indeed been a remarkably significant political development, in which anthropologists (among others) have allowed a particular representation of reality to marginalize their perspectives and so to stifle their critical contribution. They can now resist this move by historicizing and contextualizing the conventional wisdoms that have gained political ascendancy in the global arena.

Thus, for example, Arturo Escobar has explicitly embraced a "poststructuralist" position, of the kind that uninformed critics particularly charge with refusing to engage with the "real world." In point of fact, Escobar has advocated active opposition to precisely that lack of engagement – and the critics are unlikely to be happy about that, for it is their logic that comes under fire as a result. For those concerned with the cultural and social impact of "development," as for those who argue that environmentalist programs must be far more sensitive to cultural values in order to stand some chance of success, this is indeed a necessary move for anthropology. Interestingly, we also find a similarly activist perspective argued in areas of anthropology that in the past were usually relegated to the zone of the purely academic (notably kinship) studies, for which John Borneman insists we should seek a transformation that is both intellectually more defensible and politically more just. Even areas once thought to be the domain of pure aesthetics and thus to be socially epiphenomenal and politically insignificant, such as music, become sites of a political engagement. This makes the analytic separation of the intellectual from the political increasingly unconvincing.

All these arguments have to do with the distribution of power, and all in some sense reflect an uneasy awareness that globalization has reduced, or at least threatens to reduce, the arenas of choice for all societies. Anthropology thus becomes a precious resource, not only because of the esoteric knowledge of strangely different cultures that it can offer (although this is not trivial in itself), but also because its characteristic techniques of defamiliarization can be made to question the globalizing assumptions that increasingly dominate political decision-making.

This critical stance required a conscious effort to free anthropology from some of its own historically accumulated associations with nationalism, colonialism, and global economic control. Anthropologists now freely admit that their epistemology is profoundly "western" in origin – this acknowledgment must be the first stage in creating the necessary critical distance – and, as Escobar points out, the anthropological endorsement of some early development efforts in Third World countries underwrote very particular forms of order and rationality. When Escobar insists that the distinction between applied and academic anthropology has become tired and unproductive today, he challenges a part of the currently dominant symbolic order – of which the logic of development constitutes another segment. By turning the spotlight of anthropological analysis on this global cosmology, we can identify its workings more clearly and so stand back in order to make more informed decisions about the extent to which we are prepared to go along with it.

From Common Sense to Multiple Senses: Practising theory in expanded spaces

Anthropologists have good reason to be especially sensitive to the implications of visualism. Here one might see in Don Handelman's argument, discussed in some detail here and in greater detail in his *Models and Mirrors* (1990, 1998), that the modern, bureaucratic state employs spectacles – visual performances – in place of ritual, an illustration of the dramatic rise of the visual in the modern economy of power. Spectacles, in this (admittedly far from exhaustive) sense of the term, are a means by which power, especially bureaucratic power, perpetuates itself. The uncertainty that Handelman sees as an essential component of ritual is erased by the all-seeing eye, dramatically summarized in Foucault's (1975) metaphor of the Benthamite panopticon, of spectacle that reduces the citizen to the role of passive witness. Citizens may believe that they are watching the show; but Big Brother is – or may be – watching them. This is not (as in the evolutionists' view) the story of the rise of disembodied logic, but that of the historically contingent emergence of one embodied capacity – sight – that permitted an exceptionally comprehensive technology of control and thus also a fully self-reproducing teleology of power. That teleology – sometimes called "visualism" – permeates anthropology as much as it does other social sciences (note the phrase "participant observation," commonly used to describe the principal field methodology of the discipline); only by making the senses an empirical topic of anthropological appraisal, as in a chapter of this book, can we hope to regain an appropriate sense of critical distance. There is something disproportionate, as Constance Classen and others have noted, about the degree to which sight has been privileged as the locus of authoritative knowledge. There is also a danger that analyses that appear to treat bureaucracy and spectacle as spaces in which agency can get no purchase may inadvertently do the state's own work of homogenizing society. But it remains useful – indeed, vital – to remind ourselves that spectacular performances may indeed provide authoritarian regimes with the means to enact an especially pernicious form of visualism – as long as we also remember to look behind the scenes and to catch the knowing winks and cynical frowns of the spectators, as well as the nonvisual signals (such as the management of food tastes) that may convey subtler but more durable messages still. And in thus de-centering the visual, we may also gain a more critical purchase on the verbal – another beneficiary of western (or even "global") technologies of information.

The primacy of the visual in social control is a relatively recent (eighteenth century) and localized (western European) phenomenon, although in some regions (such in those south European and Middle Eastern cultures in which the "evil eye" maps patterns of individual jealousy) ocular symbolism has long been associated with malign surveillance. Anthropology, itself implicated in the colonial project, has not escaped that "visualist" bias (Fabian 1983). Indeed, it enhances the marginalization of whatever is classified as "traditional."

Because visual idioms of representation have become quite literally the common sense of the modern, industrial world, they have also become relatively invisible – a revealing metaphor in itself. Resemblance is usually construed as a resemblance of visible form. Anthropologists have not proved immune to this normalization of the visual. It is noteworthy that even though – or, indeed, because – visualism has so fully displaced other sensory preoccupations in the representational practices of anthropology, however, the discipline has only recently produced a correspondingly intense analytical concern with visual media, although the situation is now beginning to change.

The lateness of this development is not as strange as it may at first appear to be. Not only is there the curious paradox of the invisibility of the visual, but the media seemed too "modern" to fit a discipline supposedly concerned with archaic societies. Viewing was something done by active observers rather than by passive ethnographic subjects. Moreover, there was the problem of how to deal with the manifest implications of the visual for recreation and thought, which meant attributing both to exotic peoples. It also raised difficult questions about how a discipline disinclined to probe psychological inner states except as objects of representation (see Needham 1972; Rosen, ed., 1995) could address such phenomena. Yet addressing such issues is crucial to understanding the social role of visual media, as Sara Dickey has emphasized. It is also a sensitive issue because it breaches the defenses of collective intimacy in the cultures we study, our own included.

But the major shift, one that is centrally important for understanding the relevance of anthropology to the contemporary world, may not be the insight it yields into the secret spaces of national cultures, important and interesting though this is. The change that particularly distinguishes anthropological approaches to the visual and other media from those of more textually based disciplines has been a strongly intensified focus on practice and agency. The media are anthropologically important today for two principal reasons, both connected with practice and agency: first, because media often portray the actions of differentiated subjects rather than of members of a supposedly homogeneous "culture"; and second, because the same concern with agency leads to ethnographic research on how social actors relate what they encounter in the media to their own lives and social settings, thereby generating ever more unexpected fields for new forms of agency. It has become clear that the scale on which mass media operate has in no sense resulted in a homogenization of agency; on the contrary, it has provided a means of magnifying differences at many levels.

Here the new ethnographic work on the media, notably including Dickey's and Mankekar's (1993a), particularly comes into its own. This new scholarship, as Dickey notes, engages the roles of viewers as well as producers, and joins a larger and growing literature on material culture, including, but not exclusively devoted to, consumption and material culture (e.g., Miller 1987). In another dimension it should also be compared with the extensive work on self-production and its relationship to the production of artisanal objects (e.g., Kondo 1990). It is clear that mass production has not necessarily meant homogeneity of either interpretation or form, any more than the persistence of a strong sense of cultural identity necessarily entails the suppression of individual forms of agency – western stereotypes of conformist Others notwithstanding.

Examining the ways in which viewers relate to the portrayal of roles also suggests new methods for eliciting the underlying assumptions that people make about those roles. In assuming a homogeneous popular culture, we would be falling into a conceptual trap. Although it was once thought that only "archaic" societies were truly homogeneous and homeostatic, this teleological view of society, culture, and aesthetics is an invention of the modern industrial imagination about exotic "others" – and, as Handelman has indicated, it has, significantly, been most fully actualized in the aesthetic programs of such modern totalitarian ideologies as Nazism.

The myth of the homogeneous Other is deeply entrenched, and it has exercised a durable influence on anthropological theory even in such modernist arenas as the study of visual media. It has also, in recent years, generated strong reactions. Even leaving aside the sheer vastness of the Indian film industry and its complex impact on other Third World regions, the South Asian focus in this work is thus probably no accident. Ethnographers are struggling especially hard to disengage their view of this region from long prevalent social-science constructions of rigid hierarchy and ritualistic conformism. The convergence of media studies and an anthropological interest in agency thus significantly directs attention to newly empowered local voices (and to the ways in which some of them may be disenfranchised as well).

This new individuation works against the older idiom in which the Other has always been represented as homogeneous. That homogenizing process does not always concern only the colonialist view of geographically distant populations, since it may also be used of "peasants" and "the working class" closer to home, but, as a form of representation, it seems universally to serve as both the instrument and the expression of power.

That coincidence of instrumentality and meaning is an additional feature of the current intellectual landscape in anthropology. Sterile debates long pitted idealist against materialist approaches. In these confrontations, the Cartesian sense of a radical separation of the mental from the material was rigidly maintained at least until the rise of a critical Marxist structuralism (see, notably, Godelier 1984, for a major critique). Yet already at that point, in the influence of the heritage of ordinary language philosophy on both sides of the Atlantic (e.g., Ardener 1989; Bauman 1977; Needham 1972), recognition of semiotic effects as material causes – the impact of rhetoric on political action, for example – posed a productive challenge to what was, after all, the expression of a particular conceptual frame within one, admittedly dominant, cultural tradition.

Here the anthropological significance of media becomes especially clear. It is the enormous range and power of the media that turns them into something of a test case for the analysis of modern social formations. The conventional view has long been that they are forces for homogeneity and the loss of cultural autonomy. Indeed, they amplify the symbolic force of political action, serving ever larger and more encompassing forms of authority.

But by that token, as Abélès makes clear, they also magnify the power of rhetoric and symbolism to the point where these can hardly still be considered as mere epiphenomena. The performance of a ritual act on television can be an important piece of "political action." It is a demonstration of what the ordinary language philosophers had already argued in the domain of everyday inter-action: the power of words to effect change, intended or not. For this reason, the power of the media has especially shown up the artificiality of the old distinction between the material and the symbolic. But by insisting on the huge variety of audience responses to the media and on the now dramatically magnified representation of agency as much as of normativity, anthropologists have been able to go still further: they have traced the complex processes, sometimes culminating in surprisingly radical effects at the national and even international levels, whereby extremely localized reactions may come to affect the life of nations.

In this regard, it is especially useful to contrast Handelman's radical separation of ritual from spectacle with Marc Abélès's view of a modernity in which the relationship between the local and the national or supra-national is in constant flux, and in which older "referents" combine with modern "processes" to yield a modern specificity that is nevertheless analysable with the instruments developed in an older anthropology for the study of face-to-face societies exclusively. Abélès, like Benedict Anderson (1983) and Bruce Kapferer (1988), has noted the resemblance between nationalism and religious community. I would add that the Durkheimian model of religion as society worshipping itself (Durkheim 1925 [1915]) is far more apposite to the case of nationalism, as Gellner also recognized (1983: 56), than it ever was to the Australian religions that Durkheim regarded as elemental illustrations of his thesis. With nationalism, we actually know, in many cases, who the Durkheimian gremlins were. Indeed, some of them – like Ziya Gökalp, framer of the secularist constitution of modern Turkey – were his ardent admirers. The French colonial effort in Morocco similarly directly translated Durkheim's teleological reconstruction into a prescription for the government of exotic others (Rabinow 1989). Here again we see the power of a reflexivity that is historically and ethnographically grounded.

We are what we study. This is reflected in anthropological fieldwork – a process akin to problem-solving in social life, the conceptual *débrouillardise* mentioned in the Preface, in which the learning of culture largely proceeds through an "edification by puzzlement" (Fernandez 1986: 172–9). As a reaching for larger, more inclusive explanations of experience at the level of the localized and the particular, it is also and at the same time a questioning of order – and especially of claims that a given order is rooted in eternal truth, whether cosmological or scientific. It is, in a word, the critical appraisal of common sense. It is thus a fundamental source of human understanding, accessible only at moments when the categorical order of things no longer seems secure – when theory does not so much yield to practice as reveal itself as a form of practice in its own right.

Theory as practice: that insight and the intimacy of the observational scale at which it is activated largely distinguish anthropology from its closest neighbors on the map of the social sciences. It is abundantly clear that the vast increase in available topics, scale of perception, and sheer complexity of subject-matter do not seem to be compelling the discipline to an early retirement. On the contrary, it is precisely at such a moment that the more intensive focus of anthropology becomes especially valuable. The amplification of symbolic actions on a global scale gives such actions a resonance that perhaps we can sense only through the intimacy – now defined in a host of new ways – of ethnographic research.

2

Epistemologies

Circumstantial Knowledge

Social and cultural anthropology – the precise name is more of an indication of local intellectual histories than of any substantial difference, despite the fur that flew around the distinction in the 1970s – is above all an empirical discipline. Whether it is also empiricist is a very different issue. The vision represented in this book encompasses the first aspect – the principled groundedness of the discipline and its dependence on ethnographic research and description – but effectively rejects the reductionism implied by the second. It is a mediation between serious commitment to the evidence of pragmatic, on-the-spot research on the one hand, and serious engagement with the criticisms of overweening "ethnographic authority" often leveled against it (notably by Clifford 1988) on the other. Historically, this makes good sense: most of those who have expressed unease with the colonialist and ethnocentric implications of the ethnographer's gaze (e.g., Asad, ed., 1973; Clifford and Marcus 1986) have themselves been accomplished practitioners of the craft – precisely, I would argue, because their sensitivity to those implications led them to import a productively critical sensibility into their fieldwork from the start.

In his classic 1973 essay, "Thick description: toward an interpretive theory of culture," Clifford Geertz declared that the analysis of culture – with which he equated anthropology – was "not an experimental science in search of law but an interpretive one in search of meaning" (Geertz 1973a: 5). This was to deploy one of the polarities that had haunted and still haunts the discipline. To a greater degree, perhaps, than any other, anthropology has straddled the divide between the social sciences and the humanities, and been stretched uneasily between a broadly positivistic explanatory approach to social and cultural phenomena, and an empathetic exploration of communication and significance. It may be hard to imagine a synthesis of "experimental" and "interpretive" science, but neither these terms nor the "laws" and "meanings" they sought respectively to reveal appear in the same way today. Inevitably, then, anthropology must occupy a middle ground that gives the lie to those who would claim that empirical scholarship and reflexive critique are mutually incompatible.

It occupies a middle ground in yet another sense, and one that must be grasped in any approach to anthropological epistemologies. Clearly our ideas are often influenced by the people we study – even, perhaps, to the point where one could point to a direct correlation, in any given phase of the discipline's history, between the areas that were especially prominent in ethnographic description and the current theoretical predilections of anthropologists. Indeed, as I have already noted, many ostensibly central theoretical issues are not really global anthropological issues at all, but rather are problems that arise from the encounter between particular strands of the discipline and particular societies; the resulting translation problems introduce a measure of circularity that can be quite surprising – as, for example, when Latin America is reduced to a "Mediterranean" region because of the prevalence there of something glossed as an "honor" code thought to be typically Mediterranean. Anthropological texts are formed, not by a pure encounter between a theoretical language and an unmediated experience of local fieldwork, but through regional traditions of anthropological scholarship. In some cases these have long histories originating in travel writing or colonial scholarship; in others the imprint of particular, eminent professional theorists can be lasting. The stamp of India and Louis Dumont (1970) on the theory of hierarchy is a good example, as are the lineage debate in British studies of Africa, honor and shame in the Mediterranean, evolutionism in Polynesia, peasants in Latin America, and so on. There is more: absence sometimes speak louder than presences. Václav Hubinger, writing from the viewpoint of a country where anthropological models have sometimes appeared as source of legitimation for the new capitalist domination in east and central Europe, notes that anthropology was born of the project of modernity itself (much as, one might add, was the concept of "tradition"), and traces to that hegemony the exclusion of such formerly Eastern Bloc countries from the dominant idioms in "European" anthropology today.

Thus, while "anthropological epistemologies" are of two sorts – those of anthropology as a profession and academic field and those of the people anthropologists study – the discipline has increasingly had to confront the difficulty, indeed the absurdity, of separating them from each other altogether. To assume that anthropological epistemology belongs only to anthropologists is both arrogant and empirically wrong. But, as we shall see, to recognize the contributions that informants make to our theoretical formulations is to engage in a discussion that is not only epistemological but also ethical – and that resists prescriptive solutions, despite many attempts to produce them.

Anthropology, as this introductory remark should make clear, is very much a practice of theory, to invert Bourdieu's (1977) famous phrase. It must balance the advantages of both a pragmatic self-distancing and an ethical engagement that is also grounded in direct field experience. Consistently with this perspective of principled ambivalence, anthropologists have resisted disembedding the philosophy of the discipline from theoretical reappraisals and from ethnography: few monographs are devoid of reflection upon the making of anthropological knowledge, and there are fewer theoretical treatises on the subject that are devoid of primary ethnography.

This chapter is consistent with the bias of the discipline toward its own practical grounding, and sets the tone for the more topical chapters that follow. It reflects, both historically and philosophically, the discipline's basis in fieldwork. Fieldwork and its contexts have changed and continue to change, and the pragmatic character of anthropology ensures that its theoretical orientations constantly reflect that condition of flux. The very intimacy that the ethnographic encounter requires is of a different order in the European Space Agency of the 1990s than was that enjoyed by Malinowski with his Trobriand informants in the second decade of the twentieth century.

This is not to presume that anthropology is no more than ethnography; one of the discipline's strengths in recent decades has been its capacity to incorporate historical research and to extend itself to commentary upon literature and art. But anthropologists tend to work in relation to the local encounter of fieldwork even when they are doing something different, as they write ethnographically about history (e.g., Dirks 1992; Cohn 1996) and literature (e.g., A. Cohen 1994; Herzfeld 1997b; Rapport 1994; Handler and Segal 1990). The very idea of separating ethnography from anthropology is to deprive it of its distinctive method, removing the source of its sole effective answer to the common charge that its studies are not representative of larger entities: namely, that what it loses in broad statistical replicability it gains in the sheer intensity of the ethnographic encounter – as intimacy, as privileged access, as listening to voices silenced on the outside by those who wield greater power. Against the positivist view that only huge samples and the logic of western scientific rationality can provide solutions, anthropologists thus pit the prolonged intensity of field exposure (a statistical measure in its own right) and an analytical stance that is not solipsistically grounded in its own cultural milieu (or that is grounded in its own object of study but recognizes that circumstance). The resulting perspective draws its inspiration from unfamiliar ways of construing the social, natural, and material world.

For these reasons, too, anthropologists are often loath to give up their traditional concerns with marginal populations. By the same token, however, anthropology's capacity to treat in precisely the same intimate terms those centrally occupying the seats of power – as Abélès (1989, 1990, 1991, 1992) so effectively does when he describes French political life or the European Parliament, for example, or (in a very different vein) as Marcus (1992) does for the elite families of Galveston, Texas – makes the charge of obsession with the marginal and the irrelevant not only untenable but also suspiciously self-interested. For it is often precisely those who exercise power who use the discourse of marginalization as an integral part of their efforts to maintain that power, and anthropology has often been the source of hostile attention for precisely that reason.

The Epistemology of Inquiry

David Scott has suggested that the historicizing of anthropology requires an approach that raises questions of relevance. Given our concerns with marginalization and trivialization here, we must indeed ask: who benefits from these discourses? What does the response to anthropology reflect? If we conclude that the dismissal of anthropological concerns as marginal reflects a political stance, we have not only learned something (assuming we did not already know it), we have located a useful heuristic: a source of pointers to questions about who adopts that stance, why, and with what results.

While Scott is primarily interested in showing how these questions can help us refocus our understanding of the significance of colonialism for the present situation in former colonies, I would argue that the principle can usefully be expanded to the entire gamut of questions that anthropologists ask – and that others ask of them. Scott begins with R. G. Collingwood's *An Autobiography* (1939), in which the philosopher outlined what he called a logic of "question and answer." This logic, Collingwood argued, merely restated a classical principle, namely: "the principle that a body of knowledge consists not of 'propositions,' 'statements,' 'judgments,' or whatever name logicians use in order to designate assertive acts of thought (or what in those acts is asserted: for 'knowledge' means both the activity of knowing and what is known), but of these together with the questions they are meant to answer; and that a logic in which the answers are attended to and the questions neglected is a false logic" (Collingwood 1939: 30–1). On this view, says Scott, "to understand any proposition it is first necessary to identify the question to which the proposition may be regarded as an answer." And he adds: "This is an important principle for any practice of historical or philosophical understanding. Contrary to the rationalist view (as prevalent among contemporary anti-essentialist postmodernists as among the essentialists they attack) you cannot simply read off the error of a proposition without the prior labour of reconstructing the question to which it aims to respond. This is because propositions are never answers to self-evident or 'perennial' questions (for Collingwood there are no such things) and therefore you cannot assume in advance that you know the question in relation to which the text constitutes itself as an answer." Scott suggests that this principle is of prime importance to a historically sensitive anthropology. But he also extends it to what he calls "a strategic practice of criticism," which he defines as "a practice of criticism concerned with determining at any conjuncture what conceptual moves among the many available options will have the most purchase or bite." In other words, we need to know, not only what use the answer will be to someone else, but what use it will be to us. Are the questions we ask worth having answers to?

Taking Positions

This is a pragmatic view indeed. Its correlate in terms of methodology is to ask what anthropologists actually do. To that question, Geertz's essay furnished a highly influential answer – "they write" – and it was couched in appropriately pragmatic terms: he focused, not upon a formal definition of the discipline or its theories, but upon what its practitioners did, namely ethnography.

I suggest that this is an apt metonym of what anthropologists generally do, which is to focus on the uses to which people put the elements of their cultures, rather than on the objectified listing of those elements themselves. As with language, so with all aspects of culture: the elements gain meaning from their social deployment, not in the curio cabinet or the dictionary. The parallel with Scott's argument about the history of colonialism is that the elements of that history gain their meaning from the salience they have for our present-day world.

For Geertz, this stance required a nuanced account of people doing things with cultural forms – what he famously called "thick description," summarized by Nicholas Thomas as "the interpretive inscription of social discourse, primarily in its interpersonal and local rather than its institutional and global expressions." While it perhaps lacked descriptive precision, the idea of thick description proved popular and enduring. It offered an appealing portrait of an analytical style, with a bias toward localized knowledge that remains attractive today, for many anthropologists, including those who would not count themselves among Geertz's followers (although there is now an increasing preoccupation with the "local knowledge" of larger phenomena, such as nations and transnational forms). Yet, as a characterization of ethnography, it seems now to stop rather short. Ethnography is not just thick description (which as Geertz acknowledged also characterizes the novel); it refers both to fieldwork and to writing, to a practice and a genre, and both have ramifications for anthropological epistemology. It has particular resonance for the several later chapters in this book in which the idea of local understandings – "indigenous theories" – is advanced as both a necessary object of intellectual engagement and a problematic concept in itself.

The intimacy of the ethnographic encounter generally prompted ethnographers to adopt an affirmative attitude toward the people studied, and even to write accounts of their culture that were to some degree complicit in dominant local understandings. This largely arose from the idea that the anthropologist should "adopt the native point of view." This has been a powerful tenet since Malinowski, and Boas had even argued that folk narrative was a people's own ethnography – a view that has resurfaced today in the explicit genre of "auto-ethnography," which allows a measure of self-examination to the anthropologist who is also willing to listen to local theorizings of society and culture and to acknowledge them as such. It has also, more unusually, emerged in a sophisticated juxtaposition of local speech forms with anthropological theory-talk in a provocative study of the Appalachian poor by Kathleen Stewart (1996). Here the anthropologist playfully juxtaposes her own "theory-speak" with the local way of talking about events and experiences, not in order to mock either, but, to the contrary, as a way of empirically disclosing the substantial intellectual grounds shared by those who study human society professionally and those who study it because that is the only way to make sense of their very conditions of life.

Thomas, however, argues that this is a rather facile view of the relationship between anthropologists and their informants – at least in the context of cultures that are very far removed historically and linguistically from the anthropologists' own "native" experiences. (I add that proviso, because the ironic mastery of Stewart's study shows that it is in fact possible to bring local commentary to bear on the limitations of professional discourse, and to find in it also a critique of locally oppressive conditions.) Yet Thomas sounds a warning on two fronts. First, sad though this may be, it may not be a matter of much interest to local informants whether their ideas are of conceptual help to anthropologists (or other social scientists, for that matter). (I would certainly concede that my attempt to bring local concepts of meaning and Jakobsonian poetics into productive juxtaposition (Herzfeld 1985) is far more useful – if it is useful – to my professional colleagues than it is to the villagers whose ideas we are trying to understand by such comparativist means.) And second, to the extent that the anthropologists' ideas do in fact interest local people, the anthropologists may find themselves caught up, willy-nilly, in recastings of those ideas that make them acutely uncomfortable. Let us pursue each of these points in turn.

Certain forms of methodological relativism are indispensable, and no serious inquiry is possible without a certain degree of common ground and respect for local understandings. But there are profound tensions between the aspiration to grasp and share an indigenous "point of view" and the incorporation of that perspective into an analytical or theoretical discourse defined by Euro-American social science. Anthropologists are engaged in a professional activity, one that certainly gives them specific access denied to most other people who might be interested in their ideas. Notable among these is the sheer range available for comparative study: whereas villagers may be interested in comparing their own culture with that of specific others (people from the next village, the colonizers, the urban elite, the culture in which they have worked as migrant laborers), relatively few people are interested in the extraordinary tension between ethnographic detail and the search for global insights into the human condition – they may be interested in both, but they do not ordinarily connect them unless they are anthropologists themselves. The acknowledgment of informants as anthropologists (e.g., Crick 1976), while ethically attractive and respectful, must take account of this difference.

There is also a misleading simplification in the thought that the varied perspectives of local actors could be easily conflated in a representative point of view. The play of different interests was often obscured by such optimistic assessments of the ethnographer's task. Who are the experts who speak for the whole society? Who authorizes them? It is only relatively recently that anthropologists have begun to consider the epistemological problems of confronting this often discordant chorus.

If the tension between intrusive social science and indigenous concepts has long been implicit, moreover, it can only have been accentuated over recent decades, and this leads us to Thomas's second point. Anthropologists formerly presumed that the peoples they studied – whether they were European peasants or Pacific islanders – would not be among the readers of their published ethnographies. Professional scholarship is no longer contained in this way (see Brettell ed. 1993), but tends to reach diverse audiences, and be used by them. Not only anthropologists, but also a literate fraction of the people studied, will read one's work. It will also, in all likelihood, reach some in the government of the nation researched; indeed it is a condition of many research permits that publications are supplied to various institutions and departments, perhaps only to be filed away, but sometimes to receive surprising attention. In anthropologists' home countries, those in foreign affairs and official multiculturalism routinely use anthropological knowledge. Insofar as anthropological writing is drawn into these fields, and even into "area studies" such as Asian or Middle Eastern studies, it will be used in a way at odds with its anthropological reading, more for what it adds to knowledge of a place than for reflection upon a theory or an issue. Under these circumstances, the question of how, and to what effect, a particular ethnographic account colludes with or subverts local perceptions is not an abstract epistemological issue, but something subject to open contention.

The issue of the ethnographer's stance has become more acute in the wake of an overall politicization of social scientific and cultural knowledge. Thomas suggests that this trend has unproductively exaggerated the political significance of scholarly work, but that it nevertheless points to a specifically epistemological issue that was not important to Geertz, at least in 1973. Even at that date, anthropology had been accused of endorsing and tacitly or actively supporting colonialism, and Marxist analyses were gathering a following. Although that particular perspective was much diluted by the late 1970s, there was a shift toward a sense that social knowledge was inevitably political, and indeed ought to be political critique.

The understanding of knowledge as a project connected with, and justified by, efforts to reform or transform society was bolstered by the growth of feminist anthropology with its overt commitments, no doubt a desirable reaction against the bald assertion that social science could and should be value-free. Interestingly enough, however, some of the feminist criticism was directed at the very developments in anthropology that so optimistically claimed it as an effective form of cultural critique (e.g., Mascia-Lees, Sharpe, and Cohen, 1987–8). It has taken a long time for the larger lesson to sink in – the lessons of what Thomas calls "the megalomanic pretensions of politicized scholarship and theory." As he remarks: "The shifting economics of knowledge mean that no scholar today can be a Tom Paine, or is even likely to be a Margaret Mead, even if anthropological works are often appropriated locally in significant and unexpected ways. We need to define an intermediate point of view, which does not attempt to recover the pretensions of value-free neutrality, but acknowledges that research and writing take place in domains, that may have important connections for cultural policy, but are generally at some remove from the most consequential theatres of political action and transformation." And he calls for "a more localized sense of the place of the anthropologist as a commentator and critic" – a productive reversal of the Enlightenment convention that treated the anthropologist as possessed of universal vision while it was the "natives" who were "local."

This revised view of anthropology's role in the world entering a new millennium is a realistic assessment, both politically and epistemologically, and it calls for a more pragmatic engagement with the structures of power than anthropology has hitherto generally favored. It is no good bemoaning the misuse of the culture concept by nonanthropologists, for example; we must be able to show how and why its misuse is dangerous. We must be able to recognize academic discourse that essentializes "cultures" and even "civilizations" (Huntington 1996) as insidious, not because it has nothing to do with reality as people experience it, but because it takes a culturally parochial "common sense" – one could argue that western parochialism is especially pernicious because it is so well defended – and turns it into a universal truth justifying, in effect, an international structure of political and cultural apartheid. Scholars are just as likely as other people to operate on the basis of long-cherished "folk theories," and when they advise powerful security and economic interests their inability to realize how effectively they are globalizing their own "local" forms of prejudice and unreason is extraordinarily dangerous.

Huntington, for example, does use anthropological ideas about culture – but these are ideas that were current before 1960, when anthropology was itself much more critically engaged with Cold War projects, and when its customary use of terms like culture more closely resembled those of nationalistic ideologies. Cultures were like things with minds – mutually incompatible minds, guiding intractable things. This is the vision of culture that is so often reproduced today in the media, following popularizing academics who rely heavily on those anthropological discards. Those who decry "Balkan nationalism," "religious fundamentalism," and the like fail to realize the extraordinary resemblance of their own cultural fundamentalism with what they reject in exotic "others."

But what are anthropologists to do about this strange and threatening misuse of such a key concept? As Ulf Hannerz realistically points out: "However much we as anthropologists may feel that culture is really our concept, it seems doubtful that the world would now pay much attention if we abandoned it in professional discourse." (I would also add that it would be equally foolish to abandon anthropology as a discipline simply because it has a colonialist and racist past: it is precisely because anthropologists have recognized these flaws and have addressed them constructively that a rejuvenated anthropology – ever conscious of the dangers of misusing the concepts of culture and society – can serve as a useful bulwark against academically sanitized intolerance.)

There is also some urgency about this project, but there are also those who will be disappointed to see their newly raised hopes – that anthropology would salvage their "own" cultures – so firmly dashed. Nowhere, perhaps, is this more true than in what Václav Hubinger calls "post-totalitarian" states. In the words of one Slovak enthusiast: "Anthropology should understand, first of all, what is going on because so far what we have are only mythological considerations . . . there is no verifiable and methodologically sound analysis . . . It is in this sense that anthropology is the best equipped. It has the capacity to approach even a beer-drinker . . . to penetrate into his thought structure; it is able to find out why he does not believe that something can change . . ." (Chorváthová 1991: 85). Perhaps the best way to avoid disappointing such eager hopes – grounded, apparently, in a scientistic mirage – is to emphasize the limitations of anthropology up front, and to draw attention to the fact that these limitations are themselves highly instructive – again an exercise in cultural reflexivity.

Thomas's objections to the self-importance that anthropology sometimes displays, sometimes to the detriment of its actual importance in the larger scheme of things, are mostly directed at the prescriptive moralizing that turned many readers of such works as *Anthropology as Cultural Critique* (Marcus and Fischer 1986) against the very thoughtful replay in that work of the idea that the distinctiveness of another culture questions received ideas at home – that the foreign relativizes the familiar. The difficulty is that the lines between "their" cultures and "ours" are no longer clearly drawn, if indeed they ever were. Marshall Sahlins (1993: 19) has even suggested that we are witnessing a large-scale process of structural transformation: the formation of a World System of cultures, a Culture of cultures, as people everywhere, from the Amazonian rain forest to the islands of Melanesia, in intensifying contact with the outside world, elaborate self-consciously on the contrastive features of their own cultures. But this, if it is true, means that people's cultural aspirations have now become homogenized in the larger sense that everyone, everywhere, is engaged in a conceptual framework that is one of the major consequences of the historically dominant global role played by a relative handful of European powers at the height of the Romantic era – the era that "discovered" nationalism as we know it today – even though the uses to which this framework are put do vary from place to place.

This sharing of global experience has consequences. Indeed, it could now be said that any method that we find inappropriate to the study of our own social and cultural context is unlikely to satisfy at a broader, comparative level – and the old idea that anthropology must be comparative is not easy to dismiss. Indeed, the idea of a "cultural critique" logically resuscitates it.

But there are other problems with comparativism. Perhaps the most obvious is the importation of terms used in one culture to describe features elsewhere. Whether these are native terms like *mana* or *tapu* (taboo) (Crick 1976), inefficient glosses based on outmoded concepts from the anthropologist's own culture (such as "honor and shame": see Herzfeld 1987), or imaginatively decriptive neologisms such as "cargo cult," such attempts at creating cross-cultural comparisons may end up merely exoticizing – relativizing, that is, in the most condescending sense. Here is one useful illustration of the dilemma. Against the notion that there has been a distinctive moment that we can characterize as uniquely modern, we can certainly set the persistence of certain schemata that are not confined to the so-called primitive societies in which they were originally identified by anthropologists. Symbolism itself is such a property. Václav Hubinger, for example, productively invokes the idea of the "cargo cult" (originally identified in Melanesia) to explain the almost messianic appeal of capitalism to the countries of the collapsing Soviet bloc. Lamont Lindstrom, however, warns us that generalizing representations of the imitation of the West by Melanesian cultists to all the world's peoples curiously reproduces and reinforces a consumerist romance tale (Lindstrom 1995: 56–7). Yet it is surely useful to recall that symbolism is as much a feature of western industrial modernity as it is of the societies traditionally studied by anthropologists. Hubinger and Lindstrom converge in implicitly acknowledging that the discrimination between European and other societies (and then between West and East Europe) is part of a global taxonomy that serves distinct political and economic interests. Anthropologists may observe the effects of that taxonomy in the course of their fieldwork among peoples classified as "other," who often actively resist – and certainly resent – its demeaning implications. The difficulty (and this seems to be the major lesson to be learned from Lindstrom's critique) is that our own fables of global commonality can too easily seem to play into the very ideologies and hierarchies that we think we are attacking; yet our well-intended rejection of radical difference remains a powerful antidote to bigotry and domination.

The idea that the exotic relativizes the familiar is thus apt enough as a gloss on the critical logic of major recent works such as Geertz's *Negara* (1980) and Strathern's *The Gender of the Gift* (1988), in both of which the elucidation (or defamiliarization) of a domestic common sense is one explicit purpose of the analysis, or on my own attempt to treat anthropology itself as an object to be compared directly with nationalisms that share its genesis as an expression of the ideological rupture between the colonizers and the colonized (Herzfeld 1987). But such comparisons must also be able to prepare us for what Thomas calls "an unavoidable division in the ethnographer's voice." As he notes: "Because the people studied have ceased merely to be scholarly objects, and become partially incorporated within an expanded field of discussion, the anthropologist's text may be increasingly drawn in two directions, on the one hand toward a global (in fact typically a Euro-American) professional discussion, that privileges the discipline's questions, and the elevated register of 'theory', and on the other toward audiences within the nation if not the locality studied." And Thomas suggests that local people may not share the scholar's global interests in theorizing: "Scholarship may be geographically dispersed, but cannot count as universal in relation to local particulars."

Yet the divided locations of anthropological writing do have profound implications. The exoticism that structures much classic anthropological argument loses salience if the argument itself has "exotic" circulation. And the question of the presence of the "native point of view" in a particular text ceases to be a literary flourish on the part of a Malinowski, an "I was there" gesture, but becomes an assertion that may be readily tested by "native" readers who see their point of view misrepresented or appropriated. The idea that anthropology produces a "cultural critique" of relations and mores "at home" leaves us unprepared for the question of its commentary on the relations and mores actually studied. Does the discipline simply attempt to represent these, in some sense on "their own terms"? Or are they equally to be subjected to the politically deliberate scrutiny of western social science? The rhetorical strategy, moreover, too often leaves the home-point of our society unanalyzed; it is no more than a stereotypic "West." (Recent studies of "occidentalism" [Carrier, ed., 1995] serve as something of a corrective here.) As anthropological discourse circulates to a greater extent that hitherto among the communities classically studied, and turns its vision upon communities at home, the paradigm of an us-them juxtaposition seems increasingly inappropriate.

It is, in fact, a version of that conceptual habit – variously known as reification, essentialism, or objectification – against which the same moralizing rhetoric has often been directed. To be able to say that a particular ideology was essentialist provided a convenient moral cover; yet this was as essentializing as anything it opposed. As Vassos Argyrou (1996b) and Jean Jackson (1995) have pointed out, there are ethical limitations to this stance, which was in some sense born of an older tradition within anthropology of attempting to formulate an ethical posture for the discipline as a whole. That tradition arose from the application of a simplistic cultural relativism, which has now been seriously embarrassed by challenges to Western concepts of human rights. As a result, we can no longer feel sure that our moral indignation at the repressive implications of, for example, some nationalistic ideology will not in turn encourage a new repression.

Relativism Relativized

Relativism is itself an important issue. Because anthropologists championed it for so long, they have perhaps been unduly reluctant to recognize its limitations. It is, after all, a very comfortable – and comforting – doctrine: we should respect all cultures as equally moral, and therefore all systemic practices as equally valid. Yet obviously this will not do.

In practice, the principled recognition of local values does not commit us to extreme relativism, a position in which respect for all cultures is reduced to an absurd caricature: it becomes a socially impossible and logically self-contradictory argument in which all moral and empirical judgment is suspended. For how then does one deal with cultural values like ethnocentrism? How is one to confront genocide? Clearly, cultural relativism, if it is to have any meaning at all, must be resituated in a pragmatic vision. Expressed as a general ethical Diktat rather than as a socially responsible position, cultural relativism ends up defeating the purposes for which it was originally, and with the best of intentions, formulated as an epistemological creed (see also Fabian 1983). As liberal nationalists have found to their conceptual cost (Rabinowitz 1996), all social ideologies are situated in social contexts, and these contexts inevitably – if sometimes only gradually – compel acknowledgment of enormous amounts of ambiguity and contradiction in the implementation of such values.

The rethinking of relativism requires a specifically historical reconsideration of its role. And it is the specifically historical accessibility of the paths toward the present configuration of power that makes a critical "purchase," as David Scott calls it, feasible as well as desirable. By the same token, it is the demonstrable effects of documented processes of environmental and social intervention that make it absurd – Kay Milton has been especially eloquent on this – to regard all causal explanations as equally satisfactory or all outcomes as equally beneficial; but we must always ask whom they harm or benefit, thereby situating them in a particular social environment. The common reluctance of anthropologists to get involved is an abdication of responsibility, easier to sustain when we rest on a universalist form of relativism. Against this catatonic condition, a reminder that we inhabit a socially and historically specific moment, a different moment, is the best antidote.

Here, I suggest, the issue of accountability is crucial. We simply cannot predict what will be the effects of our interventions, and moral prescription is a poor substitute for accepting that responsibility. We are engaged with our informants in the work that we do; trying to devise a pat formula that will relieve us of the consequences of that cooperation is simply dishonest. But at the same time, as Thomas suggests, perhaps we should stop thinking that our actions are so consequential: it is time to get matters into proportion, and this we can only do by both downplaying the importance of our own roles and facing the engagement of our informants in the creation as well as the reception of our ethnographic accounts.

There is a certain irony in this. The issue of accountability is a very old one in anthropology: it was, for example, central to Evans-Pritchard's early work (1937). But then it concerned how "they" constructed blame and responsibility. A truly reflexive anthropology will address the same issue among practitioners of the discipline, and in equally ethnographic terms. That would invite engagement and might even increase the consequentiality of what anthropologists do – although always, as Thomas insists, in a particularistic, locally relevant sense, rather than as a global conscience.

Constituting Cultures

This is especially applicable to a line of research that flourished during the 1980s and early 1990s: the invention of tradition and identity. A global trend of signal importance has been the elaboration of explicit constructions of local custom and identity. Although related to earlier ideas of local folklore, national distinctiveness, ethnicity, and the like, and thus not wholly unprecedented as a cultural phenomenon, the objectification of culture at national, regional, and local levels has become singularly powerful over the last twenty years. Everywhere from the margins of Britain and eastern Europe to Oceania and the Amazon, peoples have become conspicuously oriented toward the rhetorical elaboration of their identity, often toward cultural affirmation, autonomy, or separatism. No doubt, these projects of identity are more heterogeneous than they appear, but the vocabulary employed is often that of a popularized anthropology: though all peoples' cultures are different, they seem to be becoming the same to the extent that they are concerned to affirm their different cultures.

Epistemologically, the question is an extremely salient one for the anthropological analyst, who confronts what in some cases turn out to be recast ethnological constructs. As Richard Handler (1985) has argued, there is indeed a historical similarity between the anthropological concept of "culture" and the self-constituted national identities first thrown into sharp relief by the Romantic ideology of the nineteenth century. As in my own comparison of anthropology with the Greek nation-state as two products of that same ideology of European distinctiveness, so in Handler's discussion we see what Thomas recognizes as an increasingly urgent concern: what is the proper response to the use of "our" concepts by the essentializers and reifiers of what we had presumed to think were "our" concepts? of what, in Thomas's terms, "we presume to call a 'folk' version of an anthropological concept – or rather, the anthropological concept, of culture." Ethnographic research has often been wittingly or unwittingly complicit in the codification of reified local "cultures" of this kind. Old ethnographies are frequently mined for customs by culture-makers; publications may be upheld as authorized versions of particular cultures. More subtly, the process of ethnographic inquiry frequently brings a new level of explication to ideas and behaviors.

Indeed, ethnography can appear as a kind of repetition or transcription, not only of what informants already know, but of the form in which they know it: "I arrived among the Kwaio announcing my intention to record their customs . . . Since [the political movement] Maasina Rule (1946–53), they had themselves, in interminable meetings with millenarian overtones, sought . . . to codify their customary law . . . the political goal . . . was to create the equivalent of colonial legal statutes . . . As a professional chronicler of "custom" . . . I could be enlisted in their cause both to write kastom and secure its legitimation. As long as I collected genealogies, recorded stories of ancestors, explored the structures of kinship, feasting, and exchange, and recorded ancestrally policed taboos . . . my work and the expectations of traditionalist (male) leaders meshed closely . . . Indeed, their politically motivated commitment to (the impossible task of) codifying customary law and my theoretically motivated commitment to (the impossible task of) writing a "cultural grammar" in the manner of Goodenough, Conklin and Frake doubtless, in retrospect, entailed a good deal of mutual co-optation" (Keesing 1985: 28–9). In this case, there is indeed what Thomas calls "a deep collusion between the anthropological account and the 'native point of view'." But in response to these codifications and affirmations, anthropologists like Roger Keesing shifted their ground, to engage the construction of culture itself, as an analytical object (Keesing 1989). If this was for a time a fertile step – there was, at least, a proliferation of studies of cultural inventions and codifications – it also temporarily deflected anthropology from a sympathetic understanding of the aspirations of the people studied. Anthropologists tended to identify their perspectives with people against governments – consider the title of Bruce Kapferer's uncompromisingly critical *Legends of People, Myths of State* (1988), a powerful comparative demonstration for Sri Lanka and Australia of how ostensibly benign ideologies can be bureaucratized into machines for the production of systematic violence and hatred. But one consequence of this development, a consequence that Kapferer's study partially anticipates, is that anthropologists sometimes find themselves ill-equipped to deal with the transformation of societies they once knew affectionately as colonial victims into states that, in the name of "national aspirations" learned too well under former oppressors, now turn violence against others within.

For Thomas, the powerful notion that another culture ought to be presented on its own terms, in some undefined sense, is morally rather than intellectually compelling. It is a consequence of the Maussian logic through which ethnographers understand the profound indebtedness incurred toward one's hosts in the field. However those people themselves understand the relationship, our sense is that there is no way their support and their patience can be reciprocated, yet we nevertheless feel the need to attempt to do so through the register of writing: our writings are sometimes morally framed as efforts to validate or help those others, yet surely more typically help us ourselves instead (cf. Fabian 1991: 264). The anthropological project will thus generally be at least Janus-faced, toward "home" and its intellectual traditions and disciplinary questions, as well as toward the presumed second home, into which one has generally invited oneself.

And one has invited oneself there as the representative of a tradition of respecting the "native point of view" – a tradition that has also allegedly given local people some tools for expressing that point of view transnationally. When, therefore, an anthropologist expresses discomfort with what has now been absorbed – "the culture" – as too essentialist, the resulting sense is often one of betrayal. Where, now, is the respect for local culture to which the visitors made such resounding claims? In these conditions, and given the common historical genesis of anthropology and nationalism, it is difficult to see how the anthropologists could avoid being accused of bad faith.

As a result, work in the construction-of-culture genre is being vigorously criticized by local intellectuals, in effect for failing to collude with the "native point of view", for insisting on, and perhaps too zealously overstating, the point that cultures are remade in and for the present. The arguments of Keesing and others have been contested by a Hawaiian scholar (Trask 1991); while F. Allan Hanson's account (1989) of the "making of Maori culture" – widely reported and excerpted in American and New Zealand newspapers – was angrily rejected by Maori scholars and Maori activists (see discussion in N. Thomas 1997). A sympathetic attitude toward indigenous reaffirmations might acknowledge that these are themselves efforts of cultural interpretation and reinterpretation, perhaps not radically unlike the anthropological project in its earlier days; and it is certainly true in historical terms that some of the materials for this kind of indigenous "cultural fundamentalism" came from anthropology itself.

Visualism

A key dimension of ethnography has been the idea of "participant observation." This concept has been absolutely central to virtually all discussions of fieldwork.

It represents the translation into field practice of a bias that has its roots in the history of "Western culture" – itself a problematic generalization, by all means, but one that at least has the virtue of having been largely self-constituted. As the balance of power shifts so that the ethnographer no longer appears in the field as the representative of a powerful colonizing force, individual habits of observation may come to seem more like unwarranted hubris than as the logical means of acquaintance with an unknown society.

For anthropology this is a heady moment – full of dangers, but also of opportunities. Robotham remarks: "From world systems theory, to interpretive anthropology, to deconstruction, reflexivity and constructivism, to 'dialogic' and 'polyphonic' writing, to orality and visuality, to the study of consumption as 'the vanguard of history,' through the 'logic of things which just happen,' back to plain homespun positivism through all the varieties of postmodernism, anthropology is experimenting with a bewildering variety of genres" (Moore 1994; Miller, ed., 1995; Drummond 1996; D'Andrade and Fischer, eds., 1996). So diverse are the studies which now fall under the rubric of anthropology that one might almost sympathize with the view that in this postcolonial period the development of anthropology has culminated in "a process which leads towards its effective dissolution today" (Giddens 1984: 97). But to accede to that perspective would mean surrendering a hard-won sense of critical engagement: it is precisely the tensions that make anthropology vibrantly resistant to easy closure.

Direct recognition of the epistemological problems brought into focus by these global processes offers a more productive path. Thus, for example, Johannes Fabian's critique of the anthropological failure of engagement with local cultures rests heavily on the charge that "visualism" – the reduction of all experience to the representational means available to only one sensory medium, that of sight – has created a strong sense of inequality, of us studying them, that objectifies "natives" as "specimens" rather than as colleagues in a negotiation of potentially shared understandings. This, obviously, does not mean that "we" should stop looking at "them," but that we should use our understanding of how this came to be viewed as a simple, commonsensical operation in order to trace its limitations – a tactic that is empirical in a fundamental sense, being grounded in a critical appraisal of what actually happens in the field and where that approach originated. In tracing the current technology of graphs and charts to its Renaissance beginnings, Fabian suggests that a serious commitment to a noncolonial anthropology – an anthropology that is seriously postcolonial – must tackle this historical burden.

In Europe, sight came to distance itself significantly from the other senses in terms of cultural importance only in the eighteenth and nineteenth centuries, when vision became associated with the burgeoning field of science. The enquiring and penetrating gaze of the scientist became the metaphor for the acquisition of knowledge at this time (Foucault 1975; Le Breton 1990). Evolutionary theories propounded by prominent figures such as Charles Darwin and later Sigmund Freud supported the elevation of sight by decreeing vision to be the sense of civilization. The "lower," "animal" senses of smell, touch and taste, by contrast supposedly lost importance as "man" climbed up the evolutionary ladder. In the late nineteenth and twentieth centuries, the role of sight in western society was further enlarged by the development of such highly influential visual technologies as photography and cinema (Jay 1993; Classen, Howes and Synnott 1994: 88–92).

As a result of this western emphasis on vision, the description and interpretation of a society's visual culture (such as may be seen in artefacts or styles of dress) is often as far as anthropologists will go in search of "sensory" meaning. As we shall see in the chapter on the senses, this has historically had the effect of relegating cultures in which the visual is given less prominence to an inferior role. Some anthropologists – basically those who are committed to an "anthropology of the senses" – now argue that we must try to understand the values of the various senses within the context of the culture under study and not within the context of the sensory model of the anthropologist's own culture. The very idea of a "native's point of view" is visualist in form, and suggests that the adoption of a broader range of understandings might at least reduce the obvious distortions arising from a relationship of political inequality. Asad, on related grounds, has recently (1993) attacked verbocentric metaphor of "translation of culture." It may well be that we cannot entirely dispense with any of these models, flawed though they clearly are, but that the pragmatic solution lies in retaining them with their deficiencies in full view, so that the discussion of what their deficiencies cause to be lost in the ethnographic encounter – a discussion in which informants are increasingly engaged, as noted – will provide the means of intensifying the understandings that ethnography is intended to generate.

Focusing on the visual, argues Constance Classen, can "introduce a rupture in the interconnected sensory system of a society." This occurs most notably with artefacts, which are frequently abstracted from a dynamic context of multisensory uses and meanings and transformed into static objects for the gaze inside the glass cases of museums or within books of photography – a point recently acknowledged in art history as well (Nelson 1989) – and it also has ethical implications. Navajo sandpaintings, for example, are much more than simply visual representations for the Navajo. Created in the context of healing ceremonies, they are made to be pressed onto the bodies of the participants, and not simply seen. From a conventional western perspective, picking up sand from the sandpainting and applying it to the body "destroys" the painting. From the Navajo perspective, this act "completes" the painting by transferring the healing power contained in the visual representation to the patient's body through the medium of touch. According to Navajo religion it is, in fact, sacrilegious to preserve a sandpainting untouched: such an act of visual hubris is said to be punished by blindness. The interest of western art collectors and scholars in the visual designs of Navajo sandpaintings, however, has led to a number of attempts to "fix" this ephemeral art form in the manner of Western paintings. Such attempts include photographing sandpaintings, gluing them onto canvases, and preserving them in airtight glass cases. The tactile element of the sandpaintings is thus suppressed and receives little or no attention in scholarly interpretations of the works (Gill 1982; Parezco 1983). It also shows scant respect for the religious preoccupations of the artists.

The visualist preoccupations of many contemporary academics are evident in the extent to which "writing" or "reading" and "texts" have been employed as models for culture and cultural analysis, notably in Geertz's famous statement: "The culture of a people is an ensemble of texts . . . which the anthropologist strains to read over the shoulders of those to whom they properly belong" (Geertz 1973a: 452). The employment of this approach across cultures by anthropologists means not only that European-derived textual ideologies are applied to societies that do not share them, but also that the dynamic multi-sensory dimensions of culture are suppressed or transformed in order to make of culture a static, visual document which can then be read using the tools of textual criticism – an act, in the terms of Fabian's critique, of both "the denial of coevalness" and "visualism."

Yet this act, too, can be replicated by local intellectuals. What is the anthropologist to do? The folklorization of peasants and pastoralists the world over represents the uses of "tradition" to glorify an emergent cultural or national entity at the expense of its constituent subaltern parts. But the latter may not take kindly to the arrival of representatives of the former colonial powers who inform them that they are being victimized. Not all minority persons are anxious to have their minority status championed. Again, the ethical response – which again is inseparable from the epistemological issue – is to accept responsibility for the consequences of one's own assessments of the merits of each case.

It is also in this context, I suggest, that we are to read David Scott's epistemological reflections on colonialism. As he remarks, "If we want our discipline to be able to recognize the extent to which it is implicated in the reproduction of a colonial problematic then the deconstruction/reconstruction of anthropological objects . . . is an indispensable exercise. But its yield is largely an internal disciplinary one." Thus far he is very much in accord with Thomas. Here, however, he takes a more ambitious and proactive turn for the field: "if we take Asad's argument seriously this deconstructive/reconstructive exercise has itself to be folded into another enterprise whose purpose is organized around a different critical yield than internal disciplinary reform. To cite Asad (1991: 322–3): 'I have been arguing that we also need to pursue our historical concerns by anthropologizing the growth of Western power, because unless we extend our questions about the cultural character of that hegemony, we may take too much for granted about the relationship between anthropology and colonialism. . . . It needs to be stressed, however, that it is not enough for anthropologists to note that [Europe's] hegemony was not monolithic, or that Western power continually provoked resistance. It is not enough because conventional political history of colonial times and places has always been a record of conflict: between different European interests, between different groups of non-Europeans, as well as between colonizers and colonized. We do not advance matters much if we simply repeat slogans about conflict and resistance in place of older slogans about repression and domination. An anthropology of Western imperial power must try to understand the radically altered form and terrain of conflict inaugurated by it – new political languages, new powers, new social groups, new desires and fears, new subjectivities.' This is the crucial argument. And one way of trying to situate it and understand its point, is by means of a contrast with aspects of the currently prevailing paradigm – what one might call the anti-colonial paradigm of anthropological inquiry and criticism." So Scott suggests that "Asad's argument registers an implicit recognition of an alteration in the cognitive-political problem-space we occupy, and therefore of the nature of the demand of (anthropological) criticism. . . . [and] that what he has done, in fact, is alter the strategic question about colonialism (and thus the description of colonial power) on the basis of which an anthropological response is solicited." The key narrative, exemplified by Frantz Fanon's *The Wretched of the Earth* (1963), is one of repression and resistance. And Scott recognizes that, especially since World War II, when anticolonial nationalist movements were gaining momentum, this master narrative gathered significant moral force. Indeed, an important dimension of its presence in anthropology was the discipline's advocacy – perhaps naïve, as Thomas suggests, but certainly the expression of a powerful academic morality – of "the native's point of view." Scott, however, now reads Asad as "saying that these are not questions to which we ought (or ought any longer) to be trying to formulate responses. They are questions whose moment has passed, or better, whose moment, over the past decade-and-a-half, has been steadily dismantled. With the collapse of the Bandung (Third World/anti-imperialist) and Socialist projects, and with the new hegemony of a neo-liberal globalisation, it is no longer clear what 'overcoming' Western power actually means." And, on the other side, there are few socialist states to be defended. "There is now, in short, a fundamental crisis in the Third World in which the very coherence of the secular-modern project . . . can no longer be taken for granted. This crisis ushers in a new problem-space and produces a new demand on anthropological criticism." The challenge for anthropology lies in recognizing this shift and responding pragmatically to it by investigating the transformations and reorganizations that were effected by the new form of power that has now, in turn, bequeathed postcolonial nationalism to the world.

Modernity at Stake

Such an exercise requires a radical rethinking – perhaps even the abandonment – of the concept of modernity. Anthropology has a complex relationship with this ill-defined notion. First, in most senses in which the term "modernity" is used, anthropology is one of its products – an attempt to place unknown worlds within a clearly defensible classification of knowledge. Second, this by now outdated (and evolutionist) view of anthropology as concerned only with societies representing the past condition of humankind raises questions about its capacity to deal with a world in which the illusion of isolated societies affording perfect laboratory conditions can no longer be sustained. And third, moder-

nity is itself a kind of identity – a contested space invested with notions of privilege, wealth, and knowledge. This is the ironic key to Václav Hubinger's wry
observation that the discipline is apparently well equipped to deal with modernity: as he tells us, "it has not been doing anything else since its very beginning – initally, however, by defining modernity as what it was not supposed to
study."

As an anthropology of "Western" inspiration moves into new spaces, it
encounters new challenges. In southern Europe there have been debates about
whether it represents a neocolonialist intrusion or an opportunity for recon-
ceptualizing subjectivity in ways that trsnscend essentialized national frontiers
(see Llobera et al. 1986; cf. Bakalaki 1993). In the former East Bloc countries,
the identification of (especially) anglophone anthropology with modernity
similarly excites both emulation and resentment. Hubinger expresses the
latter dilemma succinctly: "In the post-totalitarian societies of Eastern Europe
our discipline is seeking its raison d'être, and is trying hard to separate itself
from what it had been doing before. It is a fear both political (not to be connected with the totalitarian regime) and topical (to get involved in the discipline
as it is practiced 'elsewhere'). The protagonists take this as a process of mod-
ernizing the discipline. Clearly it has nothing in common with the recent debates
about modernism in the Western world. But it has very much to do with the
modern."

Marxism always had its own notion of how to gain modernity – a more or
less religious idea of paradise, with a just and omniscient manager. In practice,
communist regimes were frustrated by their inability to remain untouched by
influences from the outside. Socialism was presented to people who lived under
it as a society of justly distributed wealth, but it was easy to see that there was
greater wealth "out there," in the world of modern technology. The discipline
in post-totalitarian societies of Europe finds itself in a state of hesitation. There
is a very strong and, in its own way, extremely interesting tradition of classical
ethnography (more or less identical with what in German is called *Volkskunde*),
which dominates the field despite the efforts to introduce anthropology as it is
generally understood in countries where the French, British and US traditions
prevail. It is by no means surprising that the process of introducing anthropology is widely interpreted as one of modernization. Modernity, according to
many of the post-totalitarian scholars, bears greater openness, formulating
opinions and opening issues that were taboo under the previous regime.
Inevitably, along with the new possibilities of studying familiar topics, new ones
enter into the purview of more or less unprepared professionals.

The theoretical point of departure has not changed profoundly, which would
have been hard in the short time since 1989, but in eastern Europe scholars
have begun to claim that what they actually practice is social and cultural
anthropology: "The magic of the concept of anthropology is so strong in Eastern
Europe," observes Hubinger, "that it makes some colleagues believe that by
changing the name of their subject they will also liberate themselves from both
traditional ethnography (Volkskunde) and Marxism–Leninism." A Romanian
anthropologist and philosopher has remarked that apparently "cultural anthro-

pology is able to play in the larger field of social sciences the paradigmatic role which physics plays in the field of natural sciences" (Geana 1992: 313). Others are more bluntly interested in using ethnography for the pursuit of identity politics: "Croatian ethnology today writes its own history as the emancipation from hegemonic and ideological networks" (Prica 1995: 11). This is also painfully clear in widespread reports during the 1990s of a Russian ethnological establishment shot through with a virulent and recidivist anti-Semitism. Some of this concern with identity politics lurks behind "nativist" arguments in southern Europe (e.g., Moreno Navarro 1984). And anthropology has a complex interaction with the reconstitution of Maya identities in response to oppression by repressive national governments attempting to impose by force an ideology of *mestizaje* in which *indígenas* have no place (see especially Warren 1998). But the East European experience is perhaps the most revealing because the debate entails decisions about which kind of anthropology to adopt; to a lesser extent, the countries of Mediterranean Europe must confront a similar issue in deciding what to do with their departments of (national) folklore.

There is thus a process of seeking a place in a world that has changed profoundly. Old topics that dominated the discipline in eastern Europe in the last few decades are considered obsolete, antiquated, and pseudo–scientific, mostly because of their close connection with communist ideology and previous subjection to repressive control. In this crisis of identity, any discipline that can furnish reassuring stereotypes is sucked into the vacuum of uncertainty. It is a difficult and painstaking effort (see Dragadze 1995), in which old truths crumble in the wake of the regime that gave birth to them. As an example of an attempt to change as much as possible we may consider the most influential of eastern European ethnologies or anthropologies, that of the former Soviet Union: "By the mid-1980s a greater part of Soviet scholars de facto refuted Morgan's/Engels's conceptions . . . Incidentally, the current criticism of the totalitarian heritage in Russian anthropology represents additional interest. The attempts to defy remnants of Soviet ethnology are carried on in a typical Russian manner, with traditional extremes. For instance, the current Director of the Moscow Ethnological Institute asserts that Russian anthropology should be radically reshaped according to Western concepts (German, American?). Today Russian anthropology, earlier called 'Ethnography', even changed its name to 'Ethnology'" (Znamenski 1995: 186).

Here we can see with particular clarity how deeply relative our classifications are. What for Znamenski is a goal is for others a point of departure in their attempts to situate themselves in relation to the West. For some in the West, moreover, it was the East that was modern. Many Easterners, however, find this hard to understand and at odds with their own vision of modernity. Nowadays, the reality of post-totalitarian countries is sometimes considered postmodern in the sense of a dissolution of clearly defined ideological systems, with postmodernity also becoming an ideological concept. In this spatialized view of social evolution, which recalls the early anthropology of nineteenth-century Britain, modernity defines the center, backwardness the periphery.

Hubinger attributes much of this perspective to the very strong centralism of the former communist regimes and their predecessors; in that order of things, moreover, the true center of the world (and the source of political and cultural wisdom) was necessarily Moscow. A good example is the Soviet-inspired treatment of ethnicity from the 1960s on (see Bromley 1973, 1983), perhaps partly inspired by US-style sociology in the late 1950s and early 1960s. The topic, unprecedented in other socialist countries for fear of being accused of encouraging nationalist feelings, was very soon adopted all over the Soviet bloc.[1] This research stopped almost instantly in the turbulent period between fall 1989 and spring 1990, although a few works surfaced later. The collapse did not occur because the topic was exhausted; it was simply that the research idiom was too tightly associated with a now discredited political universe. The collapse of communist regimes also brought about the breakdown of this strong center-periphery bond.

And so one of the last intellectual traditions to accept a reified concept of ethnicity, which elsewhere had surrendered to the empirically grounded logic of critiques such as the celebrated collection edited by Fredrik Barth (see Barth 1969), dissolved in the collapse of other, political certainties. But this is not to say that anthropology abandoned its cherished essentialisms overnight. To the contrary, there was a marked tendency to think in terms of area studies categories – themselves, as Gupta and Ferguson (in Gupta and Ferguson 1997: 13) have observed, largely generated by geopolitical considerations. It is only in recent years that anthropologists have begun to criticize the underlying assumptions, and this has had radical effects also on the ways, and especially the kinds of places, in which they have carried out their ethnographic research. If those geopolitical considerations are associated with modernism as an ideology, this is all the more reason for anthropologists to challenge the conventional division of the world into regions, nation-states, or "culture areas," organized in cultural hierarchies with persistent overtones of survivalism.

Regions and Selves

In this spirit, Nicholas Thomas has questioned the common view of anthropology as a discipline defined by a simple tension between local ethnography and global theory. Consistent with the middle-ground perspective, however, while fully recognizing that this idealized view is complicated by all the many political and ethical entailments of the discipline, as well as by the evidence that many of its theories are more useful somewhere in the middle range between the local and the universal, we might wish to retain the idea of this tension as a goad to these same sensitivities. That tension offers us, not a credo, but an ultimately impossible goal that leads us to learn much simply in the effort of trying to reach it. This, in fact, is much like Evans-Pritchard's famous (if perhaps apocryphal) observation that social anthropology was nothing if not comparative – and that comparison was, of course, impossible.

Be that as it may, Thomas recognizes an important difficulty when he remarks: "Another sense in which the seeming complementarity of universal theory and ethnography is misleading arises from the marginalization of the regional as a frame for anthropological discussion" (redressed in an important but neglected collection, Fardon, ed., 1990). All anthropologists work, if to a varying extent, within intra-disciplinary and cross-disciplinary area studies milieux, and this produces both specialized vocabularies and seemingly esoteric preoccupations that themselves define political fields of academic discourse about "the Mediterranean," "China," or "Melanesia." There is some irony in this: if one were to compare the Mediterranean and Melanesia as they have been typecast in their respective area studies discourses, for example, one might be tempted to merge them, what with the heavy emphasis in both on strong gender ideologies and differentiations (especially aggressive masculinity), raiding, witchcraft, and a deep concern with display and the instabilities of status, not to speak of troubled forms of nationalism competing with parochial and yet fluid conceptions of local identity. Why should this be more absurd than some of the conflations that have occurred within each so-called region? Such an exercise – perhaps a book titled *Mediterranean/Melanesian: A Study in Anthropological Imagination* – would be necessarily ironic, but for that reason also useful. Thomas, perhaps rather too optimistically, remarks: "If 'area studies' debates indeed tend to be introverted and anti-theoretical, they may also be theoretically marked by engagement with the site of research, and thus reflect a more genuine compromise between a Euro-American discipline and a theatre of field research." At the moment when the global pretensions of cultural studies are becoming more evidently exhausted, the interplay between area studies and wider disciplines may suddenly provide something anthropology needs.

To be fair, however, many of those who have for so long advocated regional foci have similarly recognized the trap of viewing regions simply as natural geographic entities that frame research and professional discussion and have made efforts of varying intensity to trace their histories and particular implications (e.g., J. Davis 1977; Gilmore 1987). Yet the logical circularity remains, producing ever more conferences and learned works on "the Mediterranean," "Chinese culture," and so on, and even – in a depressing illustration of the politics of citation – leading some ambitious scholars to cite critiques of these regional foci as "evidence" of their importance!

Here the solution strikes me as lying in the provision of a political account of the significance given to the regions in question. Such studies would focus, not on Melanesia, but on "Melanesia"; not on the Mediterranean, but on the "Mediterranean." This would provide a means of contextualizing both the cultures under study and the practices of anthropologists engaged in that study, and would again be entirely consistent with a posture of reflexive mediation. It also engages productively with the rethinking of ethnographic location so eloquently advocated by Gupta and Ferguson (eds., 1997) and their collaborators: if we redesign our ethnographic projects to cross the boundaries on which anthropology and global politics have until recently concurred, we will achieve a clearer understanding of what it means for people in "local places" to find themselves designated as "Melanesians," "refugees" (Malkki 1989), "Gypsies" (Okely 1983), "stateless persons," and so on.

Reflexivity and Postmodernism

Don Robotham argues that the reflexive posture has not delivered on its promises, in part because it remains trapped in the logic of a western self-absorption. This is a challenge that we clearly must face. How do we learn from the textual critiques of anthropology without engaging in a wholly self-referential exercise in textual criticism?

The burden of the work Robotham calls "moderate postmodernism" focuses on the anthropological text as a constructed document. In other words, it challenges the claims of that text to transcendent common sense – a truly anthropological perspective. Thus, in addition to representing the people of a community in an ethnography, such work destabilizes certain principles and concepts such as culture and kinship, all taken from the cultural universe of the anthropologist. As we shall see in the discussion of caring, these categories can be challenged to productive effect.

Such critiques challenge the "scientific" authority claimed by an academic discipline and ultimately deriving from the political and economic supremacy of the West – as Weber recognized long ago (1958 [1904]). Robotham, however, also points out that the desire to create an "experimental moment" in anthropology (Marcus and Fischer 1986) "operates firmly within the paradigm of a rationalistic epistemology, seeking in time-honoured fashion to renew, re-invigorate and modernize anthropology's old role as critique of Western culture and society . . . [and] to bolster both anthropology and . . . science, between which there is no perceived contradiction, quite the contrary – a theme pursued to this day in Fischer's most recent work (D'Andrade, Fischer et al. 1996)." The aim is to point out that what is true of anthropology is also true for science, says Robotham, which then itself becomes another type of discourse, with its unique properties, but with its "poetics" also subject to critique. What we have here then is a rescue mission for anthropology to remain as a "human science" but not on the basis of the old Newtonian models.

The overwhelming focus of this "moderate postmodernism," as Robotham calls it, is on the problematic of the text and its possible (often unconscious) manipulations by its lone anthropologist. In order to avoid these pitfalls and to have accounts which are more true to their reality, proposals for "dialogic" and "polyphonic" writing are put forward. Robotham's eminently sensible point is that this is still an empirical issue – a matter, as I have said, of intensifying the ethnographic account rather than of displacing it. From this point of view, it is self-indulgent nonsense to suppose that we can somehow bypass that commitment altogether (see also D. Scott 1992: 384; 1996; Chatterjee 1986: 17).

But there is a more uncompromising postmodernism, represented especially by Stephen Tyler, as Donald Moore summarizes the matter: "The dialogic ethnography advocated by among others Clifford, as 'rendering negotiated realities as multi-subjective, power-laden and incongruent' was argued to be, like the realistic genres it was supposed to replace, 'monologue masquerading as dialogue.' 'Polyphonic' ethnography was of course susceptible to a similar critique. Similarly, rhetorical analyses of ethnographic accounts would get one nowhere under a rigorously applied poststructuralist critique, since the rhetorical analyses would be again interested and fictional meta-accounts of the initial account, themselves susceptible to yet more rhetorical analysis. Rhetorical analysis is no way to escape rhetoric. Reflexivity, finally, would also require an infinite regress, since if one accepted reflexivity in the first place, one would be obliged to admit that one's 'up-front' account of 'where I stand in writing this acknowledged fiction' would itself be a fiction, and so on, and so on" (D. Moore 1994: 349; see also C.W. Watson 1987: 35).

What distinguished Tyler from the moderate postmodernists is that, unlike the moderates, Tyler located the fundamental problem outside the text. For him the issue was one of epistemological repression. The only way out of this was to abandon any kind of rationalism at all. One had to move from representation to "evocation" (Tyler 1986: 133–4). Here, as Ahmad pointed out in his critique of Edward Said, the anti-rationalistic influence of Nietzsche is unmistakable (1992: 159–219). This is easy to ridicule from the point of view of the comfortable rationalisms of the modern world, as Robotham points out, but Robotham wants to exculpate Tyler in order to show that the unbridgeability that even his extreme position failed to resolve is not Tyler's personal failure but a consequence of the postcolonial situation: "Not even 'evocation,' no matter how therapeutic and heavenly, proved capable of bridging this postmodern, postcolonial gulf."

David Scott responds to this by turning to politics. Robotham's preferred solution is to return to an analysis, politically informed, of economic history, in order to document the transformations that today have produced, not so much a "postmodern condition," as "multiple modernities" – what he calls the "new modernities." But there is a danger here, too: that of yielding analytical primacy to a rationalism that, even within the emergent "alternative modernities (A. Ong 1996), has yet to demonstrate that its departures from western rationality are more than a matter of political rhetoric. Rather, the constant tension among competing modernities and rationalities would seem to form a worthwhile object for anthropological research – an object that includes anthropology itself as a multiply constructed object. Here we are perhaps back to "moderate postmodernism." But it is clear that the good faith of the discipline cannot be rescued by "evocation" alone, still less by self-accusing accounts of ethnographic malpractice, important those these attempts may be for alerting us to the shifting ethical grounds – the changing definition of accountability – on which our professional practice must be constantly rethought.

Empirical Reflexivity

By reflexivity, therefore, we cannot mean the kind of self-indulgent solipsism with which it has frequently been identified, and into which its self-proclaimed practitioners do occasionally slip – although not as often, perhaps, as is claimed (e.g., Spencer 1989). Although reflexivity as a technical term is associated with the "postmodern" turn in anthropology, notably since the Clifford and Marcus collection (1986) and Talal Asad's collection on *Anthropology and the Colonial Encounter* (1973), some degree of recognition of the problems of importing an alien selfhood in the field has arguably always and inevitably been an important feature of anthropological writing.

Self-accounts occur early – in Malinowski and Evans-Pritchard, for example – and to dismiss their ironies as expressions of the luxury of confident power (e.g., Asad 1986; Clifford 1988; Rosaldo 1989) is, while true and a useful insight, nevertheless perhaps also to miss the point that all reflexivity is in some sense such a luxury. Asad and Clifford show how Evans-Pritchard deftly deploys his self-deprecating humor and understatement to foster an attitude of trust in the reader in his account of Nuer life. In another essay Clifford even claims to detect 'Edenic overtones' in this book and that it is not difficult to hear a long political tradition of a nostalgia for "an egalitarian, contractual union" (Clifford 1988: 111). The problem is that this critique, which may be entirely justified, omits other aspects of these texts, which in turn represented an attempt from within the centers of academic power to gain some respect for "native peoples." But it is useful to read beyond such well-meaning intentions as well. Moreover, some accounts – such as Boehm's description of his digestive problems in Montenegro (1984) – may even simply be disingenuous devices to liven up an entirely scientist study. By the same token, however, it is no less important to emphasize that postmodernism does not have a lien on self-knowledge, and its pieties may even interfere with that virtue.

But the moralizing focus on reflexivity – pro and con – conceals an important distinction. On the whole, I agree with Thomas's gently sardonic reflection: "Although novelists and painters may write or talk in interesting ways about their own creativity, one does not look to them for the most critical or revealing account of their own moment in literature or art. Given that anthropology is predicated on the revelatory potential of the unfamiliar, we should always have known that the richest critique of anthropological writing would not be an auto-critique. What might have followed from the observation that ethnographic texts obeyed various conventions and used various devices to evoke a sense of reality and particularity could have been a historical examination of traditions in anthropological writing and anthropological knowledge" – a project Thomas sees as having indeed been taken up by Geertz (1988) and Stocking (see especially his edited series, *History of Anthropology* [from 1987]) and others.

But I would also point out what this implies at a more general level: that the most useful kind of reflexivity is not that of pure self-examination, but the kind that places the cultural assumptions of the ethnographer in question – that clarifies the ethnographic encounter and its limitations as predicated upon the imperfect meshing of two different codes, with its multiplicity of divergent identities and presuppositions. This kind of reflexivity is genuinely empirical (but not empiricist), and it is deployed to a specific purpose, that of intensifying (perhaps a better term than the progressivist "improving") the analysis.

It is a reflexivity that actually amplifies the empirical thrust of the discipline. To understand what (in the terms of current debates) might seem to be a totally paradoxical formulation, we must make a clear distinction between two quite different varieties of reflexivity: the personal and the sociocultural. Discussions of reflexivity have ranged from accusations of bad faith (it is a self-indulgent luxury at the expense of the various threatened populations we study) to passionate advocacy (only through radical self-examination can anthropology shed the taint of its colonial past).

Pragmatic considerations, however, might suggest that this is a misdirected debate and lead us to ask instead what kind of reflexivity is on offer. This is where the distinction between the personal and the sociocultural becomes especially germane. Reflexive exercises that seem merely to be a public form of psychoanalysis seem to offer far less insight than those which permit us to see our own cultural practices, anthropology prominently included, in a comparative context.

Thus, for example, the critique of functionalism in social anthropology does help us to recognize the logic adopted by the framers of rituals, constitutions, and bureaucratic systems. Indeed, the more "modern" and contemporary such systems are, the more clearly we can identify the social agents – the committees of Durkheimian gremlins, as it were – who made conscious decisions to set them up. They are real people, acting in real social spaces at specific historical moments and participating in processes rather than being suspended in timeless structures. As such, they are ethnographically – that is, empirically – accessible (see S. Moore 1987).

Moreover, viewing their actions in these terms does not entail imputing psychological motives to them. It is simply a matter of realizing that their actions give form and substance to cultural artefacts in which others – often their followers – are able to find the sense of structured order that encourages conformity and sets the standard against which rebellion acquires its identity. There is much to be gained analytically by discerning the similarities between anthropological and state functionalism, or between anthropological theories of ethnicity and myths of origin (including nationalist historiographies) (Drummond 1981), or anthropological concepts of culture and society and state-sponsored reifications of identity (Handler 1985).

The question of psychological motivation – of what is often called "intentionality" – is both a minefield and a goldmine. If we try to understand "what people are thinking," we are likely to come to grief, because our ability to "read" intentions – even assuming that we are able to get past the opacities of cultural difference – is entirely speculative. This does not mean that we are always wrong in making such guesses, but it does mean that we must specify the cultural conditions under which we feel able to make such assessments (see Needham 1972; cf. Leavitt 1996). On the other hand, those conditions may include extensive access to the cultural idioms in which emotions are represented, and these – to be found especially in some good comparative work on local psychologies (Lutz and Abu-Lughod, eds., 1990; Heelas and Lock 1981; Rosen, ed., 1995) – provide a useful baseline against which to set our own assessments. One path with which I have experimented is that of writing the life of a local novelist, setting his and his critics' views against the more collective tone of the ethnographic work already done on his home town, region, and country (Herzfeld 1997b). This device also permits a clearer view of the ways in which various forms of agency may challenge the supposed homogeneity of "a culture."

Indeed, the concept of discrete cultures is becoming increasingly problematic, not only because anthropologists are uneasy about the parallel reifications that they encounter in various ethnonationalist ideologies, but also, in an ironic inversion of the same development, because the increasing permeability of all manner of administrative borders makes the very idea of a bounded entity unpersuasive.

There are practical consequences that stem from this shift. As Arturo Escobar so eloquently writes, "Societies are not the organic wholes with structures and laws that we thought them to be until recently but fluid entities stretched on all sides by migrations, border crossing and economic forces; cultures are no longer bounded, discrete, and localized but deterritorialized and subjected to multiple hybridizations; similarly, nature can no longer be seen as an essential principle and foundational category, and independent domain of intrinsic value and truth, but as the object of constant reinventions, especially by unprecedented forms of technoscience; and, finally, nobody really knows where the economy begins and ends, even if economists, in the midst of neo-liberal frenzy and seemingly over-powering globalization, steadfastly adhere to their attempt to reduce to it every aspect of social reality, thus extending the shadow that economics casts on life and history" (see also Gupta and Ferguson, eds., 1997). Clearly, an anthropology that works against the reifications perpetuated by the logic of nation-states – and now carried forward into the overarching structure of international organizations (Gupta 1998) – must, at the very least, place concepts like "culture" under historically grounded, critical examination.

The irony is palpable: "while," as Ulf Hannerz remarks, "their old favourite concept is thus triumphantly spreading through the jungles, the streets and the conference centres of the world, some anthropologists have been having second thoughts about culture, in the sense of culture/culture differences." But the irony goes deeper still. Impelled by their good-faith desire to resist the exoticism of yore, they now worry, notes Hannerz, that "to speak of culture – especially cultures – tends to become a way of underlining, even exaggerating, difference" (see also Abu-Lughod 1991). Meanwhile, the production of "how-to" manuals for cultural "management" (e.g., Mole 1995) – often by practitioners in development and in the business world – parallels the equally destructive deployment of the culture concept in the service of international apartheid, as noted above.

In an age made increasingly aware of the possibilities of the strategic ways in which the culture concept can be invoked and deployed for political ends, therefore, anthropologists are much more reluctant to treat "cultures" uncritically as definable entities. To some extent, perhaps, they are reacting against the simplistic cooptation of "their" concept by political scientists (notably S. Huntington 1996) for purposes that seem designed more to perpetuate foreign policy stereotypes than achieve real understanding. No doubt, too, the sudden burgeoning of electronic technology has generated a new awareness of the possibilities, always present but now vastly maginified and thus more visible, for the creation of "virtual reality." In some sense identity is, and for anthropologists has long been, if not virtual, at least negotiable.

This has had a galvanizing effect on theory. Indeed, we must be careful not to underestimate either the impact of technology on theory or its capacity to adjust to the new situation. In this regard the work of Marilyn Strathern is exemplary. Not only has she shown that kinship theory can illuminate and must respond to the new reproductive technologies of in vitro fertilization (Strathern 1992; see also Ginsburg and Rapp, eds., 1996; and, for a striking variant, Kahn 2000), but she has also tackled the problem of defining culture in a world that is racing to suppress any knowledge of alternative strategies (Strathern 1988; see also Strathern 1991). She has recast culture, as Thomas notes, as something other than a field or container for actors and relations. In her analysis, Melanesians might busily be evoking collectivities through events such as ceremonial exchange, rites and dances, but these were not social systems as much as rhetorical artifacts – "insecure evocations of particular occasions, imaged entities," remarks Thomas, and "more like nations in Benedict Anderson's *Imagined Communities* (1983, 1991) than the societies of conventional anthropological and sociological reference." If older anthropological notions of culture and society were somehow much like the official formulations of nationalists, this view is much more like what is left after the deconstruction: again, it is productive to contemplate the parallels between our own intellectual activities and those we aspire to study.

But the dangers are, on the one hand, that such introspection can lead to the self-defeating despair of the positivist at the continuity between observer and observed; and, on the other, that such comparisons might become an end in themselves, validated by the moralism that currently marks the self-congratulatory rhetoric of some of those nation-states that have been especially prominent in the development of anthropology. Without them, however, it is hard to see how anthropology can make good on its claims to be empirical, for the comparisons themselves are clearly revelatory of new insights.

This reflexivity, then, regards culture rather than the ethnographer's self alone, and that is perhaps its best protection against the unattractive self-absorption with which some have charged it. In saying that reflexivity should be culture-rather than self-regarding, I do not wish to revert to the simplistic modular "cultures" imagined by earlier anthropologists and nationalists alike. Given the international character of anthropology today, as evidenced by the project that generated this book, we might more usefully think of the hybrid professional culture, with its specialized needs and preoccupations, as an appropriate object of study in its own right and as a way of shoring it up against reversion to older habits of thought. As Marilyn Strathern has similarly indicated in *The Gender of the Gift* (1988: 10), and as I have also argued in *Anthropology through the Looking-Glass* (1987: 202–5), that project has the virtue of deepening and intensifying the practice of knowledge that we call anthropological theory. Indeed, Ulf Hannerz has nicely expressed its practical implications in thinking about the fate of the culture concept in public discourse: he urges "public scrutiny of our own as well as other people's uses of the notion – whether they are interculturalists, cultural fundamentalists, or just ordinary citizens and lay people in the street." And he notes further: "There is ethnographic work in such scrutiny as well . . . We may think of it not as 'studying up' – to use an older anthropological notion – or 'down,' but as 'studying sideways,' focusing on other groups who like anthropologists make it their particular business to cross borders for the purpose of portraying what is on the other side: the travel industry, the missionaries, and not least the foreign correspondents of the news media," and the people who produce "how-to" handbooks on "survival" in other cultures as well. And in that study, the anthropologists, too, should be an object of ethnographic scrutiny: their position in the larger society, perhaps a little like that of medieval jesters or Somali smiths, is sufficiently ambivalent to serve as a touchstone for more general insights.

In Thomas's words, "descriptive ethnography can be seen as a higher-level or second-order discourse that is only intelligible by virtue of its theoretical and analytical grounding. More than any other discipline, anthropology constantly reminds its practitioners of the pretensions of our analyses, that may differ from those of our subjects, but are not obviously privileged or authoritative in relation to them. To acknowledge the formative character of 'the field' with respect to anthropological knowledge, is not only to prefer practical theory to theoretical practice: it is to realize that one works not with informants, but with co-interpreters." Every field encounter is thus necessarily a renegotiation of cultural presuppositions and identities, and the anthropological project is consequentially caught up in that process. We could not write the texts without our informants; but we could not write those texts without ourselves, either – and our practices, like theirs, have histories that are embedded in our actions and attitudes, and in the ethnographies that we write.

In that context, the attention to genres and forms initiated by the authors of *Writing Culture* (and significantly and necessarily expanded in *Writing Women's Worlds* [Abu-Lughod 1993a]) ceases to be the solipsistic self-indulgence and literary game-playing that some have found in it, and becomes instead an important part of the creation of a historical consciousness for the discipline – a topic on which many have already worked (see the series of works by Margaret Hodgen (1936, 1964), George Stocking, James Urry (1993), Henrika Kuklick (1991), and many others.

Moreover, such an approach expands the perspective to include other genres such as museum bulletins, genres that are now remote from dominant styles but remain important for their accumulations of data that are still drawn upon (cf. N. Thomas 1989). In other words, as Thomas observes, "the questions ought to have licensed not talk about ourselves, which would lead inevitably to disguised self-justifications, but a richer sense of the diversity of anthropological genres, of the strengths and limitations of descriptive modes at varying times." That would be a serious reflexivity; it already has a long and varied history of its own; and it rescues the ethnographic project from the twin solipsisms – both forms of self-admiration – of textual preening and scientistic righteousness.

The benefits of such an approach are especially substantive at this moment in history. Anthropology is firmly abandoning the (empirically untenable) vision of clearly bounded cultural isolates – the "laboratory" of Lévi-Strauss's (1966) optimistic imagination. Don Robotham, arguing from the position of the postcolonial intellectual, suggests that we move beyond both positivism and what he calls the "defensive anguish" of postmodernism to embrace the rich variety of social experience that now becomes accessible and simultaneously to reject (or at least contextualize) the western-constructed order of things implied even by such well-intentioned coinages as "postcolonialism." This is a significant change. Until now the cultural relativism of anthropology has always been relative to one constructed collective self, that of the "West" (see Carrier 1992). This expanded and variegated view of anthropology does also allow us to focus on regional entities in the critical sense I have sketched above – not, that is, in the idiom of the old culture area formulations, but in recognition of political realities that include the use of regional identity as a means for effective mobilization.

The vital task is to sustain the microscopic focus of field research at the same or even greater intensity, but to do so in ways that illuminate the overlapping, partially concentric larger entities in which it is embedded. This is possible because anthropological fieldwork itself entails experiences that coincide in instructive ways with processes that are important to informants (Jenkins 1994: 445–51). Moreover, the social intimacy of the field situation – the source of anthropologists' earliest and most fundamental reflexivity – permits a critical investigation of the cultural intimacy of the state and other supra-local entities (Herzfeld 1997a). When a fieldworker discovers that ordinary people admit to knowing about minorities and cultural traits the very existence of which is officially denied; when the anthropologist uncovers the reproduction of colonial practices at the local level under postcolonial regimes; when the official rhetoric of social and political harmony fails to blind the ethnographer to the persistence of practices deemed to be "uncivilized" (in a rhetoric that owes much to Victorian anthropology!) – at just such moments, anthropological field research can balance the sweeping generalizations of more macroscopic disciplines such as political science, economics, and cultural studies.

It is here, especially, that the reflexive critique of anthropology is conducive to a new kind of analysis of the role of the state (see also J. Scott 1998). To achieve that goal, however, reflexivity must be viewed, not as an end in itself, but as a means to the refinement of our analytic sensitivity. This makes a comparandum of anthropology itself, not because it is necessarily of special interest to non-anthropologists, but because the social and political history it shares with many of the encompassing institutional structures – nation-states, colonial empires, religious bureaucracies – can be made markedly more accessible through that discomfiting procedure. The criticism of anthropological theories as excessively based on the treatment of exotic others as living in another kind of time (see Fabian 1983), for example, leads us to the analytic dissection of similar practices in state policies on minorities and on the preservation of "tradition" in populations marginalized by their very association with its museological glories (e.g., Danforth 1984). In a similar vein, Asad's (1993) critique of the common metaphor of anthropological analysis as translation, whatever its own merits, also suggests a way of looking at the ways in which state bureaucracies reframe local traditions as national ceremonial – a pragmatic and largely non-linguistic process that resembles translation in the way it appropriates a text for a new context.

Given that anthropology, nationalism, and colonialism have complex intertwined pasts, these comparisons are less outrageous historiographically than they might appear to be from the perspective of maintaining myths of scientific detachment and transcendence. Indeed, Robotham has pointed out how the western grip on world history has relegated other "traditions" to secondary status, a phenomenon also matched in internal colonialisms such as those indexed by British discourses about "localism" (Nadel-Klein 1991). The history of anthropology is a side-show – although a very revealing one – in that larger spectacle. To take another example of the productive use of this kind of comparison, teleology may be inadmissible as an analytic presupposition, but it may also exist as an object of observation – as in the "state functionalism" described by Malarney (1996) for certain totalitarian regimes, or as in the intentional social shaping at which much state spectacle is directed.

Seeing teleology as conceived and put into operation by intending social beings takes it out of the domain of common sense and instead re-frames it as a form of social agency – in other words, as itself constituting the very phenomenon it denies, and, as such, something with which it is theoretically possible to argue. (The crudest example of this is the political rhetoric that denies that it is political. Its bluff can certainly be called! But there is often a price for doing so.) More particularly, what in modern theory would be rejected as crass essentialism appears in social practice as the outer form of a successful bid for power.

Awareness of agency in this sense reinscribes history in the analysis of the social – one of the most direct effects of the general growth of interest in agency, as Michael Roberts has noted. As Malarney (1996) wisely points out, there are limits to the functional efficiency demanded by the most controlling of regimes: the denial of agency does not mean that it has been truly eclipsed in practice, any more than – conversely – the existence of a powerful state automatically means that everyday contraventions of its authority necessarily constitute acts of deliberate resistance – although they may indeed be just that (see J. Scott 1985; cf. Reed-Danahay 1993). It is because such questions cannot be generically answered, and because they are often accessible only through non-verbal (or at least non-referential) codes – Marc Abélés's brief mention of the role of gesture in political action is especially suggestive here – that they demand painstaking, grass-roots field research. Even then they leave large areas of doubt, especially given our slow development of techniques for reading the less referential modes of meaning (on which, see Farnell 1995); but at least recognizing their significance is a step in the right direction – away from the surprisingly anti-empirical view that what cannot be measured should simply be left out of the picture. This view is usually associated with a "top-down" perspective that avoids the messiness of social reality and that dismisses ethnographic data as mere anecdotes. Such positions, always at odds with field experience, have very few adherents in social and cultural anthropology today, although a minority position expresses a disdain for fieldwork that simply serves to reinforce the external critics' deliberately uncomprehending view of both the fieldwork and of these (often self-styled postmodern) critics.

Agents and Practices

Indeed, it is the weakening of referential ideas about language in both anthropology and linguistics that probably paved the way for anthropology's hesitant but increasingly determined questioning of language-derived models for the understanding of cultures. The first move in that direction was a gradual rapprochement, largely unheralded (but see Rossi-Landi 1983; Ulin 1984) but nonetheless pervasive, between political economy and semiotics, exposing the old opposition between idealist (or "symbolic") versus materialist as an ideological dead-end. Perhaps the climax of this rethinking was Pierre Bourdieu's critique of mechanistic semiotics and affirmation of practice (1977). Hannerz nevertheless reminds us that this "close-up view" of culture in fact has an extended history within the discipline, going back at least to Edward Sapir's (1938) reflections over the significance of an early American ethnographer's report that his Omaha Indian informants were not in agreement: "Two Crows denies this." While dissension is not the sole indicator of agency, it certainly is an important one. But it has only been since the reaction to the formality of structuralism in the early 1970s that agency really began to be recognized as a central issue (see Karp 1986; Ortner 1984).

Moreover, this reaction was not a unitary theoretical effort, but rather a highly dispersed one, conducted on different fronts in different fields, against textualism and for performance in one context, and against communication and for materiality in another. Studies of embodiment, emotion, material culture, and art have all, in quite different ways, shifted away from what was previously almost axiomatic: that anything socially consequential or efficacious was perforce meaningful and significant in a primarily linguistic sense. Even if not understood as a message in relation to a code, or specifically as a text, a practice or artifact was understood to communicate. Although it would, of course, be unproductive to deny that language, iconography, and discourse are tremendously important, it has become increasingly apparent that presences as well as representations, substances as well as significances, doing as well as meaning, are of vital and constitutive importance in most domains addressed by cultural analysis. From the 1960s on, it seemed exciting when theorists in philosophy, literature, and history as well as anthropology pointed to the cultural constitution of the body, as it did when Roland Barthes and others drew attention to the semiotics of consumer goods. Yet, as Thomas remarks, "subsequent work tends to take us back to the commonsense point that critics had rhetorically distanced themselves from: the body is always more and less than a text, and the values and desires invested in consumer objects depend on their materiality as well as their imputed meaning."

My own sense has been that it is useful to think in terms of a distinction between language-based and language-derived models of meaning. The former reduce all semiotic forms to language: everything becomes a text, and is decodable because it is predictably grammatical. This is the common ground of theorists as distinct as Clifford Geertz and Claude Lévi-Strauss. In language-derived models, by contrast, the relatively immediate access one can gain to linguistic meanings – they are the ultimately reflexive ones, in that we use language to talk about language – permits the heuristic deployment of models originally worked out for language. The goal is to explore both commonalities and differences among a range of codes – architecture, music, cuisine, sports, and, indeed, language. Sometimes we confront issues that cut across these various categories: the tension between convention and invention is, to a varying degree, applicable in all of them, and permits the application of what I have called a "social poetics"; tensions between official and intimate norms may similarly undergird a whole range of semiotic domains (Herzfeld 1997a). Such models also permit the identification of practices and above all of the uses people make of the codes – they are pragmatic rather than formal, heuristic rather than predictive, and responsive to meaning rather than semantically deterministic. They play on the basic tension of all human production: the fact of structure creates illusions of fixity, but is itself a necessary precondition of invention – for all social production is necessarily also a matter of process, not of static forms (see also S. Moore 1987). In consequence, no symbolic form is immune to transformation, transmutation, or straightforward abuse (defined in terms of its prior commitments). It is also instructive to find that while anthropologists who study economics and development issues have embraced the discourse-oriented insights of postmodern or poststructuralist thinking, it is those who deal with the arts who have, in a contrary move, sought instead to rediscover structure and order. This, too, is a reversal of our conventional expectations. What these anthropologists share, however, is the empirically grounded understanding that effective knowledge is to be sought in the dialectical space in which neither positivism nor deconstruction predominates, but where the pragmatics of the field experience open up our readiness to accept and embrace surprising concatenations.

The structuralist use of linguistic models was predicated on the idea that all semiotic systems, and thus by extension all societies and all cultures, could be seen as total systems – semiotic *langues*, as it were. That tolerance for static wholes is seriously undercut by the notions of agency and practice, through which the transient sense of a permanent system or structure is continually created anew. It is, to use the current jargon, "emergent in performance" (Bauman 1977; Giddens 1984). It is, in other words, a virtual reality; but it is no less real for all that – all reality is, in this sense, virtual, since all reality is mediated by the senses. This is an insight that Giambattista Vico was perhaps the first in the West to oppose explicitly to the Cartesian worldview. Just how far the anthropological project can go in exploring the consequences of that insight, and how serious are the limitations that remain, will be evident especially in the chapter on Senses, and should already be apparent in what I have said here about the impact of the visualist bias on anthropological thinking itself. To reduce smell to a language is clearly misleading; to ask what similarities and differences might be revealed by exploiting the flaws in this model should be revealing; and to explore the role of smell, taste, and the other senses in the creation of a sense of structure is a crucially important project that remains yet ahead. It not only complicates our understanding of the present, but it also questions our often summary understanding of the past: it invites us, as I will make more explicit in the next chapter, to substitute for master narratives of a single, dominant history the rich play of multiple histories.

Note

1   See the plethora of articles published in 1970s and 1980s in periodicals such as *Sovietskaya etnografia* in the USSR, *Ceský lid and Slovenský národopis* in Czechoslovakia, *Traditiones* in Yugoslavia, and *Ethnologische und Archaelogische Zeitschrift* in the German Democratic Republic.

3

Histories

A History of Histories

Anthropology and history have danced a flirtatious pas de deux throughout the past century. While historians either seethed with irritation at what they saw as the unsystematic and anecdotal habits of anthropologists or embraced anthropological theories with an alarming dearth of critical caution, anthropologists have fluctuated between opposing their "scientific laws" to history's "idiographic" propensities (Radcliffe-Brown 1952) and claiming the historian's craft as their own, transmuted to the field (Evans-Pritchard 1963). This fluctuation has had a marked effect on the anthropological side, at least, because the suppression of temporality produces in anthropological theory a quality not unlike what Lévi-Strauss claimed for myth – a timelessness of structural form that allows investigators to ignore the fact that the people they study are actually living in the same time period as they (Fabian 1983).

Debates about what constitutes myth and history, although sometimes analytically useful to the extent that they represent informants' recognition that some stories tell of actual events while others are instead true in a symbolic and generic sense (see Hill, ed., 1988), always risk a plunge into nominalism. In this chapter, therefore, I shall recast the object of discussion as the uses of the past in the present. This is inherently a reflexive exercise: we cannot examine how various populations and interest groups use their images of the past to constitute or reinforce present interests unless we are prepared to include in our purview the question of how far anthropologists and other scholars have themselves become players in such processes. The idea that we somehow stand outside our object of study is preposterous. So is the notion, implicit in much nationalistic historiography, that a single historical narrative suffices to capture a people's past. Indeed, much of the anthropological engagement is with the multiple histories that one finds in a single social context, often articulated by the same people as they respond to the conflicting exigencies of their social, political, and cultural predicaments.

All this is now relatively familiar territory. Moreover, there are able critiques of archaeology and "Western civilization," of "orientalism" and "occidentalism," and ethnographic approaches to the local consequences of these ideologies (notable in the field of historic conservation). The Vichian paradigm of history as a series of tropes, variously revived by Hayden White (in *Metahistory* [1973]) and Edward Said (the author of *Orientalism* [1979], whose Vichian project is really laid out in *Beginnings* [1975]), have become part of the stock-in-trade; a volume on *Occidentalism* (Carrier, ed., 1995) helps to complete the critical framework. The peculiar engagement of anthropology with the past has become a topic for mature reflection.

In writing for the present project, Michael Roberts tackles the more general question of how anthropologists deal with history, while David Scott – in his extended comment, already visited in the previous chapter, on the work of Talal Asad – refocuses the discussion, specifically with regard to the history of European colonization around the world, on the criteria of relevance. As Scott remarks: "One important aspect of the discursive reality of European power concerns the relation between the objects of colonialist discourse and those of modern professional anthropology. The discourse and practice of colonial power constitutes a crucial element of the conceptual and ideological context in which anthropological objects are constructed and anthropological knowledge formed. However, despite the admirable attention to history that characterizes much contemporary anthropology it is still very poorly grasped that histories of the non-European social, cultural and political realities that anthropologists are interested in have also to be histories of the concepts through which such histories are constructed" (see D. Scott 1994; Asad et al. 1997).

One reason for which anthropologists may now be more willing to contemplate this turn is a spate of theoretical writings on the significance of the ethnography of western – and more narrowly, European – societies. Some of these address the reverse flow of immigrants from former colonial countries into "Fortress Europe" (e.g., Carter 1997), whose reaction reveals the dirty secret that it, too, has a vulnerable cultural identity. All these developments are consequences and examples of the shift to the more systemic reflexivity described in the previous chapter. As a result, the history of anthropology appears today less as a simple reflection of colonialism than as a critical commentary upon it. Yet, as Scott argues, we must go beyond even that perspective, morally appealing though it may be, for the present-day realities are such that a simple morality tale will not suffice. Instead, we must develop a history of the conditions that created the concepts of domination, which means a more exhaustive historical anthropology of colonialism (and, I would add, a more sustained ethnography of race relations as well).

That task, however, also applies to the analysis of the uses people make of the past in their everyday lives. To some extent, this is a question of method, but it is also epistemological: how do we respond to accounts of the past crafted according to criteria of relevance that do not fit our notions of truth? Does shifting the ground of investigation in the manner Scott recommends alter our own criteria? I shall begin this chapter by trying to tackle some of these issues, before returning to both Roberts's account of local, alternative readings of the colonial past and Scott's critique of the present state of postcolonial anthropology. Finally, in a question not often posed (but one that I think is a necessary consequence of these others), I shall ask what anthropologists can do to illuminate the processes that take place in the shadows of colonialism rather than under its heel – in countries that were never formally colonized, and societies whose weaker members were dragooned into the colonial project and are today confronting its consequences at home.

Methodological Issues

Are Scots songs that conflate Culloden and Bannockburn historically inaccurate? Do the Andean peasants who claim that Columbus brought the "Law of 1898" by which their lands were reorganized and sequestered simply not understand chronology (see J. Rappaport 1994)? Are the Andalusian farmers who reconstruct the events of Casas Viejas (J. Mintz 1982), or the Galicians who recall forced roadbuilding under the Franco regime (S. Roseman 1997), simply distorting a record they ought to know well? Is the account of the Inca past recorded by Guaman Poma (and discussed further in the chapter on Cosmologies) a historical text or a religious fiction?

Clearly people can and do, by the criteria of their own societies, misrepresent past events. They are judged to do so by their peers. But both the consensus and the dissenting voices are no further removed from historical accuracy than are those who, in Western society, debate the significance and morality of a war or a strike. The anthropologist's task is to determine the criteria by which accuracy (or faithfulness to an ideal of representation) is attributed, and to use these to understand the ways in which the members of a society relate the past to the present.

Questions of truth are largely predicated on relations of power, as Foucault and others have taught us. Thus, the other side of this task is to define the political context within which such assessments are made. Much of what authoritative discourse represents as "ignorant" might more precisely be seen as a form of resistance – or at least deliberate recalcitrance – in which the terms of a dominant historiography are recast by a subaltern population, for whom the capacity to decode the discourse of the powerful may be a matter of life and death. When Cretan sheep-thieves point out that the heroes of the national Greek revolution were called "thieves" (*kleftes*), are they simply distorting the truth – as the authorities would have it – or are they discerning a real historical connection now occluded by the state's careful management of categories and historical periods?

As in this example, the alleged distortions arise from the same sources as the criticism. Thus, in a very different context explored by Michael Roberts and others, Captain Cook figures in the stories related by several Aboriginal peoples in Australia. In rare cases he has been incorporated into their sacred tales of mythic origin. Among the Aboriginal people of the Victoria River Downs (VRD) region in the Northern Territory he is a central figure in more straightforward narratives, where he is "understood to be the first white fellow to invade Australia" and where his landing points and actions at specified locations along the coast of Australia are detailed (Rose 1992: 188–9). In these stories there is frequent reference to "Captain Cook's law" – a representation which Debbie Bird Rose understands to indicate "the set of rules and the structured relationships" to which the VRD Aboriginals have been subject since the late nineteenth century. In their summary view, the Whites treated them like dogs; "Captain Cook's law" must be read as one dimension within a variety of "resistance stories [seeking to] explain how certain things came to be while yet sustaining the essential moral structure of the universe." In these reviews Captain Cook is "an outlaw, morally speaking" (Rose 1992: 187–8). To the Cretan sheep-thieves, the present government is run by virtual Turks.

Among the VRD storytellers is an elderly man named Hobbles Danayarri whom Rose, in a persuasive recognition of intellectual equivalence, describes as a "political analyst." On one occasion Rose sought to reverse their roles and told Hobbles the story of Cook's death in Hawaii. Hobbles had no interest whatsoever in hearing such a tale. He said that Aboriginal people all knew that Captain Cook was dead – unlike Europeans, who refuse to allow him to die because they still "follow his law" (Rose 1993: 43–4).

Such indigenous analyses are not to be read as claims about matters of detailed fact, but as readings of the cultural and political world of the dominant Other. Captain Cook's logbook, that epitome of objectivist facticity, demonstrates that his men never set foot on Australian shores. But Hobbles, we may suppose, had other interests in mind. He clearly understood Cook as a suitable metonym for all oppressive Europeans, just as the Cumbales metonymically represented Columbus as the Hispanic oppressor and the mestizo leader Simón Bolivar as the antecedent of their own local leaders, whose seizure of land from state authorities and mestizo landowners was a metonymic act of revolution and liberation resurrecting the heroics of El Liberador. Each such act is informed by a sense of the past that derives its meaning from the present. This is the realm of what Victor Turner (1974) called "social dramas" – the infusion of present experience and action by the resurrection of key events from the past. Such reproductions of the past may not be self-conscious. Whether as invocations of long-forgotten cosmologies of chance and divine intervention in excuses or as rituals, dance, and bodily gesture, social performances may provide actors with the assurance of having a past, however inchoate it may seem to outside observers to be. That past may be reproduced in attempts to come to terms with a discomfiting present: the horror of West African slavery relived as the catastrophic disruption caused by unrestrained consumerist greed (Shaw 1997: 868–9). And there may be circumstances under which specificity is dangerous, oblivion a virtue. In the controlled spaces of totalitarian state systems, Pierre Nora's (Nora, ed., 1994) "places of memory" may be matched by "zones of forgetting" (see R. Watson, ed., 1994). The horrors of memory may overwhelm the desire for commemoration, so that the erstwhile victims of a repressive colonial regime may today show little interest in recalling such a defining phase of their collective past (Cole 1998). Given that all historical narratives are necessarily selective, those sometimes loud silences remind us that forgetting can be an active strategy.

In either case, past and present necessarily inform each other: the anthropologist's task is to identify the idioms in which they illuminate each other. Thus, for example, Andrew Shryock, to whose analysis of history-making in the context of segmentary politics I shall return more fully later in this chapter, shows how successfully a Jordanian political candidate could both claim descent from the Prophet and invoke the history of Muhammad's own rise to authority while invoking "providential cant" (about good fortune and God's will) "to protect his success . . . from the imitation of others" (Shryock 1997: 280). Social dramas have actors; and actors are the – often mutually antagonistic – agents of a process that draws in circular fashion on historical predecent in order to legitimate the present: when successful, this move in turn revalidates the specific reading of the past that has been invoked.

I emphasize the circularity of this process because it is the key to understanding history, not as a set of referential data, but as something that people use to buttress their identity against the corrosive flow of time. For it is clear that history, while ostensibly a celebration of time, often serves instead to suppress its specificity: when it becomes the discourse of any totalizing regime – whether academic or political – it acquires precisely that capacity for suppressing time that Lévi-Strauss identified as the specific property of myth.

But this does not necessarily make history static. It may provide a creative rethinking of pasts mythologized in very different fashion by previous sources of authority. While Jennifer Cole's Malagasy informants largely avoided explicit discourses about the colonial past, other peoples rework the stated facts to account for its effects in the present. Roberts has provided a fine example of the discourse of anticolonial resentment as it operates in exactly this fashion to reconstitute the facts of invasion as an exploration of its oppressive consequences. The parallel with the tales of Cook and Columbus are instructive.

Here is Roberts's account: "After Vasco da Gama sailed round the Cape of Good Hope in 1498 a number of Portuguese ships under Lourenço de Almeida turned up in the bay of Colombo in 1505. The little port was about six miles from the seat of the principal Sinhalese kingdom, the Kingdom of Kotte. A Sinhala jana kata, or folk tale, purports to describe how this arrival of exotic newcomers was received and conveyed to the Sinhalese king: 'There is in our harbour in Colombo a race of people fair of skin and comely withal. They don jackets of iron and hats of iron; they rest not a minute in one place; they walk here and there; they [gobble] hunks of stone and drink blood; they give two or three pieces of gold and silver for one fish or one lime; the report of their cannon is louder than thunder when it bursts on the rock Yugandhara. Their cannon balls fly many a gawwa and shatter fortresses of granite.'[1]

"This tale entered a palm-leaf book known as the *Alakeshvara Yuddhaya* (circa 1592) and was then incorporated in the late 16th and early 17th centuries in the various recensions of the *Rajavaliya* (*The Story of Kings*, a work written in a popular rather than classical style), from which it migrated to printed texts in English and Sinhala over the last two centuries. Among the English-educated circles in 20th-century Sri Lanka it was read as an indication of the rustic character of the indigenous people (C. R. de Silva 1983: 14). The focus in that reading is less on the Portuguese than on the Sinhalese. The result is an unintentional colonialist interpretation."

Roberts has recontextualized this story, however, in terms of the Sinhala folk poetry-cum-tales known as *teravili*, and as a local response to the brutalities accompanying the Portuguese mercantile colonization of Sri Lanka. In the Sinhala hatana (war) poems of the middle and late seventeenth century, the Portuguese emerge as "parangi, heretical evil-doers, cruel and brutal"[2] – a characterization that reflects their destructive methods and their massive assault on Buddhism through proselytization and the seizure of monastic properties. Mass conversion, notably among recent migrants on the coastal littoral, evoked the Sinhalas' especial ire in the 1560s (C. de Silva 1982: 238–41, 246). And Roberts remarks that the story of de Almeida's arrival should therefore not be read as an event that took place in 1505: "Rather, it should be treated as a parabolic representation of the Portuguese after the Sinhalese people had experienced their practices and their rule over parts of the island. Thus refigured, it can be treated as a condenzed representation of the primordial Portuguese." The reference to the Portuguese as "gobblers of stone" and "drinkers of blood" serves, Roberts argues, as a symbolic representation of the sacrament of communion and thus of the Catholic religion, linking the latter and its Portuguese bearers with the Sinhala netherworld – "whose creatures, the *yakku* and *peretayo* (demons and ancestor spirits), crave blood and flesh." Roberts deploys a series of binary oppositions to show that this cosmology "can be said to associate the Portuguese with an absence of restraint and with the forces of disorder" (see also Roberts 1989). Parentheticaly, it is worth noting the similarity of this analysis with Ossio's treatment of Guaman Poma's chronicle of the Spanish Conquista of the Andes, not only for its evidence of the way in which existing cosmologies chart cataclysmic human interventions in terms of the forces of chaos and order, but also because both analysts deploy a traditionally ahistorical methodology to elicit a historical reading not tied to the western sources. This in turn suggests that the current fad of rejecting structuralist analysis as ahistorical may turn on a culturally very limited understanding of what history should be – although, be it said, structuralism is itself beset with assumptions about human cognition that derive from a notably western philosophical tradition. Including our own theoretical perspectives in the repertoire of phenomena being compared provides a useful "reality check" for the anthropologist.

Note, too, that the Sinhala tale discussed does not mean that the Sinhalese accepted the terror with which the Portuguese tried to cow them into submission. The "restless, meat-craving, demonic beings" to which the tale assimilates them may have inspired real fear in the Sinhalese, but, as Roberts points out, they are also regarded as beings worth trying to control: "[T]hey can be tricked and subject to ridicule in ways that restore them to their proper place below humans in the hierarchical cosmos. When confronting the tale of the Portuguese arrival as a written text, the silly face of the yakku is not easy to discern. One requires the lilt and tilt of oral recitations to derive this import. In other words, the riddle would, in the past, have imparted its message most effectively in its oral form: the performance and intonation would capture a spirit of resistance at the same time that they guided the audience towards hidden plays and symbolic connections." Thus, its social embeddedness is what rescues the structural analysis from the timeless abstraction to which such analyses so often fall prey. As John McCall (1999) and Johannes Fabian (1990) both remark in other contexts, performance – not necessarily of a verbal kind – restores temporality to historical consciousness, linking the pace of presentation with the passage of the *longue durée*.

Textualizing Performances

Even when we are forced to depend on fragmentary versions appearing on paper as reported talk (e.g., Guha 1983: 100, 112, 150), oral narrative is an important source of alternative visions of the past. Moreover, the rendition of such narratives as printed text, by a huge range of agents from colonial managers to anthropologists and local intellectuals, can provide valuable insights into the relationship between text and power. The process of "entextualization" (Silverstein and Urban, eds., 1996) is itself both the expression and an important instrument of colonial and other forms of hegemony. Gloria Raheja (1996), for example, has shown in an exceptionally elegant analysis how the British colonial academic establishment entextualized proverbs about particular ethnic groups in India as a way of essentializing convenient political ineqalities as exigent cultural ones. Even the simple representation of texts as "oral" as opposed to "literate" is a form of hegemonic entextualization, especially in societies – today in the overwhelming majority – where the act of writing is itself imbued with implications of power and referentiality.

Thus, we must beware of exaggerating the contrast between literate and oral cultures (see also Barber 1989: 13). It can itself become a device for representing subaltern populations as lesser or reduced in some intrinsic way. Moreover, the separation does not entirely make sense from a literary standpoint either. Oral narrative is never completely driven out by literacy, and the relationship between oral and literate sources is not simply that of colonized and colonizer or (in folklore studies) that of peasant and savant. Recalling that "history" and "story" are etymological cognates helps somewhat, as does the fact that the Greek root of "anecdote" means "unpublished" rather than "unreliable" or "foolish." Anthropologists, operating in the intimate spaces of social life where the wisdom of official discourse is often questioned by the voice of experience, are in a position to assess the extent to which knowledge of the past is dependent on the vicissitudes of the present. Simplistic distinctions between "oral" and "literate" cultures – as though entire cultures could be defined in such single-stranded terms – occlude that key insight.

Older approaches (e.g., Vansina 1965) were an extension to oral discourse of stemmatics – the reconstruction of "original texts" from later manuscript sources. Here "objective" history was the scholars' account of the narratives' origins, rather than what the narratives themselves recounted. Because the processes of oral transmission are usually immune to close examination after the fact, and because the transmission of information is rarely unilineal, the stemmatic view of the relationship among a set of contemporaneous texts – that they constitute partial survivals of some authentic and complete original – is patently misleading.

It is made all the more so by its failure to account for the various forms of figurative language through which all narrative relates events to an overarching structure of ideas. Hayden White and Edward Said (both following Vico) have argued, albeit in different ways, that the master narratives of western historiography represent a succession of devices none of which can be said to offer a literal reading of the past (although some are literalist – that is, they make claims to literalness). By the same token, all historical narrative, including the evanescent formulae of "sound bites" media headlines, not to speak of the more obviously "symbolic" assertions of folksong and etiological myth, is to be read in terms of such interpretational devices rather than as a plain record of events.

Claims to literalness are often fiercely defended against such anthropological and historiographic agnosticism, and they carry the authority of a long imperial tradition. Their performance has a context – which, as ethnographers, we should include in any subsequent account. Michael Roberts records his own experience of such hostility meted out to his interpretation of the Portuguese arrival (K. de Silva 1990; Roberts 1994: 28), and comments, "The force of practical reason in the academic world of Sri Lanka marks the degree to which British empiricism and its epistemology have dominated its forms of knowledge." He is severely critical of the effects: "The corpus of historical publications about Sri Lanka that have been produced in recent years is quite impressive, but even a nodding acquaintance with the histories of Black Africa and the Pacific is sufficient to indicate that, broadly speaking, the work on Sri Lanka (including my own) does not match the degree of sophistication shown in the best essays on African and Pacific localities."

Roberts attributes to this difference the much greater degree of methodological innovation found in those areas where indigenous written records were not available for reduction to a European model of literate semantics. Lacking indigenous written records prior to the colonial intrusions, he argues, scholars were forced into innovative methodologies and theories. One of the pathfinders was Jan Vansina. While subsequent criticisms and other ethnographies have forced him to amend his innovative decipering of oral traditions (Vansina 1985), however, even these modifications perpetuate the idea that there are African oral texts "whose object [is] recognisably consonant with that of the European historian" (Barber 1989: 14).

In contrast to this view, Karin Barber's analysis exemplifies the approach that anthropologists bring to the historical record. In writing about the *oriki*, she argues that their performers' intention is not to chronicle events, but that they are nevertheless "intrinsically and profoundly historical" in that they "represent 'the past in the present', the way the knowledge of the past makes itself felt stubbornly and often contradictorily today. They represent a way . . . of re-experiencing the past and reintegrating it into the present." It is partly for this reason that the oriki are so valued by the Yoruba (Barber 1989: 14). It does certainly seem to be an assumption of western European historical discourse that history must be textual. Even oral historians depend on a textual model. Yet even within Europe, as for example Seremetakis (1993) has shown for Greece, historical memory may be embedded in bodily markers, "sedimented" in the body (Connerton 1989), encoded in modes of preparing food, musical forms, landscapes (K. Basso 1996), the imagery of responsibility and blame (Herzfeld 1992: 127–57), and, as John McCall (1999) has argued in detail for Ohafia (Nigeria), dance. There may be an entire series of mnemonically laden objects, embeded in a complex semiotic linking place, relationships, and history, and collectively understood by a single term – as with the Belauan *olangch* described by Parmentier (1987: 12): "These include carved narrative pictures, named ceramic and glass valuables, anthropomorphic monoliths, pre-scribed seating patterns, names and titles, ceremonial protocols, stone grave pavements, and oral narratives." Thus it is with the oriki. Their intertextual relations with other forms of oral poetry are enmeshed in a wider context of interpretation in which reference is less important as a source of meaning than are allusion, sensual recall, and relations with other genres (see also Bauman 1986, for a model of this approach, applied to Texas folklore).

Roberts has criticized the anthropological tendency to impose a textual model of coherence on forms of historical knowing, and argues that an open-ended hermeneutics more precisely fits the philosophical idiom of African societies. T. C. McKaskie (1989: 71), whom Roberts invokes in this regard, explicitly invokes the idiom of Richard Rorty: "epistemology proceeds on the assumption that all contributions to a given discourse are commensurable. Hermeneutics is largely a struggle against this assumption." McKaskie's argument is that in his field of inquiry "the Asante historical and cultural context is itself hermeneutical" and that in this respect it differs from established Western modes of analysis in history and anthropology (1989: 72).

There is, however, a danger with this approach also. What does it mean to treat our informants as theorists, as hermeneuticists, even as intellectuals, given that these terms are all grounded in their own particular histories in the West? The motivation may be benign, a principle of mutual respect, but this will only work if the Western observer relinquishes control of the meaning of such his-torically embedded terms as "theory" or "philosophy" – a task requiring her-culean efforts at detachment. As Hountondji (1983; see also Mudimbe 1988) – himself a supporter of the view that Roberts espouses – has noted, even attribut-ing "philosophy" to African societies risks representing their thought in Euro-centric terms. Similar concerns attach to the reductive implications of "oral literature" and "indigenous theory," in which the professional activities of Western intellectuals become the touchstone of excellence.

But this is the classic dilemma of an anthropology committed to respect for the intellectual and aesthetic life of all the peoples its practitioners study. Rather than simply trying to make it disappear through some inventive neologism, we should deploy this uncomfortable awareness to critical advantage, in part by recalling that our own supposedly abstract theories are a form of social practice – a concept that has been especially present in Italian social theory from Vico through Gramsci, De Martino, and Eco long before it became an integral part of a practice-oriented anthropology in politically more powerful European academies.

In this view, anthropologists themselves become the reflexive source of a critical comparativism. Instead of a purely self-indulgent narcissism, reflexivity becomes the art of keeping the assumptions of a necessarily relativistic discipline always in question. It is for this reason, too, that we cannot afford to ignore the long and sometimes shameful history of anthropological involvement in the colonial project. As Vico reminds us, forgetting the social entailments of our present knowledge undercuts that knowledge – decontextualizes it, as we would say today – and so renders it meaningless and useless. Indeed, much of what has happened to historical epistemology in postcolonial settings is, like the political life that encases it (Mbembe 1991), itself a reaction to – and parodic reproduction of – antecedent colonial forms. If we place our own assumptions about the past in direct comparison with those of other peoples, this does not mean that the gloss "history" must entail a reduction to European models.

Yet the risk of misinterpretation is always strong. Hanson's (1983) discussion of Maori historical modes of thought, while made accessible by a direct comparison with western semiotic models, shows how we may maintain the tension of analogy – between similarity and difference – against reductionism. But this did not save Hanson from considerable opprobrium when he insisted (1989) that much Maori cultural revivalism entailed a kind of strategic essentialism.

As a remarkably important experiment in broadening the category of "history" in critical fashion, we should note Shryock's (1997) remarkable deconstruction of Arabic *tarikh* as a form of history-making in which truth is locally understood to be socially embedded and therefore changeable. Here the issue is not a simplistic division of labor between oral and literary modes. Shryock shows that, just as an honest man may lie in order to expose the falsity of another's claims and so claim access to a higher truth, Bedouin historians so fully recognize the evanescence of present political alliances – which are grounded in shifting interpretations of clan genealogies – that they intensely disliked the idea of the reduction of their narratives to any form of permanent record, whether on tape or in print (Shryock 1997:16). This is the kind of historical account that works in a segmentary society; just as in my own fieldwork the denial of animal-theft fell by the wayside of interclan rivalry as each narrator became aware of his peers' access to me and wished to surpass them in tales of derring-do, so Shryock found that discord and history were often virtually the same thing. Only the official history of an institutional structure such as the nation-state will present the past as inevitably leading to unity in the present age.

Such history-making eventually yields to the unitary vision of nation-state. Indeed, informants' initial reluctance in such societies to admit to the form that events take in segmentary societies, to adopt Paul Dresch's (1986) useful phrase, suggests that the statist veneer is already in place, requiring an initial defense of the cultural intimacy of experienced differences of both opinion and alleged quality before the anthropologist's own familiarity – acquired in the field – makes such dissembling untenable. If the bland face of unity is taken to be the objective truth, as official state rhetoric usually demands, the segmentary representation of the past must logically be as mendacious as it is taken to be by the standards of a positivistic western canon.

This dilemma is especially real for those who live in societies not yet fully absorbed into a state system. History-making of the sort Shryock describes captures precisely the difficulty of knowing with certainty anything about a past that has such grave consequences for those living in the present. The goal is not to treat it as though it belonged to exactly the same mode as western historiography, but simply to compare the two idioms in order to elucidate the differences as well as the similarities between their respective sets of criteria of reliability and accountabiliy. This makes respect for both a more manageable proposition.

The kind of reflexive comparativism I am suggesting here offers precisely this advantage: instead of making "our own" mode the immovable touchstone for the evaluation of all others, we treat it as an interesting cultural object in its own right. This is surely what taking comparativism seriously and reflexively must entail. It is also the corollary of Shryock's tactical decision to engage directly in the history-making methods of his informants instead of trying to stand aloof and observe them from outside. In this manner he not only gained a fine-grained ethnographic understanding of Bedouin ideas about the past, but he also came to see his own sense of history – and of anthropology, for that matter – as the culturally located practices that they are. Note, too, that, unlike positivist historians, he does not separate his account of the data collection from the analysis proper: indeed, it is this immediate engagement that leads him to realize that, under conditions of segmentary social and political relations, "the binary rhetoric is real" (Shryock 1997: 135) – a point that also has relevance for the problems associated with the binary (structuralist) analysis of cosmologies. History, too, is refracted through such cosmological principles. Shryock deployed the field situation to achieve a measure of distance from the principles that governed official history and was thereby led to a fuller sense of how Bedouin tribal sheikhs were making theirs. Since this inevitably led him into alarming (and entirely context-dependent) discussions about who was lying and which narratives should be discarded, he also provides a vivid portrait of the fieldwork vicissitudes necessary for the achievement of this grounded understanding. And given that some Arab social attitudes encapsulate the possibility that a tactical lie may reveal a deeper truth – that one might morally subvert the truth in order to provoke worse liars into revealing themselves (Gilsenan 1976) – it is clear that we can evaluate the historicity of these sheikhly genealogies only if we are prepared to situate them in a larger moral universe in which lying in defense of one's patrilineal kin may be a high moral stance.

But the question of how we position ourselves in the quest for knowledge about "other histories" (Hastrup, ed., 1992) is not only one of methodology. It is also epistemological. One dramatic example of what happens when we insert our own historiography into the comparativist project brings us back to the case of Captain Cook. The Aboriginals who insisted that they knew better than Europeans that Cook had truly died were challenging his elevation to godhead even while, in disputing "Cook's Law," they were also pointing to a form of self-perpetuation quite different from the literal apotheosis with which Europeans thought the Tahitians had imbued him. For them Cook was the emblematic colonizer, and they certainly knew that even if he had died the oppression he represented had not. But it is among the Hawai'ians that anthropologists have most forcefully encountered their own entailment in the construction of the past.

It was among the Hawaiians, after all, that Cook was supposedly received as a god. In response to Marshall Sahlins's argument that the death of Captain Cook can be attributed to consequences of the Tahitians' conviction that he was their returned god Lono, the Sri Lankan anthropologist Gananath Obeyesekere (1992) accused Sahlins (1985) of uncritically accepting European fables that constructed the Hawaiians as incredulous primitives and inserted self-serving ideas of the Hawaiian view of Europeans into this picture. The Hawaiian myth that Cook was the god Lono, a point central to Sahlins's thesis, is, says Obeyesekere, actually a European myth – a neat and ironic reversal of epistemic categories.

Sahlins, in response (1995), charges Obeyesekere with two logical and procedural errors: on the one hand, he says, Obeyesekere has read modern (eighteenth-century) European rationalism into the Hawaiians; on the other, he has taken it upon himself to speak for all Third World victims of imperialism. Both errors, in Sahlins's view, are category mistakes, entailing ideological decisions that do as much violence to the ethnographic and historical record as does the most egregious Eurocentrism. In Roberts's words, the Hawaiians thus "become the epitome of 'practical rationality.' Through this emphasis they are assimilated to the Sinhalese; and together constitute the universal native, the homogenized Other battling the precious West."

The Sahlins–Obeyesekere debate has inspired numerous commentaries and even one fictional replay. Roberts describes it as "unresolved," but I would argue that it is, and should remain, unresolvable: the fissures may be best kept open so that we can more fully discern the ideological and political consequences of both lines of argument. Thus, for example, it is entirely clear that one key issue concerns the question of whether First World scholars are entitled to pronounce on the cultural and religious values of others; or, conversely, whether a scholar emanating from the Third World is, purely for that reason, entitled to represent that bloc in its confrontation with the West. Robert Borofsky (1997) has provided, with significant input from the protagonists, an extremely useful and dispassionate account of this debate, in the course of which Sahlins (in Borofsky 1997: 273), endorsing Borofsky's general perspective, sensibly observes: "To assume the right to speak for Hawaiians would be morally repugnant as well as epistemologically mad. Nor is the problem whether they . . . can speak. The problem is whether they can be heard and understood." This simple assertion of a principled modesty, whether followed in practice or not, restores the responsibility for interpretations to those who presume to make them, and away from the generic claims to representation from which Obeyesekere, as Borofsky (1997: 278) notes, has properly distanced himself. The debate has been useful – if for nothing else, then at least for showing up the limits on the extent to which an anthropologist – any anthropologist – can assume an authoritative voice.

Other debates, similarly embedded in the cultural politics of the late twentieth-century West, come to mind. Prominent among these is the Afrocentric claim, buttressed by the publication of Martin Bernal's magisterial but controversial *Black Athena* (1987), about the supposedly "African" (but also Semitic) genesis of western civilization (see also Lefkowitz 1996). This debate, indeed, illustrates how truth claims are filtered through differing interpretations of key cultural categories. Precisely what it means to say that the ancient Greeks owed much of their culture to "Africa" treads a dangerously ill-defined line between racial and cultural definitions of nationhood, drawing the debate into the perilous waters of ethnonational pride.

Indeed, the hostile reaction evinced by *Black Athena* among conservative Greek scholars – that is, scholars of Greek nationality – and the educated public in Greece shows that we must carefully scrutinize all claims by intellectuals to represent a national or even a broader constituency ("the Third World"). It is, after all, through the same neo-Classical elite ideology that today rejects Bernal's arguments out of hand that Greeks were taught to reject everything familiar in their vernacular culture as "foreign" to the Classical Hellenism invented by the eighteenth-century German scholars who had sired both the "autochthonous" theory of Greek ethnogenesis and, in the lineage of "Aryan" linguistics, the so-called racial science of the Nazis. This is also the ideology that has today made it necessary to specify whenever one means modern Greeks, as I have just done, because the West has made Classical antiquity the only acceptable touchstone of their cultural worth. As with the Sahlins–Obeyesekere debate, it is less interesting to take sides than it is to inspect the political implications of each position. Whatever we mean anthropologically by "the truth" must lie as much in the debate itself as in the facts marshaled by either side. And to ignore the social and cultural embedding of such debates is hardly a convincing way of being empirical.

The example of modern Greece provides a useful key to historicizing those whom Eric Wolf has ironically dubbed "the people without history" (Wolf 1982). For the modern Greeks – a people arguably plagued by an excess of history, but of a kind invented for them by more powerful others – face real-life dilemmas of self-description (for example: "are we European?") that lie at the same point of intellectual origin as the question of ancient Greek roots and as anthropology itself. Those who espouse extreme nationalist positions, claiming (as they invoke Alexander, Philip, and Aristotle) that the name of Macedonia is exclusively Greek and that there is no such thing as a Mace-

donian minority, are reacting to the exigencies of a perhaps genuinely dangerous local situation in which their country faces potentially hostile neighbors
on several fronts; but they are also resuscitating the very logic that has always
compromised their supposed independence to begin with – the logic according
to which all the country's modern claims must be evaluated by the yardstick
of ancient history. The recent furor over the publication of a relatively mild
historical and ethnographic account of the progressive hellenization of the Greek
province of Macedonia (Karakasidou 1997) exhibits both the nervousness
of the Greek establishment and the persistence of stereotypes of Greeks as
irrational, hysterical Balkan lunatics among supposedly sober commentators in
the West. It also demonstrates the neuralgia that anthropology can induce
in those who are committed to unitary myths of national origin, as it also does
the sometimes unavoidable entailment of anthropology in its object of study.
And it raises anew the question of how far anthropology should go in questioning the defensive essentialisms of weaker nations and other groups: since
these framings of identity are often grounded in a positivistic model of history,
arguments about the debatability of the past must always carry ethical overtones. While, for example, one might justify the critiques of Balkan nationalism on the grounds that they have inspired the symbolic but also very material
practice of "ethnic cleansing," one should also note the role of more powerful
international agents in promoting the logic they are so anxious to attribute
to exoticized Others.

In these terms, it should be clear that a clear adjudication of the debate
between Obeyesekere and Sahlins is probably an unrealistic goal. "The dispute
is a polemical one," remarks David Scott. "But it is not hard to see that it is
only superficially about the details, about whether eighteenth-century Hawaiians actually took Cook to be a manifestation of their god Lono. What gives
the dispute its cash-value is that it highlights the larger epistemological
question of what is (or what ought to be) entailed in the construction of knowledge of non-European peoples and places." For Scott, however, its further significance is "that the anxiety generated by the critique of colonialist discourse
often turns on mis-stated questions such as the following: When Western scholars write about non-Western societies, do they inevitably perpetuate the myths
of European imperialism? Can Western scholars ever articulate the meanings
and logics of non-Western peoples?" Dismissing such questions as misguided,
because they essentialize "the Western [or colonial] oberver" in a singularly
unhelpful fashion, he echoes Nicholas Thomas's skepticism about the real
impact of anthropological theories: "whether they do or do not perpetuate
such myths, depends neither upon their moral attitude toward the colonized or
ex-colonized (the natives), nor upon their implicit or explicit anticolonial
political sympathies. And it certainly does not depend upon whether the anthropological hermeneutic involved is Marxist, structuralist, or psychoanalytic."
Rather, he argues, their compliance in the perpetuation of such myths depends
on their ability to see these, no less than the essentialized identities of today's
struggling Third World nations, as constructions, located "in particular
conceptual and ideological histories." Colonialism is such a context. And,

as Scott observes, "it is very often the case that the objects that come to organize a professional anthropological inquiry (a religious discourse, a ritual practice, a kinship structure, a trading pattern) are first constituted as visible objects in missionary, administrative, or travel narratives, reports, and diaries." Recall Nicholas Thomas's call to look at such genres as museum reports: these, too, are documents of that particular history, that particular construction of knowledge.

It also makes very little sense, from this standpoint, to argue whether Obeyesekere or Sahlins is correct. Rather, we should attempt to describe the competing cultural logics that permit the simultaneous production of very different versions of the past even within anthropology itself – precisely, in fact, as we do for the populations we study. Here, in fact, an analogy from the study of fiction may be especially helpful: arguments about whether a work is history, a chronicle, or a novel have important consequences for the kinds of truth that are at stake, and one of the tasks the anthropologist must undertake is to explore the classification of genres in relation to concepts of truth and falsehood, or more generally to idioms and conventions of representation. This is what Shryock did with the Jordanian shaeikhs' narratives. As we examine cultures in which the genres of narrative about the past diverge in intended content from those with which we are familiar, the question of what constitutes history becomes all the more obviously embedded in the specificities of culture, politics, and pragmatic concerns ranging from the interactional to the institutional.

Roberts argues that the significance of the Obeyesekere–Sahlins debate is enhanced by the self-conscous innovativeness of Sahlins' initial work on Hawaii. Where the historian Braudel seeks to sideline event history and where Lévi-Strauss discards sequential time as irrelevant to the perduring cognitive structures he seeks to identify in all cultures, says Roberts, "Sahlins attempts to bridge anthropology and history by developing a 'structural, historical anthropology'" Or, in Aletta Biersack's words, he attempts "to recover event, action, change, and the world for structural analysis. Conversely, he [seeks] to recover structural analysis for history" (Biersack 1989: 85). In Sahlins's work, famously, we see that structured meanings "are revalued as they are practically enacted" (M. Sahlins 1985: vii); contingency and cultural form, like agency and structure, are mutually entailed and, again like agency and structure, cannot exist – that is, we cannot apprehend them – in isolation from each other.

While Biersack regards Sahlins's dialectical model as a reconciliation of structural and cultural analyses and an intertwining of "questions of genesis and meaning," others have accused Sahlins of cultural or semiotic determinism (e.g., Friedman 1987: 74; Peel 1993: 173). Peel also tackles Sahlins on his own chosen ground, arguing that "the model of history that is put forward is of transitions between given cultural orders." In the result, the Hawaiian representations of their past, with all their potentiality for contestation and reflexivity, are not given adequate attention, insofar as they are treated as an "unproblematic cultural endowment" (Peel 1993: 171). This, in other words, is mainly a question of agency. It is also a recognition that structure often only becomes apparent when it is disputed. It is the actors, moreover, who recognize analogies between events widely separated in time and space. This is the basis of the predominance, already noted, of social dramas at times of great social or cultural strain.

One consequence of this recognition of agency is that we can contextualize different kinds of text and understand that local actors use them according to shifts in context as well as intention. Of such a kind is our own distinction between academic and popularizing history, for example, or that between social and diplomatic history. Some scholars have used formal semiotic models to flush out such important internal discriminations. Hanson (1983), for example, used the notion of the syntagmatic structure (or structural sequence) to identify Maori understandings of historical experience in terms of a variable relationship with the present – which, while continuous with some aspects of the past, is not always seen as equally consequent upon it.

In a related methodological vein, Valerio Valeri found that Hawaiians used two quite distinct modes of historical text: prose narratives and genealogical chants. In the narratives the emphasis is on content and its history is argument. The genealogical panegyrics, on the other hand, are "total works of art" with magical as well as aesthetic effects. He then clarifies the mutual interplay and effect of these differing forms of indigenous history through the theoretical distinction between syntagmatic relations and paradigmatic relations in the representation of events. With syntagmatic relations, the emphasis is on events defined by their position on a temporal chain, so that they are signs presenting history as a cumulative process. Paradigmatic relations, on the other hand, establish connections "between events as members of classes of actions"; and, as such, are metaphoric. They "exemplify rules" and are memorable for this reason, thereby possessing a capacity to conflate past and present (Valeri 1990: 157, 160). They are the very stuff of social drama. In the comparison of narrative and genealogical history, "paradigmatic and syntagmatic dimensions exist in both, although for purposes of legitimation, the paradigmatic one dominates in the narratives and the syntagmatic one in the genealogies" (Valeri 1990: 174). In the genealogical chants, "the supreme value of continuity is magically reproduced out of the discontinuities represented, and justified, by narrative history" (Valeri 1990: 188). The discussion leads to the conclusion that although historical precedent may be used to legitimate change, "the relationship between past and present is never conceived as one of mechanical reproduction. It is instead analogical and thus implies difference, not only similarity, between past and present. It implies, moreover, a choice between alternatives. This is precisely what is implied by [the] use of the term paradigmatic to describe its dominant mode" (Valeri 1990: 190).

Why Does the Past Legitimate?

This question, while important, is misdirected. It should be: who gives the past its legitimating authority, and why? To ask "what the past does" is to ignore competing forms of agency – the most serious effect, in human affairs, of the logical error known as the fallacy of misplaced concreteness.

The image of origins as the source of political unity is clearly central: it is a translation of history into pragmatics. This is the sense of Evans-Pritchard's (1940) genealogical concept of "structural time," in which the degree of social distance between two groups corresponds to the number of generations that separate them from their common ancestor. Nationalist historiography renders this relativized logic absolute: if you are not of our stock, you are alien to us. It also takes over the genealogical principle of "telescoping" or "structural amnesia" to generate officially sanctioned silences about sources of internal difference: embarrassing historical interventions and invasions by "foreign" peoples are decreed not to exist. And colonialist historiography turns the process around, acknowledging difference as the justification of hegemony. Origins clearly do legitimate; Mary Helms (1988) has argued, moreover, that more distant origins – or control over more distantly produced goods – legitimate more fully: they have the ungainsayable force of inaccessibility.

But origins can also be disputed. Not only are they the direct focus of political debate; actors often use them to infuse everyday disputes with competing claims to authority, and such repeated invocation is what creates habitual respect for their significance, if not agreement as to their correct interpretation. It is this reenactment of past events in the present that gives such force to Turner's (1974) "social drama" – a recognizable type of event, corresponding to the methodological model of the "diagnostic event" (S. Moore 1987) in the study of social process, but given authority precisely because it analogically conjures up a respected past.

Social drama, sometimes in the form of major events (such as national revolutions playing themselves out as renditions of the Passion of Christ), may also subsist in relatively everyday, recurrent moments: it is then their commonplace character that makes them persuasive. Moreover, they suggest, as Roberts notes, an important reason for rejecting the functionalist view of myth (or history) as a charter for the present popularized by Malinowski (1948). Such explanations presuppose an inner purpose, a Durkheimian social genius, that decides in advance which version of the past is to be legitimated and whose interests it will serve. In practice, everything is always up for grabs: the enactment of a social drama is one of the ways in which power, precariously gained, may be kept or increased, or perhaps redirected, and to invoke a functionalist explanation is simply to collude in the just-so stories told by the victors as the instrument ("charter") of their vindication. In this sense, in fact, functionalism is a social drama in its own right.

In analyzing the fleeting social dramas of everyday life, moreover, we can correct the imbalance – the conflation of the analytic perspective with the interests of the currently powerful – by observing who uses what allusions to what past and for what purposes. Michael Roberts, drawing on recollections of his home country, Sri Lanka, nicely illustrates the fluid character of such moments: "A trivial incident from the ethnographic present of Sri Lanka illustrates the empowerment provided by historical understandings. The little drama unfolded at a cricket match in Colombo in 1981. It involved two Sri Lankan players whom I will call Laddie and Sinha. Laddie appeared to be a burgher (i.e. an ethnic label describing European descendants). But he was participating in a contest in which Sri Lanka was confronting Australia. It was as a patriotic Sri Lankan that he teased Australian fielders within earshot, with an occasional sally at local spectators. When Sinha befriended an Australian fielder, he too was subject to intermittent teasing. Amiably defensive for the most part, Sinha bore the banter – till Laddie questioned his patriotism, at which point his retort was devastatingly effective: 'I am a Sinhalese,' said he, pointing to his chest affirmatively. Laddie was silenced and after that left Sinha alone, directing his taunts elsewhere. In one stroke Laddie, the aggressor, had been disempowered" (Roberts 1994: 271–5). Sinha's retort was in restricted code. It was as evocative as lucid, its meaning fully understood by all the indigenous bystanders. He transported Laddie beyond the cricket field to the surrounding political arena of Sri Lanka. Laddie was reminded of the conventional view that Sri Lanka had been, from centuries back, a predominantly Sinhalese country; and that this claim had received a resounding majoritarian sanction at the general elections of 1956 when Sinhalese linguistic nationalism had secured the foreground of politics. And Laddie was sharply made aware of his own identity as a Sri Lankan of European descent, a newcomer with less of a lien on the place than a son of the soil. For what Sinha in effect said was: "Who are you *lansi puta* [son of a burgher] to question my loyalty?"

From our position today the incident can be deemed trivial, but its very triviality enhances its significance. Sinha and Laddie were ordinary middle-class people, not tied to a powerful party. This was an "everyday" affair, one that provides grist for those interested in the mill of popular culture. The exchange also reveals the dynamic possibilities of interpersonal interaction: namely, that specific images of the past, with their associated values and legitimations, can emerge from within the minutiae of everyday exchanges. And these images are then registered in the memory-banks of those who witness/hear such exchanges.

And in such "triviality" anthropologists play their strongest card: for the question of who defines what as trivial is itself a commentary on the politics of significance underlying the role of the social sciences in public debate (Herzfeld 1997c). Attention to the supposedly trivial can disturb the complacency of the dominant, whose construction of what constitutes common sense suddenly appears a good deal less objective, and a good deal more self-interested, than before. Common sense is the world-classifying face of power; the social dramas of everyday life forever oscillate between reproducing and disputing its authority.

Colonialism and its Reverberations

Attempting to gauge local common sense – "the native's point of view" (Geertz 1983: 55–70) – is, as we have seen, an inadequate approach if it is not thoroughly contextualized in relation to that other "native's" point of view, that of the anthropologist. The latter carries a great deal of historical baggage, and the negotiation that leads to the production of ethnography must reflect the effects of both sets of historical understandings entailed in the encounter. This is where Scott's gloss on Asad will prove particularly helpful.

In an Afterword to a recent volume of George Stocking's *History of Anthropology* series dedicated to the question of colonialism (see Stocking 1991), Asad urged a shift in preoccupations "from the history of colonial anthropology to the anthropology of Western hegemony" (Asad 1991). Whereas the former has been concerned with tracing out the role of anthropological discourse and practice (and of anthropologists) in colonialism's career, the latter, he argues, would be concerned primarily with exploring the implications of the discursive and nondiscursive transformations produced by European power (especially modern European power) upon the non-European world. The story of European colonialism, Asad argues, is now often told in terms of a dialectic of expansion and reaction, domination and resistance. This is the story that when Europe conquered and ruled non-European peoples these peoples were not mere passive victims of colonial power. They themselves responded to the colonizers in various ways, most importantly in various forms of (sometimes armed) resistance. Asad suggests, however, that the story of colonialism should also be a story of how the conditions for resistance, and for response in general, were, as he puts it, "increasingly defined by a new scheme of things – new forms of power, work, and knowledge" (Asad 1991: 314). It is toward illuminating this transformation that Asad wants to direct anthropological attention.

This view differs from its predecessors especially in its insistence on the uniqueness of the European colonial expansion. It is a call to recognize historical specificity, and especially the unique and irreversible transformation that European expansion produced in the world. No human population was unaffected by it; none can revert to the way things were before.

David Scott wants to "read this challenge along two separable but interconnected registers." One of these registers has to do with the problem of the formation of anthropological objects, with the discursive relationship, in other words, between the reflexive objects of professional anthropology and those (ideological) objects constituted as objects as such in and through colonialist knowledge. The other of these registers has to do more directly with what Asad calls an anthropology of Western hegemony – what Scott wants to call a "historical anthropology of the postcolonial present." Scott sees this register as "concerned with the transforming effects of European power in non-European (conceptual, institutional, and social) spaces, and in particular, with the transforming effects of modern European power." And he points out that this is where Asad is specifically concerned with that story of European power "not as a temporary repression of subject populations but as an irrevocable process of transmutation, in which old desires and ways of life were destroyed and new ones took their place – a story of change without precedent in its speed, global scope, and pervasiveness' (Asad 1991: 314).

Asad, providing a historical backdrop to Nicholas Thomas's deflation of the discipline's pretensions to an important role in the modern world, has pointed out that the role of anthropologists in the colonial project was, by and large, a relatively minor one. "The role of anthropologists in maintaining structures of imperial domination," he writes, "has, despite slogans to the contrary, usually been trivial; the knowledge they produced was often too esoteric for government use, and even where it was usable it was marginal in comparison to the vast body of information routinely accumulated by merchants, missionaries, and administrators" (Asad 1991: 315). He goes on to say, however: "But if the role of anthropology for colonialism was relatively unimportant, the reverse proposition does not hold. The process of European global power has been central to the anthropological task of recording and analyzing the ways of life of subject populations, even when a serious consideration of that power was theoretically excluded. It is not merely that anthropological fieldwork was facilitated by European power (although this well-known point deserves to be thought about in other than moralistic terms); it is that the fact of European power, as discourse and practice, was always part of the reality anthropologists sought to understand, and of the way they sought to understand it" (Asad 1991: 315). From this, Scott argues that "despite the admirable attention to history that characterizes much contemporary anthropology it is still very poorly grasped that histories of the non-European social, cultural and political realities that anthropologists are interested in have also to be histories of the concepts through which such histories are constructed" (see also D. Scott 1994). For Scott, the point at issue is, as he argues from his reading of Collingwood, that we must always ask questions that have some "purchase" on – relevance for – the world we inhabit. Issues of resistance and domination may no longer be as germane as they were in the immediate period of decolonization, and what is now needed, in Asad's and Scott's view, is a history of the postcolonial present. To this I would add that such a history must always also take into account the situation of places that were never explicitly colonized – or at least that claim this for themselves – and how such discourses of independence have been able to flourish.

Here the situation of the anthropologist may indeed be diagnostic. The late arrival of European ethnography as a "respectable" occupation and especially as a source of new theoretical insight is surely indicative. What anthropologists actually do may be of little interest to others. Why what they study is so often regarded as marginal ought to be of great interest to those same others: it is a question that disturbs the received wisdom about the criteria of significance. It is for this reason that the Asad/Scott project must find its counterpart in the ethnography of contemporary societies, western and non-western, for the lived consequences of the enormous transformation that preoccupies these scholars – consequences that are inscribed in the architecture, languages, and embodied daily habits of the world's peoples – do not reveal themselves easily in printed sources.

The Convergence of History and Anthropology

Detailed ethnography, then, offers daily challenges to the dominance of certain political structures, and conventional historiography has largely been impervious, even resistant, to its call. In fact, however, some historians have been open to the possibility of a "history from below." It is also noteworthy that some of this effort has come from anthropologists working on European societies (e.g., Hastrup ed. 1992): their concern has not been to reduce anthropology to the status of all the other Eurocentric cultural disciplines, but, on the contrary, to relativize the European experience while also recognizing that ordinary Europeans were also in some degree subjected to the effects of the project of world domination in ways that were not of their own making. A related theme, from the other side of the colonial relationship, has been extensively explored by John and Jean Comaroff (1991, 1997).

Anthropologists were quick to salute the rapprochement between the two disciplines.[3] While, as Roger Chartier's (1988) sharp rejoinder to Geertz's Princeton colleague Robert Darnton makes clear, generalizations about durable cultural symbols can seem simplistic to those who claim "native" knowledge, and while some uses of anthropological theory also give an impression of toolkit methodologies rather than of mutual exploration, the debates that this cross-fertilization generated only served to intensify a dialogue for which Evans-Pritchard, another devotee of the strongly Vichian R. G. Collingwood, had laid the foundations. In the "cultural history" advocated by Lynn Hunt and Chartier, one sees a partiality for modified deconstructionist and narratological theories and a full textual awareness of complex patterns of communication (Nussdorfer 1993; Hunt 1989; Chartier 1988). History acquired an ethnographic sensibility, notably in the work of Peter Sahlins's (1983) examination of the segmentary underpinnings of pre-modern French and Spanish identity formation (a fascinating counterpart to Shryock's exploration of modern Jordanian nationalism), and, rather differently, in historical sociology such as that of Charles Tilly and E. P. Thompson.

The explicitly Marxist E. P. Thompson was closely attentive to the force of religious ideas in the early phase of industrialization in Britain. Roberts writes: "Within radical circles in Britain and their extensions his work opened the door to greater significance being attached to cultural values in social analysis. From the late 1960s the availability of Gramsci's work in translation and the growing reputation of the literary scholar Raymond Williams enhanced Thompson's influence in the circuits of the *New Left Review* and *Past and Present* and promoted increasing attention to cultural domination and modes of resistance" – themes that were to yield radical departures in "cultural studies" at Birmingham, as well as to influence the "resistance theory" of James Scott and of the Subaltern Studies group (launched in India in 1982). Ranajit Guha's *Elementary Aspects of Peasant Insurgency* (1983) exemplified the work of this last group: a study of peasant insurrections in nineteenth-century British India portrays "the peasantry as a subject of history, endowed with its own distinct forms of consciousness and acting upon the world in its own terms" (Chatterjee 1993, 160). Roberts remarks that "its detailed interrogation of texts to glean peasant practices and the semiotics of resistance render the work eminently one of historical anthropology." Other parallel developments similarly challenged existing hegemonies. Feminist historians, notably Luisa Passerini and the Milan Feminist Cooperative in Italy, notably rescued the voices of those oppressed by fascism, patriarchy, and the consumerist society of late capitalism.

Roberts remarks that "it is Thompson's focus on episodic moments and subjective agents in ongoing action at such moments which merits attention." The resulting "people's history," which sought "to write an archive-based 'history from below'" and focused on the underclasses and neglected segments of society in particular (Samuel 1981: xv), matched the localized microhistories of such writers as Carlo Ginzburg in Italy. Ginzburg's influence in anthropology has meanwhile been considerable, and has influenced the production of at least one fine ethnography – a study of the modern effects of a process of "cultural disenchantment" leading to the collapse of the belief system that Ginzburg had so minutely researched in the same region of Italy (Holmes 1989).

Microhistory, a term especially popularized by Ginzburg (1980), has not been without its critics. The objections it has evinced largely parallel the charge of "anecdotalism" so often leveled against anthropology. Thus, for example, Philip Abrams has argued that it is naive to present selected moments or persons as a representation of past reality; and it is doubly naive to assume that individuals could "give the historian or sociologist unreflective but accurate accounts of the meaning of their own lives – or even reflective ones." Against such efforts, he argues that "the past . . . can only be known in terms of some conscious effort to theorize it, and that any such effort involves a recognition of the sense in which social realities are strange, relational and not directly accessible to us – a recognition of the extent to which knowledge has to be an act of estrangement" (Abrams 1982: 328–9).

The notion that knowledge is a form of "making strange" is entirely sympathetic to the anthropological imagination, and resonates also with some views of the literary art. But this does not mean that such "defamiliarization," to use the literary term, is never vouchsafed to those we study. Indeed, those who live on the political margins of state societies may be especially sensitized to the semiotics of power. It is no coincidence that destablizing forms of word play, for example, seem to flourish in precisely those liminal places (see, for example, Labov's [1972] classic study of inner-city speech in the United States). The shepherds with whom I have worked in Crete were highly aware, not only of the oddity of their own marginal situation, but also of the historical processes that had exiled them to the margins of Greek society while claiming their stereotypical virtues – courage, inventiveness, hospitality, and above all resistance to imposed authority – for the nation-state itself.

Hobbles Danaiyarri, too, a perceptive commentator if ever one existed, demands to be heard by anyone claiming not to hear the voices of the powerful alone. In the Yorubá oriki, in the Cumbales' retreading of national legal history, in the Ohafia production of historical memory through dance, and in the Cibecue Apaches' reading of the physical landscape that they inhabit, we can hear alternatives to the stories told by those with power. They, literally, speak "truth to power"; and power is thereby discomfited.

Such reversals do not only concern former colonies and Third World peoples. The rejection of history from below would also exclude significant parts of the European population as well. Just as anthropology began life as a pillar of colonialism, so folklore studies similarly supported the hegemonic goals of educated elites – precisely those people whose "invention of tradition" has been addressed by Hobsbawm and Ranger (eds., 1983). And yet their solution – to view the construction of national folk culture as purely an elite construction – is also inadequate and, ironically, elitist. It overlooks the role of ordinary people in the incessant processes of reformulation, and, much as did Hobsbawm's own earlier work on social banditry (1959), treats them as dupes of the dominant ideology rather than sometimes quite deliberate agents of their own fate.

Here anthropological fieldwork comes to the rescue. An especially brilliant example is provided by Jerome R. Mintz's ethnographic study of Casas Viejas, site of one of the bloodiest conflicts of the Spanish Civil War (1982). By concentrating on the oral accounts of survivors and situating these within his intimate knowledge of local social relations, he was able to show how far local actors were swayed by considerations of ideology and how far both official fascist and Marxist accounts of their acceptance of anarchist principles and of charismatic leadership overlooked their own active interest in recasting the tyranny of church and state in familiar principles of morality. "Free love" unions, for example, entailed a rejection of the church's control of morality, rather than a revolt against morality as such, and the sense of moral community provided a more persuasive reason for sustained resistance than did the dubious talents of local rabblerousers. Such insights bring new data to bear on the past, permitting reinterpetation that is now vastly more respectful of local memory (e.g., Maddox 1995).

Examples could easily be multiplied. Sharon Roseman's account of road-building in Galicia (1996), for example, provides an especially convincing insight into the connections between cultural separatism and resistance to the Francoist regime. In my own work on historic conservation on Crete, I have tried to illustrate the ways in which official renditions of cultural history – notably their emphasis on neo-Classical and "Western" models – run afoul of local economics, gender dynamics, family histories, and the assertion of regional at the expense of national pride (Herzfeld 1991). And in the United States Richard Handler and Eric Gable (1997) have demonstrated the tensions that lie beneath the smiling surface of a national historic site and the narratives that staff – with their different origins in colonial settler and slave populations – are expected to recount for the visitors.

An instructive result of the glorification of local "tradition" by nationalist and regionalist ideologies has been to place on a pedestal the bearers of the glorious heritage – and it is a pedestal that neatly confines them: they find their agency seriously restricted, since they can easily be dismissed as "backward" or "localist." Indeed, the discourse of localism in Britain has had precisely that effect (Nadel-Klein 1991). One result is that local people often resort to "authoritative" sources for "their traditions" in ways that index a powerfully unequal dynamic (e.g., Collier 1997). Anthropologists are not immune to entailment in this dynamic: I was once told that a young man in a nearby village was the owner of a personal "archive" on animal-theft in Crete, only to be shown, with much ceremony, my *The Poetics of Manhood* (Herzfeld 1985)! Anthropologists are far from immune to cooptation by local groups' intent on coopting them as authoritative scholars for the purpose of legitimizing specific readings of the past.

Anthropologists, however, are usually committed to resisting forms of narrative closure that would grant power to a particular faction or group. One sign of the anthropological shift away from formal sources of historical knowledge has been the current focus on memory – and forgetting – as the source of history. Of these, memory has a more august lineage in social theory, having been given especially cogent expression by Maurice Halbwachs (1980). But its negative counterpart has also had a venerable history. The analysis of genealogy, for example, has had to account for the selective devices whereby a nominally unilineal society maintains the authority and shared social capital of an apical ancestor by allowing the intervening generations to lapse – lineage "telescoping" or "structural amnesia" (Lewis 1961). Similarly systematic replications of oblivion may occur in the rhetoric of passing generations, as in my own coinage of "structural nostalgia" (Herzfeld 1997a). Indeed, nostalgia is a useful term for the crystallization of personal desire as a temporally and socially embedded representation of the past, and it takes many forms and legitimates many histories (see, e.g., Rosaldo 1989; S. Stewart 1984).

It is useful at this point to distinguish between memory, a psychological process, and remembrance, a social one; and between forgetting on the one hand and more systematic forms of obliteration ("oblivion") on the other (see Dakhlia 1990). Remembering and forgetting may be the desired ends of the corresponding social processes, but the success with which they are induced is never certain, for all psychological inner states are by definition ultimately opaque and therefore resistant to the ministrations of "thought police." Indeed, several essays in a recent and important collection of essays on memory in socialist and postsocialist societies (R. Watson, ed., 1994) show clearly that oblivion may be a strategy of dissimulation, permitting the long-term conservation of forbidden thoughts – the preservation of memories, in fact.

Monumentalization is the official face of a more general phenomenon whereby spatial arrangements are imbued with past associations. Struggles over historic conservation laws revolve around precisely this issue: particular dispositions of space encode corresponding ideas about the cultural past, so that resistance to official conservation laws may encapsulate a sense – never verbally articulated, indeed often denied – that the state's vision of history does not move local actors except, perhaps, to irritation. But that irritation is the sign of a more radical engagement, because people are well aware that the shaping of their space actually portends, through inculcation of a particularly insistent variety, the recasting of their habitual social universe; it is, so to speak, the blueprint of their reconfigured habitus (see Low 1996).

And spatial arrangements may themselves persist in memory, proving more durable therein than bricks and masonry. Thus, the startling genius of Joëlle Bahloul's (1996) account of Jewish–Muslim relations in Algeria lies in the multiple fragilities that it evokes: a curtain, easily whisked aside, represents in memory – as it once did in practice – the ritual separation of two confessional communities sharing the same domestic space and the same easy relationships, until the horrors of international conflict disrupted this symbiosis for ever. By reconstructing that space from her own refugee relatives' accounts, narrated to her in France, together with her direct observations and encounters with the Muslims still living in the compound two decades later, Bahloul was able to illuminate the complex relationships that subsist among space, memory and identity, and to provide an explanation of the nostalgic affection with which each side recalled the other despite the bitter hostilities that by now had rent them asunder. She delicately explores historical processes of fission and solidary action, showing how local actors spatialize these processes – in which the violence done to deep affections marks a seemingly indelible trajectory across the landscape of dwelling places – both in current practice and in their reconstructed memories.

Commemoration and oblivion may in fact be more closely related than is apparent. Commemorative naming practices that aim to "resurrect" earlier generations ultimately have the effect of erasing historical identities through repetition, creating a structural amnesia that corresponds, at the level of nationalist discourse, to the obliteration of individual identities in the name of a common cause (as in the Tomb of the Unknown Soldier) and to a proprietorial attitude toward a national name instead (B. Anderson 1983); indeed, where the transmission of personal names balances commemoration in the short term with the idea of ultimate reabsorption in the collective identity of the kin group, this can lead to powerful expression of possessiveness as much toward a regional name as toward the territory that it denotes (e.g., Sutton 1997).

Naming is one space in which the tension between an externally displayed unity and the internal recognition of difference and disagreement can be expressed. National symbols – a monarchy, a flag, a set of monuments – are another such space. In Shryock's ethnographic analysis of Jordanian nationalism, we see the continuing conflict that seethes around questions of commemoration just below the bland surface of the rhetoric of national unity. Shryock's analysis is also an excellent illustration of what I have called cultural reflexivity: he considers the effect of his own cultural expectations on his data and, reciprocally, that of local social values on academic and authorial practices in Jordan. This collective self-comparison is especially useful for making different modes of history-making explicit, because it challenges the assumption that all history is about recovering the most detailed factual account possible: most of it, we discover, is not. Shryock's analysis raises to the inclusive level of cross-cultural analysis a more general awareness that history is always dependent on underlying assumptions, many of them political but also ethical and social (not that these are really separate domains). These assumptions are usually so self-evident, so much a matter of "common sense," that they are locally resistant to challenge even – or, sometimes, especially – to parties whose tournaments of interpretation depend on their common acceptance of the assumptions themselves. Read in this light, accusations of violating historical truth – a favorite of nationalist leaders and litigious heirs alike – emerge as clearly dependent on some sort of agreement about what *kind* of thing constitutes "real" history.

The principles involved constitute a local, cultural classification of events, and a hierarchy of significance – of what will be considered important. We thus return here to an old anthropological staple: the analysis of classification. This time, however, the system of classification under study is not necessarily that of exotic peoples or illiterate peasants (although the analysis does not exclude those who are still sometimes so described). The modalities of history themselves become ethnographic objects, in an exercise – exemplified in one idiom by the work of Hanson and Valeri – that matches Hayden White's Vichian project of identifying the dominant trope in each phase of western historiography, in intent if not always in method.

Two further shifts away from conventional anthropology accompany this move. First, we recognize the historicizing capacities of people who may not speak like western academic historians, and indeed may not historicize by speaking at all; they may be eloquent in silence, gesture, or dance. And second, we recognize that classification is not itself the agent of thought but merely – though importantly – its immediate medium. In this way, we recognize individual agency – that of Hobbles Danayarri, for example – and its capacity, through irony or other means, to play havoc with the categories imposed on the past by those who currently hold the reins of power.

Is Past to Present as Tradition is to Modernity?

Michael Roberts sees anthropologizing history as "a general project which holds that historical knowledge is neither straightforward nor easily knowable; and which seeks to highlight voices that are neglected in the master narratives of the contemporary global order." I have followed his prescription closely here, although I shall shortly also complicate it with David Scott's insistence that we also examine the production of colonial discourse – a good illustration of what I have called "cultural reflexivity." The trick here is that of studying elites as though they were marginal: George Marcus, for example, does this with his analysis of the "dynastic uncanny" among the wealthy oil families of Galveston, Texas – a phenomenon strikingly similar to "traditional" symbolic constructions of heritable personhood in village and tribal societies (1992: 173–87). In much the same way, we can treat the discourses and practices of the colonizers, including their history, as ethnographic objects – an appropriate reversal of the visualist gaze.

I am less at ease, however, with Roberts's view of the voices of the dispossessed as expressing "those actions and cosmologies which, following Valentine Daniel, one can call the mythic ontic as distinct from the epistemic knowledges privileged today." My unease has less to do with what these two authors are saying than with the uses to which such a distinction could be put. Roberts argues that Daniel's theoretical distinction should not be confused with the usual efforts to separate myth and history to which I alluded at the beginning of this chapter. Certainly this is the logic of organizing the discussion around "cosmologies" and "histories" rather than reverting to myth and history. But to say, with Daniel, that the mythic ontic consists in ways of being in the world in participatory awe – contrasting with the epistemic ways of seeing the world, ways which have an "aboutness" to them (1990: 227–33, 243) – risks reverting to the old Lévy–Bruhlian discrimination between a primitive mentality and a rational, modern one (but see also, for a more revisionist formulation, Tambiah 1990). We can certainly rescue the distinction that Daniel is making by retaining it for industrial societies as well – that is, by rejecting the Weberian orthodoxy that modernity is a condition of disenchantment. One may wish to follow the processes of disenchantment, to be sure; that is the historical perspective that Holmes pursued in his ethnographic follow-up to Ginzburg's researches in northern Italy. But we cannot assume – and Daniel and Roberts clearly do not assume – that such developments are unilinear, logically necessary, or qualitatively evolutionary, for that would entail reducing history to the mythological structures of colonialism itself.

This, in thin disguise, is the dilemma of whether it is useful to speak of "modern" and "traditional" societies. These terms represent a characteristic difficulty for anthropology, because they are part of our own received rhetoric but they have also become increasingly important to many of the peoples we study, some of which are engaged in actively salvaging their heritage, their traditions, even their culture – terms with which earlier anthropologists, in more uncomplicated times, were once at ease. Definitional exercises necessarily do little more than affirm that modernity is "an ideological attitude, an expression of a specific way of seeing and comprehending things in time with continuity and rupture as well." As Olivia Harris (1996: 3) puts it, the "modernist moment is constituted by the idea of rupture" – but one must ask: rupture with what? And one must also ask: who defines the rupture – which for some actors, such as those who found Soviet repression no different from Czarist, may simply be "more of the same."

Indeed, the Soviet-style experiments with "really existing socialism" were in some regards no less consumerist, bureaucratic, and rationalistic than the western systems labeled "capitalist." The directions that both these movements took grew out of bourgeois intellectual concerns, which can be loosely summarized as a progressivist ideology resulting in the sense of a certain "contemporary" condition – although it has never been entirely clear what that condition was, beyond a successful emulation of western industrial achievements. Despite (or perhaps because of) its centrality to anthropology's own identity as a scholarly field, "modernity" has only started to appear recently in anthropological book titles. But it is already clear that we cannot reasonably speak of a single essential modernity, for each has its own history (Faubion 1993); even assuming for the moment that the term is susceptible of definition, it must have some kind of temporal and spatial specificity – plural modernities – if it is to be of any analytic value.

In Asia, for example, the very idea of equating "modern" with "Western" is not only understandably insulting, but is demonstrably meaningless (A. Ong 1996). Aihwa Ong recounts how notions of the special characteristics of the Chinese people are being fostered and the prestige which is now being accorded to the role of the overseas Chinese, especially from Singapore. "Capitalism with Chinese characteristics" is redefining itself as a global force, distinct from Western capitalism and rationality and deriving from a Confucian familial ethic and a range of interpersonal networks (*guanxi*). China, so the argument goes, has its own centuries old superior Confucian rationality and has no need to borrow western ones. In other words, the very factors that Weber saw as obstacles to initiating capitalist development in China are being proposed as the secret of current Chinese business success. But it is also clear that "Western" modernity is equally rooted in symbolic structures and arbitrary cultural values – and has no more successfully achieved universal transcendence. "Globalism" is itself a symbol and an ideology, not a transparent truth.

Other Asian countries are developing a similar sense of a larger, pan-Asian modernity that includes them as well. Such formulations are no less and no more ethnocentric than what they displace. Ong discusses the works of the Japanese revisionist historian Hamashita, who argues that it is a distortion to connect Japanese modernization with the bombardment by Commodore Perry. Rather, she says, this was the inauguration of a crude interruption of a development which was already underway on the basis of the tributary system of South Asian trade controlled from China but in which Japanese and Chinese merchants contended during the earlier years. Similarly, Richard Hall argues that there was a highly developed network of trade stretching from the Gulf States to China and which centered on India. It was the Portuguese, coming at the end of the fifteenth century who began the disruption of this trade and its reorientation around the interests of European nations (R. Hall 1996a and 1996b; Subrahmanyam 1990). And the situation has reappeared today in acute form, as Don Robotham, following Aihwa Ong, points out. It is clearly indicated by the failures of the former colonial powers to retain control of their own modernities – as witness the heavy Japanese investment in the City of London, Korean control of major French firms, and so on. The result is a crisis of identity matched, for the former rulers, by the crisis represented by the rising local power of "new Europeans" who hail from the former colonies or other countries once seen as safely distant and exotic.

But the crisis of modernity in Europe appears in another, no less acute form as well. It used to be that a few countries defined what modernity was: there was a hegemony internal to the European states, as powerful in its own way as the colonial, and largely mapped onto it – after all, colonialism was a major source of those few countries' extraordinary wealth. This has generated acute dilemmas for the poorer European countries. On the one side, as we have seen, is the issue of whether the East bloc's communist past should be treated as "modern" or "backward"; on the other, Greece and Cyprus – sites of one of the most protracted debates about the meaning of "Western" or "European" identity precisely because these countries, together with Turkey, constitute a geographical realization of the conceptual boundary between east and west – explore models in both emulation of and antithesis to what is seen as typical of Western Europe and North America.

The predicament of the Greeks is perhaps most revealing of all because their ambivalent position – ancestors of "Western civilization" but also "orientalized" to the margins – throws the relationship between modernity and identity into sharp relief. At least three recent studies of Greek society have addressed modernity as such: Vassos Argyrou (1996a) has documented the process of modernization on Cyprus as an investment in "Western" symbolic capital; James Faubion (1993) has argued that Greek modernity both fits the requirements of a Weberian understanding of the term and yet also possesses its distinctive cultural features, as do all other modernities; and David Sutton (1994) has documented the rhetorical play of "modernity" and "tradition" ethnographically in order to show how these epistemological questions become politicized at the level of local interaction. (It may be worth noting that the Greek-speaking world, situated in a state of great anxiety and ambiguity about the exact nature of its relationship to "Europe," experiences parallel sources of unease when confronting the equally problematic specter of "modernity.")

Thus, for example, Sutton's argument gives an intriguing twist – perhaps one that could only be revealed through the use of ethnographic methods – to Hubinger's ironic assertion that "the concept of modernization has taken on the meaning of "belonging to contemporary Western civilization," the latter a goal to which the world supposedly aspired *en masse*. Whoever does not seem to share this opinion, for whatever reason, is classified as "backward" or "remote" – locally internalized metaphors of space here reproducing the presumed temporalities of an evolutionist vision – and doomed to disappear in the foreseeable future. But modernity, thus conceived, is not an exclusive property of "the West," or even of countries claiming to be industrialized. It would not take much effort to find illustrations of this in many teleological ideologies, from ancient mythologies to present day religious and political doctrines including Marxism–Leninism (see Fukuyama 1992).

In this respect, an anthropologist might look askance at Anthony Giddens's many formulations of modernity as representing a radically unique, Western-driven rupture. That there indeed has been such a rupture is beyond question, as we see in Talal Asad and David Scott's assessment of the aftermath of colonialism, but calling it "modernity" is problematic for two reasons: it invites the conflation of many different responses to the specific causes of the rupture, especially colonialism and the sudden spread of certain technologies; and it overlooks the frequency and near-ubiquity with which such before-and-after ideologies have occurred. "For the most part it is

Western intellectuals who show themselves to be prisoners of traditional conceptions holding to a rigid and exclusive distinction between the 'traditional' and the 'modern'... We are trapped in the logic of received dichotomies" (M. Sahlins 1992: 21).

But it is not only we who are trapped there. And Hubinger observes that in a discussion of the ethics of ethnographic observation conducted at the 1992 conference of the European Association of Social Anthropologists (EASA) in Prague, "it was noted with some bitterness that in the debate that followed no Eastern Europeans took part and when the debated paper was subsequently published in Czech (Scheffel 1992), virtually nobody paid any attention to the question." He adds, "What was a burning issue in Canada and elsewhere, found the Czech anthropological (and ethnographic) community immersed in quite different problems." The political irrelevance of anthropology to some visions of modernity may itself be a sign of how people are construing modernity as an ideology: as the march of progress, measured in economic and technological terms, and as such a startling and worrisome revival of the nineteenth-century evolutionism that anthropology itself has long since abandoned.

Pervasive Dichotomies

The dichotomization of the world between traditional and modern societies – between those mired in an earlier time and those who belong in the forward flow of the present, as Fabian (1983) has noted – is part of the context in which anthropology is understood by the public at large. The discipline's struggle to escape that image may itself be educationally useful as a way of demonstrating how culturally specific the seemingly noncultural claims of self-attributed modernity really are.

For we face here a characteristic dilemma. Like Lévi-Strauss, attempting by distinguishing between "cold" and "hot" societies to recognize intellectual parity between these two forms of thought and society (Lévi-Strauss 1966), we end up reproducing the very distinction that we are attempting to dissolve. The usual procedure at this point would be to go on to a further round of deconstruction and regrouping. But I would argue that the value of such formulations lies, paradoxically, in their inadequacy. This is consistent with a critical and pedagogical model of anthropology, which helps us to see them, not only as as inadequate analytic tools, but also as a disturbingly persistent strain in popular thought around the world.

The dilemma may in any case not be amenable to resolution. This usefully conflicts with Cartesian assumptions about the nature of knowledge; it certainly risks awkward moments in the classroom, where students sometimes seem to crave authoritative answers. But to surrender to that desire would be unfair to them as well as to the people we study. For such an easy resolution obliterates the complexity of the hermeneutic task in which all anthropologists, even the most positivistically inclined, necessarily engage. It is probably anthropologists' constant discovery during fieldwork of the practical limits of their own understanding, sometimes under the most embarrassing social conditions, that encourages this resistance to intellectual closure even when their own models would have made the most convenient stance.

Tambiah (1990), like Daniel, has revived the notion of participation. But in his account – as, by extension, in Daniel's, and quite unlike what we see in the evolutionary schemata of a few decades ago – there is nothing to prevent us from seeing science and reason as immanent qualities of a social group that closely recalls the Nuer divine essence (Kwoth) or the notion of musical "talent" (Kingsbury 1988); the West here looks no different from the societies traditionally studied "in the field." This is perhaps the most useful conclusion that we can draw from studies like Shryock's. They do not come down heavily in favor of a view that divides the West from the Rest. Instead, they point up unexpected resemblances among ways of making history – resemblances that are made possible and visible only because they encompass the very possibility of difference.

Most anthropological definitions of myth can be applied quite directly to western history-making, especially of the official varieties: as a charter for the present (Malinowski), as an exploration and obliteration of social contradiction (Lévi-Strauss, Leach), as an explanation of origins (Eliade). Nationalistic historiography is especially appropriate to the Durkheimian view that religion is society worshiping itself (Durkheim 1976): when a nation-state is created, not only do political committees and legislative bodies write laws and constitutions with palpably teleological intent, but entire schools and disciplines appear in universities and schools with the purpose of teaching – and finding evidence in support of – a unitary history. Their goal is to legitimate the new status quo, exploiting the ideas of origins distant in time and space that Helms (1998) has preferred to see as sources of legitimacy only in preindustrial societies. They aim to give the new entity, usually a nation-state, a past that is, in fact, outside time – has existed, in a spectacularly revealing phrase, "since time immemorial."

As Valeri so reasonably inquires (1990: 161–2), however, "why is such importance attached to finding the rules of the present embodied in the past?" Shryock (1997: 322) inverts the question by attributing to western anthropologists a pervasive reluctance, grounded in their own ideological inheritance, to conceive of a genealogical model of the past, arguing that this attitude has not allowed them much space in which to take genealogical forms of history seriously as representations of the past in their own right. Nor have they seemed to think it necessary to explain "why legitimation [should] reside in duration" – why "time becomes a measure of value" (Roberts 1994: 202). And Roberts notes Taussig's explicit questioning of Malinowski's utilitarian functionalism, with its stress on magic (and, we may add, myth) as a form of therapeutic action: "this mode of interpretation is unacceptable because it presupposes most of what needs explaining – the richly detailed motifs and precise configuration of details that constitute the beliefs and rites in question" (Taussig 1980: 14). Roberts, like

Taussig and Valeri, rejects such explanations as too crassly teleological ("functionalist").

Indeed they are. But so, at times, is the notion of value. We have still not explained why the past appears to confer legitimacy. To answer that question, we must revert to ethnography. Only thus, in a process that resists easy assumptions about psychological or economic need, can we begin to identify the agency whereby the past is both realized and converted into a source of contestable value. Until now, the dominant mode has been to take that conversion for granted and to treat it as uncomplicated and culturally unvarying – which is why, as Shryock and others now argue, it has been so difficult to understand the sheer range of cultural idioms in which history can be made meaningful.

By the same token, we may wish to consider treating the various teleological and instrumental explanations as part of the ethnography rather than of the theory. We can, in other words, try to discover who invested utilitarian explanations with local authority. I have often been told by Cretan villagers, for example, that the blood feud is a fine deterrent to homicide, in contrast to the weak authority of the state. Whose interests do such functionalist claims serve locally? These are questions about agency – about the concealed agency of the powerful as well as the discounted agency of the weak.

This maverick analytic mode – which belongs to a larger historical project of recognizing how much anthropological theory has originated with informants' commentaries rather than solely in our own philosophies – can do much useful mischief to received prejudices. Here the anthropological study of historically documented societies becomes particularly important, because it allows us to trace through time those processes whereby encompassing teleologies are invented, not as theories (abstract explanations of what is "out there"), but as practices (pragmatic justifications of what is "in here"). Thus, when we examine societies in which the process of making history can be documented, we can seek the sources of that teleology in the expressed motives of nationalists, bureaucrats, and others: "We must have this history in place so that our authority will be secure." And the history will only stay in place – if it does – if it follows the currently regnant cultural idioms of authority.

The impermanence of the permanent: this is the challenge for secular authority, and it is also the point of intersection between history and anthropology. Although earlier anthropologists tried to stabilize their observations in terms of static systems, models, and structures, it is clear that social life is always in some sense processual (S. Moore 1987): even when nothing changes that condition is experienced in historical terms – as a lack of responsiveness, as a bulwark against immorality or contamination, as the tragedy of the neglected margins. Yet it is also in that condition that anthropologists, working in the field, often discern the first stirrings of observable change.

When massive change does arrive, it brings other temptations, notably the desire to stake out a new era, to place a fence of "posts" across the epistemological and political landscape: postmodernism, postsocialism, postcolonialism. At times this line of posts looks rather like the beginning of the end: the collapse of the socialist regimes, for example, exercised a rather sobering effect on Third World intellectuals, who had seen materially expressed in them, however imperfectly, the only viable means of combating the evils of capitalism and colonialism. The postcolonial condition looked more dismal than ever.

Don Robotham and David Scott have argued, however, that there are now new opportunities, and that these are not best understood exclusively in terms of postcoloniality. Robotham, in particular, would reject the term "postcolonial" (and with it "postmodern") in favor of recognizing, as do Aihwa Ong and James Faubion, the possibility of defining multiple modernities. While the compression of his argument here will necessarily distort its logic and conceal some of its complexity, it is important to juxtapose its Third World focus with the dynamics of emergent modernities in other places, notably eastern Europe, in which parallel incentives exist to detach "modernity" from the one particular historical formation of a dominant "West."

As he points out: "The current postcolonial pessimism springs also from internal factors connected to the external. Today, in many developing countries – Mexico and India are obvious but by no means isolated cases – there is a strong feeling of despair based on what is perceived as the failure of the local nationalist elites to be true to the cause and to realize the objectives of the nationalist movement. Whether it be the spread of Hindu chauvinism in India or the surge of crime and corruption in Mexico, Columbia or Jamaica, an internally generated malaise seems to grip many developing countries, most despairingly of all perhaps in Africa." Robotham suggests, however, that this pessimism, which is also a crisis of identity, may no longer be justified: "The true global story is appearing to be not the negative one about the fall of socialism, but the far more complicated one about the rise of Asia. It is this growth of what Ong calls 'alternative modernities,' and what I here call 'the new modernities,' that is the hallmark of the new period" – for, Robotham explains: "It is not that other forms of knowledge and ethical production were ignored. Some traditions were embraced as an enchanted garden for the alienated to find refuge from the 'iron cage' of a rationalized world, in a drama of alienation, resignation, fortitude and redemption even more heroically Western. Many (not all) occupied honored places but within a pantheon framed and dominated by the all-subsuming Enlightenment of the rationalistic, individualizing West. No matter how much they were admired for their profoundness, aesthetic harmony or ethical strength, they became marginal – at best source materials for, or a foil to, the great historical metanarrative of the all-conquering rationalistic West, enhancing its distinctive supremacy" – and the same processes were also at work within Europe, marginalizing peasants and workers to the greater glory of nationalist and socialist elites, respectively. This aspect of the story, which is too often ignored, does not invalidate the postcolonial plaint: on the contrary, by showing how localized forms of domination within the West were often the practice grounds of colonialism on the grand scale (e.g., Nadel-Klein 1991), it shows how pervasive was the entire project of hierarchizing the world once and for all.

The collapse of that project has been no less radical in its effects and poses particularly interesting challenges and opportunities for anthropology. The collapse of communism and the transition to capitalism in eastern Europe and central Asia, the ending of the Non-Aligned Movement, the crisis of Africa, the economic, social and political travails facing the European Union, the rise of east Asia (in particular Japan and China), the struggle by the United States to maintain its unique status as the single world superpower, the electronics revolution and the globalization of finance and communications, the so-called "informationalization" of society (Castells 1995) – all these processes raise new challenges for all the fields of the social sciences which have long taken for granted the validity of the "modernization equals Westernization" paradigm. If Hubinger is right that anthropology has always been in some sense about modernity, this is also an important moment for a self-examination that is cultural and political rather than personal – an exercise in cultural reflexivity, again, rather than in autobiography.

And so we find ourselves turning the critique straight back at anthropology itself. "Tradition" and "modernity," "the past" and the various posterior conditions, "myth" and "history" all emerge as meaningful categories operated for specific ends; and so we begin to make the awkwardness of received categories work for us as a productive irritant to further insight, rather than dismissing it as inefficient and inconvenient. It restores the pedagogical goal of inducing a critically productive discomfort that is so central to the anthropological enterprise. And it paradoxically, but constructively, removes anthropology from the role of referee in a game of truth in which there are no winners.

Notes

1 From the English translation in B. Gunasekera (1954: 63) – with one alteration: where *sapakanava* has been translated as "eat," Roberts has substituted "gobble" ("devour" would be another alternative). The author of this segment is not known.

2 *Culavamsa* 1953, II, 231, an update of state history written by monks written around 1780; see also the more extended commentary in the *hatana* poems (see C. de Silva 1983).

3 Such journals as *History and Anthropology* (from 1984), *Ethnohistory*, and *Comparative Studies in Society and History (CSSH)* in the 1960s all illustrate the development of this trend, as does the Culture/Power/History series of Princeton University Press, ed. Nicholas Dirks, Geoff Eley, and Sherry Ortner. Eric Wolf, an anthropologist with fieldwork experience in Latin America who was later to ironize the predicament of "peoples without history," not only served on the editorial committee of *CSSH*, but also became a joint editor in 1968. By the early 1980s the rapprochement was truly under way (Cohn 1981; Peel 1993: 162). Significant borrowings from anthropological theory were given legitimacy in Britain by the work of Keith Thomas and in USA by the writings of Natalie Davis, Robert Darnton and Rhys Isaac. Isaac expounded a dramaturgical mode of analysis that was indebted to

Victor Turner and deployed symbolic anthropology to use symptomatic as well as odd incidents as clues to value systems. Rather than tackling causality, both Darnton (1984) and Davis (1973) drew on ethnographic models of "thick description" (Geertz 1973) to explore meaning in specific situations. Thus, from the 1970s one witnesses a number of historians working as what Roberts calls "hindsight anthropologists," bringing to life the experience of subjects in the past.

4

Economies

Economies in Context

In the aftermath of the Cold War, it is hardly surprising that economics should mean, to most people, a choice between the two gargantuan ideologies of capitalism and communism. In consequence, anthropology's greatest challenge – as part of its decoction of a universalist "common sense" – has been to stand back from this narrow choice and demonstrate how much of the received wisdom of global economics is a historical accident. If orthodox Marxist economics of the type espoused by Soviet ethnologists have long seemed too deterministic in the light of the Soviet system's obvious failures, most western economic anthropologists are, as Sahlins and others have cautioned, members – in Nurit Bird-David's words – "of a bourgeois culture, whose core ideological notions are embodied in and reproduced by neoclassical economic theory" (see M. Sahlins 1996b; Dumont 1977).

This has produced several dramatic effects, all richly illustrative of the productive pedagogical inconvenience of anthropology. First, and most obvious, is the sheer difficulty of understanding economic systems that have never themselves been influenced by either dominant ideology; these, historically at least, constitute the majority of the world's economic systems. Second, there is the question of how far we an talk about "pure" economic systems (as the "formalists") argue or whether we must treat economic matters as embedded in other dimensions of the social and the cultural (as the "substantivists" argue, and as we would expect of an anthropology properly suspicious of western universalizing). Third, there is the related question of whether gifts and commodities should respectively be treated as characteristic of a grand divide between "the West and the Rest," to adopt Sahlins's (1976b) phrase, or whether they should instead be seen as aspects of both. And fourth, there is the issue of how to calculate the incalculable – on the one hand to assess the role of such imponderables as "altruism" (itself an issue of psychological rather than social import unless we treat it as as ideology, in which case it becomes material), and on the other to decide whether "2 + 2 = 7" (Ferreira 1997) is better understood as an example of bad reckoning, as evidence for poor integration into a global economic system, or as evidence for the limitations of a capitalist-embedded mathematics – for, in other words, the cultural construction of what we take to be the most bedrock kind of common sense.

In fact, even this account is a vast oversimplification. For, as Nurit Bird-David writes: "It has never been easy to write an introduction to the study of economies, and it becomes only more difficult as the field proliferates. On the threshold of the 21st century, the three common approaches previously deployed are reaching the end of their shelf life. The first anchored to the field's notorious debate between Formalists and Substantivists, which climaxed in the late 1960s. This debate is now a matter for analysis by the history of economic anthropology – not least on how the debate paved way for the present culturalist concern with 'rational man' – or, even, as a matter for cultural analysis itself (see below). The debate can no longer be regarded as the axis of state-of-the-art economic anthropology (as in Halperin 1988); the field has gone far beyond it over the past three decades. The second approach has taken as an organizing structure the division between capitalist and tribal economies, and, within the latter, divisions between 'modes of subsistence' of various ecological types (hunter-gatherer, horticulturalist, pastoralist and peasant: as partly done in M. Sahlins 1972). In today's complex state of affairs, economies are tightly interwoven (an accelerating trend, the beginning of which goes back to the 14th century, and perhaps even earlier) (Wolf 1982). Cultural communities closely interact with and mutually influence each other. People participate simultaneously in more than one economy, and often in more than one cultural community. While the traditional models are important – and some of them in diverse ways reassert and distinguish themselves in lieu of and within the global web of links (e.g., Miller, ed., 1995: Povinelli 1993) – they should nevertheless be viewed within, not as, paradigmatic frames. The third approach has centered on 'theory,' 'production,' 'consumption' and 'circulation of wealth' as its separate themes (e.g., Gregory and Altman 1989). It has dissected the world with a Western template, which renders unrecognizable many of the jigsaw's pieces, including humans themselves as cultural agents."

In this chapter, which is closely modeled on Bird-David's account, I shall especially adopt her view that much of the rationality that informs modern economics is cosmological, and that it is analyzable as such. Indeed, economics provides perhaps the richest test for the kind of anthropology advanced in this book, because, as Marshall Sahlins (1976b) has especially noted, it is the arena in which assumptions of a common sense above and beyond culture have been most prevalent. Economics offers an acid test of its own logic: if the economic assumptions of western thought truly derive from a universal logic, why do economic predictions so frequently, and sometimes so spectacularly, fail?

To contextualize this question, I propose reverting for a moment to a topic more commonly associated with issues of cosmology (in connection with which it will also appear in a later chapter): why do people appear to believe in conceptual systems that, by their own criteria, repeatedly fail? Moreover, those who espouse such absolute notions of rationality – if not a premise of pure reason, then at least that of an instrumentality in which "rational choice" is always predictable and transparent – seem no less inclined than those they despise as primitive and irrational to accept such belief as normal. I well remember a distinguished economic historian, challenged at a seminar to explain why he had compared the economic development of two American cities in entirely different periods, responding that he had never understood what historical contingency had to do with economic modeling! Rationalism, it seems, can be no less arbitrary than other cosmologies.

One of the famous debates about cosmology concerns the ability of so-called primitive peoples to thinking the abstract (Hallpike 1979; Winch 1977 [1958]) – a debate that was to echo, with practical consequences for British and North American race relations, in the parallel arguments about the logical capacities of speakers of ghetto dialects in the 1960s (see Labov 1972). The great achievement of Evans-Pritchard (1937) was to ground the entire question in social context: the validation of a claim that witchcraft had caused the rotting granary to fall on someone's head was not the generic assumption that it always must be witchcraft that makes such things happen, but that only witchcraft could explain the extraordinary fact that that granary collapsed on that person at that time. This avoids the whole question of whether people actually believed that such was the cause, although that aspect of the matter did not appear in subsequent debates about native epistemologies; Evans-Pritchard's formulation does not depend on any attribution of such a psychological condition as belief, but it does suggest that claims of this sort were socially acceptable – which is a very different matter altogether. And it helps to explain why diviners, who are supposed to anticipate mishaps and find their causes, may be proved wrong time and again without ever losing their collective authority.

I would argue that the public language of economics today has much the same character. Whatever the scholarly merits of the discipline, its clichés are readily absorbed by a public clearly anxious for order and predictability and willing to countenance repeated failure as evidence only for individual economists' failures, not for any systemic weakness in the cosmology they offer (I would not presume to judge their competence in terms internal to their calling). The very fallibility of economists (and of other representatives of the rationalist cosmology) does not threaten their continuing status as a collectivity. The ideological force of the cosmology is too strong, buttressed as it is by the aesthetics of rationalist presentation – a point that is easier to appreciate if we instead turn to non-western societies where it may be easier to recognize the importance of style even in seemingly rational calculations (see e.g., Riles 2000: 118 and *passim*). In a situation where capitalist experimentation is relatively new, as in the Shanghai Stock Exchange (E. Hertz 1998), the sense of a special aura associated with the excitement of imported novelty is especially resistant to the clear evidence of fallibility.

The notion of a totally predictive economics is a caricature, of course, because not only are many economic predictions impressively accurate but few economists would claim to be infallible in the first place. It is also unfair to judge a discipline by its image in the media – anthropologists, of all people, should be sensitive to that. But there are two good reasons to heed the caricature nonetheless. Its very exaggerations point up at least two important aspects of a widespread cultural phenomenon. First, to the extent that western economic thought represents the elaboration of a culturally distinct logic, it can usefully be placed in a comparative framework; were its premises truly extracultural, such a comparison would indeed be a fine test of the claim – and if they are not, there is no reason to scoff at the idea of such a comparison; it is only those who fear it who decry it as a preposterous idea. The second reason is more directly empirical. A significant part of the popular response to economic crisis is generated by media representations of the economy, which thus have a causal relationship with its further evolution. At the very least, then, we can say that the economy is embedded in a cosmology that partially determines its vagaries. The idea of economists as prognosticators of fortune may indeed be a caricature, but it is one that actually has a good deal of currency among the people who constitute the majority of consumers and speculators.

Bird-David defines the key issue as "the embeddedness of material life in culture, or the cultural constitution of material life." But it is important here to be clear that cultural forms are themselves material in the sense of having causal relations with features more conventionally regarded as material. To ignore the role of rhetoric, morality, or symbolism as a causative agent in economic life is as silly, from the middle ground perspective, as claiming that the concrete facts of a cash economy do not matter in our world. Terms like "political economy" and "moral economy" are not simply metaphorical fancies: they recognize that culturally salient calculations of value may seem to an outside observer to be materially disadvantageous – but that is just the point, since the outside observer does not know what "matters," a revealing term in this context. And culture here means, not – Bird-David argues – the analyst's state-like ascription of boundaries (as in Halperin 1988), nor "a package-code to market an anthropological product (made-by and for anthropologists, as in Wilk 1996)," but the value system of those whose actions are the subject of discussion, be they Colombian or Panamanian peasants (Gudeman 1986) or western economists from Aristotle to Friedman (M. Sahlins 1976b). Rescuing the materiality of such factors (or at least acknowledging the solipsistic circularity of claiming that they are not material) must be a part of the project of an economic anthropology that, as Bird-David has argued, seeks to escape the dualisms – here symbolic/material – of Cartesian epistemology.

To be sure, it is hard to escape such terms of reference; John Davis (1992), for example, insists that his is a materialist approach even as he tries to capitalize on social actors' ways of conceptualizing their economic life, pointing out that people will act in accordance with what they think is the normative meaning of a situation, whether submissively or subversively. Ideas, in short, have consequences – they are material. Bird-David, too, wisely does not attempt to dispense with this kind of terminology altogether. Instead, recognizing that materiality is an aspect of social life rather than a category of elements in it, she argues that "an underlying concern with the cultural constitution of material life unites many current studies – and not just the few works offered to date as studies in cultural economics. Such current work has to be recognized for what it is, namely, an emergent, broadly-based culturalist school in economic anthropology."

This is consistent with the overall argument of this book, in which the emergence of an empirically grounded attention to the social embeddedness of common sense is central to the emerging portrait of social and cultural anthropology. It is also consistent with a growing willingness to recognize the significance of local knowledge as the source of much of our own theorizing. It carries its own risks, of course, notably that of cultural determinism, but this can be offset by recognizing that such teleologies must be empirically documented. In practice, moreover, it is generally easier to show the cultural influences at work on what had hitherto been treated as "pure economics" than it is to find a formal model capable of explaining economic patterns in a wide range of cultures. And Western economies, in a world otherwise made up of socially embedded systems, are not the exceptions they are sometimes claimed to be. They do not follow a universal or supra-cultural logic. They do, with varying degrees of success, cover their social and cultural traces. And this does not make their exponents particularly well-disposed to inquisitive anthropologists intent on unearthing precisely those traces.

Local Theories of Material Life

The turning point for this style of analysis appears to have arrived with the insight that capitalism is itself a "local system," if this means that it cannot claim universal status except to the extent that its bearers have coerced the rest of the world to accept it. Thus, Marshall Sahlins has argued that western capitalism is a cultural system whose uniqueness "consists not in the fact that the economic system escapes symbolic determination, but that the economic symbolism is structurally determining" (1976b: 211) – and the global sway of this peculiarity is a historical accident, largely carried by the colonialist imperative. In such a system, highly localized meanings – Louis Dumont has traced the historical emergence of western economic thought as an ideology from Mandeville to Marx (1977) – take on the force of a truism because of their power-backed ubiquity. Sidney Mintz's social history of sugar production and consumption (and, indeed, the production of consumption) illustrates the phenomenon well. Mintz traces the transformation of sugar from a rare foreign luxury to a commonplace necessity of modern life, thereby changing the history of capitalism and industry (1985). James L. Watson's ethnographic purview of the global reach of McDonald's golden arches (J. Watson, ed., 1997) has added an important dimension: attention to the ways in which this globalized localism may be locally reinterpreted, hamburgers being invested with different cultural evaluations in Seoul, Beijing, and Tokyo. (Even within western societies the local may overcome the global, at least at the level of the social organization of taste: market research reputedly forced American ketchup companies to make their products sweeter in the Midwest, spicier in Texas, and sharper in the northeast

– almost a parody of stereotypes embodied and consumed.) Western assumptions about globalization have something of a flavor of ideological wishful thinking: Berdahl (1999b), however, shows how nostalgia for the outmoded local product of a bygone Soviet era may index powerful sentiments of revulsion against the ruthless march of capital in former East Germany, evoking disturbing echoes of the aftermath of Compiègne and showing up the fallibility of western economic triumphalism. All these examples suggest that local populations bring distinctive interpretational frameworks to their understanding of intrusive economic logics.

Thus, we must ask, with Bird-David: "If capitalism is a cultural system, is neoclassical economic theory (the theory currently used by most academically-trained Western economists) a Western cultural way of thinking about the economy?" If so, it traces its ancestry to Adam Smith's influential *The Wealth of Nations* (1776) and to its key notion of the "invisible hand of the market." Smith's central argument – that the pursuit of private ends works for the common good – has been central to "native Western cosmology," especially since the Smith's time (M. Sahlins 1976b, 1996), and fits with larger and still older notions of the European as a "possessive individualist" (Macpherson 1962). At the beginning of the 19th century, David Ricardo redrew this image as a more or less rationalist one, preparing the way for the shift, about a century later, toward the neoclassical representation of the individual as a rational actor who works out the best way of achieving goals by weighing alternatives against each other in terms of their utility relative to their cost. As Bird-David notes, this view is radically Cartesian: the rational mind takes care of the needful body. One might add that this is the same ideology that led early anthropologists to treat "natives" as mentally impoverished "bodies," to be led by the theorizing intellects of the colonizers – a key reason why it has been so difficult for a Western-generated discipline to accept the idea of local economic (or other social) theories.

Again, the trick would seem to be the role reversal whereby western economics appears strange in the distorting mirror of anthropological comparisons. Here is Bird-David again: "Neoclassical economic theory is deeply rooted in Western epistemology, morality and cosmology, the influence of which is apparent in methodological details, too. The idea of selfish parts, instructed each by the same 'instrumental rationality,' and making up a providential whole, has the methodological implication that multiple actions of diverse individuals can be lifted out of their respective contexts and aggregated. Neoclassical theory offers a body of logically-related concepts with which to understand, explain and predict both an individual's economic conduct and the working of the economy as a whole. The economy is doubly seen as an aggregate of individuals' operations, and an entity with laws of its own. 'Demand,' 'supply' and 'price' are some of the basic concepts, referring to the aggregates of needs for, and availability of a resource and its 'value,' as determined by the relation between these. The deeply-held cosmological notion of the providential whole that encompasses and consists of its self-interested parts assured the viability, indeed the desirability, of such an economy."

This is why Gudeman, in part following Marshall Sahlins, asks (1986) to what extent it is self-defeating to try and understand other economies using western economic "cosmology." We would be very surprised, after all, to read an investigation of western physics couched in terms of a non-western form of witchcraft. And in fact this issue emerged in the "substantivist" position of the 1960s. In this view, economies had to be investigated in terms of local social contexts and value, of which what we might now acknowledge as local theories formed an important part.

The alternative view, the older one, was that of the so-called "formalists." These anthropologists had largely used neoclassical economic theory without questioning its focus on the individual and its master trope of the "rational and needful man" – a perhaps surprising persistence of methodological individualism in a discipline otherwise so strongly marked by the sociocentric legacy of Durkheim and his disciples. They adapted it to their cases by, for example, extending the individual's need-motivated goals to include prestige and honor; having others in one's debt; and excellence in ceremonial performance. Even altruism was recast in terms of this instrumentality – a piece of circular thinking which today resurfaces also in the logic of sociobiology (see also M. Sahlins 1976a). They also short-circuited analysis by turning the monetary metaphors of their own society back on those in which cash was not yet the medium of transaction, being further protected from a realization of the circularity of such a move by the emergence of transactionalist and "negotiation" models for a host of other kinds of social interactions. Criticism of this approach was not initially epistemological – that is, concerned with the ethnocentrism of the model – but merely methodological and practical.

"Substantivism" (or "institutionalism"), by contrast, drew on the work of the economist-historian Karl Polyani (Polyani et al., eds., 1957), who intensified the distinction between securing a livelihood and calculating choices – the first involving corporeal participation in social and political processes (e.g., going to a market-place), the second, logical operations and constructs (e.g., the "market," as the aggregate supply and demand for a good). In capitalist economies, Polyani argued, the two aspects collide, with resulting ambiguity of the term "market." In other societies, however, Polanyi – who in this regard followed a well-established convention that separated "primitive" from "developed" societies – saw material actions as always "embedded" in social life. The study of noncapitalist economies there required an alternative theory without the calculative, logical dimension grafted onto the economic in capitalist society. The theory could be applied to capitalist economies too, where the institutional as well as the calculative dimension existed, but a residual sense that capitalist economies were the only ones capable of flying free of social constraints persisted. It took many more years for anthropologists to discern that this claim to transcendence was, in fact, a culturally-specific form of cosmology, grounded increasingly in the self-confirming experiences of colonialist and capitalist domination (see, notably, Gudeman 1986; M. Sahlins 1976b). Polanyi configured his version of this distinction in terms of the notion of exchange, the forms of which characterized, or so he claimed, different types of polity.

The substantivist–formalist debate was heated in the extreme. At stake was the Western claim to have transcended cultural and historical contingency. At the height of the debate, proponents even argued over whether human beings were by their nature needful and rational, a claim that, as Bird-David notes, "is only heuristically assumed by the economists." And she notes that its extraordinary intensity should alert us to "its doubling as a native feuding on core cultural convictions in native Western cosmology."

It would be absurd, from a middle-ground point of view, to deny the relevance of such western models altogether. The contribution of anthropology is to focus attention on the fact that all models are socially and culturally embedded. Academic debate is one identifiable social context. But another is economic theory. While westerners may scoff at the aesthetics of economic representation as a perversion of rationality, for example, their own frequent refusal to engage social context is surely evidence of an equally convention-bound perspective. Ellen Hertz, in her study of the Shanghai stock market (1998: 18), nicely captures the social significance of rationalist claims in economic life. Despite its obvious inability to predict stock market fluctuations, the stock market consulting industry continues to flourish worldwide, "suggesting that for investors, both expert and lay, action is not possible without this proxy of rationality separating them from their decisions" – a point that brings economic rationalizing within the sphere of accountability and cosmology, and underscoring the importance of cultural form over abstract logic. There is clearly an aesthetic and performance-based aspect to such rationalizing, a point further strengthened by the fact that economists' sometimes spectacular failures as prophets have no more cost them their personal social authority than did the failures of, say, some of the Nuer prophets studied by Evans-Pritchard.

As Hertz (1998: 16) robustly observes, moreover, "in ignoring modern economic systems traditional anthropological studies have reinforced the belief that culture is relevant to the study of economics only in exotic societies; in the West, economic institutions are merely economic." Her justification for pursuing an ethnographic approach lies in the evident failure, by its own standards, of rationalism: the logic of the stock market, as she ably demonstrates, is social rather than economic. It therefore can be opened up to interpretation: "If stocks are signs, making money means reading the signs correctly, whether one is in New York or Jakarta." And this means knowing the local cultural code, as well as the range of options open to local social actors – the play of agency and structure, rather than what we have come to see as the Thatcherite or Reaganite methodological individualism of the now politically ascendant neoclassical economics (Hertz 1998: 23; Dilley, ed., 1992).

This distinction between agency and individualism is very important here. As Carrier (1995: 101) remarks, the economically independent individual is indeed a real person – but, as it happens, "reflects at least the thinking and probably the experiences of those in particular social locations, which are treated deferentially in Western society and taken to define social identity and relationships in academic understandings of social exchange." All the more reason, then, to "study up" – to examine the peculiar cultural understandings of the economy among those so situated.

Stimulated by the work of Marshall Sahlins and Clifford Geertz, Stephen Gudeman (1986) has pursued the question of embedded cultural assumptions in more general theoretical terms. He offered the "working hypothesis" (Gudeman 1986: 37) that humans everywhere – not only professional economists – model their material life. If this is so, he argued, then in each particular case it is by their respective theories that we should try to understand both individuals' reasoning and conduct and the economy at large. Gudeman's "cultural economics" encompasses analysis of the case of capitalist economy, with its neoclassic theory, at the same time that he advocates the use of local cultural theories in the analysis of other cases. While substantivism deals with "the economy" and neglects the "individual," cultural economics – in this sense a variant of practice theory – addresses both. This, as Bird-David cautions us, is already true of neoclassic theory. What makes cultural economics different is its grounding in the kind of close attention to local values, theories, and concepts that characterizes ethnographic research and depends on the analyst's intimate acquaintance with sometimes heavily marginalized loci of opposition to globally dominant cosmologies. Moreover, it is not necessarily deterministic: recognizing cultural imperatives does not mean that actors always obey them.

Bird-David's assessment is lucid and to the point: "As a relatively young approach, it has achievements as well as growing problems. In *Economics as Cultures*, Stephen Gudeman elucidated a variety of local models, some Western (the Physiocrats and Ricardo); some indigenous (the African Bemba, Bisa and Cogo, the Dobu of New-Guinea, and the Iban of Sarawak); and some rural (peasants in Panama and Bolivia). I give a sense of these models by briefly summarizing two examples, which cannot but violate their ethnographic richness. The Physiocrats maintained that the land is economically fertile, and causes wealth to increase, while manufacturing and crafts are 'barren,' and work therein is an expenditure which gives no more return than itself. The Bemba, in comparison, maintain that agricultural prosperity 'is' an ancestral volition, and to secure a livelihood from the land one has to please the ancestors, doing what they have been doing, and distributing part of the yield to the chiefs, who are regarded [as] the living embodiment of the ancestors. Such examples provide evidence that in diverse cultures there are different conceptualizations of the logic of the economy. Furthermore, by comparing them with each other – rather than with Western theory, explicitly or implicitly – we can better map each, in greater and greater detail; the more so, the more cases are studied, providing more templates against which to 'see' further ones."

In a subsequent move, in *Conversations in Colombia* (1990), Stephen Gudeman and Alberto Rivera demonstrate the depth of understanding which can be achieved by paying attention to local models – I prefer to avoid the term "folk models," since it implicitly suggests a hierarchical distinction between ordinary people and powerful intellectuals and professionals. Suggesting that the Colombian local models resemble seventeenth-century European antecedents, Gudeman and Rivera examine the conceptual shift involved in the emergence of modern economic theory out of the latter. In parallel to this study and in part inspired by its example, Bird-David (1992) elucidated a Nayaka "hunter-gatherer" model, centered on the idea of sharing relationships with (animated) features of the natural environment (see also D. Smith 1998). This cultural–economic model renders sensible – that is, reasonable in terms of culturally-specific forms of common sense – a stance that we would otherwise find baffling: it includes a lack of acquisitiveness or much concern with the future, and satisfaction with what is available as long as it is being shared. Povinelli (1993), again, while not using Gudeman's terms, showed in analogous fashion how an Australian Aboriginal model reproduces itself through negotiation with the Australian administration's capitalistic model (cf. Gudeman 1986: 1–28).

Gudeman argues that all economic models are extensions of one or a few intersecting metaphors or conceptual schemata. Western models, Gudeman argues, draw upon abstract, logical and mathematical schemes, and on schemata taken from the domain of material objects. Models generated elsewhere, he says, are drawn on schemata taken from the social and human world. Furthermore, the western models are universalist in their claims – an outcome, we might add, of the relatively recent colonial dominance of the world by a few western powers and the consequent practical need to theorize on a much larger scale than hitherto, rather than of some inherent superiority of the models themselves. In this sense, economic anthropology partakes of the more general awareness that all human beings are capable of producing anthropological theory and often actually do so (Crick 1976), but recognizes that only the professionalization of these insights as the systematic theory of an academic discipline has made possible a far more inclusive perspective than was probably ever possible, or even needed, before.

Bird-David nonetheless finds that Gudeman's argument is, in a self-contradictory manner, reductionist: to her, it appears to offer "yet another universal theory," one that turns individual ethnographic cases into generalizations and makes grand theories "out of local ideas that are inseparably embedded in culturally-constituted economic life." There is a curious echo here of John Davis's (1992) critique of Sahlins's treatment of reciprocity. Yet Gudeman, like Sahlins, rejects the universalism of neoclassical economic theory and its various western incarnations, and it is not clear that he would expect to generalize the Colombian peasants' perspectives except in the most generic sense of wanting scholars to recognize – everywhere, to be sure – that local actors operate within their own understandings of economic process – precisely the point on which in fact all these writers agree. Why choose between universalizing particularisms, whether western or from some other cultural locality? Maintaining the tension between the specificity of these local concepts and the comparative perspective that they collectively provide locates analysis in a more productively middle-ground position that resists both kinds of closure – and is at once both heuristic and, in a provisional sense, theoretical.

Such a strategy resists the hubris of resisting the cultural embeddedness of our own perspectives or of failing to recognize that others have appropriated some of these perspectives for their own purposes (as in Gupta's [1998] model of hybridity). As Bird-David explicitly recognizes, Gudeman and Rivera themselves elsewhere disclose the organic imagery that underlies the capitalistic modeling that goes on in corporations (1990: 13) and at the same time note the derivational entailments of local metaphors, such as the Colombian "house," with its "base," "door," and with "getting things out of the door" and "keeping them inside." Sahlins, too, points out that the capitalist idea of a providential economy is similarly embedded in cosmological and religious beliefs (M. Sahlins 1996), and thus does not significantly differ in nature – but, by the same token, radically differs in its specifics – from these local models. It is itself a local model – that is, a culturally specific one – and, as Ellen Hertz's (1998) exploration of the Shanghai Stock Exchange elegantly illustrates, it is refracted around the world through a considerable range of cultural, historical, and ideological variations.

Bird-David proposes "a simple corrective": to "regard analyses by local models as a heuristic device." This avoids the risk of cultural determinism: just as neoclassical economics (as opposed to some of the more extreme formalist arguments within anthropology) adopts a heuristic strategy of positing the existence of rational decision-making individuals, cultural economics may similarly and heuristically presume model-making-and-conforming agents operating within the cultural frameworks of their economies as they understand them. A cultural-economic study, she suggests, would involve the preparatory heuristic abstraction of a model out of a cultural process and, ultimately, the production of an ethnographic account demonstrating the model's embeddedness in the complex cultural process from which it was abstracted: "The implication of this approach is that economic models are not to be compared globally, only as possibly helpful toolkits." She points out that Gudeman and Rivera analyze the Colombian "house" economy in terms drawn from modern economic theory: stock and flow, circulating and fixed capital, and so on.

Heuristically valuable the approach may be; but I would also add that this has long been the method of comparative analysis, and that the question of how far these key metaphors are universal remains open to further discussion on the basis of findings yet to come. The difficulty is to get scholars to take the local theories and concepts seriously in the first place, and to study their interrelationship with actual social practice *in situ*. Bird-David herself generalizes the epistemological status of the local. The point of a heuristic approach is not to abandon the quest for more general statements – all observations, however particularistic, at least implicitly assume some degree of selection and regularity – but to reinforce the abiding provisionality of all generalizations. In an analogous way, many scholars who distrust the grand universalism of Lévi-Straussian structuralism nevertheless have found it useful as method (e.g., Leach 1970: 120–3); yet its utility may ultimately suggest the possibility of some more general statement that nonetheless falls short of total universality. With Gudeman's work, similarly, the general principle that social actions both reveal and accord (in varying degrees) with local ideas about material matters would seem to offer precisely this kind of middle-level theory.

It might be usefully complicated by adducing the evidence of historical linkages that explain parallels that some theorists might try to universalize. Is there in their economic ideas a conceptual linkage to Aristotle, as has also, for example, been claimed for Basque notions of procreation (Ott 1979) and Latin American humoral medicine (see Foster 1987)? Some notion of an etymology of concepts might help to explain persistence that does not exist at the level of conscious traditionalizing and that does not, as Gupta (1998: 159) points out in the context of Indian agriculture, necessarily signify a wholly different way of doing things at all. Linkages of this kind would show local economic theories to overlap to a significant degree with those imposed by the bearers of intrusive logics and practices, but would also reveal many of the reasons for which development agencies are unable to understand why their recommendations are not always embraced as the exclusive path of wisdom.

One significant objection raised to Gudeman and Rivera's approach is that, while it is intuitively appealing, it rests on subjective assumptions about peasant "mentality" (Wilk 1996: 128). This line of argument includes the concern that Colombian peasants are thereby represented as all thinking alike, without any possibility of "respond[ing] to market incentives . . . or other opportunities" because they are "stuck with a restrictive and static worldview." In other words, so this objection runs, the theory denies the peasants any agency of their own.

The charge would be serious but for one detail: it has no more been tested by major events than has the model against which Wilk deploys it. It will be a matter of empirical concern to see whether, when opportunities arise, the peasants will in fact take advantage of them, or whether – and perhaps this would be the greater wisdom, if we recall the Albanian "pyramid schemes" that wrecked a faltering economy at precisely such a moment of "opportunity" – they will choose either to subvert them or to ignore them altogether, a stance that does not necessarily imply the absence of agency. Any judgment of economic action, which is a form of social practice, must necessarily be what Wilk calls "subjective," because, as his own language clearly shows, it is embedded in ideology. But to the extent that Colombian peasants themselves explain their economy in a particular way, the model is as close to an empirical fact as we can come – although, again intuitively, I find that Gupta's (1998) suggestion that such models, far from being static, are the result of long centuries of hybridization to be a useful refinement of what I take to be Gudeman's argument. To the extent that such models are viewed as invariant and overdetermining, they do indeed obscure agency; but Bird-David's discussion of this approach shows that the difficulty is easily overcome as Wilk himself would wish to overcome it – by the practice of careful ethnography focused on how agents actually use the ideas that ethnographers try to describe.

Commodities and Gifts: The social life of material things

In Bird-David's felicitous phrase: "It has been Marcel Mauss' gift to anthropologists to distinguish between 'gift' and 'commodity' as forms of circulating
things between people." In the orthodox reading, his celebrated *Essay on the
Gift* (1954) is an attempt to distinguish between commodities as alienable things
exchanged between aliens and gifts as inalienable things exchanged between
nonaliens (see, e.g., Gregory 1982: 43). Mauss, whose schema in this regard
owed a considerable intellectual debt to its evolutionist predecessors, argued an
evolution from the gift as characterizing "archaic" societies to the commodity,
which he viewed as the hallmark of modernity. Unlike the more optimistic evolutionists, however, he saw this less as evidence of progress than as the outcome
of the inexorable fragmentation of that social solidarity that marked so many
of the idealized nostalgias of late evolutionist social theory – Tönnies's *Gemeinschaft*, Engels's "primitive communism," Weber's enchanted world before the
advent of the "iron cage" of bureaucratic rationalization. Like many of his contemporaries, Mauss saw modernity as a time of loss and fragmentation, and
above all of the rupturing of balance in the mythological, edenic past of the
world as conceived by the West. In light of the preceding discussion of local and
universalizing economic theories, it is worth pointing out that this form of
"structural nostalgia" – in a time that is always just out of our reach, the world
was once a place of perfect balance and reciprocity, untouched by the corro-
sions of time – is one that these social scientists shared with many of the peoples
studied by anthropologists, and may reflect a secular reincarnation of biblical
imagery.

Mauss used the expression "the spirit of the gift," generalizing the Maori
notion of *hau* to the status of a model, and argued that it established a special
bond between giver and taker. Bird-David retrospectively reads this as "the
key cultural ideas which are embodied in the thing." But I would argue that
this does not really clarify the concept. It leaves it in the same mystical limbo
as some other recent reworkings, such as the "spirit of the commodity"
(Appadurai 1986), and "the spirit of asking" and the "morality" of money
(Bloch and Parry, eds., 1989). The application of a *hau*-like notion suffers
from the same exoticizing deficiency that Crick (1976) has noted in the
recycling of such terms as *mana* and *tapu* (taboo) into general anthropological
circulation.

On the other hand, there is considerable merit, if we are going to use such
formulations, in showing how they operate in western contexts. Then, and
only then, can they be said to be truly useful. It is not only the Chinese or Japanese stock exchanges that manifest a deep concern with the play of luck and
chance or with the aesthetics of prediction. Although Mauss, like Durkheim,
was principally concerned with exotic societies in which he hoped to discern
the "archaic" principles underlying the fragmentation of the modern age,
we should not forget that – again like Durkheim – he never conducted field
research of his own, so that the primary experiential models were to be found

at home. Even assiduous fieldworkers have not proved immune to the suggestive allure of popular models of social and political process in their home
societies (see Kuklick 1991). And armchair anthropologists never experienced
the defamiliarizing shock of field encounters. Thus, for example, Durkheim's
famous characterization of religion as society worshiping itself may thus
prove more applicable to nationalism (where the human agents who invented
the rules are knowable) than to Australian Aboriginal rituals (where they
are not).

Mauss's invocation of *hau* similarly cannot be read independently of European ideologies of gift giving, altruism, and social responsibility. This is not to
say that he necessarily misrepresented the Maori sense of *hau* – that is an empirical question – but we should recognize that he invoked an exotic model in order
to rescue something his evolutionism led him to posit as a conceptual substra-
tum of his own society's economic ideology.

Indeed, Mauss comes into his own particularly in those everyday western contexts in which the sale of objects can take on the appearance of real exchange.
As John Davis (1992: 25) observes, although in a more restricted sense than do
Gudeman and Bird-David, we should take seriously social actors' theories about
what they are doing. This courtesy, as he makes clear, should be extended to
the economic actors of our own societies as much as of those our predecessors
used to study as "primitive."

Anthropologists have begun to do just that. Gretchen Herrmann (1997), for
example, in a study of "garage sales" in the United States, has argued that the
affective value attributed by the seller to an object that has already been priced
so low as to make haggling unseemly, ensures that the buyer will be conjoined
with the seller – a person perhaps never to be seen again – in a shared sense of
participation in the affective bond. The seeming triviality of garage sales, and
other economic activities usually ignored by mainstream economists (e.g., gambling: Oxfeld 1993; Malaby 1999), reveals the powerful interests that marginalize such practices or seek to subject them to the control of the state and the
market. Gambling, for instance, may provide an important link – differently
experienced in different cultural settings – between the threatening uncertainties of social life and the regulations that govern market practices. It may also
thrive as part of the "informal" economy; and, as has increasingly happened in
Native American communities in the United States, it may provide a highly profitable and politically visible means for hitherto marginalized groups to reassert
their presence and thereby also to reveal the moral economy in which it is
embedded. But above all it is a daily practice, closely linked to cosmology as
well as economics.

The move to repatriate Mauss's model of reciprocity, moreover, finally disposes of the evolutionism inherent in his original formulation: the "archaic"
model has been there in the West all along, while commodities have circulated
elsewhere for millennia. This has indeed been one of the most notable shifts in
recent economic anthropology; James Carrier's critique of Mauss has particularly underscored and contributed to its importance (1995). Once the activities
of the household become a focus for serious economic analysis (Netting, Wilk,

and Arnould, eds., 1984), and once everyday economic actions become significant aspects of the larger picture, the rationalistic model of an autonomous economic system becomes empirically unsustainable and the invidious distinction
between "primitive" and "modern" economies, like the parallel dichotomies in
other domains of social experience, emerges in its true guise as the discursive
dimension of political inequity.

But there is a further point to note, one that is often missed in these discussions. Mauss was interested in reciprocity rather than in exchange alone. This
is a distinction between abstract potentiality and realization – an important
distinction we owe to Edwin Ardener, although he used a less user-friendly
terminology (see especially Ardener 1989). It is important in the present
context because the absence of an actual exchange can signify as much (such
as reciprocal distrust) as its presence, and because potentiality – the promise
of a reciprocation that may never actually occur, or that may be understood
to have happened even though it has no obvious realization in the movement
of concrete goods – both underlies a good deal of everyday economic action
and, at the same time, blurs the lines between economic and other spheres
of human action. When an animal is stolen within a system of reciprocal
theft, a blessing pronounced, or a courtesy extended, these are all markers –
just like the goods exchanged in Mary Douglas's (Douglas and Isherwood
1979) symbolic universe – of social relations that are themselves in flux. It is
John Davis's (1992: 22–5) failure to appreciate the exchange–reciprocity
distinction that leads him, in my view, to misapprehend Marshall Sahlins's
recognition of economies based on differing ideologies of reciprocity. Theft
is not always an act of exchange – it may indeed be a denial of the very possibility – but in ideologies of reciprocity it excites dreams (and sometimes acts)
of retribution, which is the paradigmatic form of what Sahlins calls "negative
reciprocity."

The genius of Mauss's formulation was not that he explained exchange, but
that he showed it to be embedded in the very premise of social existence – the
idea of reciprocity. To reduce reciprocity to the status of a purely economic
concept – "exchange" – dresses it in the clothing of modern capitalism, which
is only one of its possible forms. This completely subverts the special contribution of anthropology to the study of economics itself, and goes against Davis's
own professed aim of not universalizing local ideologies as grand theory (1992:
26). The answer lies in asking of "economics" what ideologies and social practices create the context in which it appears, contrary to the experience of those
who have lost all in some major financial crash, to offer a reassuring model of
reliable and rational predictability.

Commodities Un-traded

The association of the idea of the commodity with "the West" dies hard, especially because it has played such an important role for critics – notably those
of Marxist persuasion – of Western models of the economy. It is to Arjun

Appadurai (1986) that we owe a fresh perspective that reconstructs the commodity as, to quote Bird-David, "a phenomenon crossing historical sequences and economic types." Instead of assuming (as so many have done) that a thing's preexisting value is what makes it an object of exchange, Appadurai combined insights from Simmel and Marx to argue that the "value in a commodity" lay in the act of exchange, whether actual or simply imagined. (Note here again the importance of not treating exchange as logically equivalent to reciprocity: reciprocity serves as the template – the paradigmatic structure, in Ardener's terms – that allows a virtual exchange to invest objects with value.) Appadurai suggests as a heuristic measure that we should regard this value as if it were embodied in the commodity itself (describing the approach as "methodological fetishism," Appadurai [1986: 5].) In these terms, a thing can become but also unbecome a "commodity." Its status as such is situational; its exact physical properties are irrelevant except insofar as they are "overcoded" (Eco 1976) as possessing value. Exchange situations do not necessarily entail the use of money. "Commodities," thus reconceptualized, are not confined to the particular socioeconomic formation of the industrialized West.

This approach notably shifts the analysis from category to process and practice. It also provides a useful context in which to view the politics of significance more generally: it shifts the emphasis from commodities as being preconstituted as such – as being "naturally" commodities, so to speak – to the ways in which demand or desire makes commodities out of things. As a study of this process of naturalization, it may help to disembed economic theory from the cultural matrix in which it so assiduously disavows any entanglement. But this is not the kind of dissociation that most economists seek, and certainly not those whose business it is to promote the market as we generally understand it.

How do cultures produce the values that make things economic? This is what Appadurai (1986) calls the "politics of value." One of the fresh ethnographic avenues that this approach opens up is the cultural biography (or lifecycle) of a thing – the sequence of "situations" through which it progresses (see Kopytoff 1986). This takes Douglas's "world of goods" to a level of great specificity. Herrmann's analysis of garage sales fits this model, and it also allows us to trace social linkages outside the narrow confines of a conventionally face-to-face environment for ethnographic research.

Another approach is to study processes and events in which we can observe the actual creation of value – what Appadurai calls "tournaments of value" (1986: 16–29). The famous Kula cycle of the Trobriand islands is a notable non-western example of this, while western art auctions constitute a capitalist illustration (see Plattner 1996). Brian Moeran (1989) has recently shown how Japanese munificence to the British Museum informed with new meanings a reproduction of ancient coronation rituals, suggesting the transformative effects of their engagement with a voluntaristic economic ideology. Bird-David suggests, as further examples, techniques of associating things with persons in a strategic play on "gift" principles – for example, "home-made" chocolates – to be contrasted, perhaps, with the celebration of domestic-scale artisanship as a national tradition in France (see Terrio 1996) – and the personal appeal used in mail-order catalogues (see Carrier 1995: 126–45) and telephone advertising.

The status of belonging to the leisured classes may be signaled through the inverted-snobbery version of what Veblen (1965) called "conspicuous consumption," the ostentatious revaluation and acquisition of objects that cannot possibly still possess any utilitarian value in the ordinary sense; Michael Thompson (1979) has elaborated an entire "rubbish theory" to account for this phenomenon, calling, perhaps a little heavy-handedly, on "chaos theory" to provide a predictive basis for his thesis. This kind of rubbish makes excellent gifts: one would have to assume that it was expensive, because otherwise the donor could only be insulting the recipient – which always remains an implicit possibility. Services, too, can be so presented, although the greater immediacy of the interaction involved – as with flight attendants or waiters demanding rather importunately to know if there is anything further they can do to serve you (except leave one in peace, which would upset the entire transaction of value) – tends to reveal the limits of what I have called "simulacra of sociality" (Herzfeld 1997a). Indeed, such metaphors of personal engagement are further evidence, if we still need it (and as marketing specialists have long understood), that what we construe as the literal and the rational are not especially relevant to the operation of the market.

Some of those who examine the consumption of commodities even claim this topic be a successor to kinship studies as the core area of anthropology (Miller 1995), in that consumption is seen as constituting identity (see also Wilk 1996). But this development, while extremely promising, risks throwing the emphasis back on things as opposed to the practices and processes through which things gain meaning and value, and it also overlooks the remarkable centrality that kinship appears to maintain especially among those – such as North Americans (D. Schneider 1980) – among whom its significance is so often alleged to have waned. It also risks reducing analysis, once again, to a one-dimensional caricature.

Mention of kinship is suggestive also because the modern American preoccupation with genealogy suggests a fertile area for studying the confluence of both topics. The increasingly lucrative business of purveying family trees to households is no less an indication of the salience of older theoretical foci than is the garage sale, especially as it takes place in a context where "family values" are caught up in the symbolism of national identity politics. And we should not forget that baronies and coats-of-arms were also important symbolic capital in the emergence of bourgeois capitalism, which is why we speak of "railway barons" and the "lords of industry." The computerized genealogy-monger who offers his services to all comers at a stall amidst the baroque splendors of Rome's Piazza Navona is a successor, in this allegedly more democratic age, to the heraldic experts of past ages.

Conversely, however, it is indeed clear that commodities provide an area for the exploration and contestation of identity, whether in terms of kinship, gender, or nationality. Slogans like "whoever buys Greek, wins" harness stereotypical attributes of "national character" (here as the competitive individualist-patriot) for economic ends, sometimes in direct opposition to the perceived domination of the West (although the injunction to "buy American" and recent legislation to make the "made in the United States" label more restrictive show that this is no longer a one-way relationship). Studies show that commodities are "appropriated" by people to diverse cultural designs, different from place to place, and between social groups. Imported commodities, including western mass-produced ones, do not often break down local cultures, as people "tame" them, and make them part of their own cultures. In Latin America, for example, the circulation of western trade goods and the vagaries of their local imitation maps a complex history of entrepreneurship and class differentiation (Orlove and Bauer 1997), while the marketing of African ritual objects in new contexts transforms them into "art" and invests them with monetary value (Steiner 1994). Berdahl's explorations of these processes in the former East Germany show that the newcomers to German capitalism are not necessarily impressed by the gadgetry and sheen of western products; they may reject them or incorporate them into wildly different scenarios (1999a and b). The rescuing of "rubbish" as collectibles (Thompson 1979) marks the growing power of leisured classes while creating an international, often diasporic underclass of suppliers and artisans. The mass arrival of McDonald's in East Asia, again, provides a forum for expressing highly differentiated responses to the alleged cultural colonialism of the West (J. Watson, ed., 1997). The circulation of audio and video cassettes among Amazonian tribes may now be as effective a marker of their contrastive identities as were once the stylized performance of chants in each other's villages and the practice of linguistic exogamy – although it also creates problems in the face of the fetishizing of the exotic by the non-Indian wielders of metropolitan power (e.g., Conklin 1998).

Even modern money itself, a super-commodity of sorts, is "tamed." In many societies, its arrival was greeted with deep suspicion, because it subverted existing reciprocities and so threatened the social order: "money itself had an ambiguous moral value . . . [for which reason the Tolai and Duke of York Islanders of Papua New Guinea] regarded shell money to be superior to money" – not because of the western discomfort with the disjunction between social and egotistical uses but, to the contrary, because for big men to accumulate shell money was a social and therefore a reproductive act (Gewertz and Errington 1985: 171; see also Douglas 1958, on raffia currency and the tension and violence the introduction of cash generated among an African people). In Greece, to give another example, the introduction of the cash dowry represented an intrusion into well-understood social processes by larger and potentially uncontrollable forces, with the result that it has always carried implications of disapprobation and a longing for the time before such "necessities" supervened. Yet the weaving of cash into the dowry system also gave cash itself a local social meaning, which in time came to seem so dependable that the original form of cash – British gold sovereigns – came to replace the old Turkish coins used to ornament women's bodies. In time, too, these sovereigns came to be hoarded, because at least the gold was "real," in sharp contrast to the notoriously unreliable paper money produced by the banks. Here money itself became the commodity, while the everyday Greek currency was said to "fly away" on the wings of the heraldic bird on one of the coins. Foreignness enhances value, as Helms (1998) has argued, and this, in a modern context, means the direct commodification of money itself: witness the airline "sky mall" sales of ancient coins of "historic" significance (the coin that Jesus used, the last portrait of the last Czar, and so on).

In some societies in which it is a relatively recent arrival, money is sometimes incorporated into local symbolic systems with relative ease. Malaysian women, for example, "cook" the money which their fishermen-husbands earn, before it starts circulating within the community (Carsten 1989) – which in Appadurai's terms could be seen, Bird-David points out, as a gender-mediated social path that produces and places a new value on the money. But in fact the situation shares at least one key feature with what Gewertz and Errington describe for New Guinea: cash does not necessarily "mean" what its European and European-trained proponents intend it to mean. No account of a system of value should fail to take account of the impact that such revaluations might have on the actual use and importance of money in a local economy.

Less work has been done so far on the "gift" as a cross-cultural phenomenon that inhabits both capitalist and other societies, although Herrmann's article on garage sales – again by defamiliarizing a very ordinary occurrence in American society – represents an interesting new direction. Such formulations make it clear that the gift continues to play an important role, at least as an idea, in supposedly commodity-oriented societies. Jonathan Parry has indeed argued against the usual interpretation of Mauss's *The Gift* as an evolutionist progression from gift to commodity (see Parry 1986). He proposes instead that the evolution of modern society involved splitting between "persons" and "things" – entities that in primitive society are conjoined. This allows him to see in Mauss's essay a distinction between interested and disinterested transactions: in the West, in this argument, the gift is separate from the commodity because it is outside the transactional framework, just as the artist has been separated from the functions in which non-modern art is supposedly embedded. Yet this model, too, implies some kind of linear progression, and lumps societies into two discrete categories, with modernity defined by a clear separation of social functions from "pure" properties such as generosity, aesthetics, and morality.

In the Western, capitalist ideology, the gift is supposed to be totally disinterested, or "pure" (see Carrier 1995: 145–68), and as such opposed to the equally pure motivation of trade – the commodity. Carrier (1995) and Thomas (1991b) have both argued from strong evidence that this is too simplistic – indeed, for Carrier in particular, it springs from a stereotypical view of the West ("occidentalism"), couched in terms of an "orientalist" vision of Melanesians-in-general (and perhaps primitives-in-general), that Mauss shared with his Western contemporaries and successors.

This image of the pure gift, or "prestation," has been projected onto images of primitive society, eclipsing the temporal dynamics of prestation that do in fact involve calculations and strategies (Bourdieu 1977: 171). It is no coincidence, as Mauss (1954: 127) pointed out, that gift and poison are denoted by the same word in German; Bailey (1971: 23–4) extends this insight to the exchanges involved in gossip, noting that all exchange – which in his view amounted to all social life – was fraught with ambiguity and, for that reason, offered fertile ground for strategies of many kinds. Strategic gifting, as Bird-David observes, is probably a common practice in capitalist societies as much as elsewhere.

But her statement that "with very few exceptions, gifting practices in capitalist society have been little studied" (see also Carrier 1995: 145) is only applicable is we revert to a very materialistic definition of the economy – or if we mistake "ought" for "is" and overlook the numerous accounts of the role of the gift in western systems of patronage (e.g., Campbell 1964; Holmes 1989). In communist systems, too, despite their idealism, "traditional" notions of the gift seem essential to social cohesion (Yan 1996; Yang 1994). Western practices outlawing the use of gifts as sweeteners of business deals, while disguising the gifting aspect of such exchanges as "bribery," implicitly recognize the idea of the instrumental gift; indeed, the notion that they are "corrupt" points to nothing so much as the fact that an instrumental gift represents a categorical violation in terms of the prevailing ideology, rather than that such a phenomenon is nonexistent or inconceivable for westerners – which is patently not the case, as repeated political scandals have established.

Hospitality, in similar vein, often serves to give the weaker party the moral upper hand in a transaction. But is hospitality itself an economic act – a kind of exchange – or is it a strategic device intended to enhance more obviously material intentions, as in the coffee the shopkeeper offers before a bargaining session in many Middle Eastern societies? The connections revealed by these seemingly trivial acts were obscured rather than illuminated by the old division of labor between economic and political anthropology. The expansion of the language of economics into other domains – ideas like "moral economy" (J. Scott 1985), "symbolic capital" (Bourdieu 1977), and "social transaction" (Kapferer, ed., 1976) – serves to undercut such artifical separations to some degree, although it also risks "capitalizing" phenomena that may have very little to with ideas of profit and loss at all – Bourdieu, critic of "economistic" assessments of economic relations (see especially Bourdieu 1977: 172), nonetheless deploys the metaphor of capital to areas, such as the cultural and the symbolic, in which it might be seen as excessively reductionist.

A classic example of social relations in which the degree of economic entailment may be a matter for more precise definition is what Sahlins called "negative reciprocity" – especially (but not exclusively) in its institutionally reciprocal forms such as the Cretan and Sardinian practice of reciprocal animal-theft (Herzfeld 1985; Moss 1979) and Bedouin camel raiding (Meeker 1979). (In local worldviews, however, theft and the blood feud, for example, not to speak of more ludic versions such as card games and song contests, may be intricately interconnected in performances of gender identity, so that here again the separation of the economic from the political and the genealogical becomes artificial at best.)

John Davis (1992) considers the idea of negative reciprocity to be grotesque because he views it as a desperate attempt by Sahlins to preserve the universal applicability of the model of reciprocity as the basis of all economic action. But this is neither fair to Sahlins's original vision, which was mainly concerned with reciprocal theft as such, nor does it live up to Davis's own good advice about heeding native theorizing. In societies where reciprocal raiding of animals is the norm, for example, technically nonreciprocal attacks on rich families or state institutions are usually represented as vengeance for the "fact" that the latter are the true thieves, having stolen the people's birthright (e.g., Herzfeld 1985). And once again we are easily led back to the industrial West – this time by the voice of the indicted criminal pleading, "Society made me do it," again as an act of restitution. Excuses are like lies: they may offend the moral sensibilities of some observers, but, when used consistently, they reflect moral valuations in which we may find explanations for what strike us, but do not strike our informants, as irrational practices (see Austin 1971).

Lies, for example, may be a legitimate defense of a kin group's interests, and dismissing such a perspective as "amoral familism" (Banfield 1958) is a piece of self-contradictory nonsense that blithely ignores its fundamentally ethical focus. (If we recast it as "family values," the absurdity and ethnocentrism of such formulations becomes quite apparent!) Similarly, the majority of societies that practice reciprocal raiding use it creatively to formulate social relations, often to the point of creating alliances between erstwhile foes, and treat this process as the only viable basis of trustworthy friendship. In other cases – for example, smuggling on the Bulgarian–Turkish frontier – the illegal act becomes a marker of identity in the face of oppressive state systems and the basis of the negotiation of social solidarity among individuals of widely divergent backgrounds (Konstantinov 1996). The use of spells and other small rituals to avert the customs officers' interference, the incantational quality of the internal swapping in the darkened bus that allows the participants to maximize their profits, and the formulaic collusion of customs officers and smugglers – all these features suggest that reciprocity is activated in several different ways here and that, just as the Trobrianders' kula transactions encompassed some bartering of practical necessities, so here too we are seeing a concatenation of identity negotiation with economic interest and ritual activity.

"Persons" and "things" as constructs are among the important cultural notions that gift and commodity practices embody. Strathern (1988) has argued, in a study of New Guinea cultures, that the "person" in these cases is commonly constructed as a composite of social relationships. Bird-David cogently argues from this premise: "A gift embodies a particular relationship between donor and receiver and in this sense – as Mauss argued – it constitutes an inalienable 'part' of the donor. Other cultural visions of 'persons' and 'things' should be explored, in their diversity, in relation to gifting and commodity-exchange." In the context of modern national and global societies, where the commonality of participants must either be iconically "imagined" (as in nationalism:

B. Anderson 1983) or metonymically assumed (as in attributions of "typical" behavior), such phenomena as Roma trader-tourism on the Bulgarian–Turkish border provide a context in which we can see both negative and positive reciprocities being used by identifiable social actors to negotiate the meaning of identities and to situate their persons within those identities. The same is true of reciprocal animal-theft; indeed, in its evolution into what we understand today as mafia practice reciprocal violence – in respect of goods or of bodies – has become the hallmark of "Sicilianism" for those whose interests lie in supporting it (J. Schneider and P. Schneider 1994).

Bird-David partially anticipates this criticism when she points out that there are also multiple forms of transaction: "A diversity of exchange forms had been reified by anthropologists into either 'gift' or 'commodity,' while in the concreteness of social life – among indigenous people as among Westerners – there are multiple kinds. These have to be studied, too." Among these she lists barter, which, as she notes (following Humphrey and Hugh-Jones 1992: 5), "is not just a historical institution, or one peculiar to archaic or 'primitive' economies [but also] . . . a contemporary phenomenon which covers both large and small-scale transactions and occurs within and between many different types of society." Unlike Appadurai, who subsumes barter under "commodity" (Appadurai 1986: 10), Humphrey and Hugh-Jones argue that it is "a complex phenomena [sic] which, like the gift, includes ideas, values and visions of the transacting other" (Humphrey and Hugh-Jones 1992: 3). Whereas the "gift" implies some compulsion – "people must compel others to enter into debt . . . the recipient's need is forced upon him by the donor" (Strathern, cited by Humphrey and Hugh-Jones 1992: 11), however, in barter "each side decides their [sic] own needs, and the aim is to end the transaction feeling free of immediate debt" (Humphrey and Hugh-Jones 1992). Barter often bridges different "value regimes" and involves dissimilar transacted things as well as free and equal transactors.

It is perhaps not a matter of surprise, pace Bird-David, that "the study of economies in terms of the things which people use and pass among themselves, has become thoroughly culturalist." But I would argue that this should not be allowed to obscure the fact that economic relations are social as well as cultural. When the similarity of commodities is intended to reproduce a community of interest, it serves iconically (that is, in terms of resemblances) to replicate that identity – as, notably, in the sharing of standardized commodities in the (iconically) "imagined community" of the nation, and as in the search for symbolism that will make the coin of the realm truly national. At that level of inclusiveness, in the absence of face-to-face ties, common ground will largely be cultural rather than social, which is why national governments usually try to reify national culture as a common heritage. But the "social life of things" implies that their primary significance lies in the relational (or "indexical") rather than the iconic. Their generic resemblance – their membership of recognizable classes of desirable objects – may be projected as a reason for buying or hoarding or collecting, but the pathways along which they travel map the unstable nexus of relationships in which all the transactors are variously situated. They track relations of inequality, however transient, as well as alliances and enmities. What the flow of goods teaches us above all else is that social ties remain the basis of what those goods mean, no matter how stretched the metaphors of sociality may seem to be. That is perhaps the most important lesson of Herrmann's analysis of the garage sale.

Corporations and Houses: The material base of social life

The study of economies in terms of how people secure their livelihood has, according to Bird-David, begun to evolve in a culturalist direction as well. In *Stone Age Economics*, Marshall Sahlins (1972) proposed as a generalized "domestic mode of production" (DMP) what previous scholars had seen only as "modes of subsistence" of various ecological types (hunter-gatherer, horticulturalist, pastoralist and peasant). He characterized the DMP – in dichotomous opposition to the capitalist mode of production, if in some cases, leaving the contrast implicit – as economies organized by domestic groups and kinship relations. In such systems, people underutilize – as opposed to the maximizing of capitalists – their productive resources and labor capacity. Households produce for use (as opposed to exchange), or occasionally for exchange directed ultimately toward use. Each household is a microcosm of the economy at large, in terms of the division of labor.

This schema preserved the unfortunate sense of a radical split between the Rest and the West. Nonetheless, it offered several advantages. It made the separation of nonindustrial societies into discrete categories – "hunter-gatherers," "horticulturalists," "pastoralists," and "peasants" – virtually redundant, not to say misleading. In Bird-David's summary: "Ethnographers have studied groups within the same category comparatively, or just produced new ethnographies while paying attention to earlier ethnographies of the same kind, and have addressed common issues, besides those specific to their own particular study-groups. . . . For instance, ethnographers of 'hunter-gatherers' have discussed the affluence enjoyed by these peoples, their sharing practices, and their egalitarian and peaceful ethos. Ethnographers of 'horticulturalists' discussed the culturally instituted warfare practised by many of these peoples, their exchange systems and prestige economies. Students of 'peasants' addressed issues such as links with market-systems, homogeneity of households, and life-cycle determinants of household production. In many cases (if not in all of them), a particular study-group would be regarded a member of this or that subsistence category not because it exclusively pursued the subsistence activity in question, but because that activity was regarded by the local people – or the ethnographer – to be the 'significant' one, symbolically as much as practically. Sahlins elsewhere argued that the bourgeois culture uniquely singles out the economy as 'the main site of symbolic production' at the same time that it represents its economy as a separate institution (1976b: 211)." With a measure of caution, it can be said that ethnographers in the same fashion represented subsistence economies as separate spheres, at the same time as they effectively regarded them as a "privileged institutional locus of the symbolic process" (to use Sahlins' [1996] words).

If we argue that virtually no society exists in economic isolation from the rest of the world, it makes no sense to treat their economies separately from other cultural dimensions of social life. For Bird-David, there are three interconnected challenges: how to integrate cultural values and meanings into the comparative analysis of the material bases of social life; how to dissolve the orthodox reification of economy types as total systems, each homogeneous and fixed; and how to subvert the overdetermining and radical dichotomy between capitalist and noncapitalist economies. To implement this intellectual program, she turns again to Gudeman and Rivera's study of Colombian peasants (1990).

Working against the methodological individualism of orthodox economics, Gudeman and Rivera focus on people as they operate from within social groupings, distinguishing between "house" and "corporation" as ideal images. To sharpen their distinction, Bird-David suggests, "the house can be conceptualized as a socially-constituted group, which in maintaining itself engages in material actions. The corporation is viewed as a group constituted for material operations, some of which involve social engagements and relationships. The house works towards autarky, which sometimes involves exchange with others. The corporation exists for and through exchange (which principally can be infinitely extended), although its transactions are sometimes contained within the community. Both operate economically in social life, while diametrically opposed in constitution and nature."

The opposition was intended by Gudeman and Rivera to cut through historical sequences (1990: 11), but Bird-David suggests that it "can additionally cut through "subsistence types." It shifts the focus away from "modes of production" to economically-operating social groups in which cultures of livelihood-making are embodied. Contemporary economies are constitutive of houses and corporations of various kinds, from the capitalist extreme, in which corporations occupy the center but draw on houses in ever expanding margins across political and cultural domains, to the remote local extreme in which houses are central for their inhabitants but are affected by outside corporations, whose margins they represent. The extremes lie at opposite ends of a continuum of ideal types; they are not specific economic formations located at opposite ends of an evolutionist time-line.

In the Colombian peasant economy described by Gudeman and Rivera and usefully summarized by Bird-David, the corporation and the house are mutually dependent for their respective operations and reproductive capacities. The corporation predominates increasingly as we approach the political center, the house as we move away from it. But center and periphery are shifting locations; the corporation keeps expanding, pushing the house further and further to the margins. As for the Colombian rural "house," rural folk talk about its material activities in metaphors grounded in their physical homes. Economic life, as they see it, primarily involves "supporting" or "maintaining" the "base" of the house (which otherwise will fall into "ruins"; Gudeman and Rivera 1990: 11).

The "base" includes material assets such as land, livestock, and seeds as well as everything else – material and conceptual – that holds the social group together. Not least, it includes shared values and understandings – for example, the view of land as the repository of "force," created and sustained by God, a land that gives of its "strength" to people who assist its growth by the agricultural labor of their own hands. This Colombian rural "house" minimizes expenditure of money and exchange through the market (even if only for obtaining the commodities its members use), as this involves "moving [holdings] through the doors from inside to outside," thus reducing the "base." Market involvement is incorporated only as a means of reproducing the "base." The house otherwise avoids such engagement with the market by diversifying its production and by trading labor and bartering with neighbors, which amounts to "using holdings from the doors inwards." Wage labor is also minimized (except occasionally in order to secure money for unavoidable market purchases) in favor of the house production that in the local view supports and maintains the "base." The house hoards the "remainder" from its production, and "throws it forward" for future maintenance.

The corporation, unlike the house, is imagined as an organism: a "body," which must have "internal organ"-ization to "function" properly. It has "head" with a "right-hand man" and "circulating" funds that sustain its "arms," "organs," and "members." It can be "healthy" or "sick", and, when it "grows," it "issues stock" (Gudeman and Rivera 1990: 13). While the house's project is to maintain its "base," the corporation's project is to make profit. While the house is thrifty, and diversifies itself in avoidance of participation in the market, the corporation specializes in order to increase its participation therein. The house's "base" (in formal economic terms) largely takes the form of "stock," occasionally turned into "flow," only to reproduce the "stock." The corporation's "capital", on the other hand, largely takes the form of "flow," which is fictionally projected once a year as "stock" by freezing flows of income and cost against each other, in calculating the profit and its rate of increase (1990: 66–8).

Houses take various, culturally distinct forms. In Bird-David's own ethnographic work, the "hunter-gatherer" Nayaka "house" – actually a band, since the physical dwelling structure has less to do with the intimacy of coproduction than does the social unit – is a residential cluster of families, who see themselves as "us, the relatives." Their "base," which they describe as "our place", includes the forest within which they live, knowledge of its life, and companionship and sharing relationships with each other and with aspects of the natural environment seen as other-than-human "persons" (*devaru*). To maintain the "base" is to reproduce sharing relationships. Among Aboriginal Australians in Beluyen, labor is not seen as an expenditure of "force" in order to maintain the "base" but as socializing with the natural habitat and its "persons" in order to maintain companionship (Povinelli 1993). Maintaining that companionship is achieved by gathering and hunting in the forest, but also by simply spending time there, and by shamanistically keeping in touch with the forest devaru, Bird-David remarks about her own data: "A Nayaka house has no qualms about participation in the market – unlike the Colombian 'peasant' house – as long as sharing relationships are maintained in other ways among 'us, the relatives' and with the land 'our place.' Market activities which involve spending time in the forest (e.g., collecting and selling minor forest produce, wage work as forest watchmen and guides) has been a constitutive part of the Nayaka 'house' operation for a long time. The Nayaka house neither saves nor hoards material goods, which would only corrode the sharing relationships with other people, that are constitutive of its 'base.' Nor does it over-exploit the forest, which undercuts sharing relationships with devaru. Shamanistic contact with devaru continues throughout the fluctuating economic engagements of the Nayaka house."

Such relationships, which might strike the casual observer as failures to maximize, are also observable in urban settings, especially those in which the economy is a mixture of local subsistence and capitalist consumer culture. In the Cretan seaside town where I have worked, for example, an "ethos of imprecision" governs the conduct of social relations: it is unseemly for poorer residents to watch the weighing of produce too carefully – and they are in fact more likely to receive preferential treatment from equally impecunious tradespeople if, in self-conscious rejection of the ostentatious ways of the nouveaux riches, they do not do so. It is not that they are unaware of the material advantages of showing that they conform to the ethos, but it is equally clear that failure to do so makes them acutely uncomfortable. As John Davis remarks of the altruism of gift-giving, it does not really matter whether one is truly altruistic; so, here, it matters little whether one is genuinely embarrassed by excessive attention to precise weights and prices. In a society where too close attention to virtually anything at all earns one a reputation for having the evil eye, this aspect of the moral economy is as material as the cash toward which its practitioners affect such insouciance. And treating attributions of motive as part of the moral economy – rather than as factual or untrue – relieves us of having to resort to the methodological individualism that has served economic analysis so poorly. The ethos of imprecision characterizes the moral economy of houses that must socially cooperate under conditions of relative shortage, often in the face of growing pressures from what is perceived as the alien encroachment of corporations.

Moreover, house economies subsist even in the midst of the most highly industrialized polities. These are ideal types and, as with the garage sale, assumptions that flow from overdetermined theories will not help us perceive the continuities that Western economies (and cultures generally) have with very different formations. For example, along with industrial farms, which are actually "corporations," there are, Bird-David reminds us, family farms in the USA – and in all other industrial countries – that operate as "houses" in a way closer to the Colombian "house" than to the agricultural "corporation," although the extent to which the family farm is an ideological rather than an economic construct bears further investigation. (In the Balkans, the ideological adulation of the *zadruga* or residential patrilineal extended family as the local exemplar of primitive communism provides an ironic mirror for American familistic individualism.) The "consumer" of western economic discourse is often a family person, who is concerned to maintain the family "house," the "base" of which may include a house, career prospects, and various investments – including, for the upwardly mobile bourgeois, the rubbish-turned-into-antiques described by Thompson and other forms of "cultural capital" that serve as marks of "distinction" (Bourdieu 1984).

Ethnographically, houses are easier to study than are corporations, although privacy can be a daunting ethical dilemma and obstacle in investigating either. Moreover, the architectonics of house form may express an orientation to corporations in façades and to "house" economy in the interior, as when zoning laws reduce exteriors to a conformism that masks highly individualized strategies – aesthetic and economic – on the part of those dwelling within. But anthropologists are now beginning to work within business organizations, state and other bureaucracies, and international agencies. The danger here is in taking a facile view of "corporate culture" that would reduce us to the reified sense of culture from which the current on culture-as-process has so decisively moved. The idea of homogenous culture is very appealing to corporations, and to none more than the nation-state (Handler 1985). In some countries a conscious effort is made to inculcate collective company culture in employees (e.g., Janelli 1993; Kondo 1990; Moeran 1996). Sometimes ramified kinship groups, such as Chinese patrilineages, lie somewhere between the house and the corporation (J. Watson 1975), acquiring the features of each according to the exigencies of circumstance – itself a worthy topic for further research. But this is all the more reason to avoid such formulations as analytic tools. The negotiation of culture within large bureaucracies – as, for example, Stacia Zabusky has described it for the European Space Agency (1995) – is the more useful object of study because it points directly to the exercise of power and its effects. It is in observing the slippage between the ideal types of house and corporation that we may begin to achieve a better purchase on the two-way relationship between global economies and the local practices through which they are refracted, resisted, and recast.

Economies: Social, political, or cultural?

Concluding an essay on the "The Spirit of the Gift," Sahlins wrote: "the basic principles of an economics properly anthropological, includ[es] the one in particular . . . that every exchange, as it embodies some coefficient of the sociability, cannot be understood in its material terms apart from its social terms" (M. Sahlins 1972: 183). For Bird-David, this excerpt "expresses 'the spirit of economic anthropology' in past decades; a thoroughly-substantivist view, that sees perceptiveness to the social as anthropology's unique contribution to the study of economies." She herself argues that "we are in the midst of a sweeping change that should be carried through into the future. Initiated by Sahlins' study of capitalism as a cultural system, this change involves a growing perceptiveness to the cultural (ideas, symbols, world-views), which is anthropology's unique contribution to the study of economies, and a critical perspective to understanding the economic."

Brave words, and prophetic ones too: the vision that Bird-David articulates is consistent with the goals of today's anthropology, although it has been powerfully contested. But again we should be careful not to focus so heavily on the cultural as to ignore the social. Bird-David is certainly not guilty of doing so in her own ethnographic work. Nor does her own prescriptive writing suggest it. But the debate about whether anthropology should be "social" or "cultural," a silly argument that seemed mostly to serve as a proxy war for Anglo-American disputes of a surprisingly nationalistic kind, has left its scars. Moreover, as I have indicated, the relational (or indexical) aspect of the social remains the core of even the most resolutely culturalist rhetorics, such as that of the nation-state or the large corporation. Even if what we confront today is a Baudrillardian simulacrum of social experience, the fact that such simulacra persist is ample evidence in itself that economies are embedded not only in cultural values but also in the fluctuating social relations that give the lie to any reified view of culture. The house is a social unit, even if the corporation may seem to lean more toward the cultural.

But it is certainly true that economic anthropology has become increasingly substantivist. In the process, it has also become less recognizable as a separate domain of research. And today that blurring of the boundaries has begun to affect our image of "the West" (see Carrier 1992; Carrier, ed., 1995) every bit as much as it was already embryonically present in early evolutionist assumptions about a progressive specialization of spheres from "archaic" societies to "our own."

What is perhaps still missing, and may be a curious reflection of the domination of economy as a category in the western collective imagination, is an exploration of the political ramifications of the economy. While Robert Ulin (1984) has offered an important dialogue between political economy and cultural analysis, his work is particularly useful for thinking about the relationship between politics and culture, rather than about the economic dimensions as such. Much of the work on economic politics has been surprisingly tepid. Wilk (1996: 94–8) suggests that whereas the structural Marxists were generally unwilling to confront issues of agency, some aspects of world systems theory have paradoxically induced more reflection on the play of power in the relationships between agency and structure. This is an important and provocative observation. Yet here again the danger lies in ceding too much authority to the major actors and letting the voices of those whose lives are most directly affected be suffocated yet again. One of the strengths of the developments I have described in this chapter is that they provide good reasons for listening more carefully to those voices – not because they are "indigenous," but because they are so much like "our own" – because, in fact, they make nonsense of the distinction. They, too, should command our serious respect.

5

Politics

A Critical View of Power

As with economics, so, too with politics: anthropologists, committed to the study of the intimacies of everyday life, find politics in spaces where the bureaucratic state never even seeks to enter. Gender relations, kinship, reciprocal theft and vengeance, and the dynamics of the laboratory are all arenas of the political. Bringing the state into a comparative focus with these and other unlikely bedfellows may be the most promising subversion of the obvious that the discipline can perform.

This view has historical roots. Just as the history of anthropology from its evolutionist beginnings to today is a story of a revolt against its racist underpinnings and motivations, so in the specific field of political analysis the systematic unwrapping of assumptions about the state as the ideal political form has today placed the discipline in a singularly advantageous – if often underappreciated – position to challenge narrowly state-based models of the political.

Evolutionist visions of politics die hard. Thus, while few anthropologists today would willingly accept the rationalist vision of an ordered progression from "savage" through "primitive" to "civilized" society, a nostalgic image of "archaic" societies lived on even in a discipline that had managed to "rationalize" the practices of exotic peoples in "functional" terms. Archaic societies, in this view, appeared always to lack something important: they were "tribes without rulers" (Middleton and Tait, eds., 1958), practiced politics without government (Fortes and Evans-Pritchard, eds., 1940: 5–6), and enunciated law without precedent or codification (Gluckman 1963a).

Yet today, as Marc Abélès notes (see also Vincent 1990), "political anthropology has to take into account the ever closer interdependence between those societies and our own and the transformations which are affecting traditional political processes." What was once the incompleteness of "archaic" polities has today become the increasingly evident intractability to regimentation of all human societies. As a result, we have "tribes" of politicians in the industrialized nations (Abélès 1990), segmentation in the nation-state (Herzfeld 1987,

1992), and symbolism, exorcism, and principles of purity and pollution as the defining marks of some new and powerful forms of national identity politics (Hayden 1996; Kapferer 1988; Malkki 1989; Tambiah 1989). And while such attributions may have led some commentators to view these forms as new irruptions onto the world scene of archaic localism, tribalism, and blood-lust, it has become increasingly apparent that such statements are themselves fables of identity, retailed by the powerful about the weak in the ever more influential international media.

From a comparativist concern with taxonomies of political systems, anthropology has progressively moved toward a focus on the practices and codes of power and especially on the role of social actors in creating it. This approach, in which greater attention is paid to expressive forms as well as to the close links among power, ritual and symbols, necessarily also means a shift away from the privileging of the operators of structural power. By examining the intimacies of political process – of politicians but also of prisoners, of voters but also of volunteer workers, of mafia godfathers but also of village gossips – anthropologists provide a necessary corrective to structural accounts of power, treating leaders and led in a common framework that resists confusing the ideal-typical rhetoric of the modern nation-state, to take the most obvious example, with the practices that this rhetoric is used to mask.

This is especially important in dealing with authoritarian political systems, where analysts all too easily adopt as an explanation of stability the teleological certainty that regimes hope to project in their rhetoric and create in social fact. Some of these regimes even invoke social-science models to justify and perpetuate their rule and vision: Emile Durkheim became the inspiration for Turkish secular statism, while the analyses of Karl Marx have been dragooned into the service of post-revolutionary rigidity around the world. Even if these uses of the celebrated names of social science are highly selective, as indeed they are, it is the teleological components of these thinkers' work that has lent itself to political abuse. To this the only effective response is always to seek out the social actors involved – the politicians, ideologues, and popular leaders who write teleology into government. The critical focus thus now falls, not on the symbols themselves (as though they had some asocial, transcendent existence), but on the uses to which they are put – and on the people who use them (Kertzer 1988).

The obverse side of the coin of an anthropology traditionally preoccupied with the marginal and the exotic is precisely that all politics is grounded in local experience in some sense, many politicians are organized in tribes and dynasties, and the nation-state itself possesses many of the features of the segmentary polity – the type of society formerly contrasted with the state as lacking government (Fortes and Evans-Pritchard, eds., 1940). What kind of anthropology is it that cannot account for the persistence of kinship links as a key component in political succession in some of the most determinedly republican countries in the world (such as Greece [see Pappas 1999: 88] and the United States, with the latter's Tafts, Roosevelts, Kennedys, and Bushes)? Kinship in fact continues to play a major role in elite succession precisely where current assumptions would replace it with objectivist criteria of merit – in some of the most powerful industrial sectors of the American economy (see Marcus 1992). A rethought approach to politics must also, however, account for the viability of political systems where no such intimate control of power is obviously present: has rationality "really" taken over, or are new forms of consociation, only accessible at the worm's-eye level of the ethnographer, taking over? These questions go to the very heart of what anthropologists can contribute to the arena of modern politics. The power of anthropology to reframe the analysis of governmental and other modern forms of authority may well explain the nervousness with which its activities are viewed by those whose interests – intellectual and political – coincide with the larger structures of that authority.

Abélès frames the shift toward such concerns in terms of a move away from the self-classification of anthropology by topical zones such as economics, religion, politics, and the like: far from presupposing a clear-cut and virtually pre-established division between what is political and what is not, anthropologists are seeking to gain a closer understanding of the way in which power relationships are interwoven, their ramifications, and the practices to which they give rise. This entails, above all, close attention to the operation of power – to the ways in which variously situated social actors exercise it, in ways that respond to cultural and social as well as more obvious political exigencies and expectations.

This shift is part of a wider dissolution of the artificial distinction between the material and the symbolic. One might add, too, that the collapse of this distinction is nowhere more apparent than in those areas conventionally agreed to be political, where the influence of rhetoric and symbolism can be seen to be direct, recognizable, and often decisive, but where it has no meaning that is demonstrably independent of the brute facts of wealth and coercive force.

The evolutionist vision has often been phrased in terms of the increasing specialization of human activity. "Archaic" societies had no art, it was thought, independent of religion, no politics independent of kinship. This vision articulated a contrast between traditional societies, in which the political sphere is embedded in basic social structures (usually kinship); and the modern world, in which the autonomy of politics is manifested in the bureaucratic structures of states. There was little awareness that the separation of politics from kinship, for example, produced at the very core of modern political life, and under the name of "nepotism," a staple of anthropological thought – the political equivalent of the incest taboo; nor was the kinship in which virtually all nationalism has been grounded (see, e.g., Borneman 1992; Yanagisako and Delaney, eds., 1994) seen as more than a convenient metaphor. The Eurocentric assumption that a very particular kind of rationality transcended the immediacies of the cultural and the social demanded the creation of a clear demarcation between embedded and abstract systems, and anthropological perspectives on national and international political processes conflicted with the objectivist version of common sense espoused by many, if not all, political scientists.

Moreover, the adoption of ideas about culture by some political scientists in recent years has not always reflected the most recent anthropological thinking. Most notoriously, the work of Samuel Huntington (1996) reproduces the Romantic nationalism of the nineteenth-century nation-state: the ideas that some cultures can usefully be separated out as "civilizations," and that these are essentially and immutably incapable of mutual comprehension, flies in the face of everything we have learned about cultural creolization, diasporic cultural process, and even simple intercultural communication. It is thus empirically indefensible; but it does have some interest as an ethnographic object, for it reproduces in schematic form the prevailing stereotypes and folk theories through which many world leaders attempt to persuade voters to support them in pursuing divisive hegemonies overseas.

Power and Representation

The boundary between anthropology and political science is itself, in precisely this sense, both institutional and political. Some anthropologists have expanded their areas of investigation to include industrialized societies in the West, while a few political scientists have explored dimensions of politics, such as rites and symbols, that had thus far remained outside their fields of investigation (Barnett 1997; Binns 1979–80; Edelman 1971; Kertzer 1988; Sfez 1978). Anthropologists began by giving prominence to difference, taking more interest in the periphery than the center and preferring to study traditional rural societies or urban minorities which had preserved their specific features. It is true that the complex civil service, dense bureaucratic fabric, and deployment of hierarchies in the modern nation-state bear little overt resemblance to the often more diffuse workings of politics observed in other kinds of social formation. There is a substantive disparity of scale between the contemporary state and other systems habitually described by anthropologists, such as segmentary societies or chiefdoms. That disparity becomes less significant, however, when we focus on power processes and systems as these pervade institutions, and on the ways in which political action is represented.

In current anthropological thought, all politics is a dynamic phenomenon, or process. In a now well-established canon, Swartz, Turner, and Tuden saw politics as consisting in processes resulting from the choice and attainment of public objectives and the differential use of power by the members of the group concerned by these objectives (Swartz, Turner, and Tuden, ed., 1966: 7). This, as Abélès notes, clearly highlights the combination of three factors – power, determination and the achievement of collective objectives – and the existence of a sphere of public action. One weakness of this definition, as he notes, is that it ignores territoriality. Yet for Weber the state has "a monopoly on legitimate violence on a given territory," while in *The Nuer* Evans-Pritchard treats political relations as the relations that subsist, within the limits of a territorial system, among groups living in clearly defined areas and conscious of their identity and their mutual exclusivity (Evans Pritchard 1940: 19). It is also possible, however, to overemphasize territoriality. This is largely a result of anthropology's more recent focus on, but also conceptual roots shared with, colonialism and nationalism – two powerfully interlinked forces (Stocking, ed., 1991). Newer work in these areas has highlighted the territory-dissolving arrangements of power, such as those we now find in global corporations and in the increasing domination of cyberspace over economic process. Recent calls for a reconfiguration of ethnographic practice specifically address the methodological changes that this shift of focus must entail (Gupta and Ferguson, eds., 1997).

Abélès poses three vital spheres of interest for an anthropology of politics: an interest in power, in how it is acquired and in how it is exercised; an interest in the identities asserted in a given territory (and, we must now add, in nonterritorial networks) and in the areas of influence into which it has broken down; and an interest in the representations and practices that shape the public sphere. As he says, these different spheres are closely interlinked, but he argues that analytically it may be necessary to envisage these three dimensions separately and successively as we look at contemporary societies and the state.

Foucault, who, in his work on madness, sex, and prison addressed the omnipresence of norms and systems, proposed a method of analysis aimed at overcoming this central difficulty. "Analysis in terms of power should not postulate, as initial facts, the sovereignty of the State, the form of the law or the global unity of a domination; these are only the terminal forms" (Foucault 1976: 120). It is important to look beyond the most immediate facts represented by the law and the institution and to consider the power relationships and strategies that are forged within the systems. The traditional instruments of political theories prove inappropriate: "We use ways of thinking about power which are based either on legal models (what is the legitimacy of power?) or on institutional models (what is the State?)" (Dreyfus and Rabinow 1984: 298). The answer, clearly, lies in close attention to what the bearers of power actually do – how they direct institutional controls and classifications to the pursuit of particular ends, whose interests they thereby serve, and how they redistribute the authority vested in them under a system that also gives others power over them.

Rather than concretizing power by treating it as a mysterious substance, whose real nature we should endlessly seek to track down, Foucault thus asks in pragmatic terms how power is exercised. Thinking of power as an act, as a "mode of action on actions" (Foucault 1976: 316), requires from anthropologists an empirical exploration of both individual practices and the patterns that these disrupt or confirm. Trying to take into consideration the exercise of power and its roots in the complexities of everyday practice enables us to understand politics better, not as a separate sphere, but as the crystallization of activities modeled in accordance with cultural rules as these are represented and interpreted by interested actors.

Anthropologists must thus account for the conditions under which power and the capacity to govern emerge. In democratic polities, for example, they investigate what "representativeness" entails in practice. Abélès disagrees here with

Foucault on two points: on the one hand, Foucault explicitly rejects the question of representation as a metaphysical aspect of the basis and nature of power, with two blunt questions: "What is power? Where does power come from?" (Foucault 1984: 309); on the other hand, he rejects, as reflecting a legalistic attitude, any question about the legitimacy of power.

Yet to reject representation as merely metaphysical is to ignore its palpable effects on the real world; it would obviate the serious study of symbolism as a material factor in political process and make the entire question of performativity irrelevant. And to reject the issue of legitimacy as similarly epiphenomenal is, ironically, to fall into the trap of taking claims of legitimacy in a literal-minded sense – as something that does or does not "exist," rather than as something that is constituted through the exercise of social skills. Moreover, it is in the close inspection of those social skills and their discernible effects that we can more effectively heed Foucault's call not to view power as monolithic and as centered in the hands of particular persons. Separating power from performance is logically indefensible (see Fabian 1990). Representation in the sense of holding power on behalf of others – as in the sense of a "representative democracy," for example – thus emerges as a particular case of representation in the sense of portrayal, in that parliamentarians can only claim to "speak for" their constituents to the extent that their performance remains socially acceptable.

We cannot separate the acquisition of power from the way in which it is exercised. In Western democracies, where the idea of election is both a means of enabling representation and the rather undemocratic symbolic expression of a right to rule, engaging in politics means standing for election to an office that will make it possible to reach a position of real power over others. Moreover, an election is often regarded as a mysterious process that has the effect of transforming individuals into public figures – hardly the stuff of which rationality is supposed to be made. From one day to the next, people who are ordinary citizens are called upon to personify the interests of the community and speak on its behalf. This quality of representativeness gives them the right to act on the actions of other people and exercise their power over the group. It is the similarity of such attributions to the status of so-called divine kings in some East African societies that permits us to study, contrastively, the differences between these two kinds of polity.

Bourdieu regards this "alchemy of representation" as a truly circular pattern in which "representatives form the group which forms them: spokespersons with full powers to speak and act on behalf of the group and to act on the group . . . become the substitutes for the group which then exists only by proxy" (Bourdieu 1982: 101). Bourdieu interprets the phenomenon of representation in terms of "letting go" – of a transfer of authority to a third party, which then sets itself up as a unifying power and as the guarantor of collective harmony.

"In this theoretical perspective," writes Abélès, "analysing representation involves deconstructing the mechanisms which result in individuals becoming subjected to power and its symbols. The aim is to engage in a critique of this transfer by bringing to light the roots of the illusion. Anthropology does not purport to engage in a criticism of politics; it aims rather at understanding how power emerges and is asserted in a given situation." But this, it seems to me, could as easily be phrased as a critique (rather, perhaps, than "criticism") of politics: in asking how the taxonomies of a powerful state bureaucracy support the goals of reinforcing differences in access to resources, as in the case of the treatment of Gypsies in Britain studied by Okely (1983), for example, we are at one and the same time questioning the functionaries' claim to represent absolute legal clarity and subversively suggesting an analogy between this practice and the similarly categorical division of the world into non-Gypsies and Gypsies by the Gypsies themselves (or indeed by any other group of "exotic" or marginalized people traditionally studied by anthropologists). The very praxis of anthropology is, in this sense, a critique of political praxis and theory.

Political Institutions and Networks

Anthropologists working in western societies initially focused on politics in restricted communities: village politics accordingly became a key theme; and the subject of local power – its reproduction and its ramifications – came to the forefront. Anthropologists circumscribed their aims by not going beyond the bounds of the locality, which they defined as the ideal field for their investigations. There was accordingly an implicit separation between the periphery, the chosen field of ethnologists, and the center, which was bound up with national and state policy – arenas left to the attention other disciplines, such as political science and sociology. As a result, factionalism – which in a nation-state context might simply have emerged as party politics (Pappas 1999: 128–9) – comes to exemplify the kinds of political process that anthropologists study in exotic villages in, say, India (e.g., Bailey 1971). A subcategory of political anthropology dealt with gossip as micropolitics (e.g., Paine 1967).

In short, political anthropology was confined to microscopic universes; an image of authentically insular, autochthonous, and unchanging political structures in the closed world of the village community prevailed. The focus of this work was on the traditional aspects of political life. Curiously, although certain Africanists (Gluckman 1963a; Balandier 1967) had emphasized the need to think in terms of dynamics and change, the anthropologists who worked on Europe seemed to remain on the sidelines of modernity, in an extension of ancestral history. Indeed, as Andrew Lass (in Asad et al. 1997: 721–2) has noted, it has taken a self-aware critique of the concept of "the local" to force a concomitant awareness of the eligibility of elites for ethnographic inspection.

This trend has nevertheless given rise to new perspectives on phenomena that were hitherto little known – witness the monographs on patronage and power relationships in the Mediterranean world (Boissevain 1974; Campbell 1964; J. Schneider and P. Schneider 1976; Lenclud 1988). Another theme dear to anthropologists drawn to the exotic, that of the modes of devolution and transmission of political roles, has mobilized researchers; in-depth surveys have been conducted on the construction of legitimacies and on the relations among power, kinship and matrimonial strategies (Abélès 1989; Pourcher 1987; cf. also Marcus 1992). This work has the advantage of showing how dynasties of representatives are established and are reproduced even within a democratic ethos and structure, in accordance with a logic which does not always tally with a superficial view of democratic systems as transcending the social and the cultural. It also reveals that political representation brings into play a whole series of informal networks, which must constantly be taken into account in the elaboration of individual strategies.

Sensitive ethnography – always partial, because always experientially enmeshed in the political actualities it studies – entails two key steps. First, the ethnographer must view the rhetoric of fair play, democracy, human rights (S. Moore, ed., 1993), and the rest with a critical eye, because this rhetoric has itself become part of the game. Second, the ethnographer will find that the claims of opposed factions are often similarly phrased, revealing both the rules of the game and the degree to which actors are prepared to commit and tolerate deviations from the prevailing set of rules. Villagers who rail against a "non-existent" state may mean that the state has failed to act as a fair adjudicator; but they may also mean that the state has failed to be partial (that is, to the speakers' interests)! Mutual recriminations about atrocities and failure to respect human rights are evidence at least as much of a shared (and increasingly globalized) symbolism as they are of real differences in the respective fates of embattled populations. This becomes especially clear in the meticulously intimate investigations of ethnographers, whose engagement with the pragmatics of social interaction turns abstract moral judgments into the objects of critical inquiry, as well as in archival work that reveals the long-term effects of kinship connections and matrimonial strategies, inheritance practices, and moral norms.

Moving beyond the village obviously entails identifying new sites of social – that is, ethnographic – intimacy. The ability to create such "anthropological locations" (Gupta and Ferguson 1997) is crucial: on the one hand, politicians often have a great deal to hide, so that their performances will only become understandable in the light of fairly intimate knowledge of their social contexts; on the other hand, their reach extends far beyond the local community in most cases, and is usually in any case embedded in national or even (as in the case of the European Union countries) supranational political-party organizations. At the same time, the complex micropolitics that have always engaged anthropologists deserve continuing attention: gossip and factionalism within local communities may have far-reaching effects when national politicians are revealed as failures on home turf. Consider voting, for example. Candidates for political office can deliberately display the signs that are the most likely to evoke their ability to create and maintain beneficial outside contacts for the benefit of the voting community. Such connections may be real or attributed; but without them no candidate can expect to gain voters' confidence for long. This is an arena in which nation–local connections are especially accessible to ethnographic observation.

In addition to the local connection with the national, we must also consider the link between the here-and-now and the grand sweep of the past as it is represented in official discourse. Political representation, remarks Abélès, "is a phenomenon which takes on its full meaning in the long term." To illustrate this point, he uses the example of French political life, marked by the major founding events which, in addition to the French Revolution, were the separation of Church and State and the Resistance: "When, at the end of the last century, relations between the Church and the Third Republic grew increasingly bitter, the political networks organized themselves on either side of this line. Over the years, the ideological antagonism was to become gradually less sharp, but even today it is still the background to a good many electoral bouts; even in situations where there is an outward show of disregard for politics, any candidate is immediately identified by reference to this ancestral bipolarity. The founding event leaves its mark and the behavior of the electors is very much conditioned by this memory, which is handed down from generation to generation."

Political Ceremony: Rites and rights

"Power exists only 'on stage'," according to Balandier (1980). Anthropologists have succeeded in exploring the symbols and rituals of power in remote societies and it should come as no surprise that the modern world offers ample material for their analyses. The political drama takes on more familiar forms these days, but it still does not abolish the gap between the people and those who govern. Abélès suggests that, on the contrary, this gulf between the world of public figures and the daily lives of ordinary citizens is widening, "making them unassailable at the very time when media commodities enable us to capture their image with unequalled ease." But it is not entirely clear that this is always the case: the late-1990s attacks on the British monarchy – not one of the most accessible of political structures – showed how an effective marshaling of symbolic power can also fuel delegitimizing movements. The processes at work here may in fact work with much the same tension between charisma and routine as we find in small-scale societies, so that our best access will be less through speculation about the pragmatics of access and more through what Kertzer has called "the ritual construction of political reality" (Kertzer 1988: 77); "political liturgies" (Rivière 1988) are no less ceremonial than the political performances of the church – hence the conversions of religious into political symbolism, organization, and spectacle. Catholic symbolism in communist performance in post-war Italy, for example (Kertzer 1980), exhibits many of the processes whereby at a much earlier date Christianity had coopted the symbolism and especially the holy places of its pagan predecessors, and represents a pragmatic acknowledgment that familiar symbolism provides the most potent distillations of social unity.

This is familiar ground. In many societies, important rites surrounding the enthronement of the sovereign also take the form of a tour of the territory by the new monarch, each stopping-place being the occasion for ceremonial and reinforcing the link between the governors and the governed. As Geertz (1983) has shown, the ceremonial forms in which monarchs take possession of their kingdoms display significant variations, such as the peaceful and virtuous procession through England when Elizabeth Tudor assumed power in 1559, or the splendid caravan of Hayam Wuruk in fourteenth-century Java. Street demonstrations and political meetings also have a ritual aspect, although reducing them to that dimension alone does violence to the agency they are often intended to bear. While Abélès remarks that street demonstrations "are demonstrations of force which are ordered in accordance with a set scenario: improvisation is only allowed within a protocol for action which should not depart from the collectively acknowledged rules," this recognition should not be imbued with the kind of determinism that led Gluckman (1963a), for example, to argue that rituals of reversal served the teleological function of providing a reaffirmation of the need for maintaining the authority that was symbolically challenged – a view that also informs his interpretation of gossip as a reaffirmation of the prevailing moral order (Gluckman 1963b).

The same observation could be made about another rite of confrontation – the political meeting. Notes Abélès: "On the platform, there are speakers and dignitaries chosen according to the place, the circumstances and their ranking order in the movement. In the meeting hall there is the audience which has sometimes been brought in from a vast surrounding area. Everything depends on the relationship that is established between this community, whose task is to applaud and to call out names and slogans, and those officiating, who must constantly fan the flames of popular enthusiasm. The succession of announcements, promises or threats which are greeted with applause or booing make the meeting a carefully produced show. The staging, the decor, the music, the postures, all play a part in building up the candidate's distinctive identity. The meeting has to represent a highlight, where every possible means is used to create both a sense of communion around the speaker and the firm determination to 'confront' and 'beat' all the other candidates, who are portrayed to the participants as adversaries."

What political meetings and demonstrations have in common with consensual rituals, says Abélès, is that they require a physical presence on the part of the protagonists. They also employ highly conventional language, gesture, and symbolism. Political oratory has much of the redundancy that Tambiah (1968) associates with ritual formulae (see also Bloch 1977). Indeed, political meetings, like bureaucratic encounters, possess a high degree of predictability, and invoke at a relatively intimate level much larger and encompassing categories such as the nation, the people, or the working class, although I would hesitate to join Abélès in seeing such entities as transcendent except in the ethnographic sense that this is what their protagonists claim them to be.

The symbolism used is usually closely calibrated with the national or party-political historiography, which, remarkably like myth as described by Lévi-

Strauss (1955a), lays claim on eternity and parades contradictions as a way of neutralizing them – here, by suppressing evidence of past heterogeneity by re-processing them as evidence of transcendent unity, common genius, or corrupting influences from which the leaders have now provided the definitive salvation. These assimilatory processes again emerge most clearly in ethnography, where – for example – the disjuncture between the "invented tradition" (Hobsbawm and Ranger, eds., 1983; cf. Handler 1985) of the nation-state and the "local" experience of the community (see Nadel-Klein 1991) emerges precisely because this work takes place behind, not in front of, the façade of consensus and homogeneity. In key respects the exceptionalist claims of modernity do not stand up well to the ethnographic inspection of everyday life. And even the supposedly homogenizing effects of mass media have the effect of intensifying rather than of displacing the ritualistic effects of political oratory and symbolism.

From Postnational to Multicultural: New directions

The anthropological study of political arenas offers a means of seeing the state "from below" (Abélès 1990: 79). The important point to bear in mind here is that it is still often the state, or some other broadly-based entity, that commands our attention. Willy-nilly, as I have remarked elsewhere (Herzfeld 1997a), anthropologists have always worked within state structures (or colonial ones, which are extensions of states); the problem has been to provide ethnographies "of" the state and other, comparable institutional structures. Yet not to do so is to surrender insight to those structures themselves; their protagonists rarely lose the opportunity to represent them as the only viable and common-sense arrangement.

The importance of representing alternatives to state and other dominant forms of collective self-representation cannot be stated too strongly. Governments reproduce colonialism internally, often with a violence that they would rarely admit to meting out to their own citizens (e.g., Aretxaga 1997; Lavie 1990; Warren 1998). Sometimes that violence, in the form of vigilantism, is not so much orchestrated as condoned by state authorities (e.g., Warren 1999). Sometimes it take the form of bureaucratic abuse, as in the denial of minority and other human rights on essentially taxonomic grounds, or even of the reproduction of unacknowledged bias in the social practices of local communities (e.g., Rabinowitz 1997). And often it appears in the small but ultimately corrosive practices of everyday engagement rather than in acts of spectacular horror – although these, too, have not been lacking. The local perspective of the ethnographer subverts this authoritarian deceit and reminds us that the state is a two-edged sword: while it may offer substantial benefits to its citizens, it does not necessarily offer equal benefits to all its citizens, all the time.

Moreover, the state has returned to an importance many had thought it was on the verge of losing. The European Union is just that – a union, in this case a union of nation-states – and its internal disputes largely center on questions of sovereignty in the administration of law. Gupta (1998) has pointed out that the internationalist language of development cannot disguise the fact that ultimately the world order now emerging remains, or is increasingly, an order of nation-states. The break-up of the Soviet Union and of Yugoslavia has created more, not fewer, nation-states, and their constitutions represent a return to the *ius sanguinis* – the right of membership by blood (descent) – that pluralistic ideologies have tried to replace (see Hayden 1996).

Yet relations among states have certainly changed in important ways. European construction is a good illustration of the reconfiguration now taking place around the world, and the rising significance of European ethnography suggests that this will be an important area to watch for evidence of how nation-states will address the new circumstances. These processes of accelerating change, says Abélès, "are bound to give rise to in-depth reflection on political affiliations and identities." They give new resonance to terms such as territory, nation, and ethnic group (Amselle 1990), forcing us to reconsider the claims of a political discourse that represented the rising power of centralized political organizations as, in Abélès's words, "the triumph of rationality and progress."

The principle of nationalism "asserts that political unity and national unity must be congruent" (Gellner 1983: 11) – a congruence that is now exceedingly problematic. Anthropologists have been powerfully influenced in their thinking about national identities by the political scientist Benedict Anderson (1983), who shows that the government (state) of a nation, the latter imagined as a sovereign agglomeration of fundamentally similar people, appropriates the control once exercised by religious and dynastic leaders. Such thoughts require further empirical investigation of the relationship between political affiliations and cultural identities – a relationship that in Gellner's view differed only in trivial details, but that rewards ethnographic analysis with a huge variety of significant permutations. Here anthropologists and historians find common ground: the "invention" of common traditions and the symbolic construction of the nation have been the subject of far-reaching research, giving rise to such studies as that of M. Agulhon (1979, 1989) on the figure of Marianne and the symbolism of the republican nation in France. In this case, the historian highlights the vicissitudes attendant on the construction of a political community and the images it has generated. While patriotic memory remains significant, it also reveals, in ethnographic perspective, significant internal divisions, as witness the building of the memorial dedicated to the American combatants in Vietnam and the controversies to which it gave rise among veterans (Berdahl 1994, for anthropology; cf. Bodnar 1994: 3–9, for social history) or the reburial of the Hungarian leaders eliminated by the Russians during the events of 1956 (Zempleni 1996) and the repatriation of Bartok's remains after 1989 (Gal 1991). Indeed, if a nation's success can be gauged by the extent to which its citizens are willing to die for it, as Anderson suggests, the ethnographic analysis of the role of death in war and politics may reveal to what extent that consensus was coerced or faked (see now Borneman 1997).

Georges Balandier (1985: 166) has written: "The knowledge of acculturations which come from outside seems to be capable of contributing to a better understanding of self-acculturating modernity." Processes of globalization, migration, and hybridity have undoubtedly affected how the institutions and organizations that govern economy and society now work. Projects to harmonize disparate legislations are about territory, morality, and the distribution of wealth – vital issues all, now perhaps more than ever. Disputes and differences appear on a larger scale than ever before, although ethnographic approaches work best when they remain focused on specific sites of intimate access: note, for example, Zabusky's (1995) fine analysis of the uses of the rhetoric of "cooperation" in the internally tension-ridden European Space Agency in the Netherlands. Other analyses more directly tackle ongoing confrontations between different identities (McDonald 1996) and between heterogeneous languages and administrative traditions in a common political undertaking (Bellier 1995). Yet others investigate the practical and symbolic effects of deterritorialization and changes of scale in the new places of the exercise of power (Abélès 1992, 1996). Moreover, all these analyses show that the line between bureaucrats and clients is an artificial one, since it is knowledge of the shared culture that enables functionaries to function, appealing to a "secular theodicy" in order to explain away the failures of democracy as these affect specific social actors and circumstances (Herzfeld 1992).

Such a focus on everyday acts all too easily attracts the disdain of those analysts who believe that politics is only about the actions of prominent individuals and institutions operating within national or international structures of power. But this view is clearly flawed. Much as the economic pundits' failures of prediction have shown the symbolic nature of much of their rationalizing, so too the construction of political events as largely unaffected by local-level values and actions repeatedly fails to elicit much more than such obviously cosmological judgments as "electoral upset" and "electoral volatility." Such judgments suggest self-justification on the part of the analysts rather than explanations grounded in close observation of social process.

The question of "mereness" is itself a political judgment – an exercise in the "politics of significance" (Herzfeld 1997c). The role of animal-theft in determining electoral strength in key communities, for example, may briefly have influenced the selection of at least one major Greek political party leader in the 1980s, yet this possibility makes no appearance in any of the literature on electoral politics in that country. Issues of kinship structure, which provide models for the distribution of loyalty in the warring Balkan states, are ignored by political analysts who prefer instead to invoke the specter of "atavistic" hatreds in which their own, dominant national governments have no organizing role – a nice illustration of a cosmology that itself invokes a kinship idiom (cf. Latin *aves*, "ancestors") in order to attribute to supposedly innate psychological properties a violence that may largely have been generated by the play of outside interference on local ideas about kinship loyalty. The latter is a topic so "mere" as to escape mention in virtually all public political analyses. (One should again not forget that "nepotism" – from Latin *nepos*, "nephew" or "grandchild" – is symbolically construed as the political version of incest.)

Such judgments are also deeply inflected by the dominant politics of class, race, and gender. Here, feminist scholarship has been especially rich as a source of critical perspective. Lynn Stephen (1997), for example, has shown that to focus on the relationship between politics and gender does not occlude the significance of dominant social and moral values; it shows, instead, how social actors both use and find themselves operating within such values as they resist and yet also accommodate their pressing concerns to the experienced realities of a powerfully gendered authoritarian structure – her own analysis in this case being focused on a women's rights movement in El Salvador. Indeed, to dismiss such work as marginal is to participate in the same politics of significance as that dissected in Stephen's trenchant study. That the analyses themselves are often disturbingly apt to reproduce the very rhetoric they should be addressing critically is nicely conveyed in Begoña Aretxaga's (1997: 6) observation on the politics of struggle in Northern Ireland: "in the abundant social science literature on the conflict the political practices of nationalist women have either passed virtually unnoticed or been considered anecdotal to the real politics of the conflict." Indeed, analysis in this sense partially follows events: women's contributions to struggle in many parts of the world have in varying degrees been pushed aside as war receded and men took up the more pacific business of political leadership again (see Hart 1996: 235). And women, as well as male homosexuals similarly alienated by an aggressive heterosexual idiom of contest (see, e.g., Lancaster 1992: 293, on Nicaragua), may face conflicts between their support for generic political liberation and other social roles that conflict with the demands of war, thereby influencing the outcome of elections in a way that might have seemed unthinkable in the flush of initial victory: Nicaraguan women, for example, clearly played a significant role in electing a conservative and female president soon after the Sandinistas' victory and in reaction to their own style of rule. Ethnographic insights into such processes substantially alter our perspective on the reasons for "unexpected" electoral and other political developments.

In a serious sense, as I indicated at the beginning of this chapter, all anthropology is fundamentally political; the most local of social relations – for example, within the kinship group, or between genders in a small community – are infused with arguments about power. The call to focus on politics as a separate category reproduces the idea of political expertise as the prerogative of those who already hold power. It thereby risks imposing a highly particularistic "local knowledge" on the world – a form of knowledge no less radically particularistic, I would argue, than what we find in the most narrowly focused ethnography. But that risk can be averted, I think, if we refuse to cordon off a separate domain called "political anthropology," and instead concentrate on the operation of the political in all domains of society and culture. (Note that this chapter is a relatively short one: much of the work traditionally done by political anthropology informs large segments of the rest of the book, as this argument demands.) In this way, too, we break through the traditional–modern barrier, using insights gained in very recognizably "ethnographic" settings to rethink the top-down analyses that it is so easy to accept as a sound guide to modern world politics. The discommoding eye of the ethnographer disturbs more than the complacency of Eurocentric social science models, although that is a far from trivial task. It also disturbs the bland rhetoric of national and international institutions of power, opening up the often violent and disharmonious social experiences that this rhetoric conceals. Everything in social life is indeed political; every denial of political intent or significance is at once deeply suspect and, for that reason, richly ready for the ethnographer's critical insight.

6

Borders/Nodes/Groupings

Fractured Certainties

As we enter the twenty-first century, one thing is sure: the attempt to abolish uncertainty has failed. We may view the rise of bureaucratic organizations and organized communities as devices for the reduction of risk and danger, and it is true that they have proliferated; but that very proliferation – reflected in the pluralized titles of this book – has introduced new and larger areas of opacity in human affairs. Perhaps the most obvious victim of this process is the idea of the bounded human group – the "society" or "culture" of the classic anthropological imagination.

It is perhaps significant that in this context the "ethnic group," once a staple of that imagination, has come to acquire greater valency among politicians than it does among anthropologists. Ever since Fredrik Barth (1969) and his collaborators focused attention on boundary creation and maintenance rather than on some purportedly permanent "cultural stuff" within boundaries presumed to be fixed, anthropologists have steadily become more reluctant to speak of "ethnic groups" as such. While they have also noted that strategic concerns may justify the creation of fixed identities as a solidarity basis for resisting totalitarian oppression, as among some indigenous peoples in Latin America, they have been particularly prone to argue against the enshrining of such identities in the totalitarian structures themselves – as in the more genocidal ethnonationalist states and in the "cultural fundamentalism" practised by political leaders and political scientists alike. From Huntington's *The Clash of Civilizations and the Remaking of World Order* (1996) to ethnic cleansing conducted in the name of alleged historical imperatives it is not a large conceptual step, for both perspectives have a strong interest in ignoring the anthropological critique of "culture" as a product of a particular historical moment.

If the ethnic group, thus politicized, has appeared more fixed than field researchers have found it to be in practice, the city often appears to be a bounded entity whose very materiality brooks little disagreement. Cities are built environments; they are solid, and change rather slowly for the most part. Moreover, they usually have well-defined boundaries, at least in the administrative sense. Especially since Robert Redfield explored the relationship between peasant and urban societies (Redfield 1953), and under the influence of such cultural commentators as Raymond Williams (1973), anthropologists have viewed urban and rural living as mutually dependent but analytically separable forms of social existence.

Some commentators have objected to the resultant emergence of a specific subfield of "urban anthropology" on the grounds that town and country are too entangled with each other for such analytical classifications to do more than reproduce an existing social ideology (notably Hirschon 1989). There are others who would still argue that the city is a radically different place than the village or transhumant camp. Perhaps the most useful comment on this issue comes from Ulf Hannerz (1980), who suggests that urban anthropology – or, as I would prefer to say, the practice of ethnography in urban settings – can contribute significantly to the understanding of human diversity by attending to forms of life that are peculiar to the circumstances of urban living. Hirschon has accurately identified the falsity of rigid urban–rural dichotomies, especially in societies – now the majority – in which rural-to-urban migration has accelerated massively in recent years. But this does not permit us to ignore the shifts in temporality, social relationships, and much else that accompany migration into rapidly expanding urban centers. The population of Mexico City, for example, was 1,644,921 in 1940 and now exceeds 17 million. Among the main factors responsible for this expansion have been the numerous migrations from other regions of the country and the incorporation into the metropolitan area of 27 adjoining municipalities. Under such conditions, as Hannerz reminds us, some of the material circumstances of urban living force (or at least encourage) changes in lifestyle among even the most ardently and self-consciously traditionalist migrants. In this chapter, I try to take this discussion still further, by focusing instead on the human effort to spatialize and enclose in the face of the sudden, global awareness of the porosity of all borders, however physical and however vigilantly policed. Two factors have been especially decisive. One is the emergence of huge megacities, with diverse populations and enormous problems of social control (including the difficulty of controlling the authorities when, as has happened in Brazil and elsewhere, they sanction death squads as a means of "maintaining order"). The other is the logic whereby the policing of border zones itself – once places where the known world seemed to come to an abrupt halt (Berdahl 1999a) – leads to a questioning of the appropriateness and validity of electric fences and guard dogs.

Borders, especially when they traverse cities, do not produce entirely predictable effects. On the one hand the dismantling of the Berlin Wall has left few traces other than that, as Ulf Hannerz remarks, "[you] no longer [experience] those tense moments when a guard would inspect your passport, to see whether you would be allowed to make the move between city halves. You walk north from part-bohemian, part-Turkish Kreuzberg, and can just barely make out where the Wall used to be; the real, physical Wall. Recently, some say the Wall has only been in people's minds, dividing Ossis from Wessis." On the other hand, the "return" of Hong Kong to China has resulted in a determination to keep the old colonial frontier in place, as a guard against both ideological contamination to the north and the undermining of a conveniently successful capitalist venture to the south. In Cyprus, again, the visual as well as the verbal rhetoric of the border that hacks Nicosia in half violently opposes two ideologies to each other. Those on the Greek side say they "will not forget"; they expect to return to their homes, and the physical equipment of the Greek side of the border is an exercise in the rhetoric of provisionality. Those on the Turkish side, by contrast, are building for partition – permanently (see Papadakis 1993, 1998).

Maintaining order is both a practical and a conceptual issue. At the conceptual level, it starts with the question of who is to define order – who sets the boundaries? This is the question of classification. People who move around and are "of no fixed address" are bureaucratically polluting in Mary Douglas's (1966) sense of "matter out of place," and the new politics of cultural identity increasingly invests such ideas with all the virulence of racist ideology: it can be used to legitimate a politics of brutal exclusion even against settled migrants. In western Europe, as Stolcke (1995) has noted, it now often goes with a nativist version of cultural fundamentalism – an argument that has strong reverberations in western policy decisions and in some political-science analyses of international relations – and with the naturalization of xenophobia as a supposedly human characteristic (which would then "justify" it against particular populations, especially those "of no fixed abode"). Transience makes some groups an especially easy target for bureaucratic harshness (Okely 1983), even though it can also provide such populations as the Roma with high adaptability in times and places of economic shortage – a fact that hardly endears them to their sedentary "hosts" but that makes them relatively resistant to policing (Konstantinov 1996).

Douglas has elsewhere remarked (1986) that the issue is not one of scale: taxonomy remains important, no matter how large the social entity. While I fully agree with this, and suggest that this is precisely what makes such phenomena as national bureaucracies and huge conurbations appropriate objects of a specifically anthropological – as opposed, say, to a sociological or economic – analysis, we must also recognize that the change of scale that has occurred has specific historical causes, which have themselves marked the present-day culture forms we are investigating; as Talad Asad and David Scott especially have pointed out, colonialism has undoubtedly been the single most potent force in this regard – and there is no going back. García Canclini is especially clear on this: "What is meant today by city and anthropology is very different from what was understood by Robert Redfield, the Chicago and Manchester Schools and even more recent anthropologists. We need merely recall how much the significance and size of cities has changed since 1900: at that time only 4 percent of the world's population lived in cities; now half its population has become urbanized (Gmelch and Zenner eds. 1996: 188). In certain peripheral regions, such as Latin America, which were the preferred subject of earlier anthropology, 70 per cent of the population lives in urban conglomerations. Because urban expansion is due in great part to the influx of rural and indigenous populations, these social groups which have traditionally been studied by anthropologists are now found in large cities. It is here that their traditions are passed on and transformed and that the more complex exchanges arising from multi-ethnicity and multicultur-alism evolve."

The expansion has also been extraordinarily swift and sudden. As García Canclini notes, only half a century ago megalopolises were the exception. In 1950, New York and London were the only two cities in the world with more than 8 million inhabitants. By 1970 there were already 11 such cities, five of them in the so-called Third World – three in Latin America and two in Asia. According to United Nations projections, by the year 2015 there will be 33 megacities, 21 of them in Asia. These megalopolises are notable as much for their unrestrained growth as for their multicultural complexity – challenges both to assumptions about the clarity of cultural or ethnic boundaries and geographical borders.

García Canclini would like to reformulate the conventional definition of a megacity as "a phase in which neighbouring cities become part of a large urban agglomeration, forming a network of interconnected settlements." There are some cities to which this description certainly applies, and the circumstances of life in such places reinforces Hannerz's point about the specificity of urban living. In Mexico City, García Canclini notes, during the 50 years that the urban space was growing to 1,500 square kilometers, making commun-ication among its various parts extremely difficult and destroying the physical image of the whole, communications media were growing rapidly, disse-minating fresh images that renewed the connection among the disparate parts: "The same economic policy of industrial modernization which caused the city to overflow its boundaries at the same time stimulated the development of new audiovisual networks which restructured information and communica-tion practices and reconstructed the meaning of the city" through the displace-ment of the local cinema by the omnipresent television and radio and, today, internet and e-mail connections. "This reorganization of urban practices sug-gests that the socio-spatial definition of the megalopolis," remarks García Can-clini, "needs to be supplemented by a socio-communicational definition which takes into account the restructuring role played by the media in urban devel-opment."

It is this very expansion of scale that makes the anthropological intervention so urgent: phenomena associated in many people's minds with the operation of small-scale, bounded societies turn out to have a vastly magnified reach in the modern world: that reach is amplified and accelerated by technology and by increasingly widespread knowledge of what that technology can do. For example, the discrimination that once might have been most easily inves-tigated among itinerant smiths in the Horn of Africa has now become a problem for Roma in Europe and for refugees everywhere (Malkki [1989] similarly applies Douglas's model to the plight of Rwandan refugees), and the sheer magnification of taxonomic exclusion is what makes it a more, not less, commanding topic for our attention. It cannot be done without regard to economic and political factors – indeed, thus decontextualized it has no meaning – but this, I suggest, is the distinctive focus that allows us to see how large-scale decisions seep into, or sometimes violate, the closely guarded spaces of social life.

The taxonomy that defines membership in a cultural group continues to operate today in terms of essentialized characteristics. Today, amplified by a European concern with notions of possession, you must "have" a culture, just as you must "have" a fixed address; stateless persons are the new "wretched of the earth," because they have been classified out of social existence. Many of them dwell in cities: they hide in the anonymity of the crowd, creating networks of extraordinary versatility and discretion. They typify the problem of applying to the present condition of the majority of humankind the reified categories of culture and society, unless we wish to reproduce the exclusionary practices of governments.

It is in cities and at border crossings – nodes of place-ness and materialized taxonomic breakpoints, respectively – that we perhaps most fully encounter these dilemmas. Examining the processing of such dilemmas by actual bureaucrats – an ethnographic task that demands as much attention to the officially unrecognized interaction between migrants and officials as it does to the official laws and quotas (Heyman 1995) – shows that the clarity of boundaries is an ideological construct, that it has numerous uses, and that our task is to track those uses rather than to take their official representation on faith.

Official concepts of identity, which appear (and are often used) to represent bounded entities, thus have a "virtual" quality – they are adjectival rather than substantive, so to speak. It is easier to speak of "the cultural" and "the social" than of societies and cultures. The dominant imagery of many small and separate worlds, notes Hannerz, in which the Nuer, the Tikopia, the Kwakiutl and all the others seemed to exist almost as distinct species, followed a natural history tradition that turned cultures into something like animals and plants, while the subsequent experience of fieldwork kept the researchers focused on specific places. Yet truly and absolutely bounded entities have probably never in fact existed for any great length of time. There are earlier forms of anthropology in which the interconnectedness of cultural and social forms was recognized, or even (as in the case of the diffusionists who argued that all culture originated in Egypt!) exaggerated, while notions of "acculturation" may have derived some force from linguistic models of "borrowing." Ulf Hannerz emphasizes that "the sense that we are engaging with a more relative, problematic discontinuity is underlined by the fact that at the same time, other keywords of cultural and social inquiry at present emphasize more openness: fields, flows, networks." Hence, too, the title of this chapter.

Clearly, the inadequacies as well as the possibilities of the culture concept are on the line today as never before: the critique is ironically at its most explicit at a time when powerful forces are invoking the concept. At one level, then, this chapter is an ethnographic exploration of the place – physically as well as conceptually – of the culture concept in modern life. It is largely grounded in two essays already quoted here, one by Ulf Hannerz, the other by Néstor García Canclini. Both these scholars have made distinguished contributions to the study of cities, and have been, in different ways, proponents of the idea of urban anthropology (see also Kenny and Kertzer, eds., 1983; Signorelli 1996; Southall, ed., 1973). Yet both, instructively, have come to focus more on the discontinuities and apertures than on the sense of boundedness that the idea of a city conveys for many. García Canclini even suggests that much of the work done in urban anthropology is not really about cities at all: "while numerous studies on cities are to be found in the anthropological literature since the nineteenth century, anthropologists who talk about cities are often actually referring to something else. Although they deal with cities such as Luanshya, Ibadan, Mérida or São Paulo, the main purpose of many studies is to investigate cultural contacts in a colonial situation or migratory flows during periods of industrialization, working conditions and patterns of consumption, or what traditions remain under conditions of contemporary expansion."

As Hannerz (1980) has noted, urban anthropologists increasingly engaged not so much in urban anthropology as in doing anthropology in the city. As a result of such literal understandings, as García Canclini notes, "the city becomes more a locus of research than its object." This vision incorporates the attempt to discover what the idea of the city means to those who are said to live in or outside it – in other words, to probe the constructions of those boundaries that seem to take on such ironclad authority in our world, and that often only marginalized groups seem able to challenge and at the price of a sometimes terrible exclusion.

Such studies may suggest useful ways of tackling the huge practical challenge that the new social megaformations pose for the anthropologist. But they make it very clear, I would argue, that separating out a special sphere of "urban anthropology" is not the solution, all the more so because, as Robert Redfield's original formulation of the "folk–urban continuum" implicitly acknowledged, that label turns an ideal-typical distinction into an inflexible categorical straitjacket. That would be particularly ironic at the point at which we turn to the related issue of borders-as-boundaries – the realization "on the ground" of classificatory concepts of purity and defilement.

Scale and Porosity

This chapter is therefore focused on two intersecting areas in which the challenge seems to be concentrated: scale and what, for want of a more everyday term, I shall call "porosity." The latter alludes to the ease with which even – or especially – the most fiercely guarded borders can be penetrated. As Heyman (1995; see also Coutin 1995) has notably shown, ethical and pragmatic considerations give the lie to the literal-minded pretensions of bureaucrats who act as though national borders could be successfully defended even as they help their own clients to break through.

Hannerz evokes a contrast that, according to Lévi-Strauss, undergirds the entirety of human activity: the creation of boundaries between nature and culture. As Hannerz defines it, this is the contrast between what is innate and what is acquired in the experience of social life. He suggests that this notion is already under challenge because the growing capacity of human beings to remake their biology makes the distinction itself increasingly hard to sustain. Perhaps this is too literal: after all, the point of Lévi-Strauss's model was precisely to highlight the cultural use of nature and especially the expression of human identity through the deliberate deformation of culture. This can be achieved through the entire gamut of artifices available to humans, from Lévi-Strauss's own favourite of cooking (whether of foods or of "raw data," for example) to initiation rituals that inscribe "culture" on the body, and on to the patently metaphorical "naturalization" of the passport office and debates about what sexual and other behaviors are "natural." The term is always ambivalent: "others" both "live in a state of nature" and "are unnatural," a view that certainly has strongly influenced people's responses to environmental issues as well. In this sense, the moral and political ambiguities of "nature" are the logical precursors of those of "tradition" – things that the city is said to be at once the better and the worse for lacking!

Mostly, Hannerz argues, ideas of borders, when we are not concerned with state/state dividing lines, go with the culture/culture type of concern with difference. (And nation/nation borders, of course, imply that state/state and culture/culture borders go together – although for example the instance the Berlin Wall, both as a physical and as an Ossi/Wessi mental phenomenon, suggests that the assumption is questionable.) But at least in some contexts, one of those near-synonyms, "frontier," resonates with views toward the nature/culture divide. A century or so ago, the American historian Frederick Jackson Turner (1961 [1893]) offered a vision of the moving North American frontier as a region of opportunity, where wilderness could become free land and where pioneers could be self-reliant but also join together without the constraining traditions and inequalities they had left behind, and without the burden of a heritage. The wilderness, argued Turner, would master the colonist, strip off the garments of civilization, array him in the hunting shirt and moccasin. Note that the dress forms of the indigenous population (the moccasin) – another of the ways in which people convert nature into culture is clothing – constitute, for the invading settlers, a mark of "nature." This, too, is a negotiable border. But the terms of negotiation are unequal: this is the logic of western expansion, in North America, Latin America, South Africa, Australia. It is replicated in Zionist leader Theodor Herzl's famous/notorious phrase, "a land without a people for a people without a land," and is nicely captured in inverse form – that those who do not belong to the elite "have culture" in the sense of being interesting specimens – by Renato Rosaldo's (1989: 196–204) discussion of what he calls "cultural visibility and invisibility."

In these situations, then, the border, like apartheid, becomes a distancing device, and must be studied as such. Nevertheless, Hannerz maintains, "in most instances, border thought involves a recognition of greater symmetry – people and culture are recognized to exist on both sides. Even the term frontier surely allows this, as in anthropology when Leach (1960) analyzed the frontiers of Burma, or Kopytoff (ed. 1987) the African frontier."

The anthropological sense of the boundary concept, however, is generally much more flexible than that inscribed in the cartography of the nation-state. Especially since the 1969 publication of Fredrik Barth's landmark edited volume, *Ethnic Groups and Boundaries*, with its remarkable introductory chapter (Barth 1969), this difference has been explicit and significant. Apart from a certain emphasis on linkages between ecological adaptations and ethnic distinctions, Barth did not view boundaries in spatial terms. His concern was rather with the relationship between collective distinctions among people on the one hand, and the distribution of "cultural stuff" – meanings and forms – on the other. The two need not coincide. People on either side of a boundary might signal their desire to identify with their respective groups by means of diacritical markers in dress, food, language, and the like; the combination of choice and circumstance can indeed sometimes make ethnic enemies out of siblings. Ethnic boundaries thus say nothing about the sheer amount of culture that could actually be shared across those boundaries, or the amount of cultural variation that might be contained within the boundaries, within groups.

When the 25th anniversary of Barth's *Ethnic Groups and Boundaries* was honored with a conference in Amsterdam recently, Barth (1994: 12–14) suggested that although he and his 1960s collaborators "lacked the opaque terminology of present-day postmodernism," they had perhaps presented one of the first applications in anthropology of a postmodern, constructionist view of culture. Unusually at the time, they had not taken boundaries or cultural wholes for granted; they had instead argued for the situational rather than the primordial; and they had focused on contemporary rhetorics and struggles to appropriate the past. Barth also noted that in recent decades we have become more generally inclined to see global cultural variation as continuous, not easily partitioned into the kind of integrated, separate entities we have habitually been referring to as "cultures." Culture, instead, is seen as in flux, contradictory and incoherent, differentially distributed over variously positioned persons. As Hannerz so succinctly puts it, "It is not, then, that diversity is disappearing. It is just not very neatly packaged."

It has almost become a truism that identities are negotiated and reflect political realities: for example, two brothers might end up as respectively Greek and Macedonian immigrants in Australia because they had been involved in opposite sides in the Greek Civil War (Danforth 1995), or changes in subsistence mode might redefine an individual's ethnic identity within a relatively short span of years (see Burton 1980; Schein 1973; Southall 1976), or again status considerations might lead individuals to do what nation-state ideologies insist is impossible – change their identities (Shalinksky 1980). Indeed, the evidence that even "national" identity is negotiable has become so strong that some critics (e.g., Argyrou 1996b) have protested that it has tipped the balance of understanding too far the other way.

Social boundaries, then, involve memberships in collectivities, but, unless they are simply defined in terms of such social units, cultural boundaries are much more difficult to conceptualize in precise terms. Claims to "authenticity," usually based on shopping lists of culture traits or stylized artifacts (see Handler 1986; Handler and Linnekin 1984), entail the suppression of historical information, because the very idea of autochthonous origins for "a culture" flies in the face of all the evidence suggesting that identities survive, and even come into being, through the play of encounters – through the negotiation and genesis of social and cultural boundaries, in fact. Ideas, practices and artifacts may spread through social contacts across the surface of the earth according to quite diverse logics, accumulating very different histories. Old-style diffusionists had some, if limited, sense of this, and more than sixty years ago, in his parody of what it was like to be "100% American", Ralph Linton (1936: 326–7) made the point effectively: the "solid American citizen" wakes up in a bed of a type originating in the Near East, takes off his pajamas invented in India, washes with soap invented by the ancient Gauls." Linton called his account of a daily round as "merely a bit of antiquarian virtuosity", but for that very reason it reminds us that the evidence was always there had people wished to heed it. As Hannerz wrily observes, the comment "retains some value as an antidote to a mindless celebration of parochialism." And it sheds devastating light on the uses of ideas about "purity" in ideologies ranging from Nazism to Classical philology and reproduced in present-day hostility to various forms of cultural hybridity and intermarriage. Here we are back to the symbolism of difference.

This concern with the spaces in which difference is produced – anthropologically we cannot say that it "simply exists," because it is always the product of some human action – is the thread that connects Barth's work on ethnicity-as-process with current anthropological concerns. These, while not leaving ethnicity out of the equation, are now more taken up with "borderlands" – a term for a physical space that suggests something in-between, a contact zone, an area where discontinuities become somewhat blurred.

One such border zone has recently drawn more interest than any other; as Alvarez (1995) has argued, the borderland between the United States and Mexico may even be turning into the exemplary modern instance of what borderness is all about (see Rosaldo 1988; Kearney 1991). These writers, as Hannerz notes, allow an interesting comparison: "Kearney's border is rather more that fact of political geography, a state/state zone where some seek to exercise control, and others to evade it." It is a grim region of domination and terror, and at the same time the chosen habitat of the "coyotes," the people who are in the business of smuggling people; entrepreneurs to whom the border is indeed an asset.

Kearney reminds us that in indigenous Mexico and North America, Coyote is also a "supremely ambiguous and contradictory trickster and culture hero," and thus he approaches Rosaldo's more metaphorical borderlands, defined by their poets rather than by their police, and found perhaps wherever Latin America finds itself in North America. There may be a battle for survival here, but at the same time we are in a cultural zone "between stable places," with freedom, people playing, a dance of life.

Note the centrality of symbolic construction to both accounts. This is an old theme in anthropology, and arguably is one of its most distinctive contributions to social science generally. "Liminality" is another concept that comes readily to mind here, in Victor Turner's (e.g., 1982: 28) sense; "potentially and in principle a free and experimental region of culture, a region where not only new elements but also new combinatory rules may be introduced." In this view, then, borders are areas where cultures may become conspicuously unpacked: "culture+culture rather than culture/culture," in Hannerz's nicely contrastive phrase.

García Canclini, while not denying the significance of symbolic factors, turns the equation I have been describing here on its head. Where I would look for the distinctive contribution of "anthropology," he seems more concerned to show that "urban anthropology" enjoys a range of interests that take it far beyond the traditional methods of the discipline. At one level, of course, this is an argument about terminology rather than substance, although it does also concern the division of labor among the disciplines. And that is the main issue: for, while I have emphasized an approach that contrasts markedly with García Canclini's, my reasons for doing so have more to do with rescuing the particular focus of anthropology than with a desire to perpetuate the old disciplinary fiefdoms.

To balance the account, however (for his arguments answer immediate practical questions about research issues, regardless of who is to address them), I now turn in more detail to his rich methodological account of the new urban anthropology. His goal is to ask what distinguishes anthropology from other disciplines, and his answers share with others, not so much the actual methods used, as their goal – which is to recapture the diversity that so many survey methods simply erase. He does not accept the premise that contact with small groups, even in the urban context, is the defining characteristic – that "field observations and ethnographic interviews are still the specific resources of anthropology." Yet he concedes that, "in contrast to sociology, which constructs huge maps of urban structure and behavior from graphs and statistics, the qualitative and lengthy investigations conducted by anthropologists yield, in principle, a more profound understanding of social interaction." He finds the emphasis on culture that results from this localized focus to be benign inasmuch as it rescues dimensions on which more quantitative scholars focus, but he argues that "neither the tradition of anthropology as a discipline nor the indisputably economic and symbolic nature of urban processes justify limiting anthropological research to cultural factors. The growth of cities and the re-ordering (or disorder) of urban life is linked to economic, technological and symbolic changes whose inter-relationships make it essential to maintain the classic anthropological approach of considering the various dimensions of social processes all at the same time."

That has been the approach used in the 1980s and 1990s in investigations of the economic and cultural significance of urban social movements and working conditions, neoliberal de-industrialization, informal markets, and survival strategies. Brazil and Mexico are the two Latin American countries, in García Canclini's view, in which the most consistent work has been done on how economic, political, and cultural aspects are combined (e.g., Arias 1996; Dagnino, ed., 1994; Adler Lomnitz 1994; Sevilla and Aguilar Diaz, eds., 1996; Silva Tellez 1994; Valenzuela Arce 1988). The approach is used by some urban anthropologists, but García Canclini finds that these studies are "more anthropology in the city than about the city" and continues: "The field as a whole has not yet achieved the target of carrying out studies that connect the micro- and macro-social and the qualitative and quantitative in a comprehensive urban theory. The only way to capture the complexity of urban life is to understand the experiences of communities, tribes and neighborhoods as part of the organizing structures and networks of each city (Holston and Appadurai 1996; Hannerz 1992)." This means paying close attention to the everyday business of life – the domain of the ethnographer. Methodologically, the approach may be harder to manage in a city than in a village, as privacy becomes institutionalized in ways that are rare in rural settings and ethnographers cannot so easily find spaces for informal contacts. But this is precisely one of the specificities of urban living; and, as such, it becomes a topic for ethnographic investigation.

"Epistemological analysis of common sense and ordinary language is nowhere needed more than in the big cities," remarks García Canclini. Our informants encompass an enormous range of often radically divergent views; yet the places where such differences can be expressed are both more diffuse and, in many cases, less amenable to direct, interpersonal social exchange. García Canclini thus objects to what he calls "an isolated ethnographic approach to the fragmentation of the city" on the grounds that it either merely describes some form of marginality or, at best, only records the views of "the most vulnerable informants" – those, in other words, who come closest to the old colonialist model of the ideal informant. He somewhat acidulously concludes: "The methodological populism of certain anthropologists thus becomes the 'scientific' ally of political populism." While in fact work like George Marcus's study of a Texas business elite (Marcus 1992) demonstrate that this need not always be the case, the comment may be a salutary warning about the dangers of selective reporting – always an issue for ethnographic method, less for actual bias than because it attracts the easy charge of anecdotalism from those of more objectivist inclination.

Cities to Nodes

If border zones seem inevitably places of both ambiguity and definition, cities may superficially appear to possess a concreteness that would appear to make them stable objects of study. Yet their heterogeneity – which in Europe, where it was expressed in opposition to the "purity" of nature – was long the source of their reputation as sinks of symbolic pollution (Mosse 1985; Williams 1973) – actually concentrates and retemporalizes many of the features that can be directly observed at border points, dispersing them in ways that makes them initially hard to track ethnographically. At the same time, they offer new opportunities of method and perspective.

García Canclini provides a perspective that may be still more important for the way it helps to redefine the enterprise than for the immediate methodological gains and refinements it suggests. "Sociocultural heterogeneity or diversity, which has always been a basic theme in anthropology," he notes, "is today one of the most destabilizing elements for the classical model offered by urban theory." It is here that we see how unrealistic it is to view cities as made stable by their physcial concreteness: "concrete jungles" they may be, but they do not possess conceptual concreteness at all. Some theorists maintain that the parallel existence of many different functions and activities is, in fact, the defining feature of the present urban structure (Castells 1995; Signorelli 1996). Moreover, this flexibility expands as the delocalization of production weakens the historic ties between certain cities and particular types of production. Lancashire is no longer an international synonym for the textile industry; Sheffield and Pittsburgh are no longer synonymous with steel. Manufactured goods and the most advanced electronic equipment can be produced just as well in the international cities of the First World as in the cities of Brazil, Mexico and southeast Asia (Castells 1974; Sassen 1991).

The diversity of a city is usually results from distinct stages in its development. Milan, Mexico City, and Paris all provide parallel evidence at least of the following periods: historical, endowing them today with monuments that make them objects of artistic and touristic interest; industrial, entailing locally specific restructurings of land use; and a recent transnational and postindustrial architecture. The present coexistence of segments of the urban built environment representing these different periods gives rise to a sense of temporal heterogeneity in which processes of hybridization, conflict, and intense intercultural exchange occur (García Canclini 1990, 1995).

Other cities may exhibit rather different combinations of spatialized and architectonic temporality: this is a question for local research, but the heuristic value of García Canclini's suggestive comment is clear. Moreover, as immigrant populations the world over begin to restructure the urban spaces and situate them in novel networks, other and sometimes novel temporalities – those of travel, for example, especially when grounded in religious models (e.g., Carter 1997; Delaney 1990) or motivated by the market for "exotic" art (Steiner 1994) – become more important. Language becomes a crucial issue, its use a marker of new identities framed as ethnicity but experienced as class (see Urciuoli 1996).

García Canclini sees "the 'explosion' of differences" as "not just a concrete process . . . [but] also an urban ideology." But despite the emergence of what he sees as urban democracy under the new conditions, he wants to retain an analytical as well as a substantive distinction between the so-called metropolitan and peripheral countries. Such a distinction, he argues, is required by political and economic considerations: "We cannot equate the growth of self-management and plurality after a phase of planning designed to regulate urban growth and satisfy basic needs (as in nearly all European cities) with the chaotic growth of survival efforts based on scarcity, erratic expansion and predatory use of land, water and air (which are habitual in Asia, Africa and Latin America)."

To these differences he also adds the often catastrophic effects of rapid population growth in already impoverished Third World cities, adding, as he remarks, "to a disorder which is always on the verge of exploding." Citing Holston and Appadurai (1996: 252), moreover, he argues that because of the unequal power of competing interest groups and the absence of effective regulation, the popular exercise of democracy can produce especially antidemocratic results under such conditions. Official interests are also often problematic, as when governments promote massive historic conservation programs that some inhabitants regard as invasive and distorting of their locally experienced history; or when, as in Bangkok, local street markets are compressed into back alleys to make way for a gentrification of façades, an effort of dubious and unequally distributed relevance for those who live there. For those who can afford it, the solution may be to leave – people are voting with their feet (García Canclini 1995). But that process compounds the besetting inequalities.

Various studies from the 1990s address the openings for the revitalization of popular participation and organization. "When the nation-state loses the ability to convene and administer the public," García Canclini notes, "cities re-emerge as strategic sites for the development of new forms of citizenship with more 'concrete' and manageable referents than those offered by national abstractions. In addition, urban centers, especially megalopolises, have become a medium for the international flow of goods, ideas, images and people. Whatever is taken out of the people's hands by supranational decision-making appears to be recovered to some degree in the local arenas of home, work and consumption (Dagnino [ed.] 1994; Ortiz 1994). Those who today feel that they are 'voting spectators' rather than citizens of a nation are rediscovering in the new forms of recognition of difference 'compactation and reterritorialization' of the claims that make large cities possible, ways of relocating the imagination of the nation in movements of commensurable disintegrated citizens (Holston and Appadurai 1996: 192–5)."

Difference that Counts: Multiculturalists and interculturalists

These considerations indicate the dynamic relationship between urban life and the formulation of new identities not necessarily envisaged, or even approved, by the nation-state. It is this ambiguity that presumably has for so long contributed to the image of the city as a dirty – that is, symbolically polluting – place. But it is also what creates the possibility for exploring cultural difference in a pragmatic sense – that is, as a dimension of living together with a varied set of values and practices.

As a methodological insight, this suggests the importance of cities for defining the social and the cultural in an era when they occupy so large a segment of the world's population. (I would caution, however, that the persistence of non-urban features may be much more commonplace, and much more crucial to people's cultural identity, than the rush to urbanize anthropology appears to suggest.) As an object of study, the heterogeneity of the city can become a basis for new forms of political mobilization: cities, often created in part to monumentalize the permanence of the nation-state, can easily become the seat of challenges to its vision, as when the idea of cultural purity yields to the richness of multicultural experience.

The specific understanding of culture in contemporary multiculturalism, its metaculture, notes Terence Turner (1993), is that it provides a "source of values that can be converted into political assets, internally as bases of group solidarity and mobilization and externally as claims on the support of other social groups, governments and public opinion all over the globe." Multiculturalism, seen in this light, is primarily a political project, and thus it takes its central and controversial place in "identity politics" and "culture wars" – most noticeably in the United States, although certainly with counterparts elsewhere (which frequently emulate American examples to some degree). The battles are continuously fought in many arenas. For people living cheek-by-jowl in crowded conurbations, it may quite literally be a matter of life or death.

Multiculturalism, Turner notes, has tended to disappoint anthropologists. Why are they, with a long-standing expertise in cultural matters, not consulted; why do the multiculturalists reinvent the culture concept on their own, even in a form (or in several varieties) of which anthropologists may not approve? A main reason, Turner argues, is precisely that for the multiculturalists culture is a means to an end, not the end in itself. A very large part of the anthropological understanding of culture is not relevant to their political agenda – although some of it is (such as the broad relativist streak), and perhaps multiculturalism could in turn inspire anthropologists to think more about such issues as capacity and empowerment.

If multiculturalists are concerned with politics, our second group inclined to make much of borders and difference, the interculturalists, take a more technical stance. What Hannerz has facetiously but tellingly dubbed the "culture shock prevention industry" has grown rapidly in the last few decades, particularly in North America and western Europe, as an emergent profession dedicated to making it easier for people of different cultures to deal with one another. This "industry" presents anthropologists with a serious dilemma: if they refuse to participate in it they risk surrendering their already limited role as authoritative commentators on issues of culture; but if they lend it their authority, they risk becoming implicated in a process of reification that conflicts with their own professional understanding of the issues as well as with of the uses appropriate to their ideas.

Interculturalists work in different settings for different people, but in large part they operate in the marketplace, offering training and advice to clients in international business, development work, or education. Their contacts here tend to be short-term: a single lecture, a half-day workshop, a course extended over a few days. Apart from lecturing, the interculturalists often use video films and simulation games to make their points about cultural differences, and the risks of cultural clashes and misunderstandings. A fairly extensive handbook literature has developed, and through professional institutions and associations new ideas and techniques of instruction are disseminated. The notion of culture being propounded here is not necessarily that of anthropologists. Indeed, it may be much closer to the essentializings of Samuel Huntington and others, and the danger is that, because it is "applied" (we learn another culture in order to do business with it and perhaps to dominate it), and because – in limited contexts – these ethnological phrase-books may actually produce their desired short-range effects, the larger perspective that they embody may come to have an authority far in excess of their scholarly value but totally in harmony with the quick-fix philosophy that undergirds them.

Hannerz notes, in this area, "a strong tendency . . . to assume that cultures can be described at a national level." There is a certain irony in this: for, while anthropology may be said to have arisen from the same desire for cultural cartography that infuses nationalism, it has in recent years adopted a much more process and agent oriented perspective, one that allows analytic space to those who seek to change cultural forms or simply do not conform to them. Interculturalist projects do have an anthropological antecedent, and indeed, especially in the work of E. T. Hall (1959; cf. 1983, 1987), can claim direct descent from it. This is the genre of "national culture" studies thrown up by the Cold War and feeding today on the expansion of international business; it is often not very different in its proclivity for caricaturing and demonizing from the nationalist folklore literatures of the nineteenth century, with their disturbing echoes in the political punditry of our own age (on which, see, critically, Verdery [1994: 51ff]). If multinational corporations represent the new power elite, successors to colonial empires and nation-states, perhaps we should take these handbooks of culture more seriously than we usually do – not as useful sources of information (although the best of them may contain some serious analysis), but as diagnostic of new technologies of control that exploit the categorical imperative in human beings (and especially the penchant for self- and other-categorizing).

These (perhaps unduly alarmist) thoughts spring from a larger preoccupation in recent anthropology: that our preoccupation with "cultures" leads us to exoticize and to give inappropriate emphasis to difference. While the counter-vailing urge to seek commonalities – implied, for example, in the emphasis on basic symbolic attributes such as liminality and categorical systems – has also historically been at least as important as the sensationalism that the discipline has attracted, the charge is one that should be taken seriously. Again, Rosaldo's reflections on cultural "visibility" will stand us in good stead here as we seek to relate a central ethical and epistemological problem to the practical business of refashioning ethnographic practice in the more porous and populous spaces of our time.

It is presumably no coincidence, as Hannerz notes, that Samuel Huntington's dyspepsia with "other civilizations" is accompanied by his grim disapproval of multiculturalism at home: like nationalists who at one and the same time claim border territories as culturally "theirs" and deride the inhabitants of these dis-puted zones as ethnically "impure," those who have adapted the culture concept to the defense of "Western civilization" at home and abroad see no contradic-tion between models of cultural incompatibility on the one hand and calls for assimilation on the other. Yet the experience of ethnography in the border zones – where the collusion of local officials with illegal immigrants and others sus-pected of violating the law of the frontier illustrates the complexities of cultural identity in ways that such simplistic formulae simply cannot capture and must indeed distort.

Methodological Revisions

The work of studying borders and nodes presents a formidable challenge to ethnographic practice. When anthropologists were able to focus on a small local community – or even to assume that the people they knew were representative of a more or less homogeneous, larger one – they could define the research project as a matter of spending the "ritual year" in the field. Some, certainly, stayed much longer; and many went back, some re-peatedly. But the whole enterprise was conveniently circumscribed by an economy of scale that meshed relatively well with the academic apparatus of sabbatical leaves and with the anthropological preoccupation with the ritual-calendric cycle.

To some extent, what was once a convenience has become something of a problem. Does one really know, say, Tokyo, after one year? Obviously in some sense Malinowski did not really "know" the Trobrianders even to his own sat-isfaction after his sojourn, but the difficulties were arguably minor in compar-ison to those of the present-day ethnographer faced with the need for appointments, the formality of tape-recorded interviews, and the sheer haste of modern life in many places.

Yet, once again, the issue is not one of kind, but of degree. What Georg Simmel – invoked by Hannerz to comment on the complexity of modern border zones – said about interesecting fields of social action applies as much to the Nuer as to the New Yorkers: individuality grows as people come to be placed at intersections between different groups; each membership may be shared with numerous other people, yet the particular individual may have a combination of memberships shared with nobody else (Simmel 1964: 127ff). With the growth in scale, people tend to invoke patterns of common culture (which is predicated on replication and therefore can be recognized in someone one has never seen before), displacing the face-to-face emphasis on social relations (which is relational and therefore usually does require a degree of intimacy). Yet I believe that the idea of an intimate space, to be defended from outsiders (sometimes including anthropologists!) and enjoyed in the company of insiders, persists into these larger spheres, making ethnography not only possible but a matter of greater urgency than ever before.

Complexity is thus not a matter of objective conditions, but the product of inside knowledge: when a Nuer herder or a Greek villager claims to "know" another, this is a statement about intimacy that is extended to the cultural knowledge assumed by, for example, the New Yorker, who always claims to "know" other New Yorkers – to be able to "deal" with them, to predict their reactions, to understand their hopes and fears, and in general to do everything we understand by the term "identification." What we mean by "complex societies" or even by Ulf Hannerz's own phrase "cultural complexity" does represent a difference, but it is a difference that perhaps only the particularistic focus of ethnographic research can render intelligible. The alternative is recourse to the "how-to" manuals – not a happy recommendation.

It used to be, as García Canclini wryly observes, that the social sciences often pitied those people who found themselves located at social or cultural borders. The "marginal man" identified some seventy years ago by Robert Park (1964: 345), founder of Chicago urban sociology but also a forerunner in the study of race relations and human migration, was a rather tragic figure. Not so today. Now the mood is to celebrate hybridity – although this is clearly more of a trend in anthropology than it is with those who manage world affairs.

The latter, as exemplified in the case of the US–Mexican border zone (Heyman 1995), often also generate constraining structures of power and inequality. Moreover, crossing borders can also lead to misunderstandings and unease, because borders can keep shifting, complicating both our sense of categorical closure and our assumptions about agency (or even "free will"). In part, perhaps, it is because the nation-state has done its work of inculcation all too well.

The ethnography of such phenomena therefore requires sensitivity to political inequalities, a willingness to dispense with assumptions about hermetic "cultures," and a degree of facility with transportation systems and other kinds of technology. If your informants migrate, then, on the principle of participant observation, why are you not migrating with them (Deltsou 1995)?

Hannerz evokes three dramatic illustrations of modern border zones: the change in the human scenery at the Damascus gate in Jerusalem, those vanishing traces of the Wall through the middle of Berlin, and the checkpoint on Interstate 5 in southern California. These, as he says, all involve some idea of a political–geographic division, whether existing in the present, remembered from the past, or even imagined in the future. Yet what makes these three instances particularly dramatic is that they involve physical places where not just states but world religions, major military power blocs, international ideologies, even the "First World" and the "Third World", and the "First World" and the "Second World", have somehow faced each other – sometimes entailing risks of armed confrontation, at other times hopes of escape to another kind of life. Of course, not all borders share this dramatic tone. But some acquire an aura of terror and yet also of adventure because those who cross them play for particular stakes in so doing.

The Bulgarian semiotician-anthropologist Yulian Konstantinov's (1996) evocative description of Roma trader-tourists criss-crossing the Bulgarian–Turkish frontier can stand paradigmatically for this experience. The field research he describes is also an exemplary demonstration that participant observation is not confined to work on settled communities or single places: he and his fellow-researchers shared the discomforts of the cross-border bus ride, with all the attendant risks of harassment, arrest, and acute physical stress (see also Konstantinov, Kressel, and Thuen 1998 – an appropriately border-crossing collaboration by a Bulgarian, an Israeli, and a Norwegian!). As Hannerz reminds us, we are perhaps confronting the particular methodological issues involved in "multi-sited" studies, themselves a frontier of recent anthropology (see Marcus 1995; Hannerz 1988).

Nodes, Borders, and Regroupings

What should be clear from this discussion is that the urbanization of the world, while uneven in its intensity and in its practical effects, has drastically altered the object of anthropology during the lifetime of the discipline. At the same time that discipline, which in an earlier phase gave a perhaps disproportionate degree of attention to "symbolic classification," retains a perspective that allows it to resist the facile generalizations that a less intense focus on social process tends to generate.

It is probably no coincidence that anthropologists began to appreciate the porosity of borders and the negotiability of identities while this massive urbanization was beginning to accelerate ever more dramatically. Especially after World War II, more and more anthropologists situated their work within urban, or urban-dominated, research sites. These sites were small "nodes" through which processes occurring in the city were transmitted but also transformed: "civilization," in its literal sense of urban culture, became a standard, and in some countries had been for many centuries (see Silverman 1975). The large nodes, which were mostly getting ever larger (and doing so at alarming speeds), seemed to present an altogether tougher proposition.

Moreover, those nodes were located at the centers of networks that in turn defined spaces with borders; and those borders, despite their cartographic formality, turned out to be no less porous than the interactive identities that people experienced within the cities. A discipline defined only as the study of small-scale societies would have died at that moment.

Instead, there were several new adaptations, and, as the discussion in this chapter should illustrate, these are continuing to evolve. They entail considerations not only of method but also of epistemology. "The field" has become an altogether different "place." In its virtuality, in fact, it suggests that the specific focus of anthropology on the symbolic negotiation of social and cultural forms may have equipped it extraordinarily effectively to survive in this supercharged new environment.

7

Developmentalisms

Intervention as a Cultural Practice

"Few historical processes," remarks Arturo Escobar, "have fueled the paradox of anthropology – at once inextricably wedded to Western historical and epistemological dominance and a radical principle of critique of the same experience – as much as the process of development." This is practice writ large – but a practice that disguised a program of control with the benign dress of "aid." Even when that aid was intended to induce self-reliance, it was couched in the terms of a western social ideology, for its agencies – the World Bank, the IMF, and so on – were largely dominated by a handful of western powers with security concerns at stake. Indeed, for many players it was an extension of the cold war. But it took the specific form of imposing a single, technologically efficient vision of modernity on much of the Third World – which was defined by its subjection to that vision. In short, development was both a symbol and one of the most potent instruments of western hegemony, outwardly defined as assimilation, but practically intended as dominance. While we may recognize benign intentions in many of the programs carried out in its name, these cannot disguise the lack of choice with which technologically powerful nations confronted those other countries forced to depend on them in the international arena. And the effects of these interventions were often not benign at all. Indeed, as Akhil Gupta (1998) has pointed out, even the recognition of local forms of knowledge as worthy of respect has served to coopt its bearers in the schemes of international capital rather than to heed local voices decrying the spoliation of their environment and the disruption of their lives.

At the same time as we appreciate the force of these criticisms, we should be aware of two potential pitfalls. First, rejecting the essentialization of other cultures does not legitimate meting out the same treatment to "the West," a historically complex and often ambiguous term that functions in this book as a convenience to be used with extreme caution. Treating the West as a generic bogey is often misleading at best. The second caveat concerns the intentions and effects of development policies. Both, of course, can be pernicious; but it does not follow that they necessarily or invariably serve evil ends, and in any case such judgments can only be made in the context of knowing whose interests they serve. Sometimes, indeed, judgments of this sort are little more than partisanship, and may take the side of one faction against another within a local community. The present focus on agency and practice demands that we always pose this question, opening up the moral issues for debate rather than closing them down with peremptory partiality.

In this chapter, I take development as a paradigm case of what can happen when anthropology is "applied." I do not intend any rejection of the idea of making the discipline useful – a major concern of many practitioners from poorer countries – but I again insist that we must always ask: useful to whom? Who is applying the anthropology, and to what ends and with what effects? The answers, I repeat, are not always straightforward: in a courageously multivocal edited volume on the Narmada Dam in India, for example, William Fisher (1995) has sought to amplify all the contending voices in debates about immediate and long-term benefits to varying segments of the population, effects on environment and society, and compensation for the disruption experienced by often marginalized groups. That volume is indeed exemplary in its open-ended presentation of often discordant perspectives, enriching our understanding of the complexities involved by letting differently positioned social actors speak for themselves and in sometime raucous concert with each other.

In this way, we can use the paradigm of development to explore the ethical commitments and dilemmas of the discipline. In so doing, I lean heavily on the work of a handful of mostly younger scholars who have been able to show that a "poststructuralist" critique – an examination of the discourse of development – may have important practical consequences. But it should be recognized that even those anthropologists who are less interested in questions of discourse still entertain deep reservations toward the effects of much of what goes under the name of development.

Development in the sense described here perpetuates the colonial image of peoples locked in a technological childhood – an idea that was enthusiastically promoted by nineteenth-century social evolutionists and that continues to infuse much of the discourse about "underdeveloped" nations. As anthropologists turned against the colonialist underpinnings of their discipline, they not surprisingly became increasingly critical of developmentalist assumptions as well. Some were concerned with the survival of specific cultures threatened by disease, genocide, and the loss of their lands in the face of particularly rapacious forms of exploitation (such as the gold rush in the Amazon, for example). Even those who were less convinced of the premise of integral cultural identities have been critical of the impact of development on questions of self-determination.

The ideal of civil society, while itself arguably a western concept that translates into other contexts with some difficulty, at least serves to point up the double standard so often operative in development projects. As Fisher points out in his discussion of the Narmada project (Fisher 1995: 40), it entails freedom of choice – the play of human agency that anthropology, as presented in this book, examines in relation to what Fisher calls "otherwise determinant structures." As Fisher notes, such a conception of civil society is international as well as national, and indeed the activities of NGOs may usefully call the assumptions of nation-state governments into question. The notion of civil society also has limitations, and the international order represented by NGOs often, as Gupta (1998) argues, plays into and depends on the persistence of national entities. Choice is itself hardly a culture-free or ideologically neutral notion; it is a key component of neoliberal economics, for example, and is often claimed as the hallmark of western individualism. Thus, it is vitally important to examine how the idea is actually used in practice: agency may consist, in some situations, in acquiescing – and even colluding – in one's own domination by more powerful others, as Gramsci recognized in his elaboration of "hegemony."

Sometimes, then, the premise that development gives local communities the freedom to set their own agendas may actually be a means of securing that collusion, or at least that of a local elite anxious to cooperate in anything that will further its own short-term interests. One cannot consider the impact of development without also considering its entanglements with local political realities. And the only viable path to any understanding of that interaction lies through careful, on-the-spot ethnography.

On the other hand, freedom of choice – the right of self-determination – is now largely accepted worldwide as the logical antithesis of repression. It is in questioning the degree to which the rhetoric of choice corresponds to local perceptions and desires that we can begin to get some purchase on the implications of various development schemes. Often the claim that development should rise above political considerations, for example, provides a means for locally repressive regimes to subordinate political freedom to the allure of modernity; in the process, they often also, and concomitantly, subordinate their own countries to management by international organizations that do not necessarily make local interests the primary concern. James Ferguson's (1990) work on Lesotho is an excellent analysis of how the discourse of development can serve such external structures of power. Sometimes, too, local communities have often simply lacked the means to fight back effectively – a situation that is now rapidly changing as peasant-based and other activist political coalitions attack the depredations of international capital and challenge its pious expressions of goodwill. But even these movements are not uncomplicatedly virtuous. The critically engaged ethnographer must always ask who will benefit from any intervention, whether by development agencies or by local sources of opposition.

We should also note that the intentions of development agencies are less important than the effects of their work. As I have noted in the discussion of epistemology, emotions and desires are only knowable through their representation. We cannot know whether the intention of bringing freedom and modernity is genuine or not in a given case, especially because there are usually many, diverse social actors involved. As I have pointed out in discussing the anthropological uses of fiction, however, we can hear the multiple voices involved in the debates about how convincing a novel or drama is in local cultural terms. These are revealing arguments about the representation of intention, sincerity, and so forth. A collection like Fisher's *Narmada* volume (1995) is especially illuminating in this regard: it contains input from an enormous variety of persons located in key areas of the conflict, all testifying to their respective perspectives with great eloquence.

That volume represents a new kind of ethnography, one in which literate voices can be seen influencing events. But even in a more conventional sense, anthropologists' insistence on ethnographically probing the social and experiential realities created by development projects, an example in its own right of the ethnographic probing of bureaucracies, has indeed led to what Escobar calls "a more nuanced understanding of the nature of development and its modes of operation." Without doubt, anthropologists are often deeply ambivalent about their involvement in development, but at the very least their critical voices may suggest alternative paths not directly dependent on international capital. Escobar distinguishes "two broad schools of thought: those who favour an active engagement with development institutions on behalf of the poor, with the aim of transforming development practice from within; and those who prescribe a radical critique of, and distancing from, the development establishment." But Fisher, who divides the pro-development commentators into those whose objections are "tactical" and those whose concerns are more deeply "programmatic," contrasting both with the rejectionist camp he labels "ideological" (Fisher, ed., 1995: 17–18), suggests that the way out may lie more constructively with a careful examination of the interests of all the actors involved – a position consistent with the agent-oriented, middle-ground position adopted in this book, inasmuch as it recognizes that some processes of international engagement are simply not going to be reversed and that it is therefore more useful to try to understand them from within. Once again, this approach exemplifies new work being done on the anthropology of bureaucracies and other types of formal organization, in which meticulous ethnography is used to disaggregate forces too easily, and too often, lumped together in disfiguring caricatures.

For my overview of the history of these issues within anthropology specifically, I shall rely very heavily on Escobar's critical overview (see also Escobar 1995), passing from those who have opted to work within development institutions to the more recent critique of developmentalism that has emerged since the late 1980s. The latter represent what Escobar calls "the anthropology of development," thereby focusing our attention on the idea that ethnographers should look as closely at the scientists and planners as they do at the supposed beneficiaries – once again, in the spirit of "ethnographizing" bureaucracy and subjecting their supposedly universal rationality to critical scrutiny. This opens up space to consider the work of several anthropologists experimenting with creative ways of articulating anthropological theory and practice in the development field. Escobar views these authors as articulating a powerful theory of practice for anthropology as a whole; one might say that they are developing a practice of theory. Their several visions of possible forms of engagement with development work open up a vista of future prospects. While we will find that the basic dilemma – "is anthropology hopelessly compromised by its involvement in mainstream development or can anthropologists offer an effective challenge to the dominant paradigms of development?" (Gardner and Lewis 1996: 49) – remains in some degree unresolved, one constructive spin that we can put on it is by capitalizing on the productive discomfort it generates. This may lead us in turn to ask what were once unthinkable questions about the validity of the divisions between applied and academic anthropology, divisions that have come to seem awkward at best – and hopelessly inconsistent at worst – in an anthropology geared toward understanding all forms of practice and agency.

Culture and Economy in Development Anthropology

The theory and practice of development were largely shaped, in their initial stages, by neoclassical economists. That meant that local voices were rarely heard with any clarity. In his retrospective look at development anthropology at the World Bank, Michael Cernea called the econocentric and technocentric conceptual biases of development strategies "profoundly damaging" (Cernea 1995: 15) but argued that development anthropologists had done much to correct these biases. In the process, says Cernea, they also, and against precedent, carved a niche for themselves in prestigious and powerful institutions, such as the World Bank. In this view, the recognition of "culture" as something more than epiphenomenal was a major step forward in getting development agencies to take anthropology seriously (Bennett and Bowen, eds., 1988; Cernea, ed., 1985; Cernea 1995; Hoben 1982; Horowitz 1994; see also Gardner and Lewis 1996).

Development anthropologists argue that in the mid-1970s, as the poor results of top-down, technology and capital-intensive interventions became widely apparent, a new sensitivity emerged.[1] This reformulation was most evident in the shift in World Bank policy toward "poverty-oriented" programming – announced by its President, Robert S. McNamara, in 1973 – but it was being advanced at many other sites in the development establishment, including the United States Agency for International Development (USAID) and several of the United Nations technical agencies. Experts began to accept that the poor themselves – particularly the rural poor – had to participate actively in the programs if these were to have a reasonable margin of success. It was a question of "putting people first" (Cernea, ed., 1985). Projects had to be socially relevant and culturally appropriate, a view that created an unprecedented demand for anthropological skills. Even at the World Bank, the bastion of economism, the social science staff grew from the first lone anthropologist hired in 1974 to about 60 by the end of the millennium; moreover, hundreds of anthropologists and other social scientists are employed each year as short-term consultants (Cernea 1995).

Thus, from the early 1980s, when anthropologists working in development had not created an academic subdiscipline of development anthropology with "a coherent and distinctive body of theory, concepts, and methods" (Hoben 1982: 349), they moved into a much more institutionalized role administratively, educationally, and conceptually. Writing in the mid-1980s, a group of development anthropologists practitioners offered this assessment: "The anthropological difference is apparent at each stage of the problem-solving process: anthropologists design programs that work because they are culturally appropriate; they correct interventions that are underway but that will be economically unfeasible because of community opposition; they conduct evaluations that contain valid indicators of program results. They provide the unique skills necessary for intercultural brokering; they collect primary and 'emic' data necessary for planning and formulating policy; and they project and assess cultural and social effects of intervention" (Wulff and Fiske 1987: 10). Serving as cultural intermediaries ("brokers") between the worlds of development and community; collecting the local knowledge and point of view; placing local communities and projects in larger contexts of political economy; and viewing culture holistically – these all emerge as important, if not essential, anthropological contributions to the development process.

The result is supposedly development "with larger gains and fewer pains" (Cernea 1995: 9). This perceived effect has been particularly important in some areas, such as resettlement schemes, farming systems, river basin development, natural resource management, and informal sector economies. But development anthropologists of the time went further, claiming to be able to provide sophisticated analyses of the social organization that circumscribed projects that underlay local people's actions. They thus in one sense anticipated a key aspect of the later, more critical perspective on development, inasmuch as they attempted to transcend the dichotomy between theoretical and applied research. In some cases, they were even able to persuade their employers to support research that went beyond the immediate needs of particular projects, and they came to see themselves as increasingly welcome partners in project design and implementation (Cernea 1995; Horowitz 1994).

Yet this welcome came at a price, as anthropologists sometimes came to adopt the patronizing perspectives of their institutional sponsors. For example, as Escobar notes, Cernea "credits social scientists at the World Bank with changes in this institution's resettlement policies." Nowhere does he mention the role played in these changes by the widespread opposition and local mobilization against resettlement schemes in many parts of the world." That perspective began to change in part as a result of a more general legitimation within anthropology of "studying up" (Nader 1972) – that is, of treating all human agents, including anthropologists, as equally interesting and significant participants in the social phenomena under examination.

The other factor limiting development anthropologists' willingness to assess their engagement contextually lay in their epistemological preferences. Engaged as they were in practical matters determined by both the positivist orientation of much pre-1980s anthropology and the Cartesianism of government and international management styles, and beset by their employers' skepticism about the practical value of even the most positivist anthropological thinking, they rarely

managed to push critique much beyond advocating for what Escobar, following Gow (1993), calls "a firm commitment to speaking truth to power" (Gow
1993) and for enunciating a variety of responses from active interventionism to
rejectionist positions (Grillo 1985; Swantz 1985). To join or not to join: that
was the question, rather than a more nuanced consideration of what development was actually doing in the world.

Escobar calls the dominant paradigm of the time "realist." That is accurate,
but in the sense that realism consists of highly conventional forms of discourse
that work to disguise their own conventionality. (To put this in another way:
anthropologists of that time were reluctant to subject their own, supposedly
rational thinking to the sort of symbolic critique that they were just then developing for the analysis of supposedly exotic "systems of thought.") The dominant model of common sense relegated concerns with rhetoric and discourse to
the margins, thereby insulating development anthropology from a genuine critique of its cherished assumptions.

Rhetoric and the Anthropology of Development

One source of development anthropologists' resistance to the critique of their
discourse and its underlying assumptions certainly lay in their view, which was
characteristic of their conservative theoretical orientation, that rhetoric had little
or nothing to do with the realities of the work in which they were engaged.
While they did engage with issues of language, this mostly took the form of
exploring indigenous folk taxonomies in order to bring local knowledge under
their employers' (or, more generally, the Western and industrialized nations')
control (e.g., Moran 1981; cf. Gupta 1998). Their own language was of no
interest, and they generally participated in the often strident attacks on postmodernism as self-indulgent and irrelevant.

Regardless of the label one attaches to its analysis, however, scholarly rhetoric
plays an enormous role in the production of knowledge, and it is especially consequential when it is yoked to the actions of powerful development agencies. I
cannot improve on the eloquence of William Fisher (ed., 1995: 446): "Rhetoric
is not an irrelevant and easily dismissed byproduct of the development process.
Rhetoric matters in a number of fundamental ways: rhetoric can both close off
or open up new possibilities; it can mystify what is actually happening; it is also
part of and shaped by what is actually happening; and it has an effect upon
what happens. Rhetoric mystifies when it suggests consensus where there is
none, directs attention away from conflict, and obscures relationships of
inequality and power. It hides human beings behind impersonal labels like
PAPs (project-affected persons), CAPs (canal-affected persons), 'oustees,' and
'encroachers,' encouraging us to measure and comparatively weigh abstract
'things,' such as the number of PAPs against the volume of water, while overlooking, at least for the moment, the humanity behind some of these 'things'."

Fisher's analysis of the Narmada dam project and the controversies that it unleashed, on the other hand, pinpoints the materiality of the symbolism used by the developmentalists in pursuit of their goals – and it does so especially by letting all the various actors, including many of those who were committed to the project, speak for themselves.

More generally, "development" has been taken to be "really real," its rhetoric, in Escobar's words, "a neutral language that can be utilized harmlessly and put to different ends according to the political and epistemological orientation of those waging it." Anthropologically, this makes little sense, especially as the evidence suggests that the term itself has many meanings for its myriad users. To quote Escobar again: "From modernization theory to dependency or world systems; from 'market-friendly development' to self-directed, sustainable, or eco-development the qualifiers of the term have multiplied without the term itself having been rendered radically problematic" (see also Crush 1995: 2). Any new critique of what Escobar and others call the "anthropology of development" (as opposed to "development anthropology") should start by questioning the very notion of development by arguing for a critical assessment of the historical and cultural contexts in which it has appeared. As Crush puts it, "the discourse of development, the form in which it makes its arguments and establishes its authority, the manner in which it constructs the world, are usually seen as self-evident and unworthy of attention. The primary intention [of discursive analysis] is to try and make the self-evident problematic" (Crush 1995: 3). Another set of authors, more wedded to this defamiliarizing task, sought to render the language of development unspeakable, to turn the basic constructs of the development discourse – markets, needs, population, participation, environment, planning, and the like – into "toxic words" that experts could not use with such impunity as they have until now (Sachs, ed., 1992). Others showed why these discourses were problematic fro specific groups of people; notably, Chandra Mohanty (1991) found in the rapidly proliferating "women in development" texts of the 1970s and 1980s evidence of the power differentials in their depiction of Third World women as implicitly lacking what their First World counterparts had achieved. Escobar, Ferguson, Gupta, and, in a somewhat different mode, Fisher have all questioned the rhetoric of development.

Ferguson made the most general case: "Like 'civilization' in the nineteenth century, 'development' is the name not only for a value, but also for a dominant problematic or interpretive grid through which the impoverished regions of the world are known to us. Within this interpretive grid, a host of everyday observations are rendered intelligible and meaningful" (Ferguson 1990: xiii). In the terms of empirical contextualization that frame the overview of anthropology presented here, Ferguson showed how the evolutionist ring of the term "development" reinforced, in numerous practical ways, the view of "underdeveloped" countries as needing guidance in their pursuit of modernity. This in turn leads Escobar, among others, to question the construction of the "Third World" as a category that both expresses and serves the interests of "First

World" power managers. "The gaze of the analyst," remarks Escobar, "thus shifted from the so-called beneficiaries or targets of development to the allegedly neutral social technicians of the development apparatus. What are they actually doing? Are they not producing culture, ways of seeing, transforming social relations?" In particular, they introduce into Third World environments practices based on notions of individuality, rationality, economy, and the like (Ferguson 1990; Ribeiro 1994a); in this context, it may be salutary to recall the ambiguities of even such appealing values as "choice" and "civil society" as value-neutral objectives. This is not, contrary to the views of some critics, to argue that these are inappropriate goals or that Third World countries should be prevented from enjoying their benefits. It does mean, however, that we should question the uses to which such concepts are put by specific kinds of social and political actor. Discourse is never inert; development institutions do, after all, quite revealingly often call themselves "agencies," a term the broader implications of which often remain unchallenged.

Among the effects of such intervention may be radical shifts in the perception of identity. Cultural hybridization is a case in point (García Canclini 1990); as Gupta (1998) suggests, cultural hybridity in both identity and its associated practices may be especially characteristic of postcolonial societies, in which local actors – in his example, small farmers – attempt to recast the scientific knowledge made available to them in terms of their own experience, much of which may reveal serious flaws in the logic and benign rhetoric of the developers. Moreover, the circulation of concepts of development and modernity in Third World settings are used and transformed in the process of negotiating identities (Dahl and Rabo, eds., 1992; Pigg 1992). This is a special case, but an important one, of strategic essentialism, and – as Gupta's *Postocolonial Developments* (1998) shows with particular clarity – provides a framework for both channeling and challenging dominant views on the location and attribution of responsibility. Are "Third World" peasants really "responsible" for the desertification of huge tracts of land? Or is this the result of their inability to resist policies ultimately intended to feed the First World and to relocate the ecological damage to the Third? To what extent does the charge of irresponsibility simply reinforce the inequalities already created by development, and how far does a Third World identity make whole countries more vulnerable to this charge or, alternatively, provide them with a focal identity around which to conceptualize and organize their resistance? Clearly the rhetoric of accountability and blame plays a material role in the balance of international power: it induces specific political effects, as the unequal effects of the Rio Earth Summit (Gupta 1998: 326–329) show.

Escobar argues that the analysis of development as discourse "has succeeded in creating a sub-field, the anthropology of development" that is "producing a more nuanced view of the nature and modes of operation of development discourses than analyses of the 1980s and early 1990s at first suggested." He also argues that "the notion of 'postdevelopment' has become a heuristic for re-learning to see the reality of communities in Asia, Africa and Latin America." What happens, he asks, when we do not look at that reality through development agendas? Or we might ask whether there can exist "a way of writing (speaking and thinking) beyond the language of development" (Crush 1995: 18).

Yet this focus on three large areas of the world also requires some modification. The problems of "development" and "civil society" in eastern Europe, for example, might shed valuable light on the ideological imperatives, not to speak of the Realpolitik, that underlie "reconstruction" efforts (see Dunn and Hann, eds., 1996; Verdery 1996; Creed and Wedel 1997; Wedel 1998). The treatment of poverty in the First World under a separate rubric is also highly problematic. A truly postdevelopment perspective requires the ethnographic examination of the centers of decision-making as well as their impact on areas not normally included under the "developing nations" heading. It is a perspective that the work sketched here has already effectively initiated.

Anthropology and Development: Toward a new theory of practice and a new practice of theory

Development anthropology and the anthropology of development show each other their own flaws and limitations; it could be said that they mock each other. For development anthropologists, the critiques emanating from the new anthropology of development are morally wrong, because they are seen as leading to non-engagement in a world that desperately needs the anthropological input (Horowitz 1994). The focus on discourse is seen as overlooking issues of power, since poverty, underdevelopment, and oppression are not issues of language, but historical, political, and economic issues. In a similar vein, development anthropologists argue that such critiques are an intellectual conceit of privileged northern intellectuals and are irrelevant to the pressing concerns of the Third World (Little and Painter 1995); the fact that Third World activists and intellectuals have been at the forefront of these critiques, and that an increasing number of social movements find it empowering for their own struggles, is conveniently overlooked. For the critics, conversely, development anthropology is profoundly problematic: the very framework of "development," no less Eurocentric than its nineteenth-century evolutionist predecessors such as "civilization," has made possible a cultural politics of domination over the Third World that arguably reproduces the patterns of colonial expansion in the previous century. Even without such external forms of intervention, state-directed development programs are often responsible for the progressive impoverishment of populations that do not accept official forms of economic management. One effect of international intervention is to magnify the gaps between rich and poor, opening up huge spaces for the operation of clandestine economic activities and mafia-like structures (see, for example, Wedel 1998, for an excellent illustration in an area not normally considered under the "developing nations" heading). In Third World countries especially, the discourse of development is an instrument, not merely an after-effect, of this hegemony – a point that articulates with the larger theoretical argument adopted in this book about the materiality of discursive and symbolic forms.

The conventional framework of development studies and reports invokes essentially the same stereotypes of lazy, inefficient, or corrupt natives who must be brought to self-sufficiency that one encounters in nineteenth-century colonial discourse. Whether through increased dependency on market forces or through the suppression of political critique, the ostensibly benign and even liberating intentions of development agencies in practice most often induce a thinly disguised form of mass clientage which in turns feeds off local systems of patron–client relationships already in place. Development anthropologists – often, perhaps, inadvertently – are engaged in extending to Asia, Africa, and Latin America a project of cultural transformation shaped, broadly speaking, by the experience of capitalist modernity, but they are often abetted in this process by local social actors who similarly express benign intentions – for example, in the form of paternalistic programs of helping the less fortunate – while effectively making the security of their own interests their primary concern. Ferguson's study of rural development in Lesotho, for example, makes it abundantly clear that the nation-state framework adopted with consistent enthusiasm by development agencies serves both the political establishment and those who have a vested interest in concealing the country's dependency on larger neighbors and powerful market forces. In Lesotho this discourse obscured the historical emergence of dependency in a region once agriculturally self-sufficient and even capable of producing an impressive surplus, thereby protecting the interests of the national political establishment and consistently reproducing the poverty that development was supposed to "cure."

Working for institutions like the World Bank, and for processes of "induced development" in general, is thus part of the problem, not part of the solution (Escobar 1991). The anthropology of development makes visible the silent violence embodied in the development discourse; development anthropologists, in the eye of their critics, are not absolved from responsibility for this violence. Once again, we see that assigning accountability is a very material matter.

The debate between development anthropologists and the anthropologists of development is both epistemological and ethical. Indeed, it arguably brings the ethical commitments and dilemmas of modern social and cultural anthropology more sharply into focus than any other field. While development anthropologists focus on the project cycle, the use of knowledge to tailor projects to the beneficiaries' cultures and situation, and the possibility of contributing to the needs of the poor, the anthropologists of development center their analysis on the institutional apparatus, the links to power established by expert knowledge, the ethnographic analysis and critique of modernist constructs, and the possibility of contributing to the political projects of the subaltern.

These debates recapitulate an earlier argument within theoretical anthropology: for while functionalists such as Malinowski – an early advocate of development anthropology (1940) – sought to build respect for the peoples they studied by explaining away practices and concepts that colonial administrators dismissed as foolish and irrational, they eventually found themselves attacked as prejudiced because of their failure to account for historical process and agency; structuralists, too, initially praised for helping to demonstrate the mental unity of humankind, are now more often criticized for having reproduced the determinism inherent in structures of power and for denying the nonliterate peoples of the world genuine contemporaneity with themselves (see, e.g., Fabian 1983). Such debates illustrate the engagement of anthropology in its own history, and suggest perhaps the strongest case for an anthropology of development – that, despite the objections of those who treat the analysis of rhetoric as an unpardonable luxury, it is a necessary prelude to identifying the goals motivating specific development interventions and thereby also to predicting some, at least, of the effects of these interventions. Escobar argues that the political commitment of the anthropology of development is to focus constructively on local struggles for the right to be different and to identify the sources and goals of those who oppose such moves. An ethnographic view of these debates also requires us to see what the anthropologists themselves might gain. The stakes at play in the two approaches are indeed significantly different. For development anthropologists they range from high consultant fees and salaries to their desire to contribute to a better world; for the anthropologist of development, the stakes include academic positions and prestige as well as the political goal of contributing to transforming the world, sometimes perhaps in conjunction with local social movements. These are facts about the circumstances under which anthropologists make their career choices and determine their intellectual preferences. But speculation about the motives of particular actors is the one approach guaranteed not to make a serious contribution to the moral debate in which both sides are seriously engaged, and runs counter to anthropological method in any case.

It would be more constructive, instead, to focus on the areas of convergence that arise from a shared moral outrage at the often appalling conditions under which most human beings still live. This is a difficult move, and one that requires overcoming a history of mutual recrimination and distrust. There are, however, several trends that point in this direction, and Arturo Escobar has suggested ways of exploring these as a first step toward imagining a new practice.

A collection on languages of development (Crush, ed., 1995), for instance, takes on the challenge of analyzing the "texts and words" of development, while rejecting the proposition "that language is all there is" (Crush 1995: 5). "Many of the authors in this volume" – writes the editor in his introduction – "come out of a political economy tradition that argues that politics and economics have a real existence that is not reducible to the text that describe them and represent them" (Crush 1995: 6). He finds, nevertheless, that the textual turn, post-colonial and feminist theories, and critiques of the dominance of western knowledge systems provide crucial ways for understanding development, "new ways of understanding what development is and does, and why it seems so difficult to think beyond it" (Crush 1995: 4). Most of the geographers and anthropologists who contributed to the volume engage, to a greater or lesser extent, with the discursive analysis, even if most of them also remain within a tradition of academic political economy. An excellent further example of this openness to rhetorical analysis in the practical context of addressing pressing dilemmas is provided by Fisher's (1995) edited volume, already mentioned, on the Narmada Dam project. Here, the active authorial engagement of many of those directly involved works effectively to prevent the hijacking of insight by the partisans of one particular viewpoint.

An important argument for a convergence of development anthropology and the anthropology of development has been made by Gardner and Lewis (1996). Their point of departure is that both anthropology and development are facing a postmodern crisis, and that such a crisis can be the basis for a different relation between them. While accepting the discursive critique as valid and essential to this new relation, they nevertheless insist on the possibility of subverting mainstream development "both by supporting resistance to development and by working within the discourse to challenge and unpick its assumptions" (1996: 49). Theirs, like Fisher's, is thus an effort to build bridges between the discursive critique and concrete planning and policy practices, particularly in two arenas they find hopeful: poverty and gender. They conclude that "the use of applied anthropology, both within and outside the development industry, must continue to have a role, but in different ways and using different conceptual paradigms than previously" (Gardner and Lewis 1996: 153).

Such a shift entails, among other changes, the realization that attempts to reduce uncertainty and to create predictability in social life are doomed to failure. Fisher's point that changes may well be occurring even beyond the awareness of those most directly involved (1995: 40) may be especially relevant to such arenas as gender roles. One effect of the dominant developmental models in societies with strongly androcentric values, as Gupta (1998: 97) notes, may be to reinforce those values. At other times, however, development programs with the specific aim of reinforcing family values – in the most conservative and Eurocentric sense – may, simply by involving women in the active local-level management of projects and in political action of various kinds, challenge those values in quite radical ways, as Lynn Stephen (1997: 182–3) reports for Mexico. Attention to practice means recognizing that there is much in human life that is unpredictable and uncertain. While development projects usually aim in some sense to reduce that indeterminacy, unintended consequences can never be ruled out, and the best work on development acknowledges this as a key component of the empirical picture.

This may be clearest in the work of anthropologists who have dealt with development issues over long periods of time, and who thus have directly experienced the difficulty of predicting outcomes. With a body of work extending for almost four decades in the Chiapas region of Southern Mexico, for example, June Nash (1970, 1993a, 1997; Nash, ed., 1993b, 1995) has followed the dramatic changes that have occurred since the time of her first fieldwork experience in the late 1950s. Capitalism and development, as much as cultural resistance, have been constant factors during this period, and so have been the anthropologist's concern and growing involvement with the fate of the Chiapas communities. Her analyses have been not only essential to understanding the historical transformation of this region since pre-conquest times to the present, but extremely important in explaining the genesis of the reassertion of indigenous identity during the last two decades, of which the Zapatista uprising of the past few years represents only the most visible and dramatic manifestation (see also Stephen 1997: 13–15). Through her studies, as Escobar notes, Nash unveils a series of tensions central to the understanding of the current situation: "between change and the preservation of cultural integrity; between resistance to development and the selective adoption of innovations to maintain a degree of culture and ecological balance; between shared cultural practices and significant heterogeneity and internal class and gender hierarchies; between local boundaries and the increasing need for regional and national alliances; and between the commercialization of traditional craft production and its impact on cultural reproduction."

Already in her first major work, Nash redefined fieldwork as "participant observation combined with extensive eliciting" (Nash 1970: xxiii). This approach grew in complexity as she returned to Chiapas in the early 1990s – after fieldwork projects in Bolivia and Massachusetts – in many ways presaging the Zapatista mobilization of 1994, in which she also served as an international witness and as an observer of the negotiations between the government and the Zapatistas (see also Nash, ed., 1995). Her reading of the contemporary Chiapas situation, remarks Escobar, "suggests an alternative meaning of development in the making as the region's social movements press for a combination of cultural autonomy and democracy, on the one hand, and the construction of material and institutional infrastructure to improve local living conditions, on the other."

Such concerns with larger contexts in which local communities defend their cultures and rethink development, paralleled and extended in the work of Lynn Stephen (1997) and Kay Warren (1998), is also central for Brazilian anthropologist Gustavo Lins Ribeiro. Among his first works was a study on a classical development anthropology subject, the impact of a large-scale hydroelectric project on local communities, perhaps the most sophisticated ethnography of its kind to this date. Anticipating Fisher's incorporation of multiple voices, moreover, Ribeiro examined all concerned interest groups including – besides the local communities – developers, elites and government agencies, and the regional and transnational processes linking them together. Believing that "in order to understand what the development drama is" one needs to explain the complex structures laid down by the interaction of local and supra local frameworks (Ribeiro 1994a: xviii), he moved on to examine the emerging "condition of transnationality" and its impact on social movements and the environmental arena as a whole (Ribeiro 1994b; Ribeiro and Little 1996). In his view, new technologies are central to a raising transnational society that is best visualized in mega-media events such as rock concerts and UN world conferences such as the Earth Summit celebrated in Rio de Janeiro in 1992, which for Ribeiro marked the rite of passage to the trans-nation state. Along the way, Ribeiro shows how neoliberalism and globalization – while creating a complex political field – do not have uniform (and therefore predictable) effects and outcomes but are negotiated significantly by local actors. Focusing on the Amazon region, he examines in detail the kinds of agency fostered among local groups by the new discourses of environmentalism and globalization (Ribeiro and Little 1996).

Ribeiro's ethnography of the Brazilian environmental sector – from the government and the military to transnational and local NGOs and social movements – centers on the power struggles in which local agency and global forces become inextricably tied to each other in ways that defy any simple explanation. He is concerned to show both why prevailing development strategies and economic calculations do not work and, conversely, how Amazonian peoples, and others in Latin America, may emerge as powerful social actors shaping their destiny if they are able to craft and utilize new opportunities in the two-way local/global dynamic fostered by the condition of transnationality that is upon them. In many regards, this is also the message of Akhil Gupta's pathbreaking but perhaps more pessimistic work, in which the hybridity of postcolonial societies emerges as one of the causes of their marginalization – another demonstration that classic anthropological models for the analysis of rhetoric and symbolism, here the symbolism of exclusion and "matter out of place" because hybridity defies dominant classifications" (Douglas 1966), may be especially apposite for thinking in a critical fashion about the ways in which differential modes of access to resources are managed on a global scale.

The role of development discourses and practices in mediating between transnationality and local cultural processes is at the heart of Stacy Pigg's work in Nepal, which uses ethnography to ask what accounts for the continued existence of cultural difference and specificity today. The explanation of difference, in Pigg's hands, takes the form of an original account in which processes of development, globalization and modernity are interwoven in complex ways. For instance, contested notions of health – shamanic and western – are shown to be constitutive of social difference and local identities. "Beliefs" are not opposed to "modern knowledge" but both are fragmented and contested as people rework a variety of health notions and resources – again, a theme taken up by Gupta in his consideration of mixed forms of agricultural knowledge and practice. Similarly, while notions of development become effective in local culture, Pigg is also interested in showing how local people deploy these ideas to ends quite unintended by their originators and especially how they develop distinctive and locally adaptive idioms of healing (see Pigg 1996, 1995a, 1995b, 1992).

Political ecology – broadly speaking, the study of the interrelations among culture, environment, development, and social movements – is one of the key arenas in which development is being redefined. The work of Søren Hvalkof with the Ashéninka of the Gran Pajonal area of the Peruvian Amazon is exemplary in this regard. Perhaps better known for his critical analysis of the work of the Summer Institute of Linguistics (Hvalkof and Aaby, eds., 1981), in which the relativism underlying the search for "indigenous" modes of classifying the

environment was shown to incorporate a thoroughly Eurocentric and condescending vision of tutelary responsibilites held by European settlers toward
intellectually inert natives, Hvalkof has also conducted research ranging from
historical ethnography (Hvalkof and Veber, forthcoming) to local constructions
of nature and development (Hvalkof 1989), to theorizing political ecology as
anthropological practice (Hvalkof 1999). Equally important, Hvalkof's interventions, in coordination with the Ashéninka, have been very important in
putting pressure on the World Bank to stop its support of development projects
in Gran Pajonal and sponsor instead the collective titling of indigenous lands
(Hvalkof 1989), and in securing support from the Danish Agency for International Development for collective titling among neighboring communities in the
late 1980s. These titling projects were instrumental in reversing the situation of
virtual enslavement of indigenous people by local elites for centuries; they set
into motion processes of indigenous cultural affirmation and economic and
political control, as Escobar notes, almost unprecedented in Latin America.
Hvalkof's emphasis has been on the contrasting and interactive views of development at local and regional levels by indigenous people, mestizo colonists, and
institutional actors; conceptualizing collective land titling in a regional context
as a prerequisite for reversing genocidal policies and conventional development
strategies; documenting long-standing Ashéninka strategies for dealing with
outside exploiters – from past colonizers to today's military, coca bosses, guer-
rillas, and development experts; and providing an interface for the dialogue of
disparate worlds (indigenous people, development institutions, NGOs) from the
perspective of the indigenous communities. It is no coincidence that Hvalkof
also worked on missionary linguistics: in both fields, the work shows how
powerful players construct scenarios of indigenous passivity in order to justify
control over local communities' material, cultural, and spiritual lives. At their
most comprehensive, such practices constitute what we might call paternalistic
totalitarianism.

Thus, Hvalkof's work represents anthropology at its most critically inte-
grative. It calls for a recognition of local voices, not merely as interesting objects
of study, but, on the contrary, as participants in the task of analysis. Indeed,
in the work of the several anthropologists whose work has been discussed
here, three elements – a complex theoretical framework, significant ethnography, and political commitment – refocus the anthropology of development
as an engaged political practice. It recognizes the multiple forms of agency
entailed in all development situations. Some of this work seems relatively
judgmental, but this may be inevitable in situations where so much damage
has already taken place. On the other hand, Hvalkof's willingness to account
for the voices of all the social actors is, at the very least, more generous than
older approaches identifying only with the dominant at the expense of the
subaltern. And while attributions of motive may often be made (and may
indeed, scarcely less often, be plausible!), recording these charges and the
responses they elicit makes possible a more nuanced, fairer, and less predeter-
mined analysis and assessment. Escobar suggests that this will also permit
a rethinking of the troubled relationship between academic theorizing and

political practice, a distinction that rests on those old dualities that practice theory is intended to dissolve. This may, however, be the result of a more general turn toward greater epistemological self-awareness and toward the concomitant criticism of anthropology's colonialist heritage – a shift in which, nevertheless, the debates that have plagued anthropological approaches to development play an increasingly visible role.

Toward an Anthropology of Globalization and Postdevelopment?

Ethnographic research has been important in illuminating discourses of cultural, social, and economic difference among Third World and other communities in contexts of globalization and development. This research already suggests ways in which discourses and practices of difference could be used as the basis for alternative social and economic projects. It is true, however, as Escobar remarks, that neither the transformed anthropology of development nor Third World social movements predicated on a politics of difference will bring an end to development. The question that remains, however, is whether they can push the good intentions of some development practice to their logical conclusion – a radical restructuring of the entire range of development practices, one that would resist the global imposition of a single, industrially and militarily controlled structure to the benefit of the many over the few and of the weak over the strong. To put it in another way: will they be able to create a genuine self-sufficiency – a self-determination that does not rely on tutelary control but is genuinely participatory and open? The failures of development offer many lessons, but the question remains as to who will be in a position to learn them and what the outcome will be.

What this shift in the assessment of the nature, reach, and modes of operation of development entails for anthropological development studies is still unclear. Those working at the interface of local knowledge and conservation or sustainable development programs, for instance, are becoming increasingly adept at inducing a significant rethinking of development practice; they insist that successful and sustainable conservation can only be achieved on the basis of a careful consideration of local knowledge and practices of nature, perhaps in combination with certain (retooled) forms of expert knowledge (Escobar 1996; Brosius 1999; but cf. Gupta 1998). It might be the case that in the process anthropologists and local activists "become coparticipant in a project of resisting, representing and resisting" and that both culture and theory "become, in some measure, our joint project." As local people become adept at using cosmopolitan symbols and discourses, including anthropological knowledge, the political dimension of this knowledge becomes inescapable (Conklin and Graham 1995). But perhaps the clearest lesson of all is that any attempt to impose an overall "or subjection of local populations is doomed to failure. The persistence of the local in the face of "global" impulses is a clear illustration of this unpredictability (see

J. Watson, ed., 1997). The expropriation of local knowledge, while it might indeed "enrich the western intellectual tradition [rather than] destitute populations from which this knowledge was appropriated" (Karim 1996: 120), does not necessarily result in the homogenizing "monoculture" that the romantic Lévi-Strauss predicted for humankind 1955b; but it may provide the basis for localized forms of resistance that subvert both the intentions and interests of the developers.

Does this signify the end of development? In the context of this volume, rather than speculating about what such a question might mean, it might be more profitable to think about what the changing fortunes of development within the discipline of anthropology can tell us about the political and epistemological commitments of the discipline itself. If, as I have argued, our goal is to discommode hegemonic models of common sense, this does not mean that we can dispense with all of them, or even that we should try to dispense with most of them. Rather, in the spirit of an epistemology that respects agency and practice, we should always ask, "Who benefits? And do we wish to be identified with that choice?" Then, if we do not, we have a reason to speak out in which the academic and the political have at last become inseparable, because the pursuit of knowledge can no longer be said to lack material effects on the lives about whom that knowledge is compiled.

Accountability is an old theme in anthropology. From Evans-Pritchard's (1937) famous investigations of Zande witchcraft and blame, to more recent studies of gossip and the blood feud and on to still more recent investigations of bureaucracy and political rhetoric, the social organization of responsibility has been central to our understanding of how human beings account for their predicaments and burdens. In the reflexive shift that anthropology has now undergone, any refusal to turn its searching gaze – its ethnographic gaze – on our own understandings and management of development issues would be, in a word, irresponsible. That holds as true for the management of the material environment as it does for the treatment of subaltern populations. That the respective goals engaged in these two areas sometimes come into serious conflict is a key theme of the next chapter.

Notes

1   To begin with, development anthropology has developed a significant institutional basis in a number of countries in North America and Europe. A "Development Anthropology Committee," for instance, had been created in 1977 in the United Kingdom "to promote the involvement of anthropology in development in the Third World" (Grillo 1985: 2). (For a survey of development anthropology in Europe, see the special issue of *Development Anthropology Network* 10 [1], 1992, devoted to the topic.) In 1976, three anthropologists created the Institute for Development Anthropology in Binghamton, New York; since its inception, the Institute has been a leading place for development anthropology theory and applied work. Similarly, graduate training in development anthropology is now offered at a growing number

of universities, especially in the United States and Britain. But the most significant reassessment of Hoben's position has come from leading practitioners in the 1990s, like Cernea (1995) and Horowitz (1994), who consider that while the number of anthropologists in development is still small in relation to the task, development anthropology nevertheless is well on the way to becoming consolidated as both discipline and practice.

8

Environmentalisms

A Paradigmatic Practice?

Anthropologists are beset by two dualisms above all: culture and society on the one hand, culture and nature on the other. The first pair represents the twin dimensions of what anthropologists study; while the emphasis has shifted between the two terms, it is clear that they are mutually dependent in much the same degree as are "structure" and "agency." Large-scale social formations like nation-states substitute cultural identity for social relations as the basis of solidarity, but the relationship between them remains an inescapable fact of analysis.

The nature–culture pair offers challenges of another kind. Anthropologists are heirs to an old European tradition of viewing the "noble savage" in a "natural" setting that resists the corruption of urbanity and modernity. Even anthropologists of a scientist bent have also recognized the fundamentally cultural character of what we take to be "natural," from social conventions (R. Rappaport 1979: 238) to "national character" – two concepts that it has been a central task of the discipline to dissect critically. But anthropology's own distinction between nature and culture, celebrated in Lévi-Straussian structuralism (Lévi-Strauss 1963) and focalized by feminist debates about "nature and nurture" (e.g., Ortner and Whitehead eds. 1981), has a distinctive cultural history of its own. At least some anthropologists would argue that it does not exist in certain societies (e.g., P. Dwyer 1996; Ingold 1996).[1] For others, made aware of the concept's utility to advance their own agendas of self-determination and able to frame their own culture as nevertheless closer to and more respectful of "nature" (see Tweedie forthcoming), cultural self-assertion resist the demands of an often heavily western-directed environmentalism.

There is an irony in this, in that the duality of nature and culture may itself be a largely western invention. As Kay Milton points out, however, it is not even always an accurate representation of western views – in which, as Roy Ellen (1996) has emphasized, nature may both include and exclude what is human. An example of inclusion is the claim made by some environmental activists, that humanity is part of nature and human activities and their consequences are subject to natural laws. An example of exclusion is the view, popular among some other environmentalists, that human activity intrudes on a pristine (or at least "clean") nature, and that such "artificial" works are usually detrimental to its grand design. This second perspective has an evil cousin: the relegation of all urban culture and its bearers to the status of corruption and filth, a view that led to the framing of indigenous peoples as "noble savages" at first encounter, only to be condemned by their conquerors for the corrupting effects of those same conquerors' presence, and eventually to the condemnation of some urban populations – notably the Jews under Nazi rule (see Mosse 1985) – as beyond redemption, corrupted by their "nature" in quite another sense.

The case of the corrupted noble savage is especially interesting in the present context. Those who exemplified pure savagery were thought to live so close to nature that they were effectively part of it. They were wild and rude, but not fundamentally evil: they were unformed rather than unreformable. Once they had been hybridized by contact, however, they became a source of deep unease. As we shall see toward the end of this chapter, the resulting attitude has resulted in the widespread marginalization of poverty-stricken Third World peoples in our own time: their refusal to stay in a ghetto of "natives," coupled with their supposedly pernicious refusal to adopt "scientific" knowledge in an equally suppositious pure form, renders them a threat to dominant modes of classification.

Classification has long been a topic of deep interest to anthropologists (e.g., Durkheim and Mauss 1963). Its centrality to understanding human activity and the culturally specific understanding of "common sense" lay at the heart of the structuralist revolution. It also informs many of the attempts, briefly discussed in this chapter, to understand the world – natural and cultural – from local perspectives. It is the conceptual basis of the rhetoric, or symbolism, whereby people deal on common grounds with the experienced realities of their daily lives.

Anthropology, to be sure, has its own classifications. Yet anthropologists have not always been very willing to be analyzed as they analyze others. Indeed, much of the work done by anthropologists on ecological matters has, in accordance with a realist model of the material world, treated questions of rhetoric and politics as secondary. In keeping with the larger framework of this book, by contrast, I follow Kay Milton's lead here in focusing on these more conceptual and rhetorical matters (including the politics of environmentalism) rather than on assessing the methods of anthropological approaches to ecology as such. There are several reasons for this: the importance of reading various programs of reform (and the role of the anthropologists whose work informs these) in their cultural and social contexts; the fact that much of the work on "the environment" fails to account for such contextual concerns; and the relationship between the politics of environmentalism and that of development. This strategy will make possible a more critical reading of cultural approaches to the environment, and should lead to a productive questioning of anthropology's ongoing concerns in this area.

In short, this approach is an attempt to situate environmentalism and anthropology within a common framework, in order to examine the larger implications of their mutual engagement. In one major respect, modern environmentalism departs radically from anthropology. Although both ultimately emerged from the universalist philosophy of the Enlightenment, anthropology is grounded in a more particularistic consideration of local worlds and is today deeply suspicious of any claims to universal validity. On the other hand, the benign but universalizing rhetoric of environmentalism may disguise both its more exploitative aspects and may also ride roughshod over cultural imperatives seen by their bearers as no less exigent or morally compelling than those of planetary survival.

For the Makah of the Northwest Coast of the United States, for example, who recently won back the right to hunt whales in the context of traditional ritual activities, the fundamental question boils down to a choice: do the whales survive, or do we? And if we hunt whales within the constraints of our existing and traditional practices, would this actually lead to their extinction? For the Makah themselves, such questions are also inseparable from the politics of cultural repatriation (Tweedie forthcoming); so it seems at the very least unfair of those who have despoiled their culture to be using arguments about the environment in order to restrict that culture again today – a point that is echoed in Gupta's (1998) assessment of peasant reactions to development in India. Given, too, that hunting among many native peoples of North America is imbued with deep respect for the prey (see D. Smith 1998), the economistic accounting of European-derived environmentalisms may be profoundly offensive as well as inadequately calibrated to the realities of local social practice and to the actual effect on the environment. Indeed, such conflicts raise the question of what we mean by "the environment" in a compellingly cross-cultural way.

It is thus all the more important both to explore the relationship between particular societies and their environments and to treat environmentalism today as the product of a particular moment in a range of different cultural and social settings. This will enable us to avoid the evolutionist implication that we are at last arriving at a formulation of the planet's environmental needs that is supracultural and that responds rationally to the material needs of all its peoples.

The story of ways of understanding the relationship between society and environment traces out the vicissitudes of determinism in anthropological theory more generally. Early attempts to establish sweeping correlations between ecological conditions and social arrangements did not hold for long; "possibilism" (which focused on constraints rather than on causes) left too much unexplained; and Marvin Harris's (1974) attempt to explain all social institutions as rationally adaptive did not adequately either address the besetting issue of teleology or furnish clear evidence that other modes of causal explanation should be considered inferior. Indeed, his rationalization of food taboos, to take one example, nicely captured the scientistic rhetoric of much modern "folk" epistemology in western societies, but did not effectively respond to more "symbolic" explanations such as those of Mary Douglas (1966) – explanations that could in fact also explain his own model by treating "scientific" ideas about pollution as symbolic constructions. Clearly, too, such explanations can also be applied to the bureaucratic management of environmental concerns as well as to the language in which those concerns are framed.

A central reason for the latter failure is symptomatic of larger issues within the discipline. The attempt to explain the Hindu ban on beef consumption exemplifies this difficulty. From a western, economistic perspective, it is no doubt true that the conservation of the resources provided by a plow animal would seem rational. But this does not alone account for the greater inclination of some cultures than of others to practice such useful self-denial. Are we to deduce that some cultures are objectively more rational than others? Any such assumption is necessarily circular because it grants analysts the right to sit in judgment on the cultures of the world, ranking them in a hierarchy of adherence to the principles of pure reason while remaining exempt from such judgement themselves.

The cultural ecology approach is in fact flawed by the assumptions of functionalism as well as of ethnocentrism. It rests on a teleological assumption not unlike Malinowski's assumption that social institutions served the purposes of satisfying the collective psychological needs of a population: that institutional practices regulating the availability of foodstuffs and of the other necessities of life must serve the population's rational adaptation to its environmental resources. This position reproduces the teleological weaknesses of earlier functionalism by presupposing purpose where in fact only effect can be identified. Roy Rappaport (1979: 48–58) stoutly defended both this and related approaches against the charge of reproducing the biases of functionalism, but the residue of his defense would appear to be that these approaches only explain some dimensions of social life, some of the time, and always after the fact.

Not coincidentally, I suggest, these approaches are also broadly consistent with some of the most powerful forms of development intervention. From the perspective of a universalist logic, the rationality of ecological adaptation harmonized perfectly with the designs of apparently well-intentioned development agencies – much as the functionalist arguments of Malinowski, for all their circular teleology, at least had the virtue of countering colonial ideas about the fundamental irrationality of natives.

But such formulations remain flawed for one simple reason: they continue to locate the capacity for universal reasoning in the minds of authoritative interpreters, thereby reinforcing the power of international agencies to exercise control over local social actors by telling them where their interests lie, and brooking little or no disagreement (see Ferguson 1990). They effectively ghettoize local knowledge by refusing to acknowledge the experiential basis on which it fuses preexisting ideas about the natural world with imported, scientific concepts and practices (Gupta 1998: 213). That intellectual apartheid springs from the conceptual separation of "their" ideas from "ours." At least Rappaport's model of "cognized worlds," while separating native from intrusive scientific knowledge, also recognized the possibility of a considerable overlap between them (1979: 97). And we should also recognize, as Kay Milton has reminded me in the course of our discussions of this chapter, that it would be irresponsible to act as though there were no environment to be protected – an obvious point, perhaps, but one that is apt to get lost in the furor of political debate. We may ask which version of the environment should be protected from whom and what, and on whose behalf – these are, after all, fundamentally anthropological questions. But at the end a planet facing potentially devastating destruction may be a more demanding and urgent customer than those who inhabit it; for they cannot do without it. Thus, while issues of development often concern potentially negotiable distributions of wealth, the earth may not offer us that luxury. At the same time, however, we must also remember that some developmentalists will invoke the rhetoric of environmental stewardship as a justification for what we may find to be objectionable interventions. (Parenthetically, it is worth noting that in wealthy countries politicians are happy to discover the environment as a theme when this is fashionable, but tend to draw back in dismay at the first sign that the resulting policies might reduce voters' habitual comforts.)

Discussions of the environment frequently end up as debates about stewardship, and especially about who has the capacity or the right to exercise that stewardship. To understand this political dimension is not necessarily to slight the good intentions of many of those with whom I will take issue in the pages that follow, but it is to recognize that all scholarly intervention takes place in a political context – under conditions, usually, of unequal power. In that context, the classification of different forms of knowledge becomes rather more than a reflexive exercise in the ethnography of scholarship, although it is that also; it is a critical examination of the ways in which that scholarship contributes to, or undermines, the political order of specific times and places.

Ecological Puppets: The story of environmental determinism

Throughout much of its hundred-year history, as Milton observes, ecological anthropology has been dominated by one simple idea: that the features of human society and culture can be explained in terms of the environments in which they have developed. This notion, which cedes little or nothing to the possibility of agency and informed decision-making among the majority of the world's peoples, has its counterparts in widespread popular ideas about the relationship between personality and climate, for example, and harmonizes, along with ideas about blood and heredity, with the logic of Darwinian theory (Greenwood 1984). It often receives "scientific" validation in various nationalistic ideologies, where its early articulation by Hippocrates (Greenwood 1984: 74) has helped to secure the widespread notion that "national character" is in part the outcome of climate. There is some evidence to suggest that the persistence of such ideas in the popular imagination was linked to that of humoral theory – the model of bodily properties to which local-level Indian interpretations of environmental change are still sometimes attributed by scholars anxious to distinguish "indigenous" from "scientific" forms of knowledge (see Gupta 1998: 20). Such ideas die hard: southern European peoples, for example, often accuse their northern neighbors of being "cold" and champion their own "warmth" as an acceptable substitute for efficiency; the moral economy of stereotypes demonstrates the ease with which such classifications of humankind take hold and endure.

Another factor sustaining the popularity of this kind of environmental determinism lay in the possibility it afforded of sidestepping highly fraught debates, as they were in the nineteenth century, about the truthfulness of the biblical account of human genesis. Even a literal reading of Genesis could accommodate the view that climatic differences preceded the arrival of human beings on earth, and this lent climatic explanations of human difference enormous appeal. As early as the sixteenth century, for example, Jean Bodin elaborated a theory of environmental determinism that was in many respects the predecessor of later discourses about "national character." Even before the end of the sixteenth century, moreover, it even came to serve as the basis for northern – specifically, English – claims to scholarly preeminence, since a cool climate was thought to be especially conducive to intelligent reflection (see Hodgen 1964: 276–90); it seems to echo in the assumption, never entirely eradicated, that "natives" could not achieve the objectivity and detachment necessary for studying their own cultures. Given the intensification of debates about the origin of the human race in the nineteenth century and the call in early twentieth-century diffusionism to calibrate the spread of cultural influences with changes in their style and content, this variety of environmental determinism proved spectacularly hardy.

Early environmental determinism, or "anthropogeography" (Geertz 1963: 1–2), thus grew out of a popular matrix, itself formalized and elaborated by Renaissance and Enlightenment philosphers and travelers. In its academic guise, in which it emerged at roughly the same time as diffusionism, it was an attempt to gauge the type and distribution of cultural features from maps showing environmental information. Among its leading exponents, O. T. Mason (1896) sought correlations between natural features and human technologies, while Ellsworth Huntington (1924) saw climate as the main influence in the development of whole civilizations, including characteristics such as religious beliefs and rituals as well as material culture.

The emergence of sustained ethnography, especially in the work of Boas and Malinowski, made such generic determinism empirically untenable. Milton notes that numerous aspects of social life – systems of exchange, marriage rules, kinship terminologies, political institutions, and much else – varied unpredictably within areas whose topography and climate were relatively uniform. "Whatever role environmental factors played in the formation of human cultures," she remarks, "it clearly was not as straightforwardly deterministic as the early theorists had imagined." Despite the desire to put anthropology on a scientific, model-building basis, moreover, the close encounters of ethnography meant that individual variation began to belie claims of local cultural homogeneity. While concepts of agency and practice were slow to emerge,

Malinowski's *A diary in the strict sense of the term* (1967) shows that he was acutely aware of personal differences of temperament and style. Even Evans-Pritchard's (1940) notorious wisecrack about "Nuerosis" – the effects he attributed to living among a people he found to be totally committed to prevarication in responding to his questions – could not override the evidence of significant differences among the Nuer he knew, while his account of "oecology" in the same work is only deterministic in the sense that it suggests that a transhumant people had to adapt to the exigencies of climate for practical reasons of sheer survival – a perspective that had already gained widespread acceptance through Marcel Mauss's influential essay on Inuit forms of sociability and seasonal migration (1979).

This perspective, which linked particular social forms to the necessities imposed by environmental constraints, begged far fewer questions, and seemed much more compatible with the evidence of the new styles of careful, long-term ethnographic observation. As a result, environmental determinism took a weaker form. The new idiom, often called "possibilism," was more concerned with the ways in which environmental conditions restricted the range of cultural and social change than with the unprovable contention that climate actually determined such change. It seemed reasonable to point out, for example, that climatic conditions dictated the distribution of maize-growing economies in North America (Kroeber 1939), and that the presence of tsetse flies limited the distribution and migration patterns of cattle herders in Africa (Stenning 1957). Yet this very reasonableness is also the weakness of the approach: it only provides after-the-fact explanations, and thus reproduces the anemic quality of late functionalism – scientist expectations that theories would prove to have high predictive utility look rather shabby when it turns out that they can only instruct by hindsight. The specific forms of culture, as Milton notes, all remained largely untouched by possibilism. In this respect, I would add, it shared a striking limitation with experimental archaeology (the methodology of reproducing artifacts as a means of discovering the techniques through which the originals were made): its proponents could suggest what might have happened, and they could perhaps show what could never have happened, but they could not demonstrate either precisely what had in fact occurred, nor could they ever be sure that the same constraints would always produce the same or similar effects. Advocates of possibilism could thus point to its heuristic potential for suggesting – "discovering" might be too ambitious a word – specific kinds of adaptation to local environments. Having backed away from fully-fledged determinism, however, they were in no position to offer a comprehensive explanation of society and culture – the "nomothetic goal" of anthropology as conceived by Radcliffe-Brown and his admirers.

Cultural Ecology and Cultural Materialism

A more rigorous attempt to pursue this goal was not long in arriving on the scene, in the form of "cultural ecology." Julian Steward (1955), the pioneer of this approach, criticized possibilism for assigning the environment too passive a role in human affairs, and sought a more detailed and sensitive ecological analysis than earlier approaches had provided. Steward assumed that cultural features evolved as adaptations to their local environments and that, within any one culture, there was a complex of features more directly influenced by environmental factors than others, the set he called the "cultural core" (Steward 1955: 37). Reciprocally, in Milton's succinct summary, Steward "moved from the crude anthropogeographic formula of, 'environments shape cultures', to a more refined, 'specific environmental factors shape particular cultural features'." Steward's more nuanced and less heavily deterministic model called for close empirical observation, and thus also harmonized better with the now well-established centrality of ethnographic method. It called for specific observation of the use of technology in the exploitation of environmental resources as the starting-point for a comprehensive analysis of the associated patterns of behavior and the influence of these patterns on other cultural features (Steward 1955: 40–1).

Milton suggests an ethnographic illustration that reveals both the logic and the weaknesses of this approach. This is provided by Holy's analysis of changing inheritance patterns among the Toka of Zambia (Holy 1977, 1979). The Toka live in settled agricultural communities, growing millet, maize, and other crops, and, in those parts of their territory where the tsetse fly is not a problem, they also keep cattle. This enables them to cultivate their fields using a plow drawn by oxen, a form of technology introduced in the 1920s and 1930s. This observation corresponds to the first stage in Steward's methodology: a specific environmental factor, the absence of the tsetse fly, permits the use of a particular type of technology, the ox-drawn plow.

The use of the plow requires a team of people each of whom is skilled in a different task. One person drives the oxen from behind, one leads them from in front and one operates the plow itself. A fourth person, always a woman in Toka tradition, walks behind the plow sowing the seed. In addition, the oxen themselves have to be trained, a task for which the villagers lend oxen to each other and which takes three years. Efficiency in plowing thus requires access to several scarce resources: a plow, a team of skilled individuals, and a team of trained oxen. A large and comparatively wealthy household is able to provide these resources for itself, and is therefore able to maintain a degree of independence from kin and neighbors. More commonly, however, households cooperate with each other, creating plowing teams the composition of which is more or less stable from one season to the next. This observation corresponds to Steward's second step: the use of a particular type of technology, the ox-drawn plow, has generated a specific pattern of behavior, cooperation among households in the formation of plowing teams.

The third element in the Toka story is a shift away from their traditional matrilineal norm of inheritance (in which wealth was passed from mother's brother to sister's son), to a situation in which patrilineal inheritance (from father to son) has become acceptable. This has resulted from the cooperation of fathers and sons in plowing. A son may become a member of his father's plowing team at quite an early age, beginning with the simpler tasks. By the time he marries and establishes an independent household (usually close to that of his father), he may be competent at the most difficult task of operating the plow. This is a marketable skill, and he may prefer to plow other people's fields for money than to continue as part of his father's team. In order to get his own fields plowed for as little cost as possible, it is in a father's interest to keep his son's cooperation; one way of doing this is to promise that he will eventually inherit the plow and the oxen needed to drive it. Such a promise, while it conflicts with the traditional norm of matrilineal inheritance, is in accordance with another guiding principle in Toka culture: that those who contribute to the production of economic wealth should share in its benefit. Thus the third step in Steward's methodology is the observation that the behavior patterns required to operate a particular form of technology have affected another cultural feature – in this case, the pattern of inheritance.

In examining this case study, we encounter the major problems with Steward's concept of the cultural core. He apparently wished to deny that the lines of environmental determinism ran through whole cultures. For Steward, only those cultural features that are determined by environmental factors were of primary significance. But in the Toka case it is hard to see where the cultural core would end and what Steward called "secondary features" (Steward 1955: 37) begin. It appears, as Milton acknowledges, that the use of the plow, the formation of plowing teams, the changing relationships between fathers and sons, and the changing patterns of inheritance can all be traced back to the absence of the tsetse fly. As she goes on to argue, however, the changing inheritance norms will almost certainly have had further impacts, on relationships between mothers' brothers and sisters' sons, for instance, and consequently on relationships between siblings. Do these features, also apparently traceable to the same environmental influence, belong to the cultural core? It is easy to see, once the interconnectedness of cultural features is taken into account, that the core is always in danger of dissolving into the whole (Ellen 1982: 61).

Marvin Harris's "cultural materialism" retained the concept of adaptation as the central explanatory, but it does so in a reductionist fashion: for Harris, all cultural practices serve this fundamentally functionalist teleology (M. Harris 1968). Harris's argument may certainly help to explain why some practices and professions of belief were retained: for example, in his famous analysis of the Hindu taboo against eating beef (M. Harris 1974), his argument that it conserves resources vital to collective survival – cattle are important in providing milk, as labor for plowing and carrying loads, and in providing dung for fertilizer, fuel, and floor coverings – may indeed suggest a key reason for its durability. Here again, however, this type of explanation can never be more than an after-the-fact rationalization. In this sense, Harris's approach belongs to a category of folk explanation that is widespread in the West, where its legitimation as "science" has earned it considerable currency. This is the view, which also has its roots in social Darwinism (the survival of the adaptively fittest), that only those societies that practice rational management of their resources will be able to survive in their local environments.

It is, to be sure, entirely possible that some societies may have observed the benefits of conserving a key resource just as they may have noted the ill effects of consuming prohibited foods. The parallel with pseudomedical explanations is revealing, for such piecemeal analyses of specific cases will not serve to explain why, for example, pork is forbidden to Jews and Muslims but not to other peoples who dwell in equally hot and perhaps more humid climates and who appear to have suffered no ill effects. Similarly, they fail to account for supposedly "irrational" practices that deplete environmental resources. Ponting, for example argues that the inhabitants of Easter Island endangered their own survival by using up their timber resources for the erection of large stone statues for ritual purposes. This ritual activity apparently intensified as the danger increased – thereby, so the argument goes, hastening their demise (Ponting 1991: 1–7). This may indeed have been the causal connection in this specific instance, but it undermines Harris's rather extreme claim that all cultural phenomena can be explained in terms of rational choices.

To take an example that nicely bridges the dietary and ecological examples just discussed, the Fore of New Guinea were being seriously depleted by a form of encephalic disease (*kuru*), which was spread through the ritual practice of eating the brains of deceased relatives. The Fore did not adapt to the threat by abandoning this tradition; they only did so when central authority forced the issue (see Keesing 1981). Lest this be taken as evidence that such people are in fact irrational, let us also note the serious medical effects of mid-twentieth century American food preferences for fatty beef, the ecological consequences of the industrial demand for fluorocarbons, and the high risks associated with "safe" nuclear power – all cases in which large segments of the population, informed of the risks, chose to support continuing with the same practices. It is a strange claim to universal rationality that would explain these instances away as "acceptable risk."

Any attempt to push Harris's mode of analysis beyond an ad hoc explanation of specific cases must by definition be deterministic in a sense that, as Milton notes, exceeds the more modest explanatory role proposed for ecology by Steward. It also suffers from the weakness – as the earlier discussion of epistemology suggests it must be – of positing a universal rationality, accessible to wise anthropologists even when the people they were studying could not perceive it. Such objections undermined the claims of cultural ecology, and led to more nuanced approaches. Milton explains this shift in terms of the growing interest in individual and collective choice, a move initiated by, among others, Edmund Leach, and largely explicit in the "transactionalism" (e.g., Kapferer, ed., 1976) of some other researchers and in the shift away from the search for universal laws and toward an appreciation of historical process. The gradual emergence of an orientation toward practice – toward the emergence of structure in the actual performance of social relations and cultural forms – led anthropologists to perceive (as we see in the chapters on politics and cosmologies) that determinism was more often a fact of authoritarian politics than of either social relations or physical environment. This becomes especially germane when we examine developers' and environmentalists' claims to represent the march of progress, since anthropologists are in an especially critical position to ask who stands to benefit from such inbuilt teleologies.

In the next phase of ecological anthropology, scholars appeared to pay closer attention to the hearts and minds of local actors. True, as Milton says, the focus now shifted to understanding local conceptual systems. Here, in fact, the danger lay in a more concealed form of determinism: it was as though the desire to understand local forms of knowledge gave analysts direct access to what local actors were actually thinking. But note that this is a confusion of thought (an internal psychological activity) with its exterior representation (a public, or social, act). Social actors were not recognized as individuals, but were treated as though their thought was entirely determined by preexisting modes of thought. Ecological anthropology converged on this point with the rapidly developing study of systems of classification by linguistic anthropologists (see Fabian 1983: 98). It is no accident that one of the key critics of this approach to classification, Søren Hvalkof, proved to be no less scathing in his view of development programs and their appropriation of the natural environment.

Reactions and Divergences

On the other hand, some scholars – notably Emilio Moran (1981, 1990) – have argued passionately for the recognition that local societies are engaged in ongoing processes of mutual adaptation with the environment. Their approach has the virtue of emphasizing the specificity of local worlds and of showing serious respect for local knowledge, and grows out of a commitment to integrating the results of ethnographic research with the larger-scale analyses conducted by agronomists and environmental scientists. Thus, for example, Moran was able to demonstrate that top-down, government-directed projections for the development of agriculture along the Transamazon Highway were sometimes disastrously optimistic, but discerned at the local level "numerous success stories of individuals who, with limited means, achieved remarkable results, and who provide insight into the strategies that may work in creating productive environmental systems" that do not require continuing and dangerous deforestation or the genocidal destruction of aboriginal peoples (Moran 1981: 229).

Of particular importance here is the acknowledgment that most environmental issues are affected by quite small-scale activities and natural events. For Moran (1981: 227), many of the failures of conservation along the Amazon have arisen as a result of overgeneralization – a failure to recognize the inapplicability of locally generated insight to large-scale environmental protection and development. In an ironic anticipation of recent anthropological work that attacks the older model of remote and isolated societies, Moran suggests that macro-level analysis can capture some of the larger effects of environmental change without either reducing it to the sum of all local processes or reducing local circumstances to a mere reflection of the larger picture (Morań 1981: 228). Moran also correctly identifies the resistance of authoritarian bureaucracies to the kinds of local-level concern that careful ethnography can more effectively represent (Moran 1981: 226).

Moran's approach is an extension of the "ecosystem model" as developed by Roy Rappaport (1971: 238), who preferred to view the human–environment relationship, not as a unidirectional determinism, but as a system of material exchanges leading, as some tried to show, to a situation of "homeostasis" – that is, of environmental equilibrium (see Ellen 1982: 74). This required ecological anthropologists to measure and compare such things as the dietary values of different foods, the impact on soil fertility of different modes of cultivation, the energy expended in types of human activity, the environmental impacts of domestic animals, and so on. Unfortunately, however, Rappaport's approach meant that culture largely lost its distinctive significance: the killing of a deer by a lion and its death at the hands of human hunters become virtually identical because their effects are identical. "It does not, from the eco-systemic point of view, matter that the behavior of the men is cultural and the behaviour of the lion is not," remarks Rappaport (1971: 242). While he later came to acknowledge the importance of individual strategies in the performance of culturally defined roles – "if only," as he somewhat testily remarked, "to avoid fruitless argument" – his specifically ecological explanations of cultural phenomena largely concerned quantitative issues, such as the pig herd size his Tsembaga Maring informants deemed sufficient to perform a ritual involving sacrifice and food distribution (1979: 51). While he was quick to reject the label of functionalist, and while he was deeply interested in the semiotic aspects of ritual, his classic study of ritual and warfare among this highland New Guinea people was heavily oriented toward material and quantitative concerns.

In that it explores the relationships among ritual activity, food production and consumption, and the constraints and possibilities of a local ecology, his work (R. Rappaport 1968) is a major demonstration – perhaps the most comprehensive to have been attempted – of the ecosystem approach to cultural values and especially to the ritualized political practices associated with war and peace. Tsembaga communities had experienced alternating periods of peace and hostility with their neighbors. During hostilities, each community was assisted by its allies from the surrounding area. When the hostilities ended, pigs were sacrificed and their meat distributed to the allies in thanks for their help. Bigger ceremonies of thanks preceded the resumption of hostilities a few years later. What triggered these ceremonies was the size of the pig herds. Heavily reduced by the sacrifice that ended the hostilities, the herds increased again during the subsequent peace. Eventually they would become so numerous that the women found it difficult to look after them or to prevent them from damaging neighbors' gardens and eating crops intended for human consumption. The community would then decide to hold its final feast of thanks, triggering the next period of hostility. This cycle of alternating periods of hostility and truce, with transitions marked by pig feasts, facilitated the distribution of resources, including energy derived from both plant and animal food, among the human population and between humans and pigs.

In the ecosystem approach, Rappaport and his followers treated humans as organisms engaged in material exchanges with other components of their ecosystems. This called for new skills: "a generation of anthropologists, trained in ecology and systems theory, [now] went to the field to measure the flow of energy through the trophic levels of the ecosystems of which humans were but a part" (Moran 1990: 13). At the same time, Rappaport and Moran both recognized the relevance of understanding how local actors made decisions that affected actual outcomes. The conceptual and the material emerge in a dialectical relationship – what we might more appropriately call dynamic feedback – that foreshadows the mutual entailment of agency and structure in contemporary theories of practice. In Moran's work especially, this becomes the groundwork for trying to develop sustainable futures through the ethnographic enlightenment of those charged with that task (Moran 1981: 213–30; see also R. Rappaport 1971: 264).

Although Milton is inclined to see them as separate and divergent developments, the ecosystems approach shared considerable common ground with the study of local systems of knowledge ("ethnoecology") that emerged at roughly the same time. That common ground, at which I have already hinted, is ideological and political as much as it is epistemological: the study of "emic" categories – also known as "cognitive anthropology" (Tyler 1969) – created an invidious distinction between univeralist, scientific "ecology" and a set of "ethnoecologies" that belong to particular cultural traditions and are valid only in the context of those traditions.

Milton raises an important methodological objection to this distinction: "to ask how a particular category of things is classified is to assume that it is classified." Even though later work focused more on the actual uses of such terms than on their formal elicitation, however, the assumption that the organization of local knowledge can be mapped in its entirety from linguistic cues is misleading. Some anthropologists, revealingly all scholars with a powerful commitment to the ecosystems concept (e.g., Boehm 1984), labeled it as the "elicitation" of "natural" usage, thereby betraying their enduring entanglement to the logic of Enlightenment theories about the noble savage and their equally enduring commitment to a scientistic mode of anthropological analysis.

Moreover, earlier ethnolinguistic scholarship also presupposed a passive population that needed enlightened westerners to lead it to full understanding. This view, which has discernible points of origin in missionary ideology and practice, was in fact especially notable in the work of linguists exploring native languages in order to translate the Gospels into them – an activity closely linked, in Latin America, with hegemonic development programs (Hvalkof and Aaby 1981; see also Fabian 1983: 97–104; Herzfeld 1987: 87). The separation of "material" from "symbolic" approaches thus cloaked their sometimes common purpose. Some of the more sensitive scholars recognized that this separation was artificial and intellectually suspect (e.g., Rappaport 1979: 45). But that did not prevent others from perpetuating it in the defense of a scientistic vision of anthropology – a vision that in practice, if perhaps not always in intent, was grounded in the politics of religious and economic domination.

Cultural Relativism and its Implications

The investigation of emic principles was a by-product of one of the key principles guiding anthropological thought ever since it began to turn against the racism of the armchair evolutionists early in the twentieth century. That principle was cultural relativism, of which Kay Milton writes: "Like many key ideas, it has several meanings, two of which have had particular theoretical significance. First, cultural relativism has been taken to mean that cultures can only properly be understood 'in their own terms' (Holy and Stuchlik 1981: 29), in other words, that a culture cannot be properly understood in terms of ideas imported from another culture. Second, cultural relativism has been taken to mean that all cultures are equally valid interpretations of reality, that they are all equally true." The latter perspective, which in its extreme forms also means accepting such horrors as genocide as acceptable if they can be shown to be culturally grounded, is problematic at best. It would appear, as Milton shows, to be a misreading of the idea that all worldviews are socially constructed; the idea that even facts are representations, a concept rooted in the writings of Vico, does not necessarily lead to the conclusion that all facts correspond to our perceptual experience of the world around us in the same degree.

Milton points out that anthropology – with its commitment to comparative analysis – cannot afford to accept this extreme rendition of cultural relativism. As she says, "if anthropology is to be able to study the contemporary world, it has to be able to address global issues, but it would have little chance of doing so if it were tied to the idea that cultures are separate entities (cf. Appadurai 1990; Hannerz 1990)." This is the same reasoning that, in linguistic anthropology, has undermined the more extreme forms of the so-called Sapir–Whorf hypothesis, the view that language provides the forms that enable and constrain thought: if we extend that argument to the view that (a) we cannot understand another culture unless we grow up speaking its language, so that (b) only a "native" of the culture can ever understand it, the whole anthropological enterprise collapses, and the very possibility of intercultural understanding with it. Yet it is clear that this has not happened.

It is central to the argument of this book that all the observable aspects of human life are material. While it is true that we only know reality through the mediation of signs, this does not mean that there is no reality there. A pragmatic approach demands rejecting as irrelevant the hypothetical possibility that the realities we experience might not be "really there." This is where anthropology perhaps most dramatically departs from philosophy, with its broad – and often culturally narrow – generalizations. Ingold (1982) argues that the logic of social constructivism is flawed because constructions require raw material. To make his argument work, however, we must also recognize the materiality of such supposedly epiphenomenal matter as speech, ritual, and symbolism. The speech act theory of language, extended to the whole range of human expression, sidesteps this false dichotomy between the real and the ideal, or the material and the symbolic. And it makes demonstrably good sense: rhetoric clearly does have effects in the world of politics, as I have already noted.

The extreme constructivist doctrine, says Milton, thus "recognizes no mechanism through which the external environment can enter people's knowledge." Ingold (1992) has suggested that we solve this problem by distinguishing between perception and interpretation. People perceive their environment directly, as they engage with it in various ways (by walking through a forest searching for food plants, by harvesting a crop, by looking at the moon). They then reflect on that information, and share it – or refuse to share it – with others. The variation in the degree of effectiveness with which the information is conveyed then might in turn explain how some scholars came to give up on the possibility of genuinely empirical knowledge.

The challenge to extreme cultural relativism is particularly important for the practical application of anthropological knowledge. Even extreme cultural relativists, like idealists who doubt the existence of a material world, act as if their particular worldview were true; they must do so in order to act at all. Recognition of this ironic predicament, Milton reminds us, equips anthropologists to make a serious contribution to understanding the practical problems of the social and material environment – and to do so, we might add, in ways that nonetheless resist silly reductionism of the kind that politicians so often favor as a "quick fix."

This point can be illustrated with reference to a contemporary environmental issue. In Milton's words: "Scientists say that the world is getting warmer, and that human activities, specifically those which release certain gases into the atmosphere, are causing this to happen. But, as we know, the scientific view is just one among many cultural perspectives on the world. Other cultural perspectives may deny that global warming is happening, or, if they accept it, may attribute it to the actions of spirits, or a divine creator. Or, accepting some degree of human responsibility, they may regard it as retribution, imposed by some higher authority, for the failure of their society to maintain its ancient traditions. Each interpretation suggests a different solution: to reduce carbon emissions, to appease the spirits or to revive the ancient traditions. An approach which treats all cultural perspectives as equally true has no basis for choosing between them, and therefore cannot select a solution. In the face of global warming, and in the face of any problem, an extreme cultural relativist is paralysed by logic. By taking a different approach and choosing, for practical purposes, to accept the scientific arguments, anthropologists might play a role in effecting a solution."

At the same time, their approach will be empirical in another sense: it will attend to the consequences of environmental degradation as these are differentially filtered through enormous economic and social inequalities. Gupta (1998) has cogently drawn our attention, for example, to the ways in which the declaration that resulted from the Rio de Janeiro Earth Summit failed to address a central concern: while the effect of fluorocarbon emissions on the atmosphere (and especially on the ozone layer) was not sufficiently reduced because capitalist and consumer nations were unwilling to scale back their luxuries to the extent that real control required, other forms of environmental degradation such as desertification were being blamed on cultural practices in farming and fishing to which the poorer Third World peoples had few alternatives. Even within industrialized nations such as the United States, local populations may claim that their cultural heritage entitles them to activities on which environmentalists – for reasons often no less embedded in a particular set of cultural values – resolutely frown, and the ethics of environmentalism clashes with the ethics of cultural self-determination, as in the case of Makah whaling. This group recently won the right to hunt a restricted number of whales in the context of a cultural revival that is also fueled by the recent establishment of a legal regime (NAGPRA) for the repatriation of cultural patrimonies (Tweedie forthcoming).

But the issue of major deforestation and desertification is perhaps a more threatening one to the poorer populations of the world. In the Middle East, for example, it is clear that a major basis of ongoing conflict – often obscured by the rhetoric of nationalism and religious revival – concerns the dwindling and already scarce supply of water. It is easy for wealthy countries to criticize the religious, dietary, agricultural, and other practices and prohibitions that have exacerbated the situation, or to argue against religious prohibitions of birth control. A moral economy of responsibility is at work here, a product of specific cultural and political processes that anthropologists can illuminate. The problem will be to persuade those who have a vested interest in ignoring that message to heed it instead.

What is "Natural"?

Anthropologists appear to agree that the manner in which people understand their environment derives from the way they use it and live within it. P. D. Dwyer has suggested that a fully integrated view of the environment, in which no break is recognized between the human and nonhuman worlds, is consistent with an extensive pattern of resource use in which people become familiar with every part of their environment. Conversely, a perspective which separates the human and non-human worlds is consistent with a more intensive pattern of resource use which spatially concentrates human activity and so creates spaces that are not used and that therefore remain unfamiliar (Dwyer 1996).

Others have suggested that modes of plant cultivation and ways of interacting with nonhuman animals are significant in shaping people's environmental perspectives. Coursey, for example, has argued that vegetative cultivation, propagation by roots, tubers and cuttings, generates a noninterventionist attitude to the environment, in which human activities are seen as part of the same system as nonhuman processes. Seed cultivation, on the other hand, requires a more interventionist approach, one that separates human activities from the processes in which they intervene (Coursey 1978). More recently, Ingold has drawn attention to a fundamental difference in the manner in which subsistence hunters and pastoralists engage with and think about nonhuman animals (Ingold 1994). Subsistence hunters interact with their prey on the basis of mutual trust, whereas pastoralists control the lives of their animals, removing the autonomy on which trust depends. Thus, while subsistence hunters think of animals as beings of the same kind as themselves, herders are likely to see animals as objects of human domination.[2]

While they raise the risk of determinism again, theories such as these do suggest that the type of subsistence in which a group engages will at least influence its view of the environment. Milton uses this insight to extend the anthropological perspective to modern industrial societies. Having multiple ways of interacting with the environment, she suggests, such societies will hold multiple and complex perspectives on it: "For example, intensive agriculture in industrial societies has taken intervention in natural processes to spectacular lengths. Crops are grown in vast monocultures. Pests that might destroy them are wiped out with chemicals. More chemicals are used to replenish the soil deprived, through these practices, of fertility. In view of the ideas described above, it is not surprising that such activities are found alongside worldviews that oppose nature and culture and see human progress as the domination of the former by the latter. But industrial societies encompass many other ways of engaging with the environment. Less intensive ways of farming crops and animals are widespread. Many people grow their own food and ornamental plants in domestic gardens. Hunting, fishing, watching wild animals, keeping pets, visiting zoos and walking in rural landscapes all provide different experiences of the environment and can be expected to generate different perspectives on it. So it is also unsurprising that concepts of nature in industrial societies are complex and ambiguous, as they will be, to varying degrees, in any society whose members engage with their environment in diverse ways." The vastly intensified communications to which some people now have access is certainly an important factor in allowing people to develop these perspectives in convergent ways: it is not that the type of subsistence necessarily determines a specific group's attitude to the environment, but that the exchange of information may globalize ideas once held only in very restricted parts of the world. This does not make them more accurate, but it does increase the authority of an industrially and economistically driven version of common sense.

The weakening of extreme cultural relativism may also be making it easier for anthropologists to become actively engaged in environmental issues (see Paine 1986, and Milton 1993b). Where anthropologists provide a unique expertise, Milton argues, is in their understanding of the role of culture in human–environment relations. She suggests, for example, why in the United States the perception that automobiles are damaging the environment seems to have had relatively little effect. The reasons, she argues, are cultural – that cars are more than practical tools; that they symbolize status and personal freedom; that they offer protection and privacy; and that they make statements about subculture allegiance and personal preference. In Italy, considerations of social performance appear similarly to stiffen resistance (or at least indifference) toward car pooling.

Against this background, it becomes much easier to understand why Greek villagers dump their litter in rivers (in an agonistic society it is acceptable to let nature dump the litter in the next village down, especially when anti-litter campaigns seem to serve the interests of a western-oriented elite rather than the villagers themselves) (see Argyrou 1997); why desperately starving aid recipients in Muslim parts of Africa rejected food that they thought would be polluting; why Sardinian villagers regard the creation of a "national park" as an affront to their local identity and a threat to their livelihood (Heatherington 1999); and why Indian villagers prefer a socially appealing nonchalance to the precise measuring of topsoil that might serve their crops better in the short run (Gupta 1998: 237–46). If these stances offend environmentalists as much as does the American defense of the private automobile, perhaps the answer is to substitute for cultural relativism a new idiom – environmental relativism – that recognizes that injustice can pollute the world as much as fluorocarbons and smog.

Environmental Discourse and the Anthropological Perspective

These insights clearly entail a critique of much of the industrialized nations' aid and environmental policy. Anthropology can help in the search for sustainable ways of living, but anthropologists – even when they reject the extremes of cultural relativism (which may in any case be a form of condescension) – prefer to do so in ways that redress serious injustices often perpetrated in the name of environmental protection. What is more, old-fashioned cultural relativism could not solve the question of how to address injustices systematically perpetrated by some against other members of the same society. Gupta's (1998) discussion of the differential effects of development and environmental policies on an Indian village, for example, shows how power – as Foucault has taught us – is quite diffusely distributed. Upper-caste villagers may be able to garner some advantages from their status, and males in this community seem always to exercise almost total power over females; but all of them, in turn, are forced to respond ceaselessly to the competing appeals of politicians who may be able to ease their lot but who are equally likely to exploit them to the full if they can get away with it.

Milton argues that "anthropology's role in environmental discourse is a technical one; it is about means rather than ends. The problems – how to live sustainably, how to reduce carbon emissions, how to conserve biodiversity – are defined outside the discipline. Anthropologists, however, must acquire that knowledge with a sufficient degree of competence if they are to offer an informed perspective on social and political aspects. Then indeed they may raise the thorny questions about who the real beneficiaries are, or who makes the decisions and why. It is the latter component that then serves as the anthropologists' defining "systematic doubt" (Morgan 1991) – or what I have called 'productive discomfort' – applied, through the self-alienating practices of field research, "to the ways in which problems and solutions are identified, and to the fundamental assumptions on whose basis they are seen as problems and solutions."

In so doing, they may upset everyday assumptions as much as they challenge grand policy. We might, for example, be tempted applaud many of the declarations that emanated from the Rio Earth Summit. But, as Gupta shows in deftly connecting that rhetoric with the actual experiences of Third World villagers, these addressed the skin cancers of wealthy First Worlders already well connected to medical establishments far more generously – if not generously enough – than they offered solutions to the starvation occurring in destitute regions throughout Asia and Africa (1998: 312, 327). The brute juxtaposition of official rhetoric with daily life is the one arena in which the intimate access of ethnography, uniting anthropologists as different in approach and ethical stance as (say) Gupta and Moran, creates the space for a critical appraisal.

"Although it is a not a practical proposition to assume that all cultural perspectives are equally true," writes Milton, "it is a requirement of anthropology to treat them all as equally open to question. This is, perhaps, the most constructive starting point for any 'sensible' cultural relativist; not to seek to understand each culture entirely in its own terms, but to attempt to understand all cultures in the same terms, as ways of seeing the world and not as the way things are (even though some cultures may correspond very closely to the ways things are)." Equipped also with the requisite technical knowledge, necessary to any genuinely informed critique, anthropologists can frame debates about the environment in terms of complex local as well as global effects. Gupta, for example, was clearly able to use his knowledge of agronomy and environmental economics to complicate the environmental "common sense" promulgated by powerful political interests in the name of scientific and social progress. Like Gupta, Milton – who emphasizes the importance of technical knowledge in assessing environmental issues – advocates "asking what kinds of activities and relationships – economic strategies, political structures and so on – sustain and are sustained by" the particular choices made by environmentalists today.

There is a major rift, in the public environmental debate, between those who argue that the earth's resources should be controlled at a global level, through international agreements, and those who argue that local communities should have control of their own resources (see Milton 1996). Anthropologists are not, in any sense, obliged to enter this debate or to adopt a particular stance, but they do so, as Milton shows, through their attacks on Cartesian dichotomies and the universalizing frameworks of western science. She sees the technical role of anthropologists as deriving from their moral commitments both to the people they study and to the environment at large, and, unlike some anthropologists, she rejects the forms of cultural relativism that would allow indigenous peoples to continue activities such as whaling in the name of traditional values. Certainly the engagement of such groups in public discourses that reify their cultural identities also entitle them to the respect that is implied by engaging them in serious debate about the ethical divergences such arguments reveal. But such debates may also not result in agreement or compromise, and difficult questions remain about who makes the final decisions and under what conditions. Distinctions made in western culture are not universal in human thought. Different ways of engaging with the environment generate and are sustained by particular worldviews. These, combined with a respect for all cultures that is not contingent on some criterion of truth value in their claims about the world, bring to the fore voices that might otherwise be lost in the environmental debate – the voices of those whose concerns are otherwise most easily suppressed. But, in being heard, they may also be contested.

It is not clear, however, just how effective anthropologists will be in making these voices heard. The discipline works against a dominant commonsense vision of the world that rests on some very powerful interests indeed – as the Rio Earth Summit made all too clear. Those interests, engaged in the politics of significance from a position of indisputable political and economic strength, can all too easily scoff at anthropological insights as a romantic return to "primitivism," or they may coopt older anthropological definitions of culture in order to "prove" that the scientific–rational world of the West is fundamentally incompatible with the superstitious Rest. They can serve up a caricature of the extremes of cultural relativism in defense of a specific cultural vision that claims to have achieved transcendent, universal validity.

In the realm of practical politics, then, anthropologists should take care to distance themselves from the more extreme versions of cultural relativism. It can only become a source of ridicule, and it no longer represents where most of them stand. To assume the right to make moral judgments does not mean that one has the right to impose them, while to refuse to discuss them with one's informants at all is surely condescending. Local interlocutors, too, are full participants in the dialogue anthropologists are interested in promoting. Disagreement, moreover, is the basis on which we construct possibilities for choice – and the future of the global environment affects the entirety of the world's population. Cultural sensitivity, rather than uncritical and factional cultural complaisance with the values of the West or of the Rest, would seem to be the order of the day.

Notes

1   Thus, for example, Holy (1977) aimed to understand why the Toka had chosen a patrilineal mode of inheritance, at least some of the time, in favor of the traditional matrilineal form. He showed that individuals pursued personal strategies in the pursuit of power and prestige: by promising inheritance, some men induce their sons to cooperate more fully, but their ability to control the situation is far from absolute and may depend in part on the sons' own personal strategies and needs. The son is not compelled to act in this way, however, and does so only if it suits his own per-

sonal strategy. Holy's description is thus incompatible with all forms of environmental determinism.

2 Ingold suggests that hunter-gatherer communities do not have a concept of nature because "the world can only be 'nature' for a being that does not belong there" (Ingold 1996: 117). Peter Dwyer (1996) has argued that the capacity to develop a concept of nature depends on whether people view their environment as an integrated whole or divide it into familiar and unfamiliar spaces, and this in turn depends on how they live in and use their environment. He demonstrated this by comparing the New Guinea communities in which he conducted fieldwork. The Kubo-speaking residents of Gwaimasi village draw extensively on the resources of their environment, combining cultivation with hunting, gathering and fishing. The way in which they use their landscape makes it thoroughly familiar to them; there is no part of which it is not endowed with memories of some kind. The Siane-speaking residents of Leu village, several hundred kilometers to the east, use their environment in a different way. They live mainly off the products of intensively cultivated gardens, and have little need to enter unoccupied areas. Dwyer suggested that, in the fully integrated world of the Kubo, there is no sphere sufficiently distinct from the human world to merit the label "nature," while the Siane environment contains unused and unfamiliar spaces that might be so labeled. But since the very term "culture" and words used to translate it are often a response to intrusive western models, it is not clear how useful such distinctions really are. In Signe Howell's assertion that the Chewong of the Malay rainforest treat the jungle as "cultural space, not natural" (1996: 132), the distinction is a scholarly framing rather than a local device.

9

Cosmologies

Living in the Cosmos

Cosmology is about our place in the universe. It is thus crucially concerned with defining the boundaries, critically visited in the last chapter, between nature and culture. When anthropologists were more concerned with supposedly simple or primitive ways of thought, it meant everything that was included in the realm of religion and that derogatory category, "superstition." Yet the term technically encompasses both religion and science, and thus serves more usefully the goals of a comprehensive anthropology – as the study of all human societies – than do those categories treated separately. When Malinowski wrote his celebrated essay, "Magic, Science and Religion" (1948), his very endorsement of this division of conceptual labor opened the road to its eventual dissolution: by recognizing the functionality and intellectual integrity of magic and religion, treating these domains as the practical and theoretical dimensions of a prescientific worldview, he implicitly raised critical questions about the claims of rationality to be a transcendent virtue – common sense made scientific, as it were. For rationality was itself very much the product of a particular cultural moment, and, as such, proved to be inadequate as a description of some universal logic (see also Tambiah 1990). Thus, the term "cosmology" emerges as a more useful and encompassing term and tool for the comparative project of anthropology.

Let us begin with science. For physicists, the cosmos or universe represents the totality of physical things – not only matter, but also space and time and, in general, all that is physically relevant. Moreover, physicists play a role in the modern world that invests them with a special status: "The physicists' calling is awesome: memories and biographies often present this corps d'elite as unique, Promethean heroes of the search for truth. Traditionally the mysteries of the universe have been the province of theologians and priests. Physicists of course do not see themselves as writing the cosmology of some secular religion: for them, religion is about belief rather than knowledge. But they do see their own profession as the revelation and custody of fundamental truth, and to a surprising degree Western culture confirms them in this privileged role" (Traweek 1988: 2).

Once the emphasis shifts from the structure of ideas to the roles of culturally defined social agents in this way, distinctions between different sorts of reasoning emerge, not as objective assessments, but as expressions of the peculiar, Cartesian cosmology that gives us the concept of objectivity – Bourdieu's (1977) "objectivism" – in the first place. Physicists also "believe" that, while the distribution of rationality among humans is uneven, nature obeys immutable laws to which humans can adapt their ideas to the extent that they possess this capacity to be rational (Traweek 1988: 123–4). This search for heroic intellectual perfection, in which pure and disinterested knowledge transcends the here-and-now of social life, contrasts with what we have actually known for some time now about the social production of science (e.g., Latour and Woolgar 1986). It is a view of the universe, a cosmology, that does not necessarily command belief, but does command pragmatic acceptance of the process by which scientists isolate their work from any concern with "meaning" or the social and political consequences of what they do (see Rabinow 1996: 22–3). Those who are employed in such domains as the defense industry must recalibrate not only their alleged scientific detachment but also their religious beliefs concerning the moral dimensions of "truth" – an adjustment with which religious ministers have made a surprising peace, perhaps soothed by the ritualistic character of the arms industry's self-presentation itself (see Gusterson 1996). Even those who live near potentially dangerous nuclear sites develop new ways, grounded in old idioms, of dealing with the threat (Zonabend 1993).

But if this seems unduly cynical, it is also true that anthropologists who in the past claimed to be talking about "belief" in small-scale societies were actually describing collective representations – for, in the Durkheimian tradition within which they worked, such psychological questions as belief were held to be ultimately unfathomable (Needham 1972). It was not so much that anthropologists questioned the sincerity of belief, as that they declared themselves unable to judge it, or at least disinclined to do so. And once we accept that ethnographers of small-scale "exotic" societies and of science laboratories alike are concerned with the organization of ideas about the universe, the distinction between rational and "prerational" states of the collective mind – a key concept since the writings of Lévy-Bruhl (1927) and by now widely disseminated in the wake of the global march of a rationalist cosmology – falls disconcertingly away. Moreover, once we recognize the role of choice and agency, cosmology no longer serves as the determinant of action, but instead as a rich source of imagery and argumentation that individuals and groups can creatively mine as they search for explanations and justifications of their activities.

Apart from physics, cosmology in science is nurtured by different specialities that fall within the generic term of natural sciences, including astronomy, geology, and palaeontology. In Juan Ossio's words, "its subject is the universe as a systematic totality and, correspondingly, its aim is to construct a comprehensive image of its structure and evolution. . . . Although cosmology as a scientific field is generally seen as pertaining to a secular realm, its holistic approach and its concern for order are not far from views about the cosmos more closely associated with religious considerations." As Rabinow (1996: 25) cautions, however, the development of science as well as of its organizing technologies and contexts may be leading us in the direction of new formulations of the social world as well. Clearly, the religious, the scientific, and the social dimensions of understanding cannot easily be disentangled from each other, and efforts to do so often seem more like the expressions of a cosmology than serious attempts to read that cosmology in an analytic fashion.

Crucial to our understanding of what scientific cosmology might have in common with religious doctrine is the central concept of order, which is fundamentally a social construct. Through cosmology, people treat the universe as organized: rather than a collection of random physical components, it is a highly ordered disposition of matter and energy structured in different levels of size and complexity. This, especially as a context for thinking about the relationship between the here-and-now and what lies beyond the grave and horizon of our understanding, is what is meant by "the order of the world." Central questions then concern the origin of this order, how it is maintained, and whether eventually it is destined – note the quasi-religious implications of this phrasing – to disappear. It incorporates understandings of time, chance, and probability, and among its more mundane realizations are weather forecasts, actuarial tables, the Dow Jones, high-rise buildings oriented according to the principles of *feng shui* (geomancy) in Hong Kong or lacking a thirteenth floor in the United States, and casinos around the world. In all these arenas, the attempt to reduce the apparent randomness of the universe to a sense of order is grounded in assumptions about nature. And if pollution – religious as well as sanitary – is usefully to be viewed as "matter out of place" (Douglas 1966), then claims that "nature abhors a vacuum" or that "we have a 70 percent chance of rain" must similarly be seen as demonstrations of the human propensity (or need?) for deriving order from the apparent chaos of existence. At an intermediate level, we can also say that nationalism and its attendant bureaucracies similarly represent a collective attempt to impose political order by grounding it in etiological myths of origin and in ritualistic practices that demand disciplined conformity.

Order, then, is the major concern of cosmological systems from the religious schemata of temporally and geographically distant people to the argumentation of modern physics and chemistry. That scientific practices are themselves subject to social and political constraints has been the subject of sustained ethnographic investigation. In our world, these cosmological issues remain central: we have not escaped the central dialectic between nature and culture that Lévi-Strauss has identified as the defining characteristic of human self-realization. From one perspective, environmental and other political debates are disputes over the predominance of one or another type of order, so that, as Kay Milton has astutely pointed out, arguments about the relationship of nature to culture – which increasingly take cognizance of various indigenous ways of framing that relationship – extend this concern right into the heart of anthropological theory. Much the same can be said about the significance of economic models derived from the populations to which they are applied. A world deprived of these "other" views would be a truly impoverished world – and we must ask whose interests are served by so depleting its conceptual resources. Even (or especially) the reduction of all kinship to "the family" reduces the space for alternative arrangements that would make possible compassion and care for those who do not fit in – for those whom the prevailing cosmology defines as "polluting" – and universalizes a set of values that was hitherto perhaps quite peculiar in the comparative global terms in which anthropologists work. We talk about the need to recognize and preserve cultural diversity in the world; intellectual diversity is surely a critical dimension of this, in that it may help us avoid the trap of self-serving "solutions" to which no alternatives are allowed to exist, and here anthropology perhaps both has its own most important "applied" role and is the most appropriately equipped of disciplines to address it.

To put this in another way, we might say that the very possibility of comparison, essential to any notion of ethical choice, is critical. There is an obvious analogy with the plight of biodiversity in the world. An economistic version of survivalism does not offer much hope of alternative futures. That model, like the related sociobiological perspective, derives from the bourgeois, western milieu that informs so much of the global culture of today (see especially the critiques in Sahlins, 1976a, 1976b). Ironically, this makes the vaunted universalism of such "rationalities" seem dangerously parochial.

The radical move for anthropology now – and one that is a prerequisite for gaining respect for non-western and nonindustrial "rationalities" – is to go beyond what Juan Ossio, following the dominant tradition, separates out as "pre-modern and non-western cosmologies and religion" that "tend to be studied together and somewhat exclusively," with the result that cosmology is generally treated in introductory anthropological texts or in those of history, phenomenology, or the sociology of religion in a chapter entitled "Religion." In this book, I have instead attempted to transcend the distinction. The tactic is to take a supposedly "pre-modern" Andean system as laid out by Ossio (and some comparable materials from the Balkans) and juxtapose these materials with a set of current scientific projects raising crucial questions about kinship as well as the divine order and therefore embedded in observable sociopolitical processes of reinterpretation (Strathern 1989; Kahn 2000; Ginsburg and Rapp, eds., 1995; Rabinow 1996).

John Middleton (1967: ix–x) long ago acknowledged an already venerable history of cosmological studies, some of them of considerable range and sensitivity. Anthropologists, according to Middleton, have approached cosmology as a cultural phenomenon – or, in Durkheim's words, as "collective representations" or "social facts." It is indeed with Durkheim and his collaborators that the comparative and comprehensive study of cosmologies as a specific area of research properly began in the early years of the twentieth century – although, tied as they were to a view of science as a triumph of rationality, they do not appear to have realized the full comparative import of their insights. The point of departure is the assertion that "there are no religions which are false" because "all answer, though in different ways, to the given conditions of human existence." In other words, Durkheim implies that "a human institution cannot rest upon an error and a lie." His reasoning was grounded in an assumption of common, universal human powers of ratiocination, thereby anticipating the comprehensive treatment of cosmology that is emerging today: "If it were not founded in the nature of things, it would have encountered in the facts a resistance over which it could never have triumphed." Durkheim thus undertook the study of primitive religions "with the assurance that they hold to reality and express it" (Durkheim 1964: 2–3; 1960: 3). Moreover, "the first systems of representations with which men have pictured to themselves the world and themselves were of religious origin". This leads Durkheim to observe, "There is no religion that is not a cosmology at the same time that it is a speculation upon divine things" (1976: 9; 1960: 12).

According to Durkheim (1976: 9–10; 1960: 12–13), certain key ideas dominate our intellectual life; they are what philosophers since Aristotle have called the categories of understanding – ideas of time, space, class, number, cause, substance, personality, and so on. These categories, Durkheim assumed, were a product of religious thought; and this meant that they were fundamentally social (Durkheim 1976 [1964]: 10). Durkheim and his followers also rejected the idea that religion and the categories of thought could be reduced to ontologies such as nature or psychology rather than the social. In accordance with Durkheim's "rules of sociological method," the determining cause of a social fact should be sought among the social facts preceding it and not among the states of individual consciousness (Durkheim 1964).

According to Steven Lukes, Durkheim's claim that "concepts are collective representations . . . can be seen as equivalent to the simple but fertile idea, rediscovered a century later by Wittgenstein, that concepts operate within forms of social life, according to rules" (Lukes 1973: 436–7). This perspective not only contributed to a vision of society as a system of social relationships but to viewing society itself as what Mary Douglas would call a "prototype for the logical relations between things" (Douglas 1973: 11). This perspective undermined the evolutionist view of myth and ritual, since it made it possible to view both as the products of a social order every bit as logical as that of modern human groups.

There remained, however, the crucial difficulty that this exegesis was not a conscious one. Indeed, Lévi-Strauss's (1963) by now notorious suggestion that informants' conscious models are less useful than the unconscious ones laid bare by the scholar's pure and disinterested analysis springs from a persistent reluctance, which in this respect can be traced back to the Durkheimians and their evolutionist predecessors, to acknowledge the local sources of "our" theoretical insights. The formalism of Durkheimian approaches to cosmology precluded, in its unmodified form, the recognition of these sources and their similarity to the social scientists' own conceptual framework – the very conditions, as we must now acknowledge, that made mutual understanding, the essence of field research, at all feasible. This condescension has only begun to collapse with the serious challenge mounted against the uncritical use of such Eurocentric concepts as "religion" and "translation" (Asad 1993).

But serious attention to local exegesis presupposes a turn to meaning in place of function. Ossio, following Pocock (1961: 72), attributes the eventual emergence of such an interest to Evans-Pritchard in Britain and Lévi-Strauss in France. According to Evans-Pritchard, "social anthropology studies society as moral, or symbolic, systems and not as natural systems, [so] that it is less interested in process than in design, and that it therefore seeks patterns and not laws, demonstrates consistency and not necessary relations between social activities, and interprets rather than explains" (Evans-Pritchard 1963: 62). This was an important early statement of the comparativist focus of anthropology, and one that allows space for the exploration of the uses and interpretation of cosmology as much as of its formal properties.

Ossio also argues for the long-overdue recognition of the Dutch anthropologists of the Leiden school, who had started to incorporate this perspective some time earlier, and argues that the Leiden perspective "was promoted by a colonial policy, which instead of being influenced by functional considerations emphasised the learning of the rules of etiquette of the dominated in order to have a more fluid interaction with them as well as a more successful system of indirect rule." Given that etiquette itself means "label," hence a category in a system of classification, Ossio finds that "it is not strange that some of the best descriptions of the cosmologies of different people of the world derive from these three European countries, as well as the most relevant theoretical issues in the fields of anthropology and history of religion. In the case of Holland it is enough to recall people such as Henri Frankfort and his notable study on divine kingship, or Johan Huizinga and his analysis of the late medieval history, or Van der Leeuw, in the field of phenomenology of religion, without even mentioning celebrated anthropologists such as Van Wouden or Josselin de Jong." Ossio emphasizes these contributions to the description of total cosmological systems; I would also, however, underscore, once again, their interactional and interpretive elements, an aspect that tends to get lost in the excitement of recognizing systemic regularities.

That more nuanced perspective, however, did not emerge quickly. Indeed, early studies of cosmology by anthropologists were far more notable for their ingenious exploration of systemic properties. Their achievement lay, rather, in pushing that agenda beyond the limits of "primitive society," and in recognizing analogous principles in societies held to be "high cultures" or even ancestral to the West itself. In France, Marcel Granet's essay on Chinese thought (1934) is a classic attempt to understand the thought and cosmology of a high civilization not rooted in the western tradition. More recently, Jean-Pierre Vernant and Marcel Détienne developed a similar approach to ancient Greece. For small-scale societies the list is extensive, but particularly relevant are anthropologists such as Maurice Léenhardt, recognized for his book *Do Kamo* (1947); Marcel Griaule, for his studies of the Dogon; Lévi-Strauss for his contributions to Amazonian ethnography and to the development of structuralism (1949); and Louis Dumont for his studies of India (especially Dumont 1970). In Great Britain, Oxford, under the influence of Evans-Pritchard, and Cambridge, under that of Edmund Leach, Jack Goody, and classicists such as Moses Finley, through promoting the study of conceptual levels of societies, offered important contributions to the understanding of the cosmologies of different human groups. An early example of their efforts can be seen in Darryl Forde's *African Worlds* (1954), which groups together a number of interesting essays on the cosmologies of different African cultures. In the United States, this influence is perhaps most strongly represented in the work of Thomas O. Beidelman (1993) and, especially, Ivan Karp (1980) – who has also brought it to bear on the postmodern production of packaged culture itself (e.g., Karp and Levine 1991), but whose work is also notably alive to the issues of social agency and daily practice that inform the uses of cosmology.

But here, in fact, lies the greatest departure from the Durkheimian tradition, which in this respect remained rooted in the evolutionist assumptions from which its proponents tried so hard to distance themselves. For Durkheim and Mauss, the lack of role differentiation in so-called "primitive societies" – the "mechanical solidarity" whereby art, politics, and belief were all embedded in a single social structure that completely determined the ways in which these domains of experience were given collective expression – allowed no space for the role of individual agency.

For the cosmology of the post-Enlightenment West, by contrast, the exercise of individual agency required the liberation of the intellect, and western thinkers generally assumed this to be an achievement of relatively few peoples. The discourse of social science thus became the vehicle of discrimination between the intellectual activity of the colonizer and the supposed passivity of the colonized – like all cosmologies, a self-fulfilling prophecy, and one that was also reproduced in other hierarchies such as those of gender, caste, class, bureaucracy, and educational systems.

This followed a well-trodden path. Durkheim and Mauss, while pointing to the similarities between religious and scientific knowledge systems and classifications, had highlighted the differences between them. For Durkheim, in a situation of mechanical solidarity religion "pervades the whole of social life but this is because social life consists almost exclusively in common beliefs and practices which derive from unanimous adherence of a very special intensity" (Lukes 1973: 152). The specialization of roles and domains of cultural activity was, by contrast, the product of modernity, a phase of human development in which the creation of separate domains such as art, the economy, political activity, and religious practice supposedly reflected a corresponding diversification of social structures beyond the fundamental one of kinship. It is not hard to see reflected in this schema the evolutionist cosmology that presented the emergence of the romantic figure of the genius as the purest flowering of western individualism.

But this should not blind us to the fact that Durkheim and Mauss's essay on primitive classification, together with Robert Hertz's essay on the right hand (1960), Van Gennep's *The Rites of Passage* (1965), and Hubert and Mauss's disquisition on sacrifice (1964) have proved seminal for the anthropological study of cosmologies. Rather, we should read these texts as an early stage in the process, documented in several other chapters of this book, whereby anthropology began to document the sources of its own entailment in the cosmological grand scheme that underlay and legitimized western colonial domination over much of the world. Especially in the work of Mary Douglas, a self-styled Durkheimian whose work equally embraces ritual pollution (1966) and economic and industrial risk (1982, 1992, 1995), anthropological analysis can always be turned back on its sources. To treat international bureaucracies as symbolic systems masking various exercises of power, as has recently been undertaken in several contexts (see Barnett 1997; Herzfeld 1992; Malkki 1989; Zabusky 1995), is to release the analytic perspective from the constraints of a reified notion of culture; while to show how the principles of kinship itself are still operational within the complexities of modern reproductive technology and of self-styled rational nation-states (see Delaney and Yanagisako, eds., 1995) is to belie the Durkheimian separation of folk or primitive society from those of modern nation-states. Doubtless there are significant differences among societies, and some of those differences may be directly related to differences of technological expertise, but it is also equally clear today that these differences cannot be credited to a unilinear evolution of society – or to a progressive rejection of cosmology.

Indeed, the seeds of undermining this discrimination were sown by the Durkheimians themselves. By arguing that society took precedence over individual choice and action, they shook the very foundations of the romantic concept of the individualistic genius. But this logic eventually came to expose their argument to its own critical insight. In the absence of any recognition of agency, the teleological image of "society" so construed itself came to seem impossibly mystical – indeed, cosmological. Take, for example, the celebrated explanation of religion as society worshipping itself (Durkheim 1976 [1964]). This model entailed either a mystical recognition of something greater than the sum total of the individuals comprising a society, as Durkheim argued on the basis of crowd psychology (1964), or it meant that, like an audience watching a marionette performance, observers would have to posit committees of concealed Durkheimian gremlins – which in fact, in the case of some modern nationalisms as well as of certain well-planned quasireligious cults (see Binns 1979–80), is well documented for the secular world of politics. Scholars became critically interested in the relationship between power and knowledge, and epistemology and cosmology emerged as inseparable from each other.

With regard to the methods appropriate to the identification and analysis of cosmologies, Ossio takes a view that betrays its affiliation with the earlier separation (but that could easily be extended to science and modern politics): "In the study of a cosmology three kinds of information are given pre-eminence. First, the oral or written narratives, which are considered as myths; second, the rituals, which are generally perceived as the enactments of those myths; and third, the visual representations of those myths either in architecture or in iconography." Some scholars – notably James W. Fernandez in his monumental *Bwiti* (1982) – have pursued the analogies among these zones of cultural organization, showing that they are at once conceptual and spatial, and that they permeate all aspects of a society's existence. Nothing precludes the application to the study of supposedly "modern" social forms. Renée Hirschon

(1989: 233) has shown how predominantly communist Greek urban dwellers organize their living spaces according to principles laid down in Orthodox Christian cosmology; while Fernandez has also (1986) demonstrated how the church architecture of South African sects reproduces the spatial organization of dances charged with cosmological implications. Clearly even a more conservative understanding of what is meant by cosmology still allows us to locate it in contexts of modernity – which is itself a cosmological notion expressing Western present-day understandings of the meaning of time.

Popular and Doctrinal Theodicies

Perhaps the explanation for this persistence lies in the fact that human beings must always allocate responsibility and blame. This is not simply a matter of legality, although legal anthropology has been largely preoccupied with the question. It is also an important aspect of making the world livable for ourselves: if we must always accept the blame for the horrendous condition of our world, or if we are unable to explain the large and small tragedies that befall us in ways that do not preclude hope for a better future, we would find life intolerable. Even if blame is not invoked, misfortune demands explanation: humans apparently seek reassurance in the face of chaos. Attempts to predict the likelihood of air crashes, hurricanes, and illness all play this intellectually reductionist but socially creative role. People in many societies construct that exegetical aspect of cosmology known as "theodicy" – literally, "divine justice," but more specifically the doctrinal explanation of what strikes us as the pervasive injustice of the world we inhabit.

Another way of looking at this topic is in terms of accountability. This is a fundamentally political issue. Building in part on Talal Asad's (1993: 7) recognition that the control of uncertainty lies at the heart of whatever we understand by power, Thomas Malaby (1999) has articulated a "politics of contingency" that encapsulates the social repercussions and significance of chance from petty gambling to cataclysmic events. That power is centrally at stake in all assessments of probability becomes especially clear when we consider the role of excuses. As the linguistic philosopher J. L. Austin (1971) pointed out, excuses presuppose a set of ideas about causation that allow an individual to evade direct responsibility for the effects of actions (or inaction) on that person's part; in more anthropological terms, we might say that the right to assign and to evade responsibility is a fundamentally political phenomenon.

Many of the explanatory devices for evading blame come under the heading of "witchcraft," which, in its classic definition, permits people to blame unspecified others: witchcraft, unlike sorcery, does not entail evil volition (Lienhardt 1964: 122), and in many societies generic claims that it has been exercised – in the form of the evil eye, for example – are not always accompanied by accusations against specific persons. This allows people to evade blame for their various misadventures while more generally avoiding disrupting social harmony, should they so wish; they can always resort to specific accusations of sorcery as well. Argyrou (1993) has pointed out that these charges, too, by appealing to a social convention, serve as a social strategy, regardless of whether we wish to claim that individual actors actually "believe" in the idea of evil magic. As already noted, blame is not the whole story: the idea that "these things were sent to test us," while perhaps provoking the outrage of some against a cruel destiny, and offering cold comfort for the immediate moment, nevertheless offers reassurance about the general predictability of the world. In this social sense, the promise of order is the most inclusive form of hope.

Witchcraft accusations rest on a bedrock of theodicy: there is general evil in the world, and some individuals are unfortunate enough to be its carriers. Those who deliberately ensorcel others are of course to be condemned, but those so accused will usually claim instead that they were innocent of such intentions. In many versions of Christianity, too, some version of the doctrine of Original Sin provides a generic theodicy to explain the persistence of such evil presences in social life as envy, gossip, and witchcraft (e.g., Campbell 1964): precisely because others' real motives are ultimately unfathomable, a generic theory explaining the presence of random, inherent evil in this world is an appealing way of avoiding deep culpability while not placing others entirely outside the moral community either. While the formal notion of theodicy is generally associated with doctrinal religious forms, Obeyesekere (1968) showed for Buddhism that it also appears in popular forms of worship; indeed, as a specifically social phenomenon, that is precisely where one would expect to find it most comprehensively elaborated, in social strategies of individual and collective self-exoneration. In this sense, it also has a more secular counterpart in societies that clearly fail to match their own ideals, as, for example, when bureaucrats sworn to serve the citizenry display unpleasantly dictatorial tendencies, so that human weakness can be blamed for the manifest failures of "democracy" and the like.

But each is a specific case of disorder, and it is as much the unpredictability of the experienced world as it is to some specific moral flaw to which theodicy is more generally addressed. Why do things – good or bad – actually happen? How do we explain those things that so often "just happen" (Drummond 1996: 267)? Even that phrase represents a minimalist theodicy: the ontology implied by words like "just" – and indeed "mere" – is a way of cutting wayward experience down to a controllable size, what Kathleen Stewart (1996: 31) calls a "local epistemology." Can we make the pleasurable things that just happen recur? Can we avoid the nasty ones?

One readily available answer is that the people simply avoid the issue: they are fatalists. This may be true at an individual level. It may also be the case that some religions teach greater resignation to the supernatural than do others. But these matters are more complex than they seem. While the world abounds in conventions for attributing personal failures to fate, such attributions are usually retrospective – they are made after disaster has already occurred. In many cases, they are in fact highly proactive attempts to avoid the social consequences of failure. The people of modern Rome, for example, describe themselves as resigned to the difficulties of living in a complex metropolis, yet their record of activism, as well as of vocal protest at the daily indignities they feel they have to suffer, is impressive. Greek bureaucrats and their clients alike, in the same vein, blame "the system," yet that does not stop them from fighting it every inch of the way; after the fact, however, it is useful to have something to blame for the failure, especially when bureaucrat and client are neighbors. The cosmology of predestination in such cases is an instrument, not a straightjacket, of personal agency. Once we shift the focus from the narrative content and structure of ideas to the uses to which these are put, cosmology appears much more deeply embedded in the practicalities of people's everyday lives.

Mythology and Cosmology

In the same way, it is useful to ask, not only how myths are organized, but who uses them and for what ends. The concept of myth is a deeply troubling one for modern anthropology. Because the term is often associated with notions of fiction or false belief, the distinction between historical and mythical narratives turns, as we have already seen, on ideological choices as much as on operational definitions. Is the official history of a nation-state best treated as history or as myth? What of narratives asserting racial superiority or individual genius? Because we tend to dismiss as mythical that which we do not wish to accept, the terminology – in English, at least – comes laden with prejudicial assumptions. Hill (ed., 1988) and others have usefully raised the question of how far it is useful to distinguish between myth and history, suggesting that attempts to treat myth as representing a "symbolic" rather than a "historical" truth may be less benign than they appear.

European interest in myth grew out of the Renaissance preoccupation with the classical Greek and Roman past, in which the category of myth was a respected body of lore about cosmology – about the creation of the world and of humanity, and about the (often highly personalized) causes of natural phenomena. For Vico, the idea of myth was associated with the images that he claimed had existed before humans learned the use of language. Indeed, he derived the Greek *mythos* from the same root as Latin *mutus*, "mute," arguing that from the earliest days, when knowledge took the form of myth, humans have striven for ever greater precision – but that, if they failed to recognize how conditional their newly acquired knowledge was, they would fall back into a state of ignorance. This perspective, cloaked as it was in the seemingly incomprehensible idea that mythology could be expressed in something other than words, has only recently begun to make sense again, as anthropologists have explored the expression of cosmology in spatial arrangements and in organized sensory experience – what Classen (1998: 2), thinking of the combination of the olfactory (incense), musical, and oral in much Christian ritual, calls a "multisensory iconology."

Vico's perspective was grounded in ideas about human progress, albeit in a mode very different from that of his contemporaries. In the nineteenth century, the early anthropologists also saw myth in evolutionary terms. This, however, was a specifically colonialist evolutionism: they saw myth primarily as the encapsulation of "superstition" – a derogatory term that, in the following century, gradually faded from use as functionalism demanded greater intellectual respect for native institutions. From the tradition established by Durkheim and by his followers associated with the journal *Année sociologique* emerge two main approaches to the study of myth. One, developed by Bronislaw Malinowski and expanded by the historian of religions, Mircea Eliade, apart from repeating the idea that myths are sacred and true stories, emphasizes that they are social charters, and thereby act as models for the behavior of individuals. The other, agreeing in several points with the first (particularly as a device for distinguishing between traditional and modern societies), focuses on the intellectual procedures behind myths.

The functionalist view of myth as a charter for social or political realities has yielded pride of place to a series of no less functionalist assertions – for example, Lévi-Strauss's contention that myths were "machines for the suppression of time" (1964: 24), or Leach's elaborations on the inverse idea that myths paraded the internal contradictions of society to the point of rendering them immune to critical dissection (1961). Note that these definitions, precisely like Durkheim's generic characterization of religion, provide a much more persuasive account of modern (especially nationalistic) historiographies, where, once again, the role of an inbuilt and institutionalized functionalism – sometimes even as the self-serving pragmatics of statecraft (as Malarney [1996] has demonstrated for ritual practices in Vietnam) – can be traced to the specific agency of known and identifiable actors. I would suggest that many of these theories appealed to anthropologists precisely because they reproduced the Realpolitik of modern western state societies. In this sense, the distinction between the sacred and the profane itself takes on the character of a legitimizing device, so that myths come to "describe the various and sometimes dramatic breakthroughs of the sacred (or the 'supernatural') into the World" (Eliade 1963: 5–6).

The separation of the sacred from the profane is very much a heritage of the Durkheimian tradition. It becomes virtually irrelevant in the more formal approaches to myth that begin with Vladimir Propp, the publication date of whose *Morphology of the Folktale* is exactly coterminous (1909) with the original publication of Arnold Van Gennep's *The Rites of Passage* (1965). Formalist analysis was concerned with such dichotomies only insofar as they belonged to – and revealed – the larger arrangement of conceptual forms in what Claude Lévi-Strauss, especially, came to argue was fundamentally grounded in the binary structure of human cognition.

Eliade dedicates some pages to explaining how some natives distinguish myth from fable in terms of true versus false. This was irrelevant for Lévi-Strauss because it distracted attention from what he saw as the more interesting intellectual problem of how narrative was structured. Although Eliade was concerned with indigenous attributions of truth and falsehood rather than with imposing his own evaluation, the distinction itself is highly problematic also in the way in which it still reproduces the myth-history split. Juan Ossio's work on the chronicler Guaman Poma (1977), to which we shall turn shortly, illustrates how such distinctions disrupt the study of cosmology by reproducing a cosmological binarism (truth/falsehood) as a tool rather than as an object of analysis.

For Lévi-Strauss (1978: 17), "to say that a way of thinking is disinterested and that it is an intellectual way of thinking does not mean at all that it is equal to scientific thinking. Of course, it remains different in a way, and inferior in another way. It remains different because its aim is to reach by the shortest possible means a general understanding of the universe – and not only a general but a total understanding. That is, it is a way of thinking which must imply that if you don't understand everything, you don't explain anything. This is entirely in contradiction to what scientific thinking does, which is to proceed step by step, trying to give explanations for very limited phenomena, and then going on to other kinds of phenomena, and so on."

"Agreeing with Eliade," observes Ossio, "Lévi-Strauss argues that one of the main characteristics of myths is their timelessness. In contrast to history, both claim that myth deals with reversible events, whereas history deals with irreversible ones. According to Lévi-Strauss, 'Mythology is static, we find the same mythical events combined over and over again, but they are in a closed system, let us say, in contradistinction with history, which is, of course, an open system'" (see Lévi-Strauss 1978: 40). For Eliade this distinction is expressed in a geometrical image: myth is cyclical whereas history is lineal. Yet this will not do: from Vico through Spengler and Toynbee, not to speak of Hegel and Marx, various western commentators have "discovered" a systemic cyclicity in the past. And what gives linearity greater truth-value than other schemata possess? Here is a perfect illustration of the cultural specificity of common sense.

For both Lévi-Strauss and Eliade, the myth–history distinction reproduces a larger social distinction between "primitive" or "archaic" and modern societies on the one hand, and industrial, and above all literate societies on the other. As was also so true of Durkheim, this Eurocentric perspective limited the utility of their analyses (see especially Fabian 1983: 53; Hill, ed., 1988: 4). Yet – again as with Durkheim – we may use their perspectives to gain insight into the cosmology of the West itself, and thence perhaps also into the cosmological systems of some of the societies that these authors regarded as so alien. In the debate about Captain Cook, for example, Sahlins claimed to be elucidating Hawaiian mythic structures in action, while Obeyesekere saw in Sahlins's argument a specifically western myth according to which European conquerors were often received as gods by impressionable natives. There is at least an ironic confirmation in Obeyesekere's argument of Lévi-Strauss's (1955a) claim that every interpretation of a myth, including academic ones, is another variant of that myth – although he was particularly talking about Freud's reading of Oedipus.

Whatever the weaknesses of functionalist arguments, they at least had the virtue of removing narratives classified as myths from the domain of the irrational and superstitious. Eliade, starting from the essentially Malinowskian view that myths provide models for human behavior (1963: 2), argues that in primitive societies there is a fear of history that leads people to cope with suffering by developing explanations which situate the cause of that suffering in a sacred realm. In other words they make misery bearable by arguing that it is not arbitrary. This is the principle of theodicy, expressed as a problem of order. In this view, misery has a meaning, accessible through archetypes that perdure despite the corrosive – because unpredictable – influences of time and individual action (Eliade 1949: 143). Failures of order require explanation, especially when they cause others to suffer – a point that will provide the basis for rethinking some priorities in anthropology itself in the chapter on Sufferings.

But note: this way of thinking is not restricted to "archaic" societies in any sense, although those who view rationality as supracultural may be less willing to confront it close to home. We may recognize it in appeals to science as a legitimation for a seemingly disordered universe, to nationalism as a reordering of threatened and confused identities, and to bureaucracy as both the explanation and the flawed instrument of civil order. We shall return to the theme of theodicy in examining issues of suffering and care. There we will be concerned with the place of human agency in a world that our cosmologies – religious and political alike – show us to be flawed in ways that call for immediate, as well as abstract, explanation.

For the moment, let us simply note that cosmologies must always account for the failures in the systems they describe, and that this leads to much more complex ambiguities than can be described by simple structural schemata. Veena Das, quoting the great Bengali poet Rabindra Nath Tagore (who had written that the tremendous power of the goddess Kali, the goddess of time and death in Hindu mythology, moves not only through the veins of life but also in the presence of death), has noted: "The image of Kali with her four-armed body, huge eyes and lolling red tongue with a garland of skulls around her, holding a cleaver in one hand and a severed head in another, has often been identified with the terrors of the sacred. Yet her devotees experience her as full of grace and one who protects them against the terrors of life." A local oracle, in becoming the embodiment of the goddess, is able to encounter the terrors of those who have been subjected to brutal violence and the uncertainties of living in a world of war, insurgency, disappearances, and torture (P. Lawrence 1995). The theologian and scholar of comparative religions, Diana Eck (1993), in moving reflections on the meaning of the goddess for her devotees, says that there was something in this seemingly violent image that was profoundly true. She claims that it was the truth of divine power claiming the terrain of both life and death, for while it may be easy to recall the divine in the tranquillity of life, it is not so easy to evoke the presence of the divine when one is looking in the face of death. Eck goes on to describe a personal tragedy relating to the violent death of her brother, and how at the moment of seeing his body lying in the morgue she could understand the Hindus who seek the goddess in cremation grounds. We again see the profound contradictions in addressing the question of what it means to see meaning in suffering, a topic that some anthropologists have found it most appropriate to address autobiographically (notably Rosaldo 1989).

Moreover, the distinction between "modern" and "traditional" societies does not stand up well here. The former no less than the latter appeal to what Eliade views as the imperative of returning to origins, often through ritual acts: "there is everywhere a conception of the end and the beginning of a temporal period, based on the observation of biocosmic rhythms and forming part of a larger system – the system of periodic purifications . . . and of the periodic regeneration of life. . . . [and] a periodic regeneration of time presupposes, in more or less explicit form – and especially in the historical civilizations – a new Creation, that is, a repetition of the cosmologic act. And this conception of a periodic creation, i.e., of the cyclical regeneration of time, poses the problem of the abolition of 'history'" (Eliade 1954: 52–3). Yet precisely for this reason we must now also recognize that what is presented as history, sometimes in explicit contrast to a category called "myth," is often no less an exercise in the suppression of time in the name of time, producing such timeless temporalities as national origins and "age-old tradition."

Time and Temporalities

Ossio sees in this pattern of temporal regeneration the rationale of the systems of ages that are to be found in numerous mythologies – especially when, perhaps as a result of literacy and the sustained self-awareness that it enables, the history of literacy itself becomes an issue. (Once again, the pattern is reproduced in the writings of Western humanism, from Vico to Ong and even Derrida.) Clearly the issue of temporality itself – now the subject of some philosophical and historical self-examination in the West (e.g., Hawking 1988) – underlies much of what people take to be common sense.

Ossio writes: "Although the division of time into ages is not universal, many societies, particularly those regarded as 'high' civilisations, have developed this pattern. They may vary in the number of ages, in the content of each age, in their sequence, and in other aspects, but what all have in common is that they are timeless and consequently mythical. An interesting example of these variations and of the ways these ages are organised to oppose history can be seen in the contrasts between those systems which belong to the Indoeuropean tradition and those from the Andean culture." For even though we may properly be suspicious of the Lévi-Straussian division of the world into "cold" and "hot" societies, cultural differences clearly do affect the specific forms, in both nonliterate and literate contexts, taken by this evolutionist narrative – one important subset of which comprises the various 19th-century anthropological evolutionisms, from Tylor to Marx.

According to Hesiod, remarks Ossio, "the Greeks believed that before their present moment four ages had elapsed. The first was golden and was described as a period when humanity was perfect. The second was symbolised by silver, and the third by copper. The fourth one was that of heroes and was not associated with any metal, and the last one, which corresponded to their contemporary period, was symbolised by iron. The whole sequence was characterized as a process of decay from an initial state of perfection. Correspondingly, the last one, that to which the living humanity belonged, was conceived as a period in which humanity was condemned to suffering." And he draws a comparison with ancient India, where the whole cycle, or *Mahayuga*, includes four ages, each preceded by a rising and followed by a setting. Each successive age was shorter; for human beings each also entailed a reduction in lifespan, a relaxation of behavior, and a decline in intelligence. This process of decadence ended in the *Kali-yuga* age, the name of which carries the connotation of "shadows" because in this age the shadows became thicker. The whole cycle ended in a total dissolution, after which a new cycle started.

In the cultures of the historic pre-Conquest Americas, the past was similarly schematized as a sequence of ages (or "suns"), each associated with a specific level of human evolution. Instead of posing the sequence in terms of descent as in the schema recorded by Hesiod, these systems represented full humanity as attained, and then without the suffering attributed to it in the Indo-European theodicies, only in the last (variously the fourth or the fifth) age. The rupture that ended the previous periods was represented as especially fearsome inasmuch as it suggested ominous parallels likely to be realized in the present. Among Mesoamerican cultures, such as those of the Aztecs and Mayas, these ruptures were seen as the product of cataclysms caused by the intervention of each of the natural elements: one age was overcome by water, the next by fire, another by air, and yet another by earthquakes. To prevent something similar, such as the cessation of the sun's movement, the Aztecs resorted to large-scale human sacrifice.

In the Andean area, although the information derives from sources already strongly influenced by western thought, it is possible to recognize that a conception similar to that of the Mesoamerican cultures also existed. Living humanity was located in the last of five "suns." Each of these "suns" was said to have lasted one thousand years, subdivided into two equal halves. The breaking points of each division were called *pachacuti*, which connoted "world transformation" or cataclysm. Nine such breaks had already preceded the time of the chroniclers, who nevertheless held that yet another was about to occur.

Regarding the nature of the forces that produced the rupture between one period and the other there are unfortunately few references. Ossio notes, however, that some sources, such as Father de Murua's chronicle (1964), also mention the four natural elements and note that the Christian deluge was translated into Quechua language as *uno yacu pachacuti* or the "water pachacuti." Today's Andean populations still talk about previous humanities that were destroyed by water and by fire.

The Incas and other Andean groups sought refuge to avert such a catastrophic outcome, not by means of human sacrifice as did the Aztecs, but by constructing instead an elaborate divine kingship, which included as its main attribute the restoration and maintenance of order; the concept of pachacuti was associated not only with the cataclysm that produced the rupture between periods but also with the divine king (Inca) who alone was capable of restoring order. To enhance the divinity of the Inca and the position's role as a unifying principle, he was represented as the mediator of complementary opposites derived from a dual conception of the world and society.

Here is Ossio again: "Because of this capacity for ordering the world, not only the kings but also their ethnic groups were seen as a paradigm for organised society. Before them the existing social groups were seen as barbarians, engaged in endemic wars. Some chroniclers, such as Guaman Poma de Ayala, re-elaborating this conception and that of the ages of the world, organised the latter in an evolutionary sequence, one which began with a first age, where human beings clothed themselves with tree leaves and inhabited caves, and ended with a fifth age, that of the Incas, where they were seen as paradigms of full socialization."

This role of Inca kingship as a device to defy history through its capacity to introduce order, Ossio argues, later became an important framework for the incorporation of Christianity among indigenous populations. Seen also as a divine king, Christ was assimilated into the figure of the Inca. Consequently the attraction that Christianity exerted on the indigenous populations was mostly due to its association with an idea of order and also to the eschatological ideas it proclaimed. This selectivity partly explains why the temporal linearity of Christianity was hardly understood as such, since it was encapsulated within a static conception of time. The importance attached to divine kingship, its association with a cyclical view of time, and its endogamous orientation within a hierarchical social organization, Ossio thinks, also explain in part the importance granted to messianism as a recurrent religious phenomenon in this part of the world with its emphasis on the return of the Inca. These arrangements are indeed "machines for the suppression of time." According to Tom Zuidema (1989), the fact that each of the names attributed to Inca kings as well as the social groups linked to them occupy fixed positions within a closed system – such as in the *ceque* system of Cusco, which integrated time, space, social organization, religion, and, in general, the integrity of society – constitutes strong evidence of their ahistoricity. Yet they are ostensibly grounded in a concept of time, and in this respect, at least, they provide yet another example of the relationship between power and time – a relationship in which any suggestion of a unique and unrepeatable temporality, always corrosive of institutional stability as much as it is of human life itself, poses a perpetual threat. That threat was to reappear in Central and South America as a challenge to history as written by the conquistadores in significant local-level refashionings (see J. Rappaport 1994).

Mortality, that inescapable feature of individual life, is the fulcrum on which much cosmology turns. As early a writer as Frazer noted that divine kingship was set up so that the figure of the symbolic monarch died but was replaced by a simulacrum. Indeed, individuation and difference are bought at the price of mortality: the story of Adam and Eve, for example, is to a significant degree a morality tale about the corrosion that results with the introduction of temporality. But mortality also means that there are dead people – ancestors – access to whom may mean an enhancement of power. Helms (1998) has argued that those who are outside the house – affines (in-laws) – may be associated with funerary practices precisely because, coming from outside, they represent the authority that is derived from temporal distance, which is in turn analogous to the geographical distance that lends a special aura to goods traded from afar. Death being the ultimate distance, control over access to the dead may confer enormous symbolic power. We should note, too, that the mausolea of past leaders have played a central role in the symbolic consolidation of totalitarian power in the twentieth century.

Ritual and the Cosmological Order

Rituals may be seen as a way of resisting that corrosion by means of routine. Repetition and redundancy, as well as the simplification of language and a very low degree of reference to the things of the real social world, characterize most forms of what we would regard as ritual (Tambiah 1979). While some rituals aim to change specific situations – curing rituals are an obvious case in point – they are, in the cosmological sense, about the reassertion of order. Greek cures for the evil eye, for example, involve restoring an ideal balance, symbolized by exercising symbolic control over the orifices of the body – the points at which disorder, entering into individual lives, leaches into the body politic as well (Herzfeld 1986).

Rites are thus a domain of cosmological fixity: the changes they encompass are a recalibration of local detail to the grand order of things. This makes them an ideal vehicle for mythological knowledge. More than this, however, "ritual is a special moment with a beginning, a middle and an end, a full story or a chapter in an endless book which is society. This possibility allows us to rid ourselves, even if briefly, of the terrible indifference encapsulated in the continuous line that springs from societal routines without beginning or end" (Da Matta 1991: 23). It thus provides a means to bring under some kind of collective control the human attempt to defer mortality, to create unique moments in the dead stretches of experience – routine, boredom, regimentation – that serve the interests of power. It provides – as in naming practices, for example – a space in which to individuate one's own life, but, in many societies, only in terms that are already authorized by the religious or secular hierarchy. It is hard to avoid functionalist explanations of ritual, given that ritual is usually invested by its performers with specific aims – sometimes highly personal, sometimes generic, but always entailing some degree of instrumentality. Even explanations of ritual that focus on the production of meaning may have this functionalist cast, from which we can only rescue them – as, for example, Argyrou (1993) does in his discussion of magical practices – by examining the agency of those involved.

Ritual is also inevitably about time – its passage, its meaning, and its inexorable association with decay and death as well as with images of rebirth, reincarnation, or regrouping. In a sense, therefore, all rituals are about passage. I recall the late Edwin Ardener once demanding, "When is a rite not 'of passage'?" Arnold Van Gennep's (1965) famous (and very Aristotelian) tripartite division of rituals into a beginning ("separation" from a preceding phase), middle ("transition"), and end ("incorporation" into the new phase) set the scene for narratological and dramaturgical analyses of ritual, but perhaps also had a rather overdetermining influence. Indeed, while Victor Turner (1974) turned Van Gennep's scheme into a more social mode of analysis by showing how the transitional phase corresponded to conditions of definitional ambiguity ("liminality," "anti-structure," and "communitas") and to the symbolic dangers of uncertainty and categorical lack of fit (cf. Douglas 1966), the basic schema remained largely unchallenged. Only Goffman's work (e.g. 1959), meanwhile, undermines the Durkheimian barriers between the sacred and the profane and between the social and the individual.

Rituals may expose the weaknesses or contradictions of society. Indeed, Max Gluckman and his followers often wrote as though this were the teleological function of ritual – that, by exposing authority to rebellious insubordination within a ritual frame, rituals actually served to maintain the status quo; the interactional equivalent was gossip, in which morality was maintained by a constant, indeed ritualistic, harping on its inevitably frequent infractions (Gluckman 1993a, 1963b). This view of ritual as a mechanism of stability dies hard, while Lévi-Strauss's treatment of myth faithfully reproduces the teleology of these old functionalist arguments. Such a logic can indeed be discerned in the rituals created by the agencies of totalitarian state systems, which thereby attempt to inculcate a sense of inevitable purpose into the populace at large. As an analytical account of other ritual forms, it remains – at best – unproven.

For similar reasons, we must beware of the temptation to see carnivals and other ritual extravaganzas as simply a variety of "release mechanism." Bakhtin's observation that laughter offers a release "from all religious and ecclesiastic dogmatism, from all mysticism and piety" (Bakhtin 1984: 7), is a fine description of what often actually happens, but it is not an explanation of the initial genesis of rites of rebellion. Victor Turner's (1974) argument that rituals provided a space for the experiencing of communitas – the realm of antistructure and the leveling of differences – provides a more socially grounded explanation that does not preclude, and indeed encompasses, the ritual inversions that so intrigued Bakhtin. Carnival, for example, disrupts the formality of much of daily life. It is a moment when the social norms are suspended to allow individuals to express their spontaneous humanity, but still as part of a collective entity: "The people do not exclude themselves from the wholeness of the world . . . This is one of the essential differences of the people's festive laughter from the pure satire of modern times. The satirist whose laughter is negative places himself above the object of his mockery, he is opposed to it. The wholeness of the world's comic aspect is destroyed, and that which appears comic becomes a private reaction. The people's ambivalent laughter, on the other hand, expresses the point of view of the whole world; he who is laughing also belongs to it" (Bakhtin 1984: 12).

The crucial point here is that in Carnival, and in other rites of symbolic inversion, there is ample space for play. It is here that people can explore the tensions inherent in the fact that they belong to a community, yet may not share equally in its benefits. In these rituals, cosmology comes to incorporate the experiential worlds of ordinary people, so that their ways of understanding and dealing with it take center stage. These are moments not only for the assertion of order, but also for the exploration of alternative possibilities. We shall return to this aspect of ritual in the chapter on Displays of Order.

Cosmology and Representation

Cosmology may sometimes be accessible through an analysis of iconography. That iconography may be verbal, as in the blasphemous invocation of scurrilous images, or it may be more directly pictorial. The divisibility of Nuer notions of divinity, for example, appears never to take visual form – indeed, it is hard to imagine how one would pictorially represent an infinitely divisible concept of deity. Its social significance is that the idea of a transcendent divine being is fractured by the actual divisions of social life: the *Kwoth* (supreme supernatural being) of all the Nuer is refracted into numerous *kuth* (pl.), each associated with a subdivision of the social or natural world. By contrast, while the refraction of divine essence is not made visible in Eastern Orthodox iconography, it is made palpable in social practice – through the reverence paid to particular, preferred items. The logic here rests on an aesthetic theory, itself grounded in Orthodox theology, that all icons are social and localized renditions of an original pictorial image: even photographic copies of famous icons are imbued with refractions of the same grace. This logic also takes verbal form in a negative sense: one may curse the divine figures "of" one's enemies as though they were, at that moment, different figures of (for example) the Virgin Mary.

In studying iconography, structuralists sometimes realize their dream of a binarily organized universe. In pre-conquest Mesoamerican cultures such as those of the Aztecs and the Maya, for example, the world was divided into four parts and a center, and each in turn was associated with specific divinities and different symbols (Florescano 1987). The fact that those divinities and symbols occupied a fixed position within this interrelated closed system lent specificity to their meaning and enabled the reconstruction of wider structured complexes, finally disclosing the basic premises of the cosmological system.

For the Andean world, Ossio (1977) has undertaken a similar analysis, using such illustrated texts as the chronicle of Guaman Poma, dating from the end of the sixteenth and beginning of the seventeenth century. In Guaman Poma's map of the Indian realm, space is divided by two intersecting diagonals which delimit the four parts of the world with Cusco at its center. From different representations of the Inca surrounded by the kings of the four parts of the world, from the representation of time as divided into five ages with that of the Incas as the last, and from other internal evidence, Ossio has suggested that – although superficially hispanicized – Guaman Poma was very much a part of his indigenous society in which, as among the Aztecs and Mayas, the cosmos and society were together conceptualized as an integrated whole organized in accordance with dualistic principles. Ossio's structuralist analysis also revealed that the Inca, like the Chinese Tao or the Egyptian Pharaoh, was represented as a unifying principle that mediated between complementary opposites and that, within a cyclical conception of time, he was conceived as the restorer and sustainer of order. In this way, the mundane and the divine were integrated into a single cosmology.

The difficulty with such representations is, once again, their heavy focus on system at the expense of agency. It is important to know how people actually use cosmologies and their representations. The latter can be quite subversive, and in ways that are so everyday as to be pervasive: consider, for example, the restructuring of ideas about divinity that is necessarily implied in the forms of blasphemy. Both sides of the abortion debate in the United States claim to be concerned with the protection of human life; they disagree, however, on how to define it. Their common ground highlights the differences that divide them (see Ginsburg 1989). In a classic, Evans-Pritchardian sense, such interpretations represent refractions through the social universe of commonly held values made, for the purposes of debate, to look irrevocably irreconcilable. It is of course difficult to know what Guaman Poma was trying to achieve: the historical distance denies us the luxury of the ethnographic interview, or the contextual observation. But surely, at a time of painful readjustment to the new realities of Spanish rule, the consistencies so delicately disinterred from the text by Ossio were deployed to very specific, political ends? One would like to have been able to witness the arguments that the text itself may have provoked.

Cognition and Cosmology

On the other hand, it is true, Guaman Poma's chronicle offers rich material for the consideration of Lévi-Strauss's structuralist view of humankind. That position holds that all culture is based on a binary logic the roots of which appear to be located in the physiology of the human brain. It was, in fact, a late rendition of a theory that had already gained wide currency in linguistics and literary studies. As Ossio observes, dualism "has long attracted the attention of social scientists. Particular emphasis has been given to its materialisation in space in divisions that have come to be known as moieties and their association with a kind of prescriptive marriage alliance called either restricted or direct exchange. From a symbolic perspective another feature that has sparked the interest of scholars is the use of this classificatory device to underscore an image of totality and to enhance the unifying qualities of an entity thought of as divine." Moreover, such observations can be extended beyond the immediate reach of conventional field studies: thus, John Borneman (1992) treats the long-

term symbiosis of two mutually opposed political and philosohical regimes of
law by treating the two Berlins of the pre-1989 cold war era as moieties, engaged
in a structural pas de deux that leads to their eventual mutual assimilation at
the very moment of the collapse of the Wall that separated them. There is also
some evidence to suggest that some systems previously thought to be evidence
of this universal proclivity may in part represent importations from colonial
sources, as, for example, in the suggestion that some of the more striking aspects
of Andean symbolic dualism may have originated in Spanish ideas about social
hierarchy (Gelles 1995). The emergence of such historically critical views marks
a reaction against the ahistoricism of structuralist approaches, suggesting that
borrowing and imitation may be as much engaged in the structuring of supposedly indigenous or local cosmologies as are the supposed commonalities of
human cognition.

Even if we confine ourselves to small-scale societies of the kind most commonly studied by anthropologists in the past, the idea that dualism may take
specific forms – and may itself be a culturally and historically specific phenomenon, not to be found everywhere in the same degree – has important repercussions. In Andean society, at least, dualism is a recurrent classificatory device
since the prehispanic period; the mythology emphasizes the idea of reciprocity
and of opposition between the sexes. A myth explaining the origin of the
moieties of the community of Sarhua (Ayacucho, Peru) mentions that at
the beginning, because they were undivided they were not motivated to fulfil
the task of carrying the Maria Angola bell. To overcome this situation they
decided to organize a competition. For this purpose they developed the moieties
Qollana and Sawqa in which they are now organized (Palomino Flores 1984:
60). Is this tale simply an etiological, after-the-fact attempt to account for dual
social organization, or does it encapsulate memories of an actual historical
process? Are these necessarily mutually exclusive explanations? The tendency
to view dualistic social organization as both area-specific and an instantiation
of the universal principles of binarism may be misleading. Gelles's (1995) suggestion that its persistence up to the present may also owe a great deal to the
superimposition of similar dualistic systems of thought, present in the intrusive
Spanish culture makes dualism both more general (it is found in both the Old
and the New Worlds) and more historically specific (its importance is explained
by a particular confluence of cultural schemata). It may no longer be particularly profitable to speculate on the question of universality. Instead, the frequency of dualism – a smaller but more demonstrable claim – can be invoked
as part of the explanation of syncretism, a phenomenon once again of interest
to anthropologists as they historicize their largely contemporary and synchronic
data and explore the ways in which various peoples have tried to assimilate to
their own worldviews the cosmologies of conquering outsiders and invasive
missionizing (see Shaw and Stewart, eds., 1994).

Yet there can be little question about the frequency of dualistic representations of the universe. These are often encoded in architectural and other spatial
forms of organization. Not surprisingly, perhaps, they most commonly play on
such fundamental pairings as nature–culture and female–male (a parallelism that

has itself provoked enormous debates about universality: see Ortner and White-head 1981; Ardener 1989; Rogers 1985). Thus, cultures as far apart as the Purum of Borneo and the Kabyle Berbers of Algeria (Needham 1962; Bourdieu 1977) arrange domestic space according to principles that, to follow Bourdieu's later (1977) analysis, reciprocally structure individuals' perceptions of the right and proper placing of human bodies in architectonic space – the clothing, as it were, of the body politic. Nor are such arrangements confined to small-scale or premodern societies. The prominence of geomantic principles in architectural design among urban Chinese in Hong Kong and California suggests otherwise, as do the intense differentiations between external and internal design – roughly corresponding to neo-Classical or Western and rural or Turkish motifs, respectively – through which modern Greeks and other southern European popula-tions calibrate their lived spaces with a political hierarchy of cultural styles (Occident vs. Orient), and as do Afro-Brazilians in their management of house style decor (Vlach 1984).

Various explanations have been offered for the apparent ubiquity of dualis-tic principles. Eliade has suggested that dualism was an expression of the union of contraries, or of what Nicholas of Cusa called the *coincidentia oppositorum* – which "was the least imperfect definition of God" (Eliade 1965: 80–1; 1962: 98). It represented the mystery of totality and was considered to be "the best way of apprehending God or the ultimate reality" beyond terms of immediate experience which only have the capacity of perceiving "fragments and tensions" (1965: 82; 1962: 100). Eliade concludes (1965: 12; 1962: 141): "Ultimately, it is the wish to recover this lost unity that has caused man to think of the oppo-sites as complementary aspects of a single reality. It is as a result of such exis-tential experiences, caused by the need to transcend the opposites, that the first theological and philosophical speculations were elaborated. Before they became the main philosophical concepts, the One, the Unity, the Totality were desires revealed in myths and beliefs and expressed in rites and mystical techniques." But whether such an explanation can be applied universally to cosmological systems is dubious: it seems a rather obvious illustration of the criticism that Talal Asad (1993) has addressed to the anthropological category of "religion" more generally – that it imposes a Christian worldview on other ways of appre-hending the world.

More elegant is David Maybury-Lewis's argument suggesting a parallel between conceptual equilibrium and social and political peace (1989: 14). A similar argument is proposed by James W. Fernandez (1982, 1986), who found for the Fang of Gabon as well as for Zionist churches in South Africa that principles of opposition in one area of cosmology might be reproduced as architectural or other aesthetic detail in other arenas of everyday life, while the egalitarianism of church design echoed similar principles to be found in circle dances. Again such contrasts are not confined to the domain of the sacred: a folklorist, Gerald Pocius (1979), found that the sharp contrast between the hierarchical formality of Newfoundlanders' sitting-rooms and the informality of their kitchens, respectively, was echoed, in these contrasted spaces, in the designs of hooked rugs hung on the walls.

Such arrangements may be highly durable, particularly because they are encoded in the spaces of everyday life and so become a matter of habit. Indeed, Ossio finds the imperatives of dualistic structure to be potentially a strong determinant of identity, noting, for example, that in some Andean societies the fact that some sets of moieties (*ayllu*) maintain a structural continuity over time suggests that individuals may change group membership in order not to upset the equilibrium necessary for competition. While this view might suggest a lack of agency on the part of community members, there is no doubt that in many societies people do accommodate themselves to suit dominant structural constraints. The extent to which cosmology appears to determine action may in fact prove a valuable source of insight into the hegemonic processes whereby consciousness can be regimented to serve colonizing regimes of truth – processes that have often recurred in human history (see Jean Comaroff and John Comaroff 1991, 1997).

Cosmology and history may be read as durable versions of structure and agency, respectively. At any given moment, cosmology provides a view of the current reading of absolute truth. It is represented as static. When it incorporates time, it may develop a cyclical or teleological cast – as happened in western historiography with Spengler and Marx, respectively; it was this feature that lent such views of history their appeal to authoritarian political regimes. Cosmology places time at the service of social structure; one of the most dramatic illustrations of this lies in the representation of events in so-called segmentary societies, where truth becomes relativized by the instability of political relationships (Dresch 1986; Shryock 1997) – it is no coincidence that dictatorships, by contrast, promote unitary historical truths, while democracies seem to encourage the development of multiple, alternative readings, although the distinction is itself part of the cosmology and ideology of systems that go under both headings. Each of these arrangements also corresponds to a different, and appropriate, understanding of the place of agency in relation to the social body as a whole. Social actors within these systems then rework cosmologies in new ways; the cosmological idiom affords material for the negotiation of social change.

As we turn from cosmology to history, and from ritual to spectacle, we should resist the temptation to view these transitions as shifts from premodern to modern social formations. Rather, they represent shifts in the degree to which we address issues of agency in relation to the durable structures of social life – structures the very existence of which is nevertheless predicated on those actions that give them meaning and presence. Processes of what Weber called "disenchantment" are reversible, or may lie in the nostalgic eye of the beholder rather than in the experience of local communities. Modernity is not devoid of cosmology, and scientists admit to limits of knowledge more awesome now that we know technology not to be a panacea for all ills, including our own ignorance. This is the challenge that sends the anthropologist of today into the laboratory and the administrative office, into medical emergency rooms, and into e-mail networks (see J. Anderson and Eickelman, eds., 1999; Lozada 1998). Here, too, questions of life and death are explored in ways that might usefully compared with the divine kingship that so fascinated Frazer in the nineteenth century. Or, as we might say in terms that he would certainly have recognized: Cosmology has died: long live cosmology!

10

Sufferings and Disciplines

Discipline, Norms, and Care

The view of cosmologies presented in the previous chapter is an account of systems of thought. It says very little about those who do the thinking and acting that constitute the proper space of anthropological research in the field. In this chapter I shall draw on two remarkable essays, by John Borneman and Veena Das respectively. From contrasted perspectives, they together challenge the view of anthropology as a study of systems – of formal rules and normative practices – and show how the inscription of rules on bodies and persons demands a critical response from anthropology. I thus propose, with them, to ask the question: how can anthropology contribute to a rethinking of the social that will make it, not the space of regulation, punishment, and blame, but rather that of relief, care, and acceptance? I also want to tie this chapter back to the discussion of development, in which, as I have tried to show, a declared intention of helping populations achieve self-sufficiency has all too often induced forms of suffering of a degree hitherto experienced only at times of war and pestilence.

Finally, for those who may have wondered where in this book two of the oldest and most familiar themes of social anthropology – kinship and gender – will finally appear, this is the strategically delayed moment of emergence. In part following Borneman's critique of the representation of kinship, and in part focusing on recent discussions of the role of kinship in the constitution of larger entities such as nation-states, I shall attempt here to suggest important correspondences between the body personal and the body politic. I shall especially attend to the place of the body in the discipline associated with bureaucratic modernity, including the state, the media, and western biomedicine. And it is here, finally, that I shall sketch a possible ethical position for an anthropology that eschews both of two untenable extremes: racist and other forms of essentializing intolerance, and the kind of so-called cultural relativism that would make excuses for genocide. For here, too, we shall be inhabiting a militant middle ground: it has become apparent that it is the connection to local and personal agency that makes the social and the

cultural, even on the grandest international scale, an acceptable framework
for life itself.

It may seem curious that a discipline that has for so long boasted of its
commitment to cultural tolerance should find it necessary to face this task.
As Borneman has pointed out, however (see also Borneman 1996), anthropology has had a development strikingly parallel with that of the law, and its
practitioners have always tended to seek the norms of a society as the basis
for understanding such key categories as kinship and "the family." This
discourse must also be read in the context of the globalization of an ideology
that makes the heterosexual family (and, I would add, the male-headed household) the standard against which all other arrangements are treated as aberra-
tions. This may be something of an exaggeration, but as such it at least disturbs
the complacency of much current theory. For, as Borneman notes: "Even the
United Nations has approached this right with a special kind of reverence, des-
ignating 1975 'International Women's Year,' 1979 'The Year of the Child' and'
1994 'The Year of the Family.' Indeed, 'the sacrament of marriage,' defined in
terms of institutionalized procreative heterosexuality, is one of the few positive
rights that has attained nearly universal consensus. Because of this world ideology, the connections of marriage and the family – the principles of descent
and affinity – to the assertion of privilege, abjection and exclusion are rarely
seen and, therefore, rarely examined." Indeed, to the extent that marriage has
become an internationally recognized key symbol of stability, it would seem to
justify Talal Asad's (1993) more generic argument that the term "religion" has
featured in anthropological and other discourses as a surrogate for one particular religion, that of Christianity. But the uncritical adoption of models of
family, patriarchal authority, and the like can also reproduce the repressive
common sense of other religious systems and their social consequences – as, for
example, Gupta (1998: 100–1) shows for caste and gender in a rural Hindu
community in India.

I would interpret Borneman's position, however, in terms of a still larger problematic, in which its centrality to the tasks of anthropology – whatever one
thinks of his conclusions – becomes apparent. This has to do with the social
production of indifference (Herzfeld 1992) – the use of bureaucratic systems of
classification to justify exclusion, rejection, and some of the most callous disregard of large-scale suffering the world has ever known. The problem is not
necessarily one of intentions: many of the world's bureaucracies were created,
and may even function, to protect the interests of all their citizens. But bureaucracies are structures, and structures are operated by agents some of whom may
not be as benign as the founders of those structures. Precisely because intentions are ultimately only guessable at best, they provide an ethical discourse that
actors can exploit for an enormous variety of ends, from the compassionate to
the repressive. It is the particular task of a committed anthropology to question
the ways in which those structures get called into the service of highly localized
interests.

Veena Das acknowledges the difficulties arising from anthropology's historical engagement in the processes it is now called on to examine: "How to render

suffering meaningful remains a formidable task for social anthropology and sociology. This stems in part from the fact that a society must, to some extent, hide from itself how much suffering is imposed upon individuals as a price of belonging, and the social sciences may be in danger of mimicking society's silence towards this suffering." She also suggests that the question has so far been posed in terms of a rationalistic notion of calculation, in which "maximizing" may be the operative, if usually tacit, concept. While she rightly notes that the anthropological focus on everyday life – as opposed to an abstract metaphysics – is what enables anthropologists to address the question of what suffering and care mean to the members of a given society, Borneman's problematic shows that this orientation is no guarantee of the discipline's immunity to the kind of complicity that Das describes. Needed here is a historically grounded reflexivity of the kind discussed in earlier chapters: an understanding of the legal and political processes by which "we" have arrived at an understanding of the arrangements whereby people live together, not as grounded in a voluntary organization of affect and care, but as responses to the regulative powers of "society." It should be added that this focus on individual agency risks reproducing another kind of normativity, the self-stereotype of "the West" as individualistic; but here again, as we have already seen in the brief discussions of nationalism in earlier chapters, exploring the history of this construction, too, should render it more visible to us.

In writing of care, Borneman is also addressing the structural realities that people confront in their lives. He entertains the possibility that even in the most repressive-seeming bureaucracy, some social actors may be ready to break away (or through) the tangle of classificatory obfuscation with which less benign individuals attempt to serve themselves at others' expense. In our conversations for the present book, he has argued that this is a necessary balance against the cynicism that too narrow a focus on suffering might induce; and it is here that his contribution especially complements that of Das, who, while careful to avoid adding yet another layer to the academic and media-driven exploitation of suffering that we so often observe, refuses to speculate about a possible alternative politics of care – a term that in English has also acquired a considerable weight of ideological and political baggage.

We should also note that care has different meanings for different groups of people. Writing of efforts to stop the spread of AIDS in a Christian community of Botswana by identifying sufferers, Frederick Klaits (1998: 114) remarks, "Making a good death . . . emerges as a more pressing concern than preventing the spread of disease" for the community members and their bishop. There is much ambiguity in such situations: do we adopt a stance of muted cultural relativism, or do we condemn the hegemonic religious practices that allow a bishop to prefer maintaining a "community of the faithful" over identifying AIDS patients and so helping to combat the spread of the disease? As Klaits despairingly remarks, in his writing he was "celebrating such efforts to maintain and regenerate community, and yet as I watch my friends become sick and die I worry that it may be only a matter of time before things fall apart."

But even leaving such agonizing ethical decisions aside, the question of how to address the role of those who have power leads us into treacherous waters. Was the bishop a savior of her community or the agent of a repressive ideology? Does the system determine the ethics of those who work within it? It is very easy to confuse the medium with the message – to assume that examining the potential evils of a system of classification means rejecting the potentially benign role of some actors. That misses the point: it is the existence of a surface that can be variously interpreted that allows social actors of equally diverse intent to pursue their goals. But the error is extremely revealing: none of us – not even anthropologists! – are immune from the temptation to accept the conceptual safety of a system of classification that appears to divide the world into good and bad, agency and structure, sufferers and oppressors – a division that shows dualism to be alive and well today. In beating back that allure, the challenge for anthropology is to bring into the brightest possible focus the restless processuality of social life. In the tension but also the complementarity that leads me to juxtapose the thinking of Borneman and Das in this discussion, we can see exemplified many of the vexing questions that await an anthropology trying to make sense of its moral commitments and dilemmas.

The Classical Legacies: Theodicy revisited

The locus classicus for explaining the problem of suffering may be located in theories of theodicy, that cornerstone of the cosmological linkage between ideas about the universes and the social experiences of the here-and-now. For Weber (1963), a rationalized conception of the divine order required an explanation of the unjust distribution of suffering in the world. While Weber provides a majestic review of solutions to this problem in world religions, ranging from eschatological solutions to ones through spiritual and ontological dualisms, he was also interested in the consequences of these theories for practical action in the world, and this clearly has consequences for a practice-oriented anthropology. For instance, he argued that the translation of eschatological ideas into an interest in one's destiny after death generally arose when the most essential earthly needs had been met, and was generally limited to the elite; because, in the Protestant system, earthly success was also evidence of a predestined divine approbation, moreover, it had real consequences for the management of reputation and status in the earthly life. This also means that the grand concepts of theodicy may be translated into the everyday idioms of self-justification both by those who inflict suffering on others and by those who find themselves compelled to explain why they have apparently been singled out for disaster. It is this flexibility of the Weberian framework for the analysis of particular situations that recommends it especially to anthropologists.

The continuity and stability of the framework provided by Weber to conceptualize the problem of suffering can be seen in several studies. For instance, in a well-known essay on religion, Geertz (1973) stated that the problem of suffering is an experiential challenge in whose face the meaningfulness of a particular pattern of life threatens to dissolve. Therefore, he felt the challenge for religions was, paradoxically, not how to avoid suffering, but how to suffer. In the presence of physical pain, personal loss, and the helplessness of others' agony, how could individuals be supported by religious systems of meaning and patterns of sociality?

In this reading of the Weberian view, suffering seems necessary to a teleology of community life. This is a distinctly Christian notion, as we might anticipate (see Asad 1993), and it is not clear how easily it might be extended to other societies; but, as Borneman reminds us, so much of the framework of anthropology itself is grounded in Christian morality that this itself becomes a compelling object of further thought – an example of the constructive cultural reflexivity I am advocating here. Religious symbols allow the pain of suffering to take on a meaning that merits hope for reward and converts the personal pain of an isolated consciousness into something that is collectively shared. Pain and suffering, however, do not simply arise out of the contingencies of life. They may also be experiences that are actively created and distributed in the name of the social order itself – indeed, important studies in the anthropology of medical practice and local responses to it indicate that the medical establishment is often credited with malignant intentions, allied to the coercive powers of the state (Badone 1991; Balshem 1993). Arguments for the "social uses" of suffering assume that it is necessary for the pedagogic function of power in education, the price of reason, and spiritual refinement. But in every society the arbitrary failure of justice – often in the name of democracy or some other secular morality – calls for explanations: in a "disenchanted" world in which the divine is no longer the source of unquestioned authority (if indeed it ever was), the new immanences of "humanity," "democracy," "socialism," "common decency," and "rationality" must similarly answer the question, "Why have you forsaken us?" Sometimes, it seems, the only solution is to develop a controlled and democratized version of long-suppressed ideologies of revenge, notably in the legal confrontation of such horrors as genocide and other war crimes (Borneman 1997).

At a less grandiose level, too, everyday failures of democratic process, bureaucratic efficiency, and education have their secular theodicies. "This hurts me more than it hurts you" was the traditional cant of the English teacher inflicting corporal punishment – but such formulations are repeatedly questioned by those who have to submit to it, although not always in verbally explicit forms. (The resentment felt by craft apprentices with whom I worked on Crete, adolescent boys who were physically punished for their infractions, for example, might reveal itself through petty acts of sabotage and disobedience rather than through active defiance. Such embodied resentment – "resistance" probably implies too active a response – requires ethnographic attention to artisan–apprentice relations under conditions of considerable intimacy, since nothing is rendered explicit.) What Das calls "this dual character of suffering – a capacity to mould human beings into moral members of a society and at the same time a malignancy revealed in pain inflicted upon individuals in the name of the grand projects of society" – requires us to focus, as Weber did not, on exactly such minutiae of ethnography, in order to see how people invoke the grand design of theodicy to deal with extremely localized problems; it also invites us to consider the possibility of forms of "resistance" (see J. Scott 1985); and finally, and in a very important sense, it raises the important question of what happens when theodicy fails to provide any acceptable answers at all.

To go beyond the limitations of a normativist social science that simply recapitulates the principles of "order," it is not sufficient to invoke "practice." As Michel de Certeau (1984) noted in his trenchant critique of Bourdieu, the very idea of a "strategy" already implies a measure of structured authority. His solution is to recommend that we attend instead to "tactics" – to the one-shot, improvisatory actions that truly subvert patterned interaction. Given the capacity of formal structures to prevail through the power of excommunicating those who do not conform, however, it seems more useful to adopt a posture of "counter-strategy": to elicit those principles of the prevailing order that throw the contradictions of punishment-as-benefit into sharp critical relief. This is where Borneman's substitution of "caring" for "family structure" has important ramifications for social theory, as we shall see below, and where Das's proposal for the creation of moral communities provides the "translation device" for rendering such a substitution more generally accessible.

Note that there are practical implications in all this. It is almost as though we had merged the discussion of cosmologies with the "applied anthropology" discussed under the heading of Developmentalisms. Just as in that chapter, however, I urged a mediative position that made of critical discussion an applied project in itself, so too in the present chapter – and in accordance with my understanding of both Das and Borneman – I am less interested in generating a set of prescriptions than in proposing a pedagogical anthropology that can truly instruct the public about both the significance and the dangers of claims to "order." Within that framework there is plenty of room for disagreement, as, for example, Borneman's recent exchange with two feminist colleagues, Jane Collier and Sylvia Yanagisako (Borneman 1996), demonstrates. The discussion itself is instructive; and that is far from trivial. Their exchange is an outstanding example of the pedagogical value of anthropology's engagement with the problems of everyday life.

Suffering as Pedagogy

This is a very different type of pedagogy, however, from the more punitive variety addressed by Veena Das, who traces the genealogy of her own current perspective on suffering back to Durkheim and Weber. In these writers, specifically, she identifies the teleology of an argument that sees mutilation as the means of creating societal identification. She stands these writers on their heads by pointing out that the agents of state or industry may inflict excesses of pain that they, as agents, can then use to increase their power. Their capacity to routinize suffering grows in the making, especially in the present age of rapid and intensive media reproduction, and is backed by an elaborate exegetical apparatus – that of theodicy – offering salvàtion as the balm for present agonies and a cosmological explanation of the persistence of suffering in the world.

She introduces this important argument – which recognizes the process of translating classification into action – with a much more recent critique of the power of the state. In this study, Pierre Clastres (1974) examined the practice of what he called "torture" in so-called primitive societies – the rites of passage that define a young person's entry into adulthood. He concludes that they all teach us that torture is the essence of such rituals. For whereas many scholars had seen the rites as testing the personal courage of the initiates, Clastres argues that in addition, after the rites are completed and all suffering is over, there remains a residue – the scars that are left on the body. A man initiated becomes a man marked. The mark becomes an obstacle to forgetting: the body becomes memory through the inscription of pain. What it remembers is law, normativity, coercion. Das recommends that we compare this account with that of Durkheim (1976 [1964]) on the question of how pain becomes the medium through which memory is created and through which society establishes its ascendancy over its individual members. Two important points of difference between the Weberian account and that of Durkheim emerge: the place given to the body in internalizing the law of society through inscription of pain on the individual; and the administration of pain by society as a means for creating legitimacy for itself.

In his reflections on how the person comes to be defined through totemic beliefs, Durkheim observes that totemic images are not only represented on external things such as upon the walls of houses or the sides of canoes, they are also found on human bodies – the inscription of physical signs – and, as such, become an integral component of personhood. He goes on to describe how members of each clan seek to give themselves the external aspect of their totem: the body and its violent transformation as the most enduring witness to the consubstantiation between the social and the individual. In Durkheim's thesis, the best way of proving to oneself and to others that one is a member of a specific social (and therefore moral) community is thus to place a distinctive mark on the body. (Clastres goes further, asserting that this uniformity of the mark of sanctioned and above all collective pain preempts the emergence of more repressive forms of control such as those found within state systems.) For Durkheim, pain is a necessary condition for the existence of society, for it is only through pain that society can be objectified as an object of reverence – that is, reconstituted as the object of worship. Das nevertheless wonders what relation such ritualized infliction of pain bears to the sufferings undergone in everyday life. But it is surely here that the Weberian notion of disenchantment comes to the rescue: bureaucracy takes the place of the clerisy and the polity becomes the object of attempts to explain away the persistence of misfortune. This is what I have called "secular theodicy," in a deliberate attempt to emphasize through this oxymoron the continuities with the enchanted past – often marked by the linguistic and other traces of such antecedent forms of authority as fate and deity – of a rationalized present (Herzfeld 1992). Other scholars have accepted the Durkheimian model of the connection between pain and social control in a more unmediated form (see, for instance, Desjarlais 1992).

A striking example of how pain may be used in everyday life to create obedient wills may be found in Talal Asad's (1987, 1993) examination of the disciplinary practices of Christian monasticism. Asad discusses the pedagogic techniques used in medieval Latin Christianity to show how religious desires were formed out of practices of poverty and humiliation. If manual labor was to secure humility, says Asad, it had to be transformed into a disciplinary program, and, while this extreme evaluation of humility in the form of self-abasement has obviously fallen into disrepute, it may have colored subsequent ideas about the disciplining of secular manual labor, somewhere between the personal atelier and the factory floor, in ways that have yet to be explored. Asad, true to his refusal of the comprehensive category of "religion" as Christocentric and circular, argues that there is a conceptual and pragmatic continuity between ritual action and everyday behavior, here made visible by tracing the historical vicissitudes of European attitudes to labor (Asad 1987: 194). But certainly, in a hegemonic religious system, the authority of ritual specialists does seem to legitimize the inflicting of acute bodily suffering in the name of a divinely sanctioned social order.

If we do make a distinction between special ritual occasions and everyday disciplinary practice – and Asad recognizes that this may be appropriate to specific historical situations, including that of medieval European Christianity – we will still find that those in power use widely ranging procedures for inflicting pain and humiliation as a way of creating moral and social subjects. Yet no social theorist, argues Das, would argue that the social definition of the person completely assimilates the individual. The administration of pain bears the signs not only of the legitimacy of society but also of its illegitimacy – the oppression that Clastres identifies with the state, but that we might see as always a violation of individual identity in the interests of some kind of conformity. This illegitimacy, remarks Das, "may best be seen in recesses of everyday life when the body is deployed in labor to reproduce itself and the social order of which it is a part." And the question of whether it is indeed an illegitimacy must also be relative to the understandings of social actors: between the poles of compliance and resistance lie the many accommodations and forms of "making do" (Reed-Danahay 1993) that people have developed in order to create a bearable compromise between self and collectivity.

In Borneman's argument, illegitimacy is picked up by social theory when its exponents see the reproduction of persons as the central logic of social organization. In other words, he says, in this view people develop relationships, not in order to care for each other, but in order to reproduce. (An especially dramatic example of this – replete with a system of punishments and rewards and a blithe disregard for the consequences to persons – is the coercive policy of pronatalism enforced by the Çeauşescu dictatorship in Romania [Kligman 1989].) The possibility that sterility – freedom from the necessity of reproducing – might be a more benign reproductive right than the freedom to reproduce at will is simply not entertained: social theory here reproduces dominant assumptions. For Borneman, the major anthropological culprit is kinship theory, in all its various manifestations. Yet he does not dismiss kinship theory – to the contrary, he has made it central to his analysis of law and civic identity in Berlin, as we have seen. Instead, he seeks to detach it from preemptive assumptions about the primacy of reproduction in the definition of this fundamental area of human interrelatedness.

His emphasis on "caring" and the "voluntary" nature of relationships may strike some as utopian or as inapplicable outside the western ambit. (Indeed, the introduction of a public debate about "caring" – the English-language terminology is used – in Italy has raised such a storm of cynical protest that one might reasonably wonder whether the idea of a common western set of values had any applicability at all; but we should not forget that this was, after all, an Italian inititative that perhaps ill-advisedly used a language more often associated with colonial domination, complacent moralism, and virulent anticommunism for many Italians.) By the same token, however, it would be ethnocentric to presuppose that such benignity was exclusively the prerogative of western cultures. Rather, in the global context that anthropology now inhabits, and especially in view of his argument that the western model of "the family" has in fact already been globalized, his deployment of these ideas should prompt some productive discussion – as, in fact, it already has. Used heuristically, in the sense I have used that term in this book, the refocusing of kinship (and more generally social) theory to address questions of care will both undercut simplistic assumptions about a western monopoly of social welfare – itself very much in doubt after widespread reversals of European welfarist policy – and permit the consideration of a wider range of understandings about the nature of kinship itself.

In this century, as Borneman points out, the Durkheimian tradition produced two dominant theories of kinship: descent theory and alliance theory. Descent was organized around principles of consanguinity or shared substance, alliance around principles of affinity or marriage. Neither theory proved the autonomous field its originators had hoped for it and kinship as a topic was roundly criticized – for its nonuniversality (e.g., Needham, ed., 1971), its overformalization (D. Schneider 1980), its lack of coherence as a domain – and in the early 1970s many anthropologists turned to gender, often in the context of a largely feminist political critique. Borneman argues: "This is not to say that each object of knowledge replaced in turn the prior one" or that "marriage ever lost its centrality in analysis. Rather, each successive generation of anthropologists subsumed the prior object into a new one by making it secondary to or derivative of other units of analysis without in fact calling into question the initial object of research. In other words, sexuality became derivative of marriage, marriage of kinship, kinship of gender and gender of prestige and power."

Here, too, we see how easily the Durkheimian perspective coheres with the normativizing exercise of power – a point that was in fact already made, perhaps rather unfairly, by early critics of the potential for Durkheimian theory to support the repressive measures of midcentury fascism. To argue, as some might, that Borneman's critique insists too much on retooling the mainstream's theory to the interests of sexual minorities (or those who have voluntarily decided not to have children) is to reproduce the same normativizing argument all over again. Whatever the historical and statistical validity of such a claim, it reads revealingly like nationalistic objections to discussions of minority rights on the grounds of the numerical insignificance of the minorities in question. It is also a poor argument for an anthropology whose ability to craft a critique of dominant assumptions rests on its engagement with marginal voices and minute observation.

Let us turn first to the reproduction of objects, then return to that of persons. Recent research on artisanship suggests that these are closely related concerns (Kondo 1990). Perhaps because of Marx's interest in the capitalist control of the human body for the purposes of reproduction and accumulation, this relationship has been the focus of more explicit analysis than are the parallel implications of kinship theory.

Objects and Persons

In contrast to the centrality of sacred time in Durkheim's theory of society, the experience of time that most interested Karl Marx (1961) was the working day of the laborer. It was in the regulation of the working day and the toll taken over the body of the laborer that he found the struggles between capital and labor to be most instructive. For Marx the purpose of the rational administration of pain was to create docile bodies for capital. Marx's contribution to the understanding of suffering thus lies in the manner in which the body is placed within the political economy determining the conditions under which suffering is produced and distributed. There are several shifts here – from religion to political economy; from the sacred to the mundane; and from profound intellectual doubts about metaphysical questions to that of survival. Moreover, in the Gramscian concept of "hegemony" we begin to see how and why people are led to comply in their own subjection to such regimes, although understanding the actual techniques of inculcation – how people could be made to acquiesce – had to await the development of ethnographic interest in the minute spaces of workplace training (Coy, ed., 1989; Kondo 1990; but see also Lave 1977). Such studies are now proliferating and may even reveal historical connections between monastic and secular forms of discipline – a democratization of the privilege of suffering through rational means, in which what is rational is determined by those who have the real power.

Ethnographic perspectives allow us to glimpse, at least, the consequences of policies enacted by and for the body politic for the body personal. Under the brutal South African apartheid regime, for example, the forced subjugation of large numbers of people in overcrowded and ill-equipped areas had a devastating impact on health and mortality (Ramphele 1992). Such perspectives demonstrate, as Das argues, that "suffering cannot be seen simply as arising out of the contingencies of life but has to be conceptualized as actively produced and even rationally administered by institutions of the State." As she also notes, such deliberate brutality appears as much in everyday routines as it does in striking events such as when the police fired on a crowd of children. The fundamental resources of family and kinship, so jealously nurtured by the oppressive minority in their own lives, could not withstand the destructive pressures of apartheid. Ramphele (1996b) points out that that the architects of apartheid selected the institution of the family for deliberate destruction, with ruinous consequences at the level of local community: a high prevalence of sexual abuse, the emergence of local warlords, and young boys forced to do battle with the "fathers" who controlled squatter camps with the help of South African police. Ramphele shows how political institutions permeate the biographies of young people.

This permeation, in Ramphele's view, makes it difficult to identify resources for addressing the suffering still experienced by these witnesses of apartheid's horrendous impact. Yet people are remarkably resilient, and sometimes find those resources in their actual sufferings, or in the memory of those sufferings. Writing of the aftereffects of the Cultural Revolution in China, Arthur and Joan Kleinman (1994: 714–15) observed that the "remembrance of bodily complaints broadened into more general stories of suffering that integrated memories of menace and loss with their traumatic effects (criticism sessions, beatings, prison, exile). Bodily memory, biography, and social history merged." And they go on to note, "The memory of bodily complaints evoked social complaints which were not so much represented as lived and relived (remembered) in the body." This renewal of experience may not offer much practical relief, and this is where a rethinking of institutions might indeed be in order – and does, as in South Africa and eastern Europe, for example, appear to happen. But the ethnographic engagement with narratives about bodily suffering at least allows us to recover crucial connections between the body personal and the body politic.

Kinship and Theodicy

Ironically, it is Ramphele's focus on the family as a resource – as the very antithesis of the massive labor breeding machine for which the apartheid regime used it – that allows us to move away from the traditional understanding of kinship and the family as normative systems. Granted, the object of destruction was a system of relationships that held out an alternative normativity – to that of a terrorist state, thereby challenging its authority at base. But there are other circumstances in which kinship and marriage become instead the instruments of a repressive or expansionist state policy, as in pronatalist regimes such as pre-1989 Romania (Kligman 1998). Even in democratic societies, an intolerant majority can produce similar effects, as in the massive opposition to the legitimation of homosexual unions in the United States and elsewhere. The regulative capacities of kinship systems can also invest violence with a terrible logic: by extending the principles of the patrilineal feud to Bosnian ethnicity, at least two of the three major parties to the conflict in that country were able to countenance the rape of "enemy" women and their preservation as breeding machines for the rapists' children (as they were defined, according to the logic of patrilineal kinship); that the women recognized this is attested by their numerous attempts to kill those same children so as not to spawn a fifth column quite literally within the body politic of their own group. Reports from Kosovo, where the husbands of Albanian women raped by the Serbian forces repudiate them as polluted, suggest that this cruel logic – which only the most insensitive form of cultural relativism would defend unconditionally – will ramify through Balkan society for many years to come. The point is not to relativize it out of moral consciousness, but to understand it in order to address it.

But what of those who reject the prevailing norms of kinship and marriage in their own societies? Borneman suggests that this is the real test not only of the systems that enforce those norms, but also of the theories with which we attempt to analyze them. Arguing that "anthropology's quest for a regulative ideal for humanity has involved the repression of care and the privileging of forms of communal reproduction" and that "anthropology should focus instead on processes of voluntary affiliation: processes of caring and being cared for," he explores the relationship between anthropological and legal categories, respectively, of sex, marriage, kinship, and gender by exploring "alternatives for conceptualizing human affiliation outside reproductive ideologies and practices." The two sets of categories are closely related, and in a sense his project is to detach them for long enough for us to see how dangerously close our own framework has come to what it is supposed to analyze: "As the study of humankind, the discipline of anthropology prides itself on providing discursive frames for conceptualizing, demarcating, or understanding human affiliations and identifications across social formations and over time. Law prides itself on the moral regulation, through prescription and prohibition, of the discursive practices and forms of these affiliations and identifications."

His demonstration is resoundingly ethnographic: legal cases of adoption and of marriage in contemporary Germany. I will not repeat here his detailed accounts, but will selectively indicate those aspects of just one case he describes that speak most directly to the self-referential aspects of law embedded also in the assumptions of anthropological theory. And I will sketch the elements of the response they suggest to the problem of locating theodicy in an allegedly postreligious society – specifically, to note that structural problems built into a legal system may constrain individual action in ways that do indeed engender suffering, so that the theodicy may in fact have some basis in social experience.

A man petitioned to adopt a son, who was also his gay lover. The key question posed by the German civil court in the adoption concerned the nature of the relationship between the two men – a question the court was technically not allowed to ask: Was the relationship similar to that between a biological father and son? The younger man's mother, in agreeing to the arrangement (a precondition in law), nevertheless wrote that the relationship was "like a marriage." This set off an intensive judicial questioning, which was extended into a second hearing before a new judge. This official declared that he "had no problems" with homosexuality and then he asked the prospective son about his mother's comment. The latter responded that she had no knowledge in the matter, that the older man had "always taken care" of him, and that his own preference for young boys – he had a prior conviction for abusing minors – precluded his accepting the passive sexual role in the relationship. Moreover, the older man had been diagnosed with a terminal illness, as he himself then declared: he cared for the younger as for a son and friend and therefore wanted to leave his house and wealth to him. Adoption was the only legal means by which he could do this. All of this was true. Then, with great difficulty, he lied, as he had to in order to achieve his goal, and he denied ever having had sex with the younger man, claiming that he had for nearly a decade been involved in a sexual relationship with another man. Despite lengthy further questioning, the two men stuck to their story, and eventually the judge approved the adoption.

Borneman argues that "the logic of the adoption was in fact set up by the legal categories of kinship – which are also enshrined in anthropological theories – to which any petition must appeal. But once the petition was granted and the adoption approved, that initial legal kinship logic had been effectively stretched out of recognizable shape." Instead, what was now at stake was the legally recognized right to care – to be cared for – couched in the terms of inheritance as a continuation of that caring relationship, with all the reciprocities it entailed. This shift was explicitly acknowledged by the judge.

Traditionally, adoption in German law and in the western legal tradition establishes a legal relationship of parentage by descent. Kin rights permeate all legal domains as relations between specific categories of kin (such as husband and wife, or parent and child) and relations analogous to them are protected, supported, or forbidden. Yet the judge in this case did not begin by applying an abstract principle of descent to enable Harald to pass on his inheritance to Dieter, but acted, says Borneman, as if he had just read Lévi-Strauss's (1949) *The Elementary Structures of Kinship*, "where reproduction of societies is linked to respect for the incest taboo as the social precondition for the principles of heterosexual descent and affinity." He asked whether the two men had respected the fundamental incest taboo – no sex between parent and child. As Lévi-Strauss (1963: 50) argued, the incest taboo, or the forbidding of sex between people of the same descent, creates the possibility for and necessity of affinity (relations through marriage – "in-laws"). Thus, the two men – and the judge – were caught in a number of categorical confusions.

If the two men lived together in a relationship "like a marriage," then, by analogy with heterosexual kin relations, sex between them was a necessary if not compulsory effect, regardless of what they saw their mutual obligations as being. By analogy the judge was being asked if it might be possible to turn an affinal relation ("like in a marriage") into one of legal descent, a transformation expressly prohibited by the incest taboo. "Anthropological theory and the law are in widespread agreement that nature bestows on us the principle of descent while culture specifies the rules of affinity. In theory adults are to enjoy both principles simultaneously as privileged relationships with culturally specified (gendered, sexed and age-graded) categories of persons – so long as it is not with the same person." It was this that the two men attempted, successfully as it happened, in seeking "the subordination of the principle of a descent to a relation of care." Borneman's conclusion is blunt: "The breakdown in the ability of the categories of sex, marriage, kinship and gender to represent an affiliation based on the fundamental need of care presents anthropologists with the task of finding a way to re-present the relation" in question. For instead of accepting the rules as they found them, these two men "were asserting a particular principle of voluntary affiliation: the need to care and be cared for."

Borneman's example dramatically illustrates the cultural assumptions ingrained in the construction of standard anthropologies of kinship and gender. I have reinscribed his discussion in the context of an account of sufferings and disciplines because it shows how norms can collide with human experience, leaving the ultimate resolution to an arbitrary quirk of fate – to a human arbiter, in fact, who is as caught up in the trammels of the law as the two plaintiffs. Indeed, had the first judge also presided at the second trial, it seems likely that the matter might have ended very differently. My point is that in either case the decision would have been handed down in a form extremely resistant to appeal because it would have been couched in the ostensibly unambiguous terminology of the law: the quirk of fate, more or less, determines what "the truth" is going to be. Everyone knows, or so lawyers and anthropologists usually assume, what "the family" is.

One's response to calls for gay marriage is not at issue here. Indeed, Borneman would presumably argue that recent moves in the United States to legitimize gay unions as marriage are necessitated by the same kind of logic, which places conformity with categorical understandings before the legal recognition of caring arrangements. In that the denial of care is an imposition of suffering, moreover, it entails a theodicy: what is at stake is not whether or not the plaintiffs spoke the truth (one of them did actually lie) but, as is always socially more relevant, how successfully they calibrated their enunciation of the relationship to the formal framework required of them, and whether the judge was able – or wanted – to accept (rather than believe) what he was told. Had they failed, they and the judge alike would have appealed to a common secular theodicy by holding "society" responsible for the rules of kinship and its consequences. Adaptations of normativity usually occur on the side of the suffering and the weak: for example, we have increasing evidence

that women prisoners construct fictive families around homosexual relationships that allow them, at multiple levels, to create oases of mutual affection
and care in the face of a harsh prison bureaucracy and an indifferent society
beyond the prison walls (e.g., Cunha 1995; Suputtamongkol 2000). These
are appropriations of officially legitimated forms; they reveal to a remarkable
degree how a rethinking of kinship in terms other than those of authority
and dependence may also serve to detach anthropological theory from the vision
of the state.

A Political Economy of Suffering

In the German adoption case just described, whatever risk to caregiving
may have existed was at least to some extent protected by the possibility of
reframing the law to suit the case – of reinventing the domestic unit, in effect.
Constraining though the law was, it at least allowed the possibility of negotiating the specific case to a point that satisfied the plaintiffs' immediate needs
and intentions, although Borneman's account conveys something of the anguish
that these semantic acrobatics must have cost them. Because these events
occurred in a relatively peaceful and stable nation-state, the iron hand of
the law was at least wearing kid gloves. But Borneman's argument has a wider
application: that a focus on norms may preclude an attention to care, substituting theodicy (explanation after the fact) for caregiving (forestalling suffering). As he remarks: "Carol Gilligan began such a focus on the 'ethic of care'
back in 1982, although she attached it to a feminine voice and opposed it to a
masculine 'ethic of right.' We now know that the articulation of care and the
acknowledgment of right are neither essentially opposed nor gendered but
belong to every human voice. Not only do ethnographic accounts provide ample
documentation for the diversity of relations in which caring is expressed and of
the power matrix in which they are assigned value, but jural personnel are
increasingly interpreting kinship law in light of these diverse relations and not
in terms of putatively fixed and innocent identities of sexuality, marriage,
kinship, and gender."

To bring this single case of legal insensitivity to human needs into juxtaposition with the more obvious instances of material suffering brought about by
poverty, police brutality, or wretched labor conditions is not to trivialize either.
Sufferings of all varieties call for explanations, and the anthropologist's task is
to find a way of resisting identification of the analytic framework with the theodicy of those concerned. I turn back, now, to some of the more sensational examples of suffering with that goal in mind.

The devastating policies of apartheid, briefly discussed above, compel us to
see how political and economic factors shape the distribution of suffering in the
contemporary world. But these factors can easily be read out of local idioms of
justification and theodicy too: it is important to withstand the temptation to do
so. The logic of social space in understanding suffering is vital because this is

the space in which accountability is formulated. While the case of South Africa stands out for its systematic and planned brutality, comparable degradations of human experience also appear in many contexts of overwhelming poverty. Nancy Scheper-Hughes (1992), for example, has shown the impact of hunger on the lives of women in a Brazilian market town, questioning the popularly held notions of human emotions such as maternal love. Scheper-Hughes gives devastating descriptions of how mothers, crazed with hunger, find it difficult to harness material and emotional resources to ensure the survival of their children; babies viewed by their mothers as doomed because of their frailty are allowed to die of neglect. As Arthur Kleinman (1995: 237–9) notes in commenting on the book, these mothers are not rebels, and they are indeed skeptical of radical solutions. They tell us about an aspect of the ontology of suffering even more terrible than its pragmatism: the capacity to endure, survive, and even adapt to the most inhuman conditions. Scheper-Hughes's impressive ethnography might too easily lead one to condemn the actions of such mothers in facile terms like "maternal neglect." Kleinman in effect cautions us that we should not be lured by the idea that suffering always transforms the person and society toward greater refinement – the justification for its imposition, the appeal to theodicy, that is usually given by those in authority. This is the Christian teleology that Asad has so rightly identified in much European thinking about these matters. Between the potential of suffering for the creation of moral selves and communities, and its potential for destruction of any cosmology within which suffering could make sense, we find a space that is especially fertile for the creative exercise and even invention of theodicies calibrated to everyday experience.

The twentieth century has been described as the century of genocides. For philosophers and social scientists, as for many others, the events of the twentieth century are encapsulated in the idea of "useless suffering." In the magnitude and savagery inflicted on the Jews, the Holocaust, above all other events and also as a sign of the violence of this century, as Das (invoking especially the philosopher Emmanuel Levinas) emphasizes, meant the end of traditional theories of theodicy.

This pessimistic view takes us far from Weber's notion of the problem of theodicy, for to offer salvational hopes to those who have suffered in such extreme ways could today, in this interpretation, only be read as a case of bad faith. Furthermore, to find theories of theodicy or salvational hopes in the institutions responsible for creating those conditions is, thinks Das, "an exercise of subtle power that locks the victims of violence and injustice into frozen positions." Certainly, I would add, it sheds new light on the countless such acts that governments and other institutions perpetrate every day, taking refuge in their own theodicy – "the system" – as an ethical alibi for self-fulfilling formulations, such as, for example, bromides about the "culture of poverty," colonialist and postcolonial assertions about the "laziness" or "fatalism" of the "natives," and dictators' invocation of national traits that require "correction" (this often being reinforced by frightening surgical metaphors). Even history offers a theodicy of sorts: the previous government's legacy, the effects of colonialism, and so on.

Such causes may be real enough, but the effect of invoking them can also be to divert constructive criticism – in a partial sense this is what the critique of post-colonial studies offered by Talad Asad and David Scott is about (see also Mbembe 1992).

These are all denials, instrumental as well as symbolic, of agency. They are also debatable within the moral frameworks with which they appear, for they are perversions of those frameworks; but the issue is always that of finding both the will and the means to resist the allure of power in order to oppose them. On the other hand, and this is a point closer to Borneman's position, if we abandon any intention of intervening to make the structures of authority work for the greater benefit, does this not concede agency to those who wield bureaucratic power – does it not, as it were, yield agency to the agencies?

To be sure, as Das wisely observes the suffering of victims has all too often been appropriated in order to legitimize official or corporate control of the space of public ethical pronouncements. As corporations rise to a power equaling or perhaps even surpassing that of the state, and as the reach of the media allows the systematic reinterpretation of events for purposes that it may not always be easy to determine, the possibilities for such appropriation increase rather than fade – another consequence of the increase of scale in our experienced world, and thus also another important challenge for ethnographic practice.

Are we, then, to assume that we cannot work with the structures of the state at all in order to improve the conditions of life? That cannot be the real intention of Das's critique, since she recognizes the extraordinary achievement of South Africa in moving from the horrors of repressive violence to a state committed, in already tangible ways, to the rule of justice. Nor can it be said that states themselves are incapable of punishing their oppressive predecessors; indeed, Borneman argues that democratic leaders who fail to do so take far greater risks with the lives of their citizens: "Where there has been little or no attempt to prosecute former authorities for wrongdoing in East bloc states, these societies have been marked by a cycle of violence and counterviolence" (Borneman 1997: 4). In his commentary on my remarks about bureaucracy, Don Handelman has emphasized that one can overdraw the distinction between democratic and totalitarian regimes; indeed, I would argue further that an agency-based approach must recognize the huge range of possibilities for action, benign and malevolent, in all forms of government and administration. But the issue, which Borneman pinpoints as the key definiens of democratic process (Borneman 1997: 3), is one of accountability – that key theme again – and the means we devise to make all politicians and administrators answerable for their actions. There still, always and everywhere, remains that other question: answerable to whom? Here again, ethnographic perspectives at least provide some insight into the actual operation of accountability at the local level – precisely where Evans-Pritchard examined it when he explored witchcraft among the Azande of Sudan. We cannot simply assume that responsibility is a clearly defined, culture-

free concept. But when we know more about where the actors in any
social tragedy – victims and perpetrators alike – might agree on locating
responsibility in theory, we do have an initial benchmark for evaluating their
practice.

Judicial and Bureaucratic Appropriation of Suffering

Das is nevertheless surely right to say that those who control the bureaucracy
and the media are in a position to manipulate suffering to ends that do not
benefit the sufferers. The Union Carbide disaster of Bhopal, said to be the worst
industrial disaster in history, exemplifies the judicial and bureaucratic appropriation of suffering (see Das 1995). (The way in which the scientific evidence
was brought into courts of law in the Bhopal case was similar to what happened in the Agent Orange case in the United States.) In many cases of this sort,
the dominant issue in the courts of law or commissions instituted by the state
is the legitimacy of the state itself – a secular theodicy, orchestrated by the state
for the purposes of its own self-preservation – rather than a search for a means
of redressing the suffering.

The Agent Orange case is especially important, Das suggests, for our understanding of what precisely secular theodicy could usefully mean at this level.
This case represented the attempts of thousands of Vietnam veterans to
seek legal redress for grievous and debilitating illnesses they believed to have
been caused by their exposure to Agent Orange, a herbicide used by the
United States Army to defoliate Vietnam's jungle cover. This herbicide was
initially considered harmless to humans and animals. Yet as veterans spread
over different parts of the United States began to suffer from similar symptoms
including delayed onset of cancer, some began to suspect that the impact
of Agent Orange on human health had been severely underestimated. Easily
understood evidence was hard to find, in part because the chemical industry
did not release all the information at its disposal. After the judge had fashioned
an out-of-court settlement, since he felt that legal uncertainties would
create further hardship for the victims, more than a thousand veterans
came forward to testify in the fairness hearings. Even the words of the presid-
ing judge captured the enormous sense of grief and suffering of the victims
when he spoke of "broken-hearted widows who have seen their strapping young
husbands die of cancer, wives who must live with husbands wracked with
pain and in deep depression, mothers whose children suffer from multiple
birth defects and require almost saint-like daily care" (quoted in Schuck
1987). Yet he also felt that the scientific evidence was not conclusive and
thus expected the lawyers to understand the limited powers of the court in the
matter of establishing proof. Das (1995: 129) has commented: "It was assumed
by both sides to the dispute that courts of law are spaces in which a victim
becomes a plaintiff by acquiring the means of proving that damage has
been done to him. But the very certainty demanded by the judges, within
a context where the toxic hazards of chemicals were either not known or

not revealed by the chemical industry, robbed the victims of the means by which the damage done to them could be *proved*. Victims were in effect being told to learn how to transform their suffering into the language of science in order for it to be judicially recognized. But if both plaintiffs and defendants were obliged to speak *only* in the language of science, then surely it has to be conceded that proceedings in the court were being conducted on two different registers: one, the register of scientific speech; the other, an anguished expression of victims in a case by case enumeration. If the second kind of evidence was finally to turn out not to be evidence at all, then why was this suffering exhibited as display?"

In the case of the Bhopal disaster, the victims were not allowed to appear individually in court while an out-of-court settlement was being negotiated between Union Carbide and the Government of India with the mediation of the Supreme Court. The Court reasoned that the primary motive behind the settlement, which many considered grossly inadequate, was to cut short the legal delays and redress more rapidly the sufferings of the victims. Why do courts of law evoke the suffering of the victims in this manner? Das's argument was that the display of the victim's sufferings performed an ornamental function for the legal text which could now appear appropriate to the occasion. The use of metaphors, stylistic distensions, and analogies in effect acted as shears with which the victims were cut off from their own suffering, which appeared now as ornamental display in another discourse. While the courts' action actually intensified the suffering of the victims, the rhetoric of consideration and restitution, and their elaborate defense of the purported need to protect the interests of the corporation in order to secure the long-term benefit of the body politic (the argument of the greatest good for the greatest number), reproduces the state's arrogation to itself of the right of punitive action – but, in this case, as a means of reinforcing the courts' own authority rather than of finding practical ways of alleviating, as far as possible, the horrible sufferings of the disaster victims.

As Das remarks: "Secular theodicies of the State add a new dimension to visions of future. In the case of chemical hazards, the courts have repeatedly argued in many different countries that some risks to the population have to be tolerated as a condition for future production of wealth. In the case of biomedical technologies, new and experimental technologies are often tested in such populations as terminally ill patients, prison populations, prostitutes – in other words those who are defined as a social waste – in the hope that the technologies would increase the well-being of people in the future. These practices, which result from what Margaret Lock (1996) calls a violence of zeal, assume that lesser harm can be inflicted for future greater good. In giving precise definitions to harm and good, however, science and state may end up in making an alliance in which the suffering of those defined as a social waste is appropriated for projects of a good society in the future."

Authorities may later recant, as, for example, has happened in the case of the Tuskegee experiments, in which African American patients were subjected to "experimental treatments" that subjected them to intense – and often fatal –

doses of radiation. But such reversals usually come only in the wake of political mobilization, calling for a revision of the self-congratulatory histories that institutions, left unchecked, tend to write about themselves. The state is of course not the only such institution; nor, as Das admits, "can it be said that such appropriations for the cause of the community always violate the individual." But social movements themselves all too easily reduce actors to stereotypical images. Let us consider two examples from the same society. Reynolds (1996) shows has young black activists in Cape Town, who were subjected to torture, police firings, and solitary confinement were able to engage this past to find resources for the political transformation of one of the most brutal regimes in history. In her autobiographical account on the other hand, Ramphele (1996a) shows how political widowhood leads to a transposition of the widow from the role of personal to that of public loss. The struggles in South Africa over funerals of the political activists were occasions for reinterpreting, reenacting, and shaping social memory; on that very account, however, they were also deeply disturbing for the bereaved. We should also remember that the sufferers as well as the freedom fighters of one era may well be the rulers – repressive or benign – of the next.

Offering Testimony

Personal tragedy may thus be transmitted into, and sometimes overwhelmed by, collective representation. Far more pervasive in many people's lives are sensationalist media accounts of horrible human tragedies. That these are manipulations of others' sufferings is often masked by the rhetoric of the public's "right to know," certainly a moral stance in its own right (and, like all moral stances, devastating in the hands of a skilled cynic). It is not always clear, moreover, precisely why such appropriations should be objectionable: people have become so used to them that even those who might be thought the most likely to resent them often hardly seem to notice amid their grief. Does the commodification of suffering in the media today – "as if it were passing scenery for the view," as Das remarks – render it less authentic? I suggest that this is not a helpful question: it surrenders too much to the realist or objectivist fantasy of a truth knowable in noncultural terms. Das wisely addresses instead the social effects of this commodification by the media, concluding, with Arthur and Joan Kleinman (1996), that it has the effect of neutralizing the horror that it portrays. The media, however benign their intentions (and the same applies to bureaucracy), too easily routinize what for those who must bear it is appalling pain and degradation. These consequences are ethnographically observable – a further reason, in addition to those to be discussed later in connection with the media, to insist on close observation of the actual engagements of audiences with these forms of representation.

The effects of media viewing are not predictable, although we may feel we know them all too well. The realist conventions of television do nevertheless lend considerable force to Das's implication that packaging in effect becomes knowledge, and that in the process its ability to stir the conscience dwindles cat-astrophically. These realist conventions, which are tied to the spectacular power of industrial technology to reach into every home, are enhanced beyond any-thing we have seen happen with the parallel objectivism of newspaper report-ing. Yet people do resist, and not always benignly: some Greek viewers of television reporting on atrocities committed by their Serbian coreligionists in Kosovo dismissed these as mere propaganda, thereby refracting events – note the force of that metaphor once again – through the partisan divisions of regional politics. After all, if moon landings can be seen as American fabrica-tions, why not the justification of massive air strikes as well? By engaging with this aspect of the struggle, moreover, these viewers have been able to maintain their own unyielding hostility to the "other side," consisting of Catholics, Muslims, and all Americans. These are social actors who understand just how conventional realism is, and are prepared to fight it with its own criteria of proof.

But mostly objectivism and realism do their work all too well: they are the aesthetic counterpart to what we mean conceptually by "common sense" in the industrialized West, and take visual as well as textual form on television. In other words, they are a historically and culturally specific set of conventions. Because they are backed by such massive communicative power, moreover, they furnish the "logical" basis for dismissing claims made in other modes. A dra-matic illustration of this is the attack on the truthfulness of the Guatemalan Maya activist Rigoberta Menchú, which was couched in entirely objectivist terms (Stoll 1999). At one level, this might appear to be a replay of the Sahlins–Obeyesekere debate about Captain Cook. In that dispute, however, even though Obeyesekere claimed to speak for Third World peoples, his discourse was very much that of a United States academic. Shryock's Jordanian tribal chroniclers similarly trade charges of mendacity within a common discourse they all understand in the same way. In the case of Menchú, by contrast, we are dealing – as Kay Warren (2000) has powerfully argued – with a difference of genre, embedded in contrasted cultural styles, that makes nonsense of objec-tivist attempts to dismiss Menchú's accounts as untruthful. Rather they are, as Warren suggests, *testimónios* – acts of witnessing that "attempt to make the abstractions of violence, poverty, and degrading living conditions starkly immediate."

Because suffering is socially produced (Kleinman, Das, and Lock 1996), it must take cultural form, and this may result in its being pitted against hegemonic versions of common sense. Within a community, the idiom is likely to be understood: Guatemalan Indians who had suffered under the repressive regime had no difficulty in understanding Menchú's testimonies as an appropriate response; but overseas media were scandalized. This is not an unfamiliar scenario for anthropologists, who often find themselves called on to explain what strike uninformed observers as exotic, bizarre practices. More to the point, anthropologists – without necessarily attributing to such practices the teleological motivations so beloved by the functionalists of yore – see them as a substantial resource for those culturally equipped to use them.

Das emphasizes the collective nature of the ways in which "individuals seek to understand their experiences and to work toward healing. This is evident in the large number of healing cults to be found in every society. But we also find extraordinary transformations of the healing institutions of a society when it is faced with collective disaster." As evidence of how "resources for regeneration may be found in the different spiritual traditions of local communities," she cites the case of Saktirani, a woman seer from eastern Sri Lanka (P. Lawrence 1995). Women come to Saktirani, who enacts the embodied state of the goddess Kali, and seek advice, redressal, or simply solace. As mothers of children who have disappeared, or wives who think their husbands have been tortured, visit Saktirani, she presents their pain to them through both her speech and her body and thus "divines" the fate of the lost ones. When possessed by the goddess she speaks "harsh truths" (for instance she may tell a woman that her husband or son is dead, or that he has been severely tortured). The range of emotions she traverses in a single day or an hour as she enacts the fate of the disappeared is indicative of the desperate conditions in this region, but it also points to an extraordinary human ability to generate spiritual resources in the face of appalling pain (see also Trawick 1988).

Das argues that "the anthropological text may serve as a body of writing which lets the pain of the other happen to it." By this she clearly intends us to understand that the anthropologist must at all costs avoid appropriating the pain of others for any purpose, including that of scholarship, and should let the sufferer speak through the anthropological text. Here I think she is too sanguine: the meaning of a text is partly constituted by its audience, and the audience of anthropologists may often be one that seeks in turn to appropriate its texts for unintended purposes – or one that interprets the work of anthropologists as an appropriation. Indeed, for the anthropologist to argue in effect that "others may not appropriate my text" is itself an appropriation of sorts. Is the wholly disinterested ethnographer any more plausible than the objective observer?

I worry that we too easily see the production of "disinterested scholarship" as a kind of theodicy in itself, fearing a more proactive role because of the responsibility for the consequences that this may impose. Such responsibility cannot be avoided outright. Tambiah's (1992) critique of extremist Sinhala nationalism, for example, has drawn a great deal of fire; to have remained silent would, by the lights of his own commitments, have been far less responsible – and consequently far less ethical – than to risk his own reputation by taking a clear and unequivocal stance. Cultural relativism, too, offers a theodicy of its own, and this discussion exposes the limits of such refuges.

But what this discussion has revealed is that the self-criticism of anthropology, consistently with the pedagogical model outlined in the introductory chapter, can be deployed in precisely this way to open up new avenues of inquiry. It is in the moment when epistemology seems at its most frail that new insights are generated. Whether we accept the critique that Borneman brings to kinship and the family, for example, the discussion that it generates makes anthropology the kind of comparandum that illuminates its own object of study. Nowhere is this more important than in the analysis of human suffering, for it is here that "society" – anthropology's favored object – has failed its members, by almost any standard one could invoke. And it is here that the categorical brand of reflexive thinking may offer glimmers, if not of solutions, at least of understanding of the sources of that suffering.

11

Senses

Common Sense, Body Sense

Anthropology, like all academic disciplines, is primarily a verbal activity. Even the study of visual media must always be expressed in words. Recent attempts to introduce pictorial representations of human movement (notably D. Williams 1991; D. Williams, ed., 1997; Farnell 1995) suggest the inadequacy of this Cartesian commitment. We have seen already that modern representational practices are heavily dependent on visual formats, but even this restriction seems to appear most commonly as an extension of verbal texts. A diagram without a caption would not be easily understood. In consequence of this bias built into the preferred modes of representation, the role of smell and hearing, not to speak of touch, has been grossly under-represented. Can suffering, the theme of the previous chapter, be understood without reference to sensation? Especially in this chapter and in the chapter on aesthetics, I shall try to suggest paths along which anthropologists have been trying for some years now to rectify this pervasive absence.

The technical difficulties of recording smell and taste are formidable, and have certainly inhibited progress. Much of the work even on the significance of gesture must proceed through verbal responses to visual cues (e.g., Cowan 1990). The possibility of knowing "what something smells like" to a member of one's own culture is remote; when we add the further problem of cross-cultural translation, the difficulties may seem to be insurmountable, especially given the intractability to analysis of psychological inner states. It is nevertheless encouraging that a few scholars have begun to broach an "anthropology of the senses" – although I would caution that this label risks marginalizing, as yet one more specialist concern, what really ought to be a central concern for the comparative study of cultures and societies.

The fundamental premise underlying the concept of an "anthropology of the senses" is that sensory perception is a cultural as well as a physical act: sight, hearing, touch, taste, and smell are not only means of apprehending physical phenomena but are also avenues for the transmission of cultural values. While the most obvious domains for this process may be the performing arts, it is also an integral part of social relations: smell, for example, creates social boundaries, not because some smells are naturally bad, but because they are culturally constituted as such. (If one considers the radical difference between most Southeast Asians' enthusiastic response to the smell of the durian fruit in contrast to the disgust it evokes from most Europeans, for example, it becomes immediately apparent that smell is as culturally relative as aesthetic judgment.) This realization is an extension, rarely recognized as such, of Mary Douglas's famous insight that "dirt" is a matter of cultural categories rather than of biological fact (Douglas 1966), as is indeed suggested by the association of the less recordable senses with concepts of pollution and cleanliness – a bad smell, a disgusting sound, a slimy touch.

Like the notion of order that defines dirt, the experience of the senses is calibrated to the "common sense" – to the accepted range of what is self-evident" (Douglas 1975) – in any given society. In this regard, the study of the senses is remarkably like that of, say, economies: it is resistant to such anthropological relativization because this relativization threatens the security of our own unconsciously cherished perceptions and thus – especially – of the idea of a transcendent "common sense." Indeed, the etymological splitting of terms like "sense" and "taste" into two streams – the cerebral and the sensual – is diagnostic of the extent to which Cartesian and even earlier western assumptions about the separation of body from mind have taken hold of our consciousness.

This chapter should be read in close association with the chapter on aesthetics. The very term "aesthetics" is derived from a Greek root connoting the subjective perception of feeling. In the West this category is freely extended to the auditory domain: music is especially prominent here. Yet this term, too, is restricted in its applications by particular cultural definitions of the sensorium. The addition of taste and smell is rare, half-humorous (calling a chef an "artist" has all the metaphorical ring of artifice), and confined to relatively few domains. Perhaps the commodification of visual art offers a clue here: given the economic significance of collecting as well as the heavy investment in monumentality made by nation-states, the difficulty of recording smell and taste in some reproducible and reasonably durable medium has marginalized these senses more than any other except touch – which, because it is primarily dyadic and thus relatively private, generally escapes social analysis altogether.

An Anthropology of the Senses?

In recent years, anthropologists concerned with the restrictive understanding of the phenomenal world that is possible using the conventional descriptive instruments of an academic discipline, have begun to explore new approaches. Some of these approaches are inspired by phenomenology (e.g., M. Jackson 1989), some by growing awareness of dominant medical paradigms of embodiment (Desjarlais 1992; Kleinman and Kleinman 1994), some by the realization that historical knowledge may as easily be embodied as objectified

(Connerton 1989; Seremetakis 1991, 1993), and some by a focus on the inculcation of social knowledge by nonverbal means (Coy 1989; Kondo 1990;
Jenkins 1994). The contribution from medical anthropology is potentially
perhaps the most radical, because this field tackles the Cartesian paradigm at
source – in the body itself.

A few anthropologists, moreover, have bravely tackled the whole gamut
of "the senses" as a key topic for the discipline. Among these, C. Nadia
Seremetakis (ed., 1994) and Paul Stoller (1989) have offered us exercises in
reflexive exploration. Others, notably a group of Canadian scholars including
Constance Classen (whose work is central to this chapter), have attempted to
synthesize a comparative "anthropology of the senses." This is an important
departure. It places the sensual in systematic analytic focus for virtually the first
time, and it substitutes methodological challenges for vague assertions.

It also, however, inevitably raises the usual difficulty associated with the
invention of any new "anthropology-of" formulation. The small number of
scholars so far engaged in this enterprise suggests, above all, the risk that the
senses – other than those already dominant – will remain marginal to ethnographic description unless, in some practical fashion, all of anthropology can
be recognized as necessarily shot through with alertness to the entire gamut of
sensory semiosis. I use the term "semiosis" rather than "perception" here advis-
edly, for I wish to signal the importance of recognizing that what this new development offers is a specifically social, as opposed to psychological, assessment
of how the various senses are used.

Finally, I suggest that another risk is that of simply developing a catalogue
of cases. As a new awareness of the centrality of the sensory emerges, some
of this is undoubtedly inevitable, and indeed may constitute a necessary
precondition for "resensitizing" the discipline. That said, however, a slight inti-
mation of strain may appear as this chapter progresses, for my own intention
– which is surely not ultimately at odds with Classen's – is not so much to list
all the exciting new areas in which we can explore sensory semiosis, but to think
about how this might affect other domains of anthropological investigation.
We can ask, for example, how considerations of smell might affect economic
relations (a gift that smells wrong may indeed be poisoned, metaphorically
or otherwise); how the nose often provides a means of ethnic, class, and
even professional classification in ways that subvert the explicit social ideology
of a culture; or how the physical discipline of the body through intensely boring
and uncomfortable posture may not only inculcate artisanal conformity and
obedience but provide space for silent mutiny and a reallocation of loyalties.
Here again, I would emphasize the probable future contribution of what
has already been done in medical anthropology, where the issue is no longer
simply one of recognizing that culture mediates experience but has become a
focus on how such mediation is negotiated and modulated through actual
changes in the social sphere. An excessive focus on static "cultures" resists this
insight; in this chapter, I shall attempt to reverse that flow, and so to suggest
some linkages that would not necessarily accrue to an anthropology of the senses
narrowly conceived.

The senses are arenas of agency. Thus, the view that perception is conditioned by culture, while unexceptionable in itself, does not suffice. Not only do the ways in which people perceive the world vary as cultures vary, but indeed they also vary within cultures; they are negotiated. Yet it is certainly useful to begin with the local understanding of what actually can be sensed and how. As Classen has shown, perhaps the most surprising realization is the fact that even the enumeration of the senses may vary. Within western history we find, aside from the customary grouping into five senses, enumerations of four, six or seven senses described at different periods by different persons. Thus, for example, taste and touch are sometimes grouped together as one sense, and touch is sometimes divided into several senses (Classen 1993a: 2–3). Similar variations in the enumeration of the senses can be found in non-western cultures. Ian Ritchie writes that the Hausa of Nigeria, for example, recognize two general senses: visual perception and nonvisual perception (Ritchie 1991: 195). Such basic differences in the divisions of the sensorium recognized in different cultures suggest the extent to which sensation is cultural as much as it is physiological.

Scholars who are interested in the cultural patterning of sensation report a wide variety of kinds of meaning attributed to various kinds of sensory experience. The senses themselves may be linked with different trains of associations, and certain senses rank higher in value than others. The elaborate attention paid to both sight and taste in the Chinese kitchen, for example, may contrast with the Balkan preference for uncomplicated tastes and frequent indifference to the visual appearance of the food. The predominance of particular senses in symbolism also varies a great deal: smell, for example, is nowadays either neutral or slightly negative in North American culture unless the reverse is specified – as it may have to be in any attempt to generalize about "the Western sensorium," because in an older western tradition the "odor of sanctity," often marked by the attractive smell of the corpse of a saintly person, was held in high esteem. Christian mystical tradition, for example, is characterized by a strict asceticism of the body coupled with a rich sensuality of the spirit, whereby the divine is conceptualized and mystically experienced through a wealth of sensory symbols. Nonetheless, today we are more likely to say of an idea that it stinks, or that a scheme smells fishy, than to praise it as "smelling of roses" (although this, too, may happen). And a North American might regard as eccentric the behavior of a tough Greek man of military service age who plucks a flower in order to savor its smell, and then rolls a single word around in his mouth with obvious sensual relish, not because its referential meaning is remarkable, but because he wishes to share his pleasure in the pure sound of it – a revealing reversal of what we so often consider to be the "real" value of speech. (It may also be significant in this connection that the Greek term *noïma*, literally a "meaningfulness," is usually understood to mean a somewhat covert gesture that would actually be betrayed by the act of speaking, especially in the kind of pretentious way that such a gesture can be used to mock: real, social meaning inheres in action, not grandiose verbiage.)

All these examples suggest that bodily sensation and cultural value are mutually engaged at all times. Our task is to explore, not only the variety of such associations, but also their consequences for the whole range of social relations and acts. Social codes determine what constitutes acceptable sensory behavior and indicate what different sensory experiences mean. To stare at someone may signify rudeness, curiosity, flattery, or domination, depending on the circumstances and the culture. Downcast eyes, in turn, may suggest modesty, fear, contemplation, or inattention. And these are simply the possibilities for cultural coding, within which personal idiosyncrasies may produce further variation in the meanings intended – and attributed to a particular posture. Yet relatively little of this makes its way into ethnographic writing. When it does, this is often because the explicit exegesis of knowledgeable informants has legitimated it – made it "real."

Classen points out that the association between sensory faculties and kinds of meaning is surprisingly varied. Sight may be linked to reason or to witchcraft, taste may be used as a metaphor for aesthetic discrimination or for sexual experience, an odor may signify sanctity or sin, political power or social exclusion. Together, these sensory meanings and values form the sensory model espoused – more or less consistently – by the members of a society. This is what it means to say that people "make sense" of the world. Classen acknowledges the likelihood of challenges to this model from within the society – from "persons and groups who differ on certain sensory values" – but, in accordance with the respect for indigenous theories enjoined in this book, we would agree on insisting that there is usually a central paradigm to be debated, negotiated, or simply – if differentially – experienced.

Three Assumptions Challenged

Classen notes three prevalent assumptions that have impeded our understanding of the cultural construction of sense. (She herself describes that understanding as "an alternative approach to the study of culture," which suggests that one might still be able to conceive that an anthropology not fully responsive to the role of the senses could still offer a persuasive interpretation of some aspects of social life.) These assumptions are: that the senses are "windows on the world," or in other words transparent in nature, and therefore are precultural; that the most important sense is the visual; and that a more acceptable alternative to this "visualism" is the recasting of knowledge – especially about nonliterate societies – as verbal, and specifically as oral/aural.

We experience our bodies – and the world – through our senses, which we apprehend on the basis of the codes we have learned. The normative sensory model of a society thus reveals the expectations placed on individual understanding, and points up important aspects of its internal organization. For example, the gradual European abandonment of smell and increasing emphasis on vision is directly linked to the technologies of literacy and to the expansion of social relations beyond the face-to-face that these made possible.

To address the first assumption briefly, then, the view of the senses as "windows on the world" is a misleading metaphor. Unlike windows, the senses are not transparent. They are, rather, heavily encoded instruments that translate bodily experience into culturally recognizable forms. They thus frame and mediate perceptual experience in accordance with a balance of personal idiosyncrasy and socially prescribed norms. And even the idiosyncratic dimensions are variations on cultural themes. Two individuals in a given culture may not enjoy the same foods, yet they will express their respective preferences in terms of a set of preconceived categories. For example, contrary to western stereotypes, not all Thais adore spicy food (although some may "justify" their blander tastes, which are also a claim on higher social status, by wryly attributing it to their Chinese ancestry!), yet the "quality" of the food will be debated in terms of agreed-upon notions of balance, freshness, and so forth. A Greek restaurateur I know excoriated a distinguished habitué of his restaurant for demanding that the spaghetti be cooked soft; the gentleman in question, a sophisticated traveler, complained about the "hard" pasta he had encountered in Italy, where locals usually insist that it should not be cooked beyond the toughness they call *al dente* (literally, "for the tooth"). Where mutually hostile cultures abut each other, we may even find systemic discordance within a larger common code. In the Balkans, for example, Greeks view with deep ambivalence certain Turkish dishes that combine the sweet fruitiness of raisins with meat or yoghurt or add more spice than Greeks usually enjoy; the ambivalence expresses both the historical awareness of a cultural debt and the ideology of their own cultural superiority. And individual Greeks will position themselves very differently between the two extremes, sometimes varying their stance according to the social context (preferring, for example, to affect a "European" preference for blandness in a restaurant but demanding more spice at home). Note here how sensory experience intersects with performance and context.

The second assumption that has impeded the development of an anthropology of the senses is the idea that, in terms of cultural significance, sight is the only sense of major importance. This assumption reflects a western bias that associates vision with reason. Aristotle, for example, considered sight to be the most highly developed of the senses. However, while vision was usually considered the first and most important of the senses, it was still the "first among equals" (Classen 1993a: 3–4; Synnott 1991). More than that, Classen has emphasized, sight has become "something of a sensory despot," leaving little play to the other senses in the imagination. As we have also seen in other chapters, this visualist bias has dramatically influenced the way in which anthropology itself has evolved. Thus, one emergent and potentially very important aid to the refocusing of the discipline lies in attending to kinds of knowledge that have proved resistant to being coded in graphic or visual ways.

Ironically, the third problem arises precisely from the work of certain scholars who have challenged the hegemony of sight in cultural studies. These academics have suggested replacing or supplementing visual models of interpretation with models based on speech and aurality. Marshall McLuhan (1962) and Walter Ong (1967), notably, argued that the sensory model of a society is determined by its technologies of communication. According to this theory, literate – particularly print-based – societies emphasize sight because of the visual nature of writing, while nonliterate societies emphasize hearing because of the auditory nature of speech. For the latter, consequently, the notion of a "world harmony" is more appropriate than that of a "world view" (W. Ong 1969).

Classen objects, rightly, that "while such approaches have helped prepare the ground for an anthropology of the senses by proposing alternate sensory paradigms for the study of culture, they have one major drawback from the perspective of sensory anthropology. This drawback is that they do not allow for sufficient variation in sensory models across cultures." Just as we should not typecast a society by one particular kinship mode (Salzman 1978: 66) or one particular mode of subsistence (Netting 1982: 286), so "the sensory combinatories of culture are much too complex to be stereotyped as either auditory or visual according to the dominant mode of communication." The oral culture of the Hopi of Arizona, for example, places an emphasis on sensations of vibration, while that of the Desana of Colombia highlights the symbolic importance of color (Classen 1993a: 11, 131–4). Moreover, the oral–literate model assumes that societies that give priority to sight (preeminently the West) will be analytic, while those that emphasize hearing will be synthetic. Classen rightly opposes this view – "The vision which is deemed rational and analytical in the West . . . may be associated with irrationality in another society, or with the dynamic fluidity of colour" – and calls instead for "culturally-specific investigations of particular sensory orders." In fact, as Derrida (1976) mischievously noted in his famous critique of Lévi-Strauss, the absence of what westerners mean by writing does not necessarily mean, and empirically does not mean, the absence of "graphological" representation – and hence of a visual orientation. Indeed, we might add that the whole distinction between oral and literate cultures is highly prejudicial, for it all too easily creates an aesthetic hierarchy in which "oral literature" and "oral poetry" are absorbed into the canon of western written forms as lesser or "archaic" versions. This, indeed, is what happened in the history of European folklore studies.

Such biases reflect the extraordinary persistence of evolutionism in both popular and scholarly thinking in the West. The reluctance of present-day anthropologists to examine or recognize the cultural importance of smell, taste, and touch is due not only to the relative marginalization of these senses in the modern West, but also to the racist tendencies of an earlier anthropology to associate the "lower" senses with the "lower" races. As sight, and to a lesser extent, hearing, were deemed the predominant senses of "civilized" westerners, smell, taste and touch were assumed to predominate among "primitive" non-westerners.

Many early scholars were interested in depicting the "animalistic" importance of smell, taste, and touch in non-western cultures. This trend is already evident and widespread in eighteenth-century aesthetics: "as long as man is still a savage he enjoys by means of [the] tactile senses [i.e., touch, taste and smell]," rather than through the "higher" senses of sight and hearing (Schiller 1982: 195). Where Linnaeus in the seventeenth century had associated different human populations with different forms of dress, thereby yoking together supposed levels of governability with equivalent levels of bodily restraint that were sartorially expressed (Hodgen 1964), an eighteenth-century "authority" on African slaves stated that their "faculties of smell are truly bestial, nor less their commerce with the other sexes; in these acts they are as libidinous and shameless as monkeys" (Edward Long, cited by Pieterse 1992: 41). In the early nineteenth century the natural historian Lorenz Oken postulated a sensory hierarchy of human races, with the European "eye-man" at the top, followed by the Asian "ear-man", the Native American "nose-man", the Australian "tongue-man", and the African "skin-man" (Gould 1985: 204–5). In this setting, the anthropologist Charles Myers was surprised to find when he set out to explore the importance of smell among the inhabitants of the Torres Straits at the turn of the twentieth century that "the people of the Torres Straits have much the same liking and disliking for various odours as obtains among ourselves" (Myers 1903: 185). Nonetheless, Myers suggested that the strong power of evocation which odours held for the Islanders provided "yet another expression of the high degree to which the sensory side of mental life [as opposed to the rational side] is elaborated among primitive peoples" (Myers 1903: 184).

Senses and Systematic Knowledge

In its pursuit of a middle ground, as we have seen, anthropology has steered a course between several pairs of extremes. Among these is the opposition between generalization and particularism – Radcliffe-Brown's (1952) "nomothetic" and "idiographic" methods, respectively. The centrist position here is that of a heuristic approach – a probing that takes nothing for granted, but that remains firmly committed to ethnographic analysis. In the study of the senses, however, the discipline has perhaps been relatively slow to move away from gross generalizations, both because of the weight of its own Cartesian philosophical heritage and because the technological limits to investigation have seemed too daunting. While few would voice sentiments like those of Edward Long or even Charles Myers today, there has been little systematic field investigation of the ways in which meanings are invested in and conveyed through each of the senses. But a few pioneers have opened the way. Once free of the intellectualist prejudice against smell, taste, and touch as "animal" senses, the fact that the Sereer Ndut of Senegal have a complex olfactory vocabulary (Dupire 1987) or that the Tzotzil of Mexico describe the cosmos in thermal terms (Gossen 1974) no longer appears a telltale mark of "savagery" but bespeaks a sophisticated cultural elaboration of a specific sensory domain. Conversely, it also draws attention to the role of these neglected senses in societies, such as those of the anthropologists themselves, in which they have receded into the background – for they have not disappeared altogether. Indeed, the prominent recognition of the evocative powers of a "Proustian" moment of taste or smell awaits only the full emergence of what is already a nascent acknowledgment of the importance of evocation itself. A "smellscape" may encapsulate collective local histories as well as personal pasts. But there is a practical reluctance on the part of scholars to engage with what their recording equipment cannot fix in time and space. An anthropology that refuses to admit the significance of what it lacks the technical means to measure or describe would nevertheless be a poor empirical discipline indeed.

Parenthetically, it is worth making the point that both sight and writing are directly associated with power – and often with dangerous, alien, and intrusive power – in many societies, including those just mentioned. The anthropologist's role as a recorder of facts, and the frequent assumption that the anthropologist is engaged in espionage or police surveillance, largely spring from this perception. The ever-increasing domination of the world by a few industrial nations usually intensifies that association. Thus, it is a matter of political as well as epistemological urgency for the discipline to become much more sensitive to the messages couched in alternative sensory codes.

Groundwork in the Field

A number of different people have been influential in the development of the anthropology of the senses (for a fuller account see Classen 1993a). Those who see themselves as developing an "anthropology of the senses" acknowledge a debt to the media specialist Marshall McLuhan (1962, 1964) and his student Walter J. Ong (1969, 1982), who as we have seen were important prototheorists of the anthropology of the senses. Ong's largely undocumented view that, "given sufficient knowledge of the sensorium exploited within a culture, one could probably define the culture as a whole in virtually all its aspects" (1967: 6), encouraged other scholars (such as Edmund Carpenter [1972, 1973]) to explore the whole of the cultural sensorium, despite Ong's own restrictive preoccupation with the oral–literate distinction.

Within anthropology, Claude Lévi-Strauss was inspired by the synaesthetic ideals of the nineteenth-century Symbolists to pioneer exploration of the sensory codes of myths. In the first volume of *Mythologiques*, in a section entitled "Fugue of the Five Senses" (Lévi-Strauss 1969), he traces how oppositions between sensations in one modality, such as hearing, may be transposed into those of another modality, such as taste, and in turn related to various conceptual oppositions – life/death or nature/culture – and to their attempted resolution in mythical thought.

Lévi-Strauss did not, however, make the transition from analyzing the sensory codes of myths to analyzing the sensory codes of culture as a whole. His interest, as Classen perceptively remarks, "lay more in tracing the operations of the mind than with analyzing the social life of the senses." Moreover, in the absence of adequate analytic and recording technology, the structuralist penchant for breaking taste down into "gustemes" – culturally significant units of taste – has not led to any new insights, although Goody's (1982) class-based analysis of the rise of elite cuisines has at least proved suggestive and constitutes prima facie evidence for the need for further research.

Influenced by both McLuhan and Lévi-Strauss, Anthony Seeger (1975, 1981) examined how the Suyá of the Mato Grosso region of Brazil classify humans, animals, and plants according to their presumed sensory traits. He found, for example, that the Suyá characterized men as pleasantly bland-smelling, while women and children were deemed to be unpleasantly strong-smelling. This characterization is due to the association of men with the valued domain of culture, and the association of women and children with the suspect domain of nature. Seeger further found the Suyá to emphasize the social importance of speaking and hearing, while linking sight with antisocial behavior such as witchcraft – an association also made in some European societies, notably those of the eastern and northern Mediterranean (the "evil eye"), and a good illustration of why the visualism of anthropology can be methodologically self-defeating. Seeger argued, by contrast, that the importance of aurality was evident in the lip and ear discs worn by Suyá men, an instance of body decoration serving to remind individuals of the proper sensory hierarchy (see further T. Turner 1995).

The influence of Lévi-Strauss and McLuhan can also be discerned as well in the work of the ethnomusicologist Steven Feld (1982, 1986, 1991; Keil and Feld 1994), who examined the role of sound in the classificatory thought and performance art of the Kaluli of Papua New Guinea. As with Seeger on the Suyá, Feld determined that hearing, rather than sight, is the sense of greatest cultural importance for the Kaluli, providing a model for aesthetic expression, social relations, and the orchestration of the emotions. Neither Seeger nor Feld, however, follows the Ong–McLuhan ascription of the importance of aurality to the fact that the peoples they have studied belong to nonliterate cultures. In each case, the explanation for the primacy of hearing is found within the society in question in the form of indigenous theories of meaning. It does not spring from a generalized paradigm of "oral cultures" (see also Laderman 1991; M. Roseman 1991; Peek 1994).

The phrase "the cultural anthropology of the senses" was coined by the historian Roy Porter in his preface to *The Foul and the Fragrant: Odor and the French Social Imagination*, by Alain Corbin (Porter 1986). The anthropology of the senses did not, however, arise as a distinct field until the late 1980s. In 1989 Paul Stoller, arguing that "anthropologists should open their senses to the worlds of their others," called for the production of "tasteful" ethnographies with vivid literary descriptions of "the smells, tastes and textures of the land, the people, and the food" (1989: 29). In order for anthropologists to achieve this, he cautioned that they must reorient their senses away from the visualism of the West and toward the sensory landscapes of other cultures (see further Fabian 1983; Tyler 1987). In his own work among the Songhay of Niger, Paul Stoller explored the importance of such aspects of Songhay culture as perfume, sauces, and music (Stoller and Olkes 1987; Stoller 1989, 1995). As regards perfume, for example, Stoller describes in rich detail a ceremony by which a Songhay woman offers up fragrance to the spirits (1989: 128–9). Such description gives the reader a taste of Songhay sensory life.

A similar descriptive or evocative approach to the anthropology of the senses has been taken by C. Nadia Seremetakis (1991; 1994) in her work on Greece.

Seremetakis has employed multisensory imaging – the taste and feel of a peach, the smell and texture of grandma's dress – to bring to sensory life her memories of childhood in Greece: "The grandma sits on a wooden stool. . . . Her face dark, her hair tied in a bun, her hands freckled and rough. The child slips into her lap. It is time for fairy tales. Slipping into her lap is slipping into a surround of different smells and textures, sediments of her work in the fields, the kitchen, with the animals" (Seremetakis 1994: 30). Seremetakis states that her aim in undertaking an anthropology of the senses is to recover the "often hidden sensory-perceptual dispositions" of traditional societies and thereby recover the memory of culture embedded in personal recollections and material artifacts (1994: x, 9–12).

In my own work in Greece, I have suggested that the evocation of smell has the capacity to reproduce historical sequences of much longer duration. Describing the "smellscape" (1991: 3–4) of a day in the life of a Cretan seaside town, I attempted to show how the phases of this sensory succession alluded to quite different moments in the town's cultural history. While such parallels should not be overdrawn, they also offer the possibility of making explicit the often intangible-seeming sources of evocation. They do not speak to, or raise, unanswerable questions of intention and motive – we may never know whether such olfactory associations of times of the day with different segments of the larger history are ever locally conceptualized as such – but they begin to suggest how and why present-day uses of particular substances may acquire the "smell of the past" and may consequently generate affective associations between images of the past and experiences in the present. In this sense, the daily sequence of smells may recapitulate, although not necessarily in their original order, a succession of smells associated today with different periods, from an agricultural past (warming olive oil), through industrialization (the smoke from motorcycles and cars), and on to tourism and the life luxurious (colognes and sun tan creams). Such smells can also become a domain for competing agencies, as when, in that same Cretan town, a housewife tries to calculate her neighbors' economic condition from the cooking smells emanating from their houses.

At the same time as Stoller, Serematakis, and others were developing an evocative anthropology of the senses in the United States, in Canada a group of scholars was exploring how an anthropology of the senses might help to uncover the symbolic codes by which societies order and integrate the world. The members of this group, based at Concordia University in Montreal, include David Howes (1988; Howes, ed., 1991), Anthony Synnott (a sociologist) (1991, 1993), Ian Ritchie (1991) and Constance Classen (1993a, 1993b). David Howes describes the approach of this group: "The anthropology of the senses is primarily concerned with how the patterning of sense experience varies from one culture to the next in accordance with the meaning and emphasis attached to each of the senses. It is also concerned with tracing the influence such variations have on forms of social organization, conceptions of self and cosmos, the regulation of the emotions, and other domains of cultural expression . . . [It] is only by developing a rigorous awareness of the visual and textual biases of the Western episteme that we can hope to make sense of how life is lived in other cultural settings" (in Howes, ed., 1991: 4). Howes has employed this approach to examine and compare the sensory models of Dobu and Kwoma society in Papua New Guinea (Howes 1992) and to explore the elaboration of olfactory symbols and rites across cultures (Howes, ed., 1991: 128–47; Classen, Howes and Synnott 1994). In the former work Howes analyzes the social significance of diverse Melanesian sensory practices, such as the use of oil to give the body a brilliant shine, the employment of scents of mint and ginger in love magic, the bobbing motions of the dance, and the aural power of names. Throughout his writings, the emphasis is on tracing the cultural interplay of the senses, as opposed to treating a given sense in isolation.

Classen similarly examines sensory models across cultures and in western history. In *Inca Cosmology and the Human Body* (1993b), she explores the way in which the Incas ordered the cosmos and society through sensory symbols, and how this order was disrupted and reconfigured at the time of the Spanish Conquest. In *Worlds of Sense* (1993a), a key work of reference in this field, she outlined the potential breadth of a sensory approach to culture by applying it to a range of subjects, from the shifts in sensory values which have taken place at different periods of western history to the diverse sensory priorities of various non-western societies. More recently, she has examined the historical embodiment of gender ideologies through sensory codes such as the masculine gaze and the feminine touch (Classen 1998).

Those who situate their work explicitly within a self-proclaimed anthropology of the senses have cleared a great deal of ground. The real test of their contribution, however, will not be a simple proliferation of similar studies, but systematic ethnographic engagement with sensory issues as a matter of course. Some hints of things to come have already appeared. In his studies of the politics of violence in Northern Ireland, Yugoslavia and the United States, Feldman (1991, 1994) has powerfully illustrated how the senses may be employed as media for political terrorism and for "cultural anesthesia" – the use of sensory techniques and technologies to distort and efface instances of political violence. Desjarlais (1992) has explored the sensory aesthetics of pain and healing among the Tibetan Yolmo Sherpa in order to present an "embodied" analysis of emotional and physical suffering and the ritual cures used to treat them. And Taussig focuses on "understanding mimesis as both the faculty of imitation and the deployment of that faculty in sensuous knowing, sensuous Othering" within European history and Latin American colonial and postcolonial culture (1993: 68). These three avenues of research illustrate the range of subject matter amenable to a sense-based investigation. It may also be that the increased attention of anthropologists to the politics of domination has begun to require that heightened sensibility to nonverbal and nonvisual encodings of experience. The very assumption that these other sensory domains are somehow closer to nature suggests that indeed their use as avenues of indoctrination, repression, and incitement in western cultures, as well as of alienation, may have been "naturalized" to the point where their ideological charge has become all but "invisible" – a telling metaphor in this context!

Sensing the Future

The anthropology of the senses has parallels in many fields of the social sciences and humanities.[1] Historical data may prove especially important: realizing that "our own" sensorium has changed is an important first step toward decentering what we take to be, as it were, the common sensorium. In Europe, for example, the decline in the importance of the nonvisual senses from the Middle Ages to modernity (Classen 1993a) was especially accelerated by the development of photographic technology – a technology in which "anything can be separated, can be made dicontinuous from anything else," as Susan Sontag (1978: 22) remarks. We can thus see the increasing predominance of the visual in the European and European-dominated world as enhancing what Don Handelman has argued is the basis of the bureaucratic state: the power to present, over and over again in the form of uniform spectacular performances, the classification of the world that best suits the interests of those in power. Reciprocally, the intended effect of visual surveillance – the (literal) supervision of the spectators – is to drown out awareness of messages encoded in the less controllable media and senses. While this development represents the increasing sophistication of visual technology, it has occurred at great conceptual as well as political cost, so that we are now obliged to make extraordinary efforts simply to apprehend all the information that flows around us but is not encoded in the print media or the ever more exigent assault of telecast images.

The broad range of applications for a sensory analysis of culture indicates that the anthropology of the senses need not be only a "subfield" within anthropology, but may provide a fruitful perspective from which to examine many different anthropological concerns. Just as the anthropology of the senses is not ahistorical, neither is it apolitical. Indeed, the study of sensory symbolism forcefully reveals the hierarchies and stereotypes through which certain social groups are invested with moral and political authority and other groups disempowered and condemned. The use of skin color as a mark of discrimination is well known in many societies. Within the West olfactory codes have served to support the "fragrant" or "inodorate" elite and stigmatize such marginal groups as Jews and blacks. Among the Dassanetch of Ethiopia similar codes serve to distinguish "superior" cattle herders from "lowly" fishermen (Classen 1993a: 79–105). And exotic cooking smells can prompt strong reactions in neighborhoods trying to remain ethnically exclusive.

Sensory codes are likewise employed across cultures to express and enforce gender divisions and hierarchies. Anthony Seeger, as noted above, for example, has shown how the Suyá negatively characterize women as "strong-smelling" in relation to "bland-smelling" men. Women are furthermore associated with disruptive touch by the Suyá while men are deemed to possess superior powers of hearing (Seeger 1981). In the West, women have traditionally been associated with the "lower" "sensual" realms of touch, taste and smell, the realms of the bedroom, the nursery and the kitchen. Men, on the other hand, have been linked with the "higher" "intellectual" realms of sight and hearing, the sensory domains of scholarship, exploration, and government (Classen 1997).

Issues of politics and gender are penetrated with sensory values, as are all issues of importance to a culture, from religious beliefs and practices to the production and exchange of goods. With regard to the latter, examples include the precautions taken by certain New Guinea peoples to avoid offending "the sense of smell" of their garden-grown yams (Howes 1992: 289–90), the ritual exchange of differently flavored ants (representing different moieties) by the Tukano of Colombia (Reichel-Dolmatoff 1985), and the concern of western marketers to imbue their products with exactly the right look, feel and taste to appeal to (and manipulate) the consumer's sensory imagination (Howes, ed., 1996).

Classen calls for "an increase in the number of scholars pursuing a sensory approach to culture" and she deduces from the widening influence of sensory anthropology that this increase is likely to occur. While I share her enthusiasm for the topic, I would be more reassured by a pervasion of ethnographic writing by such interests. In a later chapter dealing with Aesthetics, we shall discover that this has in fact been happening. But the study of smell and taste in particular is still very undeveloped. For this, the careful scholarship of the Concordia group and others will be essential, all the more so as it increasingly intersects with a medical anthropology no longer tied to Cartesian models of causation but sensitive to the needs of an anthropology that is attuned at once, as Michael Jackson (1989) and Timothy Jenkins (1994) have especially shown, to both empirical and phenomenological concerns. The older mode of sense-less description indeed now begins to smell rather fishy.

Note

1 Within sociology Anthony Synnott, among others, has been concerned with examining the sensory codes of the contemporary West, from the symbolism of perfumes to the tactile intricacies of childcare (Synnott 1993; Classen, Howes, and Synnott 1994). A sensuous geography has been elaborated by Yi-Fu Tuan (1995) and Paul Rodaway (1994). Historians such as Alain Corbin and Roy Porter have delved into the cultural shifts in sensory values which have taken place at different periods of Western history (Corbin 1986; Porter 1993). These parallel investigations help to supplement and inform the anthropology of the senses, placing it within a multidisciplinary movement to explore the life of the senses in society.

12

Displays of Order

Instruments of Order

Our determined passage from system to action now allows us to reconceptualize system. For order is not only the means of organizing action; it is also produced through it. Thus, the turn to practice actually raises new questions about the appearance of order: who is responsible for it? Why does it take particular forms? How is it rendered effective? How does it change? And how durable is it? Not coincidentally, we also revert here for a while to the visual, this time to inspect more critically its entailment in the actual play of power.

A major challenge for modern anthropology is to move from the analysis of local ritual – although this, too, may be accessible in national celebrations such as coronations and military parades – to the performance of messages about a culture in which it is simply unimaginable that all the participants should know each other socially. The ability of nation-state governments and even imperial administrations to engage the citizenry in collective activity relies heavily on this expansion of the role of ritual, in which audience passivity and mass conformity are achieved on a scale made possible only by the explosive development of the technologies of representation. If small-scale societies operated on the basis of collective representations that could be enforced through social interaction, the coercive technology of the modern state faces a vastly larger task. Yet the lessons we have learned in the societies traditionally studied by social anthropologists serve us well in these enormously expanded contexts. If we read "bureaucracy" for "folk classification" and "cultural performances" or "spectacles" for "ritual," both the similarities and the differences become apparent, and enrich the comparative range of the anthropological imagination.

Cultural performances, in John MacAloon's words, are "occasions in which as a culture or society we reflect upon and define ourselves, dramatize our collective myths and histories, present ourselves with alternatives, and eventually change in some ways while remaining the same in others" (MacAloon 1984: 1); they range from rituals to films to sports. MacAloon's (1981) work on the Olympic Games exemplifies the ways in which such spectacular productions provide the grounds for exploring sometimes conflicting understandings of collective identity. Beginning with the work of Milton Singer, who depicted performances as "exhibiting" elements of culture (see Singer 1972), and continuing with the work of scholars who have focused on the use of museums and staged folklore (e.g., Bauman, Sawin and Carpenter 1992), "the cultural performance approach has encouraged viewing 'performance' as a whole – attending to audiences, performers, and creators as well as the place, style and text of the performance," remarks Sara Dickey. She continues: "It also attends closely to the ways in which consumers and producers communicate images of themselves to themselves and others – processes that, as Victor Turner (1986) and Clifford Geertz (1973) demonstrated, cannot always be read as straightforwardly as Singer first believed. It should be noted, however, that most of these studies, to use Geertz's familiar words, generally view performances as stories people 'tell themselves about themselves' (Geertz 1973: 448), and assume that producers and consumers are, if not identical, at least members of the same relatively homogeneous group."

One advantage of reading modern cultural performances through the prism of anthropological writings on ritual and classification is that it allows us to recover the link, in national and global contexts, between cultural performances or media representations and the imperatives of bureaucracy. The author of the article in which the present chapter is grounded, Don Handelman, has labored long and hard to establish that bureaucracy, as a taxonomic exercise and an expression of a cosmological vision, is an appropriate object of anthropological analysis, which can indeed offer a valuable corrective to the mechanistic "top-down" formulations that have for too long characterized its study. He has shifted the ground of anthropology in a useful and revealing way: and it is revealing that he has also been more attentive than many ethnographers of nation-state social formations to the forms and effects of standardized performances, from the intimate inculcations of kindergarten play to the steel-clad flexings of national military might. In the compartmentalized vision of much that goes under the rubric of cultural studies or political science, such connections are either ignored or dismissed. Handelman's work is especially useful in showing why this is misleading.

But his insight also undercuts a significant aspect of his position. For whereas Handelman sees a shift between historically differentiated types of social formation, the premodern and the modern, I prefer to treat the archaic–modern distinction as a matter of degree rather than of kind.[1] The argument is thus methodological rather than fundamentally theoretical, for we are both concerned to see what anthropology can offer the study of state societies in today's world. On the other hand, where I have tended to treat bureaucratic interaction as ritualistic in its focus on repetition and discipline, Handelman's vision of the "bureaucratic logic" that informs virtually all modern organizational practices as well as rituals of a more conventionally religious sort offers generous possibilities for developing wider comparative perspectives. Handelman has also revealed many of the peculiar systemic features of state bureaucracies by insisting on the distinction. From his own perspective he nevertheless also emphasizes structural similarities, a viewpoint that contrastively reveals the play of agency across a wide variety of social situations. Where he emphasizes structural properties, I have been more interested in agents' interests and practices; but it is clear that we both employ approaches that require the full recognition of both.

Handelman argues that there is a radical break between ritual – the religious practice of "traditional" societies – and the spectacles mounted by bureaucratic polities. Here is his own summary: "Ritual and spectacle are informed by radically different metalogics, called here respectively, transformation and presentation. Ritual in traditional social orders is perhaps the sole cultural form designed to deliberately make predictive, directed, controlled change through its own internal operations. These changes have direct effects on the social orders that encompass such rituals. The metalogic of transformation through ritual that is used here is one of systemic organization that controls the production of its effects." Ritual manipulates taxonomies, in his view, but these are immutable, and integral to the "natural" order of things. In contrast to rituals, modern spectacles, as Handelman uses the term, are public masks of the bureaucratic ethos. Bureaucracy is perhaps the paradigmatic form of organization in the modern state: Handelman has recently pointed out that no state – indeed no political system – can exist without it, and that its logic affects even the logics of oppositional discourses (such as New Age practices) if only by inversion or distortion (Handelman 1998). Bureaucrats deliberately invent taxonomies and operate them systemically. "These taxonomies are under the control of human volition. Bureaucracy makes planned, predictive changes and tries to control their effects on modern social orders. In the modern state, spectacles have developed in profusion together with the growth of bureaucratic infrastructures. Spectacles are mirrors that present and reflect impressive statist visions of social order. These visions mask the formative power of statist bureaucracies to shape, discipline, and control social order."

Our debate lies at the heart of much of what is being discussed in current anthropology. Handelman wishes to maintain a distinction between two types of society, more or less those described by Tönnies's famous distinction between *Gemeinschaft* and *Gesellschaft*. In the former, we have rituals (and their persistence in the latter can be treated as a kind of archaism); in the latter, media spectacles. Yet Handelman is able to make the crucial anthropological move across that boundary, finding in modern state taxonomies an object as exotic and astonishing in its arbitrariness as any non-European determination that "the cassowary is not a bird" (Bulmer 1967) or that the shrimp is not a fish (Douglas 1966). Others have noted that modernity has its rituals: an anthropologically oriented political scientist, for example, has analyzed Soviet state "ritual" while another has tackled the United Nations peacekeeping bureaucracy (Binns 1979–80; Barnett 1997) – although it is revealing that both had to publish their work in anthropological journals, and that it has been conspicuously absent from the bibliographies of those political scientists who continue to play an active role in policy-making. One might well conclude that the resistance of (especially "Western") political experts to any analysis that treats them in a common framework with "natives" has its own political motivations.

There is a further and related aspect that places Handelman's work firmly within the anthropological vision of this book, and that is his insistence on respecting the conceptual framework of the social actors under study. He is interested in the role of particular logics in relating the effects of agency (whether of individuals or of groups) to the forms of regulation, and in the role of what I am here calling "displays of order" – as a way of avoiding the ritual–spectacle dichotomy – in articulating such change. Displays of order both reflect and, in the sense of their performative capacity, serve to shape social transformations. As Handelman succinctly remarks: "Rituals, themselves shaped by cultural orders, shape the very orders that produce them. In order to comprehend the effects that rituals are thought to have within cultural orders, one must be open to indigenous theories that form these highly specialized contexts of action. If peoples say, for example, that through rituals they are healing illness or making rain, then we accept these goals in order to approximate how they are put into practice. These are the internal, cultural logics of rituals whose appreciation should precede any scholarly analysis of, say, the social functions of ritual." This is a very different perspective from either the late functionalism of Gluckman or the ecological systems analysis of Rappaport; it comes closer to the symbolic anthropology of Victor Turner (1974, etc.) in recognizing the always tense relationship between action and form, but it takes Turner's intermittent interest in modern nation-states to a much more comprehensive level. Indeed, while acknowledging his debt to Turner, Handelman (1998) notes a certain aridity in Turner's attempt to subordinate all rituals to a preexisting schema that is especially crude when dealing with the massive happenings staged by modern bureaucratic states.

Where we part company is over Handelman's apparent reluctance to see the practitioners of ritual as willing agents of change and caprice to an extent comparable with the manipulation of official forms carried out by state and other functionaries of "modern" systems. (Similar criticisms have been made of the thought of Pierre Bourdieu, for whom social actors are often quite unaware of the ways in which they both respond to a reshape their cultural milieux [see, e.g., Reed-Danahay 1995; Herzfeld 1987: 83–6].) Handelman appears to locate agency in the rituals rather than in their practitioners: "Rituals . . . shape the very orders that produce them." Moreover, he also argues that they are in turn governed by a "metalogic" that may not be accessible to the social actors performing or witnessing the rituals. To a certain extent this restrictive view of the social actors' agency fits with Handelman's representation of ritual as a highly formalized activity, a view that is also very much in accord with Tambiah's celebrated definition of ritual as marked by features of extreme formalism as well as redundancy and ambiguity. But Handelman sees these features as offering special opportunities for creative reinterpretation. This is a great advance on the old confusion of surface conformity with the supposed social conformity of the actors, for it recognizes the possibility of creative redefinition from within the most rigidly prescriptive performances, and it bypasses unproductive arguments about whether "primitive" people are capable of think-ing through the consequences of ritual action in the abstract – change occur-ring as a result of ritual action is accessible to the descriptive powers of the observer, including those of the local community members bringing local theo-ries of ritual causation to bear on what happens. But not to see the same pos-sibilities in state spectacles, for example, is to concede to officialdom the coercive power that the analyst has just denied the ritual practitioner in a local or "tribal" society.

I concede that it may be useful to reserve the term "ritual" for highly for-malized activities. But my argument, which also addresses moral systems in the most general sense, is, like Handelman's, that the more formal a system is the more its skilled practitioners are able to adopt its very formality as a mask for all manner of subversions and subornings. I would then suggest that the greater scale of modern spectacle simply increases the scope for dissembling, and that some of this may be deliberate. Whether it actually is deliberate or not in spe-cific situations may be beyond our ability to know, however, for we are not mind-readers and we are also reluctant to offer generalizations about "mental-ities" – a staple of the vocabulary of stereotypes (as in: "you have to know their mentality in order to get along with them").

The partial disagreement I have just sketched may be instructive for the reader of this book for a number of reasons. First, as I have said, it speaks to a key question in current anthropology: to what extent do older formulations deny agency to non-European peoples – those who in earlier writings were often called "primitive" or "archaic"? And to what extent does the evidence justify retention of such formulations? Second, it shows that there is still plenty of room for refining our terms of reference: this speaks to the pedagogical mission of this project, and I single out Handelman's argument as particularly well suited to that goal as well as because of my partial disagreement with it, set off con-trastively by an equally strong agreement with the rest of it. Third, no matter where the reader ends up in the debate, it projects anthropological theory into a consideration of modernity in a particularly constructive way – something that has long characterized Handelman's work. Finally, it represents a rare engage-ment by anthropologists with both the exotic and the familiar in the context of a single analysis. Despite Horace Miner's (1956) famous spoof about the "Nacirema," with their very exotic bathroom rituals conducted each in front of a mirror every morning, this kind of juxtaposition has run afoul of a perva-sive fear among anthropologists of lending too much support to popular deri-sion of their discipline. Perhaps they should relax: a recent anthropological study of McDonald's in East Asia has had a notable success (Watson, ed., 1997). And what could be more serious than ritual and bureaucracy? This juxtaposition has real immediacy.

This theme of the anthropology of modernity will also allow us to return, in the closing paragraphs of the chapter, to a centrally important theme that is also taken up in the chapters on Economies and Cosmologies. It is the problem of origins. Who created the various cultural manifestations with which we are concerned? How did they start? We can certainly make a good stab at tracing to source the invention of the hamburger, the toothbrush, and the medical discourse of personal hygiene. But what about cultural phenomena that predate literacy (for that seems to be the basis of the division)? Early folklorists were consumed with curiosity about such questions, either because this served nationalist attempts to find historical sources of legitimacy in the antiquity of the nation or because it served the encompassing legitimation of evolutionism – the doctrine that left Europeans in charge of the world conceptually as their military expansions had done so politically. But even after such issues went out of fashion, they lurked in the background of even the most socially grounded theories. Durkheim, for example, thought that ritual was the way in which societies paid homage to themselves as societies. Lévi-Strauss thought that they expressed a fundamental generative capacity of the human mind, filtered through enormous networks of cultural transmission. But the difficulty has always been to determine whose sage hand lay behind such inventions of religion, if indeed it was designed for such teleological purposes. And Durkheim expressly denied the possibility of individual action as a primary cause. I fully endorse Handelman's comment: "the Durkheimian claim that ritual generically generates 'social solidarity' is utterly open to question," because such a view removes the social actors from any role in the constitution of their own social realities (see Giddens 1984). As a result of such assumptions, social theory remained for far too long mired in images of a primitive world guided by the power of the (undifferentiated) social, in opposition to a modernity in which all could speak with individual voices and act with individual volitions.

There is certainly a hint of this kind of evolutionism in Handelman's own argument:

> Historically, the cultural worlds of ritual turn into those of spectacle. The practice of ritual is integral to cultural worlds that are organized holistically, worlds in which "religion" constitutes the whole through comprehensive, taxonomic classifications of the cosmos, and from which the organizing premises of moral and social order derive. These taxonomies are perceived as "natural," in the sense that they are not to be changed through human volition. When one category in a holistic religious taxonomy fails, another replaces it, so long as the horizons that enable secularism have yet to occur. When people lost faith in the efficacy of their traditional gods in ancient Rome, they deified their emperors (Momigliano 1986). A shift in classification enabled the ritual continuation of the cosmic whole. In early modern Europe, however, when people lost faith in the efficacy of ritual (Burke 1987), they were well on their way to fragmenting cosmic holism, and to organizing secular social orders. But, I would counter, they produced new totalities – political ones that demanded a worship no less absolute than the religious cults of yore.
>
> The historical fragmentation of cosmological holism enabled a host of relatively separate secular domains to emerge – political, economic, scientific, bureaucratic – each with its horizons (Dumont 1977). The public events of modern spectacle emerge from these formations, reflecting their division. Through the present day, the logics of spectacle lack the capacity to act on these ruptures in unifying ways.

By contrast, through their logics, rituals practice both the fragmentation and the reconstitution of holism. Thus the internal processes of rituals often move from conditions of holism – of self, community, health, the human and the transcendent – to their shattering, in order to regenerate a healed self, a new social being, a rejuvenated community, and so forth. The processes of ritual manipulate cultural, taxonomic categories. Taxonomically, ritual makes infinite distinctions, giving value to the slightest differences. But ritual does this in order to produce controlled change through logics of operation that are internal to the ritual event. It is to these ends that the manipulation of taxonomic distinctions are put.

This is the purpose behind Handelman's reassessment of the *chisungu* ritual of the Bemba of Zambia, originally studied by Audrey Richards, to which we shall turn later. Handelman seeks thereby to illustrate his thesis: "In traditional worlds, ritual may be the only way of deliberately making controlled changes that impact on social order." He sees modern spectacle, by contrast, as a way of reaffirming the status quo maintained by those in power – a mirror for the type of reality they wish to preserve. As he succinctly describes the contrast: "The internal logics of spectacle, taxonomize and present; those of ritual, taxonomize and transform."

But the evolutionism in Handelman's argument is not the old progressivist metaphor. It is, rather, the pessimism of Weber's "iron cage" of a bureaucracy increasingly oppressing the modern world. Instead of a march toward emancipation through an increasing self-aware agency, Handelman's contrast seems to credit modern humanity with decreased control over the potential transformations of society. He may very well be right in certain cases – perhaps in many. But such an argument ignores the possibility that resistance (J. Scott 1985) may occur within the modern arenas of state display. Handelman has remarked to me, consistently with the critique of the concept of resistance that appears at other points in this book, that it fails to deal with the largest bureaucratic spectacle of all: highly publicized wars, such as those in Iraq and Serbia, in which killing is reduced to a display of statistical and technological virtuosity. As he remarks: "This is not a disenchanted world . . . but rather one in which the 'haves' have enchanted themselves into a virtual approximation of the have-nots in ways that limited relationships to any reality." On the other hand, we cannot ignore the efforts, whatever their results (if any), of those who work from within on the formal displays of power in state rituals, rethinking their meanings and perhaps eventually subverting the intentions of their organizers – a point that I have also made in connection with media more generally. Such displays are indeed carefully scripted, and one supposes that the organizers do not usually want to see any transformations other than those enjoining obedience and conformity. But these inducements to conformity are themselves transformations of past conditions, given that most nation-states have originated in liberation struggles – a dilemma for the establishment of authority, in that the model of the original struggles always lurk in the background and may sometimes erupt unexpectedly to the fore (see J. Rappaport 1994).

Handelman's analytic distinction between ritual and spectacle lies especially in a contrast between two metalogics he identifies in these: "transformation" in traditional ritual and "presentation" in modern spectacle, the latter being closely associated in his usage with the bureaucratic nation-state of today. Indeed, this categorical discrimination leads Handelman to exclude from analysis some intermediate forms, such as opera and theater on the one side and "media events" (Katz and Dayan 1992) – those one-time events that are telecast live to enormous audiences, like the Pope's first visit to Poland and the first moon landing. The genre of the western circus is perhaps the most independent of the relationship between bureaucracy and statism, in that the circus marginalizes the appropriation of the performing body for statist purposes (Handelman 1991: 222), and in that historically the circus often flees from the institutionalizing, bureaucratic powers of the state (see Carmeli 1988).

It may be, however, that the methodological decision to exclude these other forms from his analysis has given too rigid a cast to Handelman's ideal-typical opposition between rituals and spectacles (but see 1990: 55–6 for an example of a ritual that engaged with the emergence of class relations in Zambia). Take opera, for example, a genre little investigated by anthropologists. Performances of Verdi's operas were the site of popular resistance to foreign rule in Italy; while Verdi was forced to submit to the heavy hand of censorship, both his music and the librettos he used invested with irony and ambiguity such attacks on state authority as regicide and the corruption of power. Other, still more conventional performance genres offer simlar possibilities: Beeman (for Iran, 1981) and Danforth (for Greece, 1983) have both documented the subversive potential of popular forms of puppet theater. Also excluded from Handelman's analysis are the sometimes spectacular media of cinema and television that exist only through modern technologies, and whose metalogic is often that of never-ending, or continually recycled, stories that utilize near-bureaucratic forms of classification. Precisely because, as he insists, the classification of public displays should reflect the historical circumstances of their emergence and the peculiar logics that these circumstances favored, I prefer to frame the distinction as one that particularly reflects the common western intellectual conviction that modern logic is purely rational and scientific, as opposed to the supposed religiosity of yesteryear (and of elsewhere).

Certainly some nation-states have developed extraordinarily effective technologies of control, both exhibiting and sometimes brutally utilizing their – literally – spectacular technological virtuosity. Even within idioms sanctioned by a repressive state, however, it is possible for actors and their audiences to invest particular performances with subversive force, sometimes precisely by appropriating the rules in a deadpan manner. This can even be done with literature: during the military dictatorship in Greece (1967–74), the one effective piece of resistance literature – *Eighteen Texts* – could be openly published in Athens because its authors had obeyed with stunning precision the censors' antisubversion law that required all book titles to describe the contents of each book literally (Van Dyck 1997: 19–20)! Meanwhile, of course, the colonels hoped to change the entire social order precisely by means of the production of spectacles.

Handelman, who has written skillfully about these other genres elsewhere (1992), does not consider them germane to his argument contrasting ritual with spectacle. Indeed, his argument works best if we treat these two categories as Weberian ideal types, much as Bird-David has proposed for the economic categories of house and corporation (see the chapter on Economies). It is on this provisional assumption that we can now proceed.

Transformation: A metalogic of ritual

Rituals are in some sense self-perpetuating: their repetitive character means that a ritual that is not performed with some degree of predictability and punctuality simply dies out. (Greenwood's example of a Basque ritual the temporal structure of which was disrupted by its commodification for the tourist industry in Francoist times [1989] nicely illustrates how brusquely this can in fact occur.) But if the operation of ritual is not entirely addressed by indigenous theory, as Gerholm (1988: 197–8) suggests, so that local explanations themselves require further explanation, Handelman argues that the metalogic of transformation plays an important role. He does not attribute this to all rituals, but proposes to recognize it in "all rituals that change one kind of being or condition into another by creating temporary microworlds that are predicated on the potential for change, while each microworld of this kind answers to its own horizons of cultural possibility." And he adds: "Within these temporary micro-worlds of ritual, participants are re-embodied in all their senses, their bodies becoming sites of the transformation of being. The visual sense, the gaze, does not necessarily have primacy in embodiments of ritual, as it so frequently does in spectacle." We have seen, in the chapter on the Senses, that the current predominance of the visual is largely an outcome of the extent to which western technology has imposed its own perspective on the rest of the world. I suggest that the truth of what Handelman claims here lies in the need for modern global organizations, stretched far beyond the possibility of face-to-face interaction as the basis of all identities, to turn to the most capturably iconic basis for representing the homogeneity of a performance as an iconic model of a hoped-for unity. That basis is visual – perhaps the most relentlessly "naturalizing" of all the senses, and enhanced today by a technology in which the reproducibility of the visual image far outstrips what for many would be the far more evocative senses of smell and taste.

It is in his *Models and Mirrors* (Handelman 1990: 23–41) that Handelman schematically lays out seven premises that may inform us about how at least some rituals work. I reproduce his extremely useful summary here in full:

"First, a ritual of transformation is intentional and purposive. It is organized according to a posited relationship of means to ends. The ritual is teleological. Second, within itself the ritual of transformation makes change that has specified outcomes. Third, this kind of ritual is anticipatory: it pre-views a hypothetical condition and it provides procedures that will actualize this act of the cultural imagination. As such, this kind of ritual has predictive capacities: it contains particular futures within itself. Therefore, fourth, the ritual of transformation has stipulated control over processes of causality (however these are conceptualized in indigenous theories). Fifth, the ritual of transformation regulates itself, to a degree: The ritual monitors its own progression, as this is being made. This tells the participants, for example, whether to repeat certain procedures, or when to cease particular steps and initiate others. Sixth, this kind of ritual has built into itself contradictory or conflicting conditions of being that in the course of its working the ritual must solve. Thus, a Sinhalese exorcism begins with a person who is ill, whose consciousness is possessed and occluded by the demonic, and who in the course of the ritual is made well (Kapferer 1983). The *Isoma* ritual of the Ndembu peoples of Zambia turns an incomplete person (an infertile woman) into a complete one (a fertile woman) (V. Turner 1969). Sick/healthy, infertile/fertile – the terms of each of these sets are mutually negating. These are qualities that should not coexist within the same person. The cultural designs of such rituals are premised to transform one term of each set into the other. Therefore, seventh, transformation requires the introduction of uncertainty (often perceived indigenously as a dangerous quality) into the presumed stability of the phenomenon that is to undergo this radical transmutation. Uncertainty dissolves this stability, thereby opening the way for the reshaping practices of transformation."

This is an extremely important as well as succinct statement. If we adopt Handelman's typology as an array of ideal types, it allows us to assess intermediate forms. Thus, for example, the funeral rites now officially countenanced by the communist rulers of Vietnam and briefly mentioned elsewhere in this book only partially fit the model. The rituals have been invested with a new teleology – not that of religious observance, but that of the bureaucratic state. On the other hand, the causality of the ritual is explicitly at odds with the official atheism of the state, which therefore must invest it instead with a more psychological role, consistent with its own functionalist view of such performances. The effect of closure, which seems to have been one motivation for the state's decision to tolerate such persistent strains of "superstition," can thus be justified as serving the state's utilitarian ends – but the officials who sanction and even attend such performances have no way of knowing whether this is the interpretation to which the parties involved actually subscribe. On the face of it, this would seem improbable – and so the uncertainty (that of the effects of death upon the bereaved) envisaged by the state may in fact escape the constraints of ritual intention.

In short, the opposition between ritual and spectacle has considerable heuristic value. It is especially helpful as a means of examining rituals that have been recontextualized – for example, religious practices that have been turned into the "folklore" of state ceremonial (e.g., Kligman 1981, on the Căluş rituals of Romania). But to appreciate its full range of application, we should follow Handelman's analysis of the *chisungu* – supposedly a girls' initiation ritual – of the Bemba as Richards (1982) described its occurrence around 1931 (see also Handelman 1990: 31–8). The purpose of chisungu, in Bemba theory, was to turn an immature girl into a mature woman, one who would be ready for marriage and capable of undertaking the dangerous tasks of purifying her husband and herself, following the pollution of intercourse and menstruation. Contacts with ancestral spirits were vital to the well-being of the household, but contact could be made only under conditions of purity. Chisungu was held just before a young woman's marriage. Upon its success depended the viability of future households, and so too that of the Bemba peoples.

Handelman describes the ritual, summarizing Richards, and then offers his demonstration: "The older women who supervised the ritual said that its purpose was to 'grow' the girls, and thereby make them into women. A girl who had not had her Chisungu remained 'rubbish,' an 'unfired pot,' in other words, less than a complete woman. The older women were certain that within the practice of the ritual they were causing changes to be made in the girls, transforming them from an alarming condition of immaturity to one of fertile womanhood."

In Handelman's terms, Chisungu is purposive and goal-directed, and these attributes are integral to the ritual itself, making the ritual process teleological. Moreover, he adds, "the ritual encompasses contradictory categories in the world of Bemba women, but one is turned into the other: an immature woman enters, and a mature woman exits. But the change that is deliberately made to occur in the interim is more profound than one that results merely from the reclassification of immature girls to mature women, and the social validation of this shift. The change that the ritual accomplishes is an essential one, in the being of each and every girl. The ritual transforms the girls. To do this, the ritual process must solve the taxonomic contradictions that it posits as incompatible: the candidate for change cannot leave the ritual as some amorphic conglomeration of immaturity and maturity."

On the first day of Chisungu, the girls were covered with blankets and made to crawl backward on all fours into the ritual hut – the action of passing through a dark tunnel, concealed from others, forsaking their old way of life. During the following days, teasing highlighted the girls' categorical immaturity, while their crying supposedly demonstrated their acceptance of this classification and the weakness it implied: "The degrees of crying by the girls embodied their relative openness to be reshaped and then reclassified into mature women. The relationship between teasing and crying (that is, unlearning) is teleological and adjustable. Teasing brought the girls to tears, while this weeping was itself a monitor of the success of the teasing. The older women could increase or decrease teasing, in order to achieve the desired results." Or, as we might say today, this was a system of inculcation of attitude, reinforced as it was (very much as in apprenticeship practices in Europe) by stylized ordeals and accompanied by the learning of adult knowledge, and it was designed to incorporate the initiands into adult society as conforming members – quite literally, since the bodily afflictions carried lasting associations of disobedience with humiliation and pain. One woman stated that through the ordeals, "They [the older women] try to find out if the girls have grown up" (Richards 1982: 76). The successful passing of ordeals showed, remarks Handelman, "that the being of the girls was being shaped, changed essentially, and embodied anew." This is, in his view, a teleological operation, "one of self-regulation integral to the ritual." If a girl failed an ordeal, then the ritual process was slowed down until she passed. Within the framework of the ritual, then, some measure of creativity in pacing – what Bourdieu calls the tempo of social interaction (1977: 6) – related individual propensities to a sense of overarching determination. But here, as Handelman points out, Bemba women had their own theories about the unlearning of immaturity and the learning of adulthood, and calibrated the pacing of the ritual to the initiands' responses accordingly. We would not otherwise be able to make sense of the ritual rhythm, in which the unlearning of old certainties – ridicule as a means of breaking down the initiands' sense of self-confidence – gradually gives way to learning new certainties. And it is on this basis that Handelman remarks, "The logic of Chisungu is that of a causal, predictive scheme that makes directed change. The prediction of transformation – growing the girls – and its direction and actualization, are done within the ritual itself. To a degree, Chisungu is self-regulating in its processuality: it monitors its own progression, to check whether this is having the desired effects."

For Handelman, then, ritual, through the operation of its causal relationships, makes controlled transformations that effect the world outside the ritual. Other examples support his description of the ritual metalogic. Lincoln (1981: 101, 103), in discussing a ritual that is done at menarche for girls among the Tukuna of the Northwest Amazon, notes the metaphorical use of insect metamorphosis. The Tukuna liken the candidate to a caterpillar who enters the cocoon and emerges a butterfly. Transformation is made within the cocoon/ritual. Lincoln emphasizes that rituals of this kind take up ontological issues, changing the fundamental being of women. Like the Chisungu intiand, the Tukuna girl is remade from the inside out, in terms of the potentials for maturity that have been dormant and hidden within her. In some western societies, the hazing of military cadets and fraternity brothers, as well as degrading rituals of symbolic birth among students crossing the International Dateline by ship (Brain 1981), offer similar opportunity for adjustment to individual cases, while guild and apprenticeship induction ceremonies in many places, while similarly subjecting individuals to collective discipline, can also be adjusted in this way.

Small-scale domestic rituals partake of this logic also. Thus, for example, southern European exorcisms against sorcery and the evil eye redress a balance that has been disturbed, leading a marginalized member of the community back into the fold – sometimes by direct analogies with the control of body parts by measurement or counting (Herzfeld 1986). These are not life crisis rituals like chisungu. But they share some of the transformative power of the more predictable rituals, causing the patient to accept a symbolic enactment of bodily control as the price of reintegration. I shall argue below that such rituals have their counterpart in the modern bureaucratic state, and that they have a relationship to spectacles not unlike that between small domestic rituals and the grand life-cycle rituals that Handelman attributes to "traditional" societies.

Handelman, by contrast, carefully distinguishes rituals of transformation, with their inner logics of change, from other "public events" (Handelman 1990), whose inner logics are closer to what he understands by "spectacles." The latter are "organized like mirror-images to reflect especially composed visions of social order." And he adds: "The spectacle symbolizes the turn to modern social order – the rise of the state, its bureaucratic infrastructure, and the turn to totalism." Even those responses that develop ostensibly in opposition to bureaucratic logic find themselves compelled to engage with that logic; many such movements – liberation armies are a dramatic illustration – end up reproducing the forms and logic of their erstwhile oppressors with uncanny precision.

Bureaucratic Order and the Spectacle

According to Handelman, "The rise of the spectacle occurs together with that of the power of taxonomy, the latter freed from its immutable, 'natural' embedment in religious cosmology." There is, he argues (following Foucault 1973b: 54–5), an intimate relationship between the development of modern science and that of bureaucratic ethos as a hegemonic structure of consciousness and especially of visual surveillance (see also Handelman 1995). In this development, the premises of taxonomy were used to make visible everything of the phenomenal world. In Foucault's terms, the eye was connected to discourse through the catalog – the itemizing and preserving of all items of knowledge, through comparison and contrast. The language of (Linnaean) science could no longer be "badly constructed" (Foucault 1973b: 158), in that taxonomy filled, ordered, and controlled all the space of discourses of classification, which were extended beyond science into understandings of society and polity. Thus, radical political visions of the perfectly governed society depended on invented schemes of classification (Eliav-Feldon 1982: 45).

Handelman posits two radical departures with the rise of the nation-state. First, he says, the state took control of the system of classification; no longer treating it as a passive reflection of the "natural" order of things, the bureaucracy utilized it as an increasingly flexible system of control, in which the meanings of the taxonomic units were determined with utilitarian ends in view: "taxonomic schemes must be made autonomous of the natural order of things – then structures of consciousness not only become conscious of structures, but invent them, thereby organizing their worlds anew" and the act of classification itself "becomes independent of the 'natural,' immutable cosmos, and therefore independent from the practice of ritual as the ongoing re-creation of this cosmos." This is what Handelman has called "the bureaucratic means of production." And Handelman's second point is that "taxonomic work is organized as a bureaucratic system, in the self-correcting sense." Bureaucratic classification is teleological – "bureaucracy posits causal relationships between goals and the means to accomplish these ends" – to the point also of becoming, in its most self-serving forms, tautological (see also Herzfeld 1992). Bureaucrats expect to control the effects they produce, so they must constantly be prepared to reinterpret the classification accordingly. Bureaucracy, remarks Handelman, "continually makes change by altering taxonomic categories or by creating new ones" – although, we should add, this processual dimension is often masked by the constant reassertion of bureaucratic omniscience, as is the role of individual agents by their insistence on invoking a collective ethos.

But this masking is precisely what the adoption of formal idioms of classification makes possible, raising an intriguing comparative question: if the glib assurances of consistency and immutability are what enable bureaucrats to recast the pragmatic meanings of the categories to suit their own or their masters' convenience, why should we assume that the adepts of chisungu-like rituals are not able to be equally creative? Here I suspect that there is a confusion of form with content. For I do not disagree with Handelman's view that the rise of modern bureaucracy introduces something novel. I do not think, however, that this new dimension necessarily represents a change of underlying principles. Rather, I suspect that it has always and everywhere been possible to use taxonomy as a means of implementing individuated goals, and that it is precisely the surface homogeneity of systems of classification – the assurance they seem to offer that the "natural" world is a stable place – that allows bureaucrats to "naturalize" the most arbitrary decisions and allocations. It is on a similar logic, after all, that a wide variety of actual deeds would be glossed as morally correct – as examples of virtue in the defense of the Italian or Greek rural family, for example; success or failure in securing such an interpretation from the larger public is always a complex matter comprising individual skill and particular local circumstances. This, as we shall see, has important consequences for the relationship between spectacles and state power.

There is no question but that bureaucracy is above all else a classifying structure. Much of its work lies in classifying – sometimes, it would seem, for classification's sake; hence the abiding sense of tautology. Yet much bureaucracy is also directed to the service of the citizenry, from whose ranks its staff is indeed drawn, and it would be both empirically unsound and morally ungenerous to focus only on its failures and excesses. Weber's ambivalence toward it presaged, I believe, its true capacity for good and evil: its sheer size, in today's nation-state, amplifies the uses that specific functionaries make of its esoteric codes.

Above all, the real terror lies in its arbitrariness. All signs, linguistic and other, are arbitrary, in that they have no necessary relationship with nature. They may acquire a sense of being "natural," as Bourdieu, Foucault, and others have observed. The "naturalization" of a citizen is in fact as purely cultural an act as it is possible to imagine. But it is above all the uniformity of bureaucratic symbols that shifts the locus of the "arbitrariness of the [bureaucratic] sign" from the sign itself to its operator – the bureaucrat. It is in the bureaucrat that agency is situated, even when this person invokes "the system" as part of what I have called the "secular theodicy" that bureaucrats, as citizens themselves, share with their clients – the system of explaining away the experienced deficiencies of what is ideally a benign, democratic institution in a way that both will understand and find it convenient to accept.

With this in mind, I now return to Handelman's analysis of the relationship between the bureaucratic state and the spectacles that it promotes. He certainly acknowledges the common ground of ritual and spectacle and the role of taxonomy in both, as I have noted, but prefers to treat them as related by analogy rather than as endpoints on a continuum. He writes; "In terms of their metalogics of possibility, rituals and spectacles have virtually nothing in common. (For a contrary view, see Ben-Amos and Ben-Ari 1995). Rituals (like bureaucracy) create realities that are consequential in their effects. But spectacles are the other face of bureaucracy, paralyzed by a stroke of the pen (or today, by computer command), hiding their frozen countenance behind colored spectacles that reflect spectacular fictions. These fictions mask the face of bureaucracy."

The basis for this association of spectacle and bureaucracy is the visual emphasis that both share. Visual classification – tables, charts, and spatial arrangements like the Benthamite Panopticon – is especially popular in the West, where it serves a Cartesian ideology that would relegate other senses to a very secondary intellectual role. Handelman, like Foucault, takes the Panopticon as paradigmatic: "Gone are social networks and multiple exchanges among persons. Present is the human being as reduction, as residue: separated, numbered, supervised, and put to productive tasks with rational intentionality. Who exercises power, and with what motive is not relevant: whoever occupies the tower, the center, the office, the apex of hierarchy, controls the taxonomic gaze of systemic control. Indeed, the Panopticon design has been called a 'materialized classification' (Jacques-Alain Miller, cited in Bozovic 1995: 24)." From this eighteenth-century perspective to the twentieth-century bureaucratic claims to omniscience is a short path: it is within the modern, bureaucratic state that invented taxonomies proliferate and flourish as never before, fragmenting, dividing, and classifying the humanity of human beings and reshaping it from partial fragments (Shamgar-Handelman 1981). The type of bureaucracy found in today's industrialized nation-states is certainly unique in its sheer scale as well as the ways in which it has adapted fundamental taxonomic principles to the needs created by modern technology, the internationalization of trade and some forms of political action, and the vastly increased speed and conmprehensiveness that these conditions impose on any system of classification.

Handelman, however, also argues that the spectacles provided by state governments and similar organizations are of a radically different type – not only scale – than what is represented by the Chisungu. Obviously in some sense this is simply a matter of definition: scale can be as much a determinant of difference as anything else. And there can be no doubt about the huge difference in the scale of virtually any human activity that modern technology has made possible.

But it is significant that Handelman's examples are drawn primarily from the extreme ends – the most brutal of the "iron cages" – created by modern bureaucratic state societies, the Nazi and Stalinist dictatorships. If no bureaucracies ever served citizens' needs, no bureaucracy would ever be charged by those same citizens with violating the terms of civil relationships. Handelman argues that "the other side of this furious invention of taxomonies is the statist search for aesthetics that reflect and magnify the precision and exactness of taxonomic division and combination, and so of their categorical inclusion or exclusion from the state." Here, indeed, his observations are incisive, and the contrasting cases of Nazi Germany and the USSR under Stalin are truly instructive. I again quote his discussion in full:

"For example, the leaders of the Nazi and Soviet states demanded that there be ideological purpose in public aesthetics. Nonetheless, they did this in obverse directions. Hitler thundered that 'Art is a mighty and fanatical mission,' insisting that aesthetics have a clarity of color and form, and be accessible, comprehensible, logical, true, and created for the people, whose arbiter he was (Wistrich 1996: 78–80). Ugliness and pain were banished from publicly visible, aesthetic productions. Aesthetics were characterized by utilitarian relationships between ends and means. In the workplace, technical rationality was glorified through aesthetics that made utility into a 'religion' in which 'The worker, like all the subjects of National Socialism, becomes an ornament of technically preconceived and constructed environments' (Rabinbach 1976: 55, 68). Indeed, the Nazi regime intended that true Germans would themselves be made into such aesthetic uni-forms, turning everyday life into the ongoing, totalized spectacle of Nazi social order.

"The reformulation of aesthetics in the Soviet Union was embedded in the Stalinist project to make all humanistic disciplines serve the practices of building socialism. Stalin, the political-ideological chief of the party, totalized Marxist philosophy, making it utterly subservient to ideology; and he was installed as Communism's first philosopher, the successor to Marx, Engels, and Lenin. History followed, as Stalin made himself the premier historian of the party (Tucker 1979: 350–6). So, too, aesthetics were totalized and standardized in terms of Socialist Realism, which explicitly rejected the concept of beauty. Instead, aesthetics was reclassified as a branch of science and (social) engineering, that operated under strict ideological control. Utterly without autonomy, aesthetic domains were made wholly didactic, holding up visions of how Soviet society was to be realized (Blasko 1999). In both Nazi Germany and the Soviet Union, the spectacle implemented such visions on a mass scale; while both vision and implementation were pervaded by the logic of a taxonomic, bureaucratic ethos."

Presentation: A metalogic of spectacle

Above all, the spectacle is visual, the movement and play of images that attract and appeal to the eye. In this regard, spectacle concretizes the western insistence on the visual and should be read as the Cartesian triumph over everything else described in the chapter on Senses. For the spectator, indeed, the spectacle is made distant from the self, since color and image are objectified "out there" by the seeing eye. In the sense that iconicity – the relationship of resemblance – is the semiotic relationship that seems most "natural," and vision often its most accessible register, spectacle does indeed serve the goals of national and political homogenization.

This is the aspect that Handelman (1990: 41–8) calls the metalogic of "presentation." In his words, spectacles "are declaratives, sometimes imperatives, but rarely interrogatives." They reproduce the bureaucratic concern with the outward replication of order: in their extreme precision and attention to detail, in their evocation of uniformity, and in their excess (but recall that redundancy is also a feature of ritual in the most conventional sense), they are performances of bureaucratic exactitude. Even "in the orderliness of their disorder, as for example, in numerous carnivals, there is again a plenitude of over-signification, but now of striking, clashing contrasts and the precision of inversions. The similarities of presentation in these extremes of state spectacle and carnival mark a powerful presence hidden from the gaze of the spectator. This is the presence of the bureaucratic ethos, the fulcrum of power on which the spectacle exhibits itself."

According to Handelman, spectacles "are the holidays of bureaucracy that mask this ethos of social order, celebrating this ethos while pretending to do something entirely different. Spectacles reproduce bureaucratic logic in the form of large-scale aesthetic productions that seemingly deny the taxonomic and processual power of this logic. Spectacles deny their formation in bureaucratic ethos by filling space/time with their often alluring, colorful, intricate, and complicated surfaces. Indeed, spectacles are intended to persuade spectators that these surface visions are significant or meaningful refractions – serious, profound, playful, fantastic – of social order. In other words, spectacles intend spectators to relate to surface as depth, thereby ignoring the deeper power of bureaucratic premises that striate and inform these occasions." In other words, they are concretized ideology – a mystification of political might and an opiate for those suffering under a cruel hegemony.

Again, I find myself agreeing with this characterization insofar as it is applied to totalitarian regimes. Under such regimes, naked power and deception replace patronage and débrouillardise, and the need for a secular theodicy is small – no one expects dictators to behave reasonably or benignly (except their admirers, for whom their actions are in any case axiomatically both reasonable and benign). But this works less well for democracies, where imperfection is acknowledged, faced, and negotiated day by day. This is not to argue for an absolute contrast between dictatorships and democracies; but the rhetoric of states that have attempted to cast themselves as democracies is such as to allow a more open contestation of underlying rigidities, for the most part. Some national rituals – for example, the British monarch's speech from the throne – are statements of a government's intentions, not an act of closure, and the monarch has no further role to play in what happens to the ideas laid out in that initial, programmatic declaration. This difference has material consequences for the ways in which ordinary citizens experience bureaucracy: one expects different treatment in a totalitarian state's army-run prison, for example, than one is likely to receive in a system that permits access to lawyers and a public trial with the right of appeal.

Handelman's excellent account of the totalitarian situation helps to make this point clearly. In the Nuremberg Rallies (the annual Nazi Party Day), for example, "hundreds of thousands of marchers participated in strict accordance with conscious taxonomic planning, the divisions between their units clearly visible. The directives for a Rally, concerning the order in which the formations of various party groups were to enter the parade, showed the extent of symmetry and synchronization in choreography that went into its planning. Time, space, place, body, and position, were totally coordinated, according to functional categories of participation. 'The required formations had to be formed on the approach route to the main square, where Hitler reviewed the parade. By the time the ranks moved into his sight, they were to be twelve men deep, the distance between the marchers 114 cm (30 inches). (Diagrams of the distances to be kept between individuals, between rows of men, and between the hundreds of standard bearers are attached to the document). The left hand of the marcher was to be placed on the belt buckle; the thumb was to be inside, behind the buckle, and the other fingers slightly bent, with the finger-ends at the right edge of the buckle. The document gives the exact timing of the cues for the hundreds of bands to begin to play – when they reached a certain distance from Hitler. The exact order in which the huge parade was to disband, after each formation had passed Hitler, was also carefully prearranged' (Burden 1967: 119)."

Similar care was taken in the Soviet march-past of the Great October Socialist Revolution of the Soviet Union in Moscow's Red Square. "In receiving the march-past, the political and military elites of the state stood on top of the tomb of the embalmed Lenin, above the marchers, centrist and rooted, as it were, in space and during time. The design of the spectacle was stratified with clarity, the elites at the mid-point of the parade – pillars and icons of the state, supported by the founding ancestor of the Revolution – and at the apex of the living hierarchy." And in this careful "artifice" of the Soviet political aesthetic, national, state, and party identities were "cathected" in a manner designed to naturalize their internally uncomfortable conflation for the populace. There is no space for public conversation about those messy aspects that, in a more democratically organized society, might become spaces for rethinking the rights and duties of citizens. And it is dangerous to assume that the difference is unimportant; that is not the same as saying that it is partial or fragile.

Handelman emphasizes the modular aspect of such displays of power: "All categories of presence point to the overwhelming consistency of taxonomic supremacy; and so, each module, and each component within each module reflect and replicate one another." This is the imagined community made manifest. Yet again we must ask: is this phenomenon confined to totalitarian societies, or is a looser version of it available in societies with less bluntly implacable sources of political control? Does not the Soviet or the Nazi rendition simply take to its absurd (and vicious) extreme the logic of bureaucratic organization, and is not the greater uniformity of the resulting spectacles simply a reflection of the state's more ruthless means of control? Handelman argues that "the presentations depend on the bureaucracy for their existence (as does the existence of the state itself)" and suggests further that "present day British rituals of royalty, with their polished aesthetics of beauty, affect, and synchronization (including of course the fairy tale wedding of Charles and Diana) are all the products of bureaucratic logic which changed their sloppy predecessors into exemplars of discipline and dignity." Yet this example actually seems to subvert Handelman's model, for two reasons. First, the greater efficiency of the modern model accompanied a progressive devolution of monarchical authority. And second, hindsight now allows us to appreciate that the vagaries of the royal family's misadventures, culminating in the extraordinary events of Diana's death and funeral, show how weak the actual control may be: Tony Blair's personal intervention and deft management seems to have safeguarded the monarchy for the time being – and to have effected a transformation of the role of the monarchy at the same time. There is indeed a nice irony in the fact that this particular prime minister often relies on the advice of that theorist of social practice, the sociologist Anthony Giddens; although the citizens had already effectively forced his hand, his political skill lay in presenting himself as a mediator who could persuade them to return, eventually, to their professions of affection for the monarchy, while admiring his capacity for so persuading them.

Even the most scripted spectacles contain within themselves the possibility of reverting to Handelman's ideal-typical ritual, with its transformative capacities awaiting activation by a skilled operator. True, Blair was the head of the bureaucratic machine behind the orchestration of the wedding and the funeral alike, but what is striking is that he had to interpret the meaning of the spectacle in order to bring about the changes that the populace appeared to desire. The result was a sudden restoration of the monarchy's popular standing – but it is arguably not the same monarchy as before. Moreover, Blair's own standing was palpably enhanced. Handelman recognizes such shifts in modality; his view of structure does not preclude – indeed, it demands – an interpreting social actor whose actions call that structure into social actuality.

Especially interesting in Handelman's analysis is his treatment of spectacles of inversion – Carnival and the like. There is a long tradition in anthropology – initiated by one of Handelman's early mentors, the Manchester anthropologist Max Gluckman – of treating certain rituals in which authority was mocked or threatened as teleological devices, intended to maintain the power of the leadership and its institutions in the face of popular discontent (e.g., Gluckman 1963a). This argument, the so-called "equilibrium model," has a long history, although Handelman finds it "doubtful" that his own thinking partakes of it to any significant degree. As with so many of the arguments in this Durkheimian lineage, it works more effectively when we can identify powerful agents capable of deciding that, yes, this is why they want to have such practices instituted – as a safety valve, to use one common metaphor (although not one, with its functionalist overtones, that Handelman favors). Malarney's (1996) analysis of funerary ritual in Vietnam offers a fascinating example of such "state functionalism," in which an avowedly antireligious national government controls the expression of piety as a means of satisfying the populace – allowing it, so to speak, to produce its opiate at home, although under careful supervision.

Handelman himself, emphasizing agency more explicitly than Gluckman and his immediate circle, does not particularly favor the idea of a self-sustaining equilibrium, which indeed has had a much more lively (if also modified) career in the work of ecological anthropologists concerned with humankind's place in "natural" systems (e.g., R. Rappaport 1979: 67).

Handelman is less concerned with such rituals in the so-called "traditional" societies than the somewhat similar kinds of spectacle that state societies seem willing to tolerate, even encourage. His example is the Rio carnival: "Inversion is a form of representation that offers alternative visions of social order, and so perhaps of change (Handelman 1990: 49–57). Carnival, as a limiting case of spectacle, may be less pervaded by bureaucratic logic. Indeed, in countries with carnival traditions, urban carnivals were frequently perceived by the authorities as hotbeds of sedition, subversion and potential rebellion, and often were outlawed." But he adds that "inversion is a highly limited case of change, and . . . carnival in the modern state is re-taxonomized, reorganized, and disciplined through bureaucratic logic." Such, he argues, is the case of the Rio Carnival, where "inversion revalidates and reinforces order [and] . . . keeps to the mold, the foundation-for-form of the inversion, of whatever it inverts. Therefore, inversion makes its foundation relevant and is a discourse about the validity of the latter. For instance, the inversion of a stratified social order is still a discourse about that very order of stratification. The inversion of gender remains a discourse on gender, and so forth. Inversion maintains mode of discourse, and the order that is inverted remains the normative mold for the inversion. So long as there is consensus on the greater value of the foundation-for-form, the inverted order is not self-sustaining. The inversion is invalidated as an inauthentic version that reverts to the normative foundation from which it derived." This sounds suspiciously like the equilibrium model.

In the Rio Carnival, forms of social existence that are normatively undervalued are given pride of place: public space over private space, the openness of the body over modesty and restraint, equality over hierarchy, and so forth (Da Matta 1991: 61–115). The highlight of carnival is the parades of the dancing samba schools (a form of voluntary association), especially the parade of the schools of the highest league which takes place in the center of the city, from dusk through the following midday. These competitions between schools that in principle are the equals of one another is itself an inversion of the mundane preoccupation with moral and social hierarchy (Da Matta 1991: 112). Although most members of the schools are poor, they are the focus of the parade spectacle, of the gaze of wealthier spectators who pay admission to see the show from high grandstands on either side of the route. In its presentation, each school uses costume, music, and dance to elaborate on its chosen theme.

All this seems far from the bureaucratic ethos. Nonetheless, Handelman argues, the state has in fact "domesticated" the schools through a system of applied classification: "In the past the municipality legalized the participation of the schools in carnival, in exchange for an array of regulations that stress nationalism, unity, and control over the parades and their routes. Themes for the great parade must be taken from Brazilian history; no satire, parody, or criticism of politics and current events are permitted. Within the parades, schools are penalized if they overstep the time allotted for their appearance, or if the discipline of their musical rhythms and dance steps are less than perfect (Queiroz 1985: 5, 16). So, too, the shift to a spectacle of grand scale has produced vast contingents of more uniform dancers, dressed in similar costumes; doing highly synchronized, simple, and more curtailed dance steps that destroy the art of the samba as a lower-class, innovative, dance form (Taylor 1982: 306). In the parades, order is the underlying foundation of the realization of the carnival celebration (Queiroz 1985: 31). Through bureaucratic classification, the parades have been separated and isolated from the rest of carnival, regulated and controlled. Disorderly order has vanished within the spectacle. The soul of carnival has become a partial entity that depends for its existence on statist premises of order. Despite its colorful, exciting allure, the distance between carnival and the totalitarian spectacles discussed earlier has narrowed severely."

This sobering assessment leads Handelman to ponder the constraining effects of modern bureaucracy on the performance of ritual. Its conversion into spectacle, he remarks, serves the visualist imperatives of the bureaucratic state, and these are now accentuated by television with its global reach: "In making a spectacle of ritual, we kill it." (This, perhaps, supplies part of the answer's to Constance Classen's concern with the reasons for which the visual has come to dominate so thoroughly.) But has ritual really become something so very different? Moreover, as Jerome Mintz (1997) has shown for the Carnival in post-Franco Spain, the process of government control can also be reversed: the collapse of the regime was indirectly presaged by changes in Carnival practices – changes that restored older and less formal modes of celebration back into play at a much accelerated rate after the restoration of democracy, only more recently to succumb to the conformities that this time largely arose from tourist commodification. One could argue, naturally, that Carnival was never primarily a state celebration, but the Franco regime did its best to turn it into one. And if now it shows signs of again becoming spectacle, this has little to do with state control.

Sites of Resistance, Sites of Conformity

In an interesting inversion of the older anthropological tradition, in which exotic societies were represented as bound by custom, Handelman suggests that rituals in what he calls "traditional" societies are more likely to serve as sites of resistance to authority than are the organized spectacles of bureaucratic nation-states. This reversal saves his argument from the charge with which I began the discussion: that his approach deprives the members of non-industrialized societies of agency. To the contrary, it accords them a greater degree of power over events than modern bureaucratic polities grant their citizens.

But it turns out to be a limited kind of agency: "If a metalogic of ritual is transformative, mobilizing uncertainty to question the validity of cultural form, this would seem a likely medium for the mobilization of opposition. However, this metalogic also systemically eliminates questions raised by uncertainty. Ritual, then, would seem relatively impervious to the redirection of its causality. In order to be more accessible to the mobilization of resistance, a particular ritual should be organized in the first instance as a weapon of attack, as are, for example, rituals of sorcery. Otherwise, a new ritual would have to be invented, perhaps according to the form that resistance would be expected to take (as was the case, for example, in Kikuyu, Mau Mau rituals of initiation in colonial Kenya)." This implicitly suffers from the same weakness as arguments set forth by Eric Hobsbawm, for whom "primitive rebels" (1959) are incapable of creating their own ideologies, requiring leadership, just as the peasants whose traditions are chartered by nationalistic elites seem, in his view, to be the dupes of the latter (Hobsbawm and Ranger, eds., 1983).

One might reasonably respond to this by arguing that the flaw in this argument lies in the label of "traditional" societies, for they are not at all alike – and particularly as regards the degree and direction of the agency accorded to individuals and groups. (Handelman in fact recognizes this when he retorts that my interpretation entails "conflating the logics of form, of organization, with particular instances that themselves are emergent products of possible variations" that result from particular historical conditions.) It is at least as true of modern societies that they are not all alike, despite the surface claims of globalization and "monoculture." If all bureaucracies served totalitarian regimes, Handelman's argument would be wholly persuasive, especially when he argues that spectacles offer a form of certainty that is much less amenable to the mobilization of resistance. The whole point of Nuremberg rallies and Red Square parades is to perform – in the transitive sense of a display that brooks no disagreement – the impossibility of dissent within a society of uniform persons. And of course he is right to imply that the distinction between totalitarian regimes and democracies is simplistic, if only because many states exercise what we might call "preferential democracy" – mistreating one body of citizenry (immigrants, refugees, nomads, ethnic minorities) in the name of a perverted vision of majority rule.

Perhaps Handelman's gloomy vision, the downside of Weber's more ambivalent understanding of the march to modernity in an iron cage, is a valid prophecy. Until it is shown to be so, however, I would prefer to frame it much as Bird-David has suggested for the forms of economy – as a play of ideal types. Indeed, the image of the bureaucratic monstrosity has already developed a respectable literary presence in the West, in Joseph Haller, Franz Kafka, George Orwell and Aldous Huxley, while writers suffering in the shadows of postcolonial regimes (e.g., Mbembe 1992) have pointed to its failures in terms of a larger ideology of democratic government. The kind of repressive classification that we find in totalitarian states represents but one rendition – close, perhaps, to the ideal-typical model – of a rigid bureaucracy at work.

In closing, I would like to mention a further difficulty entailed in overdrawing the ritual–spectacle opposition. This concerns the pervasiveness of small-scale ritual in bureaucratic practice. Even if we confine the argument to national bureaucracies, as Handelman and I have both largely done, we find that functionaries and clients engage together in a variety of small ritual actions that satisfy most conventional definitions of the genre: formalism, redundancy, and so forth. I have argued that we may view nationalism itself as a form of religion the teleological origins of which have historically identifiable authors and sources of inspiration; the acts of oath taking, signing, and rubber-stamping that accompany, say, the acquisition of a passport confirm the citizen's adherence to the rules of the game, although the citizen may in fact be resisting (as when that citizen uses the passport to go to a friendly state in order to continue on to a forbidden country, having just sworn to abjure any such intention). Most ritual, like chisungu, entails inculcation of norms, but that fact itself implies an ever-lurking potential for subversion and creative disobedience.

While I am thus not persuaded that a simple opposition between rituals in "traditional" societies and spectacles in "modern" ones even begins adequately to describe the range of possible formations, as an ideal-typical model it does have considerable heuristic value. It would be strange if, at this stage in the evolution of anthropology when such then-and-now formulations as gift-versus-commodity (see the chapter on Economies) are losing favor as an adequate basis for the division of the world's economic systems, we were to restore the same basic model in the arena of ritual. In Handelman's formulation there is something of a Weberian nostalgia: spectacles, in his formulation, are the self-representation of a disenchanted world. In many instances, I fear, he is right. Anthropologists will nevertheless do well to treat each case on its own merits. As I have pointed out in the chapter on Epistemologies, following Nicholas Thomas rather than Don Handelman in this regard, we should now prefer heuristic to grand predictive schemata. This does not mean that we should necessarily avoid propositions of a theoretical nature, but it does mean that our approach must necessarily reflect the provisionality of our own understanding. Vico warned in the eighteenth century that when we lose sight of that provisionality, we become entrapped in the self-reference of our own knowledge systems – a stance that may serve the more repressive kinds of state bureaucracy admirably, but that discards the self-inflicted defamiliarization essential to creative anthropological thought. Leach (1962) many years ago decried the dangers for anthropologists inherent in what he saw as conceptual "butterfly-collecting." It might seem that this is where a fundamentally heuristic orientation would lead us – as Handelman warned me in reading an earlier version of this chapter, "a straightbackward retreat to what anthropologists have excelled in for decades – piling case upon case, insisting that each has a nugget of theoretical significance," with no palpable accumulation of new insight. (This is also the burden of his one major criticism of Victor Turner's work.) But theory is an explanatory device even when its explanations are clearly provisional, and to call it heuristic is not to deny the hope of some more inclusive level of generalization. Too many scholars have tried to entrap all ritual activity in a single, inflexible framework – ironically, precisely the quality of action that both Handelman and I have both treated as a type of action characeristic of bureaucrats who have mastered the practical logic (if not the civic ideology) of their trade.

This becomes especially dangerous when we apply these insights to the ritualistic activities of nation-states, for there, more than in any other social domain, we risk becoming entrapped in precisely the phantasmagoria of bureaucratic rigidity that the totalitarian states would cheerfully foist on us all.

Note

1 Handelman has recently, and forcefully, responded to the various criticisms of his work as summarized in *Models and Mirrors*, in a lengthy introduction to the new edition of that work (1998). Some of the discussions in which he engages in that piece will further clarify the arguments that inform this chapter, especially on the type of logic peculiar to modern bureaucracies and its relationship to the distinction between ritual and spectacle.

13

Aesthetics

The Sound of Art

Perhaps the most opaque region of anthropological investigation concerns questions of taste. Not only do we lack sufficient understanding of sensory issues, as we saw in an earlier chapter, but the observer's bias so often seems natural rather than cultural that discussion is practically impeded. Indeed, anthropologists of an older era questioned the very existence of "art" as a separable category in "primitive societies," while – paradoxically – insisting that "primitive peoples," in their greater dependence on bodily sensation, were "more musical." This is a stereotype that often still surfaces as a superficially "benign" expression of racial prejudice, and anthropologists' attempts to refute such ideas have often been misconstrued as offering support for them.

It seems useful to pursue the topic of art in general through the domain of music. The anthropological study of music is relatively well developed, with its own journals (such as *Ethnomusicology*) and a significant presence in universities around the world and a well-documented, complex history. Moreover, the paradox that I have just outlined will serve as a useful goad to thinking about the nature of aesthetics in non-western as well as western societies. If music is "art" in the western sense, yet the more musical people supposedly "lack art," we see the pernicious influence of naturalizing discourses on much western thinking about these matters. So, although I shall return to the question of visual art at the end of the chapter, much of this discussion will be taken up with music as both a paradigmatic and a provocative case, and one that also works against the prevailing idiom of visualism – already critically discussed in these pages – in anthropological thought and representational practice.

Perhaps because music is something that moves quickly, changes, and is hard to "pin down," ethnomusicologists have led the way into this examination of the principles of what Silver (1982) has called ethno-aesthetics – the indigenous principles of aesthetic value. Questions about the constitution of "art" as a category have nonetheless come to play an important role (see Steiner

1994). They are especially useful in that they force us to regard value attributed to "the West" with a critical eye, and to see the individual genius, not as someone deserving of special respect in any universal sense, but as the expression of a shared but historically specific value system that may now be changing – a change to which, indeed, anthropology's critical scrutiny may have contributed decisive force.

Music first, then. Music – which David Coplan defines as the cultural practice of arranging stabilized sonic pitches for expressive purposes – has always attracted the interest of social scientists. Early folklorists and comparative mythologists had an especial interest in music, more specifically the verbal aspects of song and chant, because this mode of expression, inseparable from the drama, appeared bound up with the prehistoric origins and development of religion, a focus of the evolutionists in the mid to late nineteenth century (and persisting in the prejudice that some racial groups are "more musical" than others). Music and dance, as ancient and universal as language itself, appeared in their function and development as profound expressions of the operation of evolutionary principles in cultural life. The tradition remained stronger in ethnomusicology than elsewhere in anthropology, perhaps because "comparative musicology" in Europe was always anchored in the study of "art music" and thus served as the first chapter of a persistent evolutionary narrative. The organological ethnology of Percival Kirby (1934), for example, still unsurpassed for sheer range and detail in the ethnomusicology of southern Africa, is clouded in this way by his commitment to evolutionary concepts of musical development.

The social context of music reveals an impressive range of uses. The organization of healing, war, work, political process, ideologies of identity, the recording of history, the relationship of human beings to one another, to nature, and to the supernatural are all domains in which music, at various times and places, has played a central role. Thus, for example, the Nuer – made famous in anthropology by Evans-Pritchard's ethnographic researches (1940) – chose as their war captain the most inspiring singer of martial anthems. The discourse of chieftaincy in nineteenth-century Hawaii was unintelligible without the hula. Sometimes these phenomena have diachronic aspects: we can track the changes in their significance and forms through time. Ralph Austen, a historian of African royal epics, has demonstrated how the form and focus of heroic narrative songs changed over time in Africa in response to the waxing and waning of state power (Austen 1995) – although this suggests that the words were no less important than the music. Praise singers not only added to the ceremonial, performative awe of office; they also provided an historical record and a social mediation of power relations, and a necessary vertical channel of communication within structures of political inequality. And sometimes musical and other aesthetic practices become a diacritic marker of difference: in southern Africa, where Coplan has conducted most of his research, people of European background commonly expressed puzzlement as to why local Africans apparently could not engage in civil protest without the performance of "menacing" songs and dances.

Further, western aesthetic concepts, genre definitions, and performance categories are naturalistically imposed on non-western musics. Yet one of the first things that field research into expressive domains reveals is that other cultures do not classify them into the familiar categories of performing and visual arts, or performance into dance, music, drama, verbal recitation and so forth. Even among European societies, there are enormous differences. Any of these categories may be classed together; or separately from one another but together with forms of spectacle, rhetoric, games, historical recounting, and work.

While personal experience and popular consciousness are suffused with musical associations and images like those recalled above, many anthropologists have been reluctant to consider the possibly crucial articulation of music with other domains of practice because they lack training in formal musical analysis. Ethnomusicologists, as musicologist Joseph Kerman once noted, must "struggle to make themselves heard in the seemingly tone-deaf conclaves and enclaves of anthropology" (Kerman 1985: 181). (An analogous problem concerns the recording of gesture [Williams, ed., 1997; Farnell 1995].) One would find it hard to imagine anthropologists today operating without some knowledge of local languages; it is surely a mark of persistent ethnocentrism that this standard is not maintained in other expressive domains that may be more important – as we saw in the chapter on Senses – to the local population than to the visitor.

This reluctance has been reinforced by professional musicologists who, having studied other-than-western music, who cogently argue that the search for musical meaning must necessarily involve sonic analysis. For musicology, musics are first of all self-referential systems of tonal organization equivalent to syntax in language, and only secondarily an expression of socially semantic or pragmatic influences. Indeed, early philological musicologists such as Erich von Hornbostel (1928) had strong inclinations toward psychology and neurology. Working with the sensory evidence for cultural diversity, they hoped to discover in music insights into the workings of the mind, heart, and brain. An echo of this is perhaps to be found in Lévi-Strauss's fondness for musical metaphors.

Musics are indeed like spoken languages in some regards, especially in the infinite variability that their highly disciplined structures – like syntax – are capable of carrying (what linguists call "recursiveness"). But there are differences, too. Among these we should note the absence of even the semblance of referentiality: music can allude (connote), but it is rarely if ever used to refer (denote) – even the *Leitmotiv* is indexical and allusive rather than directly referential. Admittedly, the referentiality of language is also highly contingent on context, but music usually possesses more of what Jakobson (1960) called the "poetic function" in language – the capacity to convey meaning by creatively playing with a recognizable form, as indeed poetic language does (often without meaning anything referentially specific at all).

Music is, says Coplan, a universal practice; but it is not a universal language – a concept, he observes, that is ineradicable from popular consciousness even though musical "languages" may be as mutually unintelligible as English and Japanese (as any first-time visitor to a performance of unfamiliar musical idioms can attest). Like food, music can alienate as well as charm, and it can charm for reasons that would completely puzzle its performers. Much the same can be said about other art forms; indeed, the incorporation of non-western art forms into the western aesthetic is a process that has complex economic and political ramifications – colonialism, the tourist trade, and the international art market have all redefined the principles of many a local aesthetic (Graburn, ed., 1976; Steiner 1994). In the case of music, the most obvious failures of interpretation are those in which emotion is misread.

That said, we should not ignore those cases in which a more precise parallel between language and music emerges. In the classical music of Hindu India, for example, sonic elements have explicit semantic, ideational, and emotional referents. In European classical art, in the songs of Schubert and Schumann, it is a matter of some controversy as to whether song assimilates verbal text into a fundamentally musical mode of expression, or whether the composer begins with the reading of a poetic text that inspires and shapes its musical setting (Coplan 1994: 9). The mutual constitution of literary and musical processes is even more characteristic of songs composed in sub-Saharan African languages, with their semantic dependence on syllabic tone, alliterative and assonantal parallelisms, ideophones (images and ideas in sound), and rhythmic and reduplicative vocalizations. Such languages inescapably influence the shape and direction of melody, polyphony, and rhythm.

The search for universal meanings in music, a quest of which Weber's (1921) volume bespeaks the great significance it held for western scholars, may have been misguided; but it helped to lay the groundwork for its own undoing. Although they wasted many learned pages debating the false, misdirecting dichotomy between the "borrowing" and "independent invention" of musical and other cultural traits, nevertheless, armed with their ideas of "culture circles" and "culture areas," the industrious Weberian musicologists provided invaluable empirical descriptions and comparisons of the musical languages of non-western peoples, and mapped the salient features of local musical styles on to an ethnicized historical geography of the world. Weberian scholarship can sometimes produce its own brand of iron cage.

Yet this was also a highly disciplined tradition, and it generated an enormous range of technical knowledge and comparative data. Among the many outstanding figures who emerged from this comparativist movement was Bruno Nettl, originally known for his work on Native American musical culture, who went on not only to study the music of the Near East, but also to realize in four decades of writing, teaching, and institutional leadership at the University of Illinois a cross-disciplinary balance between anthropology and musicology. A contemporary and friend of Nettl's at nearby Indiana University, Alan Merriam, tipped the balance in favor of anthropology in *The Anthropology of Music* (Merriam 1964). Merriam, an empiricist trained in the cultural functionalism of Melville Herskovits, was uncompromising in his efforts to make music – as sonic system, as cultural artifact, as social process, and as human experience – as fit an object of anthropological description and theorization as any other form of social action. This enterprise encountered an unrelenting resistance from mainstream ethnomusicologists and mainstream anthropologists, who, Coplan suggests, thought that the study of any music was a technically specialized affair that belonged to schools of music and that anthropologists were unjustifiably forcing their own extra-musical concerns upon them.

Folklorists and departments of folklore have played possibly a more significant role in the advancement and institutionalization of the anthropological study of music than have departments of anthropology themselves. The direct concern of folklore with aural genres of cultural expression makes an anthropology of music a necessary and central disciplinary concern, although the textual bias of nineteenth-century European folklore studies often kept the music out of publications. In eastern Europe, moreover, the desire to eradicate "Oriental" cultural elements enhanced this bias against music; it was easier to edit, say, the texts of Greek folksongs to demonstrate their alleged affinity with ancient Greek prototypes than it was to explain away the "Turkish" sound of much of the music. In the twentieth century, folklorists have certainly worked hard to rectify that suppression. Perhaps the most sweeping exercise, albeit one that rests on scientistic premises that are no longer widely shared, is Alan Lomax's *Folk Song Style and Culture* (1968). His attempt to identify measurable structures in music and dance ("choreometrics") anticipates later work in which formal patterning came to be recognized as shared between domains – by music and embroidery, for example, or by dance and architecture.

In this view, certain kinds of social relations and relations of production produce social psychologies that are then expressed in certain kinds of musical sound patterning and ethno-aesthetics. Similar ideas began to appear in other domains of research. There is, for example, nothing intrinsically surprising about the idea that a culture that cherishes highly agonistic social relationships is likely to exhibit oppositional motifs in its visual art. Gerald Pocius (1979), as I have already noted, pointed out that the distribution of social space between formal and informal domains in Newfoundland houses was directly illustrated by the choice of hierarchical and nonhierarchical designs, respectively, in the hooked rugs that people hung on the walls. In a still more detailed recognition of this kind of correspondence, as I have already noted, James W. Fernandez pointed out the reproduction of cosmology in the architecture of the Fang of Gabon and the Zionist rituals of Southern Africa, and thereby showed how aesthetic principles provided a means for expressing and even creating the form of cosmology in the routines of everyday life.

Yet these correspondences differed from those identified by Lomax in that the scholars in question did not make totalizing claims about cultural form. They simply identified correspondences that were clearly observable under ethnographically well-observed conditions. In Fernandez's work, for example, the key lies in the meticulous, exhaustive analysis of ritual practice in its social context (1982). Near the end of the 1960s, in fact, isomorphic comparisons between "folksong style and culture" began to come into serious question. True, Alan Merriam's formulation, following Kwabena Nketia, of the anthropology of music as the study of "music in culture" (Merriam 1964) remained a powerful paradigm for research and musical ethnology. Further, the work of John Blacking (1973, etc.) did much to advance our understanding of the value and meaning of music in social life. At the heart of Blacking's contribution was an ability to clarify how extramusical factors regulated the structure of music, and a refusal to oppose or separate the internal or formal analysis of music from that of its relation to life. But the relationship between formal patterning and underlying social organization emerged, in part because of detailed ethnographic work of the kind I have just mentioned, as vastly more complex and unpredictable than would appear from the earlier formulations. This move away from a rule-dominated vision of social life – from structure to process – is consistent with the development of anthropology in other domains.

Geertz's (1973) analytic concept of culture as an "ethos," not unlike Blacking's formulation, suggested the embedding of art in the core cosmological orientations (religion, philosophy, science) of a cultural group. Geertz, too, anticipated the possibility that members of a group might use its normative forms in socially creative ways. Thus, for example, in Johannesburg music and dance have been used by black South Africans as an active means to urbanize, to raise their status through the acquisition of key markers of superior class identity, to protest repression and inferior social classification, and in multiple ways to transform their social being along with their social consciousness (Coplan 1985). Still, as other studies – such as those of Waterman (1990) in Lagos – have shown, there is no straightforward relationship between the dynamics of social class and musical participation. Instead, as for example in Turino's (1993) study of rural–urban musical migration among Andean Aymara speakers in Peru, the complexities of social category and position in relation to selections in musical markers of cultural style continue to inspire research and enrich analysis.

By the mid-1980s, a series of important articles and monographs had appeared establishing an anthropology of musical meaning, notably Steven Feld's fine treatise on sonic/sensory geography, narration, aesthetics, and communication among the Kaluli of Papua New Guinea (Feld 1982). Feld's work is especially germane here because he sought to show that the aesthetic principles he observed in music were actively used in organizing social relations. Another exemplary study, Anthony Seeger's *Why Suyá Sing* (1987), showed how music was constitutive of social and cultural practice, singing "an essential part of social production and reproduction" (Seeger 1987: 128). Seeger called his study a "musical anthropology," reversing "music in culture" so as to focus on music as not merely a domain but an environment within which to understand an entire society (the Suyá number only a few thousand). Seeger effectively disposes of the theoretical split between the study of music and the study of society (Stokes 1994: 2). Others, including Steven Feld (1982) and Ellen Basso (1985) (who argues for the musical organization of social processes), have also pursued this intellectual project, which also has affinities with the study of the aesthetics of social interaction ("social poetics": Herzfeld 1985, 1997a). For it is clear that the aesthetics of self-presentation, while perhaps not always dominated by an ethos in the sense of an overdetermining configuration of cultural form, often follows principles that are given more formal expression in artistic performance. If a sheep thief cannot steal with flair, who wants him as an ally? If a politician cannot tell elegant falsehoods that are obviously just that, who would join a party made vulnerable by such weakness? Performances must announce themselves as such in order to be effective – a principle recognized in such early semiotic theory as that of the Russian Formalists and the Prague School and elaborated in Jakobzon's concept of the poetic function. Musical skill is clearly, in many societies, a persuasive accouterment to political and social savvy: the eighteenth-century European salon offers but one example. As Steven Caton (1990: 22) says of poetry, so, for different aesthetic modalities in different cultural settings, we can say that to craft a good performance "is to engage in social practice." And to engage in social practice is to commit oneself to a politics of personal value, often translatable into larger idioms of power.

While not all societies give music pride of place, Seeger's work on the Suyá is nonetheless particularly important in forcing us to recognize that music is not necessarily secondary either, as it so often is in modern industrial societies. So, too, Marina Roseman (1991) showed how music was fundamental to the healing practices of the Malaysian Temiar. And Coplan shows how the culture of Basotho migrant mine workers – and by extension the historical ethnography of Lesotho – emerges from the miners' own sung poetic autobiographies (Coplan 1994). Music is therefore not simply located in a context; its performance is itself productive of change, especially if the music is considered to be "good" (Stokes 1994: 5). If a West African Yoruba drummer cannot hold the rhythm, the god (orisha) will not descend and possess the dancers. If Roseman's Temiar cannot sing with emotional conviction, no one will be healed. Performance is not an activity apart from non-performance, but continuous with other modes of action and domains of social reality.

By virtue of the ineluctable associations among expressive media, the possibilities released by such a paradigm extended as well to the emergence of a radically new "performance anthropology" out of the anthropology of performance. The foundational text of this movement, Coplan thinks, may be Johannes Fabian's Power and Performance (1990), although an important stream of research in American folklore (see especially Bauman 1977, and, for music, especially Stone 1982, 1988) had already begun to raise some of the technical issues. Fabian observes and participates in the practice of popular musical theatre in Zaire to provide a model for what he terms a performative ethnography. This performative – as opposed to informative – ethnography is based on the recognition that much practical as opposed to discursive cultural knowledge can be illuminated only through enactment and performance (Fabian 1990: 6). The approach appears, in fact, to have some intellectual common ground,

not only with practice theory, but with the kind of engaged phenomenology –
"radical empiricism," as Michael Jackson (1989) has termed it – that insists on
this kind of engagement. Further, Fabian argues, "'performance' seemed to be
a more adequate description both of the ways people realize their culture and
of the method by which an ethnographer produces knowledge about that
culture" (M. Jackson 1989: 18). Performative ethnography, then, "is appropriate to both the nature of cultural knowledge and the nature of knowledge of
cultural knowledge," where the ethnographer does not call the tune but plays
along (M. Jackson 1989: 19).[1]

Certainly, the potential for the movement of the analytical concept of
performance to the center of the ethnographic enterprise has been demonstrated
in a range of monographs, of which a fine example is Jane K. Cowan's
Dance and the Body Politic in Northern Greece (1990). In that work, we
read of an aesthetic of daily life – an aesthetic that both reproduces gender
and other discriminations and provides an idiom for their occasional contestation. Such studies remind readers that musical and other forms of performance are the means through which "appropriate gender behavior is
taught and socialized" (Stokes 1994: 22). Within those idioms, too, differently
situated individuals may contest dominant ideologies of gender through
their subversion of performative norms, as Cowan shows for dance events in
northern Greece.

Coplan recalls how the ribald Basotho mothers' song-and-dance for a new
mother, *litolobonya*, is performed in a shuttered house from which men are
strictly excluded for the occasion: "The men gather outside the house, drinking
the women's beer and conversing dyspeptically as the women's songs and
lusty cheers filter out from behind the tightly covered windows." Coplan was
himself allowed to witness two performances of litolobonya and even to record
the occasions on film and tape, authorized by the idea that since he was not a
Mosotho, he was not really a man. He adds, wryly, "I have no evidence that
having a non-man as a non-normative male spectator added anything to the
women's fun. Some of the fun of litolobonya, though, is surely the celebration
by women, married or not, of an emerging self-sufficient female world."
This growing independence of Basotho women can be seen as part of a worldwide trend which may be irreversible and profound in its effects because it challenges both the conjugal relation and the patriarchal family structure (Coplan
1994: 168).

Should performance be identified as a discrete form of social action, as "set
apart"? People may execute dance steps in the midst of a conversation, hum a
few bars, or mimic a distinguished personage or familiar friend. Music perhaps
provides a straightforward context for asking this question: people categorize
it in different ways but everyone knows it when they hear it. (We should nevertheless remember that words like "song" may be more problematic as tools
of cross-cultural analysis: what of societies, for example, where the term we
gloss as "song" is opposed to other terms denoting "hymn," "chant," or
"dirge"?). Musical performance is set apart because it exaggerates, more dramatically than many other modes of self-expression, its own framing as a dis-

crete activity and idiom. Even the brief dance step in the middle of a conversation is a framing device in this sense.

So far we have been looking at the production of music in the contexts of more or less traditional ethnography. But music transcends the local perhaps more than any other art form – not so much because it is capable of being immediately understood beyond its area of production, but because it can be universalized – or at least "nationalized" – for the purposes of creating a sense of national unity. It can also provide a means of resisting the homogenizing imperatives of the nation-state (see Askew 1998). But, conversely, as happened in Greece in the post-World War II years, it can provide a means of reconciling bourgeois distaste for "Turkish" elements in the vernacular culture with the realization that these are, after all, the familiar idioms of everyday life. The music of Mikis Theodorakis, composer of *Zorba's Dance* and a huge corpus of songs, was threatening to right-wing governments because it undercut their attempts to create a rigid separation between "oriental" and "European" aesthetics, and because it popularized poetry – the lyrics were often taken from the works of well-known writers – that these governments regarded as subversive. In brief, it challenged the official monopoly of "Greek music" (Holst-Warhaft 1979). In other situations, learning a musical heritage may be a means of asserting ethnic self-determination, as has happened with Mexican American resistance to the "melting pot" (see Parédes 1958).

The sense of place, musically created and performed, always involves notions of difference and social boundary (Stokes 1994: 3–5). Because the role of musician has become increasingly professionalized, it is easy to accept the idea that music somehow transcends the particularities of time and place. This is clearly not so; supposedly "universal" music like Mozart symphonies, while attractive to educated Japanese for whom it constitutes a form of cultural capital, leaves many other listeners – including many Europeans – quite uninterested, because they cannot link it to that sense of place. The claim that a particular music is universal, which has often been used to justify or explain its professionalization in today's transnational conditions, denies the specificity of cultural experience. Coplan offers an intriguing observation: "People who live and work amidst non-musical activities and only perform on weekends have less technical capacity to play but more to play about than professional popular musicians who have had to grapple with bus and plane schedules as well as master their instruments. Hence the rough beauty and power of Zulu sugar refinery workers singing and dancing their 'regimental' and district identities at their Durban hostels on Sundays. Compare that to the sense of place evoked by a Swedish rock star performing memorized lyrics in English describing how love . . . hasn't lasted forever."

Other Aesthetics

The ability to play a piece of music clearly does entail technical mastery. The degree to which such mastery may be shared in a given social context, however, varies enormously. In the Cretan mountain village where I did fieldwork, few indeed were the men who could not sing the rhyming couplets with which they joyfully insulted each other. The technical mastery lay, not in the music (which would have been noticeable only by its absence – by "speaking," *militondas* (an inferior activity!), but in capping a good verbal phrase. But when players of the three-stringed lira and the bass lute took up their instruments, the words – which were often conventional – became relatively immaterial; it was the virtuosity of the instrument playing that counted.

Thus, it becomes clear that even Coplan's amiable observation about Zulu sugar workers displays a somewhat Eurocentric bias. He may indeed appreciate the beauty of the songs – one should be able to learn something of an aesthetic not one's own, after all – but his assessment of the relative merits of performances would have to be evaluated in terms of audience re-actions in both cases. This is a point to which we shall return in the chapter on Media.

Now one of the features that plays a great role in the western evaluation of performance, and is indeed implicit in Coplan's remark, is the idea of personal "talent" – a version of the notion of "genius," as this was elaborated by Thomas Carlyle and others as the pinnacle of individualism in the Romantic era. In western music, talent is a hotly debated "property." I use "property" here in the sense of an immanent quality, although, again, it is a feature of the "pos-sessive individualism" – something one "has" – that marks the ideology of western identity (C. B. Macpherson 1962; see also Handler 1985). Apparently most modern nation-states have by now adopted this ideology, since it provides an efficient justification for the identification of statehood with culture and ter-ritory – with property writ large. In a converse move, an ethnomusicologist (and former music school administrator) turned his sights on the production of western "art" music. Henry Kingsbury found that the distribution of "talent" in the conservatory he studied followed fairly predictable lines of power and alliance, rather than measurable aesthetic criteria. In a very ingenious study (Kingsbury 1988), he argued that "talent" was very much like the "divine spirit" of Evans-Pritchard's Nuer: it was "refracted" through the social divisions of the community – a thoroughly Durkheimian formulation, but one that seemed well supported by the ethnographic evidence. In other words, in a community of "talented people," individuals had differential access to this common property according to their relationships with those who exercised authority within the school. Here, necessarily, we must broaden the discussion beyond the specific domain of music.

The ability of the artist in any domain is more a matter of what Bourdieu (1984) calls "the social judgment of taste" than it is of some objective set of criteria. Social position at least partially determines value: for example, leisured people may take pride in treating now useless but formerly utilitarian objects as aesthetically pleasing, in part because this demonstrates their freedom from the need to labor (Douglas and Isherwood 1979; Thompson 1979). Producers, for their part, have a great deal of "identity" – a specific form of social or cultural capital – bound up in their work and are willing to endure the consequences of risk and exploitation in order to maintain that "property" (Plattner 1996). In this, they are gambling their livelihoods on the same processes of social embedding that we have noted in Herrmann's analysis of garage sales: the sentimental or aesthetic "value added" can be used to keep them from earning much material profit from their own work.

Others' evaluation of their ability is also embedded in those sometimes inscrutable social processes, and may have tremendous consequences for whole careers. Kingsbury's discussion of "talent," for example, illustrates how supposedly absolute values of taste are, in social practice, vehicles for an elaborate form of discrimination – and indeed it is surely no coincidence that in the West a person who is thought to have good taste can be described as "discriminating." The European ideology of romanticism, with its exaltation of absolute values, disguises the social processes through which expressions of value are filtered. Such ideologies are usually expressed in forceful terms. They ordinarily only give way to a more critical perspective when the context of use is studied under conditions of close intimacy – harder, perhaps, to do in a massive institutional setting such as an art museum or a conservatory than in a peasant village, but an all-important counterweight to the universalizing claims of these formal institutions.

Does this mean that "there is no such thing as talent" – or that all aesthetic criteria are really just diacritica of power? I think not. The lesson shared by Kingsbury's and Plattner's very different analyses is more important and far subtler than that: it is that the analysis of aethetic criteria cannot be described in isolation from the social relations among those who are using those criteria to judge each other. But inasmuch as we are committed to taking our informants' claims seriously – and, after all, they often do tell us that judgments are politically motivated – we must see the operation of aesthetics as a calculus of the formal and the social; and we must recall, too, that the social is also calibrated to aesthetic criteria (manners, elegance, and so on).

These criteria may be quite specific to local cultures. There are many studies, for example, that show that evaluations of color, hue, and intensity affect both perception and production (e.g., Gell 1998; Morphy 1989). Forge (1970) even argued that the iconic qualities of a photograph were not immediately apparent to the Abelam of New Guinea, who had never previously seen – in other words, had never been socialized into decoding – the two-dimensional conventions of the photographic image. Once we realize that aesthetic principles may also guide such ubiquitous aspects of social life as ordinary manners, we can more easily appreciate how radically the analyst must resist prior assumptions about "art" as a set-apart domain – perhaps the most common device for maintaining a boundary between cerebral high "art" and manual vernacular "craft."

Anthropologists not only view aesthetics as a dimension of social life rather than as an absolute domain in its own right; they must treat the claim of absolute value as itself socially embedded. There are certainly many societies where "art for art's sake" is appreciated. There are also societies, such as Kitawa in Papua New Guinea, where apprenticeship in the specialized production may lead to the development of an aesthetic sensibility that is removed from both practical and symbolic notions of function: young men engaged in carving ritual wooden objects learn a language of form that is quite opaque to ordinary people and yet has no obvious religious or functional meaning (Scoditti 1982).

But one does not have to argue for a separate domain of aesthetics in order to recognize the local appreciation of beauty, form, or dramatic effect. Distinctions between beauty and moral worth may be differently organized than in western society, but some sense of value and appropriateness is often present. Questions of function – including the possibility of a separate aesthetic function, and distinctions between "art" and "craft" (or between artists and artisans) – are empirical, and the answers vary culturally. Craftsmen in a southern Italian town may use the idea of being "artists' (*artiri*) to keep less skilled workers at a social distance (Galt 1992: 59). Originality is an especially thorny issue, since ideas of ownership and personhood are deeply invested in it – at least for western observers. Thus, for example, the western concern with avoiding "fakes" – now the object of some ironic reflection (e.g., Baudrillard 1981; Eco 1995 [1986]) – is the reflection of both the political significance of "authenticity" (Handler 1985, 1986) and the economic scarcity of "originals" (Thompson 1979). When West African middlemen encounter the New York art market, they must learn this language of authenticity in order to maximize their advantages (Steiner 1994): they become practical ethnographers of the New York scene. When Cretan women cease weaving hunting-bags for their sons and brothers to present to patrilineal kinsmen, they are thereby taking them out of the local social context in order to devote their time to weaving generic "Greek bags" for the tourist trade; the patterns become simpler and cruder because all that is required of them is that they be "Greek" and recognizable tokens of a familiar type (Herzfeld 1992: 99). ("Zorba's Dance" has been similarly "nationalized," in the process losing the specific association with particular places and social settings associated with the dance types from which it component parts are drawn.) And when Chambri ritual objects from Papua New Guinea are relocated to tourist consumption, they may move from being unique in their significance to becoming prototypes for mass production (Gewertz and Errington 1991: 53) – an ironic riposte to western tourists' normative conviction that they alone come from a culture that values the uniqueness of true art objects an the individuality of their producers.

Note that the changes involved in each of these examples occur in the use to which the objects are put. This conversion of a Durkheimian principle into a concern with aesthetic practice carries forward Fabian's and Bauman's concerns with performance, but it also allows us to examine more static art forms within this larger framework of performance and poetics. Once we determine what particular objects and designs are used for, without prejudice as to whether they are "socially embedded" or not, the relationship between aesthetic judgment and social life becomes clearer. Even national anthems are socially embedded: they are supposedly calibrated to ideals of social unity, which explains the remarkable appeal beyond South Africa's borders of a Methodist hymn – itself a local borrowing of comparatively recent vintage – that eventually became the anthem of several other African nations, in expression of solidarity with those suffering under the oppression of apartheid. At the other end of the scale, the trills and grace notes of the concert violinist speak to the ideology of individuated genius that requires enormous technical mastery but also apportions "talent" in ways that are surprisingly predictable once the idea of immanence is shown to be ideological also. Like the calculating "spontaneity" associated (especially for tourist consumption) with the stereotype of "Mediterranean people," or like the originality claimed by a journalist who nevertheless resembles the folksinger in operating within the conventions of a genre, the western art performer must display mastery over a shared idiom. Otherwise, audience members will not applaud, because they will not know what they have heard. Andy Warhol's soup cans were effective as art precisely because they ironized the idea of genius by making its social basis embarrassingly obvious.

This example shows that the more static art forms, like those involving transient performance, express a relationship between form and use – between convention and invention, as I emphasized earlier – in terms of ideas about social relations. This is the point of Fernandez's work on Fang architectonics – and, indeed, of much of the "anthropology of space" (Lawrence and Low 1990). If architecture is the clothing of the body politic, here it is especially probable that notions of immanence will be operative. But it is also here that politics will drive aesthetics. When a historic conservation bureaucrat dismissed the makeshift house decorations of the poor residents of a Greek town as "not particularly pleasing aesthetically," she was contesting their resistance to government directives that entailed a high degree of conformity while alluding to a reconstructed past that meant little to them (Herzfeld 1991: 37). They, in turn, did everything they could to contest the conformist official model on the grounds that it conflicted with their understanding of the aesthetics (as we would say) of being Greek – it was too much of a straitjacket for people who prided themselves on their individualism and spontaneity, values that were themselves constrained by socially embedded ideas about how best to exhibit them.

This example also raises questions about the relationship between cultural ideas about the role of the individual in society and the representation of the individual, both as artist and in portraiture. Westerners assume that portraiture represents a "person." But if the notion of personhood follows a different model, one may assume that portraiture will be invested with different meanings as well. According to Orthodox Christian aesthetic principles, for example, every icon was a reproduction of an original, which was thereby refracted through the body politic: my icon is better than your icon (or more miracle-working, for instance), because I am better (or more powerful) than you are. Thus, a principle enunciated in the highest echelons of the Orthodox semi-

naries appears to find a responsive echo in the extremely competitive social relations of a modern Greek or Serbian village (see Herzfeld 1990). As an art historian has pointed out, the removal of icons to museum displays radically alters
the context in which they are interpreted (Nelson 1989). Ethnographic exhibits
of "art" are surely open to the same critique. Only an ethnographic reconsideration of the museum itself – in the spirit of what I have been calling "cultural
reflexivity" rather than "self-indulgent reflexivity" – can provide solid grounds
for further analysis of these changing meanings (see Karp and Levine, eds.,
1995).

One effect of the ethnographic museum has been to perpetuate the distinction between "high" and "popular" art forms. Curators commonly assume that
the anonymous "folk" produce "craft," while literate genius is the source of
"art." Within western society, this distinction – often phrased as setting "folklore" against "art and literature" – reproduces the colonial hierarchy of
"ethnography" versus "(high) culture." These discriminations are clearly of a
political nature, and often operate at the level of the state. Liza Bakewell, for
example, has shown how the Mexican government's interest in promoting a
national culture leads to a fusion, in Oaxaca, of "folk" events (including the
somatic stimulation of food) with "art shows," while the bourgeois basis of
support for this agenda leads to the spatial separation of the events into two
discrete areas (in Bright and Bakewell, eds., 1995: 47–50). The Greek novelist
Andreas Nenedakis uses the art-craft distinction to explore the multiple functions of the writer, but his critique is more acerbic: for him the bourgeois system
of values is represented by the picture-frame rather than the picture – by the
rigid classification that seeks to constrain flights of fancy (see Herzfeld 1997b:
170). Because he respects the craftsperson's self-confident understanding of
work embedded in practical necessity as well as the artist's desire for freedom
from political and aesthetic regimentation, he sees the real enemy as the
bourgeois state and its adulation of value for value's sake – for him, an arid
abstraction.

This point is important because it represents yet another, and far from uncom-
mon, oppositional stance within the increasingly global discourse about
"culture." As a localized commentary on national character and its incommensurability with imported western models of discipline, it suggests that the
western conventions of treating art and craft as necessarily opposed to each
other in some absolute and universal sense, a discourse that has gained increasing currency among bourgeois cosmopolitans the world over, may be quite
restrictive and misleading. It also warns us about the dangers of treating our
own political discourse, however opposed to the dominant world order it may
be, as necessarily the best guide to understanding the motives of those who have
become quite identifiable as "artists," yet who may not follow the cultural dic-
tates that western observers bring to an understanding of their work. In this
context, as Kenneth M. George (1997) cogently notes, there is no substitute for
ethnography – in this case, direct engagement with the artist in the sites of production, exhibition, and criticism, much like my own work with Nenedakis in
this respect.

George himself illustrates this point in a striking analysis of a painting by the Indonesian artist A. D. Pirous. Operating in a context where political repression has been severe, Pirous has resisted the idea, articulated by a western art critic, that a painting he executed in the aftermath of the violent events that brought the Suharto regime to power should be read as a pessimistic or dissident work. He insists that the painting is pure landscape; he does not object to others seeing in it a series of suffering human figures, but distances himself from any political interpretation of this sort. George builds on his response to make the crucial point that a politics of dissidence and hope may satisfy the agenda of an outside observer but does little to clarify the artist's own desires and reactions, which seem to include a relatively benign view – shared by many Indonesians – of the suppression of communism during the crisis in question. Pirous, says George, "has a vested interest in putting up with the way things have been dictated by the New Order" (George 1997: 629); that interest may incorporate the possibility of eventual change, but not through immediate, explicit opposition. The rapidly changing political scene in Indonesia also makes any generalized expectation of "resistance" far too simplistic an interpretation of this artist's, or other citizens', responses. Yet George also acknowledges that the art critic's interpretation now enters the social history of the work – an example of "the social life of things" (Appadurai 1986; Kopytoff 1986) – and must be confronted as such in the global context of her discipline. It is all the more important, in this context, to ensure that our perception of the world as "globalized" does not automatically lead us to assume the absence of local interpretations that differ from the dominant discourse. Indeed, it would be a supreme irony if the newly globalized political awareness of repression were to obliterate the traces of local nuance.

Aesthetic judgment, like moral evaluation, is located in sets of culturally received values. As in other areas of social life, aesthetic values are not necessarily static, and the assumption that the objects of material culture represent a fixed set of values is surely a case of the logical error of misplaced concreteness. It is through the production and critique of objects and texts in their social settings that we can understand aesthetic concerns as part of the same gamut of social process as gossip – which, far from being the regulator of social equilibrium it was thought to be by earlier anthropologists, is both the space for asserting "traditional" values and the locus of challenge and change.

It is for this reason, too, that we should be careful with static models of "ethno-aesthetics." Since performance and production themselves produce change, an assessment based on the structure of a taxonomy introduces us only to the tools, but not to the processes, of aesthetic exploration and invention in cultures around the world; and it suggests a zone of collective practice, opposed to the individualistic genius claimed by the Romantic ideologies of the West, that does not correspond to what we know of the experimentation with texture and form that seem to characterize artistic production in many parts of the world. A practice-oriented view of aesthetics thus departs from the static neoclassicism of Winckelmann and the European aesthetic, and focuses instead on the social processes through which aesthetic values are contested and reformulated. Once again, a received common sense is confounded – by the evidence of the senses.

Note

1   This is David Coplan's paraphrase of a remark made many years ago by Barbara Babcock-Abrahams to Richard Bauman. Both these scholars are renowned performance anthropologists.

14

Media

Intimacy on the Grand Scale

I have intantimally juxtaposed the chapters on Aesthetics and the Media in order to pose a direct challenge to another convention of western "high culture" – that whereby these two domains are considered to be mutually distinct. While studies of mass media have proliferated in recent decades, anthropologists are in fact only beginning to turn their attention and their methods to this arena. Following Sara Dickey's lead, I consider the reasons for our past reticence about the media and its entailment in our own system of aesthetic and social values; the force that media representations carry in the construction of contemporary imaginations, identities, and power relations; the insights anthropologists have begun to offer into these processes; and further directions we could profitably pursue. I shall also follow Dickey's ethnographic illustrations from her work with Tamil cinema in southern India, borrowing also from the work of Purnima Mankekar elsewhere in India. The focus on India is not the result of pure chance. While many countries have produced impressive film industries, the confluence in India of both a local and a foreign community of anthropologists and perhaps the largest cinema industry in the world has been especially fertile for thinking about how the media are altering our sense of what ethnography is all about.

Note that this chapter is about mass media rather than about the use of film and other visual media as tools rather than objects of study in anthropological research. Yet these categories are not entirely separable. Indeed, the relationship between them remains an area for further study and analysis. Video is used in ethnographic research, not only as a tool for recording, but also as an elicitation device – following Jane Cowan's lead, I have employed it to persuade local observers to provide simultaneous feedback on their interpretations of a specific genre of interaction involving a great deal of gesture and bodily posturing (Cowan 1990: 137–8; Fernandez and Herzfeld 1998: 99–100). Methods that focus on human movement provide a valuable corrective to the wordiness of academic interests and practices (see Farnell 1995).

We should also be aware that – like fiction before it – the film medium, in particular, is a source of valuable information about how people collectively define identities. Lee Drummond (1996), in a recent exploration of box-office successes in the United States, has shown how the most phantasmagoric imaginings of science fiction films extend and play with the idiom of kinship, itself a symbolic and pragmatic expression of ideas about social belonging. His critique of anthropology – that it draws too strong and ideologically motivated a line between the popular culture of its own world and the exotic matters with which it has traditionally been preoccupied – is an ironic illustration of the encompassing anthropological concern with boundaries in general, ultimately leading to the most important distinction of all for a supposedly globalizing world: that between human intelligence and all other forms of existence. Thus, the central theme that he teases out of American box office hits turns out not to be so very different from what we also find in the South Asian or Melanesian contexts (see Ginsburg 1991, 1993). It is clear that for anthropology today a key task is to recover the traces of human boundary-making even in the broadest of international contexts – a task to which the discipline is still sensitized by its earlier, ethnographically grounded preoccupation with the much more intimate scale of kinship and local identity.

We may define the mass media as communications media that are, or can be, widely distributed in virtually identical form; these include not only film, video, television, radio, and print periodicals – the forms that most commonly come to mind when we talk about "the media" – but also lithographic prints, advertising billboards, and the World Wide Web. The trick lies in refusing to be deceived by the significance of scale. In certain respects, mass media resemble some of the most localized of cultural productions. Newspapers, for example, are as apt as folksongs to reduce broadly similar events to a formulaic – but symbolically laden – sameness, as in the representation of Islamic others during periods of demonization in the western press (see Said 1981). Indeed, the term "demonization" is itself indicative of the symbolic and homogenizing character of this process. Conversely, descriptions of international and national events may be refracted through locally identifiable language styles and other markers of political orientation: a set of newspaper reports on a single incident will then exhibit segmentary properties – radical diversity of opinion within an apparent unity of experience – that closely parallels the effects oral recitation among some nonliterate peoples. The tribal histories written by Jordanian historians similarly refract "truth" and "falsehood" in the same way (Shryock 1997). The conventionality of journalistic language is also a means of conveying the sense of "objectivity" that, as Malkki (1997: 98) perceptively notes, is the conformist refrain of those who manage the business of news production. Indeed, journalism here exhibits one of the more generic features of bureaucratic discourse, in which, through an active deployment of the fallacy of misplaced concreteness, the standardization of the rhetoric creates the illusion of bedrock factuality – of, in other words, pure reference. Here, surely, in the mass-media production and projection of partisan common sense, is a rich arena for anthropological research.

The creation of a common public language, broadcast over potentially vast areas and infinitely reproducible, is characteristic of public media. With the advent of electronic media, the scale of operation was expanded beyond the confines of all previous experience, reproducing but also radically amplifying the potential for mobilization that led Benedict Anderson (1983) to attribute the rise of nationalism to "print capitalism." More recently still, digital and compact-disk technologies have intensified the illusion of permanence: the former permits repeated copying without significant loss of information, while the latter does hugely increase durability over all previous media. It is easy to see how both the vast difference in the scale of representation and, now, the sense of ineradicable recording might create the impression of a radical shift in significance.

In fact, however, it perpetuates a split that we see in much earlier phases of technological change. The democratization of literacy forced elites to create, through obscure styles and other conceits, a zone of "high art." Low art, by contrast, was considered unworthy of the name of culture (see Bright and Bakewell, eds., 1995). The result has been that media-borne art forms have often been deemed aesthetically uninteresting. Clearly history has not taught its lessons thoroughly enough: one of the classic "high" forms, grand opera in the hands of such composers as Verdi, both drew on and in turn inspired popular music, and in Italy still enjoys considerable popular appeal. Such examples show how contextual judgments of taste must always be. With opera, it has at least been possible to consider audience response and composition, although much remains to be done in this area. In the case of modern mass media, the practical difficulties are proportionately enormous: it has not always been clear how one would go about studying them ethnographically – that is, under conditions of social intimacy with real informants. But the payoff for making that effort, which is represented here by a few daring experimenters, is correspondingly impressive.

The methodological issue is a principal focus of this chapter. Addressing it entails shifting focus away from the media themselves and toward consumers and producers as social actors. Nor is the huge scale of operations necessarily so daunting as to make ethnography impossible. Consider, for example, the Web and e-mail: the relative sense of privacy and informality that these devices appear to generate clearly allow access to the hidden dimensions of public production. Examining e-mail exchanges among members of the Hakka diaspora, a Chinese group that has suffered considerable discrimination in the past, Lozada (1998: 163) shows that these display a sense of intimacy that permits users to discuss questions of Hakka culture that they would hesitate to discuss with outsiders. By entering into communication with them, he was able to conduct participant fieldwork that revealed attitudes normally concealed from the gaze of other Chinese and of foreigners. Such exchanges constitute a new kind of community – a "community of imagination" (Malkki 1997: 99) – with its own, constantly evolving processes of boundary construction. The challenge for ethnography now is to develop ways of responding to these processes through active engagement.

There should thus be ways of studying popular media ethnographically, and we shall return to some of these later in the chapter. But the other obstacle to this area of study deserves some additional comment as well. This is the social attitude, defined by those whose power allows them to determine what will count as cultural capital, according to which popular culture is not culture at all. In a world where scarcity defines value this attitude presupposes that the mass media must be pandering to the least reputable or most common desires in order to attract large audiences. It reproduces the western, capitalist adulation of scarcity value and represents it as a universal aesthetic.

The popular media, for precisely this reason, conform to the more general concern of anthropology with cultural products that permeate everyday life – that are so common, in other words, that they usually escape critical notice or intellectual dissection, and thus offer a more reliable index of culture than do more cerebral or controversial forms of art. Inaccurately dismissed as a more or less exclusively western product and relegated to the category of "mereness" that defines the everyday, popular media – like fast food products (J. Watson, ed., 1997) – are so pervasive that they absolutely demand serious treatment for their ubiquity and for their consequent centrality to people's lives. As Drummond (1996: 18) points out, their marginalization in scholarly discourse is the result of an intellectual elitism that illogically makes their very popularity the reason for ignoring them.

Anthropologically, their importance is increasingly difficulty to gainsay. In order to appreciate this, one need only – for example – watch a group of Cretan mountain women passionately identifying with (and even advising) the television characters in a series about an American boy who is befriended by an Indian boy of his own age and their adventures with a tame elephant (*Maya*). To be sure, the narrative is "refracted" – to reiterate the classic anthropological metaphor – through the social experiences of local actors. But that refraction is exactly what makes such encounters anthropologically interesting: it reveals the interplay of practice and structure. Moreover, these media are largely continuous with everyday experience, which they also help to shape and through which they are interpreted. I once watched a home video of wedding celebrations in Crete while seated in the home of Australian relatives of friends from the village on Crete. To dismiss such electronic expansions of the local community is ethnographically dishonest, as well as wasteful of the opportunity to understand processes of cultural transmission and change; the proliferation of videocassette recording technology for the dissemination of both political messages and aesthetic forms in the Amazon (e.g., Conklin 1997) and occasional music in India (Manuel 1993), or of fundamentalist Islamic sermons in Egypt (Starrett 1998), will not wait for anthropologists to catch up.

A sudden decentralization – or even democratization – of control comes with new technologies such as sound and video recording as well as photography and photocopying, the fax, and e-mail (Manuel 1993: 2; see also J. Anderson and Eickelman, eds., 1999). This may be upsetting to romantic purists, whose "imperial nostalgia" (Rosaldo 1989) accompanies a loss of control over technological innovation and often takes the form of attacks on cultural hybridity. To regard the influence of television as corrupting "traditional" practices, for example, reproduces an aesthetic hierarchy whereby a few well-educated elites in industrially powerful nations remain firmly in control of the economy of value, and offers a striking parallel with the international development community's discomfort with the technological bricolage conducted by Third World peasants. Through an expanded range of ethnographic practice, anthropologists are uniquely situated to provide a critical assessment of, and response to, the impact of such attitudes on the worldwide management of cultural heritage.

Indeed, pressing questions about the social and cultural roles of these newly accessible media "are applicable to virtually every field research site, as mass media in some form or another have touched most societies" (Spitulnik 1993: 294; see also Ginsburg 1991: 93). The long anthropological silence is distinctly odd since, as Michael Fischer notes, "film, for instance, was brought to India and was produced and disseminated not only in urban cinemas but also in the rural traveling shows" (1991: 531). In recent years, too, media representatives of cultural heritage have contributed to the objectification and commoditization of culture. This is not always conducive to the maintenance of cultural forms for the local community because it transforms implicit and intimate meanings into public performances, transmitted far beyond the borders of shared sociability. Greenwood (1989: 172–80), discussing the emergence of this process from the immediate commercial demands of tourism in a Basque town, suggests that it should contribute to the rethinking – which we have already visited in the discussion of environmentalisms – of cultural relativism. If he is right, anthropology ignores commoditization and the media at its peril, since these twin forces have already begun to reshape anthropology itself even as they reshape the communities anthropologists study.

That these two forces are conjoined, and sometimes cannot be analytically separated, is evident both in their forms and in their social impact. The standardization of beauty pageants, for example, owes much to the pressure of corporate sponsorship by the media; the ethnographic task is to detect the rifts that such mass-produced homogeneity masks (Cohen, Wilk, and Stoeltje, eds., 1996: 5–8). Here, the media serve to channel the pressures that shape the performances and bring them into some semblance of homogeneity. While discord may lurk beneath the surfaces thus produced, however, it is also true that the cultivation of consumerist desire may also lead to massive imitation. Mills (1999: 83) shows how the conversion of "traditional" forms into "modern" allure works its magic on impoverished rural Thai youths: "Popular serial dramas frequently focus on the romantic trials and tribulations of one or more pairs of youthful heroes and heroines. This is also a formula common to traditional folk tales and operas, but the plots of contemporary broadcasts almost always place the story and its protagonists in identifiably up-to-date settings, where the architecture, landscapes, and the characters' activities emphasize associations between youth, romance, and *thansamay* [up-to-date] style." One consequence of this allure is to send young people scurrying to Bangkok in search not only of money but also of glamour and excitement.

This brief sampling shows that anthropologists have now begun to take the media – both as broadcast fiction and as information – much more seriously than hitherto. But the tone of this work is instructively different from its early – and sparse – predecessors such as the culture-at-a-distance approach, inaugurated in the US during World War II. That approach served as a means of studying cultures that could not be visited directly (including those thought to be critical to national defense). Films, novels, and newspapers were all grist to this ideologically powered mill, the intellectual background of which was a strongly psychological orientation usually associated with the "culture and personality" school. Films in particular were examined for the "variables of dynamic psychology" revealed in recurrent themes (Wolfenstein 1953: 267). Many of these anthropologists were also involved in visual anthropology, which has usually emphasized ethnographic film (an endeavor that began very shortly after the invention of film), but has also addressed other topics, including indigenous film-making, and recently, a variety of visual media. Of special note are the rare ethnographies of media industries, including Hortense Powdermaker's precocious cultural analysis of Hollywood filmmakers (Powdermaker 1950). This work is exceptional in that it addressed the taken-for-granted aspect of much media production at an early date, although, perhaps significantly, still older forms of media such as newspapers were largely ignored – perhaps because journalists' rhetoric of facticity ("objectivity") discouraged scholars trained in a scientistic mode from treating them in the same framework as more obviously "formulaic" idioms such as folklore and gossip.

Nonanthropological analyses of the content and effects of media have burgeoned since the 1920s and 1930s, beginning in the US with government and private studies addressing the effects of radio and film, and continuing (more or less chronologically) in the academic fields of sociology, psychology, communications (and later, film and media studies), critical theory, literary criticism, and psychoanalytic theory. These predominantly text-oriented approaches (see Morley 1989) paid little attention to the complexities of audience reception and understanding that, as Dickey points out, have formed the focus of recent ethnographic work. But partly thanks to the work of Raymond Williams (e.g., 1977) and others (e.g., S. Hall 1980), interest in popular culture among working-class populations came to include a serious rethinking of the composition and reactions of audiences (see Morley 1980; Radway 1984; Pribram, ed., 1988).

Anthropologists, although relatively late to jump on the audience-response bandwaggon, logically came to pay particular attention to this aspect of the media. The trick was to get past the bland face of consensus and homogeneity in order to understand the factionalism and negotiation inherent in social process. Ethnography provides an ideal access to the point of conjuncture between local perceptions and practices on the one hand and mass-produced forms of representation on the other. Cinema and television, with their widely varying audiences, have been key arenas here, although the wide circulation of audio and video cassettes, which has also had an enormous impact worldwide, may similarly provide a common discourse for people who actually diverge in their opinions and tastes. But it is not only audiences that are internally diverse, and anthropologists have turned their attention to producers as well, noting the divisions among different creators and the distinctions in their relation to ideologically or politically dominant bodies of various kinds (see Spitulnik 1993).

Sara Dickey, whose terminology I follow here, employs standard terms such as "producer" and "consumer," or "creator" and "recipient," but with a critical resistance to the popular habit of using these terms as completely discrete, unambiguous categories. By "production" she intends any shaping part in the creative process, including direct creation as well as, for example, financial sponsorship. The term "consumption" is used in its multiple senses of ingesting, using, and purchasing. Neither production nor consumption is a unitary category. Nor are producers and consumers necessarily distinct, since producers are almost always consumers of the very media they create, as well as of other media, while consumers play a role in shaping the final product, including (perhaps especially?) commercial productions. "Media participants" covers consumers and producers together. "Text" similarly covers all media, since the process of "reading" (or interpreting) shares significant features across genres. We should be aware, however, that the popular metaphor of reading has important limits: viewing a film, for example, is socially as well as technically a different activity from reading a book. Viewing a film together does not take place only in the "lair of the skull," as Hegel famously remarked of reading a newspaper, so that it opens up to close analysis the larger social and cultural implications of fleeting reactions, both normative and dissenting. It is thus a particularly rich terrain for ethnographic research, linking the momentary immediacy of the ethnographic encounter to the large historical sweep in which it is embedded (see Mankekar 1999 for an especially insightful demonstration).

It is also, as Dickey has reminded me, an area in which the visual combines with the verbal in ways that make the usual metaphor of the text interestingly problematic. We can discern the nature of the problem by reverting briefly to the use of video as an elicitation device. In my work on Crete, I asked respondents to tell me what they thought the gestures and postures of mastercraftsmen and their apprentices could tell us about the quality of their social relationships. This entailed verbal explanations and even the possibility of substituting words or putting them into the artisans' mouths. Respondents were quick to point out that in fact very little verbal exchange actually took place. In their culture, "meaning" was not necessarily verbal, although they appreciated verbal dexterity. The technical social science vocabulary in English, however, is replete with textualist metaphors: we "inscribe" ideology on bodies, and we "read" social actions. To insist on treating films as texts thus risks a measure of reductionism; to refuse to do so may risk relegating them to a secondary category for analysts whose primary mode of communication is the written word. Films are both less and more than texts in the strict sense of the term. When we emphasize their textual properties, therefore, we shall get more purchase on these if at the same time we also point out the limitations of the metaphor. And this can best be done by emphasizing differences between reading and viewing as these are experienced by real audiences; illiterate but cinematically experienced viewers may possess enhanced competence in their creative responses to films in ways that readers of books do not ordinarily encompass. And these are questions to which ethnography provides direct, empirical access.

This is because audiences are active interpreters of the material they read, see, and hear, and because they can often wax eloquent about their responses. (It nevertheless remains an irony of our own epistemological predicament that we remain heavily dependent on verbal channels to gain access to these responses.) People come to media from the perspectives of their many subjectivities, which have been influenced by the whole "multitude of discursive practices" (Mankekar 1993b: 486) encountered during their lifetimes. Thus, Purnima Mankekar's statement that popular culture is "a contested space in which subjectivities are constituted" (Mankekar 1993b: 471) indicates two key points: first, that media can indeed help to form subjectivities, but, second, that the ground each medium covers is a contested one, involving multiple participants whose ends often compete but occasionally coincide. (We have already seen the importance of this point in an earlier chapter, in the discussion of history: people bring different histories to their understanding of the present, of which the media are today often a major element.) The message is not to be found in the text itself in any simple sense, nor is it created directly by the text's producers; consumers have a vital role in producing meaning. The larger scale of modern media does not obliterate the importance of individual agency; on the contrary, it makes its recognition all the more central to our understanding of social and cultural change, since an argument about the content of a television show or the significance of an advertisement may well both initiate and reinforce debates that eventually undermine received ideas.

When Dickey first decided in the mid-1980s to investigate the significance that popular cinema held for South Indian filmgoers, the notion that we should actually talk to audiences about how they respond to what they see was not yet the commonplace it has become. For examples of this development, see Mankekar's (1993a, 1999) study of viewers' interactions with a serialized production of the Hindu epic *Mahabharata* and Lila Abu-Lughod's (1993b) analysis of regional audiences' readings of the political ideologies portrayed in Egyptian television serials. In order to recognize the agency of audience members, and to avoid simplistic assumptions about domination, compliance, and resistance, Mankekar opts for a model of negotiation between audience and medium that begs no questions about the direction of control (Mankekar 1993b: 488). She contends that gender has a significant impact on viewers' interpretations, and that viewers use crucial moments of the serial "to confront and critique their own positions in their family, community, and class" (Mankekar 1993b: 479). Abu-Lughod also examines viewers' reactions to television, and concludes that audiences may interpret television content quite differently than its creators intended. Rural Egyptians, for example, may differ from producers in substituting for the producer's rather manichaean opposition between middle-class urban secularism and Islamic fundamentalism a perspective that treats these as "twin aspects of a national urban identity" that differs from "the local regional identity of villagers" (Abu-Lughod 1993b: 508).

There is nothing particularly surprising in this awareness that audiences do not always follow intended interpretations, unless it is the fact that it took anthropologists – with their professed interest in everyday experience – so long to follow it to its methodological conclusion. Anthropologists' reluctance to address psychological inner states may have been partly responsible for the delay. It must in any case be emphasized that this attention to audience response is perhaps the most important area in which anthropologists can complement the work of other scholars, and it also provides a major arena in which to link the analysis of social process to the complexities of mass cultural production and consumption. In literary studies, reader-response theorists (e.g., Iser 1978) usually assume that emotional responses to a text are cued by the genre label it bears, especially inasmuch as readers make a distinction between fiction and truth. But that distinction is not necessarily universal – recall, again, Shryock's example of the competing Jordanian histories – and arguments among consumers can reveal the prevailing frameworks of interpretation as well as the ways in which people constantly subvert and reformulate these.

If consumers may differ among themselves, so too can producers. Indeed, that category has also come under critical scrutiny. When Dickey was writing about Tamil cinema, she "solved" the problem of how to categorize various creative personnel by using the overarching term "film-makers" for producers and directors alike (Dickey 1993); similarly, Mankekar treats the director, researcher, and scriptwriter of an Indian television serial as the "crew" (1993a). Ethnographically, however, as Dickey has persuasively argued, it now seems preferable to develop more subtle discriminations of role and activity, much as we recognize that the bureaucrats responsible for legislating and enforcing historical and environmental conservation may hold views as divergent from each other as those entertained by the public on which they are trying to impose a supposedly common code.

In this spirit, Abu-Lughod examines the divergence between the ideologies of producers (serial directors and writers) and those of the state, arguing that although "television can be a powerful national cultural force, . . . it never simply reflects or produces the interests of the nation-state" (Abu-Lughod 1993b: 509–10). Similarly, Arlene Dávila (1997) – in a move that parallels that of the contributors to the East Asian McDonald's study (Watson, ed., 1997) – investigates actors' insertion of distinctly local values in the popular Puerto Rican television program "El Kiosko Budweiser," which was created as an advertising vehicle for an American product (Budweiser beer). She finds that the weekly program presents no unitary message but, rather, an "amalgam" of meanings. Recent studies have also begun to examine the experiences and ideologies that producers bring to their work. Further investigations of different producers, not to mention their relationships to consumers, are necessary. Other personnel who influence the shape of a medium, in addition to the directors, writers, researchers, financial producers, actors, and corporate sponsors already mentioned, include publishers, critics, censors, regulatory legislators, and fan club leaders. These are all important recognitions of the role of agency in shaping social structure and cultural form, a shift of emphasis that does not return analysis to the atomized vision represented by methodological individualism.

This new emphasis on agency carries with it a further advantage. It moves attention away from text as an inert representation, and toward the uses that differently situated social actors make of such representations. Indeed, it is arguably in the arena of film and radio that the metaphor of "social actor" becomes most cogent: the poetics of production and acting engage with the social poetics of everyday life, lending it meaning but also drawing on it for the familiarity that informs its own claims to meaning. There are also multiple levels of interpretation: an Indian viewer, for example, interprets the fictional narrative in part by drawing on the "parallel text" of well-known actors' lives – the product of a whole industry devoted to publicizing and elaborating those lives (Mishra, Jeffery, and Shoesmith 1989).

But rather than reducing all these intertwined forms of representation as texts, we might instead find it more fruitful to see "entextualization" as a social strategy deployed, in widely divergent fashions and with differing degrees of intentionality, as the means of pursuing particular interests within the embrace of a popular collective representation. To the extent that the production of the stars' public images – like those of politicians – become part of public cultural knowledge, they have been successfully entextualized. There is a striking parallel here with the ways in which, in earlier generations, proverbs and other forms of folklore were "entextualized" by scholars in the employ of the colonial regime (see Raheja 1996). In both cases, role models are produced for large-scale consumption. Whereas the older entextualizations of folklore were a means of promoting idealized ethnic stereotypes in the service of the imperial or nationalistic management of "the people" as a collective subject, modern personality cults feed a ravenous and highly profitable industry.[1] Both, however, are immediately subjected to contestation and reinterpretation in local contexts; and in this locus of cultural and social change there is no analytic or descriptive substitute for close ethnographic observation of the kind offered by such scholars as Dickey and Mankekar.

Imagination, Identity, and Power

The media image is less a pacifying substitution for reality, as Guy Debord (1983) laments in his discussion of modern spectacle, than what Dickey instead calls "a critical constituent of it." That statement needs some clarification, because, while an anthropologist would normally assume that reality is a contingent product of social experience ("it"), this clashes with the prevailing, realist common sense that creates a sharp and absolute distinction between reality and fiction. As soon as we observe audience responses to engaging television drama or cinematic realism, however, it makes very little sense to argue about what representations come closer to reality – especially once we recognize that cinematic realism (with its precursors in operatic verismo and aesthetic "socialist realism," for example) its itself intensely conventional and culturally specific.

The reality is, instead, constituted by the medium and its consumers, or, as Dickey has nicely expressed it in response to an earlier version of this chapter, "the media . . . become part of their consumers' constructions of reality." Indeed, anthropological writing itself has benefited from a critical appraisal of its own peculiar claims to "realism" (see Clifford 1986: 24–5). Yet the distinction between the real and the fictional, like that between the material and the symbolic, is itself an important part of the social reality and cultural myth that guides, in many cultures, the appreciation of media representation and academic discourse alike. The trick, for the anthropologist, is to show what a historical and cultural oddity that now-prevalent commonsensical perception is. It is, in the terms of an older canon of literary theory, to "defamiliarize" obviousness. And given the global reach and increasingly homogenized conventions of cinematic realism, that is becoming an ever harder task – until we watch those audiences.

In the kind of anthropology represented by this book, we attempt to climb out of the circular debates that continue to swirl around such beguiling dichotomies between reality and fiction. We ask instead: for whom, and under what circumstances, does a particular reality come into existence? The frequent evidence that media are experienced "as" real – the passionate conversational engagement of viewers with the soaps furnishes a familiar example – provides a useful empirical arena for understanding just how anti-empirical it is to refuse to consider the social importance, rather than the ontological "reality," of such dichotomies, and suggests that the ethnography of the media will play an increasingly important role in making an interesting analytic problem out of what was hitherto largely taken for granted. (Even for an anthropologist of a more positivistic stripe, Roy Rappaport [1979: 138–41], the way in which people "cognized" the world is reality for them; arguing whether there exists a "really real" to be so cognized is hardly productive, since, if we do not assume such a reality, there is really not much to discuss!)

Studying the media brings these issues of perception and its relation to different cultural "realities" and varieties of common sense into particularly sharp focus. Their scale intensifies our awareness of this focus, but the problem has existed ever since framed performance became a part of culture. To take a case in point, the term "soap opera" suggests an interesting continuity with grand opera: these are both "popular" forms of entertainment that are usually managed by individuals of often considerable status and power, and they both also tweak and beguile their aficionados' understanding of where reality and pretense shade into each other.

The media provide a space for the play of imagination and the construction of identities – an arena in which claims to reality are often exercises in competing rhetoric, as when one nation-state denies another's legitimacy. Proof of this lies in the extensive use of the media for propaganda purposes: massive repetition has its own rhetorical force. But nation-states do not have a monopoly of the media. To the contrary, as Arjun Appadurai argues, the contemporary displacement of huge numbers of people has given the imagination – or, as we might perhaps more accurately say, the exercise and representation of imagination – "a singular new power in social life," for which the mass media are a primary source, providing a "rich, ever-changing store of possible lives" (Appadurai 1991: 197). Moreover, as Dickey observes, "media provide the imagination not just with content but also with possibilities of form" – that is, aesthetic and narrative conventions. This is an effect that will prove immediately striking to those whose cinematic "mother tongue" is Hollywood the first time they watch a popular South Asian film, or to those who grew up with British cricket when they see the Trobriand version "objectified" in an ethnographic film (*Trobriand Cricket* [n.d.]). Dickey has noted, in response to this example, that cricket is not a mass medium in itself and therefore perhaps does not lend itself to direct comparison with film. But the fact that she is nevertheless "drawn . . . by the parallel" suggests that a spectator sport, while indeed "a performance that is not a mass medium," remains comparable in the sense that it provides a means of displaying to a large number of people the possibilities of playing creatively with shared, borrowed conventions.

News reports, novels, radio dramas and films all provide us contact with experiences, realities, and aesthetic canons that differ from our own. They create both the awareness of actual and potential differences, and the "stuff" with which to imagine those differences. Allowing for the difference in scale, spectator sports – even small-scale performances like card-games watched by a group of club members – offer similar ways of testing the capacity of conventions to frame creativity and meaning. Cretan shepherds do this with card-games: they talk about the cards in ways that are not determined by the rules of the game, but that allow the players to use the latter as a way of indirectly but clearly expressing inter-male antagonisms and competition over women and material resources (Herzfeld 1985: 149–62). In that sense, surely, Lévi-Strauss's bricoleur is far from dead; his apocalyptic vision of "monoculture," by contrast, appears as far away as ever. To the contrary, as Lee Drummond (1996) so exhaustively shows in his exploration of commercially successful American films exploring fictions about alien creatures, the bricoleur has new opportunities and operates on a grander scale than ever before. The standardization of logos, products, and advertising conventions similarly offers ever grander opportunities for the ironic manipulation of meaning.

Much anthropological work on mass-mediated "imagining" focuses on the process of constructing identities in interaction with media. Identities, like subjectivities and modes of interpretation, are formed throughout our lives through a variety of sources, and the most successful work on identity construction will examine the impact of media in conjunction with other sources. Jo Ellen Fisherkeller (1997) has sensitively examined the different contexts of identity construction among middle school students in New York City. Fisherkeller examines the uses that these young adolescents make of television shows, and especially of particular characters, in creating and buttressing their identities.

Focusing on the ways that "television culture" is used in conjunction with "local cultures," including home, neighborhood, school and peer cultures, she argues that the content of the lessons learned from these different sources is generally complementary – especially in their treatments of social power and gender, racial, ethnic, and class identities – but the way that adolescents learn from television differs. In particular, she contends, these youths gain "guiding motivations" from their local cultures, which help to define their aspirations, and they simultaneously deduce "imaginative strategies" from television for attaining these aspirations.

While Fisherkeller investigates a process in which the media that are consumed essentially originate in the viewer's own culture, Brian Larkin and Mark Liechty examine media products whose value and influence resides in their origination outside the culture in which they are consumed. Larkin (1997) focuses on the "parallel realities" that Hausa people in northern Nigeria have come to imagine by watching imported Indian films, and the echoes the films have produced in Nigerian popular literature. Even though Indian cinema is based largely on Hindu culture and the Hausa are Muslim, the films are enormously attractive in northern Nigeria because they explore tensions and desires that are also central to Hausa society. Particularly resonant are conflicts over arranged versus love marriages, and the authority of elders (or society) over youths (or individual desires) that these conflicts represent. A highly successful genre of mass-produced literature, *littatafan soyayya* (love stories), has developed during the last few years of the twentieth century, and adopts the themes of Indian cinema; these stories have themselves been read on the radio and made into videos. The soyayya authors are young Hausa men and women who contest social restrictions such as arranged marriages. But whereas Indian films are popular because they are crucially similar to and different from Hausa society, presenting familiar problems but in a society that is not Nigerian, the same images that are unthreatening when expressed by Indian families on screen are vehemently attacked when they appear in Hausa voices in soyayya. Indian cinematic productions have provided Nigerians with ways of envisioning, articulating, and countering social protests – a move that is perhaps not so far removed from nineteenth-century European operatic composers' evasion of censorship by relocating the action into mythical time or by changing key historical references. But Larkin's work is also important in that it demonstrates the folly of assuming that imagined modernities necessarily come from the West. The phenomenal worldwide popularity of karaoke and kung-fu films may indeed help us to reconceptualize western markets as a site of consumption as well as of the production of such modernities.

Western observers used to assume that Third World consumers would more or less automatically desire their trade goods and technological wonders. Indeed, Lamont Lindstrom has argued that the image of Melanesian "cargo cults" as symbolic expressions of such collective consumer envy represent precisely such ethnocentric perspectives (1995). Sometimes, of course, the technology serves only the commodification of local cultural products, although even here it creates opportunities of entrepreneurial domination. The literature is full of examples of the ways in which such commodification has occurred with video and audio cassettes, for example, and also illustrates ways in which such mass production lends itself to political and religious activism. New cultural hybridities – for example, Muslim hip-hop in Berlin (Soysal 1999: 142–69, 178–220) – reflect new sociopolitical realities.

Sometimes, however, the sheer scale of the technology introduces remarkable tensions. Liechty, working among urban Nepali youths, argues that media commodify identities, and that "the logic of consumer modernity promotes a material conception of self such that persons are encouraged to purchase their identities in the form of consumer goods" (Liechty 1995: 169). Youths find these identities, and the new "commodities" they are structured around, in imported movies and Nepal teen magazines. Liechty finds that the representations in media and the desires they spawn create "contradictions between ideologies of progress and mediated images of abundance on the one hand, and the real world of scarcity and precarious claims to social standing on the other" (Liechty 1995: 170), placing consumers in a highly alienating situation. Youths appear to feel not so much connected to a wider world as marginalized from it; Liechty argues that "while forces such as mass media now guarantee that local experience almost anywhere will be permeated by transnational cultural processes, . . . this same cultural 'deterritorialization' has a very real 'territoralizing' effect on the minds of people," creating "an acute sense of marginality" (Liechty 1995: 188).

I have already noted Mary Beth Mills's comments on the effect of media on the desires and trajectories of young rural Thai workers; here, the marginalization comes when these young people, arrived in Bangkok and yearning for the bright lights, find their hopes dashed and their persons exploited – although the stereotypical representation of their own humble status in the media was already in place (Mills 1999: 42–3). And official Thai involvement in the international beauty contest industry clearly exploited both Thai women and the all-too-willing international television in order to promote a favorable image, as it was thought to be, of the country (Van Esterik, ed., 1996: 207) – an inversion of the intimacy effect of e-mail noted by Lozada, and one requiring a careful study of local as well as overseas reactions to the shows.

Power and the response to it cannot be reduced to simple formulations of resistance-versus-domination (see also Abu-Lughod 1990; Reed-Danahay 1993). The very massiveness of the mass media creates an aura of brute fact, but it would be a mistake to allow our analyses to absorb that quality, for then the subtlety and precision of ethnographic observation would be lost, and, with it, the realization that, as Dickey remarks, "any expressive form has the potential to be emancipatory, revitalizing, divisive, and repressive, perhaps all at the same time" (see also Manuel 1993: 4). On the other hand, ethnographers can and should document the processes by which such simplification takes place – a feature that, along with redundancy, reproduces key aspects of religious ritual (see Tambiah 1981) – because these reveal the operation of the prevailing structures of power. Commercial media, as Ayşe Öncü argues in her discussion of attempts to make Turkish television more issues-oriented (1995), "provide simplified ways of organizing meanings" by packaging complicated information into "positions for or against." Like many other media, television provides a new means of acquiring knowledge, "transgressing the established borders of literate culture" (Öncü 1995: 54). Some other studies have focused on indigenous and grass-roots groups' exploitation of the new technologies – especially those that cost relatively little – to address their problems in a larger forum (e.g., Conklin 1997; Ginsburg 1991, 1993).

In this genre, Juanita Mohammed and Alexandra Juhasz (1996) write of their collaborative work through the Women's AIDS Video Enterprise, a "video support group" created in 1990 by New York City women (mostly women of color) whose lives had been affected by AIDS. Juhasz writes that such activist videomaking "enacts not another field of dominance begging for resistance or negotiation but instead a site for intimate and local identification and consolidation" (Mohammed and Juhasz 1996: 196) – a comment that nicely captures the current focus of anthropological method on the achievement of intimacy and the critical reappraisal of comprehensive models of "resistance." Videos created by WAVE have been distributed to thousands of organizations around the US and elsewhere, thus allowing the sharing of locally produced work with a widely dispersed, diverse, decentralized community of people who do not feel adequately or fairly represented in the dominant media. Given the stigma that people with AIDS often face, this creation of social intimacy beyond the bounds of the face-to-face encounter represents, as it does for minority cultures, and as it does for groups fighting for survival and desperate to revitalize their cultural existence in an alienating world (Ginsburg 1991: 92; 1993: 559), a space for the creative retooling of social identity. The importance of this move becomes more fully apparent if one thinks back to the chapter on Sufferings, in the context of attempts to pathologize cultural, sexual, and medical difference. Shared media may provide some relief from the degrading inequalities that they document, and perhaps also some hope of redressing them, by providing a platform for voices too long unheard. This effect, not necessarily an intended one, is consistent with the commitments of anthropology itself.

Media Contexts

Theories of agency are about the uses people make of cultural artifacts – language, symbols, material resources, and, of course, media and its associated technologies. Dickey's contention that "the variations of meaning imputed to media depend not only on producers' positions and consumers' subjectivities, but also on the contexts of use" is thus entirely consistent with that orientation. On this basis, she calls for a recognition of the plethora of contexts in which audiences respond: "Media are not consumed in uninflected spaces, but in theaters, living rooms, tea stalls, and subways, each of which refracts the meaning of the medium through the experience of consumption." And she adds: "Moreover, just as a medium's significance lies not only in its texts, so also it lies not simply in what people do with or to the text, but in the activities that grow out of, contribute to, and often reproduce the medium as a whole. Consumption is not limited to the moment of viewing, reading and listening. Notable examples of adjoining activities include fandom, political activities, and the consumption of media artifacts (including the purchase and display of such articles as clothing, toys, and travel based on media figures or places)."

Fandom has received little attention from anthropologists, but a few are now addressing its potential as a particularly rich and often consciously oppositional sphere of cultural production. John Fiske argues that "fandom is typically associated with cultural forms that the dominant value system denigrates ... It is thus associated with the cultural tastes of subordinated formations of the people, particularly with those disempowered by any combination of gender, age, class and race" (Fiske 1992: 30). Dickey finds Fiske's ideas about fandom as the site of actual cultural production especially useful for her own work in South India, "where mainstream film is derogated as a lower-class entertainment medium, and the young Tamil men who join fan clubs are sharply aware of their social and cultural distance from the upper class." These youths, she argues, "use their club membership to address and redress that distance, relying on a production of an 'alternative cultural capital' that ranges from fan magazines, to film star decals and T-shirts, social service ceremonies held in the streets, and insider gossip about movie stars and films. In the process of producing verbal and visual images of their heroes as generous, compassionate and virile men, and of carrying out social service activities to enact those images, these fans also produce class images" in which they "create an ambiguous place for themselves that simultaneously partakes of the attributes they glorify in the poor, and raises them above the poor through their association with the admirable attributes of their heroes, whom fans sharply distinguish from the rest of the upper class" (see Dickey, forthcoming). Here the emphasis is on the use of media images; the fans deploy them to specific ends in their local worlds, and may eventually find in them the performative capacity to transform these worlds in directions as yet only imagined (or, better, imaged).[2]

As Christian Bromberger (1998: 306) observes, sports – he writes specifically about football – provide fans with an open text, which they can fill with meanings according to need and desire: "The football match ... offers a privileged space for the affirmation of collective belonging, builds a bridge between the singular and the universal, recalls words and bonds, symbolizes life's dramas as it does the cardinal values of our societies." But sometimes a subaltern class, as in the example just discussed, can reverse that warm sense of fellowship; violent British football fans, for example, are widely believed to be expressing a sense of class alienation. Implicitly or explicitly, such uses of fandom have political significance. In South India, as also in Cyprus and elsewhere, fan clubs have been used as the basis of grass-roots political parties. In Cyprus, football matches become a staging-ground for responses by the Greek side to the continuing Turkish occupation of the north, and the political affiliations of the clubs furnish an arena in which political debate is enacted as confrontation (Papadakis 1998). Even without the involvement of fan clubs, interested actors may use media to initiate political action; in Bolivia, for example, CONDEPA, a populist and influential political party developed from a social movement organized by viewers of the television program "The Open Forum of the People." Jeff Himpele (forthcoming) argues that this highly popular program of testimony from individuals facing a wide variety of dramatic problems relies on "realist" strategies of "perceptual directness, immediate social action, and open access to the mass media" to create an impression of potent address and action. It has certainly achieved visibility for itself: the host and creator of the program, and of the radio show that preceded it, became a presidential candidate leading a significant party in the context of national consensus politics. The affective bonds that the program has created between its host and viewers have provided these viewers with a new sense of participation in the country's representational democracy – although, as Himpele points out, the realist strategies of "The Open Forum" may simultaneously contribute to the social hierarchies they appear to dismantle. Dávila's (1998) analysis of Puerto Rican responses to a local Budweiser advertising campaign raises simlar concerns: contested in a local idiom is a mainland American drink that suffuses the domain of taste and the very bodies of its consumers.

The Political Scene: Viewers and voters

In a generic sense, all communication has political implications. If the print media were vital to creating the image of homogeneous nationhood (B. Anderson 1983), however, new "communities of imagination" that may be larger than national identities are sometimes quite local or cut across existing allegiances receive enormous reinforcement from the use of media to lay claims to honesty and truthfulness and to excoriate the mendacity of one's opponents. In the United States, where "sincerity" is widely understood to be a matter of performance (so that one may be asked in a questionnaire about the "sincerity" of a company's staff, for example), the most prominent politicians today live in fear of having every detail of their private lives stripped bare. While gleeful pundits speculate about the political effects of such stories, the outcome will often depend on public displays of what are – to an anthropologist – formally impenetrable emotions like "remorse." What matters, consistently with the prevailing models of performance, is not what actually happened, not whether the accused politician is guilty or not, but how effectively that charge is deflected by an appealing display of appropriate contrition. Experienced criminals facing sentencing count on their ability to produce a fine display of remorse.

This observation has more general implications for any theoretical explanation of the role of media in political life. An electoral campaign, as Marc Abélès (drawing in part on the work of Yves Pourcher) reminds us, has a full impact only if its main actor is effective on television; and that actor can only be effective by providing culturally appropriate and palpably well-managed displays of emotion and personality – an exercise in social and cultural management. Ronald Reagan billed himself as the "great communicator," thereby using one performative utterance to confirm and validate all the other rhetorical strategies that he and his campaign managers had deployed. Knowing how to "sell" a political "product" is all-important. Knowing how to deploy the metaphors of kinship and other intimate social realities is a crucial part of political sloga-neering. The familistic claims of nationalism are perhaps the best illustration of this, but detailed attention to the forms of political rhetoric can reveal many other connections between national and local levels of ethnographic analysis (see Paine, ed., 1981).

One of the most conspicuous effects of media inflation is that all events become ordinary – commonsensical, in fact. Elections, according to Abélès, increasingly resemble television series in which personalities rather than ideas are at stake. If this is true, it at least shows once again that the personal and familial, far from becoming irrelevant in the mass media market of ideas, is central to the production of political common sense. An empirical question nev-ertheless remains: are political debates really so ideological, so context-free, in the more traditional arenas of political debate? Or are political ideas – like "talent" in the music conservatory – refracted through the existing divisions of society, the differences among them a result of social rather than conceptual contrasts? If so, the increase of scale opens up more, not fewer, possible responses. Just as increasing communication around the world brings, not homogenizing "globalization," but enriched possibilities for debating the mean-ings of shared forms, so an increasingly widespread repertoire of political models may be subject to ever greater variation in their application and inter-pretation. For their significance is set by audiences as well as producers; and those audiences are increasingly diverse.

To be sure, the media are not simply a passive arena for the conduct of politi-cal and social differences. They have performative force: they may create as much as they refract or reflect the events taking place in the larger society. In Abélès's view, for example, Pope John Paul II's journey to his homeland in 1979 brought about a dramatic confrontation between two images – the assassina-tion of Saint Stanislas and the creation of the communist state. The Pope's visit, a "social drama" in Victor Turner's (1974) sense, rocked the very foundations of the state's legitimacy by encouraging people to imagine another, very differ-ent model of legitimacy. This type of public demonstration forms an integral part of political action. The Pope's actions and words in Poland produced a strong message that destabilized communist authority through what Marc Augé (1994: 94) has described as an "expanded ritual arrangement" – an arrange-ment in which sheer scale may enhance the effects of ritual to produce actual change. It turned the static binarism of cold war confrontation into a dynamic performance with substantial material consequences. The narrative, sequentially organized "presentation of the Pope as a traveller" (Dayan, 1990), illustrates the performative impact of the media and shows that symbols, far from being epiphenomenal to political action, can achieve vastly heightened effect through their mass production in millions of homes.

The rhetorical character of so much political representation in the media further blurs the experiential gap between fact and fiction. Not only do we see the constitution of events before our eyes – the role of CNN in the Gulf War has often been portrayed in these terms, while the skepticism of those in opposition (for example, of pro-Serbian Greeks confronting the Kosovo massacres) can similarly appeal to the one seemingly indisputable fact: that "everyone knows" how easily the media can generate events, either by provoking them or simply by staging them. The newscasters' rhetoric of facticity thus splits into sharply opposed categories of "immediacy" (a realist notion) and "propaganda," while the fictional dramas of cinema and television screen alike are judged by their faithfulness to local criteria of experiential genuineness. In both cases, anthropologists can tell us a great deal about the culturally quite variable conventions of realism and the ways in which social actors can both engage and change these rules, explaining why images that persuade one group fall flat for another. Not only is reality differently experienced and represented according to culturally divergent conventions, but, as Dickey has rightly reminded me, realism may not always be what an audience even desires. Because the various kinds of media, ethnographically studied in context, can provide a very close look at the interaction of the local, the national and the international, work on media conventions and their uses should furnish the basis of an empirically grounded understanding of phenomena all-too-airily subsumed under such unhelpful descriptive labels as "globalization" and "cultural influence." It will illustrate how such links are created, maintained, undercut, and transformed. The idea of globalization is itself a realist fiction, as the subversive localism of anthropological field research makes increasingly clear.

Pleasure and Seriousness: In praise of mereness

In concluding, I return to two of the questions with which I opened this chapter: the costs of our uneasiness about pleasure and the mass media, and the gains we may achieve by posing the mass media as a socially significant category of experience and study. And I return, too, to the link between pleasure and various kinds of facticity.

Dickey argues that it is pleasure that draws most consumers to partake in most of what westerners would call "entertainment media." Yet this seems also to be the basis on which many anthropologists have avoided dealing with them: not only are they are not obviously "local" in the classic ethnographic sense, but they represent the "ordinary" pleasures in which westerners typically indulge. Within the debate on subordinate appropriations of media, some discussion has addressed questions of pleasure and escape, particularly with regard to cinema and television (e.g. Mulvey 1989; Ang 1985), but anthropologists, ever careful to avoid passing judgment, have largely avoided engaging with the topic at all. That silence is a judgmental stance in itself (R. Thomas 1985: 120). It also entails uncritically dismissing the agency of viewers as unimportant, and so reproduces a political phenomenon that it should instead take as a critical topic of reflection (see Ang 1985: 19).

We are back to the "mereness" issue – the question of why anthropologists so often seem to take up for study topics that strike others as "merely" trivial, anecdotal, marginal, statistically atypical or insignificant. At least those who suffer in remote places get some credit for their sense of adventure, although it is thought to have little relevance for major policy decisions. My own decision to conduct fieldwork in the heart of Rome raised not a few eyebrows. To take the pleasurable as a topic may strike some as unnecessary provocation. But in fact there is good reason to do so. In speaking of pleasures, we go beyond common sense to an attempt to analyze "common senses." If, as the chapter on Senses indicates, our wordiness makes us reluctant (or incompetent) to engage embodied experience at all, the hedonism of entertainment – including, for example, food – might seem to discourage serious investigation altogether, especially given the culturally specific definition of seriousness that sometimes afflicts the dominant centers of theoretical production. Doing such work either in our home cultures or in a more cosmopolitan setting seems especially difficult, a challenge to the established politics of significance. Yet if we take pleasure as a given – as something that is "naturally" produced by certain media – we not only assume the standard western interpretation of the media as primarily sources of entertainment, we simply reproduce the process whereby specific actors reinforce our assumption that this is what the media are all about – especially when they are clearly marked as fictional.

Fiction, in this sense, is rather like nature: it is good when it is "pure," but becomes dangerous when it is not tamed into a safe and privileged category. The mass media have disseminated fiction, and have also threatened the boundaries of factuality – of objectivity, to recall the epistemological terms of Malkki's (1997) discussion of journalism. And just as elites – at least western-derived elites – tend to treat nature as something that must be controlled, so that sculpted trees are acceptable in the suburbs but weeds are not, they also experience deep unease with the democratization of fictionality that the mass media have brought about. Their response is to dismiss popular fiction as "lowbrow" because it is supposedly pleasurable – and because the pleasure that it gives is not cerebral. But why accept that distinction? In thinking over the paper on which so much of this chapter is based, Dickey began to ponder the entertainment value of nonfictional media – data on the Web, for example – and to puzzle over the discrimination that many of us make between the fictional and the serious: could surfing the Web not furnish an intermediate (dare I say "hybrid"?) kind of pleasure? and what would that do our carefully tended taxonomic hedges? This is the kind of defamiliarizing reflection that grows out of an unremitting commitment to fieldwork.

As the example of the beauty pageants demonstrates, both the rejection of the media as "mere" entertainment and the opposite stance – condemning them as unthinking exploitation – refuses the actors concerned any voice in the interpretation of their actions. Bromberger (1998: 34) points out, moreover, that the "everyday passions" are precisely those through which individuals anchor themselves in collective identities of participation, debate, and the pleasurable sharing of a common hobby. A passion for the cinema would certainly fit this description; sports fandom is an outstanding example; and so, too, and for more obvious reasons, is participation in an e-mail network such as that described for the Hakka diaspora by Lozada (1998). No doubt we should, as Appadurai (1991: 208) advises, "incorporate the complexities of expressive representation (film, novels, travel accounts) into our ethnographies." But this, I suggest, is not so much an invitation to study the media for their own sake, whatever that would mean. It is, rather, because they have become an inseparable component of most people's lives, and because their permeation of those lives – their very ordinariness – makes them crucially significant.

Moreover, Dickey cautions, we should not thereby assume that everything associated with the modern media technology is itself novel. I have mentioned the links, through realist conventions and what we might now call a kind of fandom, of grand opera with the soaps. Studies of the media are not discontinuous with analyses of small-scale performative arts. Dickey, for example, adduces an older study in which James Peacock (1968) demonstrated "the social and political power embedded in the imaginative possibilities posed by ludruk drama in Java" and points out that this was "an exemplary study that, with its attention to actors, producers, audiences, texts, and their symbolic, political, and economic contexts, fulfilled the standards called for by contemporary anthropological work on media." He was thus investigating questions that, far from becoming irrelevant with the fading of traditional performance genres and locales, have been amplified by the new technology. Both the insights and the phenomena have gained, not retreated, in importance.

This is not to argue, of course, that there is nothing new in either the idiom of performance or the way we go about studying them anthropologically. But it does mean that the models for our methods are embryonically present, and perhaps more easily described, in what were "traditional" settings as much for our informants as for ourselves as ethnographers – "traditional," that is, in the old-fashioned sense of not yet having undergone massive technological transformation, but also in the sense that these were the small-scale settings in which anthropologists had "traditionally" worked.

It also means that we should be as specific as possible about what is new. Scale may as easily amplify existing patterns and structures as it can change or replace them. What is certainly quite new is the scale of comparison that now becomes possible. While fieldwork in the modern sites of disenchanted urbanity may be technically more difficult – intimacy is harder to attain when the ethnographer cannot simply visit the teashop or coffeehouse and strike up a casual conversation – the compensation lies, surely, in the ways in which we can compare similar phenomena over vast arrays of culturally distinctive settings. Some media may be conducive to superficial homogeneity. But that does not mean that nothing stirs beneath the surface.

The techniques of ethnographic fieldwork provide one strong response to the risks of becoming analytically coopted by that superficial vision, which assumes that there is only one modernity and that it wears a western face. This boring vision is neatly encapsulated in Lévi-Strauss's gloomy prognostication, surely reflecting Eurocentric romanticism rather than ethnographic acuity, of "monoculture." When American or German tourists in Bangkok or Lagos view an Indian film and discuss it in exactly the same terms, or experience exactly the same reactions, as those sitting around them, perhaps monoculture will have arrived. But the likelihood is that monoculture will only afflict those who are willing to accept a bland surface as the sum total of culture in general – the Golden Arches rather than the political tensions they both provoke and mask; the universalism of environmental policy rather than the arguments of local victims of so-called development; "family values" instead of the messy complexity of real living arrangements and their infinitude of transformations. One hopes that even those newly in power will appreciate and respect these complexities. But will they listen to the intimate voices, revealed by ethnographers, that reveal a world of hopes and desires? And if not, why not? Can they, too, be placed under the critical anthropological lens? For the success of our enterprise, and the humanity of our understanding of the world, demands no less.

Notes

1 Some of these media productions are described as "indigenous," a highly problematic term. Spitulnik finds that it may be used rather flexibly of "the producers, owner, subjects, locales, and/or audiences of these various mass media" (Spitulnik 1993: 304), with a predictable complexity of attendant power relations among participants. Gupta's (1998) critique of this term suggests the risks of ghettoization that often accompany it, with attendant implications of inferiority. But at least the term has the advantage, in the context of media technology, of reminding readers that First World experts no longer have a monopoly of its use.

2 Fiske contends that Bourdieu's (1984) model of cultural capital is poorly equipped to deal with fandom because it ignores the heterogeneity of proletarian culture and underestimates "the creativity of popular culture and its role in distinguishing between different social formations within the subordinated." Instead, he contends, fans "create a fan culture with its own systems of production and distribution," through which they construct an alternative cultural capital that is parallel to that produced by the dominant cultural systems, and differentiates fans from other members of the subordinate group who lack this distinguishing capital (Fiske 1992: 32–3).

Bibliography

Abélès, Marc. 1989: *Jours tranquilles en 1989*. Ethnologie politique d'un département français. Paris: Odile Jacob.

——. 1990: *Anthropologie de l'Etat*. Paris: Armand Colin.

——. 1991: *Quiet Days in Burgundy: A Study of Local Politics*. Cambridge studies in social and cultural anthropology; 79. Cambridge and New York: Cambridge University Press; Paris: Editions de la maison des sciences de l'homme.

——. 1992: *La vie quotidienne au Parlement européen*. Paris: Hachette.

——. 1996: *En attente d'Europe*. Paris: Hachette.

Abrams, Philip. 1982: *Historical Sociology*. Somerset: Open Books.

Abu-Lughod, Lila. 1990: Romance of resistance: tracing transformations of power through Bedouin women. *American Ethnologist*, 17 (1), 41–55.

——. 1991: Writing against culture. In R. G. Fox (ed.), *Recapturing Anthropology: Working in the Present*. Santa Fe, NM: School of American Research Press, 137–62.

——. 1993a: *Writing Women's Worlds: Bedouin Stories*. Berkeley: University of California Press.

——. 1993b: Finding a place for Islam: Egyptian television serials and the national interest. *Public Culture* 5 (3), 493–513.

Adler Lomnitz, Larissa. 1994: *Redes sociales, cultura y poder: ensayos de antropología latinoamericana*. Mexico City: FLASCO/Miguel Ángel Porrúa.

Agulhon, Maurice. 1979: *Marianne au combat: L'imagerie et la symbolique républicaines de 1789–1880*. Paris: Flammarion.

——. 1989: *Marianne au pouvoir*. Paris: Flammarion.

Ahmad, A. 1993: Orientalism and after. In P. Williams and L. Chrisman (eds.), *Colonial Discourse and Post-Colonial Theory: A Reader*. Hemel Hempstead: Harvester Wheatsheaf.

Alvarez, Robert R., Jr. 1995: The Mexican–US border: the making of an anthropology of borderlands. In *Annual Review of Anthropology* 24, 447–70.

Amselle, Jean-Loup. 1990: *Logiques métisses: anthropologie de l'identité en Afrique et ailleurs*. Paris: Payot.

Anderson, Benedict R. O'G. 1983: *Imagined Communities: Reflections on the Origin and Spread of Nationalism*. London: New Left Books.

——. 1991: *Imagined Communities: Reflections on the Origin and Spread of Nationalism*. Revised Edition. London: Verso.

Anderson, Jon W. and Eickelman, Dale F. (eds.). 1999: *New Media in the Muslim World: The Emerging Public Sphere*. Bloomington: Indiana University Press.

Anderson, Perry. 1980: *Arguments within English Marxism*. London: Verso.

Ang, Ien. 1985: *Watching Dallas*. Trans. Della Couling. London: Methuen.

Apffel-Marglin, Frédérique. 1998: Secularism, unicity and diversity: the case of Haracandi's grove. In *Contributions to Indian Sociology* 32 (2), 217–35.

Appadurai, Arjun. 1986: Towards an anthropology of things. In A. Appadurai (ed.), *The Social Life of Things: Commodities in Cultural Perspective*. Cambridge: Cambridge University Press.

——. 1990: Disjuncture and difference in the global cultural economy. In *Public Culture* 2 (2), 1–24.

——. 1991: Global ethnoscapes: Notes and queries for a transnational anthropology. In R. G. Fox (ed.), *Recapturing Anthropology: Working in the Present*. Santa Fe, NM: School of American Research Press, 191–210.

——. 1995: Playing with modernity: the decolonization of Indian cricket. In C. A. Breckenridge (ed.), *Consuming Modernity: Public Culture in South Asian World*. Minneapolis: University of Minnesota Press, 23–48.

Ardener, Edwin. 1989: *The Voice of Prophecy and Other Essays*. Oxford: Basil Blacwell.

Aretxaga, Begoña. 1997: *Shattering Silence: Women, Nationalism, and Political Subjectivity in Northern Ireland*. Princeton: Princeton University Press.

Argyrou, Vassos. 1993: Under a spell: the strategic use of magic in Greek Cypriot society. In *American Ethnologist* 20 (2), 256–71.

——. 1996a: *Tradition and Modernity in the Mediterranean: The Wedding as Symbolic Struggle*. Cambridge studies in social and cultural anthropology; 101. Cambridge: Cambridge University Press.

——. 1996b: Is "closer and closer" ever close enough? Dereification, diacritical power, and the spector of evolutionism. In *Anthropological Quarterly* 69 (4), 206–19.

——. 1997: "Keep Cyprus clean": littering, pollution, and otherness. In *Cultural Anthropology* 12 (2), 159–78.

——. 1999: Sameness and the ethnological will to meaning. In *Current Anthropology* 40 (suppl), S29–S41.

Arias, P. 1996: La antropología urbana ayer y hoy. In *Ciudades* 31 (July–Sept.), Mexico City: RNIU.

Asad, Talal (ed.). 1973: *Anthropology and the Colonial Encounter*. London: Ithaca Press.

——. 1986: Concept of cultural translation in British social anthropology. In J. Clifford and G. Marcus (eds.), *Writing Culture*. Berkeley: University of California Press, 141–64.

——. 1987: On ritual and discipline in medieval Christian monasticism. In *Economy and Society* 26 (2), 159–203.

——. 1991: Afterword: from the history of colonial anthropology to the anthropology of Western hegemony. In George Stocking (ed.), *Colonial Situations: Essays on the Contextualization of Ethnographic Knowledge*. Madison: University of Wisconsin Press, 314–24.

——. 1993: *Genealogies of Religion: Discipline and Reasons of Power in Christianity and Islam*. Baltimore: Johns Hopkins University Press.

Asad, Talal, Fernandez, James W., Herzfeld, Michael, Lass, Andrew, Rogers, Susan Carol, Schneider, Jane, and Verdery, Katherine. 1979: Provocations of European Ethnology, *American Anthropologist* 99, 713–30.

Askew, Kelly Michelle. 1997: *Performing the Nation: Swahili Musical Performance and the Production of Tanzanian National Culture*. Thesis (Ph.D.) – Harvard University.

Augé, Marc. 1994: *Pour une anthropologie des mondes contemporains*. Paris: Aubier.

Austen, Ralph. 1995: *The Elusive Epic: Performance, Text and History in the Oral Narrative of Jeki La Njambe (Cameroon Coast)*. N.p.: African American Studies Association Press.

Austin, J. L. 1971: A Plea for Excuses. In Colin Lyas (ed.), *Philosophy and Linguistics*. London: Macmillan, 79–101.

Badone, Ellen. 1991: Ethnography, fiction, and the meanings of the past in Brittany. In *American Ethnologist* 18 (3), 518–45.

Bahloul, Joëlle. 1996: *The Architecture of Memory: A Jewish-Muslim Household in Colonial Algeria, 1937–1962*. Cambridge studies in social and cultural anthropology; 99. New York: Cambridge University Press.

Bailey, F. G. 1969: *Stratagems and Spoils; A Social Anthropology of Politics*. The Pavilion series. Social anthropology. New York: Schocken Books.

——. 1971: *Gifts and Poison: The Politics of Reputation*. The Pavilion series. New York: Schocken Books.

Bakalaki, Alexandra. 1993: Anthropoloyikes prosengisis tis sinkhronis ellinikis kinonias. In *Dhiavazo* 323, 52–8.

Bakhtin, Mikhail. 1984: *Rabelais and his World*. Bloomington: Indiana University Press.

Balandier, Georges. 1967: *Anthropologie politique*. Paris: PUF.

——. 1980: *Le pouvoir sur scénes*. Paris: Balland.

——. 1985: *Le détour. Pouvoir et modernité*. Paris: Fayard.

Balshem, Martha. 1993: *Cancer in the Community: Class and Medical Authority*. Washington: Smithsonian Institution Press.

Banfield, E. C. 1958: *The Moral Basis of a Backward Society*. Glencoe: Free Press.

Barber, Karin. 1989: Interpreting oriki as history and literature. In K. Barber and P. F. de Moraes Farias (eds.), *Discourse and Its Disguises: The Interpretation of African Oral Texts*. Birmingham University African Studies Series 1, 13–24.

——. 1991: *I Could Speak Until Tomorrow*. Edinburgh: Edinburgh University Press for the International African Institute.

Barnett, Michael. 1997: The UN Security Council, indifference, and genocide in Rwanda. *Cultural Anthropology* 12, 551–78.

Barth, Fredrik. 1969: Introduction. In F. Barth (ed.), *Ethnic Groups and Boundaries*. Oslo: Universitets Forlaget, 9–38.

——. 1994: Enduring and emerging issues in the analysis of ethnicity. In H. Vermeulen and C. Govers (eds.), *The Anthropology of Ethnicity*. Amsterdam: Het Spinhuis.

Basso, Ellen B. 1985: *A Musical View of the Universe*. Philadelphia: University of Pennsylvania Press.

Basso, Keith H. 1996: Wisdom sits in places: notes on a western Apache landscape. In S. Feld and K. Basso (eds.), *Senses of Place*. Santa Fe: School of American Research Press, 53–90.

Baudrillard, Jean. 1981: *Simulacres et simulation: Débats*. Paris: Galilée.

Bauman, Richard. 1977: *Verbal Art as Performance*. Rowley, Mass.: Newbury House.

——. 1986: *Story, Performance, and Event: Contextual Studies of Oral Narrative*. New York: Cambridge Univeristy Press.

——, Sawin, Patricia, and Carpenter, Inta Gale. 1992: *Reflections on the Folklife Festival: an Ethnography of Participant Experience*. Special publications of the Folklore Institute; no. 2. Bloomington, IN: Folklore Institute, Indiana University: Distributed by Indiana University Press.

Beeman, William O. 1981: Why do they laugh? An interactional approach to humor in traditional Iranian improvisatory theater. In *Journal of American Folklore* 94 (374), 506–26.

Behar, Ruth and Gordon, Deborah A. (eds.). 1995: *Women Writing Culture*. Berkeley: University of California Press.

Beidelman, T. O. 1993: The moral imagination of the Kaguru: some thoughts on tricksters, translation and comparative analysis. In William J. Hynes and William G. Doty (eds.), *Mythical Trickster Figures: Contours, Contexts, and Criticisms*. Tuscaloosa: University of Alabama Press, 174–92.

Bellier, Irène. 1993: *L'ENA comme si vous y étiez*. Paris: Seuil.

——. 1995: Moralité, langues et pouvoir dans les institutions européennes. In *Social Anthropology* 3 (3), 235–50.

Ben-Amos, A. and Ben-Ari, E. 1995: Resonance and reverberation: ritual and bureacracy in the state funerals of the French Third Republic. In *Theory and Society* 24, 163–91.

Benedict, Ruth. 1946: *The Chrysanthemum and the Sword: Patterns of Japanese Culture*. Boston: Houghton Mifflin.

Bennett, John W. and Bowen, John R. (eds.). 1988: *Production and Autonomy*. Lanham, MA: University Press of America.

Bentham, Jeremy. 1995: *The Panopticon Writings*. Edited and introduced by Miran Bozovic. London and New York: Verso.

Berdahl, Daphne. 1994: Voices at the wall: Discourses of self, history, and national identity at the Vietnam Veterans Memorial. *History and Memory* 6: 88–124.

——. 1999a: *Where the World Ended: Re-unification and Identity in the German Borderland*. Berkeley: University of California Press.

——. 1999b: "(N)Ostalgie" for the present: memory, longing, and East German things. In *Ethnos* 64 (2), 192–211.

Bernal, Martin. 1987: *Black Athena: The Afroasiatic Roots of Classical Civilization*. New Brunswick: Rutgers University Press.

Biersack, Aletta. 1989: Local Knowledge, local history: Geertz and beyond. In L. Hunt (ed.), *The New Cultural History*. Berkeley: University of California Press, 72–96.

Binns, Christopher. 1979–80: The changing face of power: revolution and development of the Soviet ceremonial system. *Man* (n.s.) 14, 585–606 and 15, 170–87.

Bird-David, Nurit. 1992: Beyond "The Original Affluent Society": a culturalist reformulation. In *Current Anthropology* 33 (1), 25–47.

——. 1994: Sociality and immediacy: or, past and present conversations on bands. In *Man* (n.s.) 29 (3), 583–603.

Black, Max. 1962: "Metaphor", proceedings of the Aristotelian Society (1954–5). In N.S., 55, 273–94. Reprinted in *Models and Metaphors*. Ithaca, NY: Cornell University Press.

Blacking, John. 1973: *How Musical is Man?* Seattle: University of Washington Press.

Blasko, Andrew M. 1999: The Power of Perception: The case of Soviet-style aesthetics. In Plamen Makariev, Andrew M. Blasko, and Asen Davidov (eds.), *Creating Democratic Society: Values and Norms* (*Bulgarian Philosophical Studies*, II) (http://philosophy.cua.edu/rvp/book/series04/iva-12 htm).

Bloch, Maurice. 1977: The past and the present in the present. In *Man* (n.s.) 12, 278–92.

Bloch, Maurice and Parry, Jonathon (eds.). 1989: *Money and the Morality of Exchange*. Cambridge: Cambridge University Press.

Blum, Steven. 1975. Towards a Social History of Musicological Technique. In *Ethnomusicology* 19, 207–31.

Bodnar, John. 1994: *Remaking America: Public Memory, Commemoration and Patriotism in the Twentieth Century*. Princeton: Princeton University Press.

Boehm, Christopher. 1980: Exposing the moral self in Montenegro: the use of natural definitions to keep ethnography descriptive. In *American Ethnologist* 7 (1), 1–26.

——. 1984: *Blood Revenge: The Anthropology of Feuding in Montenegro and other Tribal Societies*. Lawrence: University Press of Kansas.

Boissevain, Jeremy. 1974: *Friends of Friends*. London: Blackwell.

Borneman, John. 1992: *Belonging in the Two Berlins: Kin, State, Nation*. Cambridge: Cambridge University Press.

——. 1996: Until death do us part: marriage/death in anthropological discourse. In *American Ethnologist* 23 (2), 215–35.

——. 1997: *Settling Accounts: Violence, Justice, and Accountability in Postsocialist Europe*. Princeton studies in culture/power/history. Princeton, NJ: Princeton University Press.

Borofsky, Robert. 1997: Cook, Lono, Obeyesekere, and Sahlins. In *Current Anthropology* 38 (2), 255–82.

Bourdieu, Pierre. 1977: *Outline of a Theory of Practice*. Trans. Richard Nice. Cambridge: Cambridge University Press.

——. 1982: *Ce que parler veut dire*. Paris: Fayard.

——. 1984: *Distinction*. Trans. Richard Nice. Cambridge, MA: Harvard University Press.

Bowen, John R. 1993: *Muslims through Discourse: Religion and Ritual in Gayo Society*. Princeton, NJ: Princeton University Press.

Bozovic, M. 1995: Introduction: an utterly dark spot. In Jeremy Bentham, *The Panopticon Papers* (ed. M. Bozovic) (London: Verso), 1–27.

Brain, James Lewton. 1981: Homage to Neptune: Shipboard Initiation Rites. *Proceedings of the American Philosophical Society* 125, 128–33.

Brettell, Caroline B. (ed.). 1993: *When They Read What We Write: The Politics of Ethnography*. Westport, CT: Bergin & Garvey.

Bright, Brenda Jo and Bakewell, Elizabeth Liza (eds.). 1995: *Looking High and Low: Art and Cultural Identity*. Tucson: University of Arizona Press.

Bromberger, Christopher (ed.). 1998: *Passions ordinaires: du match de football au concours de dictée*. Paris: Bayard.

Bromley, Yulian. 1973: *Etnosetnografia*. Moscow: Nauka.

——. 1983: *Ocherki teorii etnosa*. Moscow: Nauka.

Brosius, J. P. 1999: Locations and representations: writing in the ethnographic present in Sarawak, East Malaysia. In *Identities* 6, 345–86.

Bulmer, Ralph N. H. 1967: Why is the cassowary not a bird? A problem of zoological taxonomy among the Karam of the New Guinea Highlands. In *Man* (n.s.) 2 (1), [5]–25.

Burden, Hamilton T. 1967: *The Nuremberg Party Rallies, 1923–39*. London: Pall Mall.

Burke, Peter. 1987: *The Historical Anthropology of Early Modern Italy*. Cambridge: Cambridge University Press.

Burton, John W. 1980: Ethnicity on the hoof: on the economics of Nuer identity. In *Ethnology* 20 (2), 157–62.

Campbell, J. K. 1964: *Honour, Family, and Patronage: A Study of Institutions and Moral Values in a Greek Mountain Community*. Oxford: Clarendon Press.

Carmeli, Yoram S. 1988: Travelling circus: an interpretation. In *European Journal of Sociology* 29, 258–82.

Caro Baroja, Júlio. 1970: *El mito del caracter nacional.* Madrid: Seminarios Ediciones.

Carpenter, Edmund. 1972: *Oh, What a Blow that Phantom Gave Me!* Toronto: Bantam Books.

——. 1973: *Eskimo Realities.* New York: Holt, Rinehart, and Winston.

Carrier, James G. 1992: Occidentalism: the world turned upside-down. In *American Ethnologist* 19 (2), 195–212.

——. (ed.). 1995: *Occidentalism: Images of the West.* Oxford: Clarendon Press; New York: Oxford University Press.

——. 1995: *Gifts and Commodities: Exchange and Western Capitalism since 1700.* London: Routledge.

Carsten, Janet. 1989: Cooking money: gender and the symbolic transformation of means and exchange in a Malay fishing community. In M. Bloch and J. Parry (eds.), *Money and the Morality of Exchange.* Cambridge: Cambridge University Press, 117–41.

Carter, Donald Martin. 1997: *States of Grace: Senegalese in Italy and the New European Immigration.* Minneapolis: University of Minnesota Press.

Castells, Manuel. 1974: *La cuestion urbana.* Mexico City: Siglo XXI.

——. 1995: *La ciudad informacional.* Madrid: Alianza.

Caton, Steven C. 1990: *"Peaks of Yemen I Summon": Poetry as Cultural Practice in a North Yemeni Tribe.* Berkeley: University of California Press.

Cernea, Michael M. (ed.). 1985: *Putting People First.* New York: Oxford University Press.

——. 1995: Social organization and development anthropology. In *1995 Malinowski Award Lecture, Society for Applied Anthropology.* Washington, DC: The World Bank.

Chagnon, Napoleon A. 1968: *Yanomamö: The Fierce People.* New York: Holt, Rinehard and Winston.

Chartier, Roger. 1988: *Cultural History: Between Practices and Reprensentations.* Oxford: Polity Press.

Chatterjee, Partha. 1986: *Nationalist thought and the colonial world: a derivative discourse?* London: Zed Books for the United Nations University; Totowa.

——. 1989: Colonialism, nationalism, and colonialized women: the content in India. In *American Ethnologist* 16 (4), 622–33.

——. 1993: *The Nation and Its Fragments: Colonial and Postcolonial Histories.* Princeton: Princeton University Press.

Chorváthová, L. 1991: Rozhovors Petrom Skalníkom (An Interview with Peter Skalník). In *Slovenský národopis* 39 (1), 77–85.

Classen, Constance. 1993a: *Worlds of Sense: Exploring the Senses in History and Across Cultures.* London and New York: Routledge.

——. 1993b: *Inca Cosmology and the Human Body.* Salt Lake City: University of Utah Press.

——. 1998: *The Color of Angels: Cosmology, Gender and the Aesthetic Imagination.* London and New York: Routledge.

——. 1997: Engendering Perception: Gender Ideologies and Sensory Hierarchies in Western History. In *Body and Society* 3, 1–20.

——, Howes, David, and Synnott, Anthony. 1994: *Aroma: The Cultural History of Smell.* London and New York: Routledge.

Clastres, Pierre. 1974: *Societé contre l'Etat.* Paris: Les Editions de Minuit.

Clifford, James. 1986: Introduction: partial truths. In James Clifford and George E. Marcus, *Writing Culture: The Poetics and Politics of Ethnography.* Berkeley: University of California Press, 1–26.

——. 1988: *The Predicament of Culture: Twentieth-century Ethnography, Literarture and Art*. Cambridge, MA: Harvard University Press.

—— and Marcus, George E. (eds.). 1986: *Writing Culture: The Poetics and Politics of Ethnography*. Berkeley: University of California Press.

Cocchiara, Giuseppe. 1952: *Storia del folklore in Europa*. Torino: Einaudi.

Cohen, Anthony P. 1994: *Self Consciousness: An Alternative Anthropology of Identity*. London and New York: Routledge.

Cohen, Colleen Ballerino, Stoeltje, Beverly, and Wilk, Richard R. (eds.). 1996: *Beauty Queens on the Global Stage: Gender, Contests, and Power*. New York: Routledge.

Cohn, Bernard S. 1981: Anthropology and history in the 1980s. In *Journal of Interdisciplinary History* 12, 227–52.

——. 1996: *Colonialism and its Forms of Knowledge: The British India*. Princeton, NJ: Princeton University Press.

Cole, Jennifer. 1998: The work of memory in Madagascar. In *American Ethnologist* 25 (4), 610–33.

Collingwood, R. G. 1939: *An Autobiography*. London and New York: Oxford University Press.

Collier, Jane F. and Yanagisako, Sylvia J. 1996: Comments on "Until death do us part." In *American Ethnologist* 23 (2), 235–6.

Collier, Jane Fishburne. 1997: *From Duty to Desire: Remaking Families in a Spanish Village*. Princeton studies in culture/power/history. Princeton, NJ: Princeton University Press.

Comaroff, Jean and Comaroff, John. 1991: *Of Revelation and Revolution*, Vol. 1. Chicago: University of Chicago Press.

——. 1997: Postcolonial politics and discourses of democracy in Southern Africa: an anthropological reflection on African political modernities. In *Journal of Anthropological Research* 53 (2), 123–46.

Conklin, Beth A. 1997: Body paint, feathers, and VCRs: aesthetics and authenticity in Amazonian activism. In *American Ethnologist* 24 (4), 711–37.

Conklin, Beth A. and Graham, Laura R. 1995: The shifting middle ground: Amazonian Indians and eco-politics. In *American Anthropologist* 97 (4), 695–710.

Connerton, Paul. 1989: *How Societies Remember*. Cambridge: Cambridge University Press.

Coplan, David B. 1985: *In Township Tonight! South Africa's Black City Music and Theatre*. New York and London: Longman; Johannesburg: Ravan.

——. 1994: *In the Time of Cannibals: The Word Music of South Africa's Basotho Migrants*. Chicago: University of Chicago Press.

Corbin, Alain. 1986: *The Foul and the Fragrant: Odor and the French Social Imagination*, Trans. M. L. Kochan, R. Porter, and C. Prendergast. Cambridge, MA: Harvard University Press.

Coursey, D. G. 1978: Some ideological considerations relating to tropical root crop production. In E. K. Fisk (ed.), *The Adaptation of Traditional Agriculture: Socioeconomic Problems of Urbanization*. Development Studies Centre Monograph 11. Canberra: The Australian National University, 131–41.

Coutin, Susan Bibler. 1995: Smugglers or samaritans in Tucson, Arizona: producing and contesting legal truth. In *American Ethnologist* 22 (3), 549–71.

——. 1999: *Legalizing Moves: Salvadoran immigrants' struggle for U.S. residency*. Ann Arbor: University of Michigan Press.

Cowan, Jane K. 1990: *Dance and the Body Politic in Northern Greece*. Princeton: Princeton University Press.

Coy, Michael W. (ed.). 1989: *Apprenticeship: From Theory to Method and Back Again*. Albany, NY: State University of New York Press.

Creed, Gerald W. and Wedel, Janine R. 1997: Second Thoughts from the Second World: Interpreting Aid in Post-Communist Eastern Europe. In *Human Organization* 56 (3), 253–64.

Crick, Malcolm. 1976: *Explorations in Language and Meaning: Towards a Semantic Anthropology*. London: J. M. Dent.

Crush, Johnathan. 1995a: Introduction: Imagining Development. In J. Crush (ed.), *Power of Development*. New York: Routledge.

——. (ed.). 1995b: *Power of Development*. New York: Routledge.

Culavamsa. 1953: Colombo: Government Printer.

Cunha, Manuela Ivone. 1995: Sociabilité, "société," "cultures carcéraires": la prison féminine de Tires (Portugal). *Terrain* 24, 119–32.

Dagnino, Evelina (ed.). 1994: *Os anos 90: politica e sociedade no Brasil*. São Paulo: Brasiliense.

Dahl, G. and Rabo, A. (eds.). 1992: *Kam-ap or Take-off: Local Notions of Development*. Stockholm: Stockholm Studies in Social Anthropology.

Dakhlia, Jocelyne. 1990: *L'oubli de la cité: la mémoire collective à l'épreuve du lignage dans le Jérid tunisien*. Paris: La Découverte.

Da Matta, Roberto. 1991: *Carnivals, Rogues, and Heroes: An Interpretation of the Brazilian Dilemma*. Notre Dame, IN: University of Notre Dame Press.

D'Andrade, Roy and Fischer, Michael M. J. (eds.). 1996: Science in anthropology: transformations in science and society. In *Anthropology Newsletter* 37 (5), 9–12.

Danforth, Loring M. 1983: Tradition and change in Greek shadow theater. In *Journal of American Folklore* 96 (381), 281–309.

——. 1984: The Ideological Context of the Search for Continuities in Greek Culture. In *Journal of Modern Greek Studies* 2 (1), 53–87.

——. 1995: *The Macedonian Conflict: Ethnic Nationalism in a Transnational World*. Princeton, NJ: Princeton University Press.

Daniel, E. Valentine. 1990: Afterword: sacred places, violent spaces. In J. Spencer (ed.), *History and the Roots of Conflict*. London: Routledge.

Darnton, Robert. 1984: *The Great Cat Massacre and Other Episodes in French History*. New York: Basic Books.

Das, Veena. 1995: *Critical Events: An Anthropological Perspective on Modern India*. Delhi: Oxford University Press.

——. 1996: Language and body in the construction of pain. In *Daedalus* 125 (1), 67–93.

Dávila, Arlene. 1998: El Kiosko Budweiser: the making of a "national" television show in Puerto Rico. In *American Ethnologist* 25 (3), 452–70.

Davis, Natalie Z. 1973: *The Return of Martin Guerre*. Cambridge, MA: Harvard University Press.

Davis, John. 1977: *People of the Mediterranean: An essay in Comparative Social Anthropology*. London, Boston: Routledge & Kegan Paul.

——. 1992: *Exchange. Concepts in the Social Sciences*. Buckingham: Open University Press.

Dawkins, R. 1995: *River out of Eden*. London: Weidenfeld and Nicholson.

Dayan, Daniel. 1990: Présentation du pape en voyageur: télévision, expérience rituelle, dramaturgie politique. In *Terrain* 15, 13–28.

Debord, Guy. 1983: *The Society of the Spectacle*. Detroit: Red and Black.

de Certeau, Michel. 1984: *The Practice of Everyday Life*. Berkeley: University of California Press.

Delaney, Carol. 1990: Hajj: sacred and secular. In *American Ethnologist* 17 (3), 513–30.

Deltsou, Elefrheria P. 1995: *Praxes of Tradition and Modernity in a Village in Northern Greece*. Unpublished Ph.D. Dissertation. Indiana University.

Dening, Greg. 1980: *Islands and Beaches: Discourses on a Silent Land, Marquesas 1774–1880*. Honolulu: University of Hawaii Press.

Derrida, Jacques. 1976: *Of Grammatology*. 1st American edn. Baltimore: Johns Hopkins University Press.

Descola, Philippe and Pálsson, Gísli. (eds.). 1996: *Nature and Society: Anthropological Perspectives*. London: Routledge.

De Silva, Chandra Richard. 1982: *The Portuguese in Ceylon, 1617–1638*. Colombo: HW. Cave & Co.

——. 1983: The historiography of the Portuguese in Sri Lanka: A survey of the Sinhala writings. In *Sanskrit* 17, 13–22.

De Silva, K. M. 1990: The Burghers in Sri Lankan history: a review article. In *Ethnic Studies*, Report 8, 44–8.

Desjarlais, Robert R. 1992: *Body and Emotion: The Aesthetics of Illness and Healing in the Nepal Himalayas*. Philadelphia: University of Pennsylvania Press.

Dickey, Sara. 1993: *Cinema and the Urban Poor in South India*. Cambridge: Cambridge University Press.

——. forthcoming: Opposing faces: film star, fan clubs, and the construction of class identities in South India. In C. Pinney and R. Dwyer (eds.), *Pleasure and the Nation: The History, Politics and Consumption of Popular Culture in India* (New Delhi: Oxford University Press).

Dilley, Roy (ed.). 1992: *Contesting Markets: Analyses of Ideology, Discourse and Practice*. Edinburgh: Edinburgh University Press.

Dirks, Nicholas B. (ed.). 1992: *Colonialism and Culture*. Ann Arbor: University of Michigan Press.

Donnan, Christopher B. 1976: *Moche Art and Iconography*. Los Angeles: UCLA Latin American Center, University of California.

Douglas, Mary. 1958: Raffia cloth distribution in the Lele economy. In *Africa* 28, 109–22.

——. 1966: *Purity and Danger: An Analysis of the Concepts of Pollution and Taboo*. London: Routledge and Kegan Paul.

——. 1973: *Rules and Meanings: The Anthropology of Everyday Knowledge*. Harmondsworth: Penguin Education.

——. 1975: *Implicit Meanings: Essays in Anthropology*. London: Routledge & Kegan Paul.

—— and Isherwood, Baron. 1979: *The World of Goods*. New York: Basic Books.

——. 1982: *Risk and Culture: An Essay on the Selection of Technical and Environmental Dangers*. Berkeley: University of California Press.

——. 1985: *Risk Acceptability According to the Social Sciences*. Social research perspectives: occasional reports on current topics no. 11. New York: Russell Sage Foundation.

——. 1986: *How Institutions Think*. The Frank W. Abrams lectures. 1st edn. Syracuse, NY: Syracuse University Press.

——. 1992: *Risk and Blame: Essays in Cultural Theory*. London and New York: Routledge.

Dragadze, Tamara. (ed.). 1984: *Kinship and Marriage in the Soviet Union: Field Studies*. London and Boston: Routledge & Kegan Paul.

——. 1995: Politics and anthropology in Russia. In *Anthropology Today* 11 (4), 1 and 3.

Dresch, Paul. 1986: The significance of the course events take in segmentary systems. In *American Ethnologist* 13 (2), 309–24.

Dreyfus, Hubert L. and Rabinow, P. 1984: *Michel Foucault, Beyond Structuralism and Hermeneutics*. Chicago: University of Chicago Press.

Drummond, Lee. 1981: The serpent's children: semiotics of ethnogenesis in Arawak and Trobriand Myth. In *American Ethnologist* 8 (3), 633–60.

——. 1996: *American Dreamtime: A Cultural Analysis of Popular Movies and their Implications for a Science of Humanity*. Lanham, MD: Littlefield Adams Books.

Dumont, Louis. 1970: *Homo hierarchicus: An Essay on the Caste System*. Trans. M. Sainsbury. Chicago: University of Chicago Press.

——. 1977: *From Mandelville to Marx: The Genesis and Triumph of Economic Ideology*. Chicago: University of Chicago Press.

Dunn, Elizabeth and Hann, Chris (eds.). 1996: *Civil Society: Challenging Western Models*. London and New York: Routledge.

Dupire, Marguérite. 1987: Des goûts et des odeurs. In *L'Homme* 27 (4), 5–25.

Durkheim, Émile. 1925: *Les formes élémentaires de la vie religieuse: le système totèmique*, Paris: F. Alcan. Fourth edition. Paris: Presses Universitaires de France.

——. 1976: *The Elementary Forms of the Religious Life*. Trans. Joseph Edward Swain. London: Allen & Unwin.

——. 1964: *The Rules of Sociological Method*. Trans. S. A. Solovay and J. H. Mueller. New York: The Free Press.

——. 1967: *The Division of Labour in Society*. Basingstoke: Macmillan.

——. 1973 [1895]: *Les règles de la méthode sociologique*. Paris: Presses Universitaires de France.

—— and Mauss, Marcel. 1963: *Primitive Classification*. Trans. Rodney Needham. Chicago: University of Chicago Press.

Dwyer, Kevin. 1982: *Moroccan Dialogues: Anthropology in Question*. Baltimore: Johns Hopkins University Press.

Dwyer, Peter D. 1996: The invention of nature. In R. F. Ellen and K. Fukui (eds.), *Redefining Nature: Ecology, Culture and Domestication*. Oxford: Berg, 157–86.

Eck, Diana L. 1993: *Encountering God: A Spiritual Journey from Bozeman to Banaras*. Boston: Beacon Press.

Eco, Umberto. 1976: *A Theory of Semiotics*. Advances in semiotics. Bloomington: Indiana University Press.

——. 1995 [1986]: *Faith in Fakes: Travels in Hyperreality*. Translated from the Italian by William Weaver. London: Minerva.

Edelman, Murray J. (Murray Jacob). 1971: *Politics as Symbolic Action; Mass Arousal and Quiescence*. Institute for Research on Poverty monograph series. New York: Academic Press.

Eliade, Mirce. 1949: *Le mythe de l'éternel retour*. Paris: Gallimard.

——. 1954: *The Myth of the Eternal Return*. Trans. W. R. Task. Princeton: Princeton University Press.

——. 1962: *Mephistophélès et l'Androgyne*. Paris: Gallimard.

——. 1963: *Myth and Reality*. Trans. W. R. Task. New York: Harper and Row.

——. 1965: *The Two and the One*. Trans. J. M. Cohen. London: Harvill Press.

Eliav-Feldon, Miriam. 1982: *Realistic Utopias: The Ideal Imaginary Societies of the Renaissance, 1516–1630*. Oxford: Oxford University Press.

Ellen, Roy. 1982: *Environment, Subsistence and System: The Ecology of Small-Scale Social Formations*. Cambridge: Cambridge University Press.

——. 1996: The cognitive geometry of nature: a contextual approach. In P. Descola and G. Pálsson (eds.), *Nature and Society: Anthropological Perspectives*. London, New York: Routledge, 103–24.

Errington, Frederick and Gewertz, Deborah. 1987: *Cultural alternatives and a feminist anthropology: an analysis of culturally constructed gender interests in Papua New Guinea*. Cambridge and New York: Cambridge University Press.

Escobar, Arturo. 1991: Anthropology and development encounter: the making and marketing of development anthropology. In *American Ethnologist* 18 (4), 658–82.

——. 1995: *Encountering Development: The Making and Unmaking of the Third World*. Princeton: Princeton University Press.

——. 1996: Constructing nature: elements for a poststructuralist political ecology. In R. Peet and M. Watts (eds.), *Liberation Ecologies*. London: Routledge, 46–68.

Evans-Pritchard, E. E. 1937: *Witchcraft, Oracles and Magic among the Azande*. Oxford: The Clarendon Press.

——. 1940: *The Nuer: A Description of the Modes of Livelihood and Political Institutions of a Nilotic People*. Oxford: The Clarendon Press.

——. 1963: *Social Anthropology and Other Essays*. New York: The Free Press.

Fabian, Johannes. 1983: *Time and the Other: How Anthropology Makes its Object*. New York: Columbia University Press.

——. 1990: *Power and Performance*. Madison: University of Wisconsin Press.

——. 1991: *Time and the Work of Anthropology*. Chur and Reading: Harwood Academic Publishers.

Fanon, Frantz. 1963: *Wretched of the Earth*. Trans. C. Farrington. New York: Grove Press.

Fardon, Richard (ed.). 1990: *Localizing Strategies: Regional Traditions of Ethnographic Writing*. Washington: Smithsonian Institution Press.

Farnell, Brenda M. 1995: *Do You See What I Mean? Plains Indian Sign Talk and the Embodiment of Action*. Austin: University of Texas Press.

Faubion, James D. 1993: *Modern Greek Lessons: A Primer in Historical Constructivism*. Princeton studies in culture/power/history. Princeton, NJ: Princeton University Press.

Feld, Steven. 1982: *Sound and Sentiment: Birds, Weeping, and Poetics and Song in Kaluli Expression*. Philadelphia: University of Pennsylvania Press.

——. 1986: Orality and consciousness. In Y. Tokumaru and O. Yamaguti (eds.), *The Oral and the Literate in Music*. Tokyo: Academia Music Ltd.

——. 1991: Sound as a symbolic system. In D. Howes (ed.), *The Varieties of Sensory Experiences: A Sourcebook in the Anthropology of the Senses*. Toronto: University of Toronto Press, 79–99.

Feldman, Allen. 1991: *Formations of Violence: The Narrative of the Body and Political Terror in Northern Ireland*. Chicago: University of Chicago Press.

——. 1994: On cultural anesthesia: from Desert Storm to Rodney King. In *American Ethnologist* 21 (2), 404–18.

Ferguson, James. 1990: *The Anti-Politics Machine: "Development," Depoliticization, and Bureaucratic Power in Lesotho*. Cambridge: Cambridge University Press.

Fernandez, James W. 1982: *Bwiti: An Ethnography of the Religious Imagination in Africa*. Princeton, NJ: Princeton University Press.

——. 1986: *Persuasions and Performances: The Play of Tropes in Culture.* Bloomington, IN: Indiana University Press.

—— and Herzfeld, Michael. 1998: In search of meaningful methods. In H. Russell Bernard (ed.), *Handbook of Methods in Cultural Anthropology.* Walnut Creek: Sage, 89–129.

Ferreira, Mariana Kawall Leal. 1997: When 1+1≠2: making mathematics in central Brazil. In *American Ethnologist* 24 (1), 132–47.

Fischer, Michael M. J. 1991: Anthropology as cultural critique: inserts for the 1990s cultural studies of science, visual-virtual realities, and post-trauma polities. In *Cultural Anthropology* 6 (4), 525–37.

Fisher, William. 1995: Development and Resistance in the Narmada Valley. In William Fisher (ed.), 1995, *Toward Sustainable Development*, 3–46.

——. (ed.). 1995: *Toward Sustainable Development?: Struggling over India's Narmada River.* Columbia University seminar series. Armonk, NY: M.E. Sharpe.

Fisherkeller, JoEllen. 1997: Everyday learning about identities among young adolescents in TV culture. In *Anthropology and Education Quarterly* 28 (4), 467–92.

Fiske, J. 1992: The cultural economy of fandom. In L. A. Lewis (ed.), *The Adoring Audience: Fan Culture and Popular Media.* London: Routledge.

Florescano, Enrique. 1987: *Memoria mexicana: ensayo sobre la reconstrucción del pasado: epoca prehispanica-1821.* Contrapuntos. 1a ed. [Mexico, D.F.]: Editorial J. Mortiz.

Forde, Daryll. 1954: *African Worlds: Studies in the Cosmological Ideas and Social Values of African Peoples.* London: Oxford University Press.

Forge, Anthony. 1970: Learning to see in New Guinea. In Philip Mayer (ed.), *Socialization: The Approach from Social Anthropology.* A.S.A. monographs, 8. London, New York: Tavistock Publications, 191–213.

Fortes, Meyer and Evans-Pritchard, E. E. (eds.). 1940: *African Political Systems.* London: Pub. for the International institute of African languages & cultures by the Oxford University Press.

Foster, George M. 1987: On the origin of humoral medicine in Latin America. In *Medical Anthropology Quarterly* 1 (4), 355–93.

Foucault, Michel. 1973a: *The Birth of the Clinic.* Trans. A. M. Sheridan Smith. New York: Random House.

——. 1973b: *The Order of Things: An Archeology of the Human Sciences.* New York: Vintage.

——. 1975: *Surveiller et punir: naissance de la prison.* Paris: Gallimard.

——. 1976: *La volonté de savoir.* Paris: Gallimard.

——. 1979: *Discipline and Punish.* New York: Vintage.

——. 1984: "Questions et réponses." In H. Dreyfus and P. Rabinow Michel Foucault, *Un parcours philosophique.* Paris: Gallimard.

Friedman, Johnathan. 1987: Review essay. In *History and Theory* 26, 72–99.

Fukuyama, Francis. 1992: *The End of History and the Last Man.* New York: Free Press; Toronto: Maxwell Macmillan Canada; New York: Maxwell Macmillan International.

Gal, Susan. 1991: Bartok's funeral: representations of Europe in Hungarian political rhetoric. In *American Ethnologist* 18 (3), 440–58.

Galt, Anthony H. 1992: *Town and Country in Locorotondo: Case Studies in Cultural Anthropology.* Fort Worth, TX: Harcourt Brace Jovanovich College Publishers.

García Canclini, Nestor. 1990: *Culturas Hibridas: Estrategias para Entrar y Salir de la Modernidad.* Mexico, D.F.: Grijalbo.

——. 1995: Mexico: cultural globalization in a disintegrating city. In *American Ethnologist* 22 (4), 743–55.

Gardner, Katy and Lewis, David. 1996: *Anthropology, Development and the Postmodern Challenge*. London: Pluto Press.

Geana, G. 1992: Cultural anthropology as a paradigm of the socio-human sciences. *Slovensky náradopis* 40 (3), 311–16.

Geertz, Clifford. 1963: *Agricultural Involution: The Process of Ecological Change in Indonesia*. Berkeley and Los Angeles: University of California Press.

——. 1973a: *Interpretation of Cultures: Selected Essays*. New York: Basic Books.

——. 1973b: Deep play: notes on the Balinese cockfight. In C. Geertz, *The Interpretation of Cultures*. New York: Basic Books.

——. 1980: *Negara: The Theatre-State in Local Knowledge Nineteenth-Century Bali*. Princeton: Princeton University Press.

——. 1983: *Local Knowledge: Further Essays in Interpretative Anthropology*. New York: Basic Books.

——. 1988: *Works and Lives: The Anthropologist as Author*. Cambridge: Polity Press.

Gell, Alfred. 1998: *Art and Agency: An Anthropological Theory*. Oxford: Clarendon Press.

Gelles, Paul H. 1995: Equilibrium and extraction: dual organization in the Andes. In *American Ethnologist* 22 (4), 710–42.

Gellner, Ernest. 1983: *Nations and Nationalism: New Perspectives on the Past*. Oxford: Basil Blackwell.

George, Kenneth M. 1996: *Showing Signs of Violence: The Cultural Politics of a Twentieth-Century Headhunting Ritual*. Berkeley: University of California Press.

——. 1997: Some things that have happened to the Sun after September 1965: politics and the interpretation of an Indonesian painting. In *Comparative Studies in Society and History* 39 (4), 603–34.

Gerholm, Tomas. 1988: On ritual: a postmodernist view. In *Ethnos* 53, 190–203.

Gewertz, Deborah B. and Errington, Frederik. 1991: *Twisted Histories, Altered Contexts: Representing the Chambri in a World System*. Cambridge: Cambridge University Press.

——. 1995: Duelling Currencies in East New Britain. In James G. Carrier (ed.), *Occidentalism*, 161–91.

——. 1996: On PepsiCo and piety in a Papua New Guinea "modernity." In *American Ethnologist* 23 (3), 476–93.

Giddens, Anthony. 1984: *The Constitution of Society: Outline of the Theory of Structuration*. Berkeley, University of California Press.

Giles, W., Moussa, H., and Van Esterik, P. (eds.). 1996: *Development & Diaspora: Gender and the Refugee Experience*. Dundas, Ont.: Artemis Enterprises.

Gill, Sam D. 1982: *Native American Religions: An Introduction*. Belmont, CA: Wadsworth.

Gilman, Sander. 1988: *Goethe's Touch: Touching, Seeing, and Sexuality*. Tulane: Graduate School of Tulane University.

Gilmore, David D. (ed.). 1987: *Honor and Shame and the Unity of the Mediterranean*. Washington, DC: American Anthropological Association.

Gilsenan, Michael. 1976: Lying, honor and contradiction. In Bruce Kapferer (ed.), *Transaction and Meaning: Directions in the Anthropology of Exchange and Symbolic Behavior*. Philadelphia: Institute for the Study of Human Issues.

Ginsburg, Faye D. 1989: *Contested Lives: The Abortion Debate in an American Community*. Berkeley: University of California Press.

——. 1991: Indigenous media: Faustian contract or global village? In *Cultural Anthropology* 6 (1), 92–112.

——. 1993: Aboriginal media and the Australian imaginary. In *Public Culture* 5 (3), 557–78.

Ginsburg, Faye and Rapp, Rayna (eds.). 1995: *Conceiving the New World Order: The Global Politics of Reproduction*. Berkeley: University of California Press.

Ginzburg, Carlo. 1980: *The Cheese and the Worms: The Cosmos of a Sixteenth-Century Miller*. Baltimore: Johns Hopkins University Press.

Gluckman, Max. 1963a: *Order and Rebellion in Tribal Societies*. London: Cohen & West.

——. 1963b: Gossip and scandal. In *Current Anthropology* 4 (3), 307–16.

Gmelch, George and Zenner, Walter P. (eds.). 1996[1966]: *Urban life: Readings in Urban Anthropology*. 3rd edn. Prospect Heights, IL: Waveland Press.

Godelier, Maurice. 1984: *L'idéal et le matériel: pensée, économies, sociétés*. Paris: Fayard.

Goffman, Erving. 1959: *The Presentation of Self in Everyday Life*. Anchor Books ed. Garden City, N.Y.: Doubleday.

Goody, Jack. 1982: *Cooking, Cuisine, and Class: A Study in Comparative Sociology*. Themes in the social sciences. Cambridge: Cambridge University Press.

——. 1977: *The Domestication of the Savage Mind*. Themes in the social sciences. Cambridge, New York: Cambridge University Press.

Gossen, Gary H. 1974: *Chamulas in the World of the Sun*. Cambridge, MA: Harvard University Press.

Gould, Stephen Jay. 1985: *The Flamingo's Smile: Reflections in Natural History*. New York: W. W. Norton.

Gow, David D. 1993: Doubly dammed: dealing with power and praxis in development anthropology. In *Human Organization* 52 (4), 380–97.

Graburn, Nelson H. H. (ed.). 1976: *Ethnic and Tourist Arts: Cultural Expressions from the Fourth World*. Berkeley: University of California Press.

Granet, Marcel. 1934: *La pensée chinoise*. Paris: Albin Michel.

Greenwood, Davydd J. 1989: Culture by the pound: an anthropological perspective on tourism as cultural commoditization. In Valene L. Smith (ed.), *Hosts and Guests: The Anthropology of Tourism*. 2nd edition. Philadelphia: University of Pennsylvania Press, 171–86.

——. 1984: *The Taming of Evolution: The Persistence of Nonevolutionary Views in the Study of Humans*. Ithaca: Cornell University Press.

Gregory, C. A. 1982: *Gifts and Commodities*. London: Academic Press.

——. and Altman, J. C. 1989: *Observing the Economy* (ASA Research Methods). London: Routledge.

Grillo, Ralph. 1985: Applied Anthropology in the 1980s: Retrospect and Prospect. In R. Grillo and A. Rew (eds.), *Social Anthropology and Development Policy*. London: Tavistock Publications, 1–36.

Gudeman, Stephen. 1986: *Economics as Cultures: Models and Metaphors of Livelihood*. London: Routledge Kegan Paul.

——. and Rivera, Alberto. 1990: *Conversations in Colombia*. Cambridge: Cambridge University Press.

——. 1992: Remodeling the house of economics: culture and innovation. In *American Ethnologist* 19 (1), 141–54.

Guha, Ranajit. 1983: *Elementary Aspects of Peasant Insurgency*. Delhi: Oxford University Press.

Gunasekera, B. 1954: *The Rajavaliya*. Colombo: Government Printer.

Gupta, Akhil. 1998: *Postcolonial Developments: Agriculture in the Making of Modern India*. Durham, NC: Duke University Press.

Gupta, Akhil and Ferguson, James. 1997: "The field" as site, method, and location in anthropology. In Gupta and Ferguson (eds.), 1997, *Anthropological Locations*, 1–46.

——. (eds.). 1997: *Anthropological Locations: Boundaries and Grounds of a Field Science*. Berkeley: University of California Press.

Gusterson, Hugh. 1996: *Nuclear Rites: A Weapons Laboratory at the End of the Cold War*. Berkeley: University of California Press.

Halbwachs, Maurice. 1980: *The Collective Memory*. Harper colophon books; CN/800. 1st edn. New York: Harper & Row.

Hall, E. T. 1959: *The Silent Language*. 1st edn. Garden City, NY: Doubleday.

——. 1983: *Hidden Differences: How to Communicate with the Germans. Studies in International Communication*. Hamburg, West Germany: Stern.

——. 1987: *Hidden Differences: Doing Business with the Japanese*. Garden City, NY: Anchor Press/Doubleday.

——. 1990: *Understanding Cultural Differences*. Yarmouth, ME: Intercultural Press.

Hall, Richard. 1996a: Stirrings from the Indian Rim. In *Financial Times*, 16–17 November, I–II.

——. 1996b: *Empires of the Monsoon: a History of the Indian Ocean and its Invaders*. London: Harper Collins.

Hall, Stuart. 1980: Encoding/decoding. In S. Hall, D. Hobson, A. Lowe, and Paul Willis (eds.), *Culture, Media, and Language*. London: Hutchinson.

Hallpike, C. R. 1979: *The Foundations of Primitive Thought*. Oxford: Clarendon Press; New York: Oxford University Press.

Halperin, Rhoda H. 1988: *Economies across Cultures: Towards a Comparative Science of the Economy*. New York: St. Martin's Press.

Handelman, Don. 1990: *Models and Mirrors: Towards an Anthropology of Public Events*. Cambridge: Cambridge University Press.

——. 1991: Symbolic types, the body, and circus. In *Semiotica* 85, 205–25.

——. 1992: Passages to play: paradox and process. In *Play and Culture* 5, 1–19.

——. 1995: Cultural taxonomy and bureaucracy in ancient China: The Book of Lord Shang. In *International Journal of Politics, Culture, and Society* 9, 263–93.

——. 1998: *Models and Mirrors: Towards an Anthropology of Public Events*. With a new preface by the author. Oxford: Berghahn Books. (Preface pp. x–liii.)

Handler, R. and Linnekin, Jocelyn. 1984: Tradition, genuine or spurious. In *Journal of American Folklore* 97 (385), 273–90.

——. 1985: On dialogue and destructive analysis: problems in narrating nationalism and ethnicity. In *Journal of Anthropological Research* 41 (2), 171–82.

——. 1986: Authenticity. *Anthropology Today* 2 (1), 2–4.

——. and Segal, Daniel. 1990: *Jane Austen and the Fiction of Culture: An Essay on the Narration of Social Realities*. Tucson, AZ: University of Arizona Press.

——. and Gable, Eric. 1997: *The New History in an Old Museum: Creating the Past at Colonial Williamsburg*. Durham NC: Duke University Press.

Hannerz, Ulf. 1980: *Exploring the City: Inquiries Toward an Urban Anthropology*. New York: Columbia University Press.

——. 1981: The management of danger. In *Ethnos* 46 (1–2), 19–46.

——. 1990: Cosmopolitans and locals in world culture. In M. Featherstone (ed.), *Global Culture*. London: Sage, 237–52.

——. 1992: *Cultural Complexity: Studies in the Social Organization of Meaning*. New York: Columbia University Press.

——. 1996: *Transnational Connections*. London, New York: Routledge.

——. 1998: Transnational research. In H. R. Bernard (ed.), *Handbook of Methods in Anthropology* (Walnut Creek, CA: Altamira Press), pp. 235–58.

Hanson, F. Allan. 1983: Syntagmatic structures: How the Maoris make sense of history. *Semiotica* 46: 287–308.

——. 1989: The making of the Maori: cultural invention and its logic. In *American Anthropologist* 91, 890–902.

Harris, Marvin. 1968: *The Rise of Anthropological Theory: A History of Theories of Culture*. London: Routledge.

——. 1974: *Cows, Pigs, Wars, and Witches: The Riddles of Culture*. New York: Random House.

——. 1977: *Cannibals and Kings: The Origins of Cultures*. 1st edn. New York: Random House.

Harris, Olivia. 1996: Temporalities of tradition: reflections on a changing anthropology. In Václav Hubinger (ed.), *Grasping the Changing World: Anthropological Concepts in the Postmodern Era*, London, New York: Routledge, 1–16.

Hart, Janet. 1996: *New Voices in the Nation: Women and the Greek Resistance, 1941–1964*. Ithaca: Cornell University Press.

Hastrup, Kirsten (ed.). 1992: *Other Histories*. European Association of Social Anthropologists. London, New York: Routledge.

Hawking, Stephen. 1988: *A Brief History of Time*. London and New York: Bantam Books.

Hayden, Robert M. 1996: Imagined communities and real victims: self-determination and ethnic cleansing in Yugoslavia. In *American Ethnologist* 23 (4), 783–801.

Heatherington, Tracey Lynne. 1999: *As If Someone Dear to Me Had Died: The Orgosolo Commons and the Cultural Politics of Environmentalism*. Ph.D. dissertation, Harvard University, Department of Anthropology.

Heelas, Paul and Lock, Andrew. 1981: *Indigenous Psychologies: The Anthropology of the Self*. London and New York: Academic Press.

Helms, Mary W. 1998: *Access to Origins: Affines, Ancestors, and Aristocrats*. Austin, TX: Texas University Press.

Herrmann, Gretchen. 1997: Gift or commodity: What changes hands in the U.S. garage sale? In *American Ethnologist* 24: 910–30.

Hertz, Ellen. 1998: *The Trading Crowd: An Ethnography of the Shanghai Stock Market*. Cambridge: Cambridge University Press.

Hertz, Robert. 1960: *Death and The Right Hand*. Glencoe, IL: Free Press.

Herzfeld, Michael. 1984: The significance of the insignificant: blasphemy as ideology. In *Man* (n.s.), 19 (4), 653–64.

——. 1985: *The Poetics of Manhood: Contest and Identity in a Cretan Mountain Village*. Princeton: Princeton University Press.

——. 1986: Closure as cure: tropes in the exploration of bodily and social disorder. In *Current Anthropology* 27 (2), 107–20.

——. 1987: *Anthropology Through the Looking-Glass: Critical Ethnography in the Margins of Europe*. Cambridge: Cambridge University Press.

——. 1990: Icons and identity: religious orthodoxy and social practice in rural Crete. In *Anthropological Quarterly* 63 (3), 109–21.

——. 1991: *A Place in History: Social and Monumental Time in a Cretan town*. Princeton studies in culture/power/history. Princeton modern Greek studies. Princeton, NJ: Princeton University Press.

——. 1992: *The Social Production of Indifference: Exploring the Symbolic Roots of Western Bureaucracy*. Oxford: Berg.

——. 1997a: *Cultural Intimacy: Social Poetics in the Nation-State*. New York: Routledge.

——. 1997b: *Portrait of a Greek Imagination: An Ethnographic Biography of Andreas Nenedakis*. Chicago: University of Chicago Press.

——. 1997c: Anthropology and the politics of significance. In *Social Analysis* 41 (3), 107–38.

Heyman, Josiah McC. 1995: Putting power in the anthropology of bureaucracy: the immigration andnaturalization service at the Mexico-United States border. In *Current Anthropology* 36 (2), 261–87.

——. 1998: *Finding a Moral Heart for U.S. Immigration Policy: An Anthropological Perspective*. American Ethnological Society monograph series; no. 7. Arlington, VA: American Anthropological Association.

Hill, Jonathan D. (ed.). 1988: *Rethinking History and Myth: Indigenous South American Perspectives on the Past*. Urbana: University of Illinois Press.

Himpele, Jeff. Forthcoming: Arrival scenes: complicity and the ethnography of media in the Bolivian public sphere. In F. Ginsburg, L. Abu-Lughod, and B. Larkin (eds.), *The Social* Practice of Media: *Anthropological Interventions in the Age of Electronic Reproduction*. Berkeley: University of California Press.

Hirschon, Renée. 1989: *Heirs of the Greek Catastrophe: The Social Life of Asia Minor Refugees in Piraeus*. Oxford: Clarendon Press; New York: Oxford University Press.

Hobart, Mark (ed.). 1993: *An Anthropological Critique of Development*. London: Routledge.

Hoben, Allan. 1982: Anthropologists and development. In *Annual Review of Anthropology* 11, 349–75.

Hobsbawm, E. J. 1959: *Social Bandits and Primitive Rebels; Studies in Archaic Forms of Social Movement in the 19th and 20th Centuries*. Glencoe, IL: Free Press.

Hobsbawm, Eric. and Ranger, Terence. 1983: *The Invention of Tradition*. Cambridge: Cambridge University Press.

Hocquenghem, A.-M. 1987: *Iconografia Mochica*. Lima, Peru: Fondo Editorial de la Pontificia Universidad Católica del Perú.

Hodgen, Margaret T. 1936: *The Doctrine of Survivals: A Chapter in the History of Scientific Method in the Study of Man*. London: Allenson.

——. 1964. *Early Anthropology in the Sixteenth and Seventeenth Centuries*. Philadelphia: University of Pennsylvania Press.

Holmes, Douglas R. 1989: *Cultural Disenchantments: Worker Peasantries in Northeast Italy*. Princeton, NJ: Princeton University Press.

Holston, James and Appadurai, Arjun. 1996: Cities and citizenship. In *Public Culture* 8 (2), 187–204.

Holst-Warhaft, Gail. 1979: *Theodorakis, Myth and Politics in Modern Greek Music*. Amsterdam: Hakkert.

Holy, Ladislav. 1977: Toka ploughing teams: Towards a decision model of social recruitment. In M. Stuchlik (ed.), *Goals and Behaviour*. Belfast: The Queen's University Papers in Social Anthropology 2, 49–73.

——. 1979: Changing norms in matrilineal societies: The case of Toka inheritance. In D. Riches (ed.), *The Conceptulization and Explanation of Processes of Social Change*. Belfast: The Queen's University Papers in Social Anthropology 3, 83–105.

——. and Stuchlik, Milan. 1981: The structure of folk models. In L. Holy and M. Stuchlik (eds.), *The Structure of Folk Models*. London: Academic Press, 1–35.

Horowitz, Michael. 1994: Development anthropology in the mid-1990s. In *Development Anthropology Network* 12 (1 and 2), 1–14.

Hountondji, Paulin. 1983: *African Philosophy: Myth and Reality*. Trans. Henri Evans. Bloomington: Indiana University Press.

Howell, Signe. 1996: Nature in culture and culture in nature? Chewong ideas of "humans" and other species. In G. Palsson and P. Descola (eds.), *Nature and Society: anthropological perspectives*. London, Routledge, 127–44.

Howes, David. 1988: On the odour of the soul: spatial representation and olfactory classification in eastern Indonesia and western Melanesia. In *Bijdragen tot de Taal-, Land-, en Volkenkunde* 124, 84–113.

——. (ed.). 1991: *The Varieties of Sensory Experience: A Sourcebook in the Anthropology of the Senses*. Toronto: University of Toronto Press.

——. 1992: *The Bounds of Sense: An Inquiry into the Sensory Orders of Western and Melanesian Society*. Ph.D. Dissertation, Université de Montréal.

——. (ed.). 1996: *Cross-Cultural Consumption: Global Markets, Local Realities*. London and New York: Routledge.

Hubert, Henri and Mauss, Marcel. 1964: *Sacrifice: Its Nature and Function*. Chicago: University of Chicago Press.

Humphrey, Caroline and Hugh-Jones, Stephen. 1992: Introduction: barter, exchange, and value. In Caroline Humphrey and Stephen Hugh-Jones (eds.), *Barter, Exchange and Value: An Anthropological Approach*. Cambridge: Cambridge University Press, 1–20.

Hunn, Eugene. 1985: The utilitarian factor in folk biological classification. In Janet W. D. Dougherty (ed.), *Directions in Cognitive Anthropology*. Urbana, IL: University of Illinois Press, 117–40.

Hunt, Lynn. 1989: Introduction: history, culture and text. In Lynn Hunt (ed.), *The New Cultural History*. Berkeley: University of California Press, 1–22.

Huntington, Ellsworth. 1924: *Civilization and Climate*. New Haven: Yale University Press.

Huntington, Samuel P. 1993: The clash of civilizations? In *Foreign Affairs* 72 (3), 22–49.

——. 1996: *The Clash of Civilizations and the Remaking of World Order*. New York: Simon and Schuster.

Hvalkof, Søren and Aaby, Peter (eds.). 1981: *Is God an American? An Anthropological Perspective on the Missionary Work of the Summer Institute of Linguistics* (An anthology). Copenhagen, London: IWGIA/Survival International.

Hvalkof, Søren. 1989: The nature of development: native and settlers view in Gran Pajonal, Peruvian Amazon. In *Folk* 31, 125–50.

——. 1999: Outrage in rubber and oil: extractivism, indigenous peoples and justice in the Upper Amazon. In C. Zerner (ed.), *Peoples, Plants and Justice: Resource Extraction and Conservation in Tropical Developing Countries*. New York: Columbia University Press.

——. and Veber, H. forthcoming: *Guía Etnográfica de la Alta Amazonia*. Vol. III. Los Ashéninka del Gran Pajonal. Panama: Smithsonian Tropical Research Institute (Series editors: Fernando Santas and Federica Barclay).

Illich, Ivan. 1995: Guarding the eye in the age of show. In *Res* 28, 47–61.

Ingold, Tim. 1992: Culture and the perception of environment. In E. Croll and D. Parkin (eds.), *Bush Base: Forest Farm*. London: Routledge, 39–56.

——. 1993: Globes and spheres: the topology of environmentalism. In K. Milton (ed.), *Environmentalism: The view from Anthropology*. London and New York: Routledge, 31–42.

——. 1994: From trust to domination: An alternative history of human–animal relations. In A. Manning and J. Serpell (eds.), *Animals and Human Society: Changing Perspectives*. London, New York: Routledge, 1–22.

——. 1996: Hunting and gathering as ways of perceiving the environment. In R. F. Ellen and K. Fukui (eds.), *Redefining Nature: Ecology, Culture and Domestication*. Oxford: Berg, 117–56.

Isaac, Rhys. 1982: *The Transformation of Virginia, 1740–1790*. Chapel Hill: University of North Carolina Press.

Iser, Wolfgang. 1978: *The Act of Reading: A Theory of Aesthetic Response*. Baltimore: Johns Hopkins University Press.

Jackson, Jean E. 1995: Culture, genuine and spurious: the politics of Indianness in the Vaupés, Colombia. In *American Ethnologist* 22 (1), 3–27.

Jackson, Michael. 1989: *Paths towards a Clearing: Radical Empiricism and Ethnographic Inquiry*. Bloomington, IN: Indiana University Press.

Jakobson, Roman. 1960: Longuistics and poetics. In Thomas A. Sebeok (ed.), *Style in Language*. Cambridge, MA: MIT Press, 350–77.

Janelli, Roger L. 1993: *Making Capitalism: The Social and Cultural Construction of a South Korean Conglomerate*. Stanford, CA: Stanford University Press.

Jay, Martin. 1993: *Downcast Eyes: The Denigration of Vision in Contemporary French Thought*. Berkeley: University of California Press.

Jenkins, Timothy. 1994: Fieldwork and the perception of everyday life. In *Man* (n.s.), 29 (2), 433–55.

Kahn, Susan Martha. 2000. *Reproducing Jews: A Cultural Account of Assisted Conception in Israel*. Durham, NC: Duke University Press.

Kapferer, Bruce. (ed.). 1976: *Transaction and Meaning: Directions in the Anthropology of Exchange and Symbolic Behavior*. ASA essays in social anthropology; v. 1. Philadelphia: Institute for the Study of Human Issues.

——. 1983: *A Celebration of Demons: Exorcism and the Aesthetics of Healing in Sri Lanka*. Bloomington, IN: Indiana University Press.

——. 1988: *Legends of People, Myths of State: Violence, Intolerance, and Political Culture in Sri Lanka and Australia*. Washington: Smithsonian Institution Press.

Karakasidou, Anastasia N. 1997: *Fields of Wheat, Hills of Blood: Passages to Nationhood in Greek Macedonia, 1870–1990*. Chicago: University of Chicago Press.

Karim, Wazir Jahan. 1996: Anthropology without tears: how a "local" sees the "local" and the "global". In H. Moore (ed.), *The Future of Anthropological Knowledge*. London: Routledge, 115–38.

Karp, Ivan. 1980: Beer drinking and social experience in an African society: an essay in formal sociology. In Charles Bird and Ivan Karp (eds.), *Explorations in African Systems of Thought*. Bloomington, IN: Indiana University Press, 83–119.

——. and Bird, Charles (eds.). 1980: *Explorations in African Systems of Thought*. Bloomington: Indiana University Press.

——. 1986: Agency and social theory: a review of Giddens. *American Ethnologist* 13, 131–7.

——. and Levine, Stephen (eds.). 1991: *Exhibiting Cultures: The Poetics and Politics of Museum Display*. Washington: Smithsonian Institution Press.

Katz, Elihu and Dayan, Daniel. 1992: *Media Events: The Live Broadcasting of History*. Cambridge, MA: Harvard University Press.

Kearney, Michael. 1991: Borders and boundaries of state and self at the end of empire. In *Journal of Historical Sociology* 4, 52–74.

Keesing, Roger M. 1981: *Cultural Anthropology: A Contemporary Perspective, 2nd edition*. New York: Holt, Rinehart and Winston.

Keesing, Roger. 1985: Kwaio women speak: the micropolitics of autobiography in a Solomon Islands Society. In *American Anthropologist*, 87, 27–39.

——. 1989: Creating the past: custom and identity in the contemporary pacific. In *The Contemporary Pacific* 1, 19–42.

Keil, Charles and Feld, Steven. 1994: *Music Grooves*. Chicago: University of Chicago Press.

Kemper, Steven. 1993: The nation consumed: buying and believing in Sri Lanka. In *Public Culture* 5 (3), 377–93.

Kenny, Michael and Kertzer, David I. (eds.). 1983: *Urban life in Mediterranean Europe: Anthropological Perspectives*. Urbana, IL: University of Illinois Press.

Kerman, Joseph. 1985: *Musicology*. London: Fontana.

Kertzer, David I. 1980: *Comrades and Christians: Religion and Political Struggle in Communist Italy*. Cambridge: Cambridge University Press.

——. 1988: *Ritual, Politics, and Power*. New Haven: Yale University Press.

Kingsbury, Henry. 1988: *Music, Talent, and Performance: A Conservatory Cultural System*. Philadelphia: Temple University Press.

Kirby, Percival R. 1934: *The Musical Instruments of the Native Races of South Africa*. Johannesburg: Wiwatersrand University Press.

Klaits, Frederick. 1998: Making a good death: AIDS and social belonging in an independent church in Gaborone. In *Botswana Notes and Records* 30, 101–19.

Kleinman, Arthur. 1995: *Writing at the Margin: Discourses between Anthropology and Medicine*. Berkeley: University of California Press.

——. and Kleinman, Joan. 1994: How bodies remember: social memory and bodily experience of criticism, resistance, and delegitimation following China's Cultural Revolution. In *New Literary History* 25, 707–23.

——. and Kleinman, Joan. 1996: The appeal of experience; the dismay of images: cultural appropriations of suffering in our time. In *Daedalus* 125 (1), 1–25.

——. Das, Veena, and Lock, Margaret. 1996: Introduction. In *Daedalus* 125 (1), xi–xx.

Kligman, Gail. 1981: *Căluş: Symbolic Transformation in Romanian Ritual*. Chicago: University of Chicago Press.

——. 1998: *The Politics of Duplicity: Controlling Reproduction in Ceausescu's Romania*. Berkeley: University of California Press.

——. and Verdery, Katherine. 1999: Reflections on the "revolutions" of 1989 and after. In *East European Politics and Societies* 13, 303–12.

Kondo, Dorinne. 1990: *Crafting Selves: Power, Gender, and Discourse of Identity in a Japanese Workplace*. Chicago: University of Chicago Press.

Konstantinov, Yulian. 1996: Patterns of reinterpretation: trader-tourism in the Balkans (Bulgaria) as apicturesque metaphorical enactment of post-totalitarianism. In *American Ethnologist* 23 (4), 762–82.

——. Kressel, Gideon, and Thuen, Trond. 1998: Outclassed by former outcasts: petty trading in Varna. In *American Ethnologist* 25 (4), 729–45.

Koptiuch, Kristin. 1996: Cultural defense and criminological displacements: gender, race, and (trans)nation in the legal surveillance of U.S. diaspora Asians. In S. Lavie and T. Swedenburg (eds.), *Displacement, Diaspora, and Geographies of Identity*. Durham, NC: Duke University Press, 215–34.

Kopytoff, Igor. 1986: The cultural biography of things: commoditization as process. In Arjun Appadurai (ed.), *The Social Life of Things: Commodities in Cultural Perspective*. Cambridge: Cambridge University Press, 64–94.

——. (ed.). 1987: *The African Frontier*. Bloomington: Indiana University Press.

Kroeber, Alfred L. 1939: *Cultural and Natural Areas of Native North America*. Berkeley: University of California Press.

Kuklick, Henrika. 1991: *The Savage Within: The Social History of British Anthropology 1885–1945*. Cambridge: Cambridge University Press.

Labov, William. 1972: *Language in the Inner City: Studies in the Black English Vernacular*. Philadelphia: University of Pennsylvania Press.

Laderman, Carol. 1991: *Taming the Wind of Desire: Psychology, Medicine, and Aesthetics in Malay Shamanistic Performance*. Berkeley: University of California Press.

Lancaster, Roger N. 1992: *Life is Hard: Machismo, Danger, and the Intimacy of Power in Nicaragua*. Berkeley: University of California Press.

Langer, Lawrence. 1991a: *Holocaust Testimonies: The Ruins of Memory*. New Haven: Yale University Press.

——. 1991b: The alarmed vision: social suffering and Holocaust atrocity. In *Daedalus* 125 (1), 47–67.

Larkin, Brian. 1997: Indian films and Nigerian lovers: Media and the creation of parallel modernities. In *Africa* 67 (3).

Latour, Bruno and Woolgar, Steve. 1986: *Laboratory Life: The Construction of Scientific Facts*. Princeton, NJ: Princeton University Press.

Lave, Jean. 1977: Cognitive consequences of traditional apprenticeship training in West Africa. In Council on Anthropology and Education *Newsletter*, Pittsburgh, 8 (3), 177–80.

——. 1991: *Situated Learning: Legitimate Peripheral Participation*. Cambridge: Cambridge University Press.

Lavie, Smadar. 1990: *The Poetics of Military Occupation: Mzeina Allegories of Bedouin Identity under Israeli and Egyptian Rule*. Berkeley: University of California Press.

Lawrence, Denise L. and Low, Setha M. 1990: Built environment and spatial form. In *Annual Review of Anthropology* 19, 453–505.

Lawrence, P. 1995: Work of oracles: overcoming political silences in Mattakalapu. Paper presented to the 5th Srilankan Conference, Indiana.

Le Breton, David. 1990: *Anthropologie du corps et modernité*. Paris: Presses Universitaires de France.

Leach, Edmund. 1960: The frontiers of Burma. In *Comparative Studies in Society and History* 3, 49–68.

Leach, Edmund R. 1961: *Pul Eliya, a Village in Ceylon: A Study of Land Tenure and Kinship*. Cambridge: Cambridge University Press.

——. 1962[1961]: *Rethinking Anthropology*. Monographs on social anthropology; no. 22. London: University of London, Athlone Press.

——. 1961: Lévi-Strauss in the Garden of Eden: an examination of some recent developments in the analysis of myth. In *Transactions* (New York Academy of Sciences, series, II) 23 (4), 386–96.

——. 1970: *Claude Lévi-Strauss*. London: Fontana/Collins.

Leavitt, John. 1996: Meaning and feeling in the anthropology of emotions. In *American Ethnologist* 23 (3), 514–39.

Léenhardt, Maurice. 1947: *Do Kamo: la personne et le mythe dans le monde mélanésien*. Paris: Gallimard.

Lefkowitz, Mary. 1996: *Not Out of Africa: How Afrocentrism became an Excuse to Teach Myth as History*. New York: Basic Books.

Lenclud, Gérard. 1988: Des idées et des hommes: patronage électoral et culture politique en Corse. In *Revue Française de Science Politique* 38 (5), 770–82.

Lévi-Strauss, Claude. 1949: *Les Structures Élémentaires de la Parenté*. Paris: Presses Universitaires de France.

——. 1955a: The structural study of myth. In *Journal of American Folklore* 68, 428–44.

——. 1955b: *Tristes Tropiques*. Paris: Plon.

——. 1963: *Structural Anthropology*. New York: Basic Books.

——. 1966: *The Savage Mind*. Chicago: University of Chicago Press.

——. 1964: *Le cru et le cuit*. Paris: Plon.

——. 1969: *The Raw and the Cooked: Introduction to a Science of Mythology*, vol. 1. Trans. J. and D. Weightman. New York: Harper and Row.

——. 1978: *Myth and Meaning: Five Talks for Radio*. London: Routledge and Kegan Paul.

Lévy-Bruhl, Lucien. 1927: *L'âme primitive. Travaux de l'Année sociologique*. 2nd edn. Paris: F. Alcan.

Lewis, Ioan. 1961: Force and fission in northern Somali lineage structure. In *American Anthropologist* 63 (1), 94–112.

Liechty, M. 1995: Media, markets and modernization: youth identities and the experience of modernity in Kathmandu, Nepal. In V. Amit-Talai and H. Wulff (eds.), *Youth Cultures: A Cross-Cultural Perspective*. London: Routledge 166–201.

Lienhardt, R. G. 1964: *Social Anthropology*. London: Oxford University Press.

Lincoln, Bruce. 1981: *Emerging from the Chrysalis: Studies in Rituals of Women's Initiation*. Cambridge, MA: Harvard University Press.

Lindstrom, Lamont. 1995: Cargoism and Occidentalism. In J. G. Carrier (ed.), *Occidentalism: Images of the West*. Oxford: Clarendon Press, 33–60.

Linton, Ralph. 1936: *The Study of Man*. New York: Appleton-Century-Crofts.

Little, Peter D. and Painter, Michael. 1995: Discourse, politics, and the development process: reflections on Escobar's anthropology and the development encounter. In *American Ethnologist* 22 (3), 602–9.

Llobera et al. 1986: Fieldwork in Southwestern Europe: Anthropological Panacea or Epistomological [sic] Straitjacket? *Critique of Anthropology* 6 (2), 25–33.

Lock, Margaret. 1996. The quest for human organs and the violence of zeal. Cited in V. Das, Sufferings, theodicies, disciplinary practices, appropriations, *International Social Science Journal* 49 (154) (1997), 563–72.

Lomax, Alan. 1968: *Folk Song Style and Culture*. Washington, DC: American Association for the advancement of Science 88.

Low, Setha M. 1996: Spatializing culture: the social production and social construction of public space in Costa Rica. In *American Ethnologist* 23 (4), 861–79.

Lozada, Eriberto P., Jr. 1998: What it means to be Hakka in cyberspace: diasporic ethnicity and the Internet. In Sidney C. H. Cheung (ed.), *On the South China Track: Perspectives on Anthropological Research and Teaching*. Hong Kong: Hong Kong Institute of Asia-Pacific Studies, Chinese University of Hong Kong, 149–82.

Lukes, Steven. 1973: *Emile Durkheim, his Life and Work: A Historical and Critical Study*. London: Allen Lane.

Lutz, Catherine A. and Abu-Lughod, L. (eds.). 1990: *Language and the Politics of Emotion*. Cambridge: Cambridge University Press.

MacAloon, John J. 1981: *This Great Symbol: Pierre de Coubertin and the Origins of the Modern Olympic Games*. Chicago: University of Chicago Press.

——. 1984: Introduction: Cultural Performance, Culture Theory. In J. J. MacAloon (ed.), *Rite, Drama, Festival, Spectacle: Rehearsals toward a Theory of Cultural Performance*. Philadelphia: Institute for the Study of Human Issues, 1–15.

Mach, Z. 1994: National anthems: the case of Chopin as a national composer. In M. Stokes (ed.), *Ethnicity, Identity and Music: The Musical Construction of Place*. Oxford: Berg.

Macpherson, C. B. 1962: *The Political Theory of Possessive Individualism: Hobbes to Locke*. Oxford: Clarendon Press.

Maddox, Richard. 1995: Revolutionary anticlericalism and hegemonic processes in an Andalusian town, August 1936. In *American Ethnologist* 22 (1), 125–43.

——. 1998: Founding a convent in early modern Spain: cultural history, hegemonic processes, and the plurality of the historical subject. In *Rethinking History: The Journal of Theory and Practice* 2, 173–98.

Malaby, Thomas M. 1999: Fateful misconceptions: rethinking paradigms of chance among gamblers in Crete. In *Social Analysis* 43 (1), 141–64.

Malarney, Shawn Kingsley. 1996: The limits of "State Functionalism" and the reconstruction of funeral rule in contemporary Vietnam. In *American Ethnologist* 23 (3), 540–60.

Malinowski, Bronislaw. 1940: *The Scientific Basis of Applied Anthropology*. Roma: Reale Accademia d'Italia.

——. 1948: *Magic, Science, and Religion, and Other Essays*. Boston: Beacon Press.

——. 1962: *Sex, Culture, and Myth*. New York: Harcourt, Brace, and World.

——. 1967: *A Diary in the Strict Sense of the Term*. 1st edn. New York: Harcourt, Brace & World.

Malkki, Liisa Helena. 1989: *Purity and Exile: Violence, Memory and National Cosmology among Hutu Refugees in Tanzania*. Chicago: University of Chicago Press.

Malkki, Liisa. 1997: News and culture: Transitory phenomena and the fieldwork tradition. In Akhil Gupta and James Ferguson (eds.), *Anthropological Locations: Boundaries and Grounds of a Field Science*. Berkeley: University of California Press, 86–101.

Mankekar, Purnima. 1993a: National texts and gendered lives: an ethnography of television viewers in a North Indian city. In *American Ethnologist* 20 (3), 543–63.

——. 1993b: Television tales and woman's rage: a nationalist recasting of Draupadi's "disrobing." In *Public Culture* 5 (3), 469–92.

——. 1999: *Screening Culture, Viewing Politics: An Ethnography of Television, Womanhood, and Nation Postcolonial India*. Durham, NC: Duke University Press.

Manuel, Peter. 1993: *Cassette Culture: Popular Music and Technology in North India*. Chicago: University of Chicago Press.

Marcus, George E. and Fischer, Michael M. J. 1986: *Anthropology as Cultural Critique*. Chicago: University of Chicago Press.

Marcus, George E. 1992: *Lives in Trust: The Fortunes of Dynastic Families in Late Twentieth-Century America*. Boulder: Westview Press.

——. 1995: Ethnography in/of the world system: the emergence of multi-sited ethnography. In *Annual Review of Anthropology* 24, 95–117.

Marx, Karl. 1961[republished]: *Capital*, vol. 1. Moscow: Foreign Publishing House.

Mascia-Lees, Frances E., Sharpe, Patricia, and Cohen, Colleen Ballerino. 1987–8: The post-modernist turn in anthropology: cautions from a feminist perspective. In *Journal of the Steward Anthropological Society* 17 (1–2), 251–82.

Mason, O. T. 1896: Influence of environment upon human industries or arts. In *Annual Report of the Smithsonian Institution for 1895*, 639–65.

Mauss, Marcel. 1954: *The Gift*. Transl. by Ian Cunnison, London: Cohen and West.

——. 1979: Seasonal variations of the Eskimo: a study in social morphology. Collab. Henri Beuchat. Trans. James J. Fox. London: Routledge & Kegan Paul.

Maybury-Lewis, David. 1989: The Quest for Harmony. In D. Maybury-Lewis and U. Almagor (eds.), *The Attraction of the Opposites: Thought and Society in the Dualistic Mode*. Ann Arbor: University of Michigan Press, 1–18.

Mbembe, Achille. 1992: Provisional Notes on the Postcolony. In *Africa* 62 (1), 3–37.

McCall, John C. 1999: *Dancing Histories: Heuristic Ethnography with the Ohafia Ibo*. Ann Arbor: University of Michigan Press.

McDonald, Maryon. 1996: "Unity" and "Diversity": Some tensions in the construction of Europe. In *Social Anthropology* 4 (1), 47–60.

McKaskie, T. C. 1989: Asantesem: reflections on discourse and text in Africa. In K. Barber and P. F. de Moraes Farias (eds.), *Discourse and Its Disguises: The Interpretation of African Oral Texts*. Birmingham University African Studies Series no. 1, 70–86.

McLuhan, Marshall. 1962: *The Gutenberg Galaxy*. Toronto: University of Toronto Press.

——. 1964: *Understanding Media*. New York: New American Library.

Meeker, Michael E. 1979: *Literature and Violence in North Arabia*. Cambridge studies in cultural systems; 3. Cambridge: Cambridge University Press.

Merriam, Alan P. 1964: *The Anthropology of Music*. Evanston: Northwestern University Press.

Miceli, Silvana. 1982: *In nome del segno: introduzione alla semiotica della cultura*. Palermo: Sellerio.

Middleton, John. 1967. Introduction. In Middleton (ed.), 1967, *Myth and Cosmos*, pp. ix–xi.

——. (ed.). 1967: *Myth and Cosmos: Readings in Mythology and Symbolism*. Garden City. New York: The Natural History Press.

Middleton, John and Tait, David (eds.). 1958: *Tribes without Rulers; Studies in African Segmentary Systems*. London: Routledge and Kegan Paul.

Miller, Daniel. 1987: *Material Culture and Mass Consumption*. Oxford: Basil Blackwell.

——. 1995: Consumption and commodities. In *Annual Review of Anthropology* 24, 141–61.

——. (ed.). 1995: *Acknowledging Consumption: A Review of New Studies*. London: Routledge.

Mills, Mary Beth. 1999: *Thai Women in the Global Labor Force: Consuming Desires, Contested Selves*. New Brunswick, NJ: Rutgers University Press.

Milton, Kay. 1993a: Introduction: environmentalism and anthropology. In K. Milton (ed.), *Environmentalism: The View from Anthropology*. London and New York: Routledge.

——. (ed.). 1993b: *Environmentalism: The View from Anthropology*. London and New York: Routledge.

——. 1996: *Environmentalism and Cultural Theory: Exploring the Role of Anthropology in Environmental Discourse*. London and New York: Routledge.

Miner, Horace. 1956: Body ritual among the Nacirema. In *American Anthropologist* 58, 503–7.

Mintz, Jerome R. 1982: *The Anarchists of Casas Viejas*. Chicago: University of Chicago Press.

——. 1997: *Carnival Song and Society: Gossip, Sexuality, and Creativity in Andalusia. Explorations in Anthropology*. Oxford: Berg.

Mintz, Sidney W. 1985: *Sweetness and Power: The Place of Sugar in Modern History*. New York: Viking.

Mishra, V., Jeffery, P., and Shoesmith, B. 1989: The actor as parallel text in Bombay cinema. In *Quarterly Review of Film & Video* 11, 49–67.

Moeran, Brian. 1989: A Japanese Rite of Power. *Anthropology Today* 5 (5), 17–18.

——. 1996: *A Japanese Advertising Agency: an anthropology of media and markets*. ConsumAsiaN book series. Richmond, Surrey: Curzon Press and Honolulu: University of Hawai'I Press.

Mohammed, Juanita and Juhasz, Alexandra. 1996: Knowing each other through AIDS video: A dialogue between AIDS activist videomakers. In George E. Marcus (ed.), *Connected: Engagements with Media*. Chicago: University of Chicago Press.

Mohanty, Chandra. 1991: Under western eyes: feminist scholarship and colonial discourses. In C. Mohanty, A. Russo, and L. Tores (eds.), *Third World Women and the Politics in Feminism*. Bloomington: Indiana University Press, 51–80.

Mole, John. 1995: *Mind Your Manners: Managing Business Cultures in Europe*. London: Nicholas Brealey.

Momigliano, Arnaldo. 1986: How Roman emperors became gods. In *American Scholar* 55, 181–94.

Moore, Donald C. 1994: Anthropology is dead, long live anthropology: postcolonialism, literary studies and anthropology's "nervous present." In *Journal of Anthropological Research* 50, 345–66.·

Moore, Henrietta L. 1994: *A Passion for Difference: Essays in Anthropology and Gender*. Bloomington: Indiana University Press.

Moore, Sally Falk. 1987: Explaining the present: theoretical dilemmas in processual ethnography. In *American Ethnologist* 14 (4), 727–36.

——. (ed.). 1993: *Moralizing States and the Ethnography of the Present*. American Ethnological Society monograph series no. 5. Arlington, VA: American Anthropological Association.

Moran, Emilio F. 1981: *Developing the Amazon*. Bloomington: Indiana University Press.

——. 1990: Ecosystem ecology in biology and anthropology: a critical assessment. In E. F. Moran (ed.), *The Ecosystem Approach in Anthropology*. Ann Arbor: University of Michigan Press, 3–40.

Moreno Navarro, Isidoro. 1984: Doble colonizacion de la antropología andaluza y las perspectivas de futuro. In *Carcia de Orta Serie de Antropobiología* 3 (1–2), 27–35.

Morgan, G. 1991: Advocacy as a form of social science. In P. Harries-Jones (ed.), *Making Knowledge Count: Advocacy and Social Science*. Montreal and Kingston: McGill-Queen's Press, 223–31.

Morley, David. 1980: *The "Nationwide" Audience: Structure and Decoding*. London: British Film Institute.

——. 1989: Changing paradigms in audience studies. In E. Seiter, H. Borchers, G. Kreutzner, and E. M. Warth, *Remote Control: Television, Audiences, and Cultural Power*. London: Routledge, 16–43.

Morphy, Howard. 1989. From dull to brilliant: the aesthetics of spiritual power among the Yolngu. *Man* (n.s.) 24, 21–40.

Moss, David. 1979: Bandits and boundaries in Sardinia. In *Man* (n.s.) 14 (3), 477–96.

Mosse, George L. 1985: *Nationalism and Sexuality: Respectability and Abnormal Sexuality in Modern Europe*. 1st edn. New York: Harold. Fertig.

Mudimbe, V. Y. 1988: *The Invention of Africa*. Bloomington: Indiana University Press.

Mulvey, Laura. 1989: Visual pleasure and narrative cinema. In Laura Mulvey, *Visual and Other Pleasures*. Bloomington: Indiana University Press, 14–28.

Murua, Martin de. 1964: *Historia general del Peru*. Madrid: Instituto Gonzalo Fernández de Oviedo.

Myers, Charles S. 1903: Smell. In A. Haddon (ed.), *Reports of the Cambridge Anthropological Expedition to the Torres Straits, vol. 2: Physiology and Psychology*. Cambridge: Cambridge University Press, 169–85.

Nadel-Klein, Jane. 1991: Reweaving the fringe: localism, tradition, and representation in british ethnography. In *American Ethnologist* 18 (3), 500–17.

Nader, Laura. 1972: Up the anthropologist – perspective gained from studying up. In D. Hymes (ed.), *Reinventing Anthropology*, New York: Pantheon Press, 284–311.

Nash, June. 1970: *In the Eyes of the Ancestors*. New Haven: Yale University Press.

——. 1989: *From Tank Town to High Tech: The Clash of Community and Industrial Cycles*. Albany: SUNY Press.

——. 1993a: The reassertion of indigenous identity: Mayan responses to state intervention in Chiapas. In *Latin American Research Review* 30 (3), 7–42.

——. (ed.). 1993b: *Crafts in the World Market*. Albany: SUNY Press.

——. (ed.). 1995: *The Explosion of Communities in Chiapas*. Copenhagen: IWGIA.

——. 1997: The fiesta of the world: the Zapastista uprising and radical democracy in Mexico. In *American Anthropologist* 99 (2), 261–74.

Needham, Rodney. 1962: *Structure and Sentiment: A Test Case in Social Anthropology*. Chicago: University of Chicago Press.

——. 1963: Introduction. In E. Durkheim and M. Mauss (eds.), *Primitive Classification*. London: Cohen & West, vii–xlviii.

——. (ed.). 1971: *Rethinking Kinship and Marriage*. A.S.A. monographs; 11. London: Tavistock Publications.

——. 1972: *Belief, Language, and Experience*. Oxford: Basil Blackwell.

——. 1973: *Right & Left; Essays on Dual Symbolic Classification*. Chicago: University of Chicago Press.

Nelson, Robert S. 1989: The discourse of icons, then and now. In *Art History* 12 (2), 144–63.

Netting, Robert McC. 1982. The ecological perspective: holism and scholasticism in anthropology. In E. Adamson Hoebel, Richard Curries, and Susan Kaiser (eds.), *Crisis in Anthropology: The View from Spring Hill, 1980*. New York: Garland, 271–92.

——. 1986: *Cultural Ecology*. 2nd ed. Prospect Heights, IL: Waveland Press.

——. Wilk, Richard R., and Arnould, Eric J. (eds.). 1984: *Households: Comparative and Historical Studies of the Domestic Group*. Berkeley: University of California Press.

Nilsson, Martin P. 1954: *Religion as Man's Protest against the Meaninglessness of Events*. Lund: CWK Gleerup.

Nora, Pierre. (ed.). 1984: *Les lieux de mémoire*. Paris: Gallimard.

Nussdorfer, L. 1993: Review essay. In *History and Theory* 32, 74–83.

Obeyesekere, Gananath. 1968: Theodicy, sin and salvation in a sociology of Buddhism. In E. R. Leach (ed.), *Cambridge Papers in Social Anthropology* 5, 7–40.

——. 1992: *The Apotheosis of Captain Cook*. Princeton; Princeton University Press.

Okely, Judith. 1983: *The Traveller-Gypsies*. Cambridge: Cambridge University Press.

Ong, Aihwa. 1987: *Spirits of Resistance and Capitalist Discipline*. Albany: SUNY Press.
——. 1996: Anthropology, China, and modernities: the geopolitics of cultural kowledge. In Henrietta Moore (ed.), *The Future of Anthropological Knowledge*. London: Routledge, 60–92.
Ong, Walter. J. 1967: *The Presence of the World*. New Haven: Yale University Press.
——. 1969: World as view and world as event. In *American Anthropologist* 71 (4), 634–47.
——. 1981: Oral remembering and narrative structures. In *Georgetown University Round Table on Language and Linguistics*. Washington: Georgetown University, 12–24.
——. 1982a: *Orality and Literacy*. New York: Methuen.
——. 1982b: Literacy and orality in our times. In *Pacific Quarterly Moana* 7 (2), 8–21.
Öncü, Ayşe. 1995: Packaging Islam: cultural politics on the landscape of Turkish commercial television. In *Public Culture* 8 (1), 51–71.
Orlove, Benjamin and Bauer, Arnold J. 1997: Giving importance to imports. In Benjamin, Orlove (ed.), *The Allure of the Foreign: Imported Goods in Postcolonial Latin America*. Ann Arbor: University of Michigan Press, 1–30.
Ortiz, Renato. 1994: *Mundialização e Cultura, 2nd edition*. São Paulo: Brasiliense.
Ortner, Sherry B. and Whitehead, Harriett. (eds.). 1981: *Sexual Meanings, the Cultural Construction of Gender and Sexuality*. Cambridge: Cambridge University Press.
Ortner, Sherry B. 1984: Theory in anthropology in the Sixties. In *Comparative Studies in Society and History* 26 (1), 126–66.
Ossio, Juan M. 1977: Myth and history: the seventeenth-century chronicle of Gumana Poma de Ayala. In Ravindra K. Jain (ed.), *Text and Context: The Social Anthropology of Tradition*. Philadelphia: Institute for the Study of Human Issues, 51–93.
Ott, Sandra. 1979: Aristotle among the Basques: the "cheese analogy" of conception. *Man* (n.s.) 14, 699–711.
——. 1981: *The Circle of Mountains: a Basque Shepherding Community*. Oxford: Clarendon Press; New York: Oxford University Press.
Oxfeld, Ellen. 1993: *Blood, Sweat, and Mahjong: Family and Enterprise in an Overseas Chinese Community*. Anthropology of contemporary issues. Ithaca, NY: Cornell University Press.
Paine, Robert. 1967: What is gossip about: an alternative hypothesis. In *Man*, n.s. 2 (2), 278–85.
——. 1986: *Advocacy and Anthropology: First Encounters*. St. John's, Newfoundland: Institute of Social and Economic Research, Memorial University.
——. (ed.). 1981: *Politically Speaking: Cross-cultural Studies of Rhetoric*. Philadelphia: Institute for the Study of Human Issues.
Palomino Flores, Salvador. 1984: *El sistema de oposiciones en la comunidad de Sarhua*. Lima: Editorial Pueblo Indio.
Panofsky, E. 1985: *El significado de las artes visuales*. Madrid: Alianza Editorial.
Papadakis, Yiannis. 1993: Politics of memory and forgetting in Cyprus. In *Journal of Mediterranean Studies* 3 (1), 139–54.
——. 1998: Greek Cypriot narratives of history and collective identity: nationalism as a contested process. In *American Ethnologist* 25 (2), 149–65.
Pappas, Takis S. 1999: *Making Party Democracy in Greece*. London: Macmillan Press.
Paredes, Américo. 1958: *With His Pistol in His Hand: A Border Ballad and Its Hero*. Austen: University of Texas Press.

Parezco, Nancy J. 1983: *Navajo Sandpainting: From Religious Act to Commercial Art.* Tucson: University of Arizona Press.

Park, Robert Ezra. 1964: *Race and Culture.* New York: Free Press.

Parmentier, Richard J. 1987: *The Sacred Remains: myth, history, and polity in Belau.* Chicago: University of Chicago Press.

Parry, Johnathon P. 1986: The gift, the Indian gift and the "Indian gift." In *Man* (n.s.) 21 (3), 453–73.

Peacock, James L. 1968: *Rites of Modernization: Symbolic and Social Aspects of Indonesian Proletarian Drama.* Chicago: University of Chicago Press.

Peek, Philip M. 1994: The sounds of silence: cross-world communication and the auditory arts in African societies. In *American Ethnologist* 21 (3), 474–94.

Peel, J. D. Y. 1993: Review essay. In *History and Theory* 32, 74–83.

Pieterse, Jan Nederveen. 1992: *White on Black: Images of Africa and Blacks in Western Popular Culture.* New Haven, CT: Yale University Press.

Pigg, Stacy Leigh. 1992: Inventing social categories through place: social representations and development in Nepal. In *Comparative Studies in Society and History* 34 (3), 491–513.

——. 1995a: Acronyms of effacement: traditional medical practitioners (TMP) in international health development. In *Social Science and Medicine* 41 (1), 47–68.

——. 1995b: The social symbolism of healing in Nepal. In *Ethnology* 34 (1), 1–20.

——. 1996: The credible and the credulous: the question of "Villagers' Beliefs" in Nepal. In *Cultural Anthropology* 11 (2), 160–201.

Pinney, Christopher forthcoming: The nation (un)pictured? Chromolithography and "popular" politics in India: 1878–1995. In *Critical Inquiry*.

Plattner, Stuart. (ed.). 1989: *Economic Anthropology.* Stanford: Stanford University Press.

——. 1996: *High Art Down Home: an economic ethnography of a local art market.* Chicago: University of Chicago Press.

Pocius, Gerald L. 1979: Hooked rugs in Newfoundland: the representation of social structure in design. In *Journal of American Folklore* 92 (365), 273–84.

Pocock, David F. 1961: *Social Anthropology.* London and New York: Sheed and Ward.

Polanyi, Karl, Arensberg, Conrad M., and Pearson, Harry W. (eds.). 1957: *Trade and Market in the early Empires.* Glencoe, IL: The Free Press.

Ponting, Clive. 1991: *A Green History of the World.* London: Sinclair-Stevenson.

Porter, R. 1986: Foreword to A. Corbin, In *The Foul and the Fragrant: Odor and the French Social Imagination.* Trans. M. L. Kochan, R. Porter, and C. Prendergast. Cambridge, MA: Harvard University Press, v–vii.

——. 1993: The rise of physical examination. In W. F. Bynum and R. Porter (eds.), *Medicine and the Five Senses.* Cambridge: Cambridge University Press, 179–97.

Pourcher, Yves. 1985: Parente et representation politique en Lozère. In *Terrain* 4, 27–41.

——. 1987: *Les Maîtres de granit: Les notables de Lozère du XVIIIe siècle à nos jours.* Paris: Olivier Orban.

——. 1991: Tournée electorale. In *Homme* 119, 61–79.

Povinelli, Elizabeth A. 1993: *Labour's Lot: The Power, History, and Culture of Aboriginal Action.* Chicago: University of Chicago Press.

Powdermaker, Hortense. 1950: *Hollywood the Dream Factory: An Anthropologist Looks at the Movie-Makers.* Boston: Little, Brown.

Pribram, E. Deidre. (ed.). 1988: *Female Spectators: Looking at Film and Television.* London: Verso.

Prica, I. 1995: Between destruction and deconstruction: the preconditions of the Croatian ethnography of war. *Collegium Anthropologicum* (Zagreb) 19(1), 7–16.

Queiroz, M. 1985: The samba schools of Rio de Janeiro or the domestication of an urban mass. In *Diogenes* 129, 1–32.

Rabinbach, A. G. 1976: The aesthetics of production in the Third Reich. In *Journal of Contemporary History*, 11, 43–74.

Rabinow, Paul. 1977: *Reflections on Fieldwork in Morocco*. Berkeley: University of California Press.

——. 1989: *French Modern: Norms and Forms of the Social Environment*. Cambridge, MA: MIT Press.

——. 1996: *Essays on the Anthropology of Reason*. Princeton, NJ: Princeton University Press.

Rabinowitz, Dan. 1996: *Overlooking Nazareth: The Ethnography of Exclusion in Galilee*. Cambridge: Cambridge University Press.

Radcliffe-Brown, A. R. 1952: *Structure and Function in Primitive Society: Essays and Addresses*. Glencoe, IL: The Free Press; London: Cohen & West.

Radway, Janice A. 1984: *Reading the Romance: Women, Patriarchy, and Popular Literature*. Chapel Hill: The University of North Carolina Press.

Raheja, Gloria Goodwin. 1996: Caste, nationalism, and the speech of the colonized: entextualization and disciplinary control in India. In *American Ethnologist* 23 (3), 496–513.

Ramphele, Mamphela. 1992: *A Bed Called Home: Life in the Migrant Labour Hostels of Capte Town*. Edinburgh: Edinburgh University Press in association with the International African Institute.

——. 1996a: Political widowhood in South Africa: the embodiment of ambiguity. In *Daedalus* 125 (1), 99–119.

——. 1996b: Teach me how to be a man. Cited in V. Das, Sufferings, theodicies, disciplinary practices, appropriations, *International Social Science Journal* 49 (154) (1997), 563–72.

Rappaport, Joanne. 1994: *Cumbe Reborn: An Andean Ethnography of History*. Chicago: University of Chicago Press.

Rappaport, Roy. 1968: *Pigs for the Ancestors*. New Haven: Yale University Press.

——. 1971: Nature, culture and ecological anthropology. In H. L. Shapiro (ed.), In *Man, Culture and Society*. Oxford: Oxford University Press, 237–67.

——. 1979: *Ecology, Meaning, and Religion*. Richmond, CA: North Atlantic Books.

Rapport, Nigel. 1994: *The Prose and the Passion: Anthropology, Literature, and the Writing of E.M. Forster*. Manchester: Manchester University Press.

Redfield, Robert. 1953: *The Primitive World and its Transformations*. Ithaca, NY: Cornell University Press.

——. 1965: *Peasant Society and Culture: an anthropological approach to civilization*. Chicago: University of Chicago Press.

Reed-Danahay, Deborah. 1993: Talking about resistance: ethnography and theory in rural France. In *Anthropological Quarterly* 66 (4), 221–9.

——. 1995: The Kabyle and the French: Occidentalism in Bourdieu's *Theory of Practice*. In James G. Carrier (ed.), 1995, *Occidentalism*, 61–84.

——. 1996: *Education and Identity in Rural France: The Politics of Schooling*. Cambridge: Cambridge University Press.

Reed-Danahay, Deborah E. (ed.). 1997: *Auto/ethnography: Rewriting the Self and the Society*. Oxford and New York: Berg.

Reichel-Dolmatoff, Gerardo. 1985: *Basketry as Metaphor: Arts and Crafts of the Desana Indians of the Northwest Amazon.* Occasional Papers of the Museum of Cultural History Los Angeles: University of California.

Reynolds, Pamela. 1995: *The grounds of all making: State Violence, the Family, and Political Activists.* Pretoria: Cooperative Research Programme on Marriage and Family Life, Human Sciences Research Council.

Ribeiro, Gustavo Lins. 1994a: *Transnational Capitalism and Hydropolitics in Argentina.* Gainesville: University of Florida Press.

———. 1994b: *The Condition of Transnationality.* Brasília: Universidade de Brasília, Departamento de Antropologia, Série Antropologia No. 173.

———. 1998: Cybercultural politics and political activism at a distance in a transnational world. In S. Alvarez, E. Dagnino, and A. Escobar (eds.), *Cultures and Politics/ Politics of Cultures: Revisioning Latin American Social Movements.* Boulder: Westview Press, 325–52.

Ribeiro, G. L. and Little, Paul E. 1996: *Neo-Liberal Recipes, Environmental Cooks: The Transformation of Amazonian Agency.* Brasília: Departamento de Antropologia, Universidade de Brasília.

Richards, Audrey. 1982: *Chisungu: A Girl's Initiation Ceremony Among the Bemba of Zambia.* London: Tavistock.

Riles, Annelise. 2000: *The Network Inside Out.* Ann Arbor: University of Michigan Pres.

Ritchie, Ian. 1991: Fusion of the faculties: a study of the language of the senses in Hausaland. In D. Howes (ed.), *The Varieties of Sensory Experience: A Sourcebook in the Anthropology of the Senses.* Toronto: University of Toronto Press, 192–202.

Rivière, C. 1988: *Les liturgies politiques.* Paris: PUF.

Roberts, Michael. 1982: *Caste Conflict and Elite Formation: The Rise of a Karava Elite in Lanka, 1500–1931.* Cambridge: Cambridge University Press.

———. 1989: A tale of resistance: the story of the arrival of the Portuguese. In *Ethnos* 54, 69–82.

———. 1994: *Exploring Confrontation.* Chur: Harwood Academic Publishers.

Rodaway, Paul. 1994: *Sensuous Geographies.* London: Routledge.

Rogers, Susan Carol. 1985: Gender in southwestern France: the myth of male dominance revisited. In *Anthropology* 9 (1–2), 65–86.

Rosaldo, Renato. 1988: Ideology, place, and people without culture. In *Cultural Anthropology* 3, 77–87.

———. 1989: *Culture and Truth: The Remaking of Social Analysis.* Boston: Beacon Press.

Rose, Deborah Bird. 1992: *Dingo makes us Human: Life and Land in an Aboriginal Australian Culture.* Cambridge: Cambridge University Press.

———. 1993: Worshipping Captain Cook. In *Social Analysis* 34, 43–9.

Roseman, Marina. 1991: *Healing Sounds from the Malaysian Rainforest.* Berkeley: University of California Press.

Roseman, Sharon. 1996: How we built the road: the politics of memory in rural Galicia. In *American Ethnologist* 23, 836–60.

Rosen, Lawrence. (ed.). 1995: *Other Intentions: Cultural Contexts and the Attribution of Inner States.* Santa Fe: School of American Research Press.

Rossi-Landi, Ferruccio. 1983: *Language as Work and Trade: a semiotic homology for linguistics and economics.* South Hadley, MA: Bergin and Garvey.

Sachs, Wolfgang. (ed.). 1992: *The Development Dictionary.* London: Zed Books.

Sahlins, Marshall. 1972: *Stone Age Economics.* Chicago: Aldine.

———. 1976a: *The Use and Abuse of Biology: An Anthropological Critique of Sociobiology.* Ann Arbor: University of Michigan Press.

——. 1976b: *Culture and Practical Reason*. Chicago: University of Chicago Press.

——. 1981: *Historical Metaphors and Mythical Realities*. Ann Arbor: University of Michigan Press.

——. 1985: *Islands of History*. Chicago: University of Chicago Press.

——. 1992: The economics of Develop-Man in the Pacific. *Res* 21, 13–25.

——. 1993: Goodbye to tristes tropes: ethnography in the context of modern world history. In *Journal of Modern History* 65, 1–25.

——. 1995: *How "Natives" Think: About Captain Cook, for Example*. Chicago: University of Chicago Press.

——. 1996: The sadness of sweetness: the native anthropology of western cosmology. In *Current Anthropology* 37 (3), 395–415.

Sahlins, Peter. 1989: *Boundaries: The Making of France and Spain in the Pyrenees*. Berkeley: University of California Press.

Said, Edward. 1975: *Beginnings: Intention and Method*. New York: Basic Books.

——. 1979: *Orientalism*. New York: Vintage Books.

——. 1981: *Covering Islam: How the Media and the Experts Determine How we see the Rest of the World*. 1st edn. New York: Pantheon Books.

——. 1983: *The World, the Text, and the Critic*. Cambridge, MA: Harvard University Press.

Salzman, Philip Carl. 1978: Does complementary opposition exist? In *American Anthropologist* 80 (1), 53–70.

Samuel, Raphael. (ed.). 1981: *People's History and Socialist Theory*. London: Routledge and Kegan Paul.

Sapir, Edward. 1938: Why cultural anthropology needs the psychiatrist. In *Psychiatry* 1, 7–12.

Sassen, Saskia. 1991: *The Global City: New York, London, Tokyo*. Princeton, NJ: Princeton University Press.

Scheffel, D. Z. 1992: Antropologie a etika ve východní Evrop (Anthropology and ethics in Eastern Europe). In *Národopisný vestníkceskoslovenský* 9 (51), 3–10.

Schein, Muriel Dimen. 1973: When is an Ethnic Group? Ecology and class structure in northern Greece. *Ethnology* 14, 83–97.

Scheper-Hughes, Nancy. 1992: *Death without Weeping: The Violence of Everyday Life in Brazil*. Berkeley: University of California Press.

Schiller, Friedrich. 1982: *On the Aesthetics and Education of Man*. E. M. Wilkinson and L. A. Willoughby (eds. and trans.). German text with English translation. Oxford: Clarendon Press.

Schneider, David Murray. 1980: *American Kinship: A Cultural Account*. 2nd edn. Chicago: University of Chicago Press.

Schneider, Jane and Schneider, Peter. 1976: *Culture and Political Economy in Western Sicily*. New York: Academic Press.

——. 1994: Mafia, antimafia, and the question of Sicilian culture. In *Politics and Society* 22 (2), 237–58.

Schuck, P. 1987: *Agent Orange on Trial: Mass Toxic Disasters in the Court*. Cambridge, MA: Harvard University Press.

Scoditti, Giancarlo G. 1982: Aesthetics: the significance of apprenticeship on Kitawa. In *Man* (n.s.) 17 (1), 74–91.

Scott, David. 1992: Theory and post-colonial claims on anthropological disciplinarity. In *Critique of Anthropology* 12, 371–94.

——. 1994: *Formations of Ritual: Colonial and Anthropological Discourses on the Sinhala Yaktovil*. Minneapolis: University of Minnesota Press.

——. 1996: Postcolonial criticism and the claims of political modernity. In *Social Text* 48 (3), 1–26.

Scott, James C. 1985: *Weapons of the Weak: Everyday Forms of Peasant Resistance.* New Haven: Yale University Press.

——. 1998: *Seeing like a State: How Certain Schemes to Improve the Human Condition have Failed.* Yale agrarian studies. The Yale ISPS series. New Haven: Yale University Press.

Seeger, Anthony. 1975: The meaning of body ornaments. In *Ethnology* 14 (3), 211–24.

——. 1981: *Nature and Society in Central Brazil: The Suyá Indians of Mato Grosso.* Cambridge, MA: Harvard University Press.

——. 1987: *Why Suyá Sing: A Musical Anthropology of an Amazonian People.* Cambridge: Cambridge University Press.

Seeger, Charles. 1977: *Studies in Musicology, 1935–1975.* Berkeley: University of California Press.

Seremetakis, C. Nadia. 1991: *The Last Word: Women, Death and Divination in Inner Mani.* Chicago: University of Chicago Press.

——. 1993: Memory of the senses: historical perception, commensal exchange and Modernity. In *Visual Anthropology Review* 9 (2), 2–18.

——. (ed.). 1994: *The Senses Still: Memory and Perception as Material Culture in Modernity.* Boulder, CO: Westview Press.

Sevilla, Ampara and Aguilar Diaz, Miguel. (eds.). 1996: *Estudios recientes sobre cultura urbana en México.* Mexico City: Plaza y Valdés/INAH.

Sfez, Lucien. 1978: *L'enfer et le paradis: critique de la théologie politique.* Paris: PUF.

Shalinsky, Audrey C. 1980: Group prestige in northern Afghanistan: the case of an interethnic wedding. In *Ethnic Groups* 2 (4), 269–82.

Shamgar-Handelman, Lea. 1981: Administering to war widows in Israel: the birth of a social category. In *Social Analysis* 9, 24–47.

Shaw, Rosalind and Stewart, Charles. (eds.). 1994: *Syncretism/Anti-Syncretism: The Politics of Religious Synthesis.* London and New York: Routledge.

Shaw, Rosalind. 1997: Production of witchcraft, witchcraft as production: memory, modernity, and the slave trade in Sierra Leone. In *American Ethnologist* 24 (4), 856–76.

Shiva, Vandana. 1993: *Monocultures of the Mind: Perspectives on Biodiversity and Biotechnology.* London: Zed Books.

Shryock, Andrew. 1997: *Nationalism and the Genealogical Imagination: Oral History and Textual Authority in Tribal Jordan.* Berkeley: University of California Press.

Signorelli, Amalia. 1996: *Antropologia urbana: introduzione alla ricerca in Italia.* Milan: Guerini.

Silva, Tellez, Armando. 1992: *Imaginarios urbanos: Bogotá y São Paulo: cultura y communicación urbana en América Latina.* Bogotá: Tercer Mundo Editores.

——. 1994: Sociedade civil e a costrção de espaços públicos. In Dagnino (ed.) 1994 91–102.

Silver, Harry R. 1979: Ethnoart. In *Annual Review of Anthropology* 8, 267–307.

——. 1980: The culture of carving and the carving for cultural: content and context in artisan status among the Ashanti. In *American Ethnologist* 7 (3), 432–46.

Silverman, Sydel. 1975: *Three Bells of Civilization: The Life of an Italian Hill Town.* New York: Columbia University Press.

Silverstein, Michael and Urban, Greg (eds.). 1996: *Natural Histories of Discourse.* Chicago: University of Chicago Press.

Simmel, Georg. 1964: *Conflict and the Web of Group-Affiliations.* New York: Free Press.

Singer, Milton. 1972: *When a Great Tradition Modernizes.* New York: Praeger.

Smith, Adam. 1776: *An Inquiry into the Nature and Causes of the Wealth of Nations.* Dublin: Whitestone.

Smith, David M. 1998: An Athapaskan way of knowing: Chipewyan ontology. In *American Ethnologist* 25 (3), 412–32.

Sontag, Susan. 1978: *On Photography.* New York: Farrar, Straus and Giroux.

Southall, Aidan. (ed.). 1973: *Urban Anthropology: Cross-Cultural Studies of Urbanization.* New York: Oxford University Press.

Southall, Aidan William. 1976: Nuer and Dinka are people: ecology, ethnicity and logical possibility. In *Man* (n.s.) 11 (4), 463–91.

Soysal, Levent. 1999: *Projects of Culture: An Ethnographic Episode in the Life of Migrant Youth in Berlin.* Ph.D. Dissertation, Department of Anthropology, Harvard University.

Spencer, Jonathan. 1989: Anthropology as a kind of writing. In *Man* (n.s.) 24, 145–64.

Spitulnik, Debra. 1993: Anthropology and mass media. In *Annual Review of Anthropology* 22, 293–315.

Starrett, Gregory. 1998: *Putting Islam to Work: Education, Politics, and Religious Transformation in Egypt.* Berkeley: University of California Press.

Steedly, Mary M. 1993: *Hanging without a Rope: Narrative Experience in Colonial and Postcolonial Karoland.* Princeton, NJ: Princeton University Press.

Steiner, Christopher. 1994: *African Art in Transit.* Cambridge: Cambridge University Press.

Stenning, Derrick J. 1957: Transhumance, migratory drift, migration. In *Journal of the Royal Anthropological Institute* 87, 57–73.

Stephen, Lynn. 1995: Women's rights are human rights: the merging of feminine and feminist interests among El Salvador's mother of the disappeared (CO-MADRES). In *American Ethnologist* 22 (4), 807–27.

——. 1997: *Women and Social Movements in Latin America: Power from Below.* Austin, TX: University of Texas Press.

Steward, Julian. 1955: *Theory of Culture Change.* Urbana-Champaign, IL: University of Illinois Press.

Stewart, Kathleen. 1996: *A Space on the Other Side of the Road: Cultural Poetics in an "Other" America.* Princeton, NJ: Princeton University Press.

Stewart, Susan. 1984: *On Longing: Narratives of the Miniature, the Gigantic, the Souvenir, the Collection.* Baltimore: Johns Hopkins University Press.

Stocking, George W. (ed.). 1991: *Colonial Situations: Essays on the Contextualization of Ethnographic Knowledge.* Madison: University of Wisconsin Press.

——. 1995: *After Tylor: British Social Anthropology 1888–1951.* Madison: University of Wisconsin Press.

Stokes, Martin. 1994: Introduction: Ethnicity, Identity and Music. In M. Stokes (ed.), *Ethnicity, Identity and Music: The Musical Construction of Place.* Oxford: Berg, 1–27.

Stolcke, Verena. 1995: Talking culture: new boundaries, new rhetorics of exclusion in Europe. In *Current Anthropology* 36, 1–13.

Stoll, David. 1999: *Rigoberta Menchú and the Story of All Poor Guatemalans.* Boulder, CO: Westview Press.

Stoller, Paul. 1989: *The Taste of Ethnographic Things: The Senses in Anthropology.* Philadelphia: University of Pennsylvania Press.

——. 1995: *Embodying Colonial Memories: Spirit Possession, Power and the Hauka in West Africa.* New York: Routledge.

——. and Olkes, Cheryl. 1987: *In Sorcery's Shadow: A Memoir of Apprenticeship among the Songhay of Niger.* Chicago: University of Chicago Press.

Stone, Ruth M. 1982: *Let the Inside be Sweet: The Interpretation of Music Event among the Kpelle of Liberia*. Bloomington, IN: Indiana University Press.

——. 1988: *Dried Millet Breaking: Time, Words, and Song in the Woi Epic of the Kpelle*. Bloomington, In: Indiana University Press.

Strathern, Marilyn. 1988: *The Gender of the Gift*. Berkeley: University of California Press.

——. 1989: *After Nature: English Kinship in the Late Twentieth Century*. Cambridge: Cambridge University Press.

——. 1991: *Partial Connections*. Savage, MD: Rowman and Littlefield.

——. 1992: *Reproducing the Future: Essays on Anthropology, Kinship and the New Reproductive Technologies*. New York: Routledge.

Subrahmanyam, Sanjay. 1990: *The Political Economy of Commerce: Southern India, 1500–1650*. Cambridge: Cambridge University Press.

Suputtamongkol, Saipin. 2000: *Kukkabkon: Amnat le Kantotankatkun* (Prison and the Incarcerated: Power and Resistance). Bangkok: Thammasat University Press.

Sutton, David E. 1994: "Tradition and Modernity": Kalymnian constructions of identity and otherness. *Journal of Modern Greek Studies* 12, 239–60.

——. 1997: Local names, foreign claims: family inheritance and national heritage on a Greek island. *American Ethnologist* 24 (2), 415–37.

——. 1998: *Memories Cast in Stone: The Relevance of the Past in Everyday Life*. Mediterranean series. Oxford: Berg.

Swantz, M.-L. 1985: The contribution of anthropology to development work. In Harald O. Skar (ed.), *Anthropological Contributions to Planned Change and Development*. Gothenburg: Acta Universitatis Gothoburgensis.

Swartz, Marc J., Turner, Victor W., and Tuden, Arthur. (eds.). 1966: *Political Anthropology*. Chicago: Aldline.

Synnott, Anthony. 1991: Puzzling over the Senses from Plato to Marx. In D. Howes (ed.), *The Varieties of Sensory Experience: A Sourcebook in the Anthropology of the Senses*. Toronto: University of Toronto Press, 61–78.

——. 1993: *The Body Social: Symbolism, Self and Society*. London and New York: Routledge.

Tambiah, Stanley J. 1968: The magical power of words. In *Man* (n.s.) 3 (2), 175–208.

——. 1979: A performative approach to ritual. *Proceedings of the British Academy 65*, 113–69.

——. 1989: Ethnic conflict in the world today. In *American Ethnologist* 16 (2), 335–49.

——. 1990: *Magic, Science, Religion, and the Scope of Rationality*. Cambridge: Cambridge University Press.

——. 1992: *Buddhism Betrayed? Religion, Politics, and Violence in Sri Lanka*. Chicago: University of Chicago Press.

Taussig, Michael T. 1980: *The Devil and Commodity Fetishism in South America*. Chapel Hill, NC: University of North Carolina Press.

——. 1987: *Shamanism, Colonialism and the Wild Man: A Study of Terror and Healing*. Chicago: University of Chicago Press.

——. 1993: *Mimesis and Alterity: A Particular History of the Senses*. London and New York: Routledge.

Taylor, J. M. 1982: The politics of aesthetic debate: the case of Brazilian carnival. In *Ethnology* 21, 301–11.

Tedlock, Dennis. 1983: *The Spoken Word and the Work of Interpretation*. University of Pennsylvania publications in conduct and communication. Philadelphia: University of Pennsylvania Press.

Terrio, Susan J. 1996: Crafting Grand Cru chocolates in contemporary France. In *American Anthropologist* 98 (1), 67–80.

Thomas, Nicholas. 1985: Forms of personification and prestations. In *Mankind* 15 (3), 223–30.

——. 1989: *Out of Time: History and Evolution in Anthropological Discourse.* Cambridge: Cambridge University Press.

——. 1991a: Against ethnography. In *Cultural Anthropology* 6 (3), 306–22.

——. 1991b: *Entangled Objects: Exchange, Material Culture, and Colonialism in the Pacific.* Cambridge, MA: Harvard University Press.

——. 1997: *In Oceania: Visions, Artefacts, Histories.* Durham: Duke University Press.

Thomas, Rosie. 1985: Indian cinema: pleasures and popularity. In *Screen* 26 (3–4), 116–31.

Thompson, Michael. 1979: *Rubbish Theory: The Creation and Destruction of Value.* Oxford: Oxford University Press.

Trask, Haunani Kay. 1991: Natives and Anthropologists: the Colonial Struggle. In *The Contemporary Pacific* 3, 159–67.

Traweek, Sharon. 1988: *Beamtimes and Lifetimes: The World of High Energy Physicists.* Cambridge, MA: Harvard University Press.

Trawick, Margaret. 1988: Spirits and voices in Tamil songs. In *American Ethnologist* 15 (2), 193–215.

Trobriand Cricket: An Indigenous Response to Colonialism. Film, video, directed by Jerry W. Leach; film-maker, Gary Kildea; produced by Office of Information, Government of Papua New Guinea. No date.

Tsing, Anna Lowenhaupt. 1993: *In the Realm of the Diamond Queen: Marginality in an Out-of-the-Way Place.* Princeton, NJ: Princeton University Press.

Tuan, Yi-Fu. 1995: *Passing Strange and Wonderful: Aesthetics, Nature and Culture.* Tokyo and New York: Kodansha International.

Tucker, R. C. 1979: The rise of Stalin's personality cult. In *American Historical Review* 84, 347–66.

Turino, Thomas. 1993: *Moving Away from Silence.* Chicago: University of Chicago Press.

Turner, Frederick Jackon. 1961[1893]: The significance of the frontier in American history. In R. A. Billington (ed.), *Frontier and Section.* Englewood Cliffs, NJ: Prentice-Hall, 37–62.

Turner, Terence. 1993: Anthropology and multiculturalism: what is anthropology that multiculturalism should be mindful of? In *Cultural Anthropology* 8, 411–29.

——. 1995: Social body and embodied subject: bodiliness, subjectivity, and sociality among the Kayapo. In *Cultural Anthropology* 10 (2), 143–70.

Turner, Victor W. 1969: *The Ritual Process: Structure and Anti-Structure.* London: Routledge and Kegan Paul.

Turner, Victor. 1974: *Dramas, Fields, and Metaphors; Symbolic Action in Human Society.* Symbol, myth, and ritual series. Ithaca, NY: Cornell University Press.

——. 1982: *From Ritual to Theatre.* New York: Performing Arts Journal Publications.

——. 1986: *The Anthropology of Performance.* New York: PAJ Publications.

Tweedie, Ann. Forthcoming. *"Drawing back culture": The Makah Tribe's Struggle to Implement the Native American Graves Protection and Repatriation Act* [provisional title]. Seattle: University of Washington Press.

Tyler, Stephen A. 1969: *Cognitive Anthropology.* New York: Holt, Rinehart and Winston.

——. 1986: Post-modern anthropology: from document of the occult to occult document. In J. Clifford and G. Marcus (eds.), *Writing Culture*. Berkeley: University of California Press, 122–40.

——. 1987: *The Unspeakable: Discourse, Dialogue and Rhetoric in the Postmodern World*. Madison: University of Wisconsin Press.

Ulin, Robert. 1984: *Understanding Cultures: Perspectives in Anthropology and Social Theory*. Austin: University of Texas Press.

Urban, Greg. 1993: Culture's public face. In *Public Culture 5*, 213–38.

——. 1997: Culture: in and about the world. In *Anthropology Newsletter 38*, February 2, 1 and 7.

Urciuoli, Bonnie. 1996: *Exposing Prejudice: Puerto Rican Experiences of Language, Race, and Class*. Boulder, CO: Westview Press.

Urry, J. 1993: *Before Social Anthropology: Essays on the History of British Anthropology*. Philadelphia: Harwood Academic Publishers.

Valenzuela Arce, José Manuel. 1988: *A la brava ése! Cholos, punks, chavos banda*. Tijuana: El Colegio de la Frontera Norte.

Valeri, Valerio. 1990: Constitutive history: genealogy and narrative in the legitimation of Hawaiian kingship. In E. Ohnuki-Tierney (ed.), *Culture Through Time*. Stanford: Stanford University Press, 154–92.

Van Dyck, Karen. 1997: *Kassandra and the Censors: Greek Poetry Since 1967*. Ithaca, NY: Cornell University Press.

Van Esterik, Penny. 1996: The Politics of Beauty in Thailand. In Cohen, Wilk, and Stoeltje (eds.), *Beauty Queens on the Global Stage*, pp. 203–16.

Van Gennep, Arnold. 1965: *The Rites of Passage*. London and New York: Routledge and Kegan Paul.

Vansina, Jan. 1965: *Oral Tradition: A Study in Historical Methodology*. London: Routledge & Kegan Paul.

——. 1985: *Oral Tradition as History*. London: James Currey.

Veblen, Thorstein. 1965: *The Theory of the Leisure Class*. Reprints of economic classics. New York: A. M. Kelley bookseller.

Verdery, Katherine. 1994: Ethnicity, nationalism, and state-making. In Hans Vermeulen and Cora Govers (eds.), *The Anthropology of Ethnicity*. Amsterdam: Het Spinhuis.

——. 1996: *What Was Socialism and What Comes Next?* Princeton, NJ: Princeton University Press.

Vincent, Joan. 1990: *Anthropology and Politics*. Tucson: The University of Arizona Press.

Vlach, John Michael. 1984: Brazilian house in Nigeria: The emergence of a twentieth century vernacular house type. In *Journal of American Folklore 97* (383), 3–23.

Von Hornbostel, E. 1928: African negro music. In *Africa 1*, 30–62.

Warren, Kay B. 1998: *Indigenous Movements and their Critics: Pan-Maya Activism in Guatemala*. Princeton, NJ: Princeton University Press.

——. 1999: Death squads and wider complicities: dilemmas for the anthropology of violence. In J. Sluka (ed.), *Death Squad: The Anthropology of State Terror*. Philadelphia: University of Pennsylvania Press.

——. 2000: Telling truths: taking David Stoll and the Rigoberta Menchú exposé seriously. In A. Arias (ed.), *The Property of Words: Rigoberta Menchú, David Stoll, and the Identity Politics in Latin America*. Minneapolis: University of Minnesota Press, 226–48.

Waterman, Christopher. 1990: *Jùjú: A Social History and Ethnography of an African Popular Music*. Chicago: University of Chicago Press.

Watson, C. W. 1987: *State and Society in Indonesia: Three Papers*. Cantebury University of Kent at Canterbury, Centre of South-East Asian Studies.

Watson, Rubie S. (ed.). 1994: *Memory, History, and Opposition under State Socialism*. School of American Research advanced seminar series. Sante Fe, NM: School of America Research Press.

Watson, James L. 1975: *Emigration and the Chinese Lineage: the Mans in Hong Kong and London*. Berkeley: University of California Press.

——. (ed.). 1997: *Golden Arches East: McDonald's in East Asia*. Stanford, CA: Stanford University Press.

Weber, Max. 1921: *Die rationalen und soziologischen Grundlagen der Musik*. Trans. [1958], *The Rational and Social Foundations of Music*. Munich: Drei Masken Verlag.

——. 1958[1904]: *The Protestant Ethic and the Spirit of Capitalism*. New York: Charles Scribner.

——. 1963: *The Sociology of Religion*. Boston: Beacon Press.

——. 1965: *Essais sur la théorie de la science*. Paris: Plon.

Wedel, Janine R. 1998: *Collision and Collusion: The Strange Case of Western Aid to Eastern Europe, 1989–1998*. New York: St. Matin's Press.

Weiner, James F. 1994: Myth and metaphor. In T. Ingold (ed.), *Companion Encyclopedia of Anthropology: Humanity, Culture and Social Life*. London: Routledge, 591–612.

White, Hayden V. 1973: *Metahistory: The Historical Imagination in Nineteenth-Century Europe*. Baltimore: Johns Hopkins University Press.

Wilk, Richard R. 1996: *Economies and Cultures: Foundations of Economic Anthropology*. Boulder, CO: Westview.

Williams, Drid. 1991: *Ten Lectures on Theories of the Dance*. Metuchen, NJ: Scarecrow Press.

——. (ed.). 1997: *Anthropology and Human Movement: The Study of Dances*. Readings in Anthropology of Human Movement no. 1. Lanham, MD: Scarecrow Press.

Williams, Raymond. 1973: *The Country and the City*. London: Chatto and Windus.

——. 1977: *Marxism and Literature*. Oxford: Oxford University Press.

Winch, Peter. 1977[1958]: *The Idea of a Social Science and its Relation to Philosophy*. Studies in philosophical psychology. London: Routledge & Kegan Paul; Atlantic Highlands, NJ: Humanities Press.

Wistrich, Robert S. 1996: *Weekend in Munich: Art, Propaganda and Terror in the Third Reich*. London: Pavilion.

Wolf, Eric. 1969: *Peasant Wars of the Twentieth Century*. New York: Harper and Row.

——. 1982: *Europe and the People Without History*. Berkeley: University of California Press.

Wolfenstein, Martha. 1953: Movie analysis in the study of culture. In M. Mead and R. Métraux, *The Study of Culture at a Distance*. Chicago: University of Chicago Press, 267–80.

Wulff, Robert M. and Fiske, Shirley J. 1987: Introduction. In R. M. Wulff and S. J. Fiske (eds.), *Anthropological Praxis: Translating Knowledge into Action*. Boulder, CO: Westview Press, 1–11.

Wuthnow, Robert. 1983: Cultural crises. In A. Bergesen (ed.), *Crisis in the World System*. Beverly Hills: Sage.

Yanagisako, Sylvia, and Delaney, Carol. (eds.). 1995: *Naturalizing Power: Essays in Feminist Cultural Analysis*. New York: Routledge.

Yan, Yun-xiang. 1996: *The Flow of Gifts: Reciprocity and Social Networks in a Chinese village*. Stanford, CA: Stanford University Press.

Yang, Mayfair Mei-hui. 1994: *Gifts, Favors, and Banquets: The Art of Social Relationships in China*. The Wilder House series in politics, history, and culture. Ithaca, NY: Cornell University Press.

Zabusky, Stacia E. 1995: *Launching Europe: An Ethnography of European Cooperation in Space Science*. Princeton, NJ: Princeton University Press.

Zempleni, A. 1996: Les marques de la 'nation' sur quelques propriétés de la 'patrie' et de la 'nation' en Hongrie contemporaine. In Fabre, D. (ed.), *L'Europe entre culture et nations*. Paris: Editions de la Maison des Sciences de l'Homme.

Znamenski, Andrei A. 1995: A household god in a socialist world: Lewis Henry Margan and Russian/Soviet Anthropology. In *Ethnologia Europaea* 25, 177–88.

Zonabend, Françoise. 1993: *The Nuclear Peninsula*. Cambridge: Cambridge University Press; Paris: Editions de la maison des sciences de l'homme.

Zuidema, R. T. 1989: Significado en el arte Nasca. In R. Tom Zuidema (ed.), Reyes y guerreros: ensayos de cultura andina. Lima: Fomciencias.

Index